An Introduction to International Economics

SECOND EDITION

This book is designed for a one-semester course in international economics, primarily targeting non-economics majors and programs in business, international relations, public policy, and development studies. It has been written to make international economics accessible to both students and professionals. Assuming a minimal background in economics and mathematics, the textbook goes beyond the usual trade–finance dichotomy to address international trade, international production, and international finance, and takes a practitioner point of view rather than a standard academic one, introducing students to the material needed to become effective analysts in international economic policy. This new edition features such additional topics as global production and global capital flows, migration, the Ricardian model, and international organizations such as the IMF. Examples have been updated to include recent developments (Brexit, for example) and all charts include the latest data.

Kenneth A. Reinert is Professor of Public Policy at the Schar School of Policy and Government of George Mason University, where he won a Distinguished Teaching Award. He has held past positions as Senior International Economist at the US International Trade Commission and Associate Professor of Economics at Kalamazoo College. Professor Reinert has published over 80 papers in professional journals and edited volumes in the areas of international trade, economic development, and environmental policy. He is also author of *No Small Hope: Towards the Universal Provision of Basic Goods* (Oxford University Press, 2018) and co-author of *Globalization for Development: Meeting New Challenges* (Oxford University Press, 2012). He is editor of the *Handbook of Globalisation and Development* (Edward Elgar, 2017) and co-editor of *Applied Methods for Trade Policy Analysis: A Handbook* (Cambridge University Press, 1997) and the two-volume *Princeton Encyclopedia of the World Economy* (Princeton University Press, 2009).

An Introduction to International Economics

New Perspectives on the World Economy

SECOND EDITION

Kenneth A. Reinert

George Mason University, Virginia

CAMBRIDGE
UNIVERSITY PRESS

University Printing House, Cambridge CB2 8BS, United Kingdom

One Liberty Plaza, 20th Floor, New York, NY 10006, USA

477 Williamstown Road, Port Melbourne, VIC 3207, Australia

314–321, 3rd Floor, Plot 3, Splendor Forum, Jasola District Centre, New Delhi – 110025, India

79 Anson Road, #06–04/06, Singapore 079906

Cambridge University Press is part of the University of Cambridge.

It furthers the University's mission by disseminating knowledge in the pursuit of education, learning, and research at the highest international levels of excellence.

www.cambridge.org
Information on this title: www.cambridge.org/9781108470056
DOI: 10.1017/9781108555838

First published 2012

6th printing 2019

Second edition 2021

Printed in the United Kingdom by TJ International Ltd, Padstow Cornwall, 2021

A catalogue record for this publication is available from the British Library.

ISBN 978-1-108-47005-6 Hardback
ISBN 978-1-108-45516-9 Paperback

Additional resources for this publication at www.cambridge.org/reinert

To Gelaye, Oda, and Ayantu

Summary Contents

Preface *Page* xvii
List of Abbreviations xviii
List of Symbols xxiii

1 Introduction 1

Part I. International Trade

2 Absolute Advantage 27
3 Ricardian Model of Comparative Advantage 44
4 Heckscher–Ohlin Model of Comparative Advantage 60
5 Intra-Industry Trade 80
6 The Political Economy of Trade 97
7 Trade Policy Analysis 121
8 The World Trade Organization 145
9 Preferential Trade Agreements 173

Part II. International Production

10 Multinational Enterprises and Foreign Direct Investment 203
11 Global Value Chains 232
12 Engaging International Production 256
13 Migration 283

Part III. International Finance

14 Accounting Frameworks 311
15 Global Capital Flows 334
16 Exchange Rates and Purchasing Power Parity 355
17 Flexible Exchange Rates 376

18 Fixed Exchange Rates **399**

19 The International Monetary System **421**

20 Crises and Responses **451**

21 Monetary Unions **479**

22 Growth in the Open Economy **508**

Glossary 534

Index 544

Detailed Contents

	Preface	*Page* xvii
	List of Abbreviations	xviii
	List of Symbols	xxiii
1	**Introduction**	**1**
	International Trade	2
	International Production	6
	International Finance	9
	Impacts on International Development	12
	Larger Realms	14
	Analytical Elements	18
	Conclusion	19
	Review Exercises	20
	Further Reading and Web Resources	20
	References	21
	Part I. International Trade	
2	**Absolute Advantage**	**27**
	Defining Absolute Advantage	28
	Absolute Advantage in Supply and Demand	30
	Gains from Trade	35
	Limitations	36
	Conclusion	38
	Review Exercises	39
	Further Reading and Web Resources	39
	References	39
	Appendix 2.1: Review of Supply and Demand	40
3	**Ricardian Model of Comparative Advantage**	**44**
	From Absolute Advantage to Comparative Advantage	44
	Autarky and Comparative Advantage	48
	International Trade	51
	Gains from Trade	54
	Conclusion	55
	Review Exercises	55

Further Reading and Web Resources 56
References 56
Appendix 3.1: The Production Possibilities Frontier 57

4 Heckscher–Ohlin Model of Comparative Advantage 60
Factors of Production 60
From Factors of Production to Comparative Advantage 62
International Trade 66
Gains from Trade 70
FDI, Migration, and Comparative Advantage 71
Limitations 73
Conclusion 75
Review Exercises 76
Further Reading and Web Resources 76
References 77
Appendix 4.1: The Gravity Model 78

5 Intra-Industry Trade 80
Intra-Industry and Inter-Industry Trade 80
Global Patterns of Intra-Industry Trade 83
Intra-Industry Trade under Monopolistic Competition 86
The Smooth Adjustment Hypothesis 90
Conclusion 92
Review Exercises 92
Further Reading and Web Resources 93
References 93
Appendix 5.1: The Grubel–Lloyd Index 95

6 The Political Economy of Trade 97
Approaches to the Political Economy of Trade 98
Comparative Advantage, Trade, and Factors of Production 101
North–South Trade and Wages 104
The Role of Specific Factors 110
Globalization and Inequality in High-Income Countries 113
Conclusion 114
Review Exercises 115
Further Reading and Web Resources 115
References 116
Appendix 6.1: Endogenous Protection 118

7 **Trade Policy Analysis** **121**
Absolute Advantage Revisited 122
Trade Policy Measures 123
A Tariff 128
Terms of Trade Effects 130
A Quota 131
Anti-Dumping and Countervailing Measures 133
Comparative Advantage Models 136
Conclusion 137
Review Exercises 138
Further Reading and Web Resources 138
References 138
Appendix 7.1: The Imperfect Substitutes Model 140
Appendix 7.2: A Tariff Rate Quota 142

8 **The World Trade Organization** **145**
The General Agreement on Tariffs and Trade 146
The World Trade Organization 149
Trade in Goods 150
Trade in Services 152
Intellectual Property 155
Dispute Settlement 159
The Environment 162
The Doha Round 164
Conclusion 166
Review Exercises 167
Further Reading and Web Resources 168
References 168
Appendix 8.1: Tariff Rate Reduction Formulas 171

9 **Preferential Trade Agreements** **173**
Types of Preferential Trade Agreements 174
Rules of Origin 177
The Economic Effects of Preferential Trade Agreements 178
The European Union 181
The North American Free Trade Agreement 185
Mercosur 189
The FTAA 190
ASEAN and AFTA 191

The Trans-Pacific Partnership 192
Regionalism and Multilateralism 192
GATS-Plus and TRIPS-Plus 194
Conclusion 195
Review Exercises 196
Further Reading and Web Resources 196
References 197

Part II. International Production

10 Multinational Enterprises and Foreign Direct Investment 203
Foreign Market Entry 203
Motivations for International Production 208
Entry Mode Choice 210
Patterns of FDI 213
MNE Organizational Design 217
The Home Base 220
Joint Ventures 222
Research and Development 224
Conclusion 228
Review Exercises 228
Further Reading and Web Resources 229
References 229

11 Global Value Chains 232
Tasks and Value Chains 232
From Value Chains to Global Value Chains 236
Firm-Specific Assets and Internalization 237
Intra-Firm Trade 239
A Cost View of Internalization 241
Inter-Firm Relationships 242
Tying Things Together: The TLM Framework 243
Value Added in GVCs 246
Trade in Value Added 248
Trade Policy and Global Value Chains 251
Conclusion 252
Review Exercises 252
Further Reading and Web Resources 253
References 253

12 Engaging International Production 256
Attracting International Production 257
Benefits and Costs 259

Policy Stances 265
Entering Global Value Chains 268
Promoting Linkages 271
Governing International Production 274
Conclusion 277
Review Exercises 277
Further Reading and Web Resources 278
References 278

13 Migration 283
Types of Migration 284
The Migration Decision 286
High-Skilled Migration 290
Low-Skilled Migration 293
Remittances 298
Migration Policy 300
Conclusion 303
Review Exercises 304
Further Reading and Web Resources 304
References 304

Part III. International Finance

14 Accounting Frameworks 311
Open-Economy Accounts 311
Balance of Payments Accounts 317
Analyzing the Balance of Payments Accounts 322
Global Imbalances 324
Conclusion 327
Review Exercises 328
Further Reading and Web Resources 328
References 328
Appendix 14.1: Accounting Matrices 329
Appendix 14.2: An Open-Economy Model 331
Appendix 14.3: Gross Domestic Product and Gross National Income 333

15 Global Capital Flows 334
Types of Capital Flows 335
Foreign Direct Investment 336
Equity Portfolio Investment 338
Bond Finance 339
Commercial Bank Lending 342

Net versus Gross Flows 343
Determinants of Capital Flows 344
Capital Account Liberalization 347
Capital Controls 348
Balance of Payments Revisited 351
Conclusion 351
Review Exercises 352
Further Reading and Web Resources 352
References 352

16 Exchange Rates and Purchasing Power Parity 355
The Nominal Exchange Rate 356
The Real Exchange Rate 360
Purchasing Power Parity 362
Exchange Rates and Trade Flows 366
Hedging and Foreign Exchange Derivatives 367
Conclusion 370
Review Exercises 370
Further Reading and Web Resources 371
References 371
Appendix 16.1: Price Levels and the PPP Model 372
Appendix 16.2: The Monetary Approach to Exchange Rate Determination 374

17 Flexible Exchange Rates 376
A Simple Model of Exchange Rate Determination 376
A Trade-Based Model 378
An Assets-Based Model 382
Interest Rates, Expectations, and Exchange Rates 386
Conclusion 390
Review Exercises 390
Further Reading and Web Resources 391
References 391
Appendix 17.1: Monetary Policies and the Nominal Exchange Rate 392

18 Fixed Exchange Rates 399
Alternative Exchange Rate Regimes 399
A Simple Model of Fixed Exchange Rates 402
An Assets-Based Model of Fixed Exchange Rates 404
Interest Rates and Exchange Rates 407
The Role of Credibility 410

	The Impossible Trinity	411
	Currency Boards	413
	A Role for Fixed Rates?	414
	Conclusion	415
	Review Exercises	416
	Further Reading and Web Resources	416
	References	416
	Appendix 18.1: Monetary Policies and Fixed Exchange Rates	418
19	**The International Monetary System**	**421**
	Some Monetary History	422
	The Operation of the IMF	428
	A History of IMF Operations	432
	The Political Economy of IMF Lending	443
	An Assessment	445
	Conclusion	447
	Review Exercises	448
	Further Reading and Web Resources	448
	References	448
20	**Crises and Responses**	**451**
	Types of Crises	451
	Contagion and Systemic Risk	458
	Analyzing Balance of Payments and Currency Crises	459
	The Asian Crisis	462
	The IMF Response to the Asian and Brazilian Crises	465
	The Global Financial Crisis	467
	Prudential Regulation and the Basel Standards	470
	Capital Controls	472
	Conclusion	474
	Review Exercises	475
	Further Reading and Web Resources	475
	References	475
21	**Monetary Unions**	**479**
	The European Monetary Union at a Glance	479
	Planning the European Monetary Union	482
	Implementing the European Monetary Union	487
	Optimum Currency Areas and Adjustment in the EMU	493
	The EMU in the Global Financial Crisis	496
	Monetary Unions in Africa	502

Conclusion 504
Review Exercises 505
Further Reading and Web Resources 505
References 505

22 Growth in the Open Economy 508
Growth 508
Old Growth Theory 513
New Growth Theory and Human Capital 516
Trade and Growth 519
Institutions and Growth 523
Conclusion 527
Review Exercises 528
Further Reading and Web Resources 528
References 528
Appendix 22.1: Growth Theory Algebra 532

Glossary 534
Index 544

Preface

This new edition of *An Introduction to International Economics: New Perspective on the World Economy* is again written for one- and two-semester courses in international economics, primarily targeting non-economics majors and programs in business, international relations, public policy, and development studies. The book assumes a minimal background in microeconomics, namely a familiarity with the supply and demand diagram and the production possibilities frontier, along with basic algebra. It goes beyond the usual trade–finance dichotomy to give equal treatment to three areas of inquiry: international trade, international production (including migration), and international finance. It also largely takes a practitioner's point of view rather than a standard academic view.

This new edition to the book is significantly different from the previous edition. The previous single chapter on comparative advantage has been split into two: one on the Ricardian model and a second on the Heckscher–Ohlin model. The chapter on intra-industry trade now includes an introduction to the monopolistic competition model of intra-industry trade. Previous chapters on international production have been compressed to fewer. A new chapter has been included on global capital flows. A previous Part IV of the book on development has been eliminated, with the most popular chapters being subsumed into Parts I through III.

I have written the book to make international economics accessible to a wider student and professional audience than has been served by many international economics texts. E-mail correspondence from both instructors and students representing many countries suggests that I have been at least partly successful in this effort. I am grateful to these individuals for their support and input, as well as to the economics editorial team at Cambridge University Press.

Finally, this book went into production before the 2020 global pandemic. This event dramatically affected many aspects of international trade, international production, and international finance. These events will need to be addressed by instructors and students in their specific classes.

Abbreviations

AANZFTA	ASEAN–Australia–New Zealand Free Trade Area
AC	average cost
ACP	African, Caribbean and Pacific
AD	anti-dumping
AEC	ASEAN Economic Community
AFTA	ASEAN Free Trade Area
AGE	applied general equilibrium
AMC	American Motor Corporation
AMS	aggregate measure of support
ARERAER	IMF's Annual Report on Exchange Rate Arrangements and Exchange Restrictions
ASEAN	Association of Southeast Asian Nations
ATC	Agreement on Textiles and Clothing
BATNA	best alternative to a negotiated agreement
BAW	Beijing Auto Works
BCBS	Basel Committee on Banking Supervision
BI	Belassa index
BIS	Bank for International Settlements
BIT	bilateral investment treaty
BPM6	IMF's *Balance of Payments and International Investment Position Manual*
CAMA	Central African Monetary Area
CAP	Common Agricultural Policy
CAR	capital account regulation or capital adequacy ration
CBD	Convention on Biological Diversity
CEC	Commission for Environmental Cooperation (North American)
CEPT	Culture, environment, politics and technology or Common Effective Preferential Tariff
CET	common external tariff
CFA	Communauté Financière Africaine
CFM	capital flow (management) measure
CIG	capital intensive good
CIP	covered interest rate parity
CITES	Convention on International Trade in Endangered Species of Wild Fauna and Flora
CMA	Common Monetary Area of Southern Africa (rand zone)

CMO	contract manufacturing organization
CO	certificate of origin
CRTA	Committee on Regional Trade Agreements
CTE	Committee on Trade and the Environment
CTH	change in tariff heading
CU	customs union
CVD	countervailing duty
DSB	Dispute Settlement Body
DSM	dispute settlement mechanism
DSU	Dispute Settlement Understanding
EC	European Community
ECB	European Central Bank
ECF	Extended Credit Facility
ECOFIN	European Council of Ministers of Economics and Finance
ECSC	European Coal and Steel Community
ECU	European currency unit
EEC	European Economic Community
EFF	Extended Fund Facility
EFSF	European Financial Stability Facility
EME	emerging market economy
EMI	European Monetary Institute
EMIT	(Working Group on) Environmental Measures and International Trade
EMS	European Monetary System
EMU	European Monetary Union
EPZ	export-processing zone
ERM	Exchange Rate Mechanism (European Union)
ESAF	Enhanced Structural Adjustment Facility
ESCB	European System of Central Banks
ESM	European Stability Mechanism
EU	European Union
FCL	flexible credit line
FDI	foreign direct investment
FOGS	Functioning of the GATT System
FTA	free trade agreement
FTAA	Free Trade Agreement of the Americas
FTZ	free trade zone
G10	Group of 10
GAB	General Agreement to Borrow
GATS	General Agreement on Trade in Services
GATT	General Agreement on Tariffs and Trade
GBT	Group on Basic Telecommunications

GCIM	Global Commission on International Migration
GDP	gross domestic product
GF	gravitational force
GFC	global financial crisis
GIIPS	Greece, Ireland, Italy, Portugal, and Spain
GNDI	gross national disposable income
GNI	gross national income
GNP	gross national product
GPN	global production network
GSIB	globally systemically important bank
GTAP	Global Trade Analysis Project
GVC	global value chain
HDI	Human Development Index
HIC	high-income country
HICP	Harmonised Index of Consumer Prices
HLD	United Nations High-Level Dialogue on International Migration and Development
ICT	information and communication technology
ICU	International Clearing Union
IDA	Industrial Development Authority (Ireland)
IDM	integrated device manufacturer
IFSC	International Financial Services Centre (Ireland)
IIA	international investment agreement
ILO	International Labour Organization
IMF	International Monetary Fund
IOM	International Organization for Migration
IP	intellectual property
IPC	Intellectual Property Committee
IRB	internal ratings-based (approach)
ISDS	investor–state dispute settlement
ISF	International Stabilization Fund
ITO	International Trade Organization
ITRI	Industrial Technology Research Institute (Taiwan)
JV	joint venture
LED	light-emitting diode
LIG	labor-intensive good
LMICs	low- and middle-income countries
M&A	mergers and acquisitions
MAI	Multilateral Agreement on Investment
MAL	minimum access level
MBS	mortgage-backed security
MC	marginal cost

ME	market economy
MEA	multilateral environment agreement
MFN	most favored nation
MNE	multinational enterprise
MR	marginal revenue
MTN	multilateral trade negotiation
NAAEC	North American Agreement on Environmental Cooperation
NAALC	North American Agreement on Labor Cooperation
NAB	New Agreement to Borrow
NAFTA	North American Free Trade Agreement
NGBT	Negotiating Group on Basic Telecommunications
NGO	non-governmental organization
NINA	no income, no asset (mortgage)
NINJA	no income, job, or asset (mortgage)
NME	non-market economy
NT	national treatment
NTB	non-tariff barrier
NTM	non-tariff measure
OCA	optimum currency area
ODA	official development assistance
OECD	Organisation for Economic Co-operation and Development
OTDS	overall trade distortion support
PCA	Permanent Court of Arbitration (The Hague)
PIIGS	Portugal, Italy, Ireland, Greece, and Spain
PPF	production possibilities frontier
PPP	purchasing power parity
PRGF	Poverty Reduction and Growth Facility
PTA	preferential trade agreement
QPC	quantitative performance criterion
R&D	research and development
RCF	Rapid Credit Facility
REE	rare earth element
REER	real effective exchange rate
RFI	Rapid Financing Instrument
RIT	regional investment treaty
RMAP	Responsible Minerals Assurance Process
RMB	Renminbi (China)
RoHS	Restriction of Hazardous Substances (EU directive)
ROO	rule of origin
RORE	rate of return to education
RSCA	revealed symmetrical comparative advantage
RTA	regional trade agreement

RVC	regional value content
SAB	South African Breweries
SACU	Southern African Customs Union
SBA	Stand-By Arrangement
SCF	Standby Credit Facility
SDR	special drawing right
SITC	Standard International Trade Classification
SLIG	skilled labor-intensive good
SPS	sanitary and phyto-sanitary
SSM	special safeguard mechanism
STR	standards and technical regulations
TARP	Troubled Asset Relief Program
TBT	technical barrier to trade
TEU	Treaty on European Union (Maastricht Treaty)
TiSA	Trade in Services Agreement
TiVA	Trade in Value Added (project/database)
TLM	task, location, and mode (framework)
TNI	Transnationality Index
TPP	Trans-Pacific Partnership
TRIMs	trade-related investment measures
TRIPS	Trade-Related Aspects of Intellectual Property Rights (Agreement)
TRQ	tariff rate quota
TSMC	Taiwan Semiconductor Manufacturing Company
UIP	uncovered interest rate parity
ULIG	Unskilled labor-intensive good
UN	United Nations
UNCTAD	United Nations Conference on Trade and Development
UNDP	United Nations Development Programme
UNHCR	United Nations High Commission for Refugees
UNU-IHDP	United Nations University – International Human Dimensions Programme
URR	unremunerated reserve requirement
US	United States
USITC	United States International Trade Commission
VDR	variable deposit requirement
VEAM	Vietnam Engine and Agricultural Machinery Corporation
VER	voluntary export restraint
VNM	value of non-originating materials
WAMU	West African Monetary Union
WTO	World Trade Organization

Symbols

a	labor input coefficient
A	technology factor
B	Grubel–Lloyd index
BI	Belassa index of revealed comparative advantage
C	household consumption or IMF conditions
d	firm-level demand
D	demand or distance
DD	demand diagonal
Δ	change in
e	nominal exchange rate or exports as a percentage of GDP
E	exports or emigration
ES	emigration supply
F	Fixed costs or flow of trade/FDI
G	government expenditures or gain
h	ratio of total human capital to total labor (human capital-labor ratio)
H	Total human capital
I	Investment
ID	Immigration demand
k	ratio of total physical capital to total labor (capital–labor ratio)
K	physical capital
L	labor, liquidity, loans or loss
M	money (both supply and demand) or mass
n	natural rate of population growth
p	price or price level
q	firm-level quantity
Q	quantity
r	interest rate
re	real exchange rate
rw	relative wage
R	total return on asset
S	supply
S_F	foreign savings
S_G	government savings

S_H household savings
t ad valorem tariff
T specific tariff or taxes
θ constant
V variable costs or velocity of money
W wage
ω relative low-skilled to high-skilled wage
y real gross domestic product
Y nominal gross domestic product, gross national income or factor income
Z imports

1 Introduction

In the late 1990s I met an anthropology student who had just returned from a year in Senegal. As soon as she learned that I was an international economist, she asked, "Can you tell me about the CFA franc devaluation? Why was it necessary? It has made life very difficult in Senegal." Some years later, I met a religion student who had just returned from a semester spent in Haiti working in a health clinic. As soon as he learned that I was an international economist, he asked, "Can you tell me about structural adjustment programs? I'm concerned about how they are being applied to Haiti." Subsequently, one of my children's school bus driver quizzed me about the Doha Round of multilateral trade negotiations, and a college professor wanted to know the exact distinction between trade and foreign direct investment.

These are not rare incidents. International economists receive such inquiries from all sorts of people. Increasingly, it seems, more and more of us need to know something about the world economy—religion students and bus drivers, as well as economics and business students. Why is this? Put simply, the world economy impacts us all in increasingly significant ways. It has become very difficult to take shelter in our respective majors and professions without being knowledgeable about the basics of international economics. Increasingly, trade flows, exchange rates, and multinational enterprises matter to us all, even if we would prefer that they did not. The 2008 global financial crisis (GFC) made this apparent in the most dramatic way, as did the 2016 Brexit vote in favor of the United Kingdom leaving the European Union.

As a consequence of these changes, students and professionals, but also citizens more broadly, have significant concerns about "globalization." Shortly before the failed Seattle Ministerial Conference of the World Trade Organization (WTO) in December 1999, for example, I received a phone call from a former student. She was about to travel to Seattle to join in the protests against the WTO—the "Battle of Seattle," as it was called. She knew that I had spent a brief amount of time at the WTO, and, before she set off, she wanted to raise her concerns with me about globalization and the impact it was having on rural economies in the United States. The Seattle Ministerial was a failure in part because of the efforts of my former student and her fellow protesters. The same was true of other subsequent WTO Ministerial Conferences.

Since that time an anti-globalization movement has increased in strength.[1] It has drawn attention to the distributional impacts of increased global integration but has also at times questioned the entire integration of the world economy in broad-brush terms. Are the concerns of my former student and the anti-globalization movement well placed? Is globalization the evil that some contend it is? Or is it the unmitigated good that others contend it is (e.g. Wolf, 2004)? Most likely, the actualities of globalization are *more nuanced* than the good/evil dichotomy that is often invoked. For example, in an analysis of the effects of various globalization processes on the development processes, Goldin and Reinert (2012: 1) state: "The relationship between globalization and poverty is not well understood.... By examining both the processes through which globalization takes place and the effects that each of these processes has on global poverty alleviation, current discussions can be better informed."

Better informing students and professionals about globalization is an important component of this book, and exploring key aspects of globalization is one of the tasks we take up here. We will try to explore the world economy and globalization in as balanced a manner as possible. This will help us develop informed views and opinions, whatever they might be. Developing informed views and opinions, in turn, requires a serious study of international economics. This field of study is typically divided into two parts: international trade and international finance. Indeed, these two parts often constitute the only two courses in a standard "core course" series. In this book, however, we are going to approach things slightly differently. Acknowledging some new perspectives on the world economy, we are going to explore three different aspects or realms of the modern world economy. These are: international trade, international production, and international finance. Let us briefly consider each of these in turn.

International Trade

Our first realm of the world economy is **international trade**.[2] International trade refers to the exchange of *both* goods *and* services between the countries of the world. We typically picture international trade as taking place only in *goods*, such as steel, automobiles, wine, or bananas. This view is incomplete, however. It is important to acknowledge that a significant portion of world trade is composed of trade in *services*. For example, financial services, architectural services, and

[1] See, for example, Ayres (2004), Dunkley (2016), and *The Economist* (2016a).

[2] Every time you encounter a term in boldface in this book, you can find its definition in the glossary.

engineering services are all traded internationally. In fact, trade in services composes about one-fifth of total world trade.[3] Indeed, trade in goods and trade in services can be *intertwined*, as the process of trading in goods requires service inputs in the form of transportation, logistics, and customs clearance. Indeed, the process of manufacturing itself is becoming increasingly service-intensive.[4]

International trade in goods and services is playing an increasing role in the world economy. Consider the data presented in Figure 1.1. This figure plots two series of data for the years 1970 to 2018. The first series, represented by a dashed line, is inflation-adjusted world **gross domestic product** (GDP), a measure of world output. It has been normalized so that the value in 1970 is 100, and the values for each subsequent year are measured relative to 1970. The second series, represented

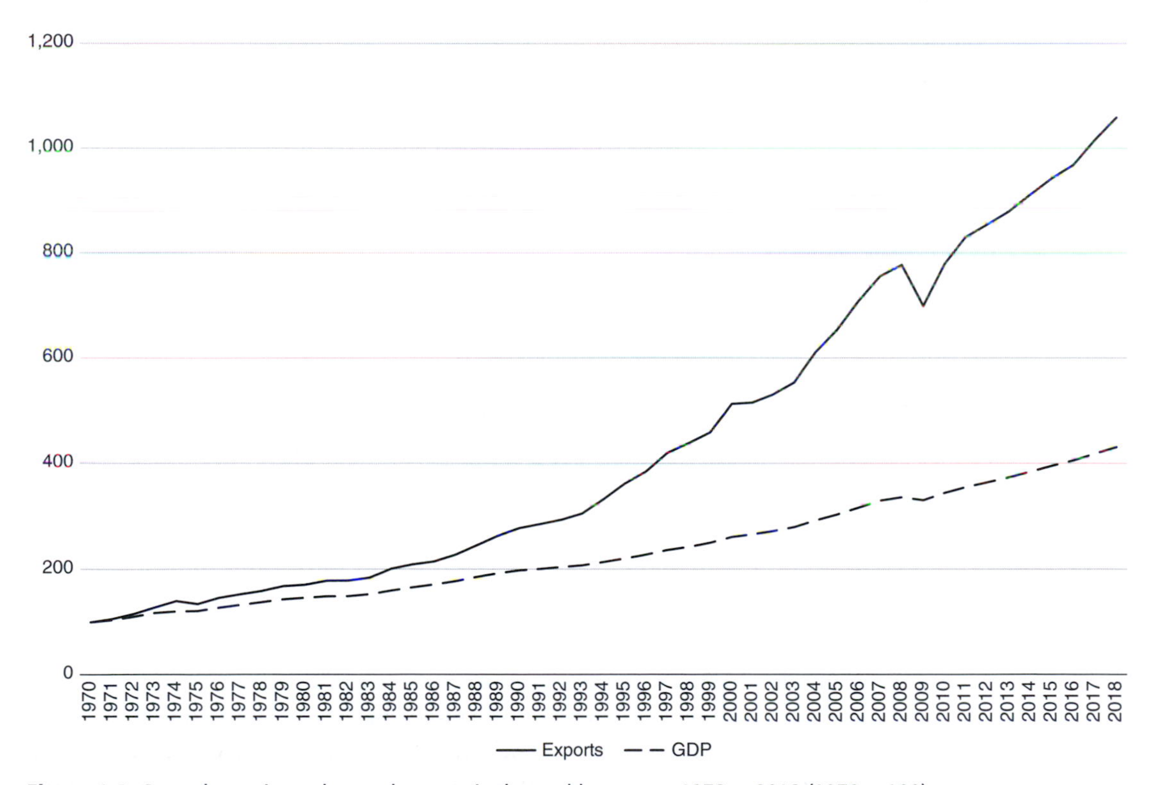

Figure 1.1 Gross domestic product and exports in the world economy, 1970 to 2018 (1970 = 100)
Source: World Bank, World Development Indicators, and author calculations.

[3] It is sometimes said that the word "goods" refers to things you can drop on your toe. Therefore, "services" refers to things you *cannot* drop on your toe! More formally, goods are tangible and storable, whereas services are intangible and non-storable. On trade in goods, see Reinert (2017b); and, on trade in services, see Francois and Hoekman (2010) and Chanda (2017).

[4] See, for example, Lodefalk (2015). Chanda (2017: 45) states: "Manufacturing firms today are buying and producing more series than ever before. 'Servicification' of manufacturing refers to the fact that services are becoming important as both inputs and outputs for manufacturing."

by a solid line, is inflation-adjusted world exports.[5] This series has been normalized in the same way as the GDP series. As you can see in Figure 1.1, over the decades considered trade activity increased more rapidly than production activity in the world economy. This is one of the main features of globalization: the expansion in the exchange of goods and services between the countries of the world. You can also see that trade decreased more quickly in 2009 than did production in response to the 2008 GFC before recovering its previous trajectory. What Figure 1.1 encapsulates is a near-half-century of the increased trade intensification of the world economy.

There are many reasons for the expansion of world trade illustrated in Figure 1.1. One way of thinking about this is in terms of "three Ts," namely transportation, technology, and tariffs. The first "T" is transportation. During the 1970s a revolution began in global goods shipping using containers, with ships being built to carry thousands of increasingly standardized containers, and ports being redesigned to efficiently handle these ships and containers. Advances in container shipping continue to this day. The largest container ships now carry over 15,000 containers, and there are ongoing experiments in new materials (e.g. carbon fiber composites), new security scanning technology, and new means of embedding container transport histories.[6] Recent statistical evidence suggests that container transport has indeed had a significant, positive impact on increased globalization via trade flows.[7]

The container shipping revolution was followed by significant changes in air freight, beginning in the mid-1980s. This mode of transportation is more expensive than container shipping. The reason air freight is important, however, is that it is so much faster. As noted by Baldwin (2016: 85), "air cargo allows manufacturers to know that intermediate goods could flow among distant factories almost as surely as they flow among factories within a nation." This new reality also helped to promote international trade flows.

The second "T" is technology, specifically in the form of **information and communication technology**, or ICT. A revolution in ICT has greatly enhanced the ability of firms to coordinate both international trade logistics and, more generally, international production systems. Advances in ICT also greatly facilitated some types of services trade via electronic commerce. ICT enhanced the development of container shipping to such an extent that we can say, to paraphrase Levinson (2006: 267), the container, combined with the computer, opened the way to modern globalization. All indications suggest that this technological transformation is still taking place.[8]

---

[5] Note that world imports track world exports very closely, so we can use the level of exports as a proxy for the overall level of world trade.

[6] On some of these new container shipping technologies, see *The Economist* (2014).

[7] See *The Economist* (2013) and Bernhofen, El-Sahli, and Kneller (2016).

[8] For example, in a review of technological change in global value chains, *The Economist* (2019) refers to artificial intelligence, cognitive analytics, deep-learning algorithms, self-learning algorithms, and 3-D printing.

The third "T" is tariffs. The time period of Figure 1.1 coincided with an era of trade liberalization, begun with the lowering of tariff barriers both unilaterally and via regional and multilateral initiatives. For example, Hoekman and Kostecki (2009: 138) report that, as a result of multilateral trade liberalization, the weighted average tariff on manufactured products imposed by high-income countries fell from approximately 20 percent to 5 percent though the 1990s. So tariffs, or trade liberalization more broadly, helped spur global trade integration.[9]

In sum, the three "Ts" of transportation, technology, and tariffs all helped to contribute to a world economy in which international trade relations have grown increasingly important.[10] They also had impacts on patterns of international production, to be discussed below.

One recent and significant change in the global trading economy has been the entry of China, as a result of its embrace of market reforms beginning in the late 1970s, as well as its joining the WTO in 2001. China's substantial increase in exports, particularly manufactured exports, was an unprecedented event that had significant implications for what we will call the *political economy of trade* throughout much of the world.[11] To gain some perspective, it is helpful to look at China's exports as a percentage of GDP and compare this with another large exporter, Germany. We do this in Figure 1.2. You can see in this figure that China's exports as a percentage of GDP are substantially *lower* than those of Germany and have been decreasing since 2006. Indeed, in 2018 China's exports as a percentage of GDP were substantially below what they had been in 2000, while Germany's increased steadily over the time period considered in the figure. Indeed, as of 2016 Germany had the largest trade surplus in the world.[12]

You will begin to understand the major factors underlying international trade in Part I of this book. We will apply standard microeconomic thinking to analyzing both trade and trade policies. In doing this, you will become acquainted with the powerful concept of **comparative advantage**. You will also be introduced to a set of key policy issues surrounding the management of international trade, including issues pertaining to the World Trade Organization and to **preferential trade agreements** such as the North American Free Trade Agreement (NAFTA) and the Association of Southeast Asian Nations (ASEAN). A full understanding of the factors underlying international trade will also require an understanding of international production, however, and this is taken up in Part II of this book.

---

[9] As we discuss in Chapters 6 and 7, there have been recent moves against global trade integration.

[10] Of these three factors (container shipping, ICT advances, and trade liberalization), Baldwin (2016) draws special attention to ICT, particularly in the decades since 1990. He sees container shipping and trade liberalization as reducing the costs of moving goods, but ICT as reducing the costs of moving ideas.

[11] See, for example, *The Economist* (2016a).

[12] See *The Economist* (2017a).

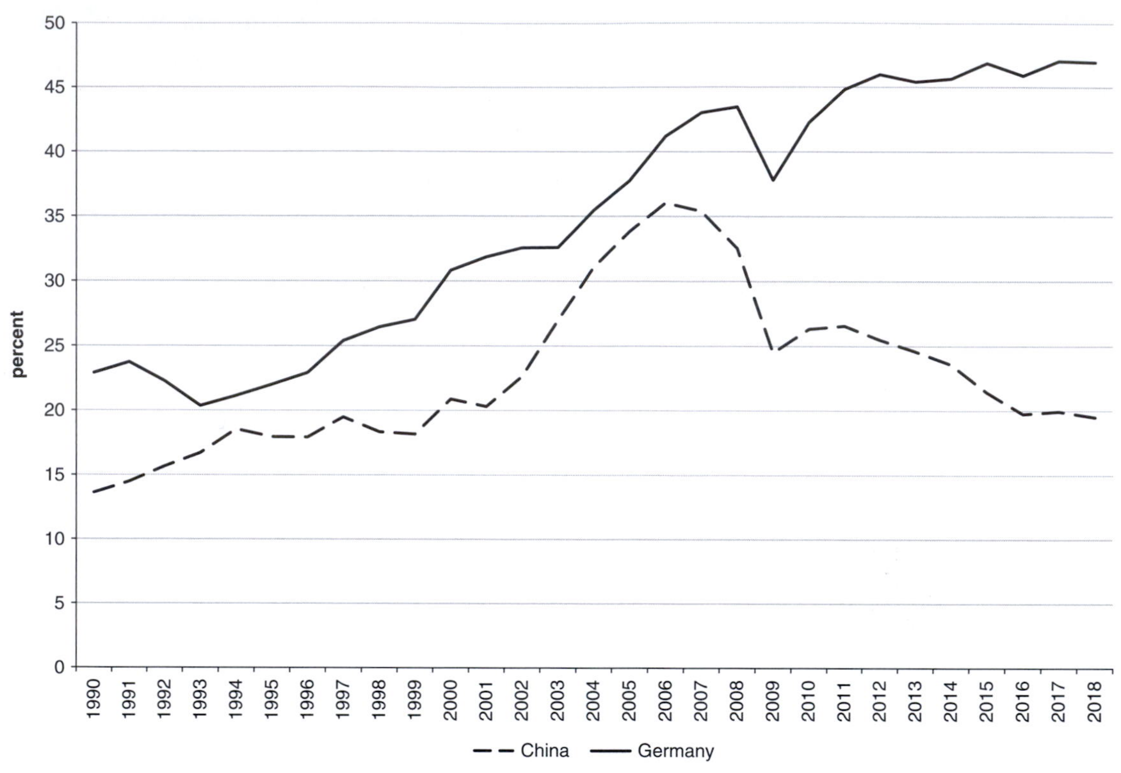

Figure 1.2 Exports as a percentage of GDP, China and Germany, 1990 to 2018
Source: World Bank, World Development Indicators.

International Production

A second important realm of the world economy is **international production**. Production patterns in the modern world economy can be relatively complex. For example, when my children were toddlers, one of their favorite books was *Bear's Busy Family*, published by the award-winning Barefoot Books. Featured in *Inc. Magazine* in 2006, Barefoot Books was founded in 1993 by Tessa Strickland and Nancy Traversy. It was initially run from their homes in the United Kingdom (where burgeoning inventory broke a table), but subsequently expanded with a flagship store in Cambridge, Massachusetts, in the United States. In the case of *Bear's Busy Family*, the color separation was done in Italy, and the actual printing took place in Malaysia. So the book my children held with such interest in their hands was a result of a production process that took place in four countries. The production of products (and their intermediate inputs) in multiple countries is what we mean by international production.

At the broadest level, international production can take place via two alternative modes. The first mode is non-equity contracting and includes foreign outsourcing, licensing, and franchising. Contracting is an arm's-length relationship across national boundaries that can be described as a low-commitment/low-control option. The second mode is equity-based **foreign direct investment** (FDI) undertaken by **multinational enterprises** (MNEs).[13] FDI involves firms based in one country *owning* at least 10 percent of a firm producing in another country and thereby exerting management influence, a high-commitment/high-control option.[14] Both these options are important in the modern world economy.[15]

MNEs are particularly important actors in the world economy. To get a sense of this, consider the following facts.[16]

- MNEs account for approximately one-fourth of world GDP.
- The sales of foreign affiliates of MNEs exceed the volume of world trade.
- MNEs are involved in approximately three-fourths of all world trade.
- Approximately one-third of world trade takes place *within* MNEs.
- MNEs account for approximately three-fourths of worldwide civilian research and development (R&D).

A series of data on global FDI inflows from 1970 to 2018 is provided in Figure 1.3. The inflows are broken down between low- and middle-income countries (LMICs: bottom) and high-income countries (top) that receive or host the FDI. FDI flows to low-income countries are miniscule by global standards, so the vast bulk of inflows to LMICs are to the middle-income countries of that group. As you can see, the 1990s were characterized by a large surge of FDI inflows, mostly into high-income countries and partly reflecting an upturn in mergers and acquisitions (M&A) activity. What is also clear, however, is that the middle-income countries of the world are hosting a growing amount of FDI. As a result of the GFC, total FDI flows decreased substantially in 2008 and 2009. They subsequently recovered to approximately US$2 trillion, a value that had been reached in the mid-2000s in the previous FDI upturn. In the most recent years of Figure 1.3, however, they have fallen again, with the decline centered on inflows to high-income countries.

[13] A formal definition of an MNE by Dunning and Lundan (2008: 3) is: "A multinational or transnational enterprise is an enterprise that engages in foreign direct investment and owns or, in some way, controls value-added activities in more than one country." For a review, see Anyanwu (2017).

[14] The 10 percent ownership threshold for categorizing FDI is, admittedly, arbitrary, but it is a widely accepted standard in balance of payments accounting, used by the International Monetary Fund (IMF) and the Organisation for Economic Co-operation and Development (OECD).

[15] The popular term "offshoring" is used in different ways in the research and policy literature. In some cases (e.g. McIvor, 2005: chap. 2) it is used to mean, essentially, foreign outsourcing. In other cases (e.g. Feenstra and Jensen, 2009) it is used to refer to FDI itself. In still other cases (e.g. Baldwin, 2016) it is used to refer to both. Given these multiple meanings, we will not use the term in this book.

[16] For further discussion of the role of MNEs, see Dunning and Lundan (2008: chap. 2).

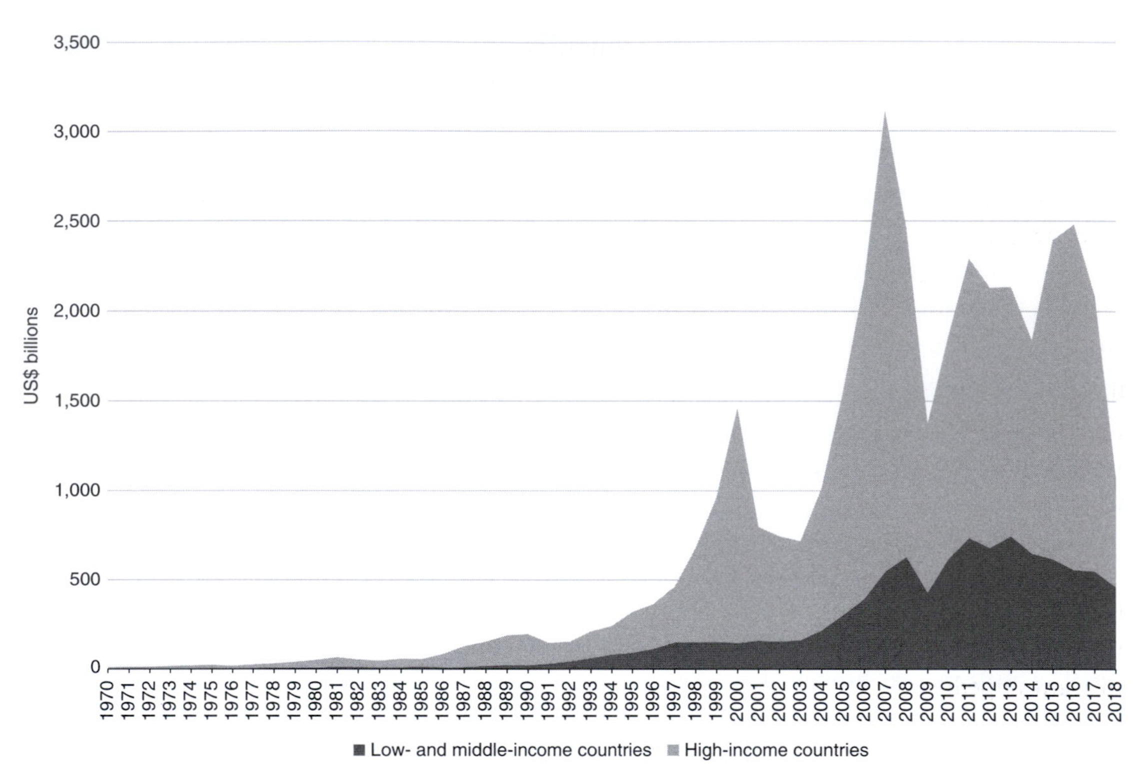

Figure 1.3 Nominal FDI inflows, 1970 to 2018
Source: World Bank, World Development Indicators.

What has accounted for the *long-term* increase in FDI activity in middle- and high-income countries? Two relevant factors are those mentioned above in our discussion of international trade, namely improvements in transportation and ICT. Add to this an expansion of global M&A activity, particularly in the services sector (finance, transport, communications). Indeed, services began to account for approximately one-half of FDI flows in the 1990s. Further, many countries in the developing world began to shift from a policy posture of antipathy towards FDI inflows to one of relative friendliness.[17] This, for example, accompanied the well-known rise of FDI flows into China, which helped spur its previously discussed export expansion.

Both contracting relationships and FDI are configured between countries in what are known as **global value chains** (GVCs). GVCs are systems of value chains linked together in buyer–supplier or ownership relationships across countries.[18] GVCs are further held together by trade relationships in both intermediate and final products. GVCs have been enabled by the innovations in container shipping

[17] See Anyanwu (2017), who notes a shift to a view of "FDI as a prerequisite and catalyst for sustainable growth and development" (134).

[18] See, for example, Gupta (2017).

and ICT described above, and their configuration affects the way countries are included or excluded from evolving patterns of modern globalization. So the lack of FDI in low-income countries in part reflects their exclusion from GVCs.

ICT-enabled GVCs have received increasing attention from researchers. Indeed, Baldwin (2016) suggests that ICT-enabled GVCs are the defining feature of modern globalization. Baldwin's observation is that ICT advances, along with advances in air cargo, made possible the coordination of production activities at a distance and, in this way, distributed factories across national boundaries. As he states, "The contours of industrial competitiveness are now increasingly defined by the outlines of international production networks rather than the boundaries of nations" (6). He and others have called this process "unbundling." By "unbundling," these researchers mean that stages of production processes are moved away from their original national location. This process is part of the modern evolution of GVCs.

Migration is also an important aspect of globalization.[19] This book considers migration to be a relevant part of international production, in that most migrants leave one country and enter into another for work purposes. Nevertheless, despite the fact that 3 to 4 percent of the world's population has migrated, there are significant impediments to this aspect of globalization. As barriers to the movements of goods, services, direct investment, and finance transactions have fallen over time, barriers to the movement of people have largely remained in place, or even increased. This has caused some international economists (e.g. Pritchett, 2006) to refer to "everything but labor" globalization. Nonetheless, migration is still an element of the world economy worth studying, and we will consider its role in international production via both low- and high-skilled migration.

As the above facts and data indicate, FDI, MNEs, GVCs, and migration are additional and important features of globalization. In Part II of the book, you will gain an understanding of these additional features of the modern world economy from both business and economic perspectives. This is a vast area of research, policy-making, and international business activity, but we will present the material in an organized and accessible manner to familiarize you with these new perspectives on the world economy.

International Finance

A third important realm of the world economy is **international finance**. Whereas international trade refers to the exchange of goods and services between the countries of the world, international finance refers to the exchange of **assets** between these countries. Assets are financial objects characterized by a monetary value that

[19] See, for example, Goldin and Reinert (2012: chap. 6) and Omelaniuk (2017).

can change over time. They make up the wealth portfolios of individuals, firms, and governments. For example, individuals and firms around the world conduct international transactions in currencies, equities, government bonds, corporate bonds (commercial paper), and even real estate as part of their management of international portfolios. The way in which the prices of these assets change in response to these international transactions impacts individual countries in important ways. Additionally, as we will see, these transactions can provide a source of savings to countries over and above the domestic savings of their households and firms.

International finance plays an increasingly important role in the world economy. We can see this by considering foreign exchange transactions. As it turns out, foreign exchange transactions are *much larger* than trade transactions. For example, Figure 1.4 plots two variables for three-year intervals between 1989 and 2016. The first variable, plotted as the vertical bars in reference to the left-hand scale (lhs), is daily foreign exchange turnover, as measured by the Bank for

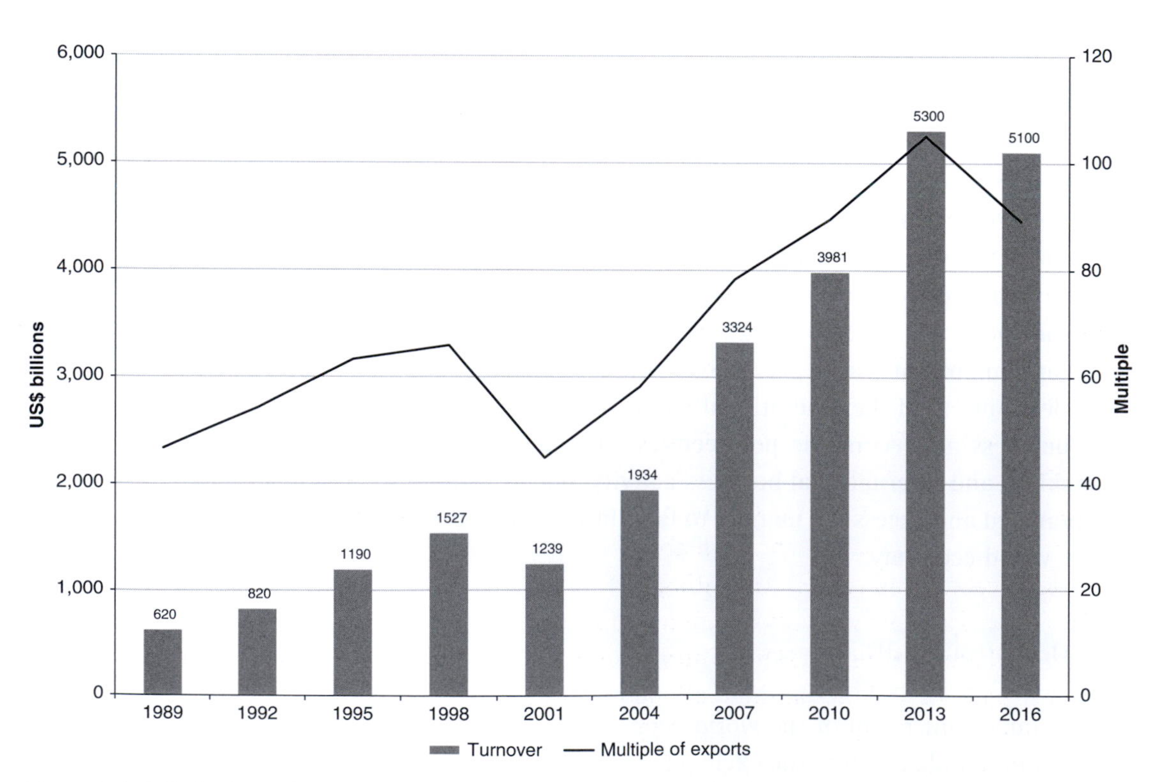

Figure 1.4 Daily foreign exchange market turnover and annualized multiple of exports, 1989 to 2016 (lhs: US$ billions; rhs: multiple of exports)

Note: The multiple of exports assumes a constant foreign exchange turnover each day of the year.

Sources: Bank for International Settlements, Triennial Central Bank Surveys, and World Bank, World Development Indicators.

International Settlements (BIS) in its triennial April surveys. Despite downturns in 2001 and 2016, the total foreign exchange turnover has increased substantially over time. Observers were amazed when it broke US$1 trillion in 1995, but in 2013 it reached over US$5 trillion! In 2016, to some surprise, foreign exchange turnover declined a little.

The second variable plots the annualized foreign exchange turnover (assuming constant turnover each day) as a multiple of total world exports in reference to the right-hand scale (rhs) also for three-year intervals between 1989 and 2016. As you can see, foreign exchange turnover can be as high as 100 times the value of exports. This makes it strikingly clear that, on an annual basis, global transactions in foreign exchange dwarf global trade transactions. International finance matters.

Another important feature of international finance has emerged in recent years. A typical expectation in the field of international finance is that LMICs will naturally receive net inflows of capital from high-income countries with relatively low rates of return and invest it at relatively high rates of return. Since 2000, however, this pattern has been reversed. Due in large part to deficits in the United States (US citizens spending in excess of national savings), LMICS (mainly middle-income countries) are now significant exporters of financial capital rather than importers. Although estimates vary, it is safe to say that the capital exports of these countries are approximately US$500 billion. This has been a major new development in international finance.[20]

Whether the foreign exchange transactions and **capital flows** of global finance are all for the best is a matter of current debate. Goldin and Reinert (2012: chap. 4) strike a note of caution in their discussion of capital flows, noting that some types of global capital flows are volatile and potentially destabilizing. This is particularly the case for bond finance and commercial bank lending. Even the International Monetary Fund has recently set a similarly cautious tone. A publication by its staff economists (Ostry, Loungani, and Fuceri, 2016) also questions the growth-promoting effects of the bond finance and commercial bank lending. Since the IMF is the central institution of global finance, this is significant. *The Economist* (2016a) summarizes these concerns by stating that "there is plenty of evidence of the trouble that floods of short-term capital can cause." Mitigating this "trouble" is an ongoing challenge.

The importance of international finance, seen in Figure 1.4, became very evident in the latter part of the 1990s. During this time investors quickly sold assets in Mexico, Thailand, Indonesia, the Philippines, Russia, and Brazil, causing **balance of payments** crises and financial crises. This was a process known as **capital flight**. Capital flight involves investors selling a country's assets and reallocating their portfolios into other countries' assets, and is part of the "trouble" of global finance.

---

[20] This phenomenon is now known as the "Lucas paradox," after Lucas (1990).

Beginning in mid-2008 the power of international finance again became evident in the form of a global financial crisis, with roots in the US housing market. Losses in housing mortgages were transmitted around the globe via a pyramid of financial instruments related to this sector. This was the result of banks taking loans that would traditionally have remained on their books, repackaging them in the form of asset-based securities, and trading these securities internationally. This provided a mechanism for a crisis related to new financial products originating in one country to take on a global profile. As the *Financial Times* noted in 2008, "the global system has shifted from financing anything, however crazy, to refusing to finance anything, however sensible." This kind of volatility is, to say the least, not desirable.

The 2008 crisis did not just affect the United States. Its most severe effects were felt in Europe, first in the United Kingdom but then in Portugal, Italy, Ireland, Greece and Spain. The crises in Greece and Ireland were particularly acute, and the European Union struggled to contain the damage to its political and economic integration. Watching the United States and the European Union succumb to financial instability has given many experts and policy-makers pause. It has even led some major players (e.g. China) to question the entire "Western model" of development.[21]

As we can see, then, international finance is a realm of increasing importance in the modern world economy. You will enter into this realm in Part III of the book. You will learn about open-economy accounting, exchange rate determination, capital flows, the international monetary system, and financial crises. Throughout Part III, the asset considerations that set international finance apart from international trade will be paramount.

Impacts on International Development

International trade, international production, and international finance make up the three areas of inquiry we will pursue in this book. The processes of international trade, production, and finance reflect the many goals of their participants. From a public policy perspective, however, it is hoped that these three processes contribute to **international development**, namely to improved levels of welfare and standards of living. Two major issues usually arise here. The first is how we *conceptualize* levels of welfare or standards of living. The second is how the processes of international trade, international production, and international finance support or undermine international development. To be truthful, neither of these issues has been fully settled, and policy debates on these matters are ongoing.

[21] See, for example, Zhao (2010).

Development has been defined in a number of ways. The most prominent is as gross domestic product per capita, the average value of production produced by a citizen of a country. This is the approach of mainstream economics. The limitation of the approach is that GDP has been explicitly developed to *not* be a measure of welfare.[22] To use it as such is very convenient, but incorrect. The main alternative to GDP per capita is the "capabilities" approach, which assesses development outcomes in terms of a range of human capabilities–things people can actually achieve, such as being healthy and literate.[23] The capabilities approach is often assessed using the **Human Development Index** (HDI), a measure devised and maintained by the United Nations Development Programme. The HDI reflects per capita income (adjusted for cost of living), average life expectancy, and average levels of education. It too has limitations, namely that per capita income is *not* a human capability.[24]

Each of these approaches leads to very different types of assessment and policy suggestions. But they have one thing in common: however we measure them, development outcomes vary *widely* across the countries of the world, from severe deprivation to relative opulence. This can be seen in Table 1.1 for just a handful of countries. Across this very small collection of countries, GDP per capita varies by a factor of almost 80, the gap in life expectancy is about 17 years, and the gap in mean years of schooling is approximately a decade. Interestingly, both South Korea and Costa Rica have higher life expectancies than the United States,

Table 1.1 Measures of living standards, 2017

Country	GDP per Capita (US$)	Life Expectancy (years)	Mean Years of Schooling (years)	Human Development Index (0 to 1) and Rank
Ethiopia	768	65.9	2.7	0.463/173
India	1,982	68.8	6.4	0.640/130
China	8,759	76.4	7.8	0.752/86
Costa Rica	11,753	80.0	8.8	0.794/63
South Korea	29,743	82.6	12.1	0.903/22
United States	59,928	78.5	13.4	0.924/13

Sources: databank.worldbank.org and hdi.undp.org.

[22] For example, Coyle (2014: 93) states that "GDP is not, and was never intended to be, a measure of welfare. It measures production."

[23] The capabilities approach originated with Sen (1989). For a more recent treatment, see Nussbaum (2011).

[24] It is also possible to measure development as the extent to which human needs are addressed through the provision of basic goods and services. The focus on human needs originated with Streeten (1979). For a more recent contribution emphasizing the provision of basic goods and services, see Reinert (2018).

indicating that it is possible to increase life expectancies to high levels at lower levels of GDP per capita. The HDI is an attempt to summarize all these gaps in a relative measure of development.

Reducing the variance in development outcomes is one of the most important challenges faced by policy-makers today. All evidence suggests that it is a challenge that will persist long into the future. Dissecting how the various dimensions of economic globalization contribute to or undermine development is an ongoing, critical area of research. Although a full treatment is beyond the scope of this book, we will definitely touch upon these issues wherever we can.[25]

Larger Realms

Each of our three realms of the world economy considered in this book—trade, production, finance—offers a different view of larger globalization and development processes. Studying each realm offers some important insights into the world economy, but these insights need to be supplemented by examining *other realms* as well. Too much specialization by focusing on one realm to the exclusion of others can be counterproductive. A few other important subjects to keep in mind are culture, the environment, politics, and technology (CEPT). The reality is that processes of international economics are strongly influenced by these CEPT factors. Let us briefly consider each in turn.

Culture has been defined in many different ways. In a discussion of the relationships between culture, globalization, and development, James (2017) defines culture as "the domain of social meaning that grounds human existence" (409), or, more informally, as "how and why we do things around here" (418).[26] We have a tendency to not notice culture until our own cultural norms have been violated in some way. Globalization, including economic integration between countries, is one means by which cultures come into contact with one another. This could be directly through migration or the movement of personnel within MNEs to support production abroad. The contact can also be indirect, through trade in cultural products such as movies and books.

It is popular to depict cultural clashes as inevitable and growing in strength in the form of various "clashes of civilizations." Such claims often reduce human identities to singular versions of what are really *multiple* identities, a process that Sen (2006) refers to as "miniaturization." Along with being multiple, cultural

---

[25] For further discussion, see Goldin and Reinert (2012) and the contributed chapters of Reinert (2017a).

[26] In a more detailed way, James (2017) defines culture as "a social domain that emphasizes the practices, discourses, and material expressions, which, over time, express the continuities and discontinuities of social meaning of a life held-in-common. Culture is thus the making or expression of meaning" (418).

identities can be somewhat fuzzy, and can change over time. Globalization can contribute to the multiple, fuzzy, and changeable nature of culture.[27] Nevertheless, the extent to which cultural conflicts are managed (at the level of international politics or within a single MNE) matters a great deal to the evolution of the world economy. For this reason, we should not discount culture's importance.

The *environment* is the second CEPT realm. The transactions of international economic integration interact in a number of different ways with the natural environment. Production processes that are part of trade and GVCs have environmental impacts. These include resource extraction, pollution, and contributions to greenhouse gasses. Illicit trade transactions impact endangered species and can involve toxic waste dumping. We should not downplay the importance of these issues. For example, increased greenhouse gas emissions impact global climate. This in turn impacts water availability and, thereby, water-intensive production processes of various kinds, both agricultural and industrial.[28] These environmental accompaniments of economic globalization are ongoing and need to be recognized and studied.

The environmental aspects of globalization need to be addressed with appropriate policies. Appropriate policies can be developed at the local, national, regional, and global levels. For our purposes in this book, the global policy responses to environmental issues are the most relevant. Indeed, a common theme related to global environmental issues is the importance of *multilateral* approaches, embodied in what are known as **multilateral environmental agreements** (MEAs).[29] Examples of MEAs include the Convention on International Trade in Endangered Species of Wild Fauna and Flora (CITES), the Montreal Protocol on Substances that Deplete the Ozone Layer (Montreal Protocol), the Kyoto Protocol to the UN Framework Convention on Climate Change (Kyoto Protocol), and the Convention on Biological Diversity (CBD). The hope of many working in this realm is that MEAs will help the world economy avoid the dangers of serious and irreversible environmental harm.

The third CEPT realm is *politics*. In an ideal world, countries would interact with one another within the multilateral framework of international law, committed to dispute resolution procedures, conflict prevention, transparency, and respect for human rights. We do not live in this ideal world: country governments do not always respect international law, and armed, non-state actors exert their own influence across national boundaries. Consequently, political events of all magnitudes continually impact the world economy. Civil and international conflicts dramatically affect the supply sides of national economies, bias government

---

[27] See, for example, Mathews (2000).

[28] For example, Wisser et al. (2010: 6) state: "Water is the principal medium through which the societal stresses of climate change will be manifested. Although the exact impacts remain uncertain, in many places, even where total rainfall increases, climate change will most likely increase rainfall variability." For a manufacturing, business perspective on water, see *The Economist* (2008).

[29] On MEAs, see Runge (2009).

expenditures towards armaments, promote the role of militaries in national governments, and undermine development. These national governments themselves are of various degrees of strength and capability, from effective to very fragile, and even failed. Political instability in struggling states affects all three realms of the world economy, but also impinges directly and negatively on international development.[30] Consequently, the best-intentioned policies in the world of international economic policy can come to naught in our less than ideal political world.[31]

In recent years the political realm has been characterized by a rise of what *The Economist* (2016b) has termed *ethno-nationalism*. The shift to ethno-nationalism is described as being "from the universal, civic-nationalism towards the blood-and-soil ethnic sort. As positive patriotism warps into negative nationalism, solidarity is mutating into mistrust of minorities, who are present in growing numbers." This type of ethno-nationalism was behind the 2016 vote in the United Kingdom to leave the European Union (a move commonly known as Brexit), the vote for Donald Trump as president of the United States that same year, and the vote for Narendra Modi's second term as prime minister of India in 2019. Such political developments are interpreted as a rejection of economic globalization in favor of ethnic identity. Managing this response to globalization, if that is what it really is, will be an important future challenge.

The fourth and final CEPT realm is *technology*. Technology of one kind or another is involved in nearly all human activities. Old economic models conceived of technology as, more or less, dropping from the sky. Newer and more relevant thinking in economics recognizes that the *process* of technological change is more complex than that.[32] We have already discussed the role of container shipping and ICT technology in the development of the modern world economy, and the accompanying box goes more deeply into the subject of ICT. But technology and technological change are part of every production process in both goods and services. They intermediate every transaction making up what we call international economics. They impact the culture, environment, and political realms of CEPT. Inversely, however, the evolution of technology is a political process in itself, with the evolution (or impediments to) technological change being outcomes of elite political processes.[33]

---

[30] This issue is potent enough to have inspired a World Bank *World Development Report* on the subject. See World Bank (2011).

[31] For one example of political considerations in the case of the Middle East, see *The Economist* (2015), which states that "the Middle East...is a valuable corrective to the Panglossian view of globalization" (66).

[32] For example, Singh (2017: 429) states: "Technology and development have come a long way from simplified suppositions about technological progress and diffusion to the complex social, political, institutional, and cultural or knowledge context within which technology is embedded."

[33] This point has been made by Acemoglu and Robinson (2006).

ICT in the World Economy

As a dynamic, driving force for global economic change, technology is central. Indeed, a large part of the globalization process can be attributed to revolutions in information and communication technology. As stated by Heshmati and Lee (2009: 628), ICT "deals with the use of electronics, computers, and computer software to convert, store, protect, process, transmit and retrieve information." There is general consensus that ICT constitutes a technological innovation on the same order of magnitude as past innovations in steam power and electricity. It thereby constitutes a revolutionary change.

It is ICT that has allowed an employee of Philips, the Dutch consumer electronics firm, to use the internet in order to adjust a television assembly line process in the Flextronics factory in Guadalajara, Mexico. It is ICT that has allowed a fund manager in London to quickly buy or sell equities on the Johannesburg stock exchange. Most recently, information and communication technologies in the area of "telepresence" have allowed teleconferencing to move into a new era, in which it appears that participants half a world away are sitting across the table, greatly enhancing global coordination and reducing the need for international travel. There is also speculation that "telerobotics" will become an increasing reality, allowing a person in one country to operate robots in another, in a form of virtual migration.

In the realm of international production, ICT has had the somewhat unusual impact of moving production in two opposing directions: towards greater global integration and towards a selective disintegration or unbundling of production systems. The communication and coordination costs of multinational production have long been a deterrent to FDI, requiring that MNEs possess offsetting advantages before engaging in successful foreign production. Advances in ICT have lowered these costs, contributing to the increased integration of global production systems. Swissair, for example, has set up an accounting subsidiary in Mumbai, India. Since close of business in Switzerland corresponds to morning in Mumbai, this accounting work is done on an overnight basis from the Swiss standpoint. This is an example of services being globalized but remaining *internal* to the firm.

At the same time, however, a second process has been at work. Improvements in ICT have resulted in firms *contracting out* on a global basis functions that they used to carry out in house, a process that has become known as "foreign outsourcing." ICT has substantially reduced the transactions costs of foreign outsourcing. For example, many US firms now contract their software development to Indian firms, notably to Tata Consultancy Services and Tata Unysys Ltd.

ICT in the World Economy (cont.)

In addition, a number of hospitals in the United States now contract with Indian firms for medical transcription services, making use of satellite technology. These are example of services being globalized while being *external* to the firm.

Both the above scenarios, FDI and foreign outsourcing, have been made possible by advances in ICT that are causing a global reconfiguration of the way work is carried out. This is a process that has not yet reached its final destination, but it has already had revolutionary impacts on the world economy, distributing production stages and tasks across the countries of the world in new ways.

Sources: Baldwin (2016), Dicken (2015), *The Economist* (2000; 2007), and Heshmati and Lee (2009).

Here is just one example of how the CEPT realms can be deeply intertwined. I once had the opportunity to talk at length with Dr. Owens Wiwa, the brother of Ken Saro-Wiwa, a member of the Ogani people of the Niger Delta. Dr. Wiwa informed me of his brother's campaign against the environmental damage resulting from oil exploration in the Niger Delta, for which he was eventually executed by the Nigerian government. One particular fact pressed upon me by Dr. Wiwa was that the gas flaring within the region takes place *horizontally* across the ground rather than vertically, as is typical practice. Despite being a handy way to dry laundry, this technology has had severe environmental and health impacts. Today one can view these gas flares on Google Images, and the Niger Delta is nearly in a civil war. Global production of petroleum in its technological aspects has gravely affected the politics, culture, and environment of this particular region of the world economy. Other examples of the way political, cultural, and environmental issues interact are common around the globe.[34]

Analytical Elements

As we begin to examine the three realms of the world economy, we will explicitly or implicitly utilize a number of *analytical elements* to improve our understanding of many complex processes. These are simultaneously actual elements at work in the real world economy and conceptual elements of the various models used by researchers to understand the world economy. We will rely on seven such analytical elements.

[34] The struggle of the Wiwa family is described in Hunt (2006).

1. *Countries.* These are the states of the world economy, their national governments, serving as "home" to both firms and residents.
2. *Sectors.* These are categories of production defined largely in terms of final goods. An example is the automotive sector.
3. *Tasks.* On occasion, we are going to need to recognize that production in a particular sector involves a number of steps or separate tasks. Automobile production moves from a chassis to engine mounting to body mounting, for example.
4. *Firms.* Production in any sector of a country is undertaken by firms, either purely local or MNEs.
5. *Factors of production.* Production in any sector of a country undertaken by a firm makes use of various factors of production. Automobile production uses labor and physical capital.
6. *Currencies.* Most (not all) countries in the world economy have a separate currency in which transactions with other countries take place through foreign exchanges.
7. *Financial assets.* Both countries and firms issue various types of financial assets, denominated in a particular currency, which can be bought to be part of wealth management portfolios by other countries, other firms, and residents of any country.

As you read through this book, keep an eye out for these seven analytical elements and the way we draw upon them in various combinations to better understand the world economy.

Conclusion

It is becoming increasingly difficult for us to ignore the ongoing, important realities of the world economy. Students and professionals of many types are finding that a basic understanding of international economics is necessary for them to operate successfully. A thorough understanding of the world economy involves the study of three realms of international economics: international trade, international production, and international finance. These are the three aspects of the world economy that we explore in this book.

International trade is increasing more rapidly than global production. International production, meanwhile, is taking on more and more complex forms, involving both contractual arrangements and foreign direct investment deployed along GVCs. FDI is undertaken by multinational enterprises, and these organizations play a critical role in the world economy. Nevertheless, as we have seen, viewing the world economy in its trade and production aspects is also incomplete. The realm of international finance is paramount, with foreign exchange transactions dwarfing trade transactions.

It is hoped that international trade, international production, and international finance will contribute positively to international development, improving welfare and living standards. Understanding how this occurs (or does not occur) will be touched upon where appropriate throughout the book in a consideration of the links between the processes of globalization and the processes of development.

These three aspects of the world economy–trade, production, and finance–must be seen as connected. Further, these three realms are strongly affected by and affect the larger factors of culture, the environment, politics, and technology (CEPT). The task of understanding how all these realms evolve over time in a system of globalization is not, to say the least, an easy one. Indeed, it takes us far beyond the scope of this book. With persistence and some patience, however, you will begin to build an intellectual foundation for understanding this system in the remaining chapters.

Review Exercises

1. Why are you interested in international economics? What is motivating you? How are your interests, major, or profession affected by the world economy?
2. What are the three realms of the world economy addressed in this book? Define each of them *carefully*.
3. What is the difference between *trade in goods* and *trade in services*?
4. What is the difference between *international trade* and *foreign direct investment*?
5. What is the difference between *international trade* and *international finance*?
6. Identify one way in which the activities of international trade, finance, and production could *positively* contribute to international development. Identify one way in which these activities could *negatively* contribute to international development. How could you demonstrate that the activities have either a positive or negative impact on development?
7. Take a look at the websites of major venues of the global business/financial press, such as *The Economist* and the *Financial Times*. Spend a little time browsing.

FURTHER READING AND WEB RESOURCES

Osterhammel and Petersson (2005) present a concise history of globalization accessible to a broad audience. Dicken (2015) and Dunning and Lundan (2008) look at foreign direct investment in recent decades, and Prahalad and Lieberthal (2008) provide a short, interesting assessment of FDI in developing countries. On international trade, see Hoekman and Kostecki (2009). Eichengreen (2008) gives an excellent history of international finance, and the *Financial Times* (2008) takes a brief look at its recent failure. Goldin and Reinert

(2012) and the chapters of Reinert (2017a) examine the relationship of a number of aspects of globalization to development and poverty alleviation. A review of globalization effects is also provided by *The Economist* (2016a; 2017b). Sen (2006) effectively addresses cultural issues in a global perspective, and Speth and Haas (2006) address global environmental issues. Szirmai (2015) provides a comprehensive consideration of economic and social development. Finally, Reinert et al. (2009) have edited a comprehensive encyclopedia of the world economy directly relevant to the three realms of the world economy examined here.

The Peterson Institute for International Economics in Washington, DC, provides timely and readable analyses of many issues in international economics. Its website is www.piie.com. Two high-quality sources on international economic issues are *The Economist* and the *Financial Times*. Their websites are www.economist.com and www.ft.com. Important institutions of the world economy include the World Trade Organization (www.wto.org), the World Bank (www.worldbank.org), the International Monetary Fund (www.imf.org), the Organisation for Economic Co-operation and Development (www.oecd.org), and the International Organization for Migration (www.iom.int).

REFERENCES

Acemoglu, D., and J. A. Robinson (2006) "Economic Backwardness in Political Perspective," *American Political Science Review*, 100:1, 115–31.

Anyanwu, J. C. (2017) "Foreign Direct Investment," in K. A. Reinert (ed.), *Handbook of Globalisation and Development*, Edward Elgar, 131–52.

Ayres, J. (2004) "Framing Collective Action against Neoliberalism: The Case of the Anti-Globalization Movement," *Journal of World Systems Research*, 10:1, 11–34.

Baldwin, R. (2016) *The Great Convergence: Information Technology and the New Globalization*, Harvard University Press.

Bernhofen, D. M., Z. El-Sahli, and R. Kneller (2016) "Estimating the Effects of the Container Revolution on World Trade," *Journal of International Economics*, 98, 36–50.

Chanda, R. (2017) "Trade in Services," in K. A. Reinert (ed.), *Handbook of Globalisation and Development*, Edward Elgar, 36–58.

Coyle, D. (2014) *GDP: A Brief but Affectionate History*, Princeton University Press.

Dicken, P. (2015) *Global Shift: Mapping the Changing Contours of the World Economy*, Guilford.

Dunkley, G. (2016) *One World Mania: A Critical Guide to Free Trade, Financialization and Over-Globalization*, Zed Books.

Dunning, J. H., and S. M. Lundan (2008) *Multinational Enterprises and the Global Economy*, Edward Elgar.

The Economist (2000) "Have Factory, Will Travel," February 12.

The Economist (2007) "Behold, Telepresence," August 24.

The Economist (2008) "Business and Water: Running Dry," August 21.

The Economist (2013) "The Humble Hero," May 18.

The Economist (2014) "Boxing Clever: High-Tech Shipping Containers," March 1.

The Economist (2015) "Beware of Sandstorms," June 20.

The Economist (2016a) "An Open and Shut Case: Special Report on the World Economy," October 1.

The Economist (2016b) "League of Nationalists," November 19.

The Economist (2017a) "Surplus War," February 11.
The Economist (2017b) "Briefing: Left-Behind Places," October 21.
The Economist (2019) "Global Supply Chains," July 13.
Eichengreen, B. (2008) *Globalizing Capital: A History of the International Monetary System*, Princeton University Press.
Financial Times (2008) "The Year the God of Finance Failed," 26 December.
Feenstra, R. C., and J. B. Jensen (2009) "Outsourcing/Offshoring," in K. A. Reinert, R. S. Rajan, A. J. Glass, and L. S. Davis (eds.), *The Princeton Encyclopedia of the World Economy*, Princeton University Press, 881–7.
Francois, J. F., and B. Hoekman (2010) "Services Trade and Policy," *Journal of Economic Literature*, 48:3, 642–92.
Goldin, I., and K. A. Reinert (2012) *Globalization for Development: Meeting New Challenges*, Oxford University Press.
Gupta, P. (2017) "Global Production Networks," in K. A. Reinert (ed.), *Handbook of Globalisation and Development*, Edward Elgar, 153–68.
Heshmati, A., and M. Lee (2009) "Information and Communication Technology," in K. A. Reinert, R. S. Rajan, A. J. Glass, and L. S. Davis (eds.), *The Princeton Encyclopedia of the World Economy*, Princeton University Press, 628–35.
Hoekman, B. M., and M. Kostecki (2009) *The Political Economy of the World Trading System*, Oxford University Press.
Hunt, J. T. (2006) *The Politics of Bones*, McClelland & Stewart.
James, P. (2017) "Culture," in K. A. Reinert (ed.), *Handbook of Globalisation and Development*, Edward Elgar, 409–25.
Levinson, M. (2006) *The Box: How the Shipping Container Made the World Smaller and the World Economy Bigger*, Princeton University Press.
Lodefalk, M. (2015) "Servicification of Manufacturing Firms Makes Divides in Trade Policy-Making Antiquated," Working Paper 2015:1, Örebro University School of Business.
Lucas, R. (1990) "Why Doesn't Capital Flow from Rich to Poor Countries?" *American Economic Review*, 80:2, 92–6.
Mathews, G. (2000) *Global Culture/Individual Identity: Searching for Home in the Cultural Supermarket*, Routledge.
McIvor, R. (2005) *The Outsourcing Process: Strategies for Evaluation and Management*, Cambridge University Press.
Nussbaum, M. (2011) *Creating Capabilities: The Human Development Approach*, Belknap Press
Omelaniuk, I. (2017) "Migration," in K. A. Reinert (ed.), *Handbook of Globalisation and Development*, Edward Elgar, 289–311.
Osterhammel, J., and N. P. Petersson (2005) *Globalization: A Short History*, Princeton University Press.
Ostry, J. D., P. Loungani, and D. Fuceri (2016) "Neoliberalism: Oversold?" *Finance and Development*, 53:2, 38–41.
Prahalad, C. K., and K. Liberthal (2008) *The End of Corporate Imperialism*, Harvard Business Press.
Pritchett, L. (2006) *Let Their People Come: Breaking the Gridlock on Global Labor Mobility*, Center for Global Development.

Reinert, K. A. (ed.) (2017a) *Handbook of Globalisation and Development*, Edward Elgar.

Reinert, K. A. (2017b) "Trade in Goods," in K. A. Reinert (ed.), *Handbook of Globalisation and Development*, Edward Elgar, 19–35.

Reinert, K. A. (2018) *No Small Hope: Towards the Universal Provision of Basic Goods*, Oxford University Press.

Reinert, K. A., R. S. Rajan, A. J. Glass, and L. S. Davis (eds.) (2009) *The Princeton Encyclopedia of the World Economy*, Princeton University Press.

Runge, C. F. (2009) "Multilateral Environmental Agreements," in K. A. Reinert, R. S. Rajan, A. J. Glass, and L. S. Davis (eds.), *The Princeton Encyclopedia of the World Economy*, Princeton University Press, 795–9.

Sen, A. (1989) "Development as Capability Expansion," *Journal of Development Planning*, 19, 41–58.

Sen, A. (2006) *Identity and Violence: The Illusion of Destiny*, Norton.

Singh, J. P. (2017) "Technology," in K. A. Reinert (ed.), *Handbook of Globalisation and Development*, Edward Elgar, 426–43.

Speth, J. G., and P. M. Haas (2006) *Global Environmental Governance*, Island Press.

Streeten, P. (1979) "Basic Needs: Premises and Promises," *Journal of Policy Modeling*, 1:1, 136–46.

Szirmai, A. (2015) *Socio-Economic Development*, Cambridge University Press.

Wisser, D., S. Frolking, E. M. Douglas, B. M. Fekete, A. H. Schumann, and C. J. Vörösmarty (2010) "The Significance of Local Water Resources Captured in Small Reservoirs for Crop Production: A Global Scale Analysis," *Journal of Hydrology*, 384:3/4, 264–75.

Wolf, M. (2004) *Why Globalization Works*, Yale University Press.

World Bank (2011) *World Development Report 2011: Conflict, Security and Development*, World Bank.

Zhao, S. (2010) "The China Model: Can It Replace the Western Model of Modernization?" *Journal of Contemporary China*, 19:65, 419–36.

PART I
International Trade

2 Absolute Advantage

Throughout most of the 1980s Vietnam imported rice. In 1989, however, Vietnam *exported* more than 1 million tons of rice. In the 1990s its annual rice exports increased to more than 3 million tons, and Vietnam's rice exports have continued to climb over the years, to about 8 million tons exported to over 100 countries. Despite being the staple consumption crop in Vietnam, the expansion of rice exports helped to alleviate poverty in that country through increased employment and wage income. This beneficial increase in rice exports represents one important aspect of Vietnam's entry into the world economy through the process of trade expansion that we discussed in Chapter 1.[1]

We stated in Chapter 1 that international trade in goods and services plays an important role in the world economy as one of the main features of globalization. We also stated that we are going to explore the factors underlying international trade in Part I of this book. It is time for us to begin this process in order to understand why a country exports or imports a particular good or service. Historically, the initial explanation for patterns of trade lay with the concept of **absolute advantage**. Subsequently, this concept was replaced with the more powerful concept of **comparative advantage**. In this chapter, you will be introduced to the absolute advantage concept, and we will take up comparative advantage in Chapters 3 and 4. In all three of these chapters you will also become familiar with one of the most fundamental principles of economics, namely the **gains from trade**.

There are two main explanations of comparative advantage. The first of these is known as the **Ricardian model**, after David Ricardo. It explores the means by which comparative advantage can be determined by differences in *technology* between the countries of the world, and is the subject of Chapter 3. The second is known as the Heckscher–Ohlin model, after Eli Heckscher and Bertil Ohlin. It explores the means by which comparative advantage can be determined by differences in *resource endowments* between the countries of the world. It is the subject of Chapter 4. As we will see, absolute advantage is more closely related to the Ricardian model of comparative advantage.

---

[1] See Goldin and Reinert (2012: chap. 3), Heo and Doanh (2009), and Bui and Chen (2017).

Let us begin our discussion of absolute advantage using Vietnam's rice exports as an example. In doing so, we also begin a consideration of what international economists call "trade theory."

Defining Absolute Advantage

The idea of absolute advantage was first presented in Adam Smith's *The Wealth of Nations*, published in 1776. We are used to interpreting *The Wealth of Nations* as a work advocating a free-market system, and this is largely the case. But Smith had another underlying purpose for his book, namely to discredit a preceding economic philosophy known as *mercantilism*. Mercantilism was a sort of zero-sum economic philosophy in which wealth was characterized as being equivalent to stocks of precious metals, usually held in royal treasuries.[2] Smith's larger purpose in his famous book was to dispute this notion in as many ways as possible, substituting a concept of wealth as the broad-based consumption of goods and services. His idea of absolute advantage was just one means of doing this, by showing the possibility of international trade being mutually beneficial rather than zero-sum.

In his famous book, Adam Smith states the following (1937 [1776]: 424): "If a foreign country can supply us with a commodity cheaper than we ourselves can make it, better buy it of them with some part of the produce of our own industry, employed in a way in which we have some advantage." In other words, a pattern of absolute advantage implies a potential pattern of trade. In modern terminology, absolute advantage refers to a country's ability to produce a good or service with fewer real resources or inputs than another country. This can also be looked at as the inverse, namely the country's ability to produce more of a good or service with the same real resources or inputs than another country.[3]

Let us formalize this a bit. Suppose that we have just one resource, *labor*. Obviously, there must be other resources as well, but we are *simplifying* here to develop our first model in international economics. The amount of labor used to produce a unit of rice will be denoted by the symbol a_R.[4] Rice is produced in many countries, but, to simplify, suppose we consider only two countries, Vietnam and Japan. The amount of labor used to produce a unit of rice in Vietnam will be a_R^V, and the amount of labor used to produce a unit of rice in Japan will be a_R^J. The principle of absolute advantage is fairly straightforward. It says that, if $a_R^V < a_R^J$, then Vietnam has an

---

[2] See, for example, Heckscher (1967).

[3] See van Marrewijk (2009).

[4] In your introductory microeconomics class, you might have been introduced to the concept of a *production function*. If the amount of labor used to produce a unit of rice is a_R, then the production function for rice is $Q = \frac{1}{a_R} L$, where Q is output and L is the labor input.

absolute advantage in the production of rice relative to Japan. Then, as suggested by Adam Smith, Vietnam should export rice to Japan, and Japan should import rice from Vietnam. Another example of absolute advantage in industrial robots is given in the box.

Robot Kingdom: Japan's Advantage in Industrial Robots

The word "robot" first appeared in 1921 in a Czech play written by Karel Čapek, based on the Czech word "robota," meaning "drudgery." The world's first industrial robot was built in the United States by the industrialist Joseph Engelberger, who founded the company Unimation in 1956 and installed the first industrial robot in 1961. Engelberger had a moment of fame in 1966 when one of his robots appeared on Johnny Carson's *Tonight Show*, opening and pouring a can of beer. In 1967 Engelberger was invited to Japan and addressed 600 Japanese scientists and business executives. As a result, Japan imported its first industrial robots from the United States. In 1969 robot production began in Japan under a licensing agreement with Unimation, and in 1972 the Japan Robot Association was founded. This was the beginning of Japan's involvement with what has been called "the most important manufacturing innovations of recent times" (Mansfield, 1989: 19).

Japan's first exports of industrial robots began in 1975. Thereafter, exports grew slowly but steadily. By the end of the 1980s Japan became the leader in most areas of the robotics industry, such as numerical controllers, machine tools, motors, and optical sensors. It accounted for one-half of the world production of industrial robots. The technological nature of Japan's advantage in robot production was captured by Porter (1990: 235): "The pace of innovation and new product introduction among the Japanese firms was feverish. Product innovations were soon imitated or upstaged by other producers." Along with faster innovation times, Japanese firms benefited from lower innovation costs and a cultivated, cultural acceptance of robots.

Accompanying and contributing to Japan's technological lead in industrial robots was the degree of competition in the Japanese industrial robot industry. With fewer than ten firms in 1968, the industry expanded to nearly 300 firms by 1987 and declined to approximately 150 firms in 2000. Another important factor has been *intra-firm diffusion*, when firms requiring the use of robots (such as the electronic equipment industry) begin producing robots for their own use. A final factor pushing the use of robots in Japan has been the presence of significant labor shortages in many areas; robots replaced humans where these shortages appeared. As of 1997 Japan used one robot for every 36 manufacturing

Robot Kingdom: Japan's Advantage in Industrial Robots (cont.)

employees, whereas the United States used only one robot for every 250 manufacturing employees. Currently, one-half of the world's industrial robots are installed in Japan, and Japan has been referred to as the "Robot Kingdom."

Despite these long-term positive factors, the Japan Robot Association (2001) has pointed to some weaknesses. The industry has had difficulty moving out of large industrial applications into biotech, medical, and consumer applications, as well as leveraging venture capital. In contrast to past models of technological innovation characterizing Japan, the Japan Robot Association called for a focus on small business and greater openness. This, it was hoped, would position the industry for a different set of robotic applications with promising future growth prospects.

Sources: The Economist (1980), Horiuchi (1989), Mansfield (1989), Porter (1990), Schodt (1988), Tanzer and Simon (1990), and Japan Robot Association (2001).

It is important to remember that the principle of absolute advantage is a *policy suggestion* that countries should import goods from other countries where they are produced more efficiently. These countries should then deploy scarce resources to produce goods that they can produce more efficiently.[5] It is also important to remember that the pattern of trade implied by absolute advantage is one determined by *technological* considerations. As it turns out, however, patterns of absolute advantage are neither necessary nor sufficient conditions for countries to either export or import a good or service. Actual patterns of trade are determined by comparative advantage, the subject of Chapters 3 and 4.

Despite the limited applicability of the absolute advantage model, it is useful to take it one step further and apply it within the standard supply and demand model of introductory microeconomics.[6] Let us do this next.

Absolute Advantage in Supply and Demand

To begin considering absolute advantage in the supply and demand model, let us first remind ourselves what the absolute advantage concept says. It says that, if $a_R^V < a_R^J$, then Vietnam has an absolute advantage in the production of rice relative to Japan. Recall that our symbol letter a_R refers to the amount of labor used to

[5] Again, see van Marrewijk (2009).

[6] If you need a review of the supply and demand model, please see Appendix 2.1.

produce a unit of rice. Thinking about this, would you characterize the absolute advantage idea as being based on the supply side or the demand side of economies? The correct answer is *supply side*. This will also be the case for the idea of comparative advantage. Indeed, most (not all) of the explanations of international trade focus on the supply sides of economies.

Given that we will focus on the supply side here, it makes sense to *simplify* the demand side. We do this for our case of Vietnam and Japan. More specifically, we will assume that *demand conditions are exactly the same in both countries*—that is, there are no differences in preferences, incomes, or the way demand responds to price changes in Vietnam and Japan. This implies that the demand curves for rice in the two countries are exactly the same as illustrated in Figure 2.1. Making this assumption will simplify things for us, but will not alter the explanation of absolute advantage.

The pattern of absolute advantage that we are considering here suggests that Vietnam has better technology in producing rice than Japan, in the sense that it uses less labor per unit of output than Japan. Let us put aside for the moment whether this is *actually* the case to consider the *implications* on the supply side of the Vietnamese and Japanese rice markets. You know from your microeconomics course that changes in technology *shift* supply curves (see also Appendix 2.1). Therefore, we will allow supply conditions for rice to differ between Vietnam and Japan and set different supply curves for the two countries. In particular, we will assume that the supply curve for Vietnam is farther to the right than the supply curve for Japan. This means that, at every price, Vietnam's quantity supplied is greater than that of Japan.

This situation is depicted in Figure 2.2. The upward-sloping supply curves reflect the positive relationship between price and quantity supplied. The difference in supply conditions positions Vietnam's supply curve farther to the right than Japan's supply curve. The intersections of the supply and demand curves determine the *equilibrium prices* of rice in the two markets. The two prices are recorded

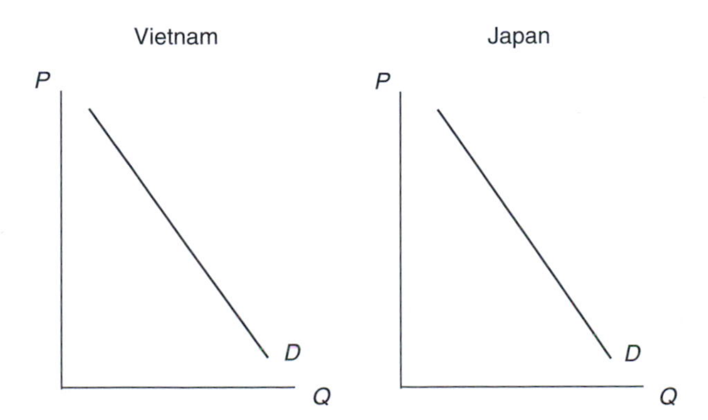

Figure 2.1 Demand for rice in Vietnam and Japan

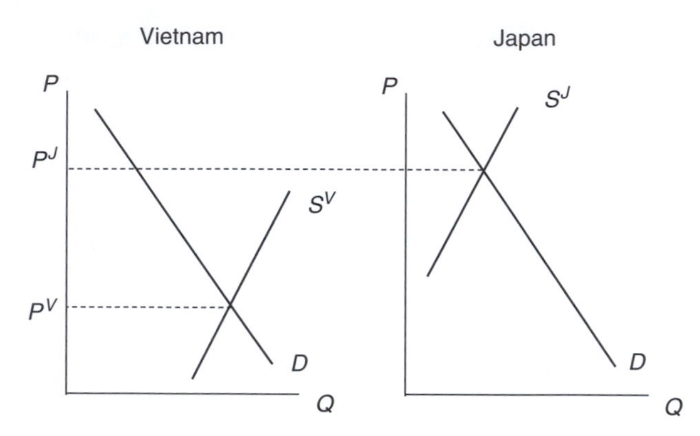

Figure 2.2 Absolute advantage in the rice market

as P^V and P^J in the figure. Since no trade is involved, these two prices are known in international economics as **autarky** prices. Autarky is a situation in which a country has no economic relationships with other countries. The autarky prices are an expression of the pattern of absolute advantage between the two countries.

Figure 2.2 depicts a situation in which the autarky price of rice is lower in Vietnam than in Japan; that is:

$$P^V < P^J \tag{2.1}$$

In international trade theory, this situation is interpreted as reflecting the fact that Vietnam has an **absolute advantage** in the production of rice vis-à-vis Japan, namely the fact that $a_R^V < a_R^J$. As we will see, the presence of absolute advantage can make international trade a possibility.

If Japan and Vietnam choose to abandon autarky and begin to trade, the world price of rice P^W will be somewhere *between* the two autarky prices, as follows:

$$P^V < P^W < P^J \tag{2.2}$$

This situation is depicted in Figure 2.3. In the movement from autarky to trade, Vietnam experiences an increase in the price of rice to the world level (from P^V to P^W). Quantity supplied will increase, while quantity demanded will decrease. The amount by which quantity supplied exceeds quantity demanded in Vietnam at P^W constitutes its *exports* of rice, E^V. Japan experiences a decrease in the price of rice to the world level (from P^J to P^W). Here, quantity supplied will decrease, while quantity demanded will increase. The amount by which quantity demanded exceeds quantity supplied in Japan at P^W constitutes its *imports* of rice, Z^J.[7] The country that has an absolute advantage (Vietnam) expands its quantity supplied

[7] We use a " Z" to denote imports throughout this book. Why Z? As we will see, "I" is used in economics to denote investment, and "M" is used to denote money. Therefore, we cannot use either of the first two letters of the word "imports."

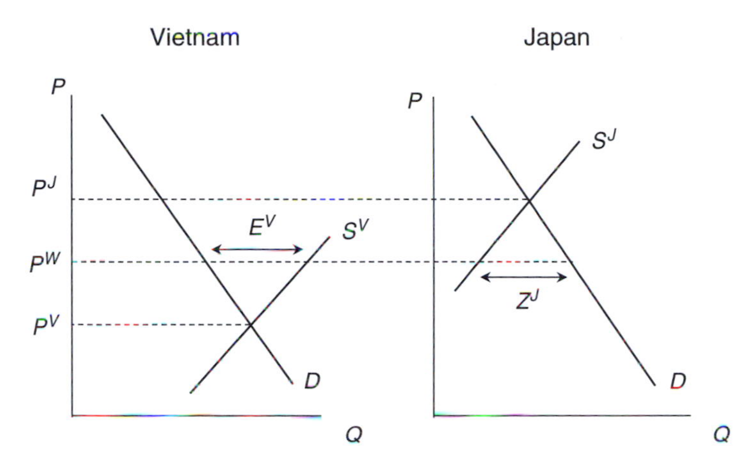

Figure 2.3 Trade in the rice market

and exports the good in question, while the trading partner (Japan) contracts its quantity supplied and imports the good.

As we have just seen, the technological differences between Vietnam and Japan, as expressed in absolute advantage, generate a pattern of trade. Vietnam tends to export rice, while Japan tends to import rice. But a question that often arises in students' minds is: what ensures that the amount exported by Vietnam is the same as the amount imported by Japan? The answer is that, if E^V were smaller than Z^J, there would be excess demand or a shortage in the world market for rice. As we know from introductory microeconomics, excess demand causes the price to rise. As P^W rose, exports by Vietnam would increase and imports into Japan would decrease, until the excess demand in the world market disappeared. Similarly, if E^V were larger than Z^J, P^W would fall to bring the world market back into equilibrium.

Absolute advantages can be found across many countries and products, both goods and services. For the peculiar case of rare earth elements, please see the accompanying box.

Rare Earth Elements

Rare earth elements, or REEs, consist of 17 elements of the periodic table. REEs are key components in some of the information and communication technologies discussed in Chapter 1 as drivers of globalization. These include liquid crystal displays, fiber optic cables, communication system magnets, wind turbines, solar panels, and rechargeable batteries used in hybrid cars. REEs are not actually rare, however. Some of them, for example, are much more common than gold. Despite this abundance, REEs are not usually concentrated enough for commercial mining, and there are consequently only a few sources.

Rare Earth Elements (cont.)

From 1965 to 1980 most REEs came from the Mountain Pass mine in the Mojave Desert in the United States. Beginning in 1985 advantage switched to the Inner Mongolia region of China. *The Economist* (2009) notes that the then Communist Party leader, Deng Xiaoping, "declaring rare earths to be the oil of China, encouraged the development of mines in the mid-1980s. Prices fell dramatically and existing mines in America were priced out of business." Subsequently, China supplied approximately 70 percent of the global market for REEs (down from 90 percent), and the Mountain Pass mine closed in 2002. For this reason, China was often described as a "monopoly" supplier of REEs.

Global exports of REEs increased from a few hundred metric tons in 1990 to over 100,000 metric tons in 2004. But, as China's own demand for REEs has grown, concern has arisen about the security of supplies. *The Economist* (2009) reports: "Sales of [REEs] add up to less than $2 billion each year. But without them, industries worth trillions of dollars would grind to a halt." In response to this situation, there has even been talk in the Chinese government about a ban of exports of some important REEs. By 2014 global exports had fallen to about 80,000 metric tons. Consequently, attention turned to alternative supply possibilities with Western Australia, North America (Alaska and Quebec), and South Africa.

China began to restrict REE exports in 2007. In 2010 REEs became part of a dispute between Japan and China over the Senkaku (Japanese) or Diaoyu (Chinese) Islands in the East China Sea, which are claimed by both countries. China barred exports of REEs to Japan as a result, and REE prices increased significantly. As a consequence, other countries began to export REEs along with China, the result of new mining projects coming into production.

In 2012 the United States, the European Union, and Japan lodged a complaint with the World Trade Organization regarding China's export restriction on REEs. In 2014 the WTO's dispute settlement mechanism (DSM) largely found against China, and China began a process of bringing its REE policies into conformity with the WTO's finding. But REEs remain a critical and sensitive trade link in global value chains of many kinds.

Just how sensitive REEs were became apparent again in 2019, when China again began to talk about restricting supply as part of a nascent trade war with the United States. China's *Global Times* reported that China was "gearing up to use rare-earth advantage." By this time, however, the Mountain Pass mine in the United States had reopened, and Japan has contracted with an Australian mining company to help meet one-third of its REE demand. As is often the case, there are limits to monopoly power that can emerge over time.

Sources: Bradsher (2010), *The Economist* (2009; 2019), Mancheri (2015), and United States Geological Survey (2002).

Gains from Trade

Up to this point we have seen that, given a pattern of absolute advantage, it is possible for a country to give up autarky in favor of importing or exporting. Japan can import rice, and Vietnam can export rice. The idea of absolute advantage suggests that countries *should* do this. Can the supply and demand model shed light on this? We can tentatively answer this question by examining Figure 2.3 from the standard economic point of view using **consumer surplus** and **producer surplus**. This is done in Figure 2.4. If you do not recall the consumer surplus and producer surplus concepts from your introductory microeconomics course, please consult Appendix 2.1.

Let us first consider Vietnam. In its movement from autarky to exporting in the rice market, producers experience both an increase in price and an increase in quantity supplied along the supply curve. This should be good for producers, and you can see in Figure 2.4 that there has been an increase in producer surplus of area $A + B$. Consumers, on the other hand, experience an increase in price and a decrease in quantity demanded along the demand curve. This should harm them, and you can see in Figure 2.4 that there has been a decrease in consumer surplus of area A.

What do these effects mean for Vietnam? Producers have gained area $A + B$, while consumers have lost area A. The gain to producers exceeds the loss to consumers. For the economy as a whole, then, there is a *net welfare increase* of area B. Vietnam gains from its entry into the world economy as an exporter.[8]

Next, consider Japan. In its movement from autarky to importing in the rice market, producers experience a decrease in price and a decrease in quantity

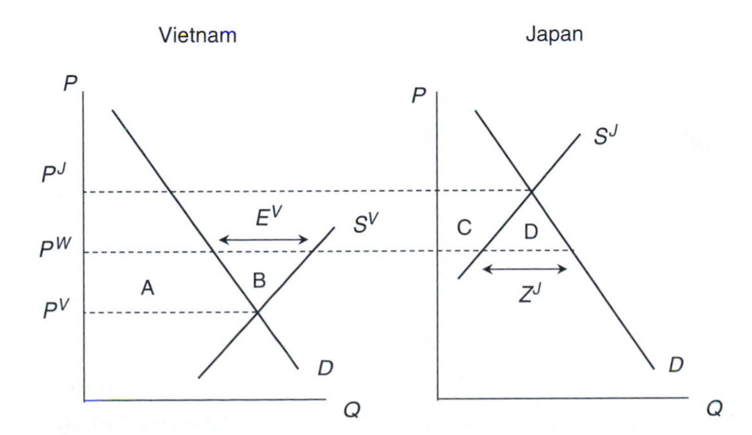

Figure 2.4 Gains from trade in the rice market

[8] Area A can be viewed as a transfer from consumers to producers in Vietnam.

supplied along the supply curve. This should harm these producers, and you can see in Figure 2.4 that there has been a decrease in producer surplus of area C. Consumers, on the other hand, experience a decrease in price and an increase in quantity demanded. These contribute to an increase in consumer surplus of area $C + D$.

What do these effects mean for Japan? Consumers have gained $C + D$, while producers have lost area C. The gain to consumers exceeds the loss to producers. For the economy as a whole, then, there is a net welfare increase of area D. Japan gains from its entry into the world economy as an importer.[9]

You can see from the above that moving from autarky to either importing or exporting based on absolute advantage involves a net increase in welfare for the country involved. This net increase in welfare is known as the **gains from trade**. Not only is it *possible* for a country to give up autarky in favor of importing or exporting but it *makes sense* to do so in most instances from the standpoint of overall welfare. Adam Smith's policy suggestion merits serious attention.

The notion of gains from trade is an important concept. To judge from the tone and content of many popular writings on the world economy, trade relationships are a win-lose proposition for the countries involved. To export is to win; to import is to lose. This is a neo-mercantilist idea that has recently gained traction among the ethno-nationalist political movements mentioned in Chapter 1.[10] The gains from trade idea tells us that trade can be *mutually beneficial* to the countries involved, however. For this reason, you need to be cautious in your assessment of some popular writing of the win-lose, neo-mercantilist variety. Although there are indeed instances in which trade can be a win-lose proposition, this is definitely not the general case.[11]

Limitations

The notion of absolute advantage, first suggested by Smith in his *The Wealth of Nations*, is useful for understanding international trade, both as a principle and in the context of the familiar supply and demand framework. It is also useful to understand that trade can improve overall welfare for the countries involved. The

---

[9] Area C can be viewed as a transfer from producers to consumers in Japan.

[10] See, for example, *The Economist* (2016), which observes: "From Warsaw to Washington, the political divide that matters is less and less between left and right, and more and more between open and closed" (16).

[11] This point was emphasized some time ago by Krugman (1996). Krugman states: "The conflict among nations that so many policy intellectuals imagine prevails is an illusion; but it is an illusion that can destroy the reality of mutual gains from trade" (84).

absolute advantage concept has its limits, however. In particular, it suggests the possibility that a country might not have an absolute advantage in *anything*, and therefore would have nothing to export at all. This, it turns out, is unlikely. We will begin to understand why this is so as we consider **comparative advantage** in Chapters 3 and 4.

The notion of the gains from trade also has its limits. It correctly suggests that countries *as a whole* can mutually gain from trade. It does not suggest, however, that *everyone within* a country will gain from trade. As you have already understood in the example of this chapter, producers of rice in Japan lose from trade, and consumers of rice in Vietnam lose from trade. Further, however, the absolute advantage principle and the notion of gains from trade do not apply to *all kinds of trade*. International trade takes place in a number of goods and services that we can in no way see as contributing to human welfare, such as arms, heroin, and prostitution services.[12] Some of this trade takes place via what is known as **illicit trade**, a subject taken up in the accompanying box.

Illicit Trade

The Organisation for Economic Co-operation and Development states: "Illicit trade involves goods and services that are deemed illegal as they threaten communities and societies as a whole." Such trade can take place in a wide variety of products, including illegal drugs, tobacco products, counterfeit brands, counterfeit pharmaceuticals, digital media, antiquities, oil, water, timber, wildlife, weapons, and child pornography. Illicit trade can even take place in human beings, an activity known as human trafficking. Because of its criminal nature, and because it can be a source of illegal funds, illicit trade has been identified as a contributor to armed conflict, weapons proliferation (including weapons of mass destruction: WMDs), environmental degradation of various kinds, and compromised health and safety. Some kinds of illicit trade are enabled by advances in information and communication technology, including via the "dark web."

There is an important political economy of illicit trade. As noted by a leading researcher on the subject:

> Illicit trade often flourishes because it is not bad for everyone. There are winners as well as losers. Governments and their corrupt high-level officials may be beneficiaries and facilitators of this illicit trade. Trade-based money-laundering allows kleptocrats and elites to move money out of the country. Non-state actors,

[12] This point has been made by Reinert (2004).

Illicit Trade (cont.)

as well as legitimate business people, may also benefit from illicit trade, both intentionally engaging with smugglers to advance their financial interests (Shelley, 2017: 101)

With such incentives, illicit trade flourishes.

Of interest to trade policy researchers, criminologists, national security professions, environmentalists, and many others, illicit trade is of growing importance in the world economy. Addressing it through appropriate policies and smart criminal investigations is therefore also of growing importance. More broadly, recognizing that not all economic globalization is sweetness and light is the intellectually honest position for both researchers and policy-makers.

Sources: OECD (2018), *The Economist* (2014), Reinert (2017), and Shelley (2017).

Conclusion

Autarky refers to a situation in which a country does not engage in either imports or exports. It is a rare situation. More commonly, countries engage in both importing and exporting relationships with other countries of the world economy. In this chapter, you have begun to understand why. In particular, we have discussed Adam Smith's notion of absolute advantage, which reflects differences between countries in technology. A country with better technology, in the sense that it uses fewer resources per unit of output, has an absolute advantage in the production of that item. In a policy suggestion, Smith said it should therefore export that item and import items in which it does not have an absolute advantage.

Deploying the idea of absolute advantage in our supply and demand model illustrates Smith's policy suggestion. It also suggests that there are potential *mutual gains from trade* in which the overall welfare of the countries involved increases. This is in contrast to mercantilist thinking, which Smith sought to overturn and which has reappeared in current ethno-nationalist thinking.

The notion of absolute advantage has its limits. First, it suggests that a country might not have anything to export at all. This, as we will see in Chapters 3 and 4 on comparative advantage, is an unlikely outcome. Second, it does not suggest that all persons in a country will gain from trade. Within any country, there can be both winners and losers from international trade, a subject we will turn to in Chapter 6 on the political economy of trade.

Review Exercises

1. Use Figure 2.5 in Appendix 2.1 to consider the following changes: a fall in incomes because of a recession; an increased preference for rice consumption; an increase in input prices for rice production; and an improvement in rice production technology. Use diagrams to analyze the effects of these changes on equilibrium price and quantity.
2. Create an example of an absolute advantage model by choosing two countries and a single product.
   a. Draw a supply and demand diagram describing *autarky* and a *pattern of absolute advantage* for your example.
   b. Show the transition from autarky to trade in your diagram, label the trade flows, and demonstrate the *gains from trade*.
   c. In a new diagram, and starting from a trading equilibrium, show what would happen to the world price if *income increased* by exactly the same, small amount in both countries.
3. Can you recall from introductory microeconomics the notions of the price elasticity of demand and price elasticity of supply? If so, can you say what would happen to the gains from trade as supply *and* demand in Vietnam *and* Japan become more and more *inelastic*?

FURTHER READING AND WEB RESOURCES

The idea of absolute advantage was first discussed in Chapter II, Book IV, of Smith (1937 [1776]). This book is available in the nonfiction section of www.bibliomania.com. A historical discussion of Smith's theory can be found in Myint (1977). A much more recent overview can be found in van Marrewijk (2009). A blog about global rice trade can be found at rice-trade.blogspot.com.

REFERENCES

Bradsher, K. (2010) "Amid Tension, China Blocks Crucial Exports to Japan," *New York Times*, September 22.

Bui, T. H. H., and Q. Chen (2017) "An Analysis of Factors Influencing Rice Export in Vietnam Based on Gravity Model," *Journal of the Knowledge Economy*, 8:3, 830–44.

The Economist (1980) "Robots," October 17.

The Economist (2009) "The Hunt for Rare Earths," October 8.

The Economist (2014) "Uncontained: Trade and Money Laundering," May 3.

The Economist (2016) "Briefing: Globalisation and Politics," July 30.

The Economist (2019) "Rare Earths: Magnetic Attraction," June 15.

Goldin, I., and K. A. Reinert (2012) *Globalization for Development: Meeting New Challenges*, Oxford University Press.

Heckscher, E. (1967) "Mercantilism," in E. R. A. Seligman and A. S. Johnson (eds.), *Encyclopaedia of the Social Sciences*, vol. 9, Macmillan, 333–9.

Heo, Y., and N. K. Doanh (2009) "Trade Liberalization and Poverty Reduction in Vietnam," *World Economy*, 32:6, 934–64.

Horiuchi, T. (1989) "Development Process of Robot Industries in Japan," *Rivista Internazionale di Scienze Economiche e Commerciali*, 36:12, 1089–108.

Japan Robot Association (2001) *Summary Report on Technology Strategy for Creating a Robot Society in the 21st Century*, Japan Robot Association.

Krugman, P. (1996) "The Illusion of Conflict in International Trade," in P. Krugman, *Pop Internationalism*, MIT Press, 69–84.

Mancheri, N. A. (2015) "World Trade in Rare Earths, Chinese Export Restrictions, and Implications," *Resources Policy*, 46:2, 262–71.

Mansfield, E. (1989) "Technological Change in Robotics: Japan and the United States," *Managerial and Decision Economics*, 10:1, 19–25.

Myint, H. (1977) "Adam Smith's Theory of International Trade in the Perspective of Economic Development," *Economica*, 44:175, 231–48.

Organisation for Economic Co-operation and Development (2018) *Governance Frameworks to Counter Illicit Trade*, OECD.

Porter, M. E. (1990) *The Competitive Advantage of Nations*, Free Press.

Reinert, K. A. (2004) "Outcomes Assessment in Trade Policy Analysis: A Note on the Welfare Propositions of the 'Gains from Trade,'" *Journal of Economics Issues*, 38:4, 1067–73.

Reinert, K. A. (2017) "Introduction," in K. A. Reinert (ed.), *Handbook of Globalisation and Development*, Edward Elgar, 1–15.

Schodt, F. L. (1988) *Inside the Robot Kingdom: Japan, Mechatronics, and the Coming Robotopia*, Kodansha International.

Sen, A. (1987) *The Standard of Living*, Cambridge University Press.

Shelley, L. (2017) "Illicit Trade," in K. A. Reinert (ed.), *Handbook of Globalisation and Development*, Edward Elgar, 100–14.

Smith, A. (1937 [1776]) *The Wealth of Nations*, Modern Library.

Tanzer, A., and R. Simon (1990) "Why Japan Loves Robots and We Don't," *Forbes*, 145:8, 148–53.

United States Geological Survey (2002) "Rare Earth Elements: Critical Resources for High Technology," Fact Sheet 087-02, United States Geological Survey.

Van Marrewijk, C. (2009) "Absolute Advantage," in K. A. Reinert, R. S. Rajan, A. J. Glass, and L. S. Davis (eds.), *The Princeton Encyclopedia of the World Economy*, Princeton University Press, 1–3.

Appendix 2.1: Review of Supply and Demand

Throughout the world, rice is exchanged in markets. Although these markets are international, let us assume for a moment that we can analyze a single domestic market in isolation. This will help orient you to the supply and demand model. Figure 2.5 illustrates such a market. The diagram has two axes. The horizontal axis

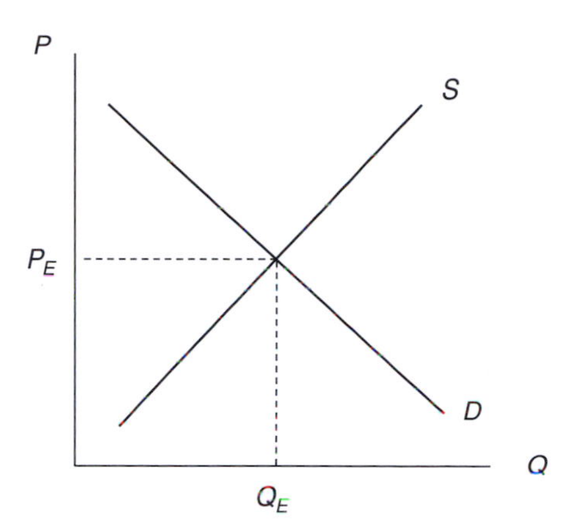

Figure 2.5 A domestic rice market

plots the quantity (Q) of rice in tons per year. The vertical axis plots the price (P) of rice per ton. There are two curves in the diagram, identified by the symbols S and D. S is the supply curve and represents the behavior of domestic rice-producing firms. D is the demand curve and represents the behavior of domestic consumers of rice, both firms and households.[13] Together, these two curves compose the visual representation of the supply and demand model.

There are a number of properties of the supply and demand curves in Figure 2.5 that are important to understand. Let us take the supply curve first. It is upward-sloping, and this indicates that firms supply more rice to the market as the price increases. Consequently, changes in price are represented in the diagram by *movements along* the supply curve, and these movements are known as **changes in quantity supplied.** There are two additional supply-side factors relevant to the supply curve. These are input or factor prices and technology. Reductions in input prices and improvements in technology shift the supply curve to the right. This means that producers supply more rice than before at every price. Increases in input prices and technology set-backs shift the supply curve to the left. This means that producers supply less rice than before at every price. We can see that changes in input prices and technology are represented by *shifts of* the supply curve. These shifts are known as **changes in supply.**[14]

Now let us take a look at the rice demand curve. It is downward-sloping, and this indicates that consumers demand less rice from the market as the price increases. Consequently, changes in price are represented in the diagram by *movements along* the demand curve, and these movements are known as

---

[13] Firms consuming rice use it as an intermediate product to produce a final product, such as rice flour or a restaurant meal.

[14] Sometimes, firms' expectations of future prices are also included as a shift factor, but we do not do that here.

changes in quantity demanded. There are a number of additional demand-side factors relevant to the demand curve. Two important ones are incomes and preferences.[15] Increases in incomes and increased preference for rice consumption shift the demand curve to the right. This means that consumers demand more rice than before at every price. Decreases in incomes and decreased preference for rice consumption shift the demand curve to the left. This means that consumers demand less rice than before at every price. Consequently, changes in incomes and preferences are represented by *shifts of* the demand curve. These shifts are known as **changes in demand**.

Finally, the intersection of the supply and demand curves in Figure 2.5 determines the equilibrium in the domestic rice market. In this diagram, the equilibrium price is P_E, and the equilibrium quantity is Q_E. Given what we have just stated about the role of input prices, technology, incomes, and preferences in shifting the two curves in Figure 2.5, you can see that any such shifts will change the equilibrium price and quantity for rice by shifting the demand or supply curves. These sorts of changes are natural parts of market processes, and the supply and demand model helps us to better understand them.

Our discussion of the gains from trade in this chapter utilized the notions of *consumer surplus* and *producer surplus*. These concepts are illustrated in Figure 2.6. As in Figure 2.5, this figure considers equilibrium in a single market. The equilibrium price is P_E, and the equilibrium quantity is Q_E. The height of the demand curve shows consumers' maximum *willingness to pay* for the good in question. For quantities between zero and Q_E, however, the willingness to pay is *greater than* what consumers actually pay—that is, the height of the demand curve is greater

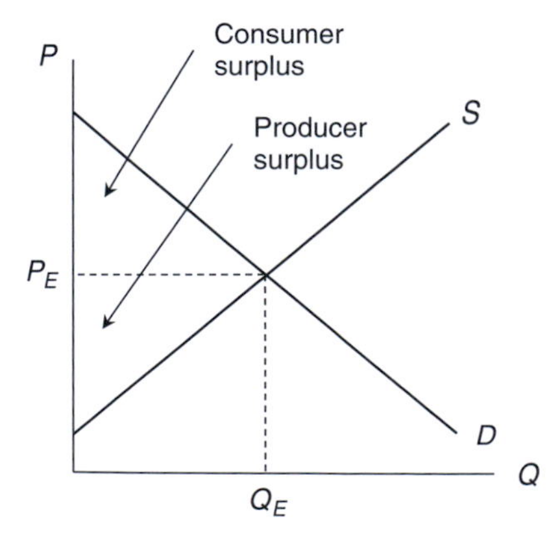

Figure 2.6 Consumer and producer surplus

[15] Other demand-side factors are prices of related products, wealth, and expectations. Changes in these factors shift the demand curve, as do changes in income and preferences.

than the market price. This gives consumers a premium on each unit up to Q_E, and the sum of the consumer premia is the upper triangle in the figure: consumer surplus.

The height of the supply curve shows the producers' minimum *willingness to accept* for the good in question. For quantities between zero and Q_E, however, the willingness to accept is *less than* what the producers actually receive–that is, the height of the supply curve is less than the market price. Producers too, then, receive a premium on each unit up to Q_E. The sum of the producer premia is the lower triangle in the figure: producer surplus.

In demonstrating the gains from trade in Figure 2.4, we considered the *changes* in consumer and producer surplus that result from the price changes brought on by the move from autarky to trade. This analysis of the gains from trade is based on the standard view of economic welfare. As discussed in Reinert (2004), this standard view does impose some limitations. It restricts our consideration of welfare to income per capita, or, more formally, what economists term the "utility of consumption." Alternative views, such as in the form of human capabilities, as argued by Sen (1987), are advocated by some economists.

3 Ricardian Model of Comparative Advantage

We stated in Chapter 1 that international trade in goods and services plays an important role in the world economy as one of the main features of globalization. We also stated that we were going to explore the factors underlying international trade in Part I of this book, and we began this process in Chapter 2 with a consideration of **absolute advantage**. That chapter explained Adam Smith's concept and applied it within the context of the supply and demand model, explaining the trade relationship between Vietnam and Japan in the single good rice. We also used the supply and demand treatment of absolute advantage to introduce the **gains from trade**. But Chapter 2 also struck a cautious note, reminding us that absolute advantage is a policy suggestion that can be dominated by the more power concept of **comparative advantage**. It is now time to consider this more powerful concept.

There are two main explanations of comparative advantage. The first of these is known as the **Ricardian model**, after David Ricardo. It explores the means by which comparative advantage can be determined by differences in *technology* between the countries of the world, and is the subject of this chapter. With its focus on technology, the Ricardian model is an extension of the absolute advantage concept. The second explanation of comparative advantage is known as the **Heckscher–Ohlin model**, after economists Eli Heckscher and Bertil Ohlin. It explores the means by which comparative advantage can be determined by differences in *resource endowments* between the countries of the world. It is the subject of Chapter 4.

In order to understand comparative advantage, we will use the concept of a **production possibilities frontier** (PPF). The PPF should be familiar to you from an introductory microeconomics course. If it is not, please see Appendix 3.1 for a brief introduction. You can rely on Appendix 3.1 for the material in Chapter 4 as well. Let us begin our consideration of the Ricardian model by relating it to the absolute advantage concept of Chapter 2.

From Absolute Advantage to Comparative Advantage

For Vietnam, rice is a significant component of both the country's production and its consumption. As incomes have increased in Vietnam, however, there is another product that many Vietnamese think about buying. That product is a *motorcycle*. Indeed, motorcycles have been all the rage in Vietnam. Originally the most desirable motorcycle was the aptly named Honda Dream, but subsequently attention turned to the Honda Wave. These brands have been so popular that copies of them have been made in China and exported to Vietnam. Hundreds of new motorcycles are registered daily in the city of Hanoi alone, and tourists visiting this city report being overwhelmed by the chaos of motorcycle traffic. Indeed, there is now a motorcycle for every two Vietnamese citizens. In this chapter, we will place motorcycles alongside rice so that you can begin to understand the powerful concept of **comparative advantage** and its role in generating patterns of trade between the countries of the world.

Recall from Chapter 2 that we simplified the demand side of the rice market to focus our attention on the supply side. We are going to do the same thing in this chapter, to help us in our analysis of comparative advantage. More specifically, we will assume that demand for rice and motorcycles in both Vietnam and Japan is such that these two goods are consumed in the *same, fixed proportions*. This assumption is depicted in Figure 3.1. In the diagrams for Vietnam and Japan, the quantity of rice (Q_R) is measured on the horizontal axes, and the quantity of motorcycles (Q_M) is measured on the vertical axes. Since demand for these two goods is in the same, fixed proportions, we can represent it by diagonal lines from the origins in the figure. We label both these lines *DD* for "demand diagonal." Any change in preferences for the two products would rotate the demand diagonal lines either up or down, maintaining the intercept at the origin. Changes in income would move a country up and down a given demand diagonal. As we will see below, movements up and down a demand diagonal can also be viewed as changes in economic welfare.[1]

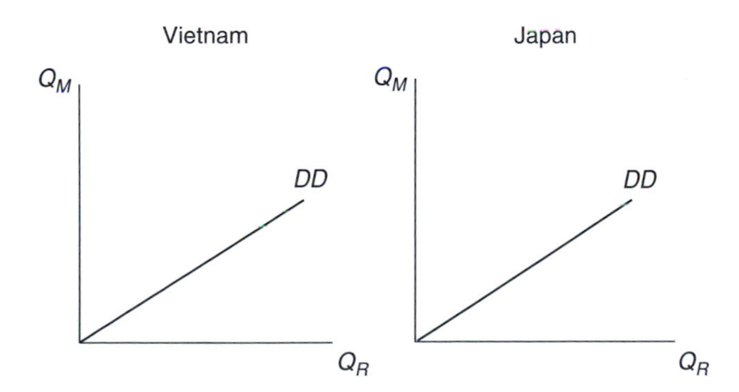

Figure 3.1 Demand diagonals in Vietnam and Japan

[1] Some caution is necessary here. The *DD* lines in Figure 3.1 are *not* demand curves. Demand curves show a relationship between price and quantity demanded, but no price appears on an axis in Figure 3.1. Furthermore, demand curves are downward-sloping, not upward-sloping as the *DD* curves are. We take the *DD* approach here to avoid using *indifference curves*, with which many students are not familiar. But the results we obtain are the same as those derived with the more advanced indifference curve concept, and the *DD* assumption can be relaxed without changing any of the results of this chapter.

In order to understand comparative advantage, we will use the concept of a **production possibilities frontier**. In this chapter, we consider a specific kind of PPF associated with the Ricardian model of comparative advantage, deviating a bit from the kind of PPF discussed in Appendix 3.1. Consider again our two countries, Vietnam and Japan. Both these countries produce two goods: rice and motorcycles. As in our consideration of absolute advantage in Chapter 2, we will assume that there is only one resource: labor. The amounts of labor required to produce each these two goods in the two countries are as follows.

Rice in Vietnam: a_R^V
Rice in Japan: a_R^J
Motorcycles in Vietnam: a_M^V
Motorcycles in Japan: a_M^J

These four terms are descriptions of *technology* in Vietnam and Japan. In order to develop the Ricardian PPF, we need to combine technology with resources in the form of economy-wide *resource constraints* for the two countries. To do this, we need to also define the quantities produced in the two sectors of the two countries, as follows.

Quantity of rice produced in Vietnam: Q_R^V
Quantity of rice produced in Japan: Q_R^J
Quantity of motorcycles produced in Vietnam: Q_M^V
Quantity of motorcycles produced in Japan: Q_M^J

If we define the total amount of labor available in the two countries as L^V and L^J, then the economy-wide resource constraints are

$$a_R^V Q_R^V + a_M^V Q_M^V = L^V \tag{3.1}$$

$$a_R^J Q_R^J + a_M^J Q_M^J = L^J \tag{3.2}$$

Equations 3.1 and 3.2 state that the labor used in rice production plus the labor used in motorcycle production must sum to the total labor available in each country. The availability of the labor resource *constrains* production possibilities in both countries.

But what do the PPFs look like in this model? How would we draw them in the equivalent of Figure 3.1? There is a simple way to get a handle on this. Let us just look at Vietnam as an example. Suppose we allocate all the labor in Vietnam to rice production. Then Q_M^V would be zero, since no motorcycles are produced in Vietnam. A little algebra (substitute $Q_M^V = 0$ into Equation 3.1) tells us that $Q_R^V = L^V / a_R^V$. This is the *endpoint* of the PPF along the rice axis in Vietnam in Figure 3.2. If we allocate all the labor in Vietnam to motorcycle production, then,

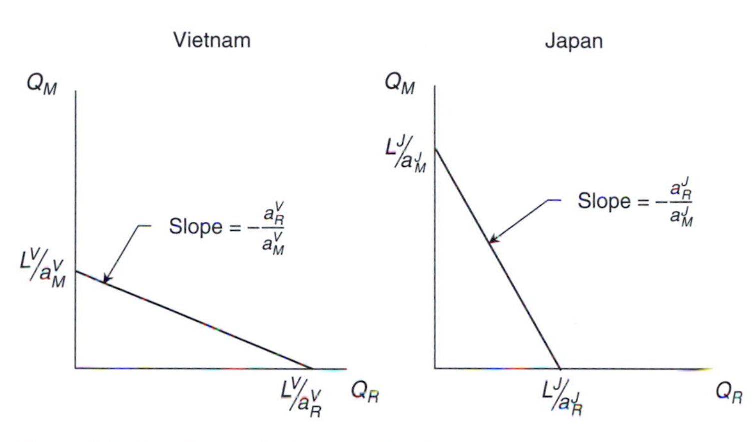

Figure 3.2 Ricardian production possibility frontiers in Vietnam and Japan

similarly, $Q_M^V = L^V/a_M^V$. This gives us the endpoint of the PPF along the motorcycle axis in Vietnam.

In the Ricardian model, all the a terms (labor requirements per unit of output) are *constant*. For this reason, the Ricardian PPF for Vietnam is *linear*, as depicted in Figure 3.2. A similar set of considerations gives us the linear PPF for Japan in Figure 3.2. Figure 3.2 is drawn so that the two PPFs have *different slopes*, reflecting different relative technological efficiencies. Given the constant a terms, the two slopes are as follows.

Vietnam: $-a_R^V/a_M^V$

Japan: $-a_R^J/a_M^J$

Let us spend some time developing the intuition of the Ricardian PPFs presented in Figure 3.2. PPFs are a special sort of *resource constraint*. What the PPF does is to recognize the resources (the Ls) and technology (the as) available to Vietnam and Japan. Given the labor resource and technology, the PPFs plot the highest potential combinations of rice and motorcycles achievable for the two countries. The PPFs themselves, along with all the points inside them, together provide *feasible production sets*. But the points inside the PPFs represent combinations of rice and motorcycle production that would imply some of the available labor being unemployed. The endpoints labeled in Figure 3.2 are on the PPFs but are special, in that all the labor has been allocated to one or the other good.

There is another property of resource constraints. It is that the slope of any resource constraint gives the **opportunity cost** of the item on the horizontal axis of the diagram. As you can see in Figure 3.2, the slopes are *negative*. This means that there are indeed opportunity *costs* of production. In Figure 3.2, rice is on the horizontal axis. So the slopes of the PPFs in the figure give the opportunity cost of rice. This is expressed as the number of units of motorcycles the countries would need to forgo or give up in order to increase rice output by one unit, or $\Delta Q_M / \Delta Q_R$. The steeper the PPFs, the more negative the slope, and the higher the opportunity costs of rice. The opportunity cost of motorcycles is the *inverse* of the opportunity cost of rice, or $\Delta Q_R / \Delta Q_M$.

So, here is the important question: which country has the lower opportunity cost of producing rice? It has to be the one with the flatter or less steep PPF: Vietnam. Since the opportunity costs of motorcycles is the inverse of the slope of the PPF, this would imply that the country with the lower opportunity cost of producing motorcycles would have the steeper-sloped PPF: Japan. So, what we see in Figure 3.2 is that Vietnam has a lower opportunity cost of producing rice, and Japan has a lower opportunity cost of producing motorcycles. These relative opportunity costs turn out to be central to the comparative advantage idea. Let us see how this works.

Autarky and Comparative Advantage

The concept of comparative advantage was first introduced in 1817 by David Ricardo in his *Principles of Political Economy and Taxation* (Ricardo, 1951 [1817]). In a footnote in chapter 7 of that book, Ricardo states:

> It will appear...that a country possessing very considerable advantages in machinery and skill, and which may therefore be enabled to manufacture commodities with much less labour than her neighbours, may, in return for such commodities, import a portion of its corn required for its consumption, even if its land were more fertile, and corn could be grown with less labour than in the country from which it was imported (136).

This country, in our example, is Japan, whose endowments of "machinery and skill" might *in principle* give it an absolute advantage in producing both rice and motorcycles. Corn in Ricardo's time was the word for "grain," and, in our example, this is rice. Ricardo therefore suggests that, given its *comparative* advantage in motorcycles, Japan can import rice even if it has an *absolute* advantage in rice production.

As it turns out, comparative advantage is elucidated in terms of the relative opportunity costs shown in Figure 3.2 or the relative slopes. It is best to do this without the negative signs included in Figure 3.2. This is as follows:

$$\frac{a_R^V}{a_M^V} < \frac{a_R^J}{a_M^J} \tag{3.3}$$

Inequality 3.3 says that, since Vietnam has the lower opportunity cost of producing rice, it has a comparative advantage in producing rice relative to Japan. This also implies a comparative advantage for Japan, which we can see by taking the inverse of Inequality 3.3:

$$\frac{a_M^J}{a_R^J} < \frac{a_M^V}{a_R^V} \tag{3.4}$$

Inequality 3.4 says that, since Japan has the lower opportunity cost of producing motorcycles, it has a comparative advantage in producing motorcycles relative to Vietnam. So Figure 3.2, with its differently sloped PPFs, embodies a pattern of comparative advantage.[2]

The demand diagonals of Figure 3.1 represent the demand sides of the Vietnamese and Japanese economies. The PPFs of Figure 3.2 represent the supply sides. We combine Figures 3.1 and 3.2 in Figure 3.3. This gives us the autarky equilibria points A. Production needs to be on the PPFs, and demand needs to be on the demand diagonals. Without trade, the only points where both these things are true are where the demand diagonals and the PPFs intersect: points A. Without trade, consumption and production need to take place at the same points in Figure 3.3.

There is something else we need to understand, and this requires a few assumptions. With full employment (which puts the economies *on* rather than inside the PPF), profit maximization, and perfect competition, opportunity costs of production are fully reflected in *relative prices* (see Appendix 3.1). Therefore, the constant slopes of the two PPFs where the demand diagonal crosses it are the relative prices of rice in the two countries, $\left(P_R/P_M\right)^V$ and $\left(P_R/P_M\right)^J$.

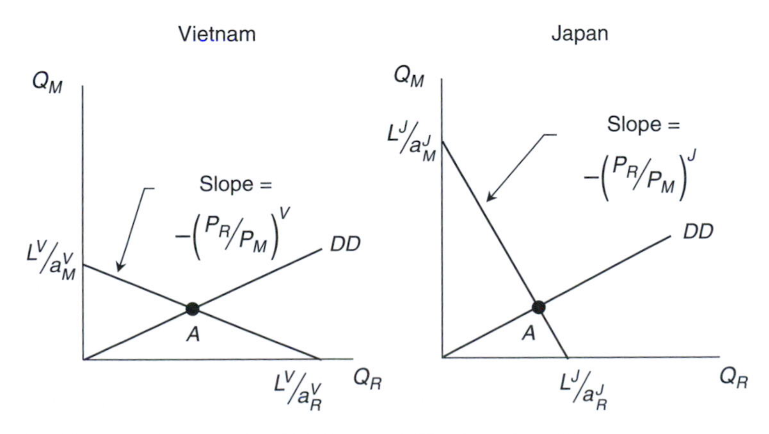

Figure 3.3 Autarky in the Ricardian model in Vietnam and Japan

[2] Samuelson (1969) refers to the four a terms in Inequalities 3.3 and 3.4 as the four "magic numbers" of comparative advantage.

Looking at points A in Figure 3.3, you can see that the PPF line giving relative prices is flatter in Vietnam than in Japan—that is, the opportunity cost of rice is lower in Vietnam than in Japan. In other words, under autarky

$$\left(\frac{P_R}{P_M}\right)^V < \left(\frac{P_R}{P_M}\right)^J \tag{3.5}$$

This equation says that the relative price of rice is lower in Vietnam than in Japan. Since Vietnam is the country that has a lower opportunity cost of producing rice, Inequality 3.5 makes sense. This inequality is an expression of a pattern of comparative advantage. Differences in economy-wide supply conditions cause differences in relative autarky prices and, thereby, a pattern of comparative advantage. It is these differences that make trade possible.

We need to note one very important thing about Inequality 3.5. This comparative advantage inequality involves *four prices* rather than *two prices*, as in the absolute advantage inequality of Equation 2.1. This difference has an immediate and important implication: a country can have a *comparative advantage* in a good in which it has an *absolute disadvantage*. This is one reason why the comparative advantage concept is more powerful than the absolute advantage concept.

Ricardo's Larger Project

Recall from Chapter 2 that Adam Smith's notion of absolute advantage was developed as part of his larger criticism of mercantilism. Something similar was the case with David Ricardo's notion of comparative advantage. Ricardo was born in London in 1772, just before Smith published *The Wealth of Nations*. At a very early age he began to work on the London stock exchange, following in the footsteps of his father. He became acquainted with *The Wealth of Nations* in the very late eighteenth century. In the early nineteenth century Ricardo met James Mill, the father of the philosopher and economist John Stuart Mill, discovering their mutual interests in the issues of their day. The elder Mill encouraged Ricardo to begin to write on these issues, and Ricardo began to do so, beginning with newspaper articles and moving on to pamphlets.

In 1817 Ricardo published an important book, *On the Principles of Political Economy and Taxation*, which took its place among the most important books in the history of economic thought. Evidence suggests that he had "discovered" the comparative advantage concept in late 1816. In 1819 he was elected to the British Parliament at James Mill's urging, and he served there until illness forced him out in 1823. This illness led to his death in that year.

Ricardo's Larger Project (cont.)

In all these activities, Ricardo had a *larger project*. This was to provide intellectual and policy support to the capitalist sector in Britain relative to the agricultural sector. In class terms, he favored the capitalists over the land owners. In about 1815 debate began over what were known as the "Corn Laws," the word "corn" meaning grains. At that time Britain introduced high tariffs and other restrictions on imports of gain, and this helped the landowning class maintain high rents. Since food costs were a main factor in wage costs, the Corn Laws suppressed capitalist profits. As Heilbroner (1953: 89–90) expresses it, "The capitalist, who worked and saved and invested, found that all his trouble was for nothing: his wage costs were higher, his profits smaller, and his landed opponent far richer than he. And the landlord, who did nothing but collect his rents, sat back and watched them increase." Ricardo opposed this situation and argued for a repeal of the Corn Laws.

Ruffin (2002: 744) notes that "Ricardo had an uncanny knack for addressing himself to the big questions." The comparative advantage principle was just one part of Ricardo's larger project—a big question indeed. The argument in favor of "free trade" was used to support his position in favor of the industrial capitalist class of his day. After his death he eventually prevailed. The Corn Laws were finally repealed in 1846.

Sources: Heilbroner (1953), Ruffin (2002), and Spiegel (1991).

International Trade

With the principle of comparative advantage established, it is now time to consider *international trade* in the Ricardian model. Let us do this. If Vietnam and Japan abandon autarky in favor of trade, the world relative price of rice $\left(P_R/P_M\right)^W$ will be somewhere *between* the two autarky price ratios:

$$\left(\frac{P_R}{P_M}\right)^V < \left(\frac{P_R}{P_M}\right)^W < \left(\frac{P_R}{P_M}\right)^J \tag{3.6}$$

This situation is depicted in Figure 3.4. The world price ratio here is depicted with dashed lines that have the slope $\left(P_R/P_M\right)^W$. In the "normal" PPFs you encountered in your introductory microeconomics course, there were increasing opportunity costs reflected in their increasingly negative shape. In this case, the world price lines would be tangent to the PPFs, so that the relative world prices and

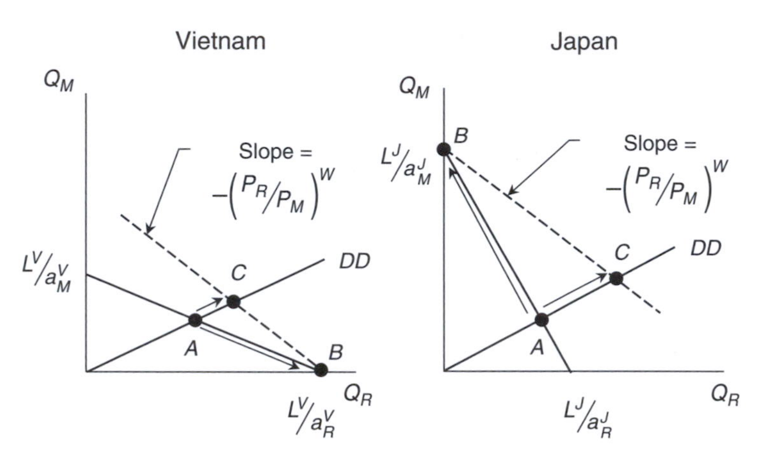

Figure 3.4 Autarky and comparative advantage in Vietnam and Japan

opportunity costs are one and the same. This does not happen in the Ricardian model, with constant opportunity costs and linear PPFs. Instead, the world price lines rest on the far corners of the PPFs.

The change in relative prices has an effect on production in each of the two countries, moving the production points from A to B. In the case of Vietnam, the relative price has *increased* from autarky to trade, and this provides an increased incentive to produce rice. In Japan, the relative price has *decreased*, and this provides an increased incentive to produce motorcycles.

One thing that characterizes trade in the Ricardian model and that can be seen in Figure 3.4 is that the movement from autarky to trade (from A to B) involves *complete specialization* in production according to comparative advantage. Vietnam moves from producing rice and motorcycles to producing only rice. Japan moves from producing rice and motorcycles to producing only motorcycles. This is a result of the fact that the opportunity costs of production are constant.

In a "normal" PPF, such as in Appendix 3.1, as trade moves a country to specialize in the production of the good in which it has a comparative advantage, the opportunity costs of producing more of that good increase. This increase in opportunity cost acts as a sort of brake on complete specialization. In the Ricardian model with constant opportunity costs, there is no such brake, and specialization in accordance with comparative advantage becomes complete. This is an extreme result that indicates that we are leaving some relevant features out of the picture by focusing only on technological differences between countries.[3]

[3] This complete specialization result will not be present in the Heckscher–Ohlin model of comparative advantage considered in Chapter 4. There, opportunity costs of production will be increasing, as in the typical textbook PPF.

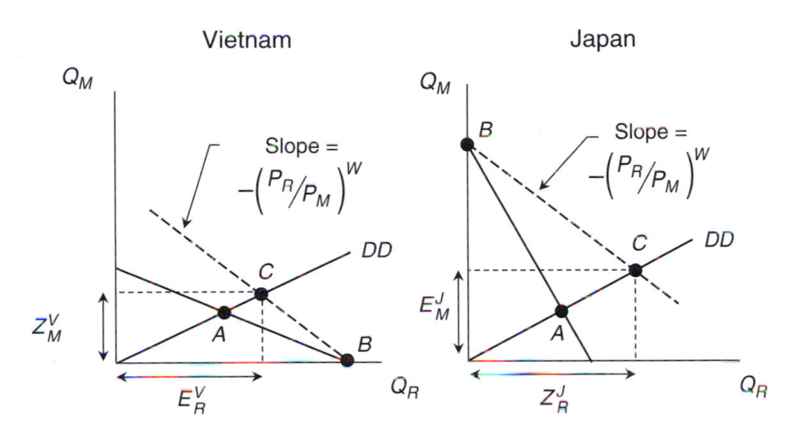

Figure 3.5 Trade in the Ricardian model between Vietnam and Japan

With the production impacts of moving out of autarky understood, let us next consider *consumption*. Consumption points for Vietnam and Japan must be along our demand diagonal lines. These points, labeled *C* in Figure 3.4, occur where the dashed world price lines intersect the demand lines. Why is this? Both consumption and production must respect world prices—that is, *both* points *B* and *C* must be on the world price lines. In contrast to autarky, the consumption and production points are now *different*. How can this be so? Through trade.

Look at Figure 3.5. In Vietnam, production of rice exceeds consumption of rice, and the difference is exported (E_R^V). Production of motorcycles falls short of consumption of motorcycles, however, and this shortfall is imported (Z_M^V).[4] In Japan, production of motorcycles exceeds consumption of motorcycles, and the difference is exported (E_M^J). Production of rice falls short of production, however, and this shortfall is imported (Z_R^J). What we see in Figure 3.5 is that a pattern of comparative advantage, based on differences in supply conditions (technology) between two countries, gives rise to a complementary pattern of trade.

We mentioned in Chapter 2 that the absolute advantage concept can leave the impression that a country might lack an advantage in anything, and therefore have nothing to export. The concept of comparative advantage clears up this problem. Having an *absolute* disadvantage in a product does not preclude having a *comparative* advantage in that product. Vietnam could have an absolute disadvantage in rice, but still export this product because of its comparative advantage.[5]

[4] As in Chapter 2, we use Z to denote imports, since the symbols I and M are taken up by investment and money, respectively.

[5] The reader who is not convinced of this can work with the following example: $a_R^V = 2$, $a_R^J = 1$, $a_M^V = 4$, $a_M^J = 1$. Here, you will see that Japan has an *absolute* advantage in producing both goods ($a_R^J < a_R^V$ and $a_M^J < a_M^V$), but Vietnam has a *comparative* advantage in producing rice.

This is why comparative advantage is a more powerful concept than absolute advantage. Indeed, comparative advantage is perhaps the most central concept in international economics.

Before moving on to discuss the gains from trade, another key concept in international economics, let us summarize what we have shown this far in a box.

> Differences in technology-determined supply conditions between the countries of the world give rise to complementary patterns of comparative advantage. These patterns of comparative advantage, in turn, make possible complementary patterns of international trade.

Gains from Trade

To this point, we have seen that, given a pattern of comparative advantage, it is possible for a country to give up autarky in favor of importing and exporting. But *should* a country actually do this? We can answer this question by examining Figure 3.5 once again. Notice that the post-trade consumption points *C* are to the "northeast" of the autarky consumption points *A*. This directional relationship between points *A* and *C* means that the movement from autarky to trade increases consumption of *both* rice *and* motorcycles. Increased consumption of both goods, in turn, implies that economic welfare has increased. Vietnam and Japan have experienced mutual **gains from trade** based on comparative advantage.[6]

As in Chapter 2, caveats are in order. First, like all economic models, the Ricardian model employs a set of assumptions. There is only one resource: labor. There is perfect competition, full employment, and profit maximization. The one resource, labor, cannot move from one country to another–that is, there is no international migration (as considered in Chapter 13). Countries differ from one another in only one way: technological efficiency. The model is powerful, but we always need to keep an eye on the assumptions that go into it.

Second, the gains from trade occur for the country *as a whole*. The fact that a country as a whole benefits in the aggregate from trade does *not* mean that every individual or group within the country benefits. Indeed, as you will see in Chapter 6, there are good reasons to expect that there will be groups that *lose* from

[6] Ricardo himself was very much aware of the possibility of gains from trade, stating: "Foreign trade [is] highly beneficial to a country, as it increases the amount and variety of the objects on which revenue may be expended" (1951 [1817]: 133). The implicit assumption here is the standard one in economics, namely that welfare is determined by consumption levels. For a well-known challenge to this assumption, see Sen (1987).

increased trade, and these groups might oppose increased trade despite the overall gains to their country. To foreshadow our discussion in Chapter 6, for example, rice producers in Japan have a long history of opposing imports of rice.

Third, as we mentioned in Chapter 2, some goods are traded that do not contribute to increased welfare. Land mines, heroin, and prostitution services are all traded internationally, but their consumption significantly *reduces* welfare rather than increases it. For this reason, you need to be careful not to generalize the gains from trade concept too far.[7]

Conclusion

Differences in technology between the countries of the world can generate patterns of comparative advantage and, thereby, patterns of trade. Although patterns of comparative advantage and trade can be *influenced* by patterns of absolute advantage, they are not *determined* by them. Indeed, a country can have a comparative advantage in a good or service in which it has an absolute disadvantage. There is empirical evidence that the relative technological differences at the center of the Ricardian model *do affect* patterns of trade.[8] Further, patterns of trade based on comparative advantage can generate gains from trade. The trade policy implications of comparative advantage are significant.[9]

As with our analysis of absolute advantage in Chapter 2, it is important to remember that the gains from trade arising from comparative advantage are for countries *as a whole*, and not for all individuals and groups within a country. Within any country, there can be both winners and losers from international trade. This is the issue of the political economy of trade, which we take up in Chapter 6.

Review Exercises

1. What is the difference between *absolute* and *comparative* advantage?
2. Create an example of a comparative advantage model by choosing two countries and two products.

---

[7] See, for example, Reinert (2004).

[8] See, for example, Trefler (1995) and Costinot, Donaldson, and Komunjer (2012).

[9] It is for this reason that Ruffin (2002) states that comparative advantage "may be the single best illustration of the power of economic analysis to defeat the forces of foolishness" (728). By "forces of foolishness," he means mercantilism and neo-mercantilism.

a. Draw a diagram describing *autarky* and a *pattern of comparative advantage* for your example.
b. Show the transition from autarky to trade in your diagram, label the trade flows, and demonstrate the *gains from trade.*

3. Think about the movements along the PPFs in Figure 3.4 from points A to B. What is actually happening in these economies to allow these specialization processes to take place? Are there any institutional realities that you can think of that would get in the way of these specialization processes?

FURTHER READING AND WEB RESOURCES

A concise introduction to comparative advantage can be found in Maneschi (2009) and a historical perspective can be found in Maneschi (1998). An oft-cited piece on Ricardo's idea of comparative advantage is Paul Krugman's (1998) "Ricardo's Difficult Idea." A Google search will turn up copies of this. A more technical review is in Deardorff (2009) and an historical consideration can be found in Ruffin (2002).

REFERENCES

Costinot, A., D. Donaldson, and I. Komunjer (2012) "What Goods Do Countries Trade? A Quantitative Exploration of Ricardo's Ideas," *Review of Economic Studies*, 79:2, 581–608.

Deardorff, A. V. (2009) "Ricardian Model," in K. A. Reinert, R. S. Rajan, A. J. Glass, and L. S. Davis (eds.), *The Princeton Encyclopedia of the World Economy*, Princeton University Press, 973–80.

Heilbroner, R. L. (1953) *The Worldly Philosophers*, Simon & Schuster.

Krugman, P. (1998) "Ricardo's Difficult Idea: Why Intellectuals Can't Understand Comparative Advantage," in G. Cook (ed.), *Freedom and Trade: The Economics and Politics of International Trade*, vol. 2, Routledge, 22–36.

Maneschi, A. (1998) *Comparative Advantage in International Trade: A Historical Perspective*, Edward Elgar.

Maneschi, A. (2009) "Comparative Advantage," in K. A. Reinert, R. S. Rajan, A. J. Glass, and L. S. Davis (eds.), *The Princeton Encyclopedia of the World Economy*, Princeton University Press, 198–205.

Reinert, K. A. (2004) "Outcomes Assessment in Trade Policy Analysis: A Note on the Welfare Propositions of the 'Gains from Trade,'" *Journal of Economic Issues*, 38:4, 1067–73.

Ricardo, D. (1951 [1817]) *On the Principles of Political Economy and Taxation*, vol. 1 of P. Sraffa (ed.), *The Works and Correspondence of David Ricardo*, Cambridge University Press.

Ruffin, R. J. (2002) "David Ricardo's Discovery of Comparative Advantage," *History of Political Economy*, 34:4, 727–48.

Samuelson, P. A. (1969) "The Way of an Economist," in P. A. Samuelson (ed.), *International Economic Relations: Proceedings of the Third Congress of the International Economic Association*, Macmillan, 1–11.

Sen, A. (1987) *The Standard of Living*, Cambridge University Press.

Spiegel, H. W. (1991) *The Growth of Economic Thought*, Duke University Press.
Trefler, D. (1995) "The Case of the Missing Trade and Other Mysteries," *American Economic Review*, 85:5, 1029–46.
Van Marrewijk, C. (2009) "Absolute Advantage," in K.A. Reinert, R.S. Rajan, A.J. Glass and L.S. Davis (eds.) *The Princeton Encyclopedia of the World Economy*, Princeton University Press, 1–3.

Appendix 3.1: The Production Possibilities Frontier

The purpose of this appendix is to describe the "normal" PPF for your understanding and use in both Chapters 3 and 4. As we stated in the beginning of this chapter, PPFs are economy-wide resource constraints that reflect available resources and technology. Let us consider an economy that produces two goods, rice and motorcycles. The quantities in these two sectors we will call Q_R and Q_M, respectively. We will depict the supply side of this economy using a production possibilities frontier diagram. The PPF depicts the combinations of output of rice and motorcycles that the economy can produce given its available resources and technology.

The PPF is depicted in Figure 3.6. It is depicted as *concave* with respect to the origin in this figure. Given the available resources and technology, the economy can produce anywhere on or inside the PPF. Point *A*, on the PPF itself, is one such point. If the economy were at point *A* on the PPF, it would be producing Q_{RA} of rice and Q_{MA} of motorcycles. If the economy were to move from point *A* to point *B*, the output of rice would increase from Q_{RA} to Q_{RB}. The output of motorcycles would *fall* from Q_{MA} to Q_{MB}, however. The fall in motorcycles output is an example of a very general and very important concept in economics: **opportunity cost**. Opportunity cost is what must be forgone when a particular decision is made. If

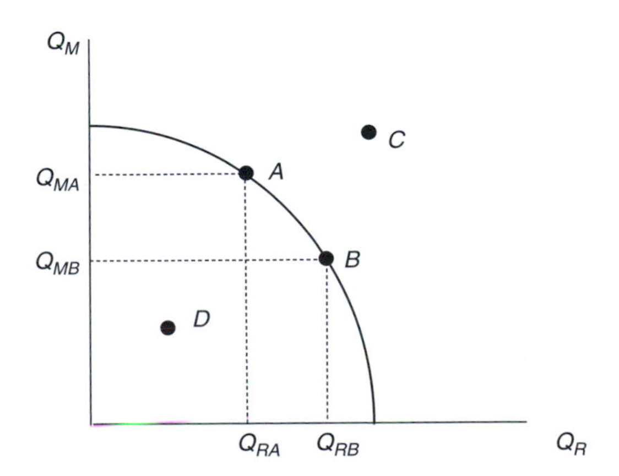

Figure 3.6 The production possibilities frontier

this economy chooses to move from point A to point B, the decreased production of motorcycles is the opportunity cost of the increased production of rice.

Point C is another production point in Figure 3.6. It is more desirable than either point A or point B, since point C provides more of both rice and motorcycles compared to A and B. Point C is *infeasible*, however, given the resources and technology of the economy. Point D, inside the PPF, is feasible. In comparison to points A and B, however, it offers less of both rice and motorcycles. Points A and B are said to be *efficient*, in that, at these points, the economy is getting all it can from its scarce resources. This is not true at point D, and, consequently, point D is *inefficient*.[10]

How are the relative prices we use in this chapter determined in a PPF? We consider this in Figure 3.7 using the following steps.

Step 1. The slope of the PPF $\left(\Delta Q_M / \Delta Q_R\right)$ is the opportunity cost of the good on the horizontal axis, rice. It indicates how many motorcycles must be given up to produce an additional unit of rice.

Step 2. In a perfectly competitive market system, when resources are fully employed and firms maximize profits, the opportunity costs are *fully reflected* in relative prices. The relative price of rice, the good on the horizontal axis, is $\left(P_R / P_M\right)$.

Step 3. A tangent line to the PPF shares the same slope of the PPF, namely $\left(\Delta Q_M / \Delta Q_R\right)$.

Step 4. Given Steps 1, 2, and 3, we can see that a tangent line to the PPF has a slope equal to the relative price of the good on the horizontal axis: $\left(P_R / P_M\right)$.

Does the result of Step 4, that the slope of a tangent line represents the relative price of rice, the good on the horizontal axis, make any sense? Let us look at this a bit further in Figure 3.8. Suppose that, from point A, we want to *increase* the output of rice from Q_{RA} to Q_{RB}. Since there are opportunity costs of production represented by the PPF, this implies a *decrease* in the output of motorcycles from Q_{MA} to Q_{MB}. As production moves from point A to point B, the slope of the PPF increases, reflecting increasing opportunity costs of rice production. To offset these increasing opportunity costs, the relative price of rice *must rise*. Therefore, increasing the output of rice requires increasing its relative price from $\left(P_R / P_M\right)_A$ to

[10] Recall that the concept of efficiency in economics refers to *allocative efficiency*, not technological efficiency.

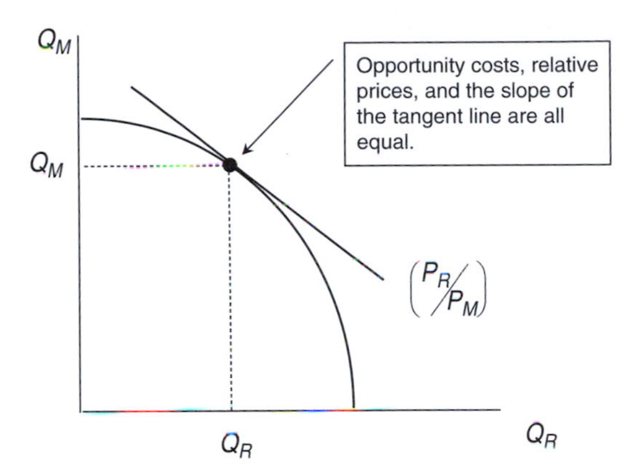

Figure 3.7 Relative prices and the production possibilities frontier

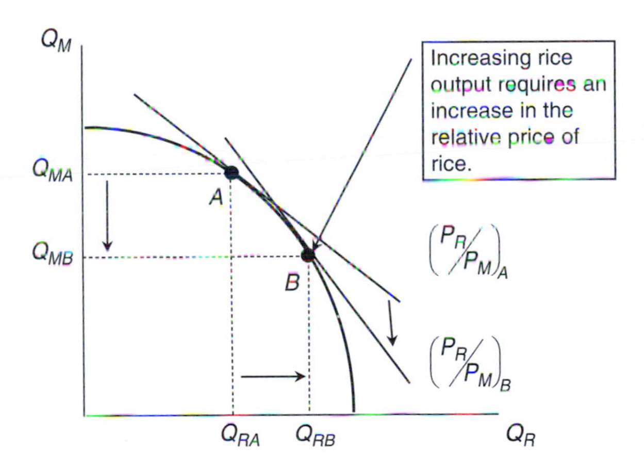

Figure 3.8 An increase in rice output

the steeper $\left(P_R/P_M\right)_B$. This supply relationship, equivalent to the upward-sloping rice supply curve of Chapter 2, indeed makes economic sense.

In the Ricardian model of this chapter, we end up with a restricted version of the PPF considered in Figures 3.6 to 3.8 in which the opportunity costs of production are constant and the PPF is therefore linear. As discussed in this chapter, this tends to lead to *complete specialization* when a country begins to pursue trade with other countries. This property is not fully realistic, however.

4 Heckscher–Ohlin Model of Comparative Advantage

In Chapter 3 we noted that there are two different models of comparative advantage: the Ricardian model, based on differences in technology, and the Heckscher–Ohlin model, based on differences in factor endowments. With an understanding of the Ricardian model in Chapter 3, it is now time to consider the Heckscher–Ohlin model. We need to again keep in mind that we are investigating the determinants of patterns of trade between the countries of the world and, in so doing, examining the underlying forces of the trade aspects of economic globalization.

The Heckscher–Ohlin model of comparative advantage is every bit as important as the Ricardian model.[1] It lies at the heart of the field of trade theory and has been shown to have empirical relevance. It will also be one of the sources of our analysis of the political economy of trade in Chapter 6. It opens up the consideration of comparative advantage to more than one factor of production (such as labor and physical capital or labor and land), but in the process suppresses the role of technology. In order to maintain a comprehensive view of global trade, applied trade policy analysis draws on the insights of *both* the Ricardian and the Heckscher–Ohlin models.[2]

Factors of Production

The notion of "factors of production" is a central part of microeconomics and reflects the field's recognition of resource scarcity. Factors of production are types of resources that are used in production processes. They appear as independent variables in production functions, with firms' outputs as the dependent variables. Commonly used factors of production are labor, the more inclusive human capital, physical capital, and natural resources such as land. Physical capital consists of produced goods that are, in turn, used over some significant length of time in the production of other goods. It includes things such as buildings, equipment, and machinery. Although it is not an explicit part of the Heckscher–Ohlin model,

[1] This model originated in the work of Heckscher (1949) and Ohlin (1933).

[2] This is the case, for example, with applied general equilibrium models. For a brief introduction to these models, see Reinert (2009a). For an introduction to the gravity model of international trade, which is also agnostic on the source of comparative advantage, see Appendix 4.1.

intangible capital can also be an important factor of production, and we will discuss this in Part II of this textbook.[3]

A basic observation is that countries of the world differ significantly in their *endowments* of these factors of production. To see an example of this, consider the data compiled by the *Inclusive Wealth Report 2014* and presented in Figure 4.1. This presents the long-term average of the percentages of total resource endowments broken down between natural capital (natural resources of various kinds), physical capital, and human capital. Human capital here includes not just labor but the value of education, training, and skills. You can see that endowments differ between the various regions of the world. For example, Africa has the greatest relative amount of natural capital, and Europe has the greatest relative amounts of both physical capital and human capital. Figure 4.1 reports these data by regions. Looked at on a country basis, the differences are *even greater*. The conclusion here is that countries do differ significantly in their factor endowments, and this reality is captured by the Heckscher–Ohlin model.

Given this reality, the Heckscher–Ohlin model of international trade begins with *factor endowments* in its explanation of comparative advantage. But, along with factor endowments, there is a second factor-related concept at the center of the

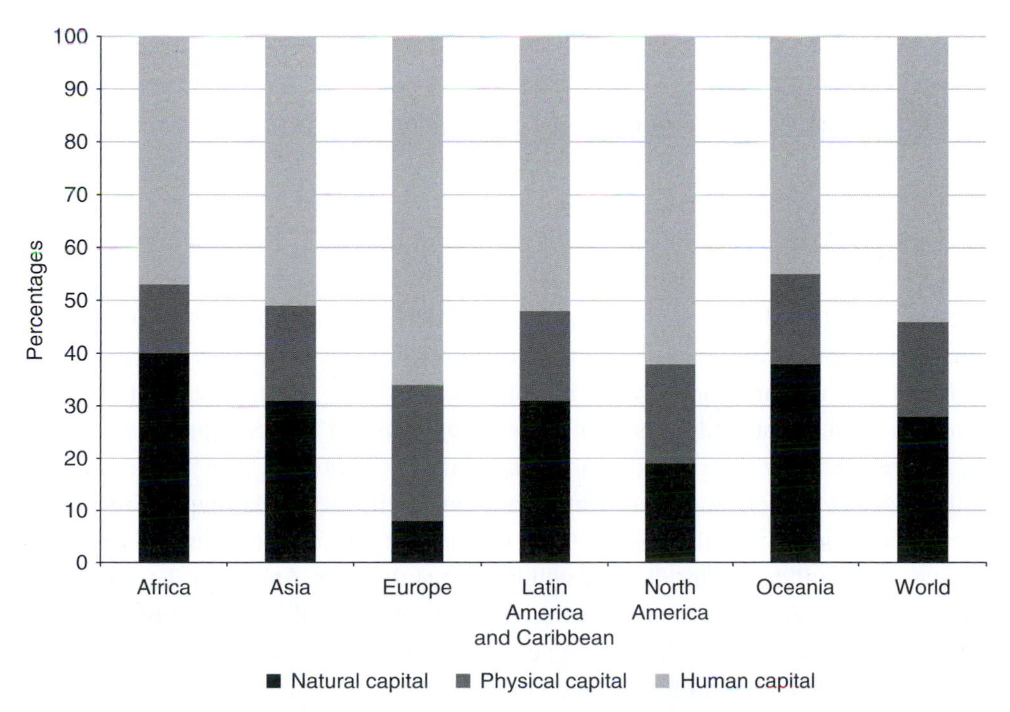

Figure 4.1 Endowments of natural capital, physical capital, and human capital by region (percentages)
Source: UNU-IHDP and UNEP (2014).

[3] See, for example, Haskel and Westlake (2017).

model. This is *factor intensities*. Factor endowments are features that characterize *countries*. In contrast, factor intensities characterize *sectors*, reflecting the technology associated with *sectors* across *all countries*. So, for example, production in the chemicals sector tends to be intensive in physical capital, production in the clothing sector tends be intensive in labor, and production in the agricultural sector tends to be intensive in natural resources, particularly land. Whereas factor intensities recognize differences in technologies across *sectors*, technologies in the Heckscher–Ohlin model are assumed to be *identical across countries*. In the Heckscher–Ohlin model, it is the interaction of country-based factor endowments with sector-based factor intensities that determines patterns of comparative advantage.

It is easy to forget or mix up the association of endowments with countries and intensities with sectors, so here is something you can refer to as you read the remainder of this chapter:

factor endowments ⇔ countries
factor intensities ⇔ sectors

Now let us begin to examine the Heckscher–Ohlin model in some detail, keeping in mind the important difference between factor endowments (countries) and factor intensities (sectors).

From Factors of Production to Comparative Advantage

Let us again use Vietnam and Japan as our two countries. Recall from Chapter 3 that we simplified the demand side of these countries in order to focus our attention on the supply side, where the most important explanatory variables are found. We are going to do the same thing in this chapter to help us in our analysis of the Heckscher–Ohlin model of comparative advantage. Again, we will assume that demands for rice and motorcycles in both Vietnam and Japan are such that these two goods are consumed in the *same, fixed proportions*. This assumption is depicted in Figure 4.2 using the same demand diagonals of Chapter 3.

In order to understand comparative advantage in the Heckscher–Ohlin model, we will also again use the concept of a production possibilities frontier. Unlike in Chapter 3, the PPFs of this chapter will be "normal," as in Appendix 3.1. That is to say, the slopes of the PPFs will be increasingly negative, indicating that **opportunity costs** are increasing.[4] In the Heckscher–Ohlin model, the increasing opportunity costs reflect the fact that the two sectors represented have different factor intensities and therefore benefit differently from additional units of the two factors considered.

[4] Remember from Chapter 3 that PPFs are resource constraints and that the slope of any resource constraint gives the opportunity cost of the item on the horizontal axis of the diagram.

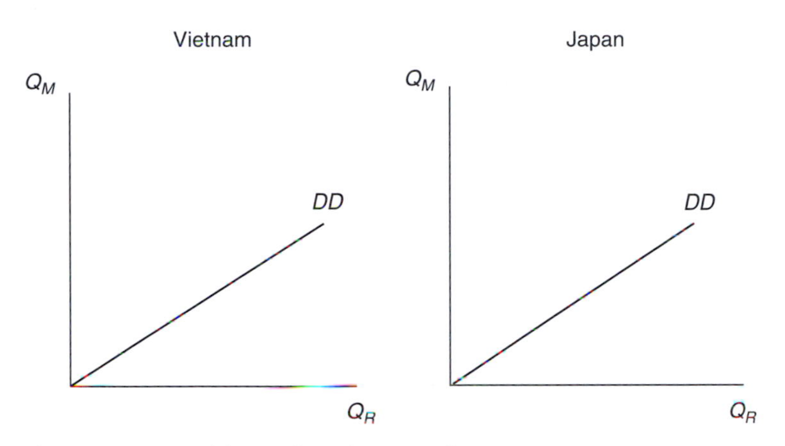

Figure 4.2 Demand diagonals in Vietnam and Japan

Consider again our two countries, Vietnam and Japan. Suppose that Vietnam has a relatively large endowment of land. In the language of international trade theory, Vietnam is relatively *land-abundant*. By this, we mean that the ratio of land to physical capital is larger in Vietnam than in Japan. As we will see, this relative abundance of land gives Vietnam a comparative advantage in producing rice, a *land-intensive* good. Similarly, suppose that Japan has a relatively large endowment of physical capital. In the language of international trade theory, Japan is relatively *capital-abundant*. By this, we mean that the ratio of physical capital to land is larger in Japan than in Vietnam. As we will see, this relative abundance of physical capital gives Japan a comparative advantage in producing motorcycles, a *capital-intensive* good.

We can get a better sense of this chain of causation using Figure 4.3. The top two boxes of this figure concern factor endowments. As we have said, Vietnam is relatively land-abundant, and Japan is relatively capital-abundant. The next two boxes concern the pattern of comparative advantage. Vietnam has a comparative advantage in rice (land-intensive), and Japan has a comparative advantage in motorcycles (capital-intensive). The third level of boxes in Figure 4.3 concerns trade flows. In accordance with the pattern of comparative advantage, Vietnam exports rice to Japan, and Japan exports motorcycles to Vietnam. More generally, the Heckscher–Ohlin model of international trade gives the following result with regard to trade.[5]

> A country exports the good whose production is intensive in its abundant factor. It imports the good whose production is intensive in its scarce factor.

[5] This result is known as the *Heckscher–Ohlin theorem* in trade theory. We will consider a second theorem of the Heckscher–Ohlin model in Chapter 6.

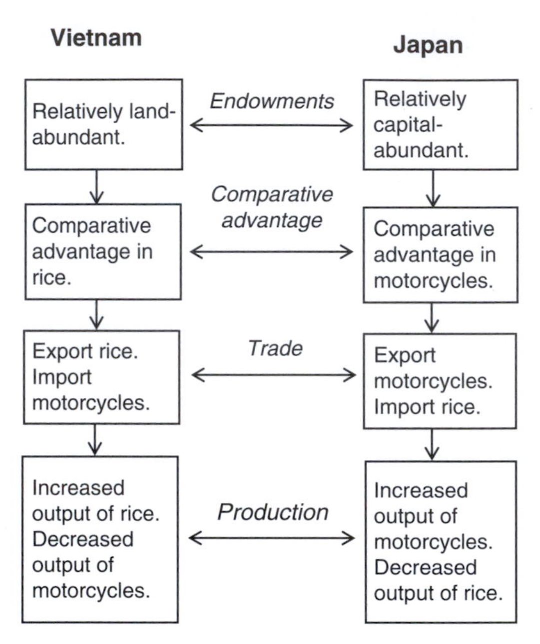

Figure 4.3 The Heckscher–Ohlin model of comparative advantage

The last set of boxes in Figure 4.3 concerns production. In Vietnam, the comparative advantage in rice causes an increase in the output of rice at the expense of motorcycles. This is the specialization in production that we saw in Chapter 3, but, as we will see, the specialization will not be complete, as in the Ricardian model. In Japan, the comparative advantage in motorcycles causes an increase in the output of motorcycles at the expense of rice. Again, this specialization in production will not be complete.

Figure 4.3 is a preview of what we will be doing in this chapter. In this section, however, we are focusing on comparative advantage itself. As in Chapter 3, we are going to do this using production possibilities frontiers in order to focus on supply conditions. These PPFs are presented in Figure 4.4. Since Vietnam is relatively *land-abundant*, this causes a bias in its PPF towards the *land-intensive* good rice. Similarly, since Japan is relatively *capital-abundant*, this causes a bias in its PPF towards the *capital-intensive* good motorcycles. The biases in the PPF in Figure 4.4 correspond to the first four boxes in Figure 4.3. They are an expression of comparative advantage.

In order to complete our discussion of comparative advantage, we need to take the demand side of Figure 4.1 and combine it with the supply side of Figure 4.4. This is done in Figure 4.5. The *DD* lines represent the demand sides of the two economies, and the PPFs represent the supply sides of the two economies. How do we determine prices, though? As we have said, the slopes of the PPFs show how many motorcycles must be given up to produce an additional unit of rice. These

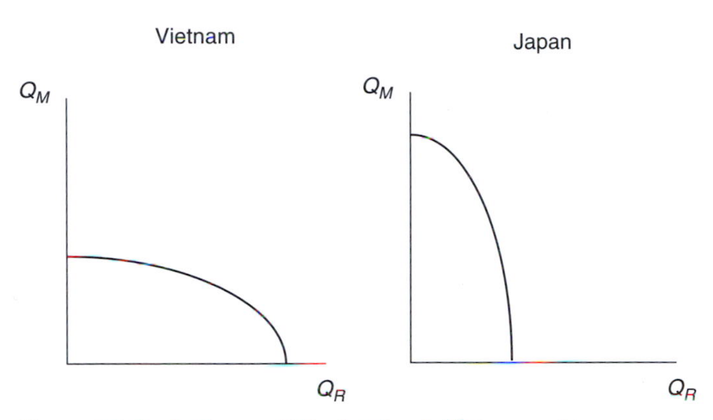

Figure 4.4 Production possibility frontiers in Vietnam and Japan

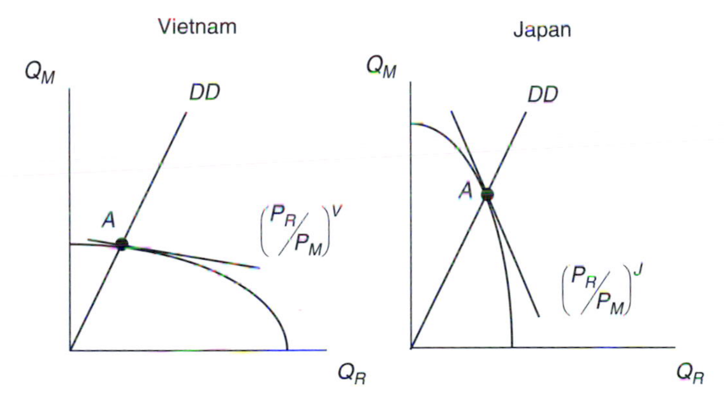

Figure 4.5 Relative autarky prices in Vietnam and Japan

slopes measure the opportunity cost of producing the item on the horizontal axis, rice, expressed in terms of how many units of the item on the vertical axis, motorcycles, must be given up or not produced because resources have switched to rice. Therefore, the slopes of the PPFs in Figures 4.4 and 4.5 represent the opportunity costs of rice in Vietnam and Japan.

As discussed in Appendix 3.1, in a system of freely operating markets, perfect competition, and full employment of production factors, opportunity costs are fully reflected in *relative* prices. Therefore, the slope of a PPF, where the demand diagonal crosses it, is the relative price of rice, $\left({P_R}/{P_M}\right)$. We represent this in Figure 4.5 by drawing in the *tangent* lines to the PPFs where the demand diagonals cross them at points *A*.[6] Points *A* in the two PPFs of Figure 4.5 represent the two countries under **autarky** in isolation from the rest of the world economy.

[6] This is discussed further in Appendix 3.1.

Looking at points A in Figure 4.5, you can see that the tangency line giving relative prices is *flatter* in Vietnam than in Japan—that is, the opportunity cost of rice is *lower* in Vietnam than in Japan. In other words, under autarky:

$$\left(\frac{P_R}{P_M}\right)^V < \left(\frac{P_R}{P_M}\right)^J \tag{4.1}$$

Inequality 4.1 says that the relative price of rice is lower in Vietnam than in Japan. Since Vietnam is the country that has a supply advantage in producing rice, Inequality 4.1 makes sense. It is an expression of a *pattern of comparative advantage*. Differences in economy-wide supply conditions cause differences in relative autarky prices and, thereby, a pattern of comparative advantage. It is these differences that make trade possible.

As we did in Chapter 3, we need to note one very important thing about Equation 4.1. This comparative advantage inequality involves *four prices* rather than *two prices*, as in the absolute advantage expression of Inequality 2.1. As we mentioned in Chapter 3, this difference has an immediate and important implication: a country can have a *comparative advantage* in a good in which it has an *absolute disadvantage*. Again, this is one reason why the comparative advantage concept is more powerful than the absolute advantage concept.

International Trade

With an understanding of comparative advantage, let us consider international trade. If Vietnam and Japan abandon autarky in favor of trade, as in the Ricardian model, the world relative price of rice $\left({}^{P_R}\!/_{P_M}\right)^W$ will be somewhere between the two autarky price ratios:

$$\left(\frac{P_R}{P_M}\right)^V < \left(\frac{P_R}{P_M}\right)^W < \left(\frac{P_R}{P_M}\right)^J \tag{4.2}$$

This situation is depicted in Figure 4.6. The world price ratio here is depicted with dashed lines that have the slope $\left({}^{P_R}\!/_{P_M}\right)^W$. These lines are steeper than the autarky price line in Vietnam and flatter than the autarky price line in Japan, as is indicated in Inequality 4.2. The tangencies of these world price lines with the PPFs determine the new production points in Vietnam and Japan. These points are labeled B. In Vietnam, the movement along the PPF from A to B involves an increase in the production of rice, while, in Japan, this movement involves an increase in the production of motorcycles. This is known as *specialization in production*.

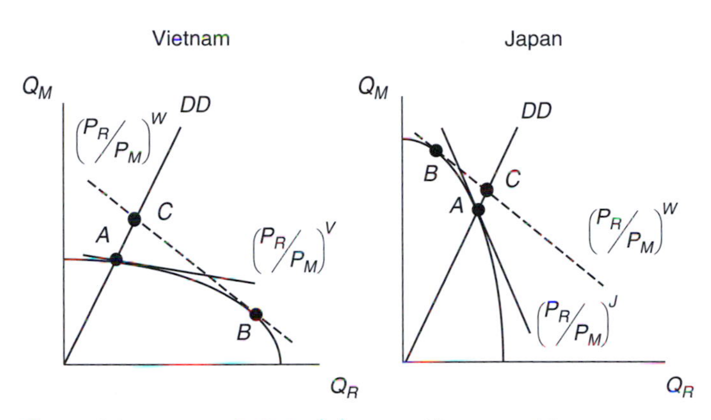

Figure 4.6 From autarky to trade between Vietnam and Japan

The important lesson you should understand here is that moving from autarky to trade restructures an economy's production towards the good in which the country has a comparative advantage. This is one reason why opening economies up to trading relations with the rest of the world can be difficult for the countries involved. Workers and other resources must be moved from one sector of the economy to another in the process.[7] This corresponds to the fourth set of boxes in Figure 4.3.

As in the Ricardian model, consumption points for Vietnam and Japan must be along our demand diagonal lines. These points, labeled *C* in Figure 4.6, occur where the dashed world price lines intersect the demand diagonals. Why is this? Both consumption and production must respect world prices–that is, *both* points *B* and *C* must be on the world price lines. In contrast to autarky, consumption and production points are now different. This separation of consumption and production points takes place through trade.

Look at Figure 4.7, which removes the autarky price lines. In Vietnam, production of rice along the horizontal axis exceeds consumption of rice, and the difference is exported (E_R^V). Production of motorcycles along the vertical axis falls short of consumption of motorcycles, however, and this shortfall is imported (Z_M^V).[8] In Japan, production of motorcycles along the vertical axis exceeds consumption of motorcycles, and the difference is exported (E_M^J). Production of rice along the horizontal axis falls short of consumption, however, and this shortfall is imported (Z_R^J). What we see in Figure 4.7 is that a pattern of comparative advantage, based on differences in supply conditions between two countries, gives rise to a complementary pattern of trade. This corresponds to the third set of boxes in Figure 4.3.

---

[7] We take up the political economy implications of these resource movements in Chapter 6.

[8] As in Chapters 2 and 3, we use *Z* to denote imports, since the symbols *I* and *M* are taken up by investment and money, respectively.

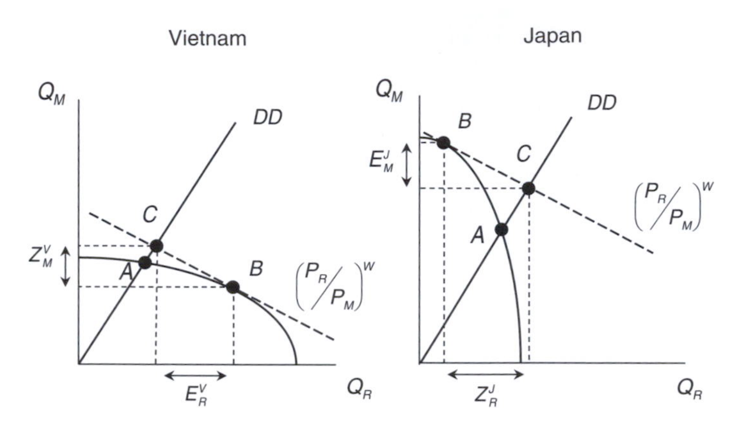

Figure 4.7 Trade between Vietnam and Japan

What ensures that the quantities imported and exported in Figure 4.7 balance? Suppose that E_R^V were smaller than Z_R^J. If this were the case, there would be excess demand for (or a shortage of) rice in the world market. As we saw in our absolute advantage model of Chapter 2, excess demand for rice would cause P_R^W to rise. Therefore, the $\left(P_R/P_M\right)^W$ lines in Figure 4.7 would become steeper. This would direct production in both countries along the PPFs towards rice, alleviating the excess demand.[9]

We mentioned in Chapter 2 that the absolute advantage concept can leave the impression that a country might lack an advantage in anything, and therefore have nothing to export. The concept of comparative advantage clears up this problem. Having an *absolute* disadvantage in a product does not preclude having a *comparative* advantage in that product. Vietnam could have an absolute disadvantage in rice, but still export this product because of its comparative advantage. This is why comparative advantage is a more powerful concept than absolute advantage and is the most central concept in international economics.

Let us summarize what we have shown this far in a box.

> Differences in factor endowments between the countries of the world give rise to complementary patterns of comparative advantage. These patterns of comparative advantage, in turn, make possible complementary patterns of international trade.

For the sake of completeness, let us look at this box alongside the equivalent box for the Ricardian model.

[9] In more advanced treatments (e.g. Markusen et al., 1995), adjustments also occur on the demand side.

Ricardian model Differences in *technology-determined supply conditions* between the countries of the world give rise to complementary patterns of comparative advantage. These patterns of comparative advantage, in turn, make possible complementary patterns of international trade.

Heckscher–Ohlin model Differences in *factor endowments* between the countries of the world give rise to complementary patterns of comparative advantage. These patterns of comparative advantage, in turn, make possible complementary patterns of international trade.

These two statements represent two primary sources of comparative advantage that operate simultaneously in the world economy. They help to determine trade patterns in the world economy, albeit in complex ways. They bring us a good distance in understanding the trade aspects of economic globalization.

Before moving on to discuss the gains from trade, another key concept in international economics, we also need to note that it is possible to get an *empirical* handle on patterns of comparative advantage in the world economy. This is done using the measure of revealed comparative advantage, described in the accompanying box.

Revealed Comparative Advantage

How is the notion of comparative advantage applied in practice? Beginning with Belassa (1965), the standard approach has been to examine actual trade flows of a country to understand what is known as *revealed comparative advantage*. This is done in relative terms to a set of comparison countries or to a single comparison country. What has come to be known as the *Belassa index* (*BI*) is calculated for sector *i* of country *j* as follows:

$$BI_i^j = \frac{\text{share of sector } i \text{ in country } j \text{ exports}}{\text{share of sector } i \text{ in reference country (or world) exports}}$$

Comparative advantage is said to be "revealed" when BI_i^j is greater than one. As is evident in this formula, however, a key question is what country or countries to use as a point of reference in the denominator. Another issue is how to handle *intra*-industry trade, a topic discussed in Chapter 5. In addition, the revealed

Revealed Comparative Advantage (cont.)

comparative advantage measure does not identify the *source* of the comparative advantage, be it technology or resource endowments. Further, revealed comparative advantage measures are affected by various barriers to trade, including the measures of protection considered in Chapter 7.

One property of the Balassa index that has troubled international economists is that it is not symmetrically distributed around the value of one. This can be corrected by computing the revealed symmetrical comparative advantage (RSCA) as:

$$RSCA = \frac{(BI - 1)}{(BI + 1)}$$

The RSCA is symmetrical around one. Sometimes researchers multiply it by 100 to make it symmetrical around 100.

Despite its limitations, revealed comparative advantage has been used for a long time by a number of researchers to understand evolving patterns of comparative advantage in the world economy.

Sources: Belassa (1965), Laursen (2015), Rodrigo (2009), and van Marrewijk (2002)

Gains from Trade

To this point, we have seen that, given a pattern of comparative advantage, it is possible for a country to give up autarky in favor of importing and exporting based on differences in factor endowments. But should a country actually do this? We considered this question in both Chapter 2 on absolute advantage and Chapter 3 on the Ricardian model of comparative advantage, and became familiar with the notion of the **gains from trade**. We can answer this question once again by examining Figure 4.7. Notice that the post-trade consumption points *C* are up and to the right ("northeast") of the autarky consumption points *A*. This directional relationship between points *A* and *C* means that the movement from autarky to trade increases consumption of *both* rice *and* motorcycles, as it did in the Ricardian model of Chapter 3. Increased consumption of both goods, in turn, implies that economic welfare has increased. Vietnam and Japan have experienced mutual gains from trade based on comparative advantage.[10]

[10] Our implicit assumption here is the standard one in economics, namely that welfare is determined by consumption levels. For a well-known challenge to this assumption, see Sen (1987).

We have now considered the gains from trade in three different contexts: absolute advantage in Chapter 2, the Ricardian model of comparative advantage in Chapter 3, and the Heckscher–Ohlin model of comparative advantage in this chapter. The principle of the gains from trade is indeed a general concept that applies to most types of trade. It is therefore worth repeating something we said in Chapter 2. To judge from the tone and content of many popular writings on the world economy, trade relationships are a win-lose proposition for the countries involved. To export is to win; to import is to lose. This is a neo-mercantilist idea that has recently gained traction among the ethno-nationalist political movements mentioned in Chapter 1.[11] The gains from trade idea tells us that trade can be *mutually beneficial* to the countries involved, however. For this reason, you need to be cautious in your assessment of some popular writing of the win-lose, neo-mercantilist variety.

FDI, Migration, and Comparative Advantage

One basic assumption that the Heckscher–Ohlin model shares with the Ricardian model is that factors of production do not move from one country to another. Another way of stating this is that there is no **foreign direct investment** and international **migration**. But, as we discussed in Chapter 1, both FDI and migration are important aspects of international economic integration or globalization. As it turns out, it is possible to get a sense of what the effects of FDI and migration are on patterns of comparative advantage on the basis of factor endowments. We do this in Figure 4.8 for FDI and Figure 4.9 for migration.

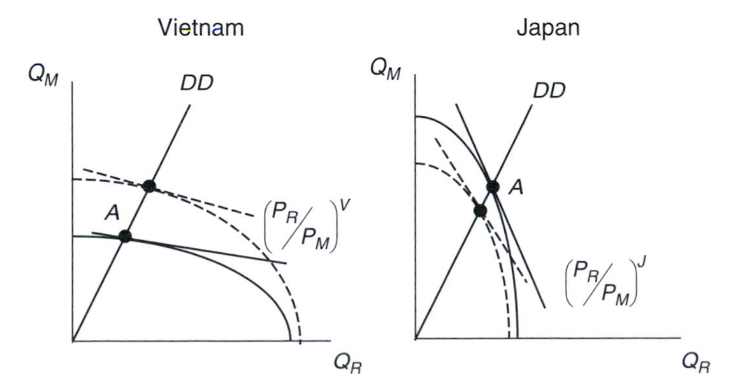

Figure 4.8 FDI and comparative advantage between Vietnam and Japan

[11] See, for example, *The Economist* (2016), which observes: "From Warsaw to Washington, the political divide that matters is less and less between left and right, and more and more between open and closed" (16).

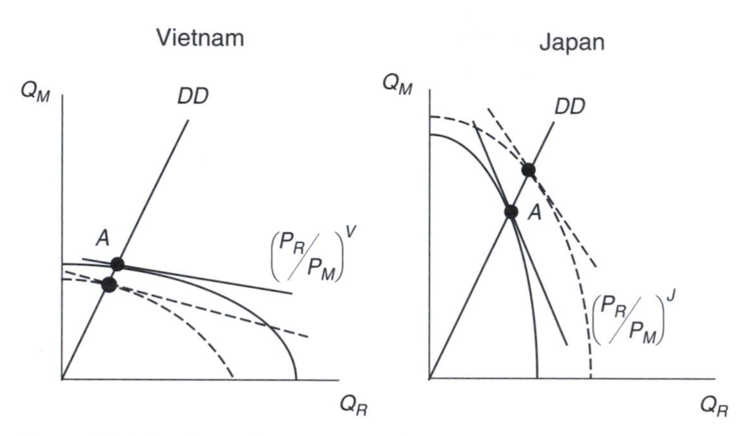

Figure 4.9 Migration and comparative advantage between Vietnam and Japan

Let us consider FDI first. Recall that we have evaluated comparative advantage by examining the relative price of rice to motorcycles, or $\left(P_R/P_M\right)$, in Vietnam and Japan. As we saw, this price ratio was lower in Vietnam, indicating that Vietnam had a comparative advantage in rice and that Japan had a comparative advantage in motorcycles. Let us see what FDI does to these relative autarky prices. We will do this in Figure 4.8.

Suppose that we allow for an FDI flow from Japan to Vietnam. To make matters simple, suppose that this is a full "offshoring," involving the closing of a motorcycle factory in Japan and the opening of a new motorcycle factory in Vietnam. This FDI flow changes the relative factor endowments of the two countries. Japan becomes less capital-abundant and Vietnam becomes more capital-abundant. These two changes have impacts on the PPFs of the two countries in Figure 4.8. The PPFs shift in a manner biased towards the capital-intensive good, motorcycles. In Vietnam, with the inflow of capital, the PPF shifts *out* to the dashed concave curve, while in Japan the PPF shifts *in* to the dashed curve. The new autarky points along the demand diagonals (*DD*) are such that the autarky price ratios change to the dashed lines. In Vietnam, $\left(P_R/P_M\right)^V$ increases, while, in Japan, $\left(P_R/P_M\right)^J$ decreases. You can see this by examining the relative slopes of the solid and dashed price lines.

What do these changes in the autarky price ratios mean? They mean that the gap between the two autarky price ratios is *narrowing*, or that the pattern of comparative advantage is weakening. This indicates that FDI can function as a *substitute* for trade.[12] Recall, however, that the assumption of the Heckscher–Ohlin model is that production technology is the same in each country of the world.

[12] This famous result was first pointed out by Mundell (1957).

This is not always the case, and, where technologies differ, sometimes FDI can be a *complement* to trade. In other words, with differing technologies, some types of FDI can strengthen patterns of comparative advantage.[13]

Let us next consider migration, in Figure 4.9. Suppose that we allow for a migration flow from Vietnam to Japan.[14] This migration flow changes the relative factor endowments of the two countries. Japan becomes more labor-abundant (less capital-abundant) and Vietnam becomes less labor-abundant (more capital-abundant). These two changes have impacts on the PPFs of the two countries in a manner affecting the labor-intensive sector, rice, most strongly. In Vietnam, with the outflow of labor, the PPF shifts *in* to the dashed concave curve, while, in Japan, the PPF shifts *out* to the dashed curve. The new autarky points along the demand diagonals (*DD*) are such that the autarky price ratios change to the dashed lines. In Vietnam, $\left({P_R}/{P_M}\right)^V$ increases, while, in Japan, $\left({P_R}/{P_M}\right)^J$ decreases. You can see this by examining the relative slopes of the solid and dashed price lines.

What is the implication of these changes in the autarky price ratios? It means that the gap between the two autarky price ratios is narrowing, or that the pattern of comparative advantage is weakening. As we have examined the process here, it indicates that migration (as well as FDI) can function as a *substitute* for trade.[15] Once again, however, recall that the assumption of the Heckscher–Ohlin model is that production technology is the same in each country of the world. This is not always the case, and, where technologies differ, sometimes migration can be a *complement* to trade. In other words, with differing technologies, some types of migration can strengthen patterns of comparative advantage.[16]

Limitations

As with our analysis of absolute advantage in Chapter 2 and the Ricardian model in Chapter 3, caveats are in order. First, like all economic models, the Heckscher–Ohlin model employs a set of assumptions. The Heckscher–Ohlin model as described here assumes that there are only two resources or factors of production.[17] There is

---

[13] This modified result was due to Purvis (1972).

[14] Pritchett (2006) estimates the relative wage between Japan and Vietnam to be approximately nine and notes that this is higher than relative wages prevalent during the "Great Migration" of the late nineteenth and early twentieth centuries. In fact, however, Japan has well-developed mechanisms to ensure that this will never occur in any meaningful way, despite its significant "birth dearth" problems.

[15] Again, this result was first pointed out by Mundell (1957).

[16] Again, this modified result was due to Purvis (1972).

[17] It is possible to relax this assumption and include additional resources, but the results become less clear.

perfect competition, full employment, and profit maximization. The two resources are generally assumed to not move from one country to another, but, as we have seen, it is possible to relax this assumption. Countries differ from one another in only one way, factor endowments, and technology is assumed to be the same everywhere. The model is powerful, but we always need to keep an eye on the assumptions that go into it.

Second, the gains from trade occur for the country *as a whole*. The fact that a country as a whole benefits in the aggregate from trade does *not* mean that every individual or group within the country benefits. Indeed, as you will see in Chapter 6, there are good reasons to expect that there will be groups that *lose* from increased trade, and these groups might oppose increased trade despite the overall gains to their country. To foreshadow our discussion in Chapter 6, for example, rice producers in Japan have a long history of opposing imports of rice.

Third, as we mentioned in Chapter 2, some goods are traded that do not contribute to increased welfare. Land mines, heroin, and prostitution services are all traded internationally, but their consumption significantly reduces welfare rather than increases it. For this reason, you need to be careful not to generalize the gains from trade concept too far.[18]

Fourth, in recent decades there has also been a great deal of discussion of the impacts of trade on the basis of comparative advantage on the *environment*. It is sometimes alleged that international trade is almost always detrimental to the environment. The situation is not this straightforward, however. Both theoretical and empirical results demonstrate that increased trade can be either good or bad for the environment, and that we need to approach the trade and environment issue on a case-by-case basis. This issue is discussed in the accompanying box.

Comparative Advantage and the Environment

Given the steady advance of the volume of trade discussed in Chapter 1 and the growing concern about environmental issues worldwide, it is natural to ask what role trade and comparative advantage play in levels of pollution and other forms of environmental degradation. Although this issue is largely empirical, trade and environmental economists have identified three means through which trade can have positive or negative environmental impacts: a scale or growth effect, an activity composition effect, and a technique effect.

The *scale or growth effect* refers to the possibility that trade can stimulate the overall level of economic activity, which can, in turn, have environmental repercussions.

[18] See, for example, Reinert (2004).

Comparative Advantage and the Environment (cont.)

This effect holds constant the composition of economic activity and production technology. For example, trade might stimulate the overall use of scarce natural resources or the overall level of pollution. It is here that we encounter the "inverted U" hypothesis: that environmental degradation first increases and then decreases with the level of economic activity or gross domestic product. This inverted U relationship is sometimes also known as the environmental Kuznets curve, or EKC.

The *activity composition effect* refers to something that we have seen in this chapter, namely that trade changes the location of countries on the PPF. This effect holds constant the overall level of economic activity and the production technology. Depending on the pattern of comparative advantage, pollution-intensive sectors such as chemicals and metals can either increase or decrease their share in the total output of a country. López and Islam (2009) state that, as a general rule of thumb, physical-capital- and natural-resource-intensive sectors tend to be more polluting than human-capital-intensive sectors.

The *technique effect* holds constant both the overall level of economic activity and the sectoral composition of that activity. It refers to the possibility that the pollutant intensity of a given level of output in a sector can change, sometimes for the better. López and Islam (2009) note: "The technique effect of trade has been found to reduce certain pollutants, particularly air pollutants, but the effects on other environmental factors [are] less significant." The technique effect also becomes applicable in the spread of green or environmentally friendly technologies, on which much hope has been placed in recent years.

The *net effect* of trade on the environment is, as we stated above, an empirical issue, and the case of NAFTA and the environment is discussed in a box in Chapter 8. But, in principle, this net effect would reflect the combined impacts of the scale or growth effect, the activity composition effect, and the technique effect. These are the lenses through which economists view the trade and environment issue.

Sources: Beghin and Potier (1997) and López and Islam (2009)

Conclusion

In this book, we have considered two models of comparative advantage, the Ricardian model of Chapter 3 and the Heckscher–Ohlin model of this chapter. The Ricardian model explains comparative advantage among the countries of the world in terms of *technological differences*. The Heckscher–Ohlin model assumes that technology is the same among all countries and focuses on differences in *factor endowments* and the way these factor endowments interact with the different factor intensities of sectors. Therefore, a question that comes to mind is: which model is right? The answer is that they *both* are: technology and factor endowments both matter to patterns of comparative advantage.[19] In applied trade policy analysis, models are used that capture the insights of both the Ricardian and Heckscher–Ohlin models.[20]

As it turns out, there is a third source of international trade patterns that is somewhat independent of comparative advantage. This is intra-industry trade, and it is the subject of the next chapter. Chapters 3, 4, and 5, then, identify three potential sources of trade: comparative advantages based on differences in technology, comparative advantage based on differences in factor endowments, and intra-industry trade. Let us next find out what the third of these is all about.

Review Exercises

1. Create an example of a comparative advantage based on factor endowment by choosing two countries, two products, and two factors of production. Make one of the factors labor.
   a. Draw a diagram describing *autarky* and a *pattern of comparative advantage* for your example.
   b. Show the transition from autarky to trade in your diagram, label the trade flows, and demonstrate the *gains from trade.*
2. For your example in Question 1 above, and in words, take yourself through the logic of Figure 4.3. Do this for both countries, describing endowments, comparative advantage, the patterns of trade, and specialization in production.
3. For your example in Questions 1 and 2 above, use the autarky PPF diagrams to describe how migration from the relatively labor-abundant country to the relatively labor-scarce country will impact the PPFs of the two countries and their autarky price ratios.

FURTHER READING AND WEB RESOURCES

A concise introduction to comparative advantage can be found in Maneschi (2009) and a fuller historical perspective can be found in Maneschi (1998). A more advanced treatment can be found in Markusen et al. (1995: chap. 5) and Brakman et al. (2006: chap. 3). For an

[19] See, for example, Trefler (1995).

[20] This is particularly true of what are known as applied general equilibrium models. See, for example, McDaniel, Reinert, and Hughes (2004) and Reinert (2009a).

introduction to the Heckscher–Ohlin model itself, see Panagariya (2009). For a balanced view of the trade and environment issue, see Copeland and Taylor (2005).

REFERENCES

Beghin, J., and M. Potier (1997) "Effects of Trade Liberalisation on the Environment in the Manufacturing Sector," *The World Economy*, 20:4, 435–56.

Belassa, B. (1965) "Trade Liberalization and 'Revealed' Comparative Advantage," *Manchester School of Economic and Social Studies*, 33:2, 92–123.

Brakman, S., H. Garretsen, C. van Marrewijk, and A. van Witteloostuijn (2006) *Nations and Firms in the Global Economy: An Introduction to International Economics and Business*, Cambridge University Press.

Copeland, B. R., and M. S. Taylor (2005) *Trade and the Environment: Theory and Evidence*, Princeton University Press.

Deardorff, A. V. (1998) "Determinants of Bilateral Trade: Does Gravity Work in a Neoclassical World?," in J. A. Frankel (ed.), *The Regionalization of the World Economy*, University of Chicago Press, 7–32.

The Economist (2016) "Briefing: Globalisation and Politics," July 30.

Haskel, J., and S. Westlake (2017) *Capitalism without Capital: The Rise of the Intangible Economy*, Princeton University Press.

Heckscher, E. (1949) "The Effect of Foreign Trade on the Distribution of Income," in H. S. Ellis and L. A. Metzler (eds.), *Readings in the Theory of International Trade*, Irwin, 272–300.

Krugman, P. (1998) "Ricardo's Difficult Idea: Why Intellectuals Can't Understand Comparative Advantage," in G. Cook (ed.), *Freedom and Trade: The Economics and Politics of International Trade*, vol. 2, Routledge, 22–36.

Laursen, K. (2015) "Revealed Comparative Advantage and the Alternatives as Measures of International Specialization," *Eurasian Business Review*, 5:1, 99–115.

López, R., and A. Islam (2009) "Trade and the Environment," in K. A. Reinert, R. S. Rajan, A. J. Glass, and L. S. Davis (eds.), *The Princeton Encyclopedia of the World Economy*, Princeton University Press, 1103–8.

McDaniel, C., K. A. Reinert, and K. Hughes (2004) *Tools of the Trade: Models for Trade Policy Analysis*, Woodrow Wilson Center.

Maneschi, A. (1998) *Comparative Advantage in International Trade: A Historical Perspective*, Edward Elgar.

Maneschi, A. (2009) "Comparative Advantage," in K. A. Reinert, R. S. Rajan, A. J. Glass, and L. S. Davis (eds.), *The Princeton Encyclopedia of the World Economy*, Princeton University Press, 198–205.

Markusen, J. R., J. R. Melvin, W. H. Kaempfer, and K. E. Maskus (1995) *International Trade: Theory and Evidence*, McGraw-Hill.

Mundell, R. A. (1957) "International Trade and Factor Mobility," *American Economic Review*, 47:3, 321–35.

Ohlin, B. (1933) *International and Inter-Regional Trade*, Harvard University Press.

Panagariya, A. (2009) "Heckscher–Ohlin Model," in K. A. Reinert, R. S. Rajan, A. J. Glass, and L. S. Davis (eds.), *The Princeton Encyclopedia of the World Economy*, Princeton University Press, 591–7.

Pritchett, L. (2006) *Let Their People Come: Breaking the Gridlock on Global Labor Mobility*, Center for Global Development.

Purvis, D. D. (1972) "Technology, Trade and Factor Mobility," *Economic Journal*, 82:327, 991–9.

Reinert, K. A. (2004) "Outcomes Assessment in Trade Policy Analysis: A Note on the Welfare Propositions of the 'Gains from Trade,'" *Journal of Economic Issues*, 38:4, 1067–73.

Reinert, K. A. (2009a) "Applied General Equilibrium Models," in K. A. Reinert, R. S. Rajan, A. J. Glass, and L. S. Davis (eds.), *The Princeton Encyclopedia of the World Economy*, Princeton University Press, 74–9.

Reinert, K. A. (2009b) "Gravity Models," in K. A. Reinert, R. S. Rajan, A. J. Glass, and L. S. Davis (eds.), *The Princeton Encyclopedia of the World Economy*, Princeton University Press, 567–70.

Rodrigo, G. C. (2009) "Revealed Comparative Advantage," in K. A. Reinert, R. S. Rajan, A. J. Glass, and L. S. Davis (eds.), *The Princeton Encyclopedia of the World Economy*, Princeton University Press, 971–3.

Sen, A. (1987) *The Standard of Living*, Cambridge University Press.

Tinbergen, J. (1962) *Shaping the World Economy: Suggestions for an International Economic Policy*, Twentieth Century Fund.

Trefler, D. (1995) "The Case of the Missing Trade and Other Mysteries," *American Economic Review*, 85:5, 1029–46.

UNU-IHDP and UNEP (2014) *Inclusive Wealth Report 2014: Measuring Progress toward Sustainability*, Cambridge University Press.

Van Marrewijk, C. (2002) *International Trade and the World Economy*, Oxford University Press.

Appendix 4.1: The Gravity Model

Gravity models utilize the gravitational force concept as an analogy to explain the volume of trade or foreign direct investment between the countries of the world.[21] For example, gravity models establish a baseline for trade or FDI *flows* as determined by gross domestic product, population, and distance.[22] The effect of policies on trade or FDI flows can then be assessed by adding the policy variables to the equation and estimating deviations from the baseline flows. In many instances, gravity models have significant explanatory power, leading Deardorff (1998) to refer to them as a "fact of life."

[21] For a concise review, see Reinert (2009b).

[22] The emphasis on *flows* here is to remind us that the gravity model does not explain FDI stocks such as those reported in Chapter 10. Distance is sometimes expanded conceptually to include linguistic and cultural distance. The origins of the gravity model go back to Tinbergen (1962).

Gravity models begin with Newton's law for the gravitational force (GF_{ij}) between the two objects i and j. In equation form, this is expressed as

$$GF_{ij} = \frac{M_i M_j}{D_{ij}} \quad i \neq j \tag{4.3}$$

In this equation, the gravitational force is directly proportional to the masses of the objects (M_i and M_j) and indirectly proportional to the distance between them (D_{ij}).

Gravity models are estimated in terms of *natural logarithms*, denoted "**ln**." In this natural log form, what is multiplied in Equation 4.3 becomes added, and what is divided becomes subtracted, translating Equation 4.3 into a linear equation:

$$\ln GF_{ij} = \ln M_i + \ln M_j - \ln D_{ij} \quad i \neq j \tag{4.4}$$

Gravity models of international trade and FDI implement Equation 4.4 by using trade flows or FDI flows from country i to country j (F_{ij}) in place of gravitational force, with arbitrarily small numbers sometimes being used in place of any zero values. Distance is often measured using "great circle" calculations. The handling of mass in Equation 4.4 takes place via at least two alternatives. In the *first alternative*, with the more solid theoretical foundations, mass in Equation 4.4 is associated with the gross domestic product (*GDP*) of the countries. In this case, Equation 4.4 becomes

$$\ln F_{ij} = \alpha + \beta_1 \ln GDP_i + \beta_2 \ln GDP_j + \beta_3 \ln D_{ij} \tag{4.5}$$

In general, the expected signs here are $\beta_1, \beta_2 > 0$ and $\beta_3 < 0$.

In the *second alternative*, mass in Equation 4.4 is associated with *both* GDP *and* population (*POP*). In this case, Equation 4.4 becomes

$$\ln F_{ij} = \varphi + \gamma_1 \ln GDP_i + \gamma_2 \ln POP_i + \gamma_3 \ln GDP_j + \gamma_4 \ln POP_j + \gamma_5 \ln D_{ij} \tag{4.6}$$

Regarding the expected signs on the population variables, these are typically interpreted in terms of market size and are therefore positive ($\gamma_2, \gamma_4 > 0$).

Whatever the specification, the gravity model has been shown to have empirical validity, and it is a part of the "toolkit" of international economics.

5 Intra-Industry Trade

Once, while visiting the World Trade Organization in Geneva, I took a three-day side trip to Clermont-Ferrand, France, in order to visit some students who were there on study abroad. At my first buffet breakfast in the hotel, I noticed an exceptional-looking blue cheese. It was as wonderful to eat as to look at, and upon my inquiry I learned that this was the famed bleu d'Auvergne from the surrounding region.[1] I sampled it as often as I could during my short trip, and, on my return to the United States, began to purchase it whenever possible. In this way, I contributed to the total volume of cheese imports of the United States. It turns out, however, that the United States also *exports* cheese, especially what is known as "food service" cheese (admittedly, less exceptional than the bleu d'Auvergne). Thus, the United States *both* imports *and* exports cheese, a phenomenon known as ***intra*-industry trade**.

In this chapter, you will begin to appreciate this important type of trade. You will also understand how it differs from ***inter*-industry trade**, two different *types* of intra-industry trade, why they occur, and their role in the world economy. In the process, you will also be introduced to one model of intra-industry trade that is part of what is known as **new trade theory**. We begin by contrasting *inter*- and *intra*-industry trade.[2]

Intra-Industry and Inter-Industry Trade

In Chapters 3 and 4, we discussed the important concept of **comparative advantage**. In our example of those chapters, we saw that Japan imported rice and exported motorcycles, while Vietnam exported rice and imported motorcycles. This is an example of how comparative advantage is associated with inter-industry trade. In inter-industry trade, a country *either* imports *or* exports a given product. Our

[1] The term "blue d'Auvergne" is one example of what is known as a *regional indicator* in international trade law. We will encounter regional indicators in our discussion of intellectual property in Chapter 8.

[2] The first use of the term "intra-industry trade" and contrast with inter-industry trade was by Balassa (1966).

example above of US cheese trade is quite different. The United States *both* imports *and* exports cheese, an example of intra-industry trade. Therefore, you should have the following associations in mind when distinguishing intra-industry trade from inter-industry trade:

inter-industry trade ⇔ either/or

intra-industry trade ⇔ both/and

As we just mentioned, and as indicated in Table 5.1, inter-industry trade has its source in comparative advantage, in the differences in technology and factor endowments of countries. Intra-industry trade and its sources are different, and there are actually *two types* of intra-industry trade. The example of trade in cheese varieties is a case of **horizontal intra-industry trade**, and has its source in **product differentiation**. The term "horizontal" refers to the fact that the products exchanged are at the *same level of processing*—that is, both the exported variety (food service cheese) and the imported variety (bleu d'Auvergne) are final goods. The role of product differentiation here is that the two varieties of cheese are different from one another. The final product bleu d'Auvergne is not the same kind of product as food service cheese or Wisconsin cheddar. Similarly, the final product Ford Focus is not exactly the same kind of product as a Honda Civic.[3]

The second type of intra-industry trade is **vertical intra-industry trade**, and has its source in **fragmentation** (again, see Table 5.1). For example, China imports computer components and assembles them into the final product computers.

Table 5.1 Types of trade

Type of trade	Phrase	Meaning	Source
Inter-industry	Either/or	*Either* imports *or* exports in a given sector of the economy	Comparative advantage
Horizontal intra-industry	Both/and/same	*Both* imports *and* exports in a given sector of the economy and at the *same* stage of processing	Product differentiation
Vertical intra-industry	Both/and/different	*Both* imports *and* exports in a given sector of the economy and at *different* stages of processing	Fragmentation (comparative advantage in some instances)

[3] As stated by van Marrewijk (2002: 183), "A satisfactory theoretical explanation [of intra-industry trade] should...be able to distinguish between goods and services which are close, but imperfect substitutes."

The imported computer components are at a previous stage of processing to the exported computers, but, from the point of view of computer products, this is intra-industry trade. The reason this has occurred is that firms have decided to break up the production process of computers into *tasks* or *fragments* and distribute them across national boundaries. This fragmentation is an example of what we called international production in Chapter 1, and vertical intra-industry trade is one area where the subjects of international trade and international production interact in important ways. Indeed, another term for fragmentation is "international production sharing."[4] This is a relatively new phenomenon, and has shown up in the increased volumes of parts and components in international trade flows.

There is another subtle issue associated with vertical intra-industry trade. Some types of fragmentation take place so that final assembly will occur where there is abundant, inexpensive labor.[5] This sounds a lot like the Heckscher–Ohlin model of comparative advantage discussed in Chapter 4. Although these issues are still being fully worked out by trade theorists, there is agreement that some part of fragmentation is comparative advantage working in a *new way*, within the realm of parts and components rather than final goods. So, although comparative advantage is not much help in explaining horizontal intra-industry trade, it is of help in explaining some types of vertical intra-industry trade.[6]

Globally, intra-industry trade is becoming more important over time.[7] In the next section we will examine global patterns of this type of trade. Then we will consider more formal explanations of how and why this type of trade occurs.

---

[4] See, for example, Arndt (2009), who notes that there are important connections between fragmentation and foreign direct investment. Indeed, some *vertical intra*-industry trade can also be *intra*-firm trade within a multinational enterprise. As the OECD (2002: 162) states, "The combination of rising intra-industry trade and high foreign direct investment inflows [in some countries] is consistent with the increasing extent to which multinational firms have located parts of their production operations in these countries."

[5] As Brakman et al. (2006: 37) note, "Technological and communication advances have enabled many production processes to be subdivided into various phases which are physically separable, a process known as fragmentation. This enables a finer and more complex division of labor, as the different phases of the production process may now be spatially separated and undertaken at locations where costs are lowest."

[6] One reason why comparative advantage does not explain *all* vertical intra-industry trade is that, for this kind of trade involving a series of tasks located in different countries, proximity to transportation and logistics hubs can also be important.

[7] So, for example, Peterson and Thies (2015: 178) observe: "Although the theory of comparative advantage and the Heckscher–Ohlin model remain relevant and useful today, scholars have noted that an increasing proportion of international trade no longer fits the expectations of these models. Since the end of World War II there has been an increasing proportion of trade within, rather than between, industries—often among states with very similar factor endowments."

Global Patterns of Intra-Industry Trade

Estimates of the amount of intra-industry trade vary and depend both on the measurement technique and the level of disaggregation of the trade data. As discussed in Appendix 5.1, the more disaggregated the trade data are, the less the measured amount of intra-industry trade. One comprehensive assessment of global intra-industry trade is that of Brülhart (2009). His estimates are presented in Figure 5.1. This figure shows that, measured at the five-digit Standard Industrial Trade Classification (SITC) level, intra-industry trade increased from 7 percent of world trade in 1962 to 27 percent of world trade in 2006. Measured at the three-digit SITC level, intra-industry trade increased from 20 percent of world trade in 1962 to 44 percent of world trade in 2006. Based on this type of evidence, an accepted rule of thumb is that intra-industry trade accounts for approximately *one-third* of world trade.

It is also clear that intra-industry trade is especially prominent in the trade in manufactured goods, especially as the degree of sophistication of the manufacturing process increases. Increased sophistication of the manufacturing process allows for both greater differentiation of final products in horizontal intra-industry trade

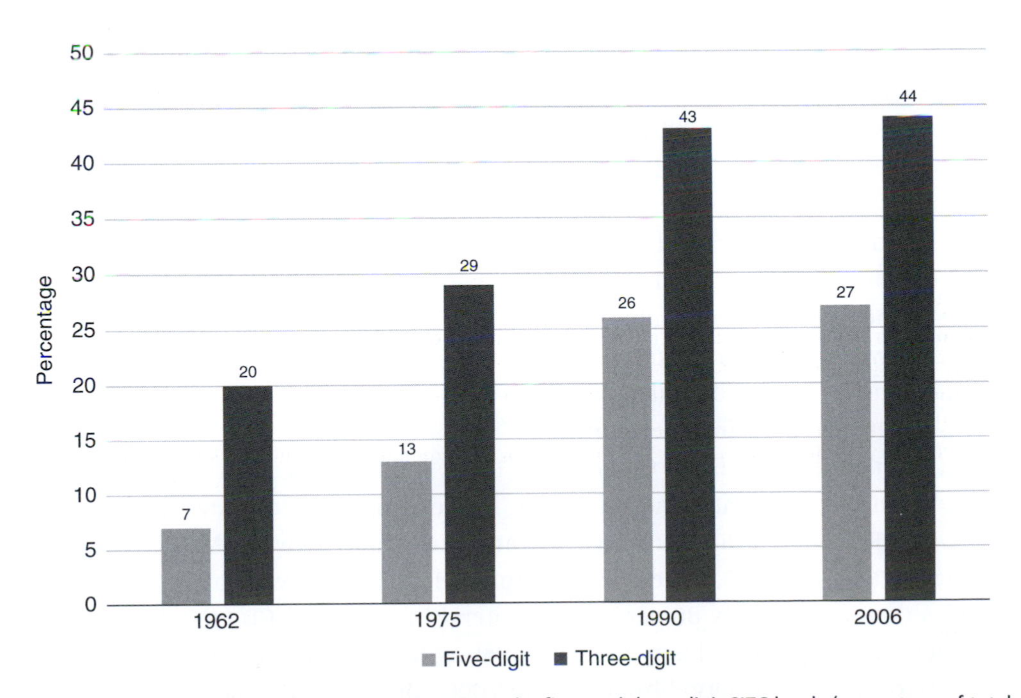

Figure 5.1 The evolution of intra-industry trade at the five- and three-digit SITC levels (percentage of total trade)

Note: SITC refers to Standard International Trade Classification.

Source: Brülhart (2009).

and greater scope for fragmentation in vertical intra-industry trade.[8] For some countries and manufactured products, intra-industry trade can exceed 70 percent of trade. Another related observation that is often made is that horizontal intra-industry trade tends to be concentrated between higher-income countries, while vertical intra-industry trade tends to be concentrated between specific pairs of countries that are at different levels of per capita incomes.

Intra-industry trade was first analyzed in the context of trade between the countries of Western Europe, as well as trade between the United States and Europe. The early study by Grubel and Lloyd (1975) focuses on intra-industry trade between ten original countries of the Organisation for Economic Co-operation and Development, an organization consisting of mostly high-income countries. These ten countries are Australia, Belgium, Canada, France, Italy, Japan, the Netherlands, the United Kingdom, the United States, and West Germany (before integration with East Germany). These authors developed an index used to measure the degree of intra-industry trade, which is explained in Appendix 5.1. Using this index, they note an increase in intra-industry trade between these ten countries during the 1960s. Subsequent studies found that this trend continued into the 1970s and beyond. For example, Baldwin (2016: 97, fig. 29) estimates that about 65 percent of trade between France and Germany is intra-industry trade.

It turns out, however, that it was a mistake to envision intra-industry trade as taking place exclusively between high-income countries. For example, I spent the early years of the 1990s analyzing NAFTA for the US International Trade Commission. As part of this analysis, I developed a database of trade between the countries of North America for the year 1988.[9] What struck me at the time was the decidedly intra-industry character of the trade flows between Mexico and the United States even before NAFTA went into effect. With the few exceptions of petroleum, nonmetallic minerals, and non-electrical machinery, sectoral trade between these two countries was quite balanced. I realized at that time that intra-industry trade could take place between low- and high-income countries as well as between high-income countries.

At about the same time, Globerman (1992) published results indicating substantial increases in intra-industry trade between the United States and Mexico between 1980 and 1988. Ruffin (1999) analyzed trade between Mexico and the United States for 1998, a decade later than the year of my database, and concludes that it was nearly 80 percent of bilateral trade. The OECD (2002) also notes Mexico's role in intra-industry trade, estimating it at over 70 percent of that country's trade during the period from 1996 to 2000. More recently, Baldwin (2016: 97,

---

[8] See OECD (2002).

[9] See Reinert, Roland-Holst, and Shiells (1993).

fig. 29) estimates it at just over 40 percent. Whatever the exact figure, it is clear that intra-industry trade is not confined to developed countries alone.

Evidence of increases in intra-industry trade in Asia also surfaced. As indicated in the accompanying box, intra-industry trade in Asia appears to be most important between newly industrialized countries (Singapore, Hong Kong, and South Korea) and newly exporting countries (Malaysia, Thailand, the Philippines, and Indonesia). Evidence has emerged, however, of increasing intra-industry trade between Japan and other Asian countries (e.g. Wakasugi, 1997), as well as in the trade of China and its major trading partners (e.g. Hu and Ma, 1999). Hence, we can view intra-industry trade as a multi-regional process that is increasing over time.[10] There are regions that have been left out of this trend, however. Evidence suggests that western Asia (including the Middle East) and most of Africa participate very little in intra-industry trade.[11] This is one of the main distinctions between these two regions and the rest of the world with regard to international trade characteristics.

Intra-Industry Trade in East Asia

The phenomenon of intra-industry trade was first noticed in the expansion of trade between the countries of Western Europe and between Western Europe and the United States that occurred after World War II. Later, however, researchers recognized its importance for the countries of East Asia, including China, Hong Kong, Indonesia, Japan, Malaysia, the Philippines, Singapore, South Korea, Taiwan, and Thailand. Early on, Hellvin (1994) provided estimates of intra-industry trade in East Asia that exceeded 20 percent in the mid-1980s. Subsequent analysis was provided by Thorpe and Zhang (2005) and Ando (2006). Thorpe and Zhang (2005) suggest that intra-industry trade increased from approximately 25 percent to approximately 50 percent between the mid-1970s and the mid-1990s. They also suggest that vertical intra-industry trade increased to about 30 percent during this period. Evidence from the machinery sector presented by Ando (2006) suggests that these trends continued through at least 2000.

The East Asian region remains a very important one for the world economy, setting trends that are later experienced in other regions. What can now be called decadal evidence on the expansion of East Asian trade suggests that *intra*-industry trade in general and vertical intra-industry trade in particular are going to be increasingly important for this region of the world economy.

Sources: Ando (2006), Hellvin (1994), and Thorpe and Zhang (2005).

[10] We revisit the case of China in Appendix 5.1.

[11] See, for example, Brülhart (2009).

Intra-Industry Trade under Monopolistic Competition

There is now a standard approach to modeling intra-industry trade, based on imperfect competition and part of what is known as "new trade theory."[12] New trade theory is "new" in that it originated in the 1980s rather than in the late nineteenth century or middle of the twentieth century. The particular type of imperfect competition used in the new trade theory approach to intra-industry trade is *monopolistic competition.*[13] The term "monopolistic competition" is a funny one. How can a monopoly be competitive? But the term actually refers to the fact that the model borrows one feature from monopoly and another from perfect competition.

The monopoly feature is that monopolistically competitive firms face *downward-sloping* demand curves. This is attributable to a fact very relevant to the intra-industry trade phenomenon, namely that monopolistically competitive firms produce *differentiated products.* The products are differentiated in the sense that they are slightly or somewhat different from one another across all the firms in the industry/sector. The competition feature is that firms have *free entry and exit* from the sector in the long run. There are many more firms in monopolistically competitive sectors than under monopoly and oligopoly. Therefore, there can be *no long-run economic profits.*

There is also a third element that is part of the monopolistic competition, intra-industry trade model. This is *increasing returns to scale* or *economies of scale.* The notion of increasing returns to scale says that, if you double all inputs into production, output *more than* doubles. Increasing returns to scale cause economies of scale. Under economies of scale, average costs fall as a firm's output increases. To understand the model, we need to combine the three elements of product differentiation, free entry and exit, and economies of scale.[14] We will begin with economies of scale.

Figure 5.2 shows the relationships between a firm's average costs (AC), marginal costs (MC), and quantity of output (q). This figure shows an AC line that is *falling* because of economies of scale. From what we know about the relationship

---

[12] For a review of new trade theory, see Krugman (1999) and Matschke (2009). Matschke (2009: 829) notes that new trade theory "is the descriptive term for theories that assume imperfect competition and increasing returns to scale...in order to explain international trade. In contrast, traditional trade theories, such as the Ricardian or the Heckscher–Ohlin model, assume perfect competition and constant returns to scale."

[13] This model goes back to the work of Chamberlin (1933). The application to intra-industry trade was made by Krugman (1980).

[14] Krugman (1999) writes: "To understand the revolution, you need to grasp two related dichotomies. One is that between constant and increasing returns; the other between perfect and imperfect competition."

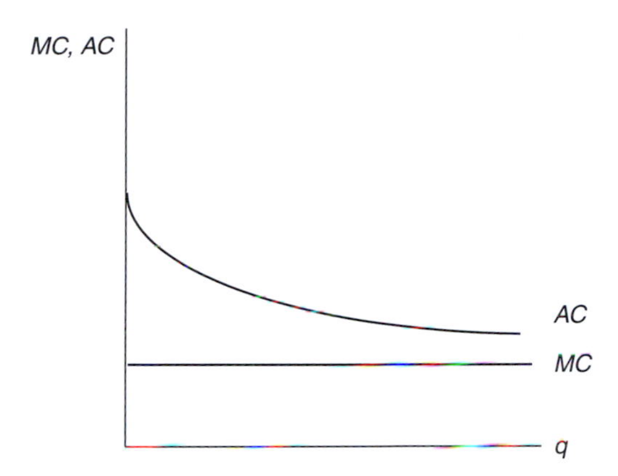

Figure 5.2 Economies of scale in the monopolistic competition model

between averages and marginals, if an average is falling, the marginal must be below it.[15] That is the case in the figure, and, for simplicity, we assume that the *MC* curve is *constant*.

Please note that Figure 5.2 and subsequent figures in this section plot *firm* quantities, not sector quantities, as in Chapters 2 through 4. Firm quantities are denoted with the lower-case q rather than with the upper-case Q. The monopolistic competition model of intra-industry trade focuses on individual firms. We would have to sum up all the firm quantities in a country's sector to get the sector quantity.[16] This firm perspective is also why the demand curves in the model will be denoted with the lower-case d rather than an upper-case D.

The *AC* and *MC* lines in Figure 5.2 describe the *cost side* of the monopolistically competitive firm. What we need to add is the *revenue side*. The centerpiece of the revenue side is the firm's demand curve (d). We need to draw this as relatively elastic (flat), because there are a significant number of close substitutes (e.g. varieties of cheese) for the good that the firm produces. Associated with the demand curve is a steeper marginal revenue (*MR*) curve. It is steeper than the demand curve because, whenever the firm increases its output, the price (p) falls. These two lines are presented in Figure 5.3.

Our next task is to put together the cost side of the firm (Figure 5.2) and the revenue side of the firm (Figure 5.3). We do this is Figure 5.4, illustrating long-run equilibrium in the monopolistically competitive sector or industry. This involves

---

[15] Imagine that you have a grade point average (GPA) of 3.0. You take on additional (marginal) course and score a 2.0. What will happen to your GPA? It will fall, but (fortunately) not all the way to 2.0.

[16] Formally, this would be $Q = \Sigma_i q_i$, where i is an index of firms.

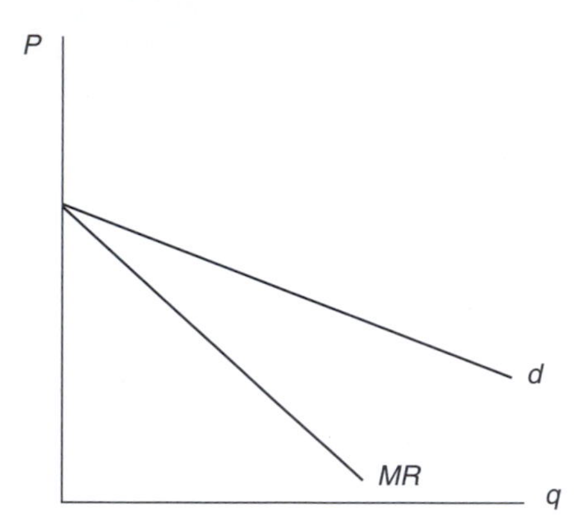

Figure 5.3 Demand and marginal revenue in the monopolistic competition model

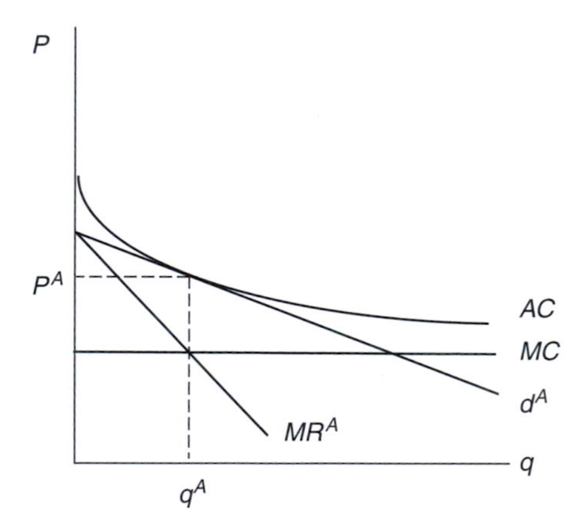

Figure 5.4 Autarky equilibrium in the monopolistic competition model

two things. First, firms must be maximizing profits. Recall from your introductory microeconomics course that this implies that they choose a level of output at which marginal revenue equals marginal cost ($MR = MC$). Second, the long-run entry and exit of firms ensures that economic profits are zero or that price equals average costs ($P = AC$). These two conditions are represented in Figure 5.4. They determine the price and quantity of the monopolistically competitive firm. Because we have not yet introduced international trade, we will refer to these as the autarky price (P^A) and the autarky quantity (q^A).[17]

[17] Formally, the monopolistically competitive sectors are allocatively inefficient, in that the price is too high and the quantity is too low. Economists do not tend to worry about this, because the effects are relatively small and are offset by gains in variety arising from product differentiation.

We next need to introduce *international trade* into the model. The main effect of trade is to *expand the market* in which firms compete. The number of firms operating abroad is added to the number of firms operating domestically, so, after trade, any one firm competes against a larger set of differentiated products that is composed of a greater number of close substitutes. This means that trade increases the price elasticity of demand for any individual firm. Consequently, the demand curve becomes *flatter*.

The consequences of trade, including the flatter demand curve, are presented in Figure 5.5. The flatter demand curve that trade brings carries along with it a flatter *MR* curve. These revenue-side effects increase the individual firm's profit-maximizing output from q^A to q^T. The new and higher profit-maximizing level of output also involves a fall in the price from P^A to P^T. This price fall takes place for all firms remaining in the sector. The fact that all remaining firms have lowered their price is the result of increased competitive pressure, and this involves some firms *exiting* from the sector in the transition to the new, long-run equilibrium illustrated in Figure 5.5. The number of *firms* in the sector is *lower* as a result of trade, but the number of available *varieties* is *higher* as a result of trade, with more varieties being imported from abroad.

This brief consideration of the monopolistic competition model of intra-industry trade shows how product differentiation can lead to two-way trade within a sector. In the case of horizontal intra-industry trade, the demand for the final products can come from both households and firms. In the case of vertical intra-industry trade, the demand for the intermediate products comes from just firms. The gains from trade come from two sources. The first is the standard gains from trade reflecting the fact that prices are lower ($P^T < P^A$). The second is due to the fact that households have access to a larger *variety* of goods, which has value in and of itself.

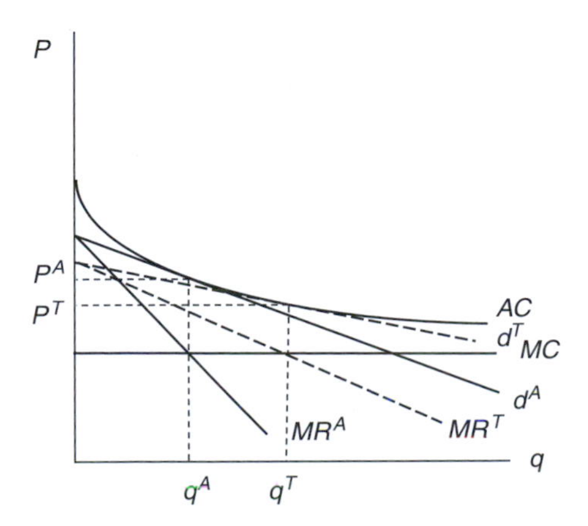

Figure 5.5 The effects of international trade in the monopolistic competition model

The Smooth Adjustment Hypothesis

The increasing extent of intra-industry trade in the world trading system has some potentially important implications for the adjustment of economies to increasing trade. Recall from Chapters 2 through 4 that increases in inter-industry trade based on absolute or comparative advantage involve import sectors contracting and export sectors expanding. In the absolute advantage model of Chapter 2, this adjustment involves movements up and down the supply curve, whereas, in the comparative advantage models of Chapters 3 and 4, adjustment involves movements along the PPFs. This, in turn, requires that productive resources, most notably workers, shift from contracting to expanding sectors in order to avoid unemployment. Workers in Vietnam must shift from the motorcycle sector to the rice sector. Workers in Japan must shift from the rice sector to the motorcycle sector. This is not always an easy process, and, as we will discuss in Chapter 6, it often gives rise to calls for trade protection.

Early investigations suggested that adjustment processes under increased intra-industry trade might be different, because increased trade in differentiated final or intermediate products would entail fewer changes in the overall structure of production.[18] The thinking was that, under intra-industry trade, a given sector could experience increases in imports and exports *simultaneously*. Therefore, workers are less likely to need to shift between sectors of their home economy. In the case of horizontal intra-industry trade, the labor market adjustment is across product market niches. For example, workers in the US cheese sector can adjust to the expansion of imports of cheese by expanding exports of a different cheese variety. In the case of vertical intra-industry trade, the labor market adjustment is across *tasks* or *stages* of production. For example, workers in a computer sector might need to shift from producing both computer components and final, assembled computers to just producing certain components. This idea became known as the *smooth adjustment hypothesis* of intra-industry trade.[19]

Since the introduction of the smooth adjustment hypothesis, there has been a great deal of empirical testing of its validity. This process began in the mid-1990s and continues to this day. These studies use a variety of measures of labor adjustment costs and consider both horizontal and vertical intra-industry trade for a number of countries.[20] About two-thirds of the studies to date support the smooth

[18] For a very early example, see Balassa (1966), who states: "It would appear that the difficulties of adjustment to freer trade have been generally overestimated" (472).

[19] Early examples included Marvel and Ray (1987), Grimwade (1989), and Thom and McDowell (1999). Ruffin (1999: 7) also notes: "One of the great benefits of intra-industry trade is that international trade need not cause the dislocations associated with inter-industry trade."

[20] For a useful review, see White (2014: chap. 9), particularly table 9.1.

adjustment hypothesis, so the hypothesis might be best seen as a *likely* but not necessarily *universal* property of intra-industry trade. Further research will continue to shed light on the smooth adjustment hypothesis.

There are more expansive conceptions of the smooth adjustment hypothesis. For example, in an introduction to an edited volume on the field of intra-industry trade, Lloyd and Grubel (2003: xxv, emphasis added) suggest: "The study of intra-industry trade has made significant contributions to our understanding of international trade in an increasingly globalized and interconnected world. It also has important policy implications since the costs of trade liberalization may be smaller and *aspirations for economic development may be more easily met* in a world where intra-industry trade plays an important role than one where inter-industry trade dominates." More recently, Peterson and Thies (2015) have examined the role of intra-industry trade within **preferential trade agreements** (PTAs), to be discussed in Chapter 9. They suggest that increased intra-industry trade within PTAs increases the likelihood of peaceful relations and cooperation between the countries involved. Although they are no doubt preliminary, results such as these suggest that the smooth adjustment process can potentially have political implications.

Computer Products Trade

As noted by Curry and Kenney (2004), the personal computer is a highly modular product. This fact has ensured that personal computer assembly is one that supports vertical intra-industry trade via fragmentation and production sharing. The tasks involved in building a personal computer stretch out along what is known as **global value chains**, ranging from raw materials to many kinds of component manufacturing to final assembly and sales. Various raw materials, such as ceramics, metals, and chemicals, are used to produce a large range of components, such as microprocessors, circuit boards, display panels, and many others. Compared to component manufacturing, assembly is very straightforward. Indeed, Curry and Kenney (2004: 118) state: "Modularity and international standardization has proceeded to such an extent that an assembler with minimal training can assemble a PC in fifteen minutes with little more equipment than a screwdriver and a socket set." Consequently, computer assembly is more of a logistics operation than a manufacturing operation.

In recent years a great deal of computer assembly has been taken on by Taiwanese firms operating in China. These firms often need to import computer components (particularly the high-end components, such as microprocessors)

Computer Products Trade (cont.)

that are then used to assemble the final computer. Despite a growing PC market in China, most of the assembled computers are then exported to major markets outside China. Thus, China imports computer products at one stage of processing (components) and exports computer products at another stage of processing (the final, assembled computer). This is vertical intra-industry trade in computer products.

Sources: Curry and Kenney (2004) and McIvor (2005)

Conclusion

In Chapters 2 through 4, we considered models of inter-industry trade. Approximately one-third of world trade consists of intra-industry trade, however. This breaks down into two types: horizontal intra-industry trade, based on product differentiation; and vertical intra-industry trade, based on fragmentation and, potentially, on comparative advantage. If, as you proceed through this book, you have trouble distinguishing inter-industry and intra-industry trade, be sure to refer back to Table 5.1. We have also considered a new trade theory model of monopolistic competition, which is often used to describe intra-industry trade, and have introduced and evaluated the smooth adjustment hypotheses associated with intra-industry trade.

Although the monopolistic competition model of intra-industry trade is sometimes applied to vertical intra-industry trade, a fuller appreciation of this type of trade needs to include an appreciation of global value chains. For this reason, we will have reason to refer back to vertical intra-industry trade in Part II of the book on **international production**. In doing this, we will reconsider the processes involved in fragmentation.

Review Exercises

1. In your own words, please explain the difference between inter-industry and intra-industry trade.
2. How is the phenomenon of horizontal intra-industry trade related to product diversification?

3. Create your own example of a horizontal intra-industry trade by choosing two countries and a product. Explain how product differentiation makes horizontal intra-industry trade in this product possible.
4. Create your own example of vertical intra-industry trade by choosing two countries and two stages of production of a product. Explain how fragmentation makes vertical intra-industry trade possible in this case.
5. Explain why the adjustment process stemming from intra-industry trade might be easier for a country to accommodate than the adjustment process stemming from inter-industry trade.

FURTHER READING AND WEB RESOURCES

The concept of intra-industry trade goes back to Balassa (1966) but see also Grubel and Lloyd (1975). For an early review, see Greenaway and Torstensson (1997). For concise, more recent reviews, see van Marrewijk (2002: chap. 10), OECD (2002), Brakman et al. (2006: chap. 4), and van Marrewijk (2009). For a longer, empirical review, see Brülhart (2009). On the political economy of intra-industry trade, see Peterson and Thies (2015).

REFERENCES

Ando, M. (2006) "Fragmentation and Vertical Intra-Industry Trade in East Asia," *North American Journal of Economics and Finance*, 17:3, 257–81.

Arndt, S. W. (2009) "Fragmentation," in K. A. Reinert, R. S. Rajan, A. J. Glass, and L. S. Davis (eds.), *The Princeton Encyclopedia of the World Economy*, Princeton University Press, 498–502.

Balassa, B. (1966) "Tariff Reductions and Trade in Manufactures among the Industrial Countries," *American Economic Review*, 56:3, 466–73.

Baldwin, R. (2016) *The Great Convergence: Information Technology and the New Globalization*, Harvard University Press.

Brakman, S., H. Garretsen, C. van Marrewijk, and A. van Witteloostuijn (2006) *Nations and Firms in the Global Economy: An Introduction to International Economics and Business*, Cambridge University Press.

Brülhart, M. (1994) "Marginal Intra-Industry Trade: Measurement and Relevance for the Pattern of Industrial Adjustment," *Weltwirtschaftliches Archiv*, 130:3, 600–13.

Brülhart, M. (2009) "An Account of Global Intra-industry Trade, 1962–2006," *World Economy*, 32:3, 401–59.

Chamberlin, E. H. (1933) *The Theory of Monopolistic Competition: A Re-orientation of the Theory of Value*, Harvard University Press.

Curry, J., and M. Kenney (2004) "The Organization and Geographic Configuration of the Personal Computer Value Chain," in M. Kenney (ed.), *Locating Global Advantage: Industry Dynamics in the International Economy*, Stanford University Press, 113–41.

Globerman, S. (1992) "North American Trade Liberalization and Intra-industry Trade," *Weltwirtschaftliches Archiv*, 128:3, 487–97.

Greenaway, D., and J. Torstensson (1997) "Back to the Future: Taking Stock on Intra-industry Trade," *Weltwirtschaftliches Archiv*, 133:2, 249–69.

Grimwade, N. (1989) *International Trade: New Patterns of Trade, Production, and Investment*, Routledge.

Grubel, H. G., and P. J. Lloyd (1975) *Intra-Industry Trade: The Theory and Measurement of International Trade in Differentiated Products*, John Wiley.

Hellvin, L. (1994) "Intra-Industry Trade in Asia," *International Economic Journal*, 8:4, 27–40.

Hu, X., and Y. Ma (1999) "International Intra-Industry Trade of China," *Weltwirtschaftliches Archiv*, 135:1, 82–101.

Krugman, P. (1980) "Scale Economies, Product Differentiation, and the Pattern of Trade," *American Economic Review*, 70:5, 950–9.

Krugman, P. (1999) "Talking about a Revolution: How Kelvin Lancaster Helped Transform Economics," *Slate Magazine*, August 19, https://slate.com/business/1999/08/talking-about-a-revolution.html.

Lloyd, P. J., and H. G. Grubel (2003) "Introduction," in P. J. Lloyd and H. G. Grubel (eds.), *Intra-Industry Trade*, Edward Elgar, xiii–xxviii.

McIvor, R. (2005) *The Outsourcing Process: Strategies for Evaluation and Management*, Cambridge University Press.

Marvel, H. P., and E. J. Ray (1987) "Intraindustry Trade: Sources and Effects on Production," *Journal of Political Economy*, 95:6, 1278–91.

Matschke, X. (2009) "New Trade Theory," in K. A. Reinert, R. S. Rajan, A. J. Glass, and L. S. Davis (eds.), *Princeton Encyclopedia of the World Economy*, Princeton University Press, 829–33.

Organisation for Economic Co-operation and Development (2002) "Intraindustry and Intrafirm Trade and the Internationalisation of Production," *OECD Economic Outlook*, 71:1, 159–70.

Peterson, M., and C. Thies (2015) "Intra-Industry Trade and Policy Outcomes," in L. L. Martin (ed.), *The Oxford Handbook of the Political Economy of International Trade*, Oxford University Press, 177–95.

Reinert, K. A., D. W. Roland-Holst, and C. R. Shiells (1993) "Social Accounts and the Structure of the North American Economy," *Economic Systems Research*, 5:3, 295–326.

Ruffin, R. J. (1999) "The Nature and Significance of Intra-Industry Trade," *Federal Reserve Bank of Dallas Economic and Financial Review*, 1999:4, 2–9.

Thom, R., and M. McDowell (1999) "Measuring Marginal Intra-Industry Trade," *Weltwirtschaftliches Archiv*, 135:1, 48–61.

Thorpe, M., and Z. Zhang (2005) "Study of the Measurement and Determinants of Intra-Industry Trade in East Asia," *Asian Economic Journal*, 19:2, 231–47.

Van Marrewijk, C. (2002) *International Trade and the World Economy*, Oxford University Press.

Van Marrewijk, C. (2009) "Intraindustry Trade," in K. A. Reinert, R. S. Rajan, A. J. Glass, and L. S. Davis (eds.), *The Princeton Encyclopedia of the World Economy*, Princeton University Press, 708–12.

Wakasugi, R. (1997) "Missing Factors of Intra-Industry Trade: Some Empirical Evidence Based on Japan," *Japan and the World Economy*, 9:3, 353–62.

White, R. (2014) *Making Sense of Anti-Trade Sentiment: International Trade and the American Worker*, Palgrave Macmillan.

Appendix 5.1: The Grubel–Lloyd Index

We mentioned in this chapter that Grubel and Lloyd (1975) completed the first important study of *intra*-industry trade. In this study, these authors developed what is now a well-known index for measuring the degree of intra-industry trade, the **Grubel–Lloyd index**. This appendix introduces you to this index and provides a brief example of its application to China.

The Grubel–Lloyd index looks at a given product category denoted by the letter i. The index of intra-industry trade in this product category is usually denoted by B_i. B_i is calculated based on the level of imports of product i (denoted Z_i) and the level of exports of product i (denoted E_i). The Grubel–Lloyd index is calculated as

$$B_i = \left[1 - \frac{|E_i - Z_i|}{(E_i + Z_i)}\right] \cdot 100 \tag{5.1}$$

Recall that $|E_i - Z_i|$ in Equation 5.1 refers to the *absolute value* of the difference between exports and imports of product or sector i. This value is always positive. The best way to make sense of the Grubel-Lloyd index is to consider the case when intra-industry trade is at its maximum–that is, when exports and imports of product i are *exactly equal* to one another. In this case, $|E_i - Z_i| = 0$ and $B_i = (1 - 0) \cdot 100 = 100$. Therefore, the Grubel-Lloyd index ranges from zero to 100. As the index increases from zero to 100, the amount of intra-industry trade in product category i increases.

We can visualize this using Figure 5.6. In cases when $E_i = Z_i$, a particular trading economy will be on the 45° line in this figure and $B_i = 100$. As the trading economy diverges in either direction from the 45° line, B_i will decline from 100. If the import and export values are such that one is zero (the pure inter-industry trade case), then the economy will be on one of the two axes and $B_i = 0$.

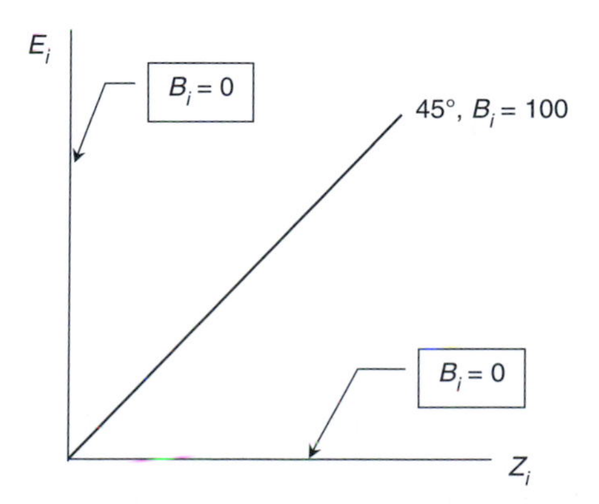

Figure 5.6 Visualizing the Grubel–Lloyd index

Table 5.2 Measuring China's *intra*-industry trade using the Grubel–Lloyd index

Year	3-digit SITC or 237 sectors	2-digit SITC or 67 sectors	1-digit SITC or 10 sectors
1980	20	30	63
1985	20	29	44
1990	36	45	60
1995	38	48	67
2000	39	48	57
2005	42	49	58

Note: SITC refers to standard international trade classification. The Grubel–Lloyd indices reported here are average, trade-weighted indices.
Source: Van Marrewijk (2009).

Table 5.2 reports a few measures of intra-industry trade for China using the Grubel–Lloyd index calculated by van Marrewijk (2009). Van Marrewijk rightly drew three conclusions from the results presented in this table. First, as we disaggregate further (moving right to left in the table), the amount of trade classified as intra-industry declines. Second, despite this decline, intra-industry trade does not disappear.[21] Third, as discussed in this chapter, the amount of intra-industry trade increases over time.

More recently, researchers have been using a modification of the Grubel–Lloyd index known as the *marginal* Grubel–Lloyd index. Recall that the notion of *marginal* refers to changes or, more specifically, to ratios of changes. So, the marginal Grubel–Lloyd index is defined as[22]

$$MB_i = \left[1 - \frac{|\ E_i - \ Z_i|}{|\ E_i| + |\ Z_i|}\right] \cdot 100 \tag{5.2}$$

Consider the case when marginal intra-industry trade is at its maximum—that is, when the change in exports and the change in imports of product i are *exactly equal* to one another. In this case, $|\ E_i - \ Z_i| = 0$ and $MB_i = (1-0) \cdot 100 = 100$. Therefore, the marginal Grubel–Lloyd index also ranges from zero to 100. As the index increases from zero to 100, the amount of marginal intra-industry trade in product category i increases. You will find researchers using both Equation 5.1 and Equation 5.2 in their analysis.

---

[21] Van Marrewijk (2009: 710) notes: "This is a general characteristic of current trade flows as intraindustry trade exists for very detailed sector classifications." For examples of the detailed sector classifications for the case of China, see Hu and Ma (1999).

[22] See Brülhart (1994) and White (2014: chap. 9).

6 The Political Economy of Trade

In previous chapters, we have seen that it is possible for countries to move from autarky to inter-industry trading relationships based on comparative advantage or to intra-industry trading relationships based on product diversification and fragmentation. In the case of comparative advantage, for example, Japan can export motorcycles to Vietnam while importing rice from Vietnam. We have also seen that movements from autarky to trade involve *improvements in welfare* for the countries involved. In other words, both Japan and Vietnam can experience gains from trade. Japan has a very long history of *restricting* imports of rice, however. This reluctance to import rice was explained some years ago by the Consulate General of Japan in San Francisco:

> Rice has been the staple of the Japanese for over 200 years and can be considered the most important element in the evolution of the Japanese culture and social structure. Therefore, a significant segment of the Japanese population expresses cultural concerns over rice imports. In addition, many Japanese rice producers have historically been strongly opposed to accepting rice imports for both economic security and cultural reasons.

Indeed, during the Uruguay Round of multilateral trade negotiations (1986–1994), the Japanese Diet (parliament) passed three resolutions opposing the proposed partial liberalization of the Japanese rice market. At the very end of the Uruguay Round negotiations Japan was given "special treatment" to continue to restrict rice imports. Even the rice that Japan has agreed to import is rarely allowed to actually enter the market, however.[1] To this day Japan offers significant protection to its domestic rice sector, such that the domestic price is two to three times the world price.[2]

Welcome to the *political economy of trade*. In Chapters 2 through 5 we were careful to mention that the improvement in overall welfare in a country that occurs because of the gains from trade does not necessarily imply an improvement in welfare for *every* individual and group in that country. In this chapter you will learn that it is both possible and likely that, in countries moving from autarky

[1] See Lewis (2015). This article also discusses the larger role of rice in Japanese society and politics.
[2] See Fukuda, Dyck, and Stout (2003) and *The Economist* (2015), for example.

to trade, certain groups actually *lose* from this change.[3] Japanese rice producers are one such politically powerful group. The fact that there are both winners and losers from international trade gives rise to the political economy of trade. This is a realm in which the field of international trade begins to merge somewhat into political science and public policy, a very exciting prospect for many researchers and practitioners. It is also a realm in which there is great deal of lobbying on the part of specific sectors and product producers.

We will begin in this chapter by considering different approaches to the political economy of trade, including country-based, factor-based, sector-based, and firm based. We will then revisit the **Heckscher–Ohlin model** of comparative advantage developed in Chapter 4. This will be the means through which we explore factor-based approaches to the political economy of trade using the **Stolper–Samuelson theorem**. Second, we will examine the application of this theorem to the topic of North–South trade. Third, we will consider a sector-based approach to the political economy of trade by introducing the **specific factors model** of trade. Finally, we will relate our discussion of the political economy of trade to the broader issue of globalization and inequality. Appendix 6.1 considers a model of **endogenous protection**.

Approaches to the Political Economy of Trade

Research into the political economy of trade takes place within a framework of a *market for protection* that draws our attention to supply-side and demand-side factors in this market.[4] The supply of protection is provided by national governments, and there are two country-based approaches in the field of international relations and political science that offer alternative perspectives of this side of the protection markets. As shown in Table 6.1, these are the perspectives of *realism* and *institutionalism*. Let us briefly consider each of them.

Realism is a school of thought in international relations that stresses the lack of global government and concludes that the inherently anarchic relations between countries must be addressed via the projection of power.[5] Realism consequently views trade through the lens of *power*, emphasizing the security and technology aspects of trade and the need to harness these to promote national "strength." For

[3] As in the cases of previous chapters, we are working in this chapter within the standard economic view of welfare. We do need to recognize, however, that there are other views that can lead to different interpretations of trade issues.

[4] Research in this vein began with Schattschneider (1935). For more modern contributions, see Rodrik (1995) and Milner (1999).

[5] For a more thorough treatment of realism, see Donnelly (2000).

Table 6.1 Approaches to the political economy of trade

Focus	Name	Insight
Country-based	Realism	There are security externalities associated with international trade that need to be managed by country governments.
Country-based	Institutionalism	Institutional structures within country governments affect trade policy outcomes.
Factor-based	Heckscher–Ohlin model Stolper–Samuelson theorem	Under factor mobility within a country, different factors can win or lose from increased trade.
Sector-based	Specific factors model	With sector-specific factors, whether factors win or lose can depend on whether they are specific to an export- or import-oriented sector.
Firm-based	Firm-based	The exposure of firms to trade or international capital mobility can influence the posture of these firms to trade liberalization.

Source: Adapted from Walter and Sen (2009).

example, trade in certain defense-related products can dissipate power and consequently be tightly controlled within established alliances. High technology can be "dual-use," potentially having defense-related characteristics. It too can be tightly controlled.[6] Access to hydrocarbons and minerals is often viewed through a realist lens by national governments, as in the case of rare earth elements, discussed in Chapter 2. More recently the realist lens has been brought to semiconductor trade.[7] Finally, illicit trade can have important national security implications.[8] Protection is often offered by governments in support of these ends, and, more generally, these governments often view trade relations through a lens of security alliances.[9]

Institutionalism is a second country-based approach, is associated with most branches of the social sciences, and focuses on the "rules of the game" within

[6] For example, *The Economist* (2018b: 25) reports that "foreign technology firms that want to sell their wares in China face at least six different security reviews, each of which can be used to delay or block market access."

[7] See *The Economist* (2018c).

[8] See Shelley (2017).

[9] These considerations have also spawned the profession of "trade compliance," in which firms ensure that they meet national-security-based trade regulations, as well as the larger field of "strategic trade."

a particular socio-political or socio-economic system. In the realm of the political economy of trade, institutional analysis emphasizes the importance of certain key aspects of national governments in supplying protection.[10] The distribution of decision-making power within national governmental systems can be important, as well as the relationship of executive and legislative branches with regard to trade policy. To generalize a little, the contrast with realism is to view national governments as non-unitary actors rather than as unitary actors in the realm of global power politics. A central insight of institutional analysis is that trade policy changes are more likely when decision-making power is more centralized within the institutional framework of a government.

Other approaches to the political economy of trade emphasize the role of demand for protection in the form of what is sometimes referred to as "pressure group models." It is here that international economists have made their most important contribution to analyzing the political economy of trade, and the rest of this chapter will consider these contributions. One approach is factor-based, in that pressure comes from *classes* composed of one factor of production or another that lose as a result of trade liberalization. Below, we will consider the Heckscher–Ohlin model and its Stolper–Samuelson theorem as a factor-based theory of the demand for protection. A second approach emphasizes pressure from *sectors* rather than classes (sector interests can cut across classes), and here we encounter what is known as the specific factors model. Together, the Stolper–Samuelson theorem and the specific factors model represent economists' contribution to the political economy of trade.

There is another strand in the analysis of the political economy of trade, which focuses on specific firms and their exposure to trade and international capital mobility. This firm-level analysis was inspired by Milner (1988), who argues that firms that are more export oriented and "multinationalized" in their production and/or ownership will tend to be less protectionist in their lobbying efforts. This is a plausible hypothesis in many circumstances, but might fall short of a general principle.[11] The point of view of firms is given a good deal of attention in Part II of this book.

Table 6.1 reveals that the political economy of trade is not straightforward but is, rather, subject to a number of influences at the levels of nations, factors, sectors, and firms. In the remainder of this chapter, we will focus on factor-based and sector-based explanations, but we should not lose sight of the fact that specific cases could be more complex than suggested by these two frameworks.

---

[10] See, for example, Milner (1997). For empirical evidence, see Henisz and Mansfield (2006).

[11] For a critique of the hypothesized relationship between firms with "multinationalized" ownership and less protectionist orientations, see Hiscox (2004).

Comparative Advantage, Trade, and Factors of Production

In order to begin talking more specifically about the factor- and sector-based approaches to the political economy of trade, it is useful to revisit the Heckscher–Ohlin model of comparative advantage we developed in Chapter 4. Figure 6.1 reproduces Figure 4.6 from that chapter. Recall that Vietnam has a comparative advantage in the production of rice (denoted R) and Japan has a comparative advantage in the production of motorcycles (denoted M). As these two economies move from autarky to trade, production in each country expands in the direction of the sector in which it has comparative advantage. In the movement from points A to B along the production possibility frontiers in Figure 6.1, rice production expands in Vietnam, and motorcycle production expands in Japan. The purpose of this chapter is to analyze these processes much more carefully.

What determines the pattern of comparative advantage illustrated in Figure 6.1? Recall from Chapter 4 that, in the Heckscher–Ohlin model, it is *factor endowments* that matter. A factor-based analysis of the political economy of trade examines the implications of the movement from points A to B along the production possibilities frontiers in Figure 6.1 for factors of production in Vietnam and Japan. What we will see is that, along with the gains from trade, there are also "pains from trade," which arise from the movements along PPFs in response to increased international trade.

To be more specific, Vietnam's comparative advantage in rice reflects the fact that it has a relatively large endowment of land. In the language of international trade theory, Vietnam is relatively *land-abundant*. By this, we mean that the ratio of land to physical capital is larger in Vietnam than in Japan. This relative abundance of land gives Vietnam a comparative advantage in producing rice,

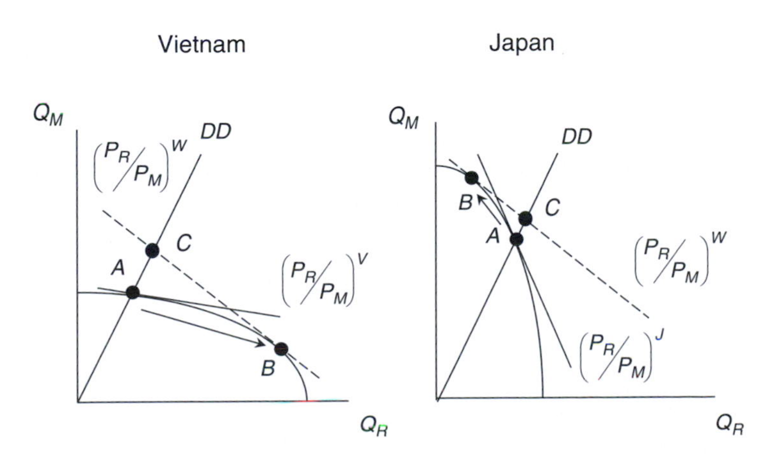

Figure 6.1 Autarky and comparative advantage in Vietnam and Japan

a *land-intensive* good. Similarly, Japan's comparative advantage in motorcycles reflects the fact that it has a relatively large endowment of physical capital–that is, Japan is relatively *capital-abundant*. By this, we mean that the ratio of physical capital to land is larger in Japan than in Vietnam. This relative abundance of capital gives Japan a comparative advantage in producing motorcycles, a *capital-intensive* good.[12]

As discussed in Chapter 4, the explanation of comparative advantage in terms of factor endowments is associated with the Heckscher–Ohlin model of international trade.[13] The logic of the Heckscher–Ohlin model was illustrated in Figure 4.3. We now need to expand this figure, as in Figure 6.2. The top two boxes of this figure concern factor endowments. Vietnam is relatively land-abundant, and Japan is relatively capital-abundant. The next two boxes concern the pattern of comparative advantage. Vietnam has a comparative advantage in rice (land-intensive), and Japan has a comparative advantage in motorcycles (capital-intensive). The third level of boxes in Figure 6.2 concerns trade flows. In accordance with the pattern of comparative advantage, Vietnam exports rice to Japan, and Japan exports motorcycles to Vietnam.

The implication of Figure 6.2 for the political economy of trade is addressed in the bottom six boxes. In Vietnam, the comparative advantage in rice causes an increase in the output of rice at the expense of motorcycles. Consequently, in Vietnam there is an increase in demand for land and a decrease in demand for physical capital. These factor demand changes have an impact on the returns to factors of production in Vietnam. As a result of trade and specialization along the PPF, land owners in Vietnam gain from trade, while Vietnamese capital owners (capitalists) lose from trade.[14]

In Japan, the comparative advantage in motorcycles causes an increase in the output of motorcycles at the expense of rice. Consequently, in Japan there is an increase in demand for physical capital and a decrease in demand for land. These factor demand changes have an impact on the returns to factors of production in Japan. As a result of trade and specialization along the PPF, capital owners in Japan gain from trade, while Japanese land owners lose from trade.

Given the results of Figure 6.2, we would expect that land owners in Vietnam and capital owners in Japan would support trade. Political opposition to trade or demand for protection would come from capital owners in Vietnam and land

---

[12] We need to interpret these statements with care. We are saying that Vietnam is relatively land-abundant in comparison to Japan. In comparison to its own population, land is in fact scarce in Vietnam. See *The Economist* (2002b).

[13] This model originated in the work of Heckscher (1949) and Ohlin (1933).

[14] Given that Vietnam is a socialist country, we need to be careful here. Institutions of ownership can be very different from those in fully market-oriented countries.

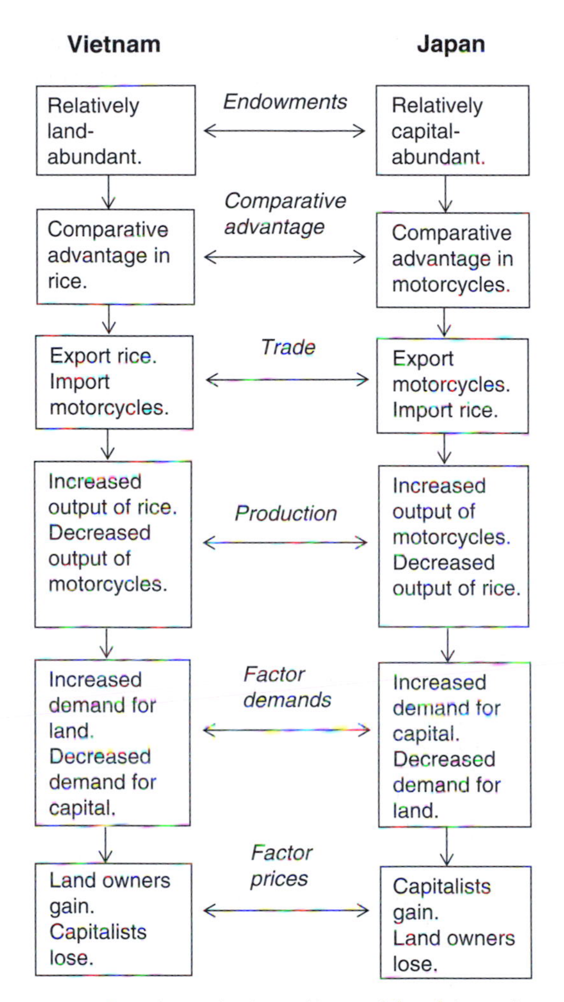

Figure 6.2 The Heckscher–Ohlin model and the Stolper–Samuelson theorem

owners in Japan. In this way, we can see why the strong and persistent opposition to rice imports in Japan discussed in the introduction to this chapter arises and persists. It reflects the political clout of Japanese land owners. The reason is not "economic security and culture," however. Rather, it is income loss.[15]

Let us summarize the above results in more general terms. In both Vietnam and Japan, the sector intensive in the country's abundant factor expands, while the sector intensive in the country's scarce factor contracts. This, in turn, causes an increase in demand for the abundant factor in each country and a decrease in

[15] The historical relevance of this result can be seen in the work of Anderson and Hayami (1986). Walter and Sen (2009: 82) note that "an electoral system that gives representation to rural districts, as in Japan, can entrench protectionist policies in agriculture." For proposed changes to this system, see *The Economist* (2011).

demand for the scarce factor in each country. These changes in demand, in turn, have implications for the *returns to* or *incomes of* the factors in question, and hence the demand for protection. Political *opposition* to trade arises from *relatively scarce* factors of production in trading countries.

The Heckscher–Ohlin model thus has an important implication for the political economy of trade, and this implication is summarized in a central result of international trade theory, namely the Stolper–Samuelson theorem.[16] In general terms, this theorem can be stated as follows in the box.

> As a country moves from autarky to trade, the country's abundant factor of production (used intensively in the export sector) gains, while the country's scarce factor of production (used intensively in the import sector) loses. Opposition to trade or demand for protection therefore arises from the relatively scarce factor of production.

In this way, the Stolper–Samuelson theorem locates the potential opposition to increased trade (and support for protection) in countries' relatively scarce factors of production. This key insight composes the lens through which many international economists and policy-makers view the political economy of trade. An extension of the model to the issue of endogenous protection is presented in Appendix 6.1. The Stolper–Samuelson theorem cannot be applied blindly, however. It applies only to *inter*-industry trade based on different endowments in factors of production. Trade based on differences in technology (as in the Ricardian model of Chapter 3) and *intra*-industry trade (as in Chapter 5) can mitigate the effects described by the theorem.

North–South Trade and Wages

There is an application of the Stolper–Samuelson theorem that has generated a great deal of interest over the years. This is the question of *North–South trade* and *wages*. The term "North" refers to the high-income countries of the world, while the term "South" refers to the low- and middle-income countries of the world. High-income countries tend to be relatively capital-abundant, whereas low- and middle-income countries tend to be relatively labor-abundant. We are painting with a broad brush here, but the results turn out to be interesting.

---

[16] This theorem originated in a famous article by Wolfgang Stolper and Paul Samuelson (1941). In the words of Deardorff (1998: 364), "One might have thought and hoped that the broader gains from trade...might have allowed both abundant and scarce factors to gain from trade.... But alas no, Stolper and Samuelson showed this is not the case."

The implications of these relative factor endowments are illustrated in Figure 6.3. The Heckscher–Ohlin model of trade would suggest that the North has a comparative advantage in capital-intensive goods (CIGs) and that the South has a comparative advantage in labor-intensive goods (LIGs). This is illustrated in the top six boxes of Figure 6.3. Furthermore, the Stolper–Samuelson theorem would suggest that *labor in the North* will *lose* as a result of trade. This is illustrated in the bottom six boxes of Figure 6.3. The possibility of Northern labor losing as a result of trade has led labor interests in the North to be, in many instances, opposed to increased trade. For example, the US labor movement opposed both the North American Free Trade Agreement and the formation of the World Trade Organization.[17]

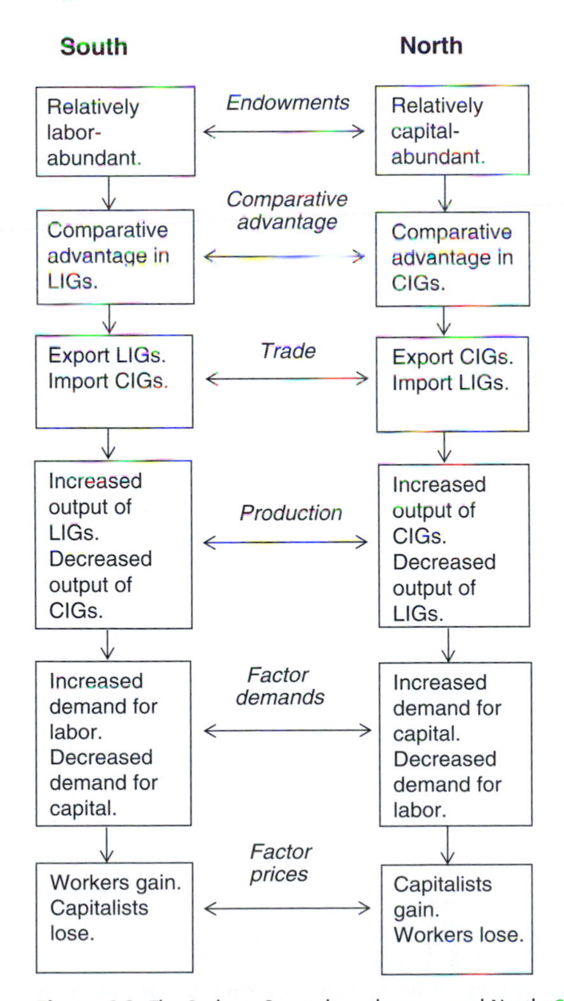

Figure 6.3 The Stolper–Samuelson theorem and North–South trade
Notes: LIGs = labor-intensive goods; CIGs = capital-intensive goods.

[17] See, for example, Dreiling and Robinson (1998).

Although the possibility of Northern labor as a whole losing as a result of increased international trade with the South is of some interest, there is a more subtle issue in the ongoing debate concerning North–South trade and wages that is very much worth emphasizing. There is evidence that countries in the South have comparative advantage in *unskilled*-labor-intensive goods (ULIGs), and that countries in the North have comparative advantage in *skilled*-labor-intensive goods (SLIGs). If this is indeed true, then, according to the Stolper–Samuelson theorem, the Northern workers who lose as a result of increased North–South trade are actually *unskilled* workers. This possibility, first introduced by Wood (1994), is of great interest and concern. For example, since the early 1980s in the United States, unskilled workers have seen their wages decline relative to skilled workers, with negative impacts for the overall income distribution. It is possible that increased North–South trade has caused this relative wage decline.[18]

Wood (2018) estimates the impact of North–South trade on employment in the North for the year 2011. These estimates are presented in Table 6.2. In this table, we can see that employment losses were indeed concentrated among the unskilled. Increased imports from the South caused declines in unskilled labor in both manufacturing and services, although the effects were larger in manufacturing. In total, North–South trade caused a decline in 17 million unskilled jobs in the North but also an increase in 5 million skilled jobs in the North. Since wage changes and employment changes are negatively related, the distinction between ULIGs

Table 6.2 North–South trade and employment in the North (millions)

	Manufacturing			Services			Total
Labor-type	*Exports*	*Imports*	*Net*	*Exports*	*Imports*	*Net*	*Net*
Skilled	2.5	−0.5	2.0	3.4	−0.7	2.7	4.8
Unskilled	3.9	−17.5	−13.6	4.5	−7.9	−3.4	−16.9
Total	6.4	−18.0	−11.5	7.9	−8.6	−0.6	−12.2

Source: Wood (2018).

[18] In the case of the United States, the concern was summarized some years ago by Krugman and Lawrence (1996: 35) as follows: "The conventional wisdom holds that foreign competition has eroded the US manufacturing base, washing out the high-paying jobs that a strong manufacturing sector provides.... And because imports increasingly come from Third World countries with their huge reserves of unskilled labor, the heaviest burden of this foreign competition has ostensibly fallen on less educated American workers." More recently Baldwin (2016: 161) has stated: "Free trade pushes the developing nation[s] to make more of the goods that involve a lot of low-skilled labor, and this is good for low-skill workers in developing nations. The resulting intensification of low-skill-intensive exports [of developing nations], however, tends to be bad for low-skill workers in rich nations."

and SLIGs, and the application of the Stolper–Samuelson theorem in this context, appear to be relevant.[19]

Such considerations have prompted ongoing empirical investigations into the effects of trade on Northern wages (see the box below on Southern wages in the case of Latin America). The number of studies is too large, and the technical issues too detailed, for a review here.[20] Suffice it to say that North–South trade appears to be complicit in relative wage declines in the North. There are a few caveats worth noting, however, regarding the causes of the decline in relative wages of Northern unskilled workers.

First, technology is at least as complicit as trade in Northern wage declines. There is clearly an ongoing process of technological change in the North that increases demand for skilled workers, and makes these workers more productive, relative to unskilled workers.[21] Some time ago Deardorff (1998: 368) aptly summarized the relevance of this process to wage changes:

> The computer revolution has made it possible for highly skilled workers, manipulating their environments with electronic devices, to produce far more than equally skilled workers could have previously, also replacing to a large extent the unskilled workers whose tasks are taken over increasingly by intelligent machines. As a result, the productivity and wages of skilled workers rise, while those of unskilled workers do not.

All evidence suggests that unskilled-labor-displacing technological changes are ongoing. There have been suggestions that trade itself plays a role in these changes, however. Increased imports from the South can cause firms in the North to engage in defensive technological innovations that are biased towards skilled labor and away from unskilled labor. Although researchers have identified this as a logical possibility, they are not yet fully sure of its empirical importance.[22]

---

[19] See also Helpman (2018: chaps. 2 & 3).

[20] For reviews, see Freeman (1995), Richardson (1995), Deardorff (1998), Wood (2002), Krugman (2008), Helpman (2018), and Wood (2018). For a more extended discussion that brings in elements of international production, see Baldwin (2016: chap. 5).

[21] This appears to be part of the shift towards flexible manufacturing systems, touched upon in Chapters 10 through 12, that has had the effect of suppressing blue-collar wages. In addition, globally, multinational enterprises often serve as conduits of technological change through their foreign direct investment activities. Therefore, it is possible that MNEs can contribute to changing wage patterns via technology.

[22] For example, Wood (2018: 982) states that "there is not enough evidence to gauge the overall impact of trade-induced productivity change." Milanovic (2016) actually casts doubt on our ability to disentangle technological change from trade: "Technological change and globalization are...wrapped around each other, and trying to disentangle their individual effects is futile" (110). For more on this issue, see Burstein and Vogel (2017) and Helpman (2018: chaps. 4 & 5).

The second caveat relates to international production, discussed briefly in Chapter 1 and taken up in earnest in Part II of this book. The operation of **foreign direct investment** and **global value chains**, partly enabled by information and communication technology and influencing trade flows, can both impact patterns of wages. We will return to these issues in Part II of the book.

There are other caveats as well. Recall that the Stolper–Samuelson theorem suggests that Northern unskilled workers lose because the North has a comparative advantage in *skilled*-labor-intensive goods. These effects tend to be smaller than the Stolper–Samuelson theorem would suggest, however. Why is this? First, there is some evidence that export-oriented industries in the North tend to pay higher wages than other industries. Consequently, the labor reallocations caused by increased trade tend to boost average wages.[23] Second, some North–South trade is based on higher labor productivity (better technology) in the North rather than differences in factor endowments. Third, some North–South trade is *intra*-industry in nature and might therefore offer more adjustment opportunities to Northern workers than *inter*-industry trade.[24] For these reasons, although trade is important, it is not the only source of the decline in relative wages of Northern unskilled workers. Technology matters as well, and intra-industry trade might mitigate the standard Stolper–Samuelson effects.

There are policy analysts (and politicians) in the North, with well-grounded concerns about the plight of unskilled Northern workers, who call for *trade restrictions* to address the effects of North–South trade on unskilled wages in the North. For a number of reasons, this is probably not the best policy approach. First, technology appears to be as important a factor as trade, and few policy analysts call for limiting technological change. Second, trade restrictions will suppress overall gains from trade in both the North and South. Third, such restrictions could violate multilateral commitments made in the WTO (see Chapter 8). Fourth, trade restrictions might harm unskilled workers in the South, who are in more dire straits than their Northern counterparts.

A more long-term and productive policy approach would be to offer other forms of support to unskilled Northern workers.[25] These could be income supports (including trade adjustment assistance) and, more importantly, support to increase human capital assets (education and training).[26] If there is one factor contributing

[23] See Bernard, Jensen, and Lawrence (1995). Some evidence suggests that firms that pay higher wages tend to end up exporting because of better productivity rather than exporting activities causing the higher wages. See Schank, Schnabel and Wagner (2010).

[24] See Reinert and Roland-Holst (1998) for the example of the North American Free Trade Agreement.

[25] This was the conclusion of a joint report by the International Monetary Fund, the World Bank, and the World Trade Organization (IMF, World Bank, and WTO, 2016), for example.

[26] See, for example, White (2014: chap. 10).

to wage and income inequality in the North, it is the failure to complete secondary (high school) education. Remedying educational failures is an important, and neglected, policy imperative in Northern countries as well as in Southern countries.[27]

Trade and Wages in Latin America

We have suggested that developing countries in the "South" have a comparative advantage in *unskilled*-labor-intensive goods. As suggested by the Heckscher–Ohlin model, this is a result of these countries being abundant in unskilled labor. If this is the case, then, according to the Stolper–Samuelson theorem, increased trade would benefit unskilled labor in developing countries, relative to skilled labor. It turns out, however, that, in a number of Latin American countries, the opposite appears to have been the case. Trade liberalization in a number of Latin America countries has been accompanied by *decreases* in the relative wages of unskilled workers. More generally, exports in the region are associated with higher premia paid to *skilled* workers. Why would the Stolper–Samuelson theorem be wrong?

One potential answer is trade in capital goods. As some Latin American countries liberalized their trading regimes, firms imported more physical capital (machines) in order to remain competitive. Embodied in these machines was a higher technology level that demanded somewhat more skilled workers than had the old technology in use previously. Consequently, as trade was liberalized, the technology effects overpowered the Stolper–Samuelson effects, and the net result was that unskilled workers lost relative to skilled workers as a consequence of trade.

This is another important case of the political economy of trade. Given that the majority of workers in Latin America are unskilled and Latin American countries already have severe inequality problems, the above results give some cause for concern. They indicate that trade can, in some instances, exacerbate existing inequalities.

Sources: Brambilla et al. (2012), Gindling and Robbins (2001), Robbins and Gindling (1999), and Wood (1997).

[27] Consider Baldwin (2016: chap. 8) on policies in high-income countries. He states: "Of the many factors of production, people and skills are perhaps the most important when thinking about a new paradigm for competitiveness policy.... Human capital has the extra attraction of being flexible. Skills that produce excellence are often transferable across sectors and stages [of production], which allows workers to adapt to changing demands" (231).

The Role of Specific Factors

As we saw in Table 6.1, a sector-based approach to the political economy of trade is associated with what is called the specific factors model. A central assumption of the Heckscher–Ohlin model and its Stolper–Samuelson theorem is that resources or factors of production such as labor, physical capital, and land can move effortlessly between different sectors of trading economies. So, for example, Japanese resources are assumed to be able to shift back and forth between rice and motorcycle production. The same is assumed to be true for Vietnam. For some types of analysis, particularly in the very *long run*, this "perfect factor mobility" assumption is reasonable. In other instances, the assumption can be at odds with reality. Instead, factors of production can be *sector-specific*, and it is this phenomenon that motivates the specific factors model and its approach to the political economy of trade.[28]

The presence of specific factors requires a *modification* of the Stolper–Samuelson theorem. To see this, let us consider the example of steel production in the United States. The United States is, without a doubt, relatively abundant in physical capital. The Stolper–Samuelson theorem would therefore suggest that capital owners in the United States should *gain* as a result of increased trade. But here is a puzzle. In its 2000 annual report the US-based Weirton Steel Corporation drew attention to what it called an "import crisis" and pledged to fight the "import war." It said it planned to "aggressively seek changes in Washington, DC to stop the devastation caused by unfair trade." This hardly sounds like capitalists gaining from trade.

Why would capitalists in a capital-abundant country oppose increased trade in violation of the Stolper–Samuelson theorem? As it turns out, the notion of specific factors helps us to address this puzzle. Weirton Steel Corporation, and many other US steel firms, are owners of large amounts of specific factors in the form of steel mills, some of them very large, "integrated" facilities.[29] These facilities cannot easily move into the production of other products, such as semiconductors. They are *specific* to the production of steel.

A modification of the Stolper–Samuelson theorem in the face of such specific factors is important to understanding the US steel and other similar cases. This specific factors modification is as follows.

[28] Von Haberler (1937: chap. 12) first emphasized the role of specific factors in models of international trade, but this model was formalized by Jones (1971).

[29] Blecker (2009: 1032) notes: "Steel production, especially in integrated mills, is capital intensive and has large economies of scale, which create a tendency toward the existence of excess capacity (except in times of strong demand)." In the short run, the large amount of capital in integrated mills constitutes a sector-specific factor.

Factors of production that are specific to import sectors tend to lose as a result of trade, while factors of production specific to export sectors tend to gain as a result of trade.

From this perspective, Weirton Steel's actions are not difficult to understand. It is a company in an import sector that is characterized by sector-specific physical capital (and perhaps even sector-specific labor). The owners of Weirton Steel therefore stand to lose as a result of increased trade. Consequently, as described in the accompanying box, the firm entered the "import war" to attempt to reduce imports and protect the incomes of its specific factors. Further, protection of the US steel sector has continued, even accelerating at the time of this writing.[30]

US Steel Protection

In September 1998 12 US steel companies, including Weirton Steel (mentioned above), filed cases with the US government alleging that the hot-rolled steel exports of Russia, Japan, and Brazil had been unfairly "dumped," or sold at "less than fair value" in US markets. The US International Trade Commission (USITC) found in favor of the US steel industry, and protection to offset the dumping was applied. In June 1999 seven US steel companies, again including Weirton Steel, filed follow-up cases involving cold-rolled steel exports from China, South Africa, Turkey, Brazil, Argentina, Thailand, Russia, Venezuela, Japan, Indonesia, Slovakia, and Taiwan (note the long list). The USITC found in favor of the US steel industry in the cases of Indonesia, Slovakia, and Taiwan. Next, in October 1999, Weirton Steel filed an anti-dumping case against Japan's exports of tin mill products, and the USITC found in Weirton's favor.

Despite the above results, capping two decades of special protection, the US steel industry felt that a more comprehensive solution was required to support the incomes of its sector-specific factors. Under the banner "Stand Up for Steel" (US-manufactured steel, that is), the industry pressed on with a campaign for further protection. This campaign, in which Weirton played a leading role, included petitions, lobbying, and even motorcycle rallies ("Ride for Steel"). The efforts were best organized in Weirton's home state, West Virginia, a state that helped secure George W. Bush's position as US president through switches in party loyalties.

[30] See, for example, Slobodian (2018).

US Steel Protection (cont.)

In June 2001 President Bush's administration instructed the USITC to undertake a *global safeguard investigation* of US steel imports. Such an investigation does not require a finding of "unfair" trade or "dumping," nor is it targeted to specific countries. In December 2001 the USITC found that the US steel industry had been subject to injury as a result of imports and recommended certain remedies. In March 2002 the Bush administration imposed a number of protection measures, including "safeguard" tariffs of up to 30 percent, on US$30 billion worth of steel imports. The European Union and Japan, both of which were targets in the protection, appealed to the World Trade Organization in Geneva. In 2003 the WTO found against the United States and ruled that the tariffs were incompatible with WTO principles.

Steel protection made a significant reappearance in March 2018, when the Trump administration imposed 25 percent tariffs, along with a 10 percent tariff on aluminum. Rather than pursuing a safeguard action, the Trump administration chose to use a national security provision in US trade law. This was a spurious argument, because most steel imports come from US allies, namely Canada, the European Union, Mexico, and South Korea. Further, the long-term issues facing the US steel industry are also affected by the use of something we discussed in Chapter 2, namely industrial robots that displace workers. At the time of this writing, the promised response from the European Union to these trade actions is developing.

Sources: Blecker (2009), *The Economist* (2002a; 2018a), Rampell (2018), Slobodian (2018), and Weirton Steel Corporation.

It is not always easy to keep the difference between specific and mobile factors in mind when assessing the political economy of trade. For this reason, we need a box to help us.

Mobile factors of production: The Stolper–Samuelson theorem applies. The abundant factor of production (used intensively in the export sector) gains, while the scarce factor of production (used intensively in the import sector) loses.

Specific factors of production: The Stolper–Samuelson theorem does *not* apply. The factor of production specific to the export sector gains, while the factor of production specific to the import sector loses. The fate of mobile factors is uncertain.

When you come upon a political economy of trade issue, in any country of the trading world, it will be very helpful to your understanding if you first try to identify the mobile or specific factors of production involved. Then glance up at the above box. The political economy of trade issue should be very much clarified by this process. If not, it is probably the case that technology, not factors of production, drives the trade involved (the Ricardian model of Chapter 3).

Globalization and Inequality in High-Income Countries

Chapter 1 mentioned the rise of ethno-nationalism as a political force, with its ire directed at specific dimensions of globalization, particularly trade and migration. There is some evidence emerging that increased trade competition might help to explain ethno-nationalist voting behavior.[31] The political processes at work here are no doubt complex, but, to the extent that a stagnant or declining quality of life for certain groups of people in high-income countries is at play, there are relevant trends. There is indeed evidence of declining living standards for less educated individuals (workers and the unemployed) in high-income countries. Citing numerous studies, for example, Wood (2018: 978) lists the qualities of this decline as follows:

> The rise in wage inequality between more and less-educated workers and between white-collar and blue-collar workers...has endured.... There has been a dramatic rise in inequality between the mass of the population and the richest 1%. Labor's share of GDP has fallen, so the average wage has grown slower than productivity. Employment in manufacturing, formerly a major provider of jobs requiring little education, has declined steeply, contributing to the polarization of employment opportunities. Casual contracts have replaced regular jobs.

In talking about labor in the United States, Moretti (2012: 6) puts it more succinctly, stating that the worker "is worse off by almost every measure." But further evidence has also been offered by Milanovic (2016: chap. 1) in terms of the global distribution of income. Milanovic examines the gains in real income between 1988 and both 2008 and 2011 for the world as a whole, broken down into groups of households rather than countries. The largest gains during these time periods were for individuals in China, India, Thailand, Vietnam, and Indonesia, as well as the "global top one percent," primarily located in high-income countries. Those who have gained the least were the lower middle class in high-income countries. Milanovic attributes these changes to "globalization" writ large, as does Baldwin (2016: chap. 5).

---

[31] See, for example, Colantone and Stanig (2018) for the case of Western Europe.

It is still difficult to *directly* attribute these changes to *specific* dimensions of globalization as opposed to technological changes, but we must acknowledge that the analytical realms of globalization and technology are now intertwined. As we noted in Chapter 1, advances in technology (mainly in the form of ICT) are a main driver of globalization. Beyond trade, changes in international production discussed in Part II of this book (FDI and GVCs) can have additional, significant effects. Indeed, Baldwin (2016: chap. 5) attributes Milanovic's results to the operation of international production over the years considered by Milanovic. We will return to these questions in Part II of this book.

Conclusion

In a recent book on global trade relations, Singh (2017: 32) states that "the economic basis for trade lies in comparative advantage, but its realization through trade policy is a political process that deals with the economic and cultural preferences of those affected positively or negatively by trade." Indeed, these preferences ensure that support for trade is *not universal*, and protection from trade is common. Country-based explanations for the supply of protection can be found in realism and institutionalism. Explanations for the demand for protection can be found in factor-based and sector-based insights from trade theory. In this chapter, we have seen that the movement from autarky to trade in any country can hurt some groups of people in that country. According to the Stolper–Samuelson theorem of the Heckscher–Ohlin model, this can be as a result of owning a factor of production that is scarce in the particular country. Alternatively, it can also be a result of owning a factor specific to an import sector.

Suppose that losing groups become unhappy with the level of trade in their country. What might they do? It is possible that they might *lobby* their government to intervene in the trade relationship, as we saw in the case of the US steel industry. This is demand for protection. It turns out that such trade policy interventions are common. Despite the gains from trade described in Chapters 2, 3, and 4, governments usually intervene in free trade in some way in response to political pressures from constituencies. This is supply of protection. Interactions in the market for protection constitute the political economy of trade.

We mentioned in Chapter 1 that there are important cultural issues that affect the world economy. At times, opposition to trade and demand for protection can be an expression of cultural issues. This is evident in the quote at the beginning of this chapter. It is important to recognize that cultural and economic factors work side by side in many national contexts. The analysis of this chapter helps us understand the economic factors.

What are the effects of the protective policies that develop in the market for protection? We will find out in the next chapter.

Review Exercises

1. Use daily news sources to identify aspects of *realism* or international power politics in trade or technology. Try to describe the issues as accurately as possible. What are the concerns of the players involved? To your mind, are they valid concerns?
2. Consider the trade between Germany and the Dominican Republic. Germany is a capital-abundant country, and the Dominican Republic is a labor-abundant country. There are two goods: a capital-intensive good, chemicals, and a labor-intensive good, clothing.
   a. Draw a Heckscher–Ohlin comparative advantage diagram such as Figure 6.1 for trade between Germany and the Dominican Republic, labeling the trade flows along the axes of your diagrams.
   b. Using the Stolper–Samuelson theorem, describe who will support and who will oppose trade in these two countries. Use a flow chart diagram like that of Figure 6.2 to help you in your description
3. As mentioned in Chapter 3, in the early nineteenth century in Britain a debate arose in Parliament over the Corn Laws, restrictions on imports of grain into the country. David Ricardo, the father of the comparative advantage concept, favored the repeal of these import restrictions. Consider the two relevant political groups in Britain at that time: land owners and capital owners. Who do you think agreed with Ricardo? Why?
4. Use daily news sources to identify a political economy of trade issue. Can you also identify the factors or production involved in this issue? Are they mobile factors as in the Heckscher–Ohlin model, or are they specific factors? Alternatively, are there any elements of technology involved?

FURTHER READING AND WEB RESOURCES

An excellent review of the subject of this chapter can be found in Walter and Sen (2009: chap. 3). Another very useful starting point for the reader interested in the political economy of trade is Baldwin (1989). A concise introduction to the Heckscher–Ohlin model is provided by Panagariya (2009), and a volume dedicated to the Stolper–Samuelson theorem has been edited by Deardorff and Stern (1994). For a review of the trade and wages debate, see Marjit and Archaryya (2009) and Wood (2018).

An interesting discussion of fairness in the political economy of trade can be found in Davidson, Matusz, and Nelson (2006). For a review of realist issues in technology between the United States and China, see *The Economist* (2018b). To keep track of the "realist" concerns in the field of strategic trade, see the journal *Strategic Trade Review*. Finally, for an excellent discussion of changing employment conditions in the United States (partly attributable to North–South trade), see Moretti (2012). Finally, for a book-length treatment of some of the issues discussed in this chapter, see Helpman (2018).

You can follow one aspect of the market for protectionism in the United States via the website for the US International Trade Commission, at www.usitc.gov. For the case of the European Union, see ec.europa.eu/trade. For the official Chinese view, see china-embassy.org/eng/zt/bps/t943740.htm.

REFERENCES

Anderson, K., and Y. Hayami (eds.) (1986) *The Political Economy of Agricultural Protection: East Asia in International Perspective*, Allen & Unwin.

Baldwin, R. (1989) "The Political Economy of Trade Policy," *Journal of Economic Perspectives*, 3:4, 119–35.

Baldwin, R. (2016) *The Great Convergence: Information Technology and the New Globalization*, Harvard University Press.

Bernard, A. B., J. B. Jensen, and R. Z. Lawrence (1995) "Exporters, Jobs and Wages in US Manufacturing: 1976–1987," *Brookings Papers on Economic Activity*, 26:Special, 67–112.

Black, D. (1948) "On the Rationale of Group Decision-Making," *Journal of Political Economy*, 56:1, 23–34.

Blecker, R. A. (2009) "Steel," in K. A. Reinert, R. S. Rajan, A. J. Glass, and L. S. Davis (eds.), *The Princeton Encyclopedia of the World Economy*, Princeton University Press, 1030–5.

Brambilla, I., R. Dix-Carneiro, D. Lederman, and G. Porto (2012) "Skill, Export, and the Wages of Seven Million Latin American Workers," *World Bank Economic Review*, 26:1, 34–60.

Burstein, A., and J. Vogel (2017) "International Trade, Technology, and the Skill Premium," *Journal of Political Economy*, 125:5, 1356–412.

Colantone, I., and P. Stanig (2018) "The Trade Origins of Economic Nationalism: Import Competition and Voting Behavior in Western Europe," *American Journal of Political Science*, 62:4, 936–53.

Davidson, C., S. Matusz, and D. Nelson (2006) "Fairness and the Political Economy of Trade," *The World Economy*, 29:8, 989–1004.

Deardorff, A. V. (1998) "Technology, Trade, and Increasing Inequality: Does the Cause Matter for the Cure?" *Journal of International Economic Law*, 1:3, 353–76.

Deardorff, A. V., and R. M. Stern (1994) *The Stolper–Samuelson Theorem: A Golden Jubilee*. University of Michigan Press.

Donnelly, J. (2000) *Realism in International Relations*, Cambridge University Press.

Dreiling, M., and I. Robinson (1998) "Union Responses to NAFTA in the US and Canada: Explaining Intra- and International Variation," *Mobilization: An International Quarterly*, 3:2, 163–84.

The Economist (2002a) "Steel: Rust Never Sleeps," March 9.

The Economist (2002b) "Vietnam: Land and Freedom," June 15.

The Economist (2011) "Electoral Reform in Japan: Breaking the Backs of Farmers," January 29.

The Economist (2015) "Rice: Hare-Grained," November 14.

The Economist (2018a) “Massive Attack: The Looming Trade War,” March 10.

The Economist (2018b) “Technopolitics: The Challenger,” March 17.

The Economist (2018c) “The Chips Are Down,” December 1.

Freeman, R. B. (1995) “Are Your Wages Set in Beijing?” *Journal of Economic Perspectives*, 9:3, 15–32.

Fukuda, H., J. Dyck, and J. Stout (2003) “Rice Sector Policies in Japan,” Outlook RCS-0303-01, Economic Research Service, US Department of Agriculture.

Gindling, T. H., and D. Robbins (2001) “Patterns and Sources of Changing Wage Inequality in Chile and Costa Rica during Structural Adjustment,” *World Development*, 29:4, 725–45.

Heckscher, E. (1949) “The Effect of Foreign Trade on the Distribution of Income,” in H. S. Ellis and L. A. Metzler (eds.), *Readings in the Theory of International Trade*, Irwin, 272–300.

Helpman, E. (2018) *Globalization and Inequality*, Harvard University Press.

Henisz, W., and E. D. Mansfield (2006) “Votes and Vetoes: The Political Determinants of Commercial Openness,” *International Studies Quarterly*, 50:1, 189–211.

Hiscox, M. J. (2004) “International Capital Mobility and Trade Politics: Capital Flows, Political Coalitions, and Lobbying,” *Economics and Politics*, 16:3, 253–85.

International Monetary Fund, World Bank, and World Trade Organization (2016) *Making Trade an Engine of Growth for All: The Case for Trace and for Policies to Facilitate Adjustment*, IMF.

Jones, R. W. (1971) “A Three-Factor Model in Theory, Trade, and History,” in J. N. Bhagwati, R. W. Jones, R. A. Mundell, and J. Vanek (eds.), *Trade, Balance of Payments and Growth: Papers in International Economics in Honor of Charles P. Kindleberger*, North Holland, 3–21.

Krugman, P. (2008) “Trade and Wages, Reconsidered,” *Brooking Papers on Economic Activity*, Spring, 103–38.

Krugman, P., and R. Z. Lawrence (1996) “Trade, Jobs, and Wages,” in P. Krugman, *Pop Internationalism*, MIT Press, 35–48.

Lewis, L. (2015) “Japan: The End of the Rice Age,” *Financial Times*, September 21.

Marjit, S., and R. Archaryya (2009) “Trade and Wages,” in K. A. Reinert, R. S. Rajan, A. J. Glass, and L. S. Davis (eds.), *The Princeton Encyclopedia of the World Economy*, Princeton University Press, 1108–12.

Mayer, W. (1984) “Endogenous Tariff Formation,” *American Economic Review*, 74:5, 970–85.

Milanovic, B. (2016) *Global Inequality: A New Approach for the Age of Globalization*, Harvard University Press.

Milner, H. V. (1988) *Resisting Protectionism: Global Industries and the Politics of International Trade*, Princeton University Press.

Milner, H.V. (1997) *Interests, Institutions, and Information*, Princeton University Press.

Milner, H. V. (1999) “The Political Economy of International Trade,” *Annual Review of Political Science*, 2, 91–114.

Moretti, E. (2012) *The New Geography of Jobs*, Houghton Mifflin Harcourt.

Ohlin, B. (1933) *International and Inter-Regional Trade*, Harvard University Press.

Panagariya, A. (2009) “Heckscher–Ohlin Model,” in K. A. Reinert, R. S. Rajan, A. J. Glass, and L. S. Davis (eds.), *The Princeton Encyclopedia of the World Economy*, Princeton University Press, 591–7.

Rampell, C. (2018) "Don't Blame China, Mr. President. Blame Robots," *Washington Post*, March 5.

Reinert, K. A., and D. W. Roland-Holst (1998) "North–South Trade and Occupational Wages: Some Evidence from North America," *Review of International Economics*, 6:1, 74–89.

Richardson, J. D. (1995) "Income Inequality and Trade: How to Think, What to Conclude," *Journal of Economic Perspectives*, 9:3, 33–55.

Robbins, D., and T. H. Gindling (1999) "Trade Liberalization and the Relative Wages for More-Skilled Workers in Costa Rica," *Review of Development Economics*, 3:2, 140–54.

Rodrik, D (1995) "Political Economy of Trade Policy," in G. M. Grossman and K. Rogoff (eds.), *Handbook of International Economics*, vol. 3, Elsevier, 1457–94.

Schank, T., C. Schnabel, and J. Wagner (2010) "Higher Wages in Exporting Firms: Self-Selection, Export Effect, or Both? First Evidence from Linked Employer–Employee Data," *Review of World Economics*, 146:2, 303–22.

Schattschneider, E. E. (1935) *Politics, Pressures and the Tariff*, Prentice-Hall.

Shelley, L. (2017) "Illicit Trade," in K. A. Reinert (ed.), *Handbook of Globalisation and Development*, Edward Elgar, 100–14.

Singh, J. P. (2017) *Sweet Talk: Paternalism and Collective Action in North–South Trade Relations*, Stanford University Press.

Slobodian, Q. (2018) "You Live in Robert Lighthizer's World Now," *Foreign Policy*, August 6.

Stolper, W., and P. A. Samuelson (1941) "Protection and Real Wages," *Review of Economic Studies*, 9:1, 58–73.

Von Harberler, G. (1937) *The Theory of International Trade*, Macmillan.

Walter, A., and G. Sen (2009) *Analyzing the Global Political Economy*, Princeton University Press.

White, R. (2014) *Making Sense of Anti-Trade Sentiment: International Trade and the American Worker*, Palgrave Macmillan.

Wood, A. (1994) *North–South Trade, Employment, and Inequality: Changing Fortunes in a Skill-Driven World*, Oxford University Press.

Wood, A. (1997) "Openness and Wage Inequality in Developing Countries: The Latin American Challenge to East Asian Conventional Wisdom," *World Bank Economic Review*, 11:1, 33–57.

Wood, A. (2002) "Globalization and Wage Inequalities: A Synthesis of Three Theories," *Weltwirtschaftliches Archiv*, 138:1, 54–82.

Wood, A. (2018) "The 1990s Trade and Wages Debate in Retrospect," *The World Economy*, 41:4, 975–99.

Appendix 6.1: Endogenous Protection

The factor-based approach to the political economy of trade as represented by the Heckscher–Ohlin model can be extended to a concept known as **endogenous protection**. This is a formal explanation of why the demand for and supply of protection interact in such a way as to result in positive levels of protection, particularly but not exclusively in the form of tariffs (see Chapter 7). Suppose that there are 100 individuals in a country described by the Heckscher–Ohlin model and that each of these individuals has one unit of labor (herself or himself). The other factor of production or resource in the Heckscher–Ohlin economy is physical capital. For each individual, the relative endowment of physical capital is the ratio of the individual's physical capital to labor. Since the labor endowment is just "1," the ratio is just the amount of physical capital she or he owns. For example, for individual 10:

$$\frac{K_{10}}{L_{10}} = \frac{K_{10}}{1} = K_{10} \tag{6.1}$$

We then rank our individuals from the lowest amount of physical capital owned to the highest amount as follows:

$$K_1 \le K_2 \le K_3 \le \cdots \le K_{100} \tag{6.2}$$

We graph these ownership ratios in the upper graph in Figure 6.4. Note that many individuals own *no physical capital* at all and are therefore at "0" in this graph.

If we place these 100 individuals in the Heckscher–Ohlin framework developed in this chapter, then a significant result emerges. Suppose that this is a capital-abundant country that will export the capital-intensive good. In this instance, Mayer (1984) shows that losses will occur for those individuals who own less capital and that gains will occur for those individuals who own more capital. We get a gain/loss ($G - L$) line something like that in the lower graph of Figure 6.4. All the individuals with "0" capital lose, but so do those with only a little capital, as well as the median individual. Gains are reserved for those with larger amounts of capital.[32]

The presence of losses for the majority of the individuals represents a significant demand for protection as a result of the Mayer/Stolper/Samuelson effects. But that is not all. There is a basic insight in public choice theory, due to Black (1948), that politicians who want to maximize the number of votes they receive will abide by the policy preference of the median voter.[33] This is voter or individual "50" in our model, and this individual suffers losses under free trade in this capital-abundant country. There is thus a *bias* in this framework towards *protectionism*. Supply of protection meets demand.

[32] Suppose that, instead of 100 individuals, there were only five, with relative endowments of 0, 0, 1, 2 and 3. The median individual has an endowment of 1 but the mean endowment is 1.2. Since our median individual has less than the mean endowment, he or she would lose as a result of trade, as is the case for individual 50 in Figure 6.4.

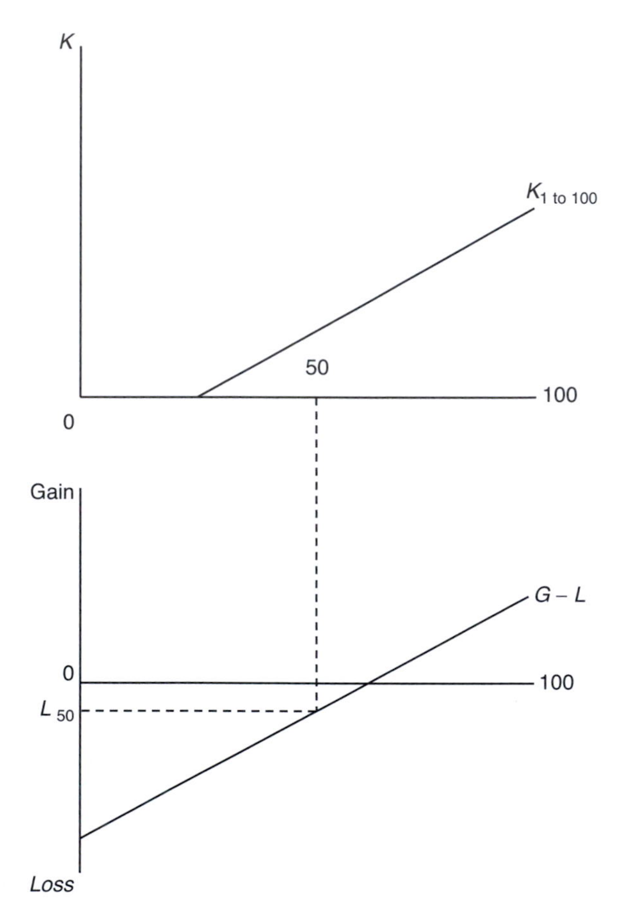

Figure 6.4 Endogenous protection: capital ownership among 100 residents

The model considered here combines a factor-based approach to the demand for protection with an explanation of the supply of protection that is a very particular and narrow example of institutionalist considerations. The model is not universal. Not all economies are best described by the Heckscher–Ohlin model. For example, as we have seen in this chapter, specific factors matter as well. In addition, politics is more complicated than that described by Black (1948). Nevertheless, the model illustrates one possibility that is commonly recognized by many trade policy analysts.

[33] This is referred to as "Black's theorem" or the "median voter model." It is not a perfect model, but it illustrates one possibility.

7 Trade Policy Analysis

In Chapter 6, you saw that there are reasons to expect that land owners in Japan might oppose the import of rice from Vietnam, or, for that matter, from any other country. This opposition to imports exists despite the *overall gains* to Japan from these imports because of a loss in land owners' income as a result of trade. Whether for these economic reasons, or for cultural reasons, demands for protection are common. For example, Ikuo Kanno, a fourth-generation Japanese rice farmer, states: "I believe that the value of agriculture can't be measured just by an economic yardstick. Japan has been a farming country for centuries, and rice farming is embedded in the culture. It should be preserved."[1] Indeed, as we mentioned in Chapter 6, rice farming in Japan has been supported through various stringent limits on imports, and these limits exist to this day.

For trade policy analysts, knowing that factor conditions lead to the demand for import protection is not enough. These individuals are often called upon to assess, both qualitatively and quantitatively, the numerous impacts of government interventions in international trade. If you pursue an international economic affairs career, it is likely that you will either be involved in making these assessments or in interpreting the assessments made by someone else. Therefore, it is important for you to understand how the assessments are made. This is the purpose of the present chapter.

We will begin our discussion of trade policy analysis by revisiting the model of absolute advantage in rice between Japan and Vietnam that we developed in Chapter 2. Next, we will consider the large variety of trade policy measures available to governments. Then we will analyze what happens when Japan introduces a **tariff** on its imports of rice. We also will consider the **terms of trade effects** of this tariff. Next, we will consider what happens when Japan introduces a **quota** on its imports of rice. Tariffs and quotas compose the basic means of protecting domestic markets from competition. It is important that you are familiar with both these policies.

Next, we will briefly consider two **non-tariff measures** in the form of **anti-dumping** and **countervailing duties**. Finally, we will briefly take up trade policy analysis using the comparative advantage model of Chapters 3 and 4. For the

---

[1] Planet Rice (2000).

interested reader, Appendix 7.1 considers the case of the imperfect substitutes model, used in many kinds of trade policy analysis, and Appendix 7.2 considers the case of tariff rate quotas (TRQs), used to protect the Japanese rice sector and other agricultural sectors.

Absolute Advantage Revisited

In Chapter 2, we developed a model of absolute advantage and applied it to trade in rice between Vietnam and Japan. This model is summarized in Figure 7.1. Recall from Chapter 2 that we assume the demand conditions in the two countries to be *exactly the same*. Consequently, we can use the same demand curve in both the diagrams of this figure. We also assume that supply conditions in the two countries are such that Vietnam's supply curve for rice is farther to the right than Japan's supply curve. Consequently, the autarky price of rice in Vietnam, P^V, is lower than the autarky price of rice in Japan, P^J. This gives Vietnam an absolute advantage in producing rice. The world price settles *between* the two autarky prices. Vietnam exports rice, while Japan imports rice. The world price will adjust to ensure that Vietnam's exports are the same as Japan's imports.

Note that, in moving from autarky to trade in Figure 7.1, there is a reduction in the domestic quantity supplied in Japan, as indicated by the downward arrow along S^J. It is possible that the firms producing rice in Japan might lobby the Japanese government to oppose this decrease in domestic quantity supplied, demanding protection from Vietnam's exports. This is exactly what has happened in Japan, given the political voice of people such as Ikuo Kanno, mentioned above.

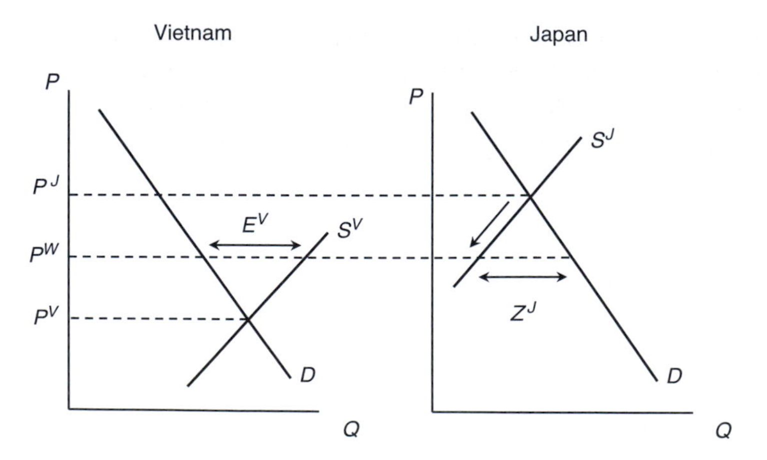

Figure 7.1 Absolute advantage and trade in the rice market

More generally, though, demands for protection are *nearly* universal. Indeed, since protective policies are so widespread in the world economy, analyzing them is an important subfield of international economics.[2]

Trade Policy Measures

When a country seeks to grant import protection to a sector of its economy, it can choose from among a number of measures, which can be broadly classified as either *tariffs* or *non-tariff measures*. A **tariff** is a tax on imports. It is a very common trade policy, used by almost all countries. There are two primary kinds of tariffs. A *specific tariff* is a fixed tax per physical unit of the import, and an *ad valorem* tariff is a percentage tax applied to the value of the import. Governments in the world trading system employ both types of tariffs.[3]

From the point of view of many trade policy analysts and the World Trade Organization, the ideal trading system would consist of only tariffs. Tariffs, particularly ad valorem tariffs, are the most transparent kind of trade policy, one that is least susceptible to political manipulation and corruption. Tariffs are far from the only type of trade policy, however. Therefore, the second category of trade policy measures we need to consider is the inclusive and large collection of **non-tariff measures** (NTMs).[4] The range of these NTMs is limited only by the imaginations of policy-makers, and the particularly strange case of used automobile imports in Latin America is discussed in the box starting on page 126.

To get a handle on the numerous kinds of NTMs, we can follow Takacs (2009) and distinguish between four categories: tax-like measures, cost-increasing measures, quantitative trade restrictions, and government procurement policies. A number of examples of these are presented in Table 7.1. *Tax-like measures* include anti-dumping (AD) duties, countervailing duties (CVDs), temporary import surcharges, and variable levies. Dumping involves the price of an exported good being lower than the price of the same good in the exporting country, and AD duties can be applied in certain circumstances when dumping takes place. CVD measures "countervail" subsidies by exporters and, again, can be applied in certain circumstances. AD and CVD measures are together often referred to as "administrative protection"

---

[2] See, for example, McDaniel, Reinert, and Hughes (2008).

[3] Bacchetta (2009) notes that there are three additional kinds of tariffs. A *compound tariff* has both an ad valorem component and a specific component. A *mixed tariff* takes on an ad valorem or a specific form depending on which is higher. Finally, a *technical tariff* depends on the products content and inputs.

[4] You might come across an older, less inclusive term of *non-tariff barriers*, or NTBs.

Table 7.1 Non-tariff measures

Category	Measure	Description
Tax-like measures	Anti-dumping (AD) duties	Tariff-like charges imposed on imports that are deemed by the imposing government to have been "dumped" or sold at "less than fair value" by the exporter.
	Countervailing duties (CVDs)	Tariff-like charges imposed on imports that are deemed by the imposing government to have been "unfairly" subsidized by the exporting country government.
	Temporary import surcharges	Extra import tariffs imposed in "emergency" circumstances of various kinds.
	Variable levies	Import tariffs whose size depends on the price of the imported good. This is usually to help maintain a certain level of domestic price, particularly in agricultural sectors.
Cost-increasing measures	Standards and technical regulations (STRs) or technical barriers to trade (TBTs)	A large set of measures, including certification guidelines, performance mandates, testing procedures and labeling requirements designed to contribute to consumer safety, environmental protection, national security, product interoperability, and other goals.
	Sanitary and phytosanitary (SPS) requirements	Technical barriers to trade in the agricultural arena designed to protect plant, animal, and human health.
	Prior import deposits	Non-interest-bearing deposits equal to a percentage of the value of an imported good that must be deposited into a central bank for a specified amount of time.
	Customs procedures	Inspection and customs clearance procedures, which can increase costs of imports and impose delays.
	Reference or minimum import prices	Official prices used to calculate import tariffs.
Quantitative measures	Import quota	A maximum import quantity set for a particular good.
	Tariff rate quota (TRQ)	Involves two tariff levels: a lower tariff for levels of imports within the quota and a higher tariff for levels of imports above the quota.
	Voluntary export restraint (VER)	An export quota that is "voluntarily" applied by the exporting country.

Table 7.1 (cont.)

Category	Measure	Description
	Import licensing	The requirement that a license be obtained from the importing country government before a product can be imported.
	Foreign exchange controls	The allocation of foreign exchange by the importing country government among potential importers as a way to limit imports.
	Sanctions and embargoes	Export bans and trade embargoes imposed on countries for political reasons.
	Local or domestic content requirements	A requirement that imported goods must contain a minimum amount of intermediate products from the importing country.
	Import or export balancing requirements	A requirement that a firm importing intermediate products must export a certain amount.
Government procurement practices		The myriad processes that governments employ in determining their contract procurements and the posture of these contracts towards imported goods.

Sources: Takacs (2009) and Laird (1997).

and form a veritable industry of trade policy analysis, spanning national governments and trade policy law firms, attempting to assure that trade is "fair." We will take up AD and CVD measures in more detail later in the chapter.

Cost-increasing measures include what are known both as standards and technical regulations (STRs) and technical barriers to trade (TBTs), sanitary and phytosanitary (SPS) requirements, prior import deposits, customs procedures, and reference or minimum import prices. STRs and TBTs are a growing area of trade policy activity and analysis.[5] It is one area where there are clear cases in which increasing protection can improve welfare in instances such as consumer health and safety. It is also an area where barriers are put in place simply for their protective effect, however. Customs procedures constitute another area that has received increased attention. This is for two reasons. First, there is a concern that slow customs clearance procedures in developing countries can be wasteful. Second, customs clearance, particularly in a "post-9/11" context, can be a real barrier for developing country exporters trying to enter developed country markets. Consequently, there is a concern with capacity building for developing country exporters in this area.[6]

[5] See Wilson (2009).

[6] See Peterson (2017).

Used Automobile Protection in Latin America

In the wake of the debt crises of the early 1980s, Latin America embarked on a process of significant trade liberalization, reducing tariffs and removing quotas. In the case of used automobiles, however, this liberalization has not, in general, taken place. Many Latin American countries retain significant restrictions on the imports of used automobiles even as liberalization has occurred in the new automobiles sector. What is more, the protective measures applied to used automobile imports have been rather creative.

As of 1999 seven relatively small Latin American countries imposed only minimal restrictions on imports of used automobiles. These countries were Bahamas, Barbados, Belize, Bolivia, El Salvador, Guatemala, and Panama. Some of these countries used "reference prices" to value the used automobiles. These reference prices were either domestically generated or published, "Blue Book" values.

Five relatively small countries imposed clear restrictions on the imports of used automobiles. These countries were Costa Rica, the Dominican Republic, Haiti, Honduras, and Nicaragua. A popular measure here was capped depreciation. For example, the Dominican Republic accepted invoices as the value of new automobiles, but it did not do so for used automobiles. Instead, the value of a used automobile was calculated using a depreciation schedule based on the price of an equivalent, new automobile in the current year. Given the depreciation schedule, however, the price of the used automobile could not fall below 50 percent of the new automobile. As we know, the market prices of used automobiles are often substantially below 50 percent of equivalent new automobiles, so this represented a discriminatory measure.

Jamaica, Peru, and Trinidad and Tobago imposed relatively severe protection measures against imports of used automobiles. Trinidad and Tobago required that used automobiles be *disassembled* before importation! Engines were often removed from used vehicles before importation and shipped separately. Peru and Jamaica both had age-delimited bans. Beginning in 1996 Peru banned automobiles over five years old and commercial vehicles over eight years old. Furthermore, imported used automobiles with fewer than 24 seats faced a "selective consumption tax" of 45 percent, while similar new automobiles faced a rate of only 20 percent, violating the "national treatment" (NT) principle, discussed in Chapter 8. In 1998 Jamaica's motor vehicle policy was tightened to allow only licensed used automobile dealers to import automobiles no older than four years old and light commercial vehicles no older than five years old.

Used Automobile Protection in Latin America (cont.)

Finally, in 1999, nine of the largest Latin American countries prohibited imports of used automobiles altogether. These countries were Argentina, Brazil, Chile, Colombia, Ecuador, Mexico, Paraguay, Uruguay, and Venezuela. In the cases of Argentina, Brazil, Paraguay, and Uruguay, this import ban was part of the Mercosur preferential trade agreement (see Chapter 9). It is clear that, when it comes to used automobiles, even "free trade" countries such as Chile choose the most severe form of protection.

Source: Pelletiere and Reinert (2002).

Quantitative measures constitute a large group of NTMs, including import quotas, tariff rate quotas, voluntary export restraints (VERs), import licensing, foreign exchange controls, sanctions and embargoes, local or domestic content requirements, and import or export balancing requirements. As will be discussed in Chapter 8, for many years import quotas were the norm in agriculture, textiles, and the clothing trade. This is no longer the case among WTO members, but can still exist in non-member countries. TRQs are still in use in agricultural sectors, however, including the Japanese rice sector. These involve two tariff levels: a lower tariff for levels of imports within the quota (the within-quota tariff) and a higher tariff for levels of imports above the quota (the out-of-quota tariff). These complexities make it complicated to administer and analyze.[7] Sanctions and embargoes are a perennial topic with regard to their effectiveness in influencing regimes deemed to be unacceptable (e.g. apartheid South Africa or, in past years, Myanmar).

Government procurement practices concern the processes that governments employ in determining their contract procurements and the posture of these contracts towards imported goods. Takacs (2009: 845) reminds us that, "[i]n most countries, regardless of the stage of development, government is the single largest purchaser of goods and services." That makes the government procurement processes and their specific posture towards imports an important matter.[8]

From this discussion and the content of Table 7.1, it is clear that trade policies are numerous. We are going to simplify greatly in this chapter and focus on the basic analysis of a tariff and quota within the absolute advantage framework. We begin with the case of a tariff.

[7] See Hertel and Martin (2000), de Gorter (2009), and Appendix 7.2.

[8] See, for example, Arrowsmith (2003).

A Tariff

As mentioned above, there are two kinds of tariffs: a specific tariff and an ad valorem tariff. For our graphical analysis in this chapter, it is much simpler to consider a specific tariff, so that is what we will do. The basic results you will learn here, however, will also apply to an ad valorem tariff. Let us introduce a specific tariff on Japan's imports of rice. This policy is depicted in Figure 7.2. The world price is P^W. At this price, Japanese rice suppliers choose to supply Q^S, and Japanese consumers demand Q^D. The difference, $Q^D - Q^S = Z^J$, is imported from Vietnam.

Suppose, then, that the Japanese government imposes a specific tariff of T on its imports of rice from Vietnam. This raises the domestic price of the imported product above the world price, to $P^W + T$. In the case of Japanese rice, the domestic price is in fact many times larger than the world price. The increase in the domestic price of rice above the world price has a number of effects. Japan's production of rice expands, from Q^S to Q^S_{tariff}. This expansion in output is what the Japanese rice farmers hoped to gain from the tariff. Domestic consumption of rice falls, from Q^D to Q^D_{tariff}. Imports fall, from Z^J to Z^J_{tariff}. The tariff has suppressed the importing relationship of Japan with Vietnam.[9]

In addition to the above quantity effects of a tariff, there are also a set of *welfare* and *revenue effects*. These involve Japan's households, firms, and government. What has happened to the *consumer surplus* of Japanese households in Figure 7.2?[10] Examining this diagram carefully, you should be able to see that the

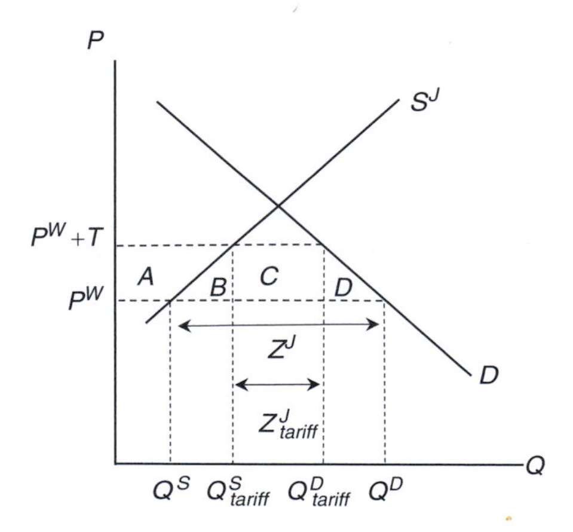

Figure 7.2 A tariff on Japan's imports of rice

[9] This makes sense. A tariff is a tax, and a tax on any activity causes the amount of that activity to decrease. In this case, the taxed activity is rice imports by Japan.

[10] Remember that the concepts of consumer and producer surplus are covered in Appendix 2.1. Please review this appendix if necessary.

tariff has caused consumer surplus to fall by area $A + B + C + D$. Since Japanese rice consumers are paying more and consuming less, this fall in consumer surplus makes sense.

What has happened to the *producer surplus* of Japanese firms? Again, examining the diagram carefully, you should be able to see that producer surplus has increased by area A. Japanese rice producers are better off as a result of the tariff. Since Japanese producers are receiving more for their product and producing more as well, this increase in producer surplus makes sense.

What about the Japanese government? It is receiving revenue from the import tax. How much revenue? The tariff is T, and the post-tariff import level is Z^J_{tariff}. Therefore, the tariff revenue is $T \times Z^J_{tariff}$, or area C in Figure 7.2.[11]

Economists and trade policy analysts are often asked to assess the *net welfare effect* of a trade policy. This standard measure summarizes the welfare impact of the policy for the country as a whole. What would the net welfare effect be? In this case, we take the gains to firms and the government and subtract the losses to households. Doing this, we have

$$N = A + C - (A + B + C + D) = -(B + D) \quad (7.1)$$

Area A is a transfer from consumers to producers, while area C is a transfer from consumers to the government. These areas cancel out with each other in Equation 7.1. That leaves areas B and D. There is a net welfare *loss* of the tariff equal to areas $B + D$. From an economic standpoint, the tariff hurts Japanese society as a whole. Although it benefits producers and government, the losses imposed on consumers outweigh these benefits. The two triangles B and D are similar to the "deadweight loss" triangle of a monopoly you learned about in introductory microeconomics. They represent economic or allocative inefficiency. In certain situations, tariffs do not necessarily cause a net welfare loss. One such situation, a *terms of trade* gain, is explored in the next section.

Please note one more thing. Figure 7.2 gives us information on what happens to Japanese rice output as a result of the tariff. As we stated above, Japanese rice output increases from Q^S to Q^S_{tariff}. Given information on the employment/output ratio in this sector, we could translate the change in output into a change in *employment*. From the point of view of Japanese politicians, this employment effect is important. Therefore, trade policy analysts often include an estimate of the employment effects of tariffs and other trade policies.

[11] There is an important public finance lesson here. An increase in the import tax (tariff) from zero to T reduces the potential *tax base* from Z^J to Z^J_{tariff}. All increases in taxes decrease the base on which the tax is assessed. For many developing countries, tariffs are an important source of government revenue, so this tax base reduction can be important.

Terms of Trade Effects

In some important cases, the analysis of the above section is incomplete. Why? We have shown that, when Japan imposes a tariff on its imports from Vietnam, the amount of these imports decreases. Looking at Figure 7.1, however, we can see that, as Japan's imports of rice decrease, there will be excess supply in the world market for rice. As we discussed in Chapter 2, this excess supply of rice will cause the world price to fall. Since Japan is importing rice, this is a good thing for this country. The fall in the price of an import good is one kind of **terms of trade effect**. It is depicted in Figure 7.3.

The main difference between Figure 7.3 and Figure 7.2 is that, in Figure 7.3, the world price does not stay constant, as the Japanese government places a tariff on imports of rice. The world price before the tariff is P^W. After the tariff the world price *falls* to P^W_{tariff}, and the tariff is placed on top of this lower world price. Therefore, after the tariff is in place, the domestic price is $P^W_{tariff} + T$. The fall in the world price of rice affects the welfare analysis of the tariff. Consumer surplus in Japan falls by $(A+B+C+D)$, as in Figure 7.2. Producer surplus in Japan rises by A, as in Figure 7.2. Japanese government revenue is now area $(C+E)$, however. Therefore, the net welfare effect is

$$N = A + (C + E) - (A + B + C + D) = -(B + D) + E \qquad (7.2)$$

The net welfare effect in Figure 7.3 is different from Figure 7.2. There is still the efficiency loss of $(B+D)$, as in the previous case. Now, however, there is a *terms of trade gain* of area E in Equation 7.2. For this reason, we cannot say whether the tariff hurts welfare in Japan or not. If the world price falls by a lot, E could be very large, even larger than $(B+D)$. Nevertheless, we should not jump to the conclusion that, given large terms of trade effects, tariffs are good for countries.

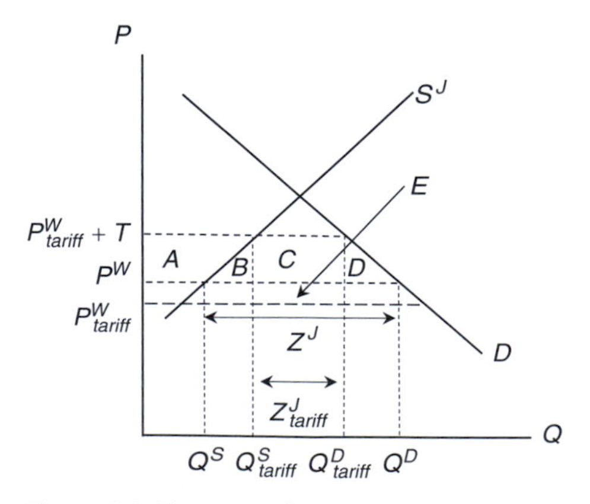

Figure 7.3 The terms of trade effect of Japan's tariff

This is because Vietnam would probably not sit idle when Japan imposes a tariff on imports of rice. Vietnam could instead *retaliate* by imposing a tariff on a product that Japan exports. This tariff would lower the world price of Japan's export good, which would hurt Japan's welfare. Japan might further retaliate in turn. This retaliation process is often known as a *trade war*, and it is always welfare-reducing in the end. It was to prevent such trade wars that the General Agreement on Tariffs and Trade (GATT) was drawn up after World War II. We discuss the GATT and its successor, the World Trade Organization (WTO), in Chapter 8.[12]

A Quota

An import **quota** is a quantitative restriction on imports, and one important type of NTM. When the Japanese government imposes a quota on rice imports, it is saying to rice exporters and domestic importers, "We will allow imports up to this amount, and no more!" Suppose that, instead of imposing a tariff, as in Figures 7.2 and 7.3, Japan imposes a quota. We examine this in Figure 7.4.

Before the quota, rice imports are $Z^J = Q^D - Q^S$. For political economy of trade reasons, the Japanese government is not satisfied with this outcome. It decides to *restrict* imports to a smaller amount: $Z^J_{quota} = Q^D_{quota} - Q^S_{quota}$. This policy induces a shortage of rice relative to the initial situation without the quota. The domestic price of rice in Japan rises from P^W to P_{quota}. The difference between these two prices is known as the **quota premium**. As with the case of a tariff, consumer surplus falls by area $(A + B + C + D)$, and producer surplus increases by area A. The new matter we must deal with in the case of a quota is the nature of area C.

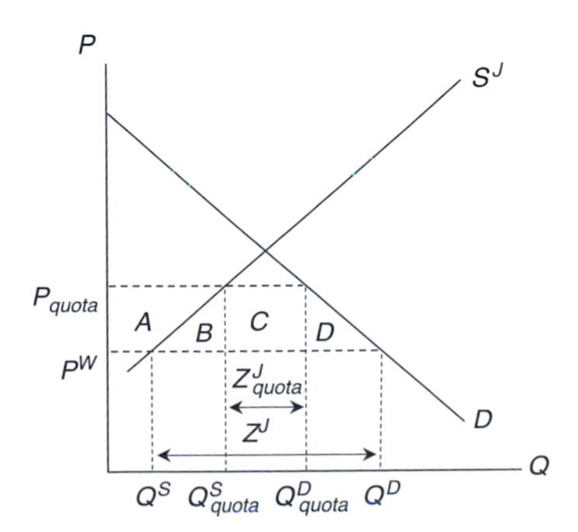

Figure 7.4 A quota on Japan's rice imports

[12] On the evolving trade war between the United States and China, see Liu and Woo (2018).

The quota policy is typically administered via a system of **import licenses**. In effect, the quota policy has restricted the supply of import licenses in the world. The area C represents the extra value of the right to import amount Z^J_{quota}. It is known as **quota rents**.[13] Who receives the rents depends on how the quota licenses are *allocated*. There are two common possibilities.[14]

1. Import licenses are *allocated to domestic (Japanese) importers*. Here, the quota rents accrue to the importers, so they *remain within* the country. They are a *gain to Japan*.
2. Import licenses are *allocated to foreign (Vietnamese) exporters*. Here, the quota rents accrue to these exporters, so they *leave* the country. They are a *loss to Japan*.

With the above in mind, we can address the question of the net welfare effect of the quota. In the case of import licenses allocated to *domestic* importers, the area C is a transfer from domestic consumers to domestic importers. Area C is a loss to consumers and a gain to importers, for a net effect of zero for Japan as a whole. Our net welfare effect is just like a specific tariff, known as the *equivalent tariff*, equal to the quota premium $P_{quota} - P^W$, which results in an import level of Z^J_{quota}:

$$N = A + C - (A + B + C + D) = -(B + D) \tag{7.3}$$

In the case of import licenses allocated to *foreign* exporters, area C is a transfer from domestic consumers to these foreign exporters. It is no longer a net loss of zero, because the loss to consumers is not offset by a gain to domestic importers. Our net welfare effect is simply the gain to firms less the loss to consumers:

$$N = A - (A + B + C + D) = -(B + C + D) \tag{7.4}$$

In this case, the quota is worse than a tariff that results in an import level of Z^J_{quota}.

Given what we have just said, suppose you were a government official administering quota policy. Which of the above two alternatives would you choose: a quota allocated to domestic importers or a quota allocated to foreign exporters? Your answer is probably the quota allocated to domestic importers, since these have the smaller welfare loss. Now, here is a puzzle: when quotas were in active

[13] Corden (1997: 127, emphasis in original) notes: "There will be quota profits...received by the lucky people who obtain the import licenses. These quota profits are *rents* because they are not received as payments for any services, and any reduction in these profits would not affect the supply of any resource."

[14] There is a third possibility, whereby the import licenses are *auctioned* to the highest bidder by the government. Since the quota auction proceeds accrue domestically (to the government), the welfare properties of this case are like that of the case in which the import licenses are allocated to domestic importers.

use, many governments chose a foreign allocated quota.[15] Why? One possibility is that these governments were uninformed about the economic implications of their choices. Another possibility is that political considerations caused such a choice. For some reason, governments perhaps found it beneficial from a political point of view to assist foreigners, particularly low- and middle-income countries, in the form of what is sometimes called a "side payment." A better approach from the viewpoint of LMIC country exporters, however, would have been to remove the quota altogether.[16]

In this and the previous two sections, we have discussed four trade policy possibilities: a tariff, a tariff with terms of trade effects, a domestic-allocated quota, and a foreign-allocated quota. Before moving on to discuss anti-dumping and countervailing measures, let us summarize these four possibilities in a box.[17]

Tariff Unambiguous net welfare loss, because of consumer surplus loss outweighing gains in producer surplus and government revenue.

Tariff with terms of trade effects Ambiguous net welfare effect, because of terms of trade gain (fall in world price) potentially outweighing the efficiency loss.

Domestic-allocated quota Unambiguous net welfare loss, because of consumer surplus loss outweighing gains in producer surplus and quota rents.

Foreign-allocated quota Unambiguous net welfare loss that exceeds that of the domestic-allocated quota case and equivalent tariff.

Anti-Dumping and Countervailing Measures

Table 7.1 included the two tax-like NTMs of anti-dumping and countervailing duties. Because these NTMs play such a significant role in systems of trade protection, it is worthwhile to consider them in some more detail.[18] The AD notion implies that a product has been "dumped" into an economy. This in turn implies that the product has been sold at less than "normal" value. Tariffs can be applied against dumped goods if the dumping causes "material injury" to the domestic

---

[15] For example, this was the case for quotas in textiles and clothing, until they were phased out at the end of 2004.

[16] This is a case of what Singh (2017) calls "paternalism" in international trade relations.

[17] Note that quotas can also involve terms of trade effects that can complicate their analysis.

[18] For a review of AD and CVD measures from a legal perspective, see Matsushita, Schoenbaum, and Mavroidis (2015: chaps. 10 & 11).

competing sector producing a "like product." The terms "dumped," "normal," "material injury," and "like product" are put in quotation marks here because they are terms of *trade law* with legal as well as economic meanings.

One reason that AD measures are so important is that they are one of only a few means of applying protection in a manner consistent with obligations under the World Trade Organization. Article VI of the General Agreement on Tariffs and Trade (GATT 1994) provides for such measures as exceptions to the general principle of most favored nation (MFN), discussed in Chapter 8. The Marrakesh Agreement, resulting from the Uruguay Round of multinational trade negotiations, includes the important Agreement on Implementation of Article VI of GATT 1994 (commonly known as the Anti-Dumping Agreement), which clarifies the legal use of AD measures.

The determination of dumping takes place via two potential means. *Price-based dumping* is determined with evidence that an exporter is selling a good in the importing country at a price below what it charges in its own country. *Cost-based dumping* is determined with evidence that an exporter is selling a good in the importing country below its costs of production. Both these determinations are allowable under Article VI of GATT 1994, but the determination is a two-part process: one to show that there is price-based or cost-based dumping, and another to show that there has been "damage" to the domestic competing sector. This damage is sometimes determined using the imperfect substitutes model described in Appendix 7.1. If dumping and damage are both shown to be present, then "anti-dumping duties" may be imposed.

The administration of anti-dumping investigations can be rather involved.[19] For example, calculating "dumping margins" requires price and/or cost information from the foreign firm. Even with this information, calculating the dumping margins can be complicated, particularly when market systems in exporting countries are not completely operational. The old saying "It's an art, not a science" can sometimes apply here.

Once this entire process is complete, the importing country can choose from three policy responses. (1) Impose anti-dumping duties equal to the found dumping margin. (2) Impose anti-dumping duties sufficient to remove "material injury" ("lesser-duty rule"). (3) Have foreign exporting firms increase their prices ("price undertakings"). Although the Agreement on Implementation of Article VI of GATT 1994 requires that AD cases be reviewed every five years, there is no stipulated time limit. That said, like most other trade policy matters, AD actions are subject to the WTO dispute settlement mechanism, discussed in Chapter 8.

[19] For a succinct description, see Moore (2009).

Among trade economists, AD actions have a lot of critics.[20] The main criticism is that AD is just protectionism in another guise, and one that is being used ever more widely. It is often pointed out that a mere AD *investigation* can suppress trade and that actual AD duties can significantly suppress or actually eliminate the affected trade flow. Another criticism is that the determinations involved in AD actions are so complicated as to render any AD actions questionable. Finally, it is often pointed out that the two indicators of the presence of dumping, price differentials and selling below average total costs, are both practices that firms adopt in their domestic markets, sometimes as part of profit-maximizing behavior. These criticisms are valid, but the fact that AD actions are subject to WTO dispute settlement offers some hope, and the use of such actions is preferable to other options, such as invoking "national security," as mentioned in Chapter 6 in the case of US steel protection.

Countervailing duties can be imposed on foreign exporters as offsets when they benefit from *subsidies* offered to them by their national governments.[21] Like AD, CVDs are also covered under Article VI of GATT 1994 and an Agreement on Subsidies and Countervailing Measures. CVDs are much less frequently used, however, and therefore less scrutinized by trade policy analysts. CVD actions are allowed if it can be shown both that the subsidies benefited the foreign exporter and that the resulting exports caused "material injury" to the domestic competing industry in the importing country. So CVD determinations must measure both subsidy levels and injury, and such measurement can be imperfect.

Like AD, CVDs have detractors, with allegations that they are simply a way of protecting domestic industries. Evidence for this came in the form of trading entities (the United States and the European Union) imposing CVDs against clusters of countries simultaneously, and even engaging in both AD and CVD actions simultaneously. The latter is known as "double remedy" and was eventually found to be inappropriate in a WTO dispute settlement case. CVDs have also emerged as an issue in the interaction between "market economies" (MEs) and "non-market economies" (NMEs) within the WTO, with the observation that NMEs are more likely to use subsidies, and MEs are therefore more likely to deploy CVDs in response.[22]

Despite the criticisms levied against AD and CVD actions, they are important parts of the international trade and protection landscape. For better or worse, their analysis will continue to occupy both trade economists and trade lawyers as central types of NTMs.

[20] See Besedeš and Prusa (2017), Prusa (2005), and Moore (2009).

[21] For reviews, see Reynolds (2009) and Coppens (2014).

[22] See, for example, Prusa (2017).

Comparative Advantage Models

Our analysis of trade policies in this chapter has been based on the absolute advantage model of Chapter 2. The absolute advantage model has taken us quite far. We have shown how one can examine trade policies to make estimates of production, consumption, trade, employment, and welfare impacts. In many instances, however, the effects of trade policies go beyond a single sector. For example, protecting a large sector such as automobiles can draw resources from other sectors into the protected automobile sector. Perhaps workers in the metal furniture sector will move into the automobile sector as it expands under protection. Moreover, protecting a large intermediate product sector, such as petroleum or steel, can raise costs for other sectors that use petroleum or steel in their production processes.

In these cases, trade policy analysts turn to models of comparative advantage, such as those we discussed in Chapters 3 and 4. As you will recall, the comparative advantage model analyzes more than one sector simultaneously (e.g. rice and motorcycles). In some instances, this is an important feature. Such models are much more complicated than the absolute advantage models we considered in this chapter, and we will not formally discuss them here. You should be aware of their use, however. At the level of basic theory, the central insights of the comparative advantage approach include the fact that a protective measure in one sector acts as an *implicit tax* on production in other sectors, reducing their output levels. This is the result of the opportunity costs of production, discussed in Chapters 3 and 4.[23]

Given the importance of the comparative advantage perspective in many trade policy issues, trade policy analysts have turned to mathematical models of comparative advantage known as applied general equilibrium (AGE) models.[24] These combine the insights of the comparative advantage models of Chapters 3 and 4, namely technology and resources, with the framework of the imperfect substitutes model discussed in Appendix 7.1. The latter allows for intra-industry trade. AGE models can therefore account for both inter-industry trade based on comparative advantage and intra-industry trade based on product differentiation.[25] Some years ago constructing an AGE model for trade policy analysis was a substantial undertaking. More recently, however, a few standard models have eased the difficulty of using them. We discuss one such standard model in the accompanying box. We will also encounter AGE models again in Chapter 9, in the context of preferential trade agreements (PTAs).

---

[23] See Markusen et al. (1995: chaps. 15 & 16).

[24] On AGE models in general, see Reinert (2009) and references therein.

[25] Formally, AGE models usually allow for product differentiation by country of origin rather than at the level of the firm, as in the monopolistic competition model of Chapter 5.

The Global Trade Analysis Project

The Global Trade Analysis Project (GTAP) began in 1993 and is based at Purdue University. It has evolved into a global network of trade policy analysts conducting research in an applied general equilibrium framework. At its core, GTAP is a source for a database of global production and trade that is combined with a standard GTAP AGE model. Around this core is a global network of users, developers, and contributors, who use the database and the model or just the database and their own model. At the time of this writing the latest version of the database is GTAP 10, describing the world economy in 2004, 2007, 2011, and 2014 with 141 regions/countries and 65 sectors. The latest version of the model was GTAP 7, released in 2017.

The GTAP network or community of trade policy analysts convene each year in an annual conference, and short courses on using the GTAP database and model are held around the world. This effort has advanced the use of AGE models of trade policy in both national governments and global organizations such as the United Nations. In addition, multilateral financial institutions, including the World Bank, often rely on the GTAP model or database for their own trade policy analysis. Interestingly, the model has been increasingly applied to environmental and natural resource issues.

Efforts such as GTAP have contributed immensely to the ease and widespread use of the comparative advantage framework in trade policy analysis. These AGE models continue to be central tool for trade policy analysis.

Sources: Hertel (1997), Van Tongeren et al. (2017), and gtap.agecon.purdue.edu.

Conclusion

In order to help protect the losers of increased international trade, most countries of the world engage in trade policies. The supply and demand analysis of the absolute advantage model allows us to discover the effects of these trade policies on production, consumption, trade, welfare, and employment. In this chapter, we have analyzed tariffs, tariffs with terms of trade effects, quotas, and AD/CVD policies. Appendices 7.1 and 7.2 consider the important cases of the imperfect substitutes model and tariff rate quotas. In addition, we briefly mentioned trade policy analysis based on comparative advantage models of trade. In general, intervention in free trade reduces the overall welfare of the intervening country. Certain groups might benefit from these policies, however, which is why they are usually implemented.

This chapter has engaged in formal, economic analysis of trade policies. In Chapter 8 we will engage in a more institutional or legal analysis of trade policies when we examine the World Trade Organization. In practice, trade policy analysis is a combination of formal economic analysis and institutional or legal analysis. The marriage of these two perspectives is what allows for a full appreciation of trade policies.

Review Exercises

1. Consider Figure 7.2. For a given T, what would be the impact of an *increase in supply* (a shift of the supply curve to the right) on government revenue? What would be the impact of an *increase in demand* (a shift of the demand curve to the right)?
2. In Figure 7.3, we introduced the terms of trade effects of Japan's tariff on imports of rice. The terms of trade effect (area E in the diagram) was positive for Japan. In a new diagram similar to Figure 7.1, show that these terms of trade effects adversely affect the welfare of Vietnam.
3. Consider our diagram of a quota in Figure 7.4. Suppose the government reduced the quota to below Z^{J}_{quota}. What would happen to the *quota premium*? Can you say with certainty what would happen to the total *quota rent*? What would this depend on?
4. Trade protection is often used to maintain employment in a sector. Given our analysis, what do you think of this approach to maintaining employment? Can you think of any other measures that might also maintain employment in a sector?

FURTHER READING AND WEB RESOURCES

For some fundamental introductions to trade policy analysis, see Vousden (1990), Corden (1997), and Francois and Reinert (1997). For the analysis of additional trade policies using the absolute advantage framework, see Hoekman and Kostecki (2009: appendix). See Anderson (2005) for the role that economics has played in trade policy analysis in the era since World War II, and an excellent set of references. Goode (2007) provides an excellent dictionary of the plethora of trade policy terms. You can visit the Global Trade Analysis Project website at www.gtap.agecon.purdue.edu. The WTO has published its own guide to trade policy analysis, at www.wto.org/english/res_e/publications_e/practical_guide12_e.htm.

REFERENCES

Anderson, K. (2005) "Setting the Trade Policy Agenda: What Role for Economists?," *Journal of World Trade*, 39:2, 341–81.

Armington, P. (1969) "A Theory of Demand for Products Distinguished by Place of Production," *IMF Staff Papers*, 16:3, 159–76.

Arrowsmith, S. (2003) "Transparency in Government Procurement: The Objectives of Regulation and the Boundaries of the World Trade Organization," *Journal of World Trade*, 37:2, 283–303.

Bacchetta, M. (2009) "Tariffs," in K. A. Reinert, R. S. Rajan, A. J. Glass, and L. S. Davis (eds.), *The Princeton Encyclopedia of the World Economy*, Princeton University Press, 1063–7.

Baldwin, R., and T. Murray (1977) "MFN Tariff Reductions and Developing Country Trade under the GSP," *Economic Journal*, 87:345, 30–46.

Besedeš, T., and T. J. Prusa (2017) "The Hazardous Effects of Anti-Dumping," *Economic Inquiry*, 55:1, 9–30.

Coppens, D. (2014) *WTO Disciplines on Subsidies and Countervailing Measures: Balancing Policy Space and Legal Constraints*, Cambridge University Press.

Corden, W. M. (1997) *Trade Policy and Economic Welfare*, Oxford University Press.

Francois, J. F., and K. A. Reinert (eds.) (1997) *Applied Methods for Trade Policy Analysis: A Handbook*, Cambridge University Press.

Goode, W. (2007) *Dictionary of Trade Policy Terms*, Cambridge University Press.

De Gorter, H. (2009) "Tariff Rate Quotas," in K. A. Reinert, R. S. Rajan, A. J. Glass, and L. S. Davis (eds.), *The Princeton Encyclopedia of the World Economy*, Princeton University Press, 1060–3.

Hertel, T. W. (1997) *Global Trade Analysis: Modeling and Applications*, Cambridge University Press.

Hertel, T. W., and W. Martin (2000) "Liberalising Agriculture and Manufactures in a Millennium Round: Implications for Developing Countries," *The World Economy*, 23:4, 455–69.

Hoekman, B. M., and M. M. Kostecki (2009) *The Political Economy of the World Trading System*, Oxford University Press.

Laird, S. (1997) "Quantifying Commercial Policies," in *Applied Methods for Trade Policy Analysis: A Handbook*, Cambridge University Press, 27–75.

Liu, T., and W. T. Woo (2018) "Understanding the US–China Trade War," *China Economic Journal*, 11:3, 319–40.

McDaniel, C., K. A. Reinert, and K. Hughes (2008) *Tools of the Trade: Models for Trade Policy Analysis*, Woodrow Wilson Center.

Markusen, J. R., J. R. Melvin, W. H. Kaempfer, and K. E. Maskus (1995) *International Trade: Theory and Evidence*, McGraw-Hill.

Matsushita, M., T. J. Schoenbaum, and P. C. Mavroidis (2015) *The World Trade Organization: Law, Practice, and Policy*, Oxford University Press.

Moore, M. O. (2009) "Anti-Dumping," in K. A. Reinert, R. S. Rajan, A. J. Glass, and L. S. Davis (eds.), *The Princeton Encyclopedia of the World Economy*, Princeton University Press, 64–8.

Pelletiere, D., and K. A. Reinert (2002) "The Political Economy of Used Automobile Protection in Latin America," *The World Economy*, 25:7, 1019–37.

Peterson, J. (2017) "An Overview of Customs Reforms to Facilitate Trade," *Journal of International Commerce and Economics*, August, 1–30.

Planet Rice (2000) "Japan to USA: Rice Farming Is Our Culture: Don't Interfere," November 26, www.planetrice.net.

Prusa, T. J. (2005) "Anti-Dumping: A Growing Problem in International Trade," *World Economy*, 28:5, 683–700.

Prusa, T. J. (2017) "NMEs and the Double Remedy Problem," *World Trade Review*, 16:4, 619–34.

Reinert, K. A. (2009) "Applied General Equilibrium Models," in K. A. Reinert, R. S. Rajan, A. J. Glass, and L. S. Davis (eds.), *Princeton Encyclopedia of the World Economy*, Princeton University Press, 74–9.

Reinert, K. A. (2014) "Sensitivity Analysis in an Imperfect Substitutes Model of Preferential Trade," *Journal of Economic Studies*, 41:5, 630–43.

Reynolds, K. M. (2009) "Countervailing Duties," in K. A. Reinert, R. S. Rajan, A. J. Glass, and L. S. Davis (eds.), *The Princeton Encyclopedia of the World Economy*, Princeton University Press, 236–40.

Rouslang, D. J., and J. W. Suomela (1988) "Calculating the Welfare Costs of Import Restrictions in the Imperfect Substitutes Model," *Applied Economics*, 20:5, 691–700.

Singh, J. P. (2017) *Sweet Talk: Paternalism and Collective Action in North–South Trade Relations*, Stanford University Press.

Takacs, W. (2009) "Nontariff Measures," in K. A. Reinert, R. S. Rajan, A. J. Glass, and L. S. Davis (eds.), *The Princeton Encyclopedia of the World Economy*, Princeton University Press, 843–7.

Van Tongeren, F., R. Koopman, S. Karingi, J. Reilly, and J. F. Francois (2017) "Back to the Future: A 25-Year Retrospective on GTAP and the Shaping of a New Agenda," *Journal of Global Economic Analysis*, 2:2, 1–42.

Vousden, N. (1990) *The Economics of Trade Protection*, Cambridge University Press.

Wilson, J. S. (2009) "Technical Barriers to Trade," in K. A. Reinert, R. S. Rajan, A. J. Glass, and L. S. Davis (eds.), *The Princeton Encyclopedia of the World Economy*, Princeton University Press, 1067–70.

Appendix 7.1: The Imperfect Substitutes Model

The absolute advantage model used in this chapter assumes that the imported good and domestic competing goods are *perfect substitutes*. In a number of instances, however, trade policy analysts want to allow for the possibility that the imported and domestic competing goods are *imperfect substitutes*.[26] This leads us to what is now known as the imperfect substitutes model, depicted in Figure 7.5.[27] This figure allows for the terms of trade effects described in this chapter.

The important difference between Figure 7.5 and those previously considered in this chapter is that there are now *two* closely related markets: one for the imported

[26] This is one type of product differentiation known as *product differentiation by country* of origin, which is related to explanations of intra-industry trade we discussed in Chapter 5. An early contribution to this approach was Armington (1969).

[27] The original contribution on this model was Baldwin and Murray (1977). A more explicit version is provided by Rouslang and Suomela (1988) and Reinert (2014).

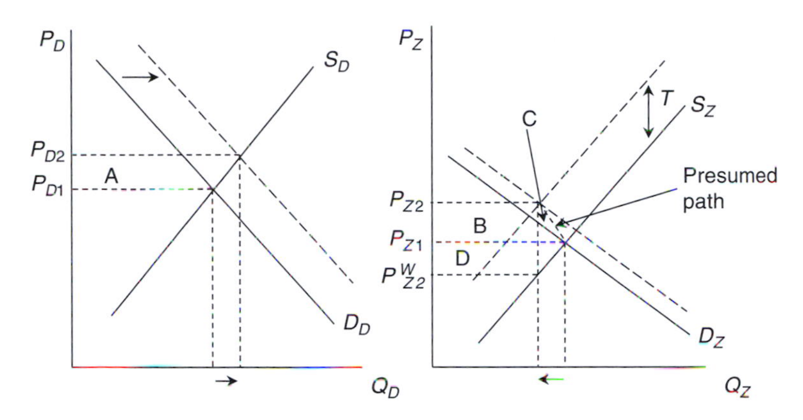

Figure 7.5 The imperfect substitutes model

good Z, and the other for a domestic competing good D. The demand curves for these two markets are related through the cross-price elasticity of demand between the two goods. The initial equilibrium in the absence of a tariff results in the two prices P_{Z1} and P_{D1}. The imposition of a specific tariff T on imports of good Z causes the supply curve of this good to shift upwards by the amount of the tariff, raising the domestic price of the imported good along the demand curve.

The increase in the price of good Z affects the demand for good D, shifting the curve out to the dashed line as households substitute towards the domestic good. This increases the domestic price of good D, which in turn causes a substitution towards good Z and a shift out of the demand curve for imports to the dashed line. These two substitution effects are *simultaneous*, and the resulting new domestic prices are P_{Z2} and P_{D2}. The world price of the imported good falls along the supply curve of the imported variety (S_Z) to P^W_{Z2}. This is the terms of trade effect discussed in this chapter.

We next consider the welfare effects of the tariff in this imperfect substitutes framework. In the market for the domestic good, there is an increase in producer surplus along the supply curve equal to trapezoid A (extending from the vertical price axis all the way to the supply curve). This entire area comes as a cost to consumers, however, with the producer gain and the consumer loss exactly offsetting each other. This nets to zero.

In the market of the imported good, there are no domestic producers to account for. The estimation of the consumer welfare effect is troubled by the fact that both the supply curve and the demand curve in the market for good Z have shifted. The standard approach to this is to measure the change in consumer surplus along the presumed path between the initial and final equilibria points. The resulting consumer surplus loss is the trapezoid $B + C$. The increase in tariff revenue as a result of the tariff is equal to $B + D$. Consequently, the net welfare effect in Figure 7.5 is $D - C$. Area D represents the terms of trade gain, and area

C represents the efficiency loss. In practice, the terms of trade gain is probably small for a single country and a single, narrowly defined product. Some modelers assume that the supply curve of the imported variety is infinitely elastic (horizontal), so that there is no terms of trade effect at all.

This might seem to be a more complicated approach to trade policy analysis than the perfect-substitutes case of Figures 7.2 and 7.3. The approach is *widely used*, however, particularly in the analysis of AD and CVD cases by national governments. For this reason, it is very much worth understanding.

Appendix 7.2: A Tariff Rate Quota

In Chapter 8 we will discuss the Uruguay Round of multilateral trade negotiations and its Agreement on Agriculture. One implication of the Agreement on Agriculture is that many high-income countries and some LMICs now impose **tariff** rate quotas on imports of agricultural goods.[28] A TRQ involves two tariff levels: a lower tariff for levels of imports within the quota and a higher tariff for levels of imports above the quota. Suppose Japan were to impose a TRQ on imports of rice. This policy can be stated as follows. Up to the quota amount Z^{JQ}, Japan applies a *within-quota tariff rate* of T^{IN}. Above the quota amount Z^{JQ}, Japan applies a larger, *out-of-quota tariff rate* of T^{OUT}. To analyze this policy, it is best to consider three cases.

Case I: $Z^J < Z^{JQ}$
Case II: $Z^J = Z^{JQ}$
Case III: $Z^J > Z^{JQ}$

We are going to consider each of these three cases in turn. For each, we are going to use a diagram set out along the lines illustrated in Figure 7.6. The quota amount, Z^{JQ}, is plotted along the horizontal axis, and this distance is indicated with a double-headed arrow. Along the vertical axis, there are three prices indicated. The first, and lowest, price is the world price of imported rice, P^W. To simplify our analysis here, we assume that Japan cannot affect this world price–that is, there are none of the terms of trade effects we discussed in this chapter. The second, higher, price is the world price plus the within-quota tariff rate of T^{IN}. The third, and highest, price is the world price plus the out-of-quota tariff rate of T^{OUT}.

We are going to use the framework depicted in Figure 7.6 to analyze the three cases mentioned above. Case I is presented in Figure 7.7. Here the level of rice

[28] See Hertel and Martin (2000) and de Gorter (2009).

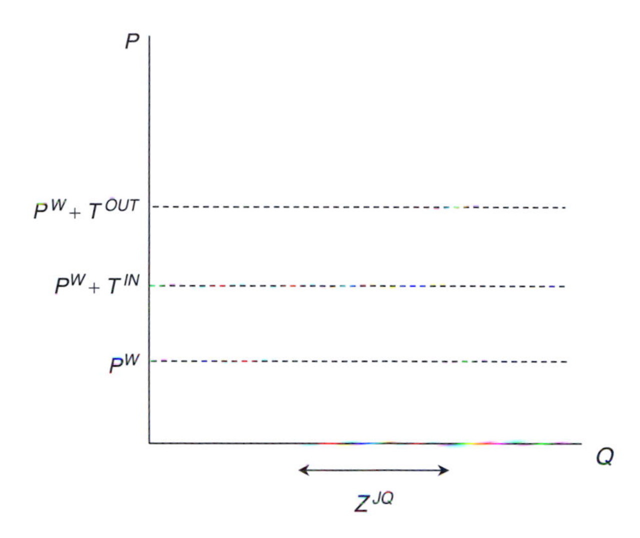

Figure 7.6 Framework for analyzing Japan's tariff rate quota on rice

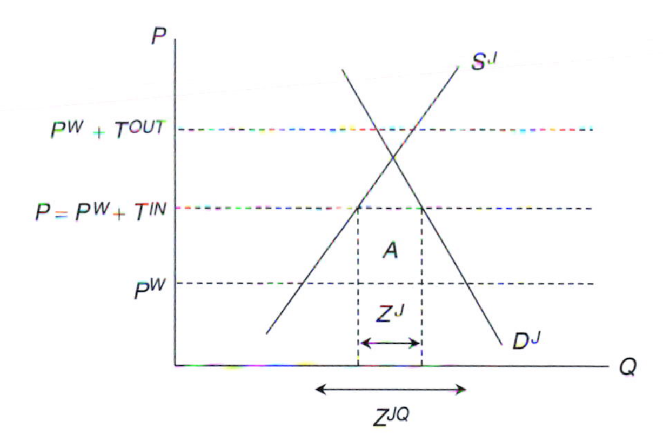

Figure 7.7 Case I of Japan's tariff rate quota on rice

imports is within the quota amount. Therefore, the domestic price P is determined by the lower tariff value, T^{IN}, and the tariff revenue collected by the government is area A.

Case II is presented in Figure 7.8. Here the level of rice imports is exactly equal to the quota amount. In this case, the domestic price is somewhere between the two tariff-inclusive prices–that is, $P^W + T^{IN} \leq P \leq P^W + T^{OUT}$. As in Case I, the tariff revenue collected by the government is area A. If the positions of the Japanese supply and demand curves for rice cause the domestic price P to be above $P^W + T^{IN}$, however, then there are also quota rents equal to area B.

Case III is presented in Figure 7.9. Here the level of rice imports exceeds the quota amount. Therefore, the domestic price P is determined by the higher tariff

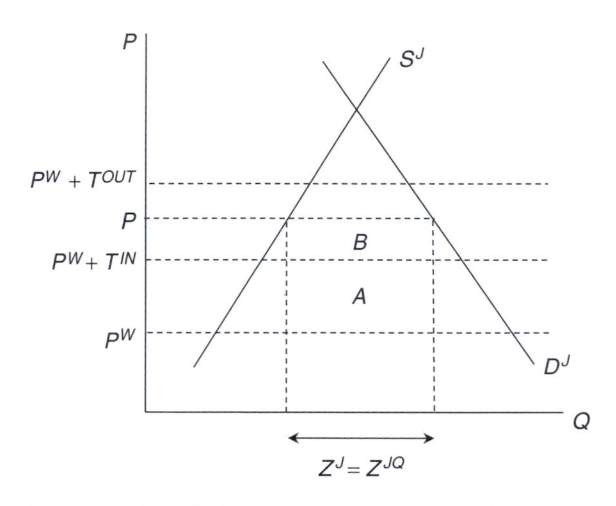

Figure 7.8 Case II of Japan's tariff rate quota on rice

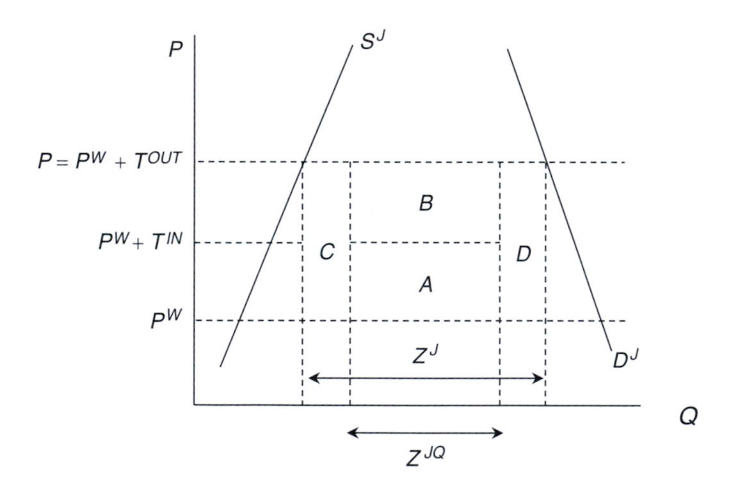

Figure 7.9 Case III of Japan's tariff rate quota on rice

value. The total tariff revenue collected by the government is composed of three areas. Area A represents the tariff revenue collected on the imports that are within the quota. Areas C and D represent the additional tariff revenue collected on the imports that are above the quota. In addition, as in Case II, there are quota rents on the quota amount equal to area B.

Readers of this appendix will no doubt get the impression that the analysis of TRQs is a little complicated. Unfortunately, it is simply a reality of the modern world trading system, and requires some patience and persistence on the part of the student or professional. The world is a complex place, and our analysis of it often needs to be complex as well.

8 The World Trade Organization

Geneva is a beautiful city, and walking alongside Lake Geneva is an activity enjoyed by many of its residents and tourists. If you begin in downtown Geneva and proceed along the northwestern shore of Lake Geneva, you will have a grand view of the beautiful water jet in the middle of the lake. Quai du Mont Blanc turns into Quai Wilson, and you will then proceed by a number of statues and pleasant, open parks. Next, you will enter into the wooded Parc Mon Repos and proceed by the Graduate Institute of International and Development Studies. Finally, you will walk between a large, gray building and the lake. If you turn to face this building, you will be looking at the **World Trade Organization**, an organization lauded and vilified with equal intensity by various groups with concerns about trade policy.

Although many individuals and groups have strong opinions about the WTO, most know very little about it. This chapter will make sure you understand key aspects of this important institution of world trade. To develop your understanding of the WTO, we will first take up its predecessor, the **General Agreement on Tariffs and Trade**, and introduce the principles it established for the conduct of international trade in goods. Next, we will turn to the WTO itself, as established by the 1994 Marrakesh Agreement. Here we will cover the main provisions of the Marrakesh Agreement in the areas of goods, services, intellectual property, and dispute settlement. We will also consider the issue of trade and the environment within the WTO. Finally, we will take up the recently failed Doha Round of **multilateral trade negotiations**.

Nobel laureate Douglass North (1990: 3) defines institutions as "humanly devised constraints that shape human interaction," a less formal definition being "the rules of the game." The WTO is the *central institution of global trade* and sets out the rules of the trading game.[1] These rules have force as public international law, and the study of the WTO takes place on the boundaries of economics, political science, and law. This, in turn, involves a subtle change in vocabulary that may appear odd at first. Trust that the terms we introduce here are widely utilized in the trade policy field.

---

[1] To be more precise, the WTO is both a global *institution* and a global *organization*. On the latter concept, see Debebe (2017).

The General Agreement on Tariffs and Trade

During World War II the United States and Britain began developing the outlines of a set of post-war economic institutions. The specifics of the plan were negotiated in 1944 at the Bretton Woods Conference. This conference set up the International Bank for Reconstruction and Development (what became the World Bank) and the International Monetary Fund. The conference also noted, however, that there should be a third international organization in the realm of international trade.

In 1945 the United States attempted to launch the idea of an International Trade Organization (ITO), and this proposal was taken up in a 1946 meeting in London to write the ITO charter. In early 1947 a draft General Agreement on Tariffs and Trade based on part of the draft ITO charter was prepared at a meeting in the United States. This led to a subsequent meeting that year in Geneva, at which 23 countries ("contracting parties") signed the Final Act of the GATT. The ITO charter itself was finalized at a 1948 meeting of 56 countries in Havana, Cuba, and this became known as the Havana Charter.[2] In 1950, however, the US government announced that it would *not* seek US congressional ratification of the Havana Charter, effectively terminating the ITO plan. Consequently, the institutional vehicle for post-war trade became the GATT itself.[3]

The GATT preamble encouraged member countries to consider "reciprocal and mutually advantageous arrangements directed to the substantial reduction of tariffs and other barriers to trade and to the elimination of discriminatory treatment in international commerce." This exhortation had some effect. Between 1946 and 1994 the GATT provided a framework for a number of "rounds" of multilateral trade negotiations (MTNs). These are listed in Table 8.1, along with the failed, WTO-sponsored Doha Round. The GATT-sponsored rounds reduced tariffs between member countries in many (but not all) sectors. As a result, the weighted average tariff on manufactured products imposed by high-income countries (HICs) fell from approximately 20 percent to approximately 5 percent.[4]

Despite these successes, the Geneva-based GATT Secretariat could not always effectively enforce negotiated agreements without the legal standing of the ITO. This and other "constitutional defects" (Jackson, 1994) limited its effectiveness.

---

[2] The Havana Charter was substantially more comprehensive than the GATT, in that it addressed restrictive business practices, international investment, and services.

[3] The decision not to seek ratification was in response to pressures from isolationist members of the US Congress. Formally, the GATT was able to exist without the ITO thanks to what was called the Protocol of Provisional Application, which had standing under international law. The 23 Geneva signatories became "contracting parties" to the GATT rather than "members" of the ITO. Jackson (1990: 15) notes: "Since the ITO did not come into being, a major gap was left in the fabric intended for post-World War II international economic institutions."

[4] See Hoekman and Kostecki (2009: 138) and Bown and Irwin (2015).

Table 8.1 GATT/WTO rounds of multilateral trade negotiations

Name of round	Years	Number of countries	Auspices
Geneva	1947	23	GATT
Annecy	1949	29	GATT
Torquay	1950–1951	32	GATT
Geneva	1955–1956	33	GATT
Dillon	1960–1961	39	GATT
Kennedy	1963–1967	74	GATT
Tokyo	1973–1979	99	GATT
Uruguay	1986–1994	117	GATT
Doha Round (*failed*)	2001–2015	Approximately 160	WTO

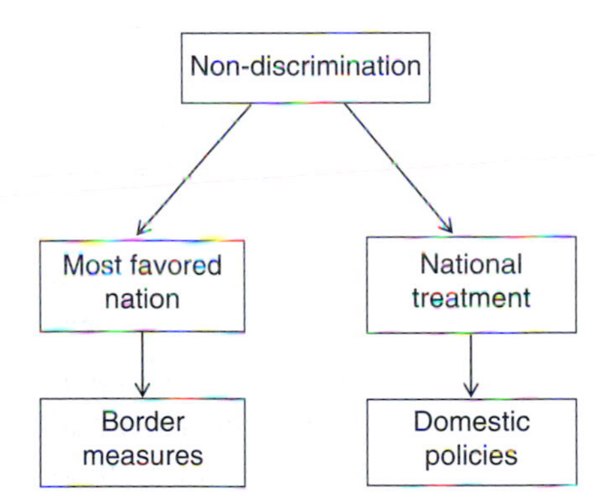

Figure 8.1 The non-discrimination principle

These limitations were finally addressed in 1994 with the end of the Uruguay Round negotiations in a signing ceremony in Marrakesh, Morocco. The **Marrakesh Agreement** provided for the creation of the World Trade Organization, which finally completed the vision of the ITO. This section of the chapter focuses on the GATT, while the following sections focus on the WTO.

The GATT covers only trade in *goods*.[5] Its most important principle is that of **non-discrimination**. As illustrated in Figure 8.1, non-discrimination has two important sub-principles, namely those of **most favored nation** (GATT Article I) and **national treatment** (GATT Article III). Under MFN, each member must grant treatment to all other members as favorable as it extends to any individual member country. If Japan lowers a tariff on Indonesia's exports of a certain product, it must also lower its tariff on the exports of that product from *all other* member

[5] For a review of trade in goods, see Reinert (2017).

countries for "like products." Exceptions to MFN treatment are allowed in the case of certain preferential trade agreements (see Chapter 9) and preferences granted to low- and middle-income countries (LMICs).

Whereas MFN addresses border measures, NT addresses internal, domestic policies. NT specifies that foreign goods within a country should be treated no less favorably than domestic goods with regard to tax policies and other regulations (e.g. technical standards), again for "like products." Together, MFN and NT compose the critically important non-discrimination principle.

A second important GATT principle is a general *prohibition of quotas* or quantitative restrictions on trade (Article XI). This reflects a longstanding view that price distortions (tariffs) are preferred to quantity distortions in international markets. It also reflects the history of GATT. During its birth, quantitative restrictions were one of the most significant impediments to trade. As always, there are exceptions allowed. Temporary quantitative restrictions on trade can be used in the case of balance of payments difficulties, but these must be implemented with the non-discrimination principle of Figure 8.1 in mind.

For many years there were sector-specific exceptions to the general prohibition of quotas in the GATT. The first was the case of agricultural products, granted to address US agricultural programs, and used for decades to reduce US imports of sugar, dairy products, and peanuts.[6] The United States also insisted that export subsidies (also prohibited) be allowed for agriculture. Eventually the European Union became the most vociferous supporter of these subsidies, under its Common Agricultural Policy (CAP).[7] A second important exemption to quota prohibition was for textiles and clothing. These began in the early 1960s and were in place through the end of 2004, the period from 1995 to 2004 being under the auspices of the World Trade Organization and an Agreement on Textiles and Clothing (ATC).[8]

Exceptions to the quota prohibitions of the GATT in the areas of agriculture, textiles, and clothing generated negative feelings on the part of LMICs with regard to the world trading system. Why? Agriculture, textiles, and clothing are three groups of products that countries first turn to in their trade and development processes. The fact that these three groups of products were taken out of the GATT framework at the insistence of HICs left the LMICs wondering how they could have a fair chance to participate in the trade and development process.[9] These sentiments have not entirely disappeared.

---

[6] See Hathaway (1987: 109).

[7] On the EU Common Agricultural Policy, see Hathaway (1987), Hathaway and Ingo (1996), and Dinan (2010: chap. 11).

[8] For the interesting history of textiles and clothing protection, see Reinert (2000) and Singh (2017: chap. 4).

[9] See Singh (2017: chap. 3).

A third important GATT principle is that of **binding**. GATT- and WTO-sponsored reductions in tariff levels have been based on the practice of binding tariffs at agreed-upon levels, often *above* applied levels. Once set, tariff bindings may not in general be increased in the future. Applied rates that are below bound rates may be increased, however. Although there are provisions made for some renegotiation of bound tariffs, such renegotiations must be accompanied by compensation. The general purpose of the binding principle is to introduce a degree of predictability into the world trading system.[10]

The World Trade Organization

When the Uruguay Round of MTNs was launched, in 1986, there was recognition that the GATT had inherent institutional flaws. This recognition evolved into a commitment to address these flaws, and by the end of 1993 the text of the Uruguay Round contained a final charter for a World Trade Organization.[11] Indeed, the 1994 Marrakesh Agreement that concluded the Uruguay Round is actually the "Marrakesh Agreement Establishing the World Trade Organization." The old GATT was updated to GATT 1994 and folded into the institutional structure of the WTO. In fact, the WTO is sometimes referred to as a "tripod" in that it stands on the following three legs:

trade in goods, governed by GATT 1994, including an Agreement on Agriculture and an Agreement on Textiles and Clothing (the latter expiring in 2005);

trade in services, as specified in the **General Agreement on Trade in Services** (GATS); and

intellectual property, as specified in the **Agreement on Trade-Related Aspects of Intellectual Property Rights** (TRIPS).

Importantly, the Marrakesh Agreement included a WTO *charter*. It established the WTO as a legal international organization, stipulating: "The WTO shall provide the common institutional framework for the conduct of trade relations between its members."[12] The charter also defined the functions of the WTO, including: to

[10] It is important to note that the MFN principle applies to *both* applied *and* bound tariff rates. Gaps between bound and applied rates are (strangely) known as "water in the tariff."

[11] The Uruguay Round included a negotiating group on the "function of the GATT system," or FOGS. Then John Jackson (1990), a preeminent trade lawyer, suggested that the Uruguay Round consider establishing a World Trade Organization. In 1991 the director general of GATT, Arthur Dunkel, released a draft agreement for the Uruguay Round, which became known as "the Dunkel text." The Dunkel text included a draft charter for the WTO.

[12] All quotations without citations are taken from GATT Secretariat (1994).

facilitate the implementation, administration, and operation of the multilateral trade agreements; to provide a forum for negotiations between members concerning multilateral trade relations; to administer disputes between members; and to cooperate with the International Monetary Fund and World Bank.

The administrative aspects of the WTO are summarized in Table 8.2. Members of the WTO send representatives to a Ministerial Conference, which meets at least once every two years and carries out the functions of the WTO. The Ministerial Conference appoints a director general of the WTO Secretariat, who, in turn, appoints the staff of the Secretariat. The Ministerial Conference adopts "regulations setting out the powers, duties, conditions of service and term of office of the Director General." Between meetings of the Ministerial Conference, the General Council meets to conduct the affairs of the WTO. The General Council establishes rules and procedures, discharges the responsibilities of the Dispute Settlement Body, and discharges the responsibilities of the Trade Policy Review Body.

When possible, the Ministerial Conference and the General Council make decisions by *consensus*. Consensus is defined to be a situation in which "no member, present at the meeting when the decision is taken, *formally objects* to the proposed decision" (emphasis added). Therefore, consensus does not necessarily imply unanimity but only the absence of formally expressed objection. This definition of consensus has proved to be important in the dispute settlement process of the WTO (to be discussed below). When consensus cannot be reached, the WTO makes decisions through a process of majority voting: one vote per member.[13]

Let us now turn to a few important aspects of the WTO.

Trade in Goods

In the realm of trade in goods, the Marrakesh Agreement contains GATT 1994 (an update of the original GATT), an Agreement on Agriculture, and an Agreement on Textiles and Clothing (which expired in 2005). The negotiated Agreement on Agriculture addressed three outstanding issues concerning international trade in agricultural goods: market access, domestic support, and export subsidies. In the case of *market access*, the Agreement on Agriculture replaced a quota-based system with a system of bound tariffs and tariff reduction commitments. The conversion of quotas into equivalent tariffs is a process known as **tariffication**.[14] In this

---

[13] This is in contrast to the International Monetary Fund and World Bank, in which voting is weighted.

[14] "Developed" country members had to have reduced average agricultural tariffs by 36 percent by 2001, and "developing" country members had to have reduced average agricultural tariffs by 24 percent by 2005. "Least developed" country members were not required to reduce their tariffs.

Table 8.2 Administrative structure of the WTO

Body	Composition	Function
Ministerial Conference	Representatives of all members.	Meets at least once every two years. Carries out functions of WTO. Makes decisions and takes actions.
General Council	Representatives of all members.	Meets between the meetings of the Ministerial Conference. Establishes rules and procedures. Discharges responsibilities of the Dispute Settlement Body. Discharges responsibilities of the Trade Policy Review Body.
Council for Trade in Goods	Representative of all members.	Oversees the functioning of the multilateral agreements of Annex 1A.
Council for Trade in Services	Representative of all members.	Oversees the functioning of the multilateral agreements of Annex 1B.
Council for Trade-Related Aspects of Intellectual Property Rights	Representative of all members.	Oversees the functioning of the multilateral agreements of Annex 1C.
Dispute Settlement Body	Representative of all members.	Establishes panels, adopts panel and Appellate Body reports, maintains surveillance of implementation of rulings and recommendations.
Dispute Settlement Panels	Three or five well-qualified governmental and/or non-governmental individuals.	Assists the Dispute Settlement Body by making findings and recommendations in dispute settlement cases.
Appellate Body	Seven persons, three of whom serve on any one case.	Hears appeals from panel cases.
Secretariat	Director general and staff.	Provides support for the activities of the member countries.

aspect, the Agreement on Agriculture represented a significant *change of regime.* In particular, non-tariff measures (quotas) were prohibited, with minimum access levels (MALs) implemented with the tariff rate quotas discussed in Appendix 7.2.

In the case of *domestic support,* a distinction is made between *non-trade-distorting policies,* known as "green box" measures, and *trade-distorting policies,* known as "amber box" measures. Green box measures are exempt from any reduction commitments. Amber box measures are not exempt, and these commitments are specified in terms of what are known as "total aggregate measures of support" (total AMSs).[15] Finally, in the case of *export subsidies,* use has *not* been eliminated. Rather, it has been limited to specified situations.[16]

Despite the above-specified commitments, the Agreement on Agriculture is best viewed as a *change in rules* rather than as a significant program for the liberalization of trade in agricultural products.[17] The hope on the part of some members was that further liberalization would take place in the subsequent Doha Round of trade negotiations, discussed below. This would prove not to be the case.

Trade in Services

As we discussed in Chapter 1, trade in services composes more than 20 percent of total world trade and has at times grown more rapidly than trade in goods.[18] The General Agreement on Trade in Services represented the first time that services were brought into a multilateral trade agreement. For these reasons, the GATS is a significant outcome of the Uruguay Round. The negotiations on GATS were somewhat difficult. Initially, LMICs were reluctant to agree to services being part of a multilateral agreement. A combination of pressure from the United States and LMICs discovering their own potential comparative advantage in some types of services eventually dissolved this reluctance.

---

[15] "Developed" country members had to have reduced total AMS by 20 percent by 2001, and "developing" country members had to have reduced total AMS by 13 percent by 2005. "Least developed" country members were not required to reduce their total AMS.

[16] "Developed" country members had to have reduced export subsidies by 36 percent by 2001, and "developing" country members had to have reduced export subsidies by 24 percent by 2005. "Least developed" country members were not required to reduce their export subsidies. The persistence of developed-country export subsidies represents a *major distortion* in global agricultural trade.

[17] Hathaway and Ingo (1996) support this view. More recently, Singh (2017) concludes that the Agreement on Agriculture "was ineffective for agricultural liberalization: The agricultural subsidies went up, and imports of commodities from the developing world may have decreased rather than increased" (122).

[18] For the role of services in the world economy, see Chanda (2017) and Francois and Hoekman (2010).

To provide a structure to trade in services, GATS defines trade in services as occurring in one of *four modes*:

Mode 1: cross-border trade;
Mode 2: movement of consumers;
Mode 3: commercial presence or foreign direct investment (FDI); and
Mode 4: movement of natural persons.

Let us consider each of these in turn. *Cross-border trade* is a mode of supply that does not require the physical movement of either producers or consumers, such as when Indian firms provide medical transcription services to US hospitals via satellite technology. *Movement of consumers* involves the consumer traveling to the country of the producer, and is typical of the consumption of tourism and health services. *Commercial presence*, or FDI, is involved for services that require a commercial presence by producers in the country of the consumers, and is typical of financial services. Finally, the *movement of natural persons* involves a non-commercial presence by producers to supply consulting, construction, and instructional services.[19]

The GATS includes the principle of non-discrimination discussed above.[20] For those sectors a member country specifies on a "positive list," the GATS prohibits certain market access restrictions. Commitments to prohibit six types of limitations can be recorded on the positive list: the number of service suppliers; the total value of service transactions; the total number of operations or quantity of output; the number of personnel employed; the type of legal entity, in the case of FDI; and the share of foreign ownership, in the case of FDI. Singh (2017: 153) notes that "the positive list approach in the GATS agreement ensured that countries did not undertake trade liberalizations that were difficult politically." This contributed to the success of GATS negotiations.

The GATS negotiations also had an understanding that subsequent periodic negotiations would be required to incrementally liberalize trade in services. These negotiations have resulted in the following protocols to the GATS.[21]

Second GATS Protocol: Revised Schedules of Commitments on Financial Services, 1995.
Third GATS Protocol: Schedules of Specific Commitments Relating to Movement of Natural Persons, 1995.

[19] GATS Mode 4 is often referred to as the *temporary* movement of natural persons, but, as Matsushita et al. (2015: chap. 16) note, GATS does not actually state that the movement of natural persons under Mode 4 must be temporary.

[20] Initially, each member was allowed to specify non-discrimination exemptions on a "negative list" of sectors upon entry into the agreement, which lasted for ten years.

[21] The list begins with the "Second Protocol" because the first protocol was the GATS itself.

Fourth GATS Protocol: Schedules of Specific Commitments Concerning Basic Telecommunications, 1997.

Fifth GATS Protocol: Schedules of Specific Commitments and Lists of Exemptions from Article II Concerning Financial Services, 1998.

The Second and Fifth Protocols on financial services were a significant outcome of the post-Marrakesh negotiations, although the negotiation process was contentious. As a result, beginning in 1999 more than 100 WTO members entered into multilateral commitments in the areas of insurance, banking, and other financial services. The important Fourth Protocol on telecommunications is discussed in the accompanying box. The Third Protocol on the movement of natural persons (Mode 4, defined above) was not significant, involving only a few countries.[22]

Telecommunication Services in the GATS

As we discussed in Chapter 1, information and communication technology has been an important driver of globalization processes. Nevertheless, the Marrakesh Agreement of 1994 contained no agreement on trade in telecommunication services. Negotiations on telecommunication services had begun in 1989 at the instigation of the United States. These negotiations broke down, however, because the United States was unsatisfied with the size of the market access concessions made by other countries of the world. The Marrakesh Agreement contained a commitment to convene a Negotiating Group on Basic Telecommunications (NGBT). The NGBT did not meet a 1996 deadline and then morphed into the Group on Basic Telecommunications (GBT), which worked through 1997.

Despite some difficult negotiations, by 1997 success was in reach, resulting in an Agreement on Basic Telecommunications, which composed the Fourth Protocol of the GATS and initially involved commitments by 69 countries. The Telecommunications Agreement contains general provisions on non-discrimination and transparency, as well as specific commitments in the areas of market access (mostly via Mode 3) and domestic regulation. The latter regulatory principles are contained in an associated reference paper, and all of this came into effect in 1998.

The Telecommunications Agreement addresses telecommunications trade in 14 telecom sectors. In principle, the Fourth Protocol applies to all forms of basic

[22] This has been a disappointment to developing countries, because Mode 4 services trade is where developing countries possess an important comparative advantage. This point was stressed by Mattoo (2000) and Winters et al. (2003).

Telecommunication Services in the GATS (cont.)

telecommunications services, all modes of transmission, and all modes of supply. All WTO members have already committed themselves to the GATS, but, as Fourth Protocol signatories, they have also committed themselves to market access and national treatment commitments and the regulatory principles of the reference paper. Subsequent accession agreements and unilateral actions have led to commitments of one type or another by over 100 WTO members at the time of this writing. Signatories include LMICs as well as HICs.

Overall, the Agreement on Basic Telecommunications represents a success on the part of the WTO. It has helped to liberalize a highly regulated and monopolized sector under an umbrella of global rules. Technical savvy was displayed not just by HICs but also by LMICs. The latter were not just acquiescing to the demands of the United States and the European Union but were also responding to their own development policy objectives. This was a positive development.

Sources: Bronckers and Larouche (1997), Cowhey and Klimenko (2000), Fredebeul-Krein and Freytag (1999), Singh (2008; 2017), and World Trade Organization

The GATS committed signatories to begin a new round of GATS negotiations beginning in the year 2000, known as GATS 2000. On the agenda of GATS 2000 were subsidies, safeguard measures, government procurement, and additional market access. Progress in these negotiations was slow, however, and it took the launch of the Doha Round in 2001 to revive them. Plurilateral requests and offers were made in 2006 and 2008, but the Doha Round ended in failure in 2015.

As will be discussed in Chapter 9, further services liberalization took place in preferential trade agreements (PTAs) in the form of what are known as GATS-Plus provisions. In addition, *secret* services negotiations in the form of a Trade in Services Agreement (TiSA) took place *outside the WTO* (but in Geneva) between 23 parties, including the European Union. These secret negotiations became public in 2014, further eroding the role of multilateral efforts in trade in services.

Intellectual Property

The most contentious aspect of the Marrakesh Agreement is to be found in the Agreement on Trade-Related Aspects of Intellectual Property Rights (TRIPS). Intellectual property, or IP, is an asset in the form of rights conferred upon a product of invention or creation by a country's legal system.[23] The TRIPS Agreement defines intellectual property as belonging to any of six categories: copyrights; trademarks; geographical indications; industrial designs; patents; and layout designs of integrated circuits.[24] It is thus quite comprehensive.

The trade-relatedness of IP refers to the fact that "theft" of intellectual property suppresses trade of the goods in question. For example, if India produces its own "off-patent" version of a foreign-patented drug, it will import substantially less of that drug, if any at all. If it agrees to honor the patent, it will import the drug or host FDI from the foreign patent holder. Similarly, if a jeweler in Dubai sells counterfeit Cartier watches in place of authentic Cartier watches, this trademark violation will suppress the imports of authentic Cartier watches.[25]

The United States and the European Union strongly pushed for the inclusion of IP in the Uruguay Round. This stance also reflected the presence of an Intellectual Property Committee (IPC) of MNEs, which spawned a position paper commissioned by IBM. This position paper was the foundation of the US approach to the TRIPS negotiations.[26] LMICs, led by India and Brazil, opposed the TRIPS negotiations. In the end, the United States and the European Union prevailed, and TRIPS became a part of the WTO. The ensuing disagreements, which have continued to this day, are well summarized by Barton et al. (2006: 140–1):

> Conclusion of the TRIPS agreement has had important legal and political implications. As a legal matter, it has taken the GATT/WTO system into uncharted territory, covering not merely border measures, but also mandating threshold national regulatory standards and means of enforcing those standards. Politically, it has placed WTO rules and negotiations into the center of domestic political battles over the appropriate scope of IP protection, and has been responsible more than any other issue area for exacerbating North–South acrimony in Geneva.

The TRIPS Agreement applies the principle of non-discrimination to IP. Any advantage a WTO member grants to any country with regard to IP must be granted to all other members. If India agrees to honor UK pharmaceutical patents, it must honor US pharmaceutical patents as well.

---

[23] See Maskus (2000). Forsyth (2017: 83) defines intellectual property rights as "rights over intangible products of the human mind, such as designs, stories, creations, inventions, processes and knowledge."

[24] Geographical indications are defined as "indications which identify a good as originating in the territory of a Member, or a region or locality in that territory, where a given quality, reputation or other characteristic of the good is essentially attributable to its geographic origin."

[25] In the past, Cartier crushed counterfeit watches with steamrollers to protest against counterfeiting.

[26] See Singh (2017: chap. 6), who notes that "the work of the IPC was directly responsible for the hardening of the IP position in the developed world" (142). This example also points to the role of MNEs in forging aspects of global economic institutions.

The TRIPS Agreement also sets out obligations for members, structured around the six IP categories listed above.

1. *Copyrights* Members must comply with the 1971 Berne Convention on copyrights. Computer programs are protected as literary works under the Berne Convention, and the unauthorized recording of live broadcasts and performances is prohibited. The term of this protection is to be 50 years.
2. *Trademarks* Trademarks of goods and services are to be protected for a term of no less than seven years. Provisions for the registration of trademarks must be made and are renewable indefinitely.
3. *Geographical indications* Members must provide legal means to prevent the false use of geographical indications.
4. *Industrial designs* Members must protect "independently created industrial designs that are new or original." This protection does not apply to "designs dictated essentially by technical or functional considerations." The protection of industrial designs must last at least ten years.
5. *Patents* The agreement states, "Patents shall be available for any inventions, whether products or processes, in all fields of technology, provided that they are new, involve an inventive step and are capable of industrial application." Exceptions to this do exist, and include the protection of public order, and human, animal and plant life. Patents are to be extended for at least 20 years, representing a harmonization to the HIC standard.
6. *Layout designs of integrated circuits* The distribution of protected layout designs, as well as integrated circuits embodying protected layout designs, is forbidden. This protection is to extend for at least ten years.

Because most IP is held by the citizens and firms of HICs, and because LMICs have historically had less IP protection, the TRIPS Agreement has raised the cost of many goods and services to the latter set of countries. This can have adverse welfare impacts on LMICs. In the short term at least, TRIPS represents a global transfer of income from lower-income individuals to high-income individuals in the world.

There is another way to state this. Although the liberalization of trade in goods and trade in services both involve standard gains from trade, this is not the case for increased IP protection in the TRIPS. Indeed, some prominent trade economists consider the TRIPS to be a welfare-worsening, "non-trade" agenda item that has no place in the WTO. In addition, the TRIPS inappropriately restricts the freedom of countries to choose the intellectual property regime that is best for them.[27]

Can LMICs potentially expect any long-run benefits from the TRIPS Agreement? Some trade economists (e.g. Maskus, 2000) have argued that they can. These

[27] See, for example, Panagariya (2004).

potential benefits can come in the form of increased inward FDI, increased technology transfer, and increased domestic innovation. In this view, the TRIPS Agreement imposes short-term costs in the hopes of generating long-term benefits.

Other economists are less sanguine. For example, Goldin and Reinert (2012: chaps. 7 & 8) have called for a *moratorium* on further IP commitments and a reevaluation of existing commitments. There has also been an ongoing issue of the role of TRIPS in public health. This issue is considered in the accompanying box.

Access to Medicines

The area in which the TRIPS Agreement has been most contentious is that of *access to medicines*. With the end of the TRIPS transition period in 2005, costs of pharmaceuticals for some notable countries rose as off-patent, generic production became prohibited. In addition, a number of practices continue to allow for the "evergreening" of pharmaceutical patents beyond the standard 20 years. The consequent increased cost of pharmaceuticals can have detrimental health impacts.

Immediately after TRIPS went into effect in 1995, the US government began to pressure the governments of Brazil, India, and South Africa to honor US patents on HIV/AIDS drugs. This pressure violated TRIPS Article 31 allowing for the use of **compulsory licensing** to produce generics in the case of public health emergencies. In reaction to this, a number of LMICs threatened to prevent the launch of the Doha Round in 2001. The compromise was a special Declaration on the TRIPS Agreement and Public Health that *reaffirmed* Article 31. The declaration stated: "Each member has the right to determine what constitutes a national emergency or other circumstances of extreme urgency, it being understood that public health crises, including those related to HIV/AIDS, tuberculosis, malaria and other epidemics, can represent a national emergency or other circumstances of extreme urgency."

Although Article 31 permits compulsory licensing, Article 31(f) limits the use of these generic drugs to the *domestic markets* of the producing countries. Matthews (2004: 78) notes that this had "the practical effect of preventing exports of generic drugs to countries that do not have significant pharmaceutical industries themselves.... For countries with insufficient manufacturing capacity, the only realistic sourcing mechanism is importation." This emerged as a limit to addressing public health emergencies in some countries.

A WTO "Decision" on this issue was adopted in 2003 that allowed the least developed WTO members to import off-patent, generic drugs. This decision had a few weaknesses, however. First, it was procedurally demanding. Second, deliberations at the TRIPS Council regarding the application of the decision could be lengthy. Third, there was a concern that HICs with pharmaceutical industries

Access to Medicines (cont.)

could take unilateral action against LMICs making use of the decision. Fourth, there was evidence of bilateral "TRIPS-Plus" activity that might undermine rights under the decision.

The 2003 decision directed the WTO TRIPS Council to prepare an *amendment* on the issue. Agreement regarding this amendment was reached in 2005 but was not fully ratified until 2017, over two decades after the advent of TRIPS. It remains for supporting legislation in WTO member countries to be fully enacted, however, and for the provisions of the amendment to be tested in practice. Indeed, the Article 31 amendment imposes a number of significant limiting conditions. These conditions are the reason why Abbas and Riaz (2017: 252) conclude that the amendment "was not likely to make the desired practical impact because of the overly cumbersome formalities that accompany it." Consequently, TRIPS can still adversely affect public health.

Sources: Abbas and Riaz (2017), Abbott and Reichman (2007), Forsyth (2017), and Matthews (2004; 2006).

Dispute Settlement

Trade economist Chad Bown (2009: 1) notes that "international trade disputes between countries are an inevitable feature of economic relations in an interdependent world." Recognizing this reality, the Marrakesh Agreement included an Understanding on Rules and Procedures Governing the Settlement of Disputes. The original GATT had been somewhat unclear about the resolution of disputes, and, in establishing the WTO, the Marrakesh Agreement attempted to clarify dispute settlement procedures. In the event of disputes, the WTO turns to a Dispute Settlement Body, or DSB, whose function is to administer the dispute settlement rules and procedures (see Table 8.2). The DSB makes decisions by "consensus." As with the WTO in general, consensus for the DSB exists "if no Member, present at the meeting of the DSB when the decision is taken, formally objects to the proposed decision."

The dispute settlement procedure is summarized in Figure 8.2. If a member of the WTO has a complaint against another member, the first step in settling this dispute is a *consultation* between the members involved. If the consultation process fails to settle a dispute within 60 days, the complaining member *may* request the establishment of a *panel*.[28] Panels are composed of three or five "well-qualified

[28] The word "may" here is important. As noted by Hoekman and Kostecki (2009: 93), consultation processes can last over 200 days.

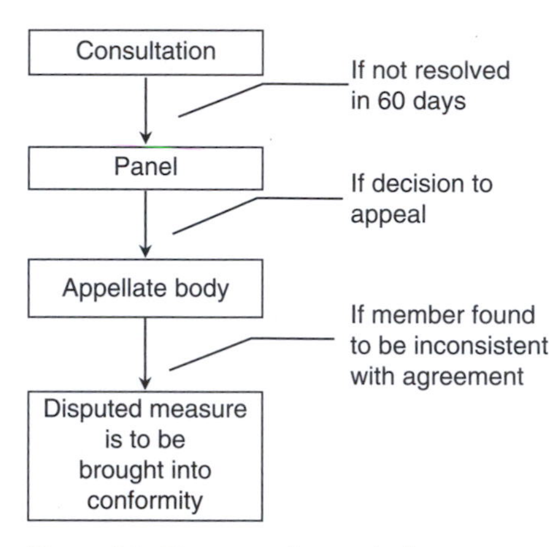

Figure 8.2 Dispute settlement in the WTO

governmental or non-governmental individuals." The function of the panel is to assist the DSB in the dispute settlement process. It consults the parties involved and provides the DSB with a written report of its findings. The DSB then has 60 days to adopt the report by consensus unless a party to the dispute decides to appeal.

An appeal of a panel report is referred to an *appellate body*, composed of seven persons "of recognized authority, with demonstrated expertise in law, international trade and the subject matter of the covered agreements generally." The appellate body reviews the appeal and submits its report to the DSB. At this point it is stipulated that the appellate body report "shall be adopted by the DSB and unconditionally accepted by the parties to the dispute unless the DSB decides by consensus *not* to adopt the appellate body report within 30 days following its circulation to the members" (emphasis added). Therefore, given the definition of consensus for the DSB, *any DSB member can effectively insist on the adoption of the appellate body report*. Renowned international trade lawyer John Jackson (1994: 70) refers to this appellate body procedure as "ingenious" and notes that "the result of the procedure is that appellate report will in virtually every case come into force as a matter of international law." The way in which this dispute settlement process evolved in the famous "bananas dispute" is presented in the accompanying box.

The "Bananarama" Dispute

Perhaps the most famous of all dispute settlement proceedings of the WTO is the "bananas dispute" between five Latin American countries and the European Union. Its roots actually go back to the GATT era, when, in 1993, Costa Rica, Colombia, Nicaragua, Guatemala, and Venezuela invoked GATT dispute resolution

The "Bananarama" Dispute (cont.)

proceedings against the EU (then EC) harmonized banana regime. This regime was put into place to support the banana exports of former colonies in the African, Caribbean and Pacific (ACP) group recognized by the European Union and consisted of a discriminatory tariff rate quota system (see Appendix 7.2). The ensuing GATT panel found against the European Union, citing the regime's violation of MFN and quantitative restriction principles. The European Union and the ACP blocked the adoption of the panel, however, under the GATT's positive consensus rule on panel reports. A similar result followed a second GATT panel requested by the five Latin American countries that addressed the specific rules of the EU banana regime, but it was again blocked.

With the creation of the WTO in 1995, the United States joined the Latin American claimants in support of US-based banana multinationals. Having acceded to the WTO in 1996, Ecuador also joined in asking for a panel that year. The panel issued its report in 1997, again finding against the European Union. The European Union appealed, and an Appellate Body was set up, but it did not significantly change the panel's findings. The WTO's negative consensus rule ensured that the Appellate Body's findings were adopted. The European Union subsequently obtained an arbitration finding allowing it time to bring its banana regime into conformity.

As a result of this, a *new* EU banana regime replacing country-specific measures began in 1999. Not satisfied, the United States, the original five Latin American countries, Ecuador, and Panama initiated further consultations with the European Union. The United States was planning to retaliate against the European Union under its own domestic trade legislation, and a WTO arbitration decision set the value of this retaliation in 1999. This complicated consultative process, as well as further subsidiary disputes, finally resulted in a *revised*, new EU banana regime in 2001. Initially, this appeared to satisfy all parties by phasing in a tariff-only regime by 2006.

What the European Union put in place in 2006, however, maintained duty-free access for ACP countries while imposing a €176 per ton tariff on bananas from non-ACP sources. In 2007 both Ecuador and the United States initiated new dispute settlement proceedings against the European Union. The same year a panel *again* found against the European Union. Parties to the dispute met in 2008 to attempt to resolve their disagreements, but it took until the end of 2009 for the matter to be resolved, with the announcement of a gradual reduction of the tariff from €176 per ton to €114 per ton by 2017. With the approval of this compromise by the European Parliament in early 2011, the "Bananarama" dispute finally came to an end.

Sources: Herrmann, Kramb, and Monnich (2003) and Salas and Jackson (2000).

Table 8.3 WTO dispute settlement complaints, 1995–2016

	1995–9	2000–4	2005–9	2010–14	2015–16	Total
Complaints	185	139	78	86	30	518
Panel reports	37	55	34	36	15	177
Appellate Body reports	25	31	22	19	10	107

Source: Leitner and Lester (2017).

The dispute settlement procedure outlined above and in Figure 8.2 applies to *all aspects* of the Marrakesh Agreement. It significantly improves the procedures of the old GATT and therefore makes a significant contribution to the conduct of international trade.[29] The effectiveness of the procedures depends on members' *commitment* to it, however. A country has the option of ignoring the outcome of the dispute settlement process. In this case, the complaining member has the right to impose retaliatory tariffs on a volume of imports from the other country determined by the DSB, as in the bananas dispute.

The WTO dispute settlement process has been utilized quite a bit over the years. As shown in Table 8.3, there were 518 complaints between 1995 and 2016 resulting in consultations. This resulted in 177 panel reports and 107 Appellate Body reports over that time period. Complaints related to GATT 1994 have featured prominently, as have anti-dumping and countervailing duty measures (discussed in Chapter 7). Interestingly, TRIPS has not featured that prominently in dispute settlement.

The Environment

The issue of trade and the environment within the GATT and WTO has largely revolved around GATT Article III, on national treatment. The question has been whether domestic environmental policies can function as grounds to treat domestic and imported goods differentially based on environmental considerations. This, in turn, often comes down to the phrase "like products" used in Article III. For, if environmental considerations allow products to be *unalike* that would otherwise be like, then NT would not necessarily apply.

In 1991 the GATT reactivated a long-dormant Working Group on Environmental Measures and International Trade (EMIT). This was in response to a dispute resolution panel issuing a controversial finding in the now famous tuna/dolphin case.

[29] For more on the WTO dispute settlement procedures, see Bown (2009), Davey (2000), Hoekman and Mavroidis (2000), and Kuruvila (1997).

The panel ruled against a US law banning imports of Mexican tuna that involved dolphin-unsafe fishing practices, issued in response to the US Marine Mammal Protection Act. The panel argued that the import ban violated the general prohibition against quotas (Article XI) and that the United States had not attempted to negotiate cooperative agreements on dolphin-safe tuna fishing. The US environmental community reacted strongly against the GATT panel ruling, casting the GATT as anti-environment.[30]

With the advent of the WTO in 1995, EMIT was replaced by the Committee on Trade and the Environment (CTE). Most LMIC members of the WTO have taken a dim view of the work of the CTE, fearing the possibility of further protection against their exports on environmental grounds, what they term "green protection." The subsequent polarization of views has inhibited the effectiveness of the CTE.[31]

In 1999 the WTO took up the trade and environment issue formally with the publication of a report on this subject (Nordström and Vaughan, 1999). As with Runge (1994; 2009) and others, this report argues that increased trade can have both positive and negative impacts on the environment. The report emphasizes, however, that trade-driven growth cannot always be counted upon to deliver improvements in environmental quality through increased incomes, as many economists claim. Consequently, these higher incomes must be "translated" into higher environmental quality through the mechanism of international cooperation. The WTO report also emphasizes that government subsidies to polluting and resource-depleting sectors such as agriculture, fishing, and energy can exacerbate the environmental consequences of trade.

The 1990s ended with another difficult case regarding the impact of shrimp fishing on sea turtles.[32] As described by Cosbey and Mavroidis (2014), the findings in this case overturned a number of the findings of the previous tuna/dolphin case, and actually led to a different outcome in a second tuna/dolphin case, which began in 2008. These authors emphasize that the trend in WTO dispute settlement of environmental issues "has been toward deference to nationally enunciated objectives and the measures chosen to achieve them, even where those measures are trade restrictive, unilateral and with extra-jurisdictional effect" (Cosbey and Mavroidis, 2014: 300). In this manner, the WTO has come a long way from the tuna/dolphin legacy.

---

[30] For a review of the tuna/dolphin case, see Runge (1994: chap. 4). Cosbey and Mavroidis (2014) strongly argue that the case should have been considered under Article III NT rather than Article XI.

[31] See Shaffer (2001). This author notes: "In light of the immense challenge developing countries face in meeting the basic needs of the majority of their human populations, southern constituencies typically place less weight on the social value of environmental preservation than on economic and social development and poverty eradication" (87).

[32] In this case, the Appellate Body overruled the panel.

The Doha Round

As mentioned in Chapter 1, the 1999 Seattle Ministerial Conference of the WTO was a failure. In part, this was because of the protests of young people against the WTO as an agent of globalization. It was also attributable to a lack of agreement between HIC WTO members and LMIC WTO members on a number of issues discussed in this chapter. As a result of this failure, WTO members were not able to launch the hoped-for new round of multilateral trade talks that year.

A second attempt to launch a new round took place at the 2001 Ministerial Conference in Doha, Qatar. This attempt was successful, though the same disputes were still simmering beneath the surface. Although, as mentioned above, progress was made on the TRIPS/AIDS issue, the European Union maintained its intransigent position on agricultural trade liberalization. Additionally, the LMICs were displeased with the introduction of new agenda items in the form of the new "Singapore issues" from the 1996 Singapore Ministerial Conference, including competition policy, transparency in government procurement, trade facilitation, and investment.[33]

The progress that did take place in the Doha Round was itself very uneven. For example, at the Cancún Ministerial Conference in 2003, the European Union insisted that the Singapore issues be included in the negotiations. Further, the European Union and the United States issued a draft text on the agricultural negotiations in quasi-bilateral fashion. Some LMICs opposed both these proposals. Indeed, a new coalition of LMICs emerged at Cancún. Known as the G20 and led by Argentina, Brazil, China, India, and South Africa, this group accounted for over two-thirds of the world population and over 60 percent of its farmers. It adamantly opposed the EU/US agricultural text, proposing more strenuous liberalization in agricultural markets. Despite predictions to the contrary, the group *held firm* during the negotiations, and the ministerial statement coming out of Cancún was only one-half of a page long.[34]

Some progress took place in 2004 with the "July 2004 Package," which reaffirmed the Doha Ministerial commitments in agriculture and acknowledged some specific concerns of the LMICs (e.g. cotton subsidies). Most important was the adoption of a "tiered approach" to reductions in tariffs and domestic support, as well as the commitment to eliminate export subsidies by an unspecified date.

---

[33] See Hoekman and Kostecki (2009: chap. 13).

[34] At the time, a representative of the Brazilian government stated: "The real dilemma that many of us had to face was whether it was sensible to accept an agreement that would essentially consolidate the policies of the two subsidizing superpowers...and then have to wait for another 15 to 18 years to launch a new round, after having spent precious bargaining chips" (Narlikar and Tussie, 2004: 951).

Despite this progress, a July 2005 deadline for progress in agricultural negotiations was missed. A small breakthrough occurred in October 2005, with proposals for domestic support being tabled using the tiered framework. In July 2006 negotiations between the United States, the European Union, Japan, Brazil, India, and Australia regarding the Doha Round broke down, and the WTO director general, Pascal Lamy, suspended further discussions, noting: "We have missed a very important opportunity to show that multilateralism works."

Although it was not appreciated at the time, the high-water mark of the Doha Round took place in July 2008 in the form of the "July 2008 Package." This package included progress in agricultural negotiations and tariffs on manufactured goods and even services.[35] Subsequent to the July 2008 Package, however, disagreement emerged over a special safeguard mechanism (SSM) in agriculture, called for by LMICs (especially India), and "sectorals," the reduction in tariffs on manufactured goods beyond what was negotiated in 2008 and called for by HICs.[36] A 2010 "stocktaking" meeting turned out to be one in which there was "no stock to take."

In retrospect, the failure of the July 2008 Package marked the end of the Doha Round. Indeed, Singh (2017: 125) states that "the breakdown of the July 2008 framework is now regarded as the breakdown of the Doha Round itself." But it took until the 2015 Ministerial Conference, held in Nairobi, Kenya, for this to be officially acknowledged and the Doha Round called to a close. Consequently, the most-recent attempt at MTNs, in the form of the Doha Round, proved to be a failure with no successful round taking place since 1994.[37]

Trade Negotiations

Trade negotiations are a both a field of practice and a field of research, with the research informing the practice. There are a set of fundamental concepts of trade negotiations recognized by both practitioners and researchers. Let us consider just a few here.

The first important concept is *best alternative to a negotiated agreement* (BATNA), namely the most advantageous alternative available to a negotiating

[35] The July 2008 Package specified tariff cut tiers in agricultural market access, as well as agricultural domestic support reductions, the latter in terms of an overall trade distortion support (OTDS) measure.

[36] The special safeguard mechanism was different from normal WTO safeguards in that there was no requirement to demonstrate injury. In the case of the often ignored sectorals, Laborde (2011) reports that HICs made unreasonable demands across nearly the entire range of manufacture goods.

[37] For a sense of what success could have looked like, see Martin and Mattoo (2010).

Trade Negotiations (cont.)

party in the event that the negotiations fail. The better the BATNA of a party, the greater is its negotiating strength.

A second important concept is *agenda setting*, the determination of issues to be included or excluded in a particular set of negotiations. This is clearly important at the beginning of a set of negotiations, but, as Singh (2008: chap. 2) emphasizes, it is also important *throughout* negotiations, with earlier-set agendas affecting agenda-setting efforts later in negotiations.

A third important concept is *coalitions*. MTNs and PTAs are complex multi-issue and multi-player games. Coalition formation over time allows individual countries to increase their bargaining power on a particular issue. Of course, the function of coalitions could also decrease these countries' bargaining power on other issues. Overlapping coalitions are a feature of modern MTNs and PTAs.

A fourth important concept is *lobbying*. Only governments have had "standing" at the GATT and WTO. But behind these governments are an array of domestic actors and interests with stakes in any trade negotiations. Additionally, actors in one country can align themselves with actors in a second country to put pressure on that second country's government. Further, some international organizations (multinational enterprises and non-governmental organizations) can engage in their own lobbying across a set of country governments.

A final negotiations concept is *forum shopping*, the name for when a member country engages in negotiations on a particular topic area (e.g. services or intellectual property) in multiple forums as a threat strategy in one forum. The most important type of forum shopping takes place across MTNs and PTAs, with the latter providing a threat to the former.

BATNA, agenda setting, coalitions, lobbying, and forum shopping are central aspects of all trade negotiations. There are others as well. In many cases, these concepts apply not only to *trade* negotiations but to many different types of international negotiations. They are therefore important to the evolving institutional structure of the world economy.

Sources: Hoekman and Kostecki (2009), Odell (2000) and Singh (2008; 2017).

Conclusion

The GATT and WTO have functioned as central institutions of international trade, and the evidence suggests that they have indeed supported the expansion of global trade relations (e.g. Goldstein, Rivers, and Tomz, 2007). If the past is any guide, however, the WTO will continue to be, as stated in the introduction to this chapter, "both lauded and vilified with equal intensity by various groups with concerns about trade policy." In general, a common fault line exists across many issues within the WTO between HIC members and LMIC members.

Regarding the old GATT agenda of trade in goods, LMICs are still at a market access disadvantage in some manufacturing sectors, with their exports facing tariff peaks in high-income markets. In agriculture, they also face the massive domestic and export subsidies of the United States and the European Union, of over US$100 billion per year.[38] The ongoing controversies over TRIPS also have a similar fault line. In the short term, most LMICs will lose from intellectual property protection by paying higher prices for goods and services. Bearing these short-term costs, these countries hope for long-term benefits of increased inward FDI and domestic innovation. Finally, at the time of this writing, the US government is holding up appointments to the Appellate Body, thereby undermining the WTO's dispute settlement process.[39]

The failure of the Doha Round, the rise of ethno-nationalism with anti-trade agendas, and the undermining of the dispute settlement system by the US government all contribute to an emerging crisis of legitimacy for the WTO. Given the irreplaceable nature of the WTO as the institution of world trade, this crisis of legitimacy is a serious development.

Review Exercises

1. What is meant by *non-discrimination* in international trade agreements? Be as specific as you can.
2. One criticism of the Agreement on Agriculture is that it involves something known as *dirty tariffication*. Dirty tariffication involves quotas being converted into tariffs that are larger than the actual tariff equivalent of the original quota. Draw a diagram like that of Figure 7.4, illustrating dirty tariffication.
3. The chapter mentioned the four modes by which trade in services can occur: cross-border trade; movement of consumers; foreign direct investment; and personnel movement. Try to give an example of each of these modes–the more specific, the better.
4. The chapter also gave an example of the way that the "theft" of intellectual property in the case of pharmaceuticals suppresses trade in this product. Try to give another example of such trade suppression in intellectual property.
5. Can you think of any ways in which trade issues and environmental issues interact? Try to be as specific as you can.

---

[38] See, for example, Peterson (2009).

[39] See, for example, *The Economist* (2017).

FURTHER READING AND WEB RESOURCES

On the GATT, see Blackhurst (2009a), Irwin, Mavroidis, and Sykes (2008), and Singh (2017: chap. 3). On the WTO, see Barton et al. (2006), Blackhurst (2009b), Hoekman and Kostecki (2009), and Lee (2016). A more legal approach can be found in Jackson (1997) and Matsushita et al. (2015). Journals covering the subjects of this chapter include the *Journal of World Trade*, *World Trade Review*, and the *Journal of International Economic Law*. Intellectual property and TRIPS are addressed by Maskus (2000) and Forsyth (2017). The subject of LMICs in trade negotiations is covered by Odell (2006) and Singh (2017). On the Doha Round, see Messerlin (2013).

To keep up with the work of the WTO, the reader will want to visit its web-site: www.wto.org. Perhaps the most useful link here is the one to "trade topics." The document dissemination facility at this website is a particularly useful resource, however.

REFERENCES

Abbas, M. Z., and S. Riaz (2017) "Compulsory Licensing and Access to Medicines: TRIPS Amendment Allows Export to Least-Developed Countries," *Journal of Intellectual Property Law and Practice*, 12:6, 451–2.

Abbott, F. M., and J. H. Reichman (2007) "The Doha Round's Public Health Legacy: Strategies for the Production and Diffusion of Patented Medicines under the Amended TRIPS Provisions," *Journal of International Economic Law*, 10:4, 921–87.

Barton, J. H., J. L. Goldstein, T. E. Josling, and R. H. Steinberg (2006) *The Evolution of the Trade Regime: Politics, Law, and Economics of the GATT and the WTO*, Princeton University Press.

Blackhurst, R. (2009a) "General Agreement on Tariffs and Trade (GATT)," in K. A. Reinert, R. S. Rajan, A. J. Glass, and L. S. Davis (eds.), *The Princeton Encyclopedia of the World Economy*, Princeton University Press, 521–8.

Blackhurst, R. (2009b) "World Trade Organization," in K. A. Reinert, R. S. Rajan, A. J. Glass, and L. S. Davis (eds.), *The Princeton Encyclopedia of the World Economy*, Princeton University Press, 1185–91.

Bronckers, M. C. E. J., and P. Larouche (1997) "Telecommunications Services and the World Trade Organization," *Journal of World Trade*, 31:3, 5–47.

Bown, C. P. (2009) *Self-Enforcing Trade: Developing Countries and WTO Dispute Settlement*, Brooking Institution.

Bown, C. P., and D. A. Irwin (2015) "GATT's Starting Point: Tariff Levels circa 1947," Working Paper 21782, National Bureau of Economic Research.

Chanda, R. (2017) "Trade in Services," in K. A. Reinert (ed.), *Handbook of Globalisation and Development*, Edward Elgar, 36–58.

Cosbey, A., and P. C. Mavroidis (2014) "Heavy Fuel: Trade and the Environment in the GATT/WTO Case Law," *Review of European, Comparative and International Environmental Law*, 23:3, 288–301.

Cowhey, P., and M. M. Klimenko (2000) "Telecommunications Reform in Developing Countries after the WTO Agreement on Basic Telecommunications Services," *Journal of International Development*, 12:2, 265–81.

Davey, W. J. (2000) "The WTO Dispute Settlement System," *Journal of International Economic Law*, 3:1, 15–18.

Debebe, G. (2017) "Global Organizations," in K. A. Reinert (ed.), *Handbook of Globalisation and Development*, Edward Elgar, 463–84.

Dinan, D. (2010) *Ever Closer Union: An Introduction to European Integration*, Lynne Rienner.

The Economist (2017) "Dispute Unsettlement: America Holds the World Trade Organization Hostage," September 23.

Forsyth, M. (2017) "Intellectual Property," in K. A. Reinert (ed.), *Handbook of Globalisation and Development*, Edward Elgar, 83–99.

Francois, J. F., and B. Hoekman (2010) "Services Trade and Policy," *Journal of Economic Literature*, 48:3, 642–92.

Fredebeul-Krein, M., and A. Freytag (1999) "The Case for a More Binding WTO Agreement on Regulatory Principles in Telecommunication Markets," *Telecommunications Policy*, 23:9, 625–44.

GATT Secretariat (1994) *The Results of the Uruguay Round of Multilateral Trade Negotiations: The Legal Text*, GATT Secretariat.

Goldin, I., and K. A. Reinert (2012) *Globalization for Development: Meeting New Challenges*, Oxford University Press.

Goldstein, J. L., D. Rivers, and M. Tomz (2007) "Institutions in International Relations: Understanding the Effects of GATT and WTO on World Trade," *International Organization*, 61:1, 37–67.

Hathaway, D. E. (1987) *Agriculture and the GATT: Rewriting the Rules*, Institute for International Economics.

Hathaway, D. E., and M. D. Ingo (1996) "Agricultural Liberalization and the Uruguay Round," in W. Martin and L. A. Winters (eds.), *The Uruguay Round and the Developing Countries*, Cambridge University Press, 30–57.

Herrmann, R., M. Kramb, and C. Monnich (2003) "The Banana Dispute: Survey and Lessons," *Quarterly Journal of International Agriculture*, 42:1, 21–47.

Hoekman, B. M., and M. Kostecki (2009) *The Political Economy of the World Trading System: From GATT to WTO*, Oxford University Press.

Hoekman, B. M., and P. C. Mavroidis (2000) "WTO Dispute Settlement, Transparency and Surveillance," *The World Economy*, 23:4, 527–42.

Irwin, D. A., P. C. Mavroidis, and A. O. Sykes (2008) *The Genesis of the GATT*, Cambridge University Press.

Jackson, J. H. (1990) *Restructuring the GATT System*, Royal Institute of International Affairs.

Jackson, J. H. (1994) "The World Trade Organization, Dispute Settlement and Codes of Conduct," in S. M Collins and B. P. Bosworth (eds.), *The New GATT*, Brookings Institution.

Jackson, J. H. (1997) *The World Trading System*, MIT Press.

Kuruvila, P. E. (1997) "Developing Countries and the GATT/WTO Dispute Settlement Mechanism," *Journal of World Trade*, 31:6, 171–207.

Laborde, D. (2011) "Sectoral Initiatives in the Doha Round," in W. Martin and A. Matoo (eds.), *Unfinished Business? The WTO's Doha Agenda*, World Bank, 277–97.

Lee, Y.-S. (2016) *Reclaiming Development in the World Trading System*, Cambridge University Press.

Leitner, K., and S. Lester (2017) "WTO Dispute Settlement 1995–2016: A Statistical Analysis," *Journal of International Economic Law*, 20:1, 171–87.

Martin, W., and A. Mattoo (2010) "The Doha Development Agenda: What's on the Table?," *Journal of International Trade and Economic Development*, 19:1, 81–107.

Maskus, K. E. (2000) *Intellectual Property Rights in the Global Economy*, Institute for International Economics.

Matsushita, M., T. J. Schoenbaum, P. C. Mavroidis, and M. Hahn (2015) *The World Trade Organization: Law, Practice, and Policy*, Oxford University Press.

Matthews, D. (2004) "WTO Decision on Implementation of Paragraph 6 of the Doha Declaration on the TRIPS Agreement and Public Health: A Solution to the Access to Essential Medicines Problem?," *Journal of International Economic Law*, 7:1, 73–107.

Matthews, D. (2006) "From the August 30, 2003 WTO Decision to the December 6, 2005 Agreement on Amendments to TRIPS: Improving Access to Medicines in Developing Countries," *Intellectual Property Quarterly*, 10:2, 91–130.

Mattoo, A. (2000) "Developing Countries in the New Round of GATS Negotiations: Towards a Pro-Active Role," *The World Economy*, 23:4, 471–89.

Messerlin, P. A. (2013) "The Doha Round," in A. Lukauskas, R. M. Stern, and G. Zanini (eds.), *Handbook of Trade Policy for Development*, Oxford University Press, 254–300.

Narlikar, A., and D. Tussie (2004) "The G20 and the Cancún Ministerial: Developing Countries and Their Evolving Coalitions in the WTO," *The World Economy*, 27:7, 947–66.

Nordström, H., and S. Vaughan (1999) *Trade and the Environment*, World Trade Organization.

North, D. C. (1990) *Institutions, Institutional Change and Economic Performance*, Cambridge University Press.

Odell, J. S. (2000) *Negotiating the World Economy*, Cornell University Press.

Odell, J. S. (ed.) (2006) *Negotiating Trade: Developing Countries in the WTO and NAFTA*, Cambridge University Press.

Panagariya, A. (2004) "TRIPS and the WTO: An Uneasy Marriage," in K. Maskus (ed.), *The WTO, Intellectual Property Rights and the Knowledge Economy*, Edward Elgar, 42–53.

Peterson, E. W. F. (2009) *A Billion Dollars a Day: The Economics and Politics of Agricultural Subsidies*, Wiley-Blackwell.

Reinert, K. A. (2000) "Give Us Virtue, But Not Yet: Safeguard Actions under the Agreement on Textiles and Clothing," *World Economy*, 23:1, 25–55.

Reinert, K. A. (2017) "Trade in Goods," in K. A. Reinert (ed.), *Handbook of Globalisation and Development*, Edward Elgar, 19–35.

Runge, C. F. (1994) *Freer Trade, Protected Environment*, Council of Foreign Relations.

Runge, C. F. (2009) "Multilateral Environmental Agreements," in K. A. Reinert, R. S. Rajan, A. J. Glass, and L. S. Davis (eds.), *The Princeton Encyclopedia of the World Economy*, Princeton University Press, 795–9.

Salas, M., and J. H. Jackson (2000) "Procedural Overview of the WTO EC-Banana Dispute," *Journal of International Economic Law*, 3:1, 145–66.

Shaffer, G. C. (2001) "The World Trade Organization under Challenge: Democracy and the Law and Politics of the WTO's Treatment of Trade and Environmental Matters," *Harvard Environmental Law Review*, 25:1, 1–93.

Singh, J. P. (2008) *Negotiation and the Global Information Economy*, Cambridge University Press.

Singh, J. P. (2017) *Sweet Talk: Paternalism and Collective Action in North–South Trade Relations*, Stanford University Press.

Winters, L. A., T. L. Walmsley, Z. K Wang, and R. Grynberg (2003) "Liberalizing the Temporary Movement of Natural Persons: An Agenda for the Development Round," *The World Economy*, 26:8, 1137–61.

Appendix 8.1: Tariff Rate Reduction Formulas

One aspect of multilateral trade negotiations or MTNs is tariff reduction. The Kennedy Round (see Table 8.1) introduced linear or proportional tariff reduction, which can be represented as

$$t_1 = at_0 \quad 0 \leq a \leq 1 \tag{8.1}$$

where t_1 is the final tariff, and t_0 is the initial or base tariff. If, for example, $a = 0.8$, then all tariffs would be reduced by 20 percent.

The Tokyo Round of MTNs (again, see Table 8.1) introduced tariff reduction via the "Swiss formula," which can be represented as

$$t_1 = \frac{b\ t_0}{b + t_0} \quad 0 \leq b \leq 100 \tag{8.2}$$

where b is the ceiling tariff.

The purpose of the Swiss formula is to reduce higher base tariffs by a greater proportion than lower base tariffs. This can be seen in Figure 8.3, which translates

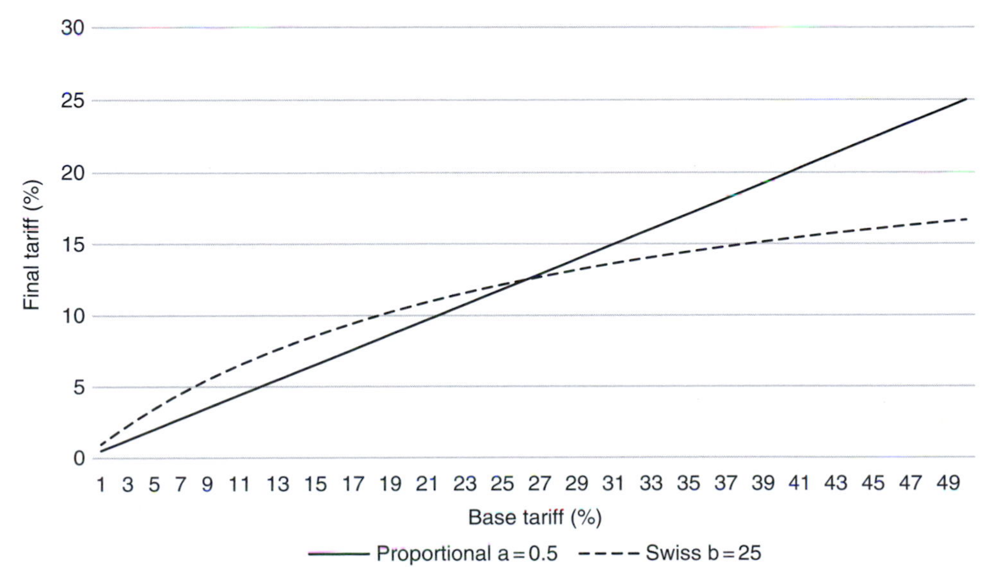

Figure 8.3 Tariff reduction formula comparison
Source: Author's calculations.

base tariffs along the horizontal axis into final tariffs along the vertical axis. The linear formula is presented as the solid line for a proportional reduction of 50 percent, or $a = 0.50$. Here you can see in the figure that a base tariff of 50 percent is reduced to a final tariff of 25 percent. The Swiss formula is presented as the dashed line with a ceiling of 25 percent, or $b = 25$. Here, for each base tariff of over 25 percent, the reduction of the base tariff is greater than in the linear case. Further, as you can see, the gap between the proportional and Swiss reductions over the 25 percent base tariff increases as the base tariff increases.

9 Preferential Trade Agreements

I once attended a talk by a Canadian trade negotiator at which he made the following potent statement: "When multilateralism falters, regionalism picks up the pace." His use of the term "multilateralism" referred to the GATT/WTO system described in Chapter 8 and its multilateral trade negotiations. His use of the term "regionalism" referred to the possibility of pursuing what is known as **preferential trade agreements**. Recall from Chapter 8 that one of the founding principles of the GATT/WTO system is **non-discrimination**, and that non-discrimination, in turn, involves the **most favored nation** and **national treatment** sub-principles. Under MFN, each WTO member must grant to each other member treatment as favorable as they extend to any other member country. PTAs are a *violation of the MFN principle*, in that one PTA member discriminates in its trade policies in favor of another PTA member and against non-members.[1] This type of discrimination has been allowed by the GATT/WTO under certain circumstances. These circumstances include the well-known cases of **free trade areas** (FTAs), **customs unions** (CUs), and interim agreements leading to an FTA or CU "within a reasonable length of time."[2]

Before we begin, we need to clarify a terminological issue. Originally, FTAs and CUs were collectively known as **regional trade agreements** (RTAs), and this is the term commonly employed by the World Trade Organization. Since the 1990s, however, an increasing number of PTAs have been between countries that are *not geographically contiguous*, such as the Canada–Chile and Japan–Mexico FTAs. Consequently, a number of leading economists and trade lawyers have recommended that the RTA nomenclature be replaced with that of preferential trade agreement.[3] In the spirit of greater accuracy, we will use this term here, but it is likely that you will encounter *both terms* and their abbreviations.

As suggested by the comment of the trade minister above, "regionalism" (or, more accurately, preferentialism) and multilateralism represent two alternative

---

[1] The history of PTAs is often traced back to the establishment of the German Customs Union (Zollverein) in 1834.

[2] All quotations without citations are from GATT Secretariat (1994).

[3] For example, Matsushita et al. (2015: 507) state: "Not all such schemes are regional, in the sense of geographical proximity. One third of FTAs currently under investigation are among countries that are not in geographical proximity."

trade policy options available to the countries of the world. When the larger countries of the world lose commitment to the multilateralism option, multilateralism "falters." This is when countries often turn their attention to the preferential option, however, and regionalism "picks up the pace." Indeed, nearly every member of the WTO is also a member of at least one PTA, and approximately 300 "physical" PTAs are in force at the time of this writing in 2019.[4] PTAs are therefore a central feature of the world trading system.[5]

This chapter will introduce you to various types of PTAs and their economic effects. These effects are analyzed in international economics in terms of the concepts of **trade creation** and **trade diversion**. We then consider some examples of PTAs, namely the **European Union**, the North American Free Trade Agreement, Mercosur and the Free Trade Area of the Americas, the ASEAN Free Trade Area, and the Trans-Pacific Partnership. Finally, we consider in more detail the relationship of "regionalism" to multilateralism, as well as GATS-Plus and TRIPS-Plus agreements in PTAs.

Types of Preferential Trade Agreements

Under the WTO, and as listed in Table 9.1, there are *four ways* in which a PTA can be "notified." Under Article XXIV of the General Agreement on Tariffs and Trade 1994, covering trade in goods, a PTA can be notified as either a free trade area or a customs union. As noted in Table 9.1, both these PTA types involve the member countries *eliminating* trade restrictions between themselves. The difference between the FTA and CU options is that the latter involves member countries establishing a *common external tariff*, or CET. Article XXIV of GATT requires that WTO members wishing to form FTAs or CUs must meet certain requirements. First, trade barriers against non-members cannot be "higher or more restrictive than" those in existence prior to the FTA or CU. Second, the FTA or CU must be formed "within a reasonable length of time." Third, the FTA or CU must eliminate trade barriers on "substantially all the trade" between the members. As can be seen in Table 9.1, the number of FTAs notified to the WTO greatly exceeds the number of CUs.

A third way in which a PTA can occur under the WTO is known as the "enabling clause." This 1979 decision (currently part of GATT 1994) allows PTAs in goods trade between low- and middle-income countries. According to this decision, the

[4] As we explain below, there is actually some double-counting involved in the way the WTO records PTAs. This leads to the distinction between "physical" and "notified" PTAs, with the double-counting characterizing the latter.

[5] Another way of interpreting the Canadian trade minister's comment is in terms of the "forum shopping" mentioned in the Chapter 8 box on trade negotiations.

Table 9.1 Types of preferential trade agreements, 2019

Type of PTA	Description	Number of notifications in force, 2019
GATT Article XXIV (FTA)	An agreement on the part of a set of countries to *eliminate* trade restrictions between themselves.	243
GATT Article XXIV (CU)	An agreement on the part of a set of countries to eliminate trade restrictions between themselves and to adopt a *common external tariff*.	21
Enabling clause	Allows PTAs in goods trade between developing countries.	57
GATS Article V	An agreement to reduce barriers to trade in services between a set of countries.	160
		Total notifications in force: 481 Total physical PTAs in force: 302

Note: This table includes double-counting between GATT and GATS notifications as well as in the case of accessions to existing agreements. Consult the WTO website for more current information.

Source: World Trade Organization, September 2019.

pursuit of a PTA within the enabling clause is for the "mutual reduction or elimination" of tariffs and non-tariff measures. There is thus less emphasis on eliminating trade restrictions than in the cases of FTAs and CUs. As can be seen in Table 9.1, there are more enabling clause PTAs than CUs, but significantly fewer than FTAs.

The fourth and final way in which a PTA can occur under the WTO is under Article V of the General Agreement on Trade in Services. FTAs or CUs under the GATS must involve "substantial sectoral coverage," language that differs from trade in goods. Importantly, most PTAs (other than enabling clause PTAs) notified to the WTO since its inception in 1995 have been under both GATT Article XXIV and GATS Article V. Therefore, there is *double-counting* in the WTO PTA system, which is reflected in Table 9.1.[6]

However notified, the oversight of PTAs by the WTO is difficult. This is because the phrases "higher or more restrictive than," "within a reasonable length of time," "substantially all trade," and "substantial sectoral coverage" are simply too vague.

[6] In the words of the WTO, its statistics on PTAs "are based on notification requirements rather than on physical numbers" of PTAs. Thus, for any PTA including both goods and services, the WTO counts two notifications (one for goods and the other services) rather than one. There is also some double-counting that takes place in the case of accessions to existing PTA agreement.

As part of the Marrakesh Agreement establishing the WTO (see Chapter 8), there was an agreed-upon "understanding" on PTAs. This understanding specified that the relevant measure to assess restrictiveness against non-members is a weighted average of tariff rates and that the length of time allowable for the elimination of trade barriers within FTA and CUs is to be no more than ten years.

Even with this understanding, however, there is still much ambiguity.[7] Further, the unfortunate fact is that *there has never been any serious evaluation or enforcement of PTAs under either the GATT or the WTO.* As noted by Matsushita et al. (2015), most PTAs are of "dubious WTO-consistency." No WTO member has the incentive to challenge PTAs through WTO dispute settlement, however, because nearly all important WTO members are themselves members of at least one PTA. This "cooperative equilibrium" has proved to be quite durable. Some small steps towards increased transparency have been taken by the WTO's Committee on Regional Trade Agreements (CRTA), in the form of an improved database of FTAs and CUs; but transparency is not enforcement.[8]

Although many PTAs are not regional, some PTAs are true attempts to build regional integration between contiguous countries. Steps on the way to regional integration are described in Table 9.2. Here we see that FTAs and CUs are the first two

Table 9.2 Steps to regional integration

Type	Description
Free trade area	An agreement on the part of a set of countries to *eliminate trade restrictions between themselves.*
Customs union	An agreement on the part of a set of countries to eliminate trade restrictions between themselves and to *adopt a common external tariff.*
Common market	An agreement on the part of a set of countries to eliminate trade restrictions between themselves, to adopt a common external tariff, and to allow the *free movement of labor and physical capital* between member countries.
Monetary union	A common market that adopts a *common currency* and adopts a *common monetary policy.*
Economic union	A monetary union that adopts a process of *domestic policy harmonization* in areas such as tax and spending policies and domestic regulation.

[7] See Serra et al. (1997).

[8] Matsushita et al. (2015: 527) state: "When judged against its original mandate [to review consistency of notified PTAs with the relevant multilateral rules], the multilateral review has been a failure by any reasonable benchmark." They also say: "Only a handful of [dispute settlement] panels have so far been established in order to discuss the consistency of PTAs with the multilateral rules, and this is certainly not many when one takes into account the sheer number of PTAs and the absence of meaningful review by the CRTA over the years" (533).

steps towards a common market in which the regional membership allows for the free flow of both labor and physical capital. A **common market** can proceed further to a **monetary union** with a common currency and common monetary policy. Finally, an **economic union** is characterized by members attempting to harmonize domestic policies in the areas of taxation and spending, domestic regulation, and competition. The most notable case of an economic union is the European Union, discussed below.

Rules of Origin

One issue that inevitably arises in the design of PTAs in the form of FTAs is how to determine whether a product is from a partner country. In an FTA, a product can be imported into a low-tariff member and then resold in a high-tariff member, a process known as *tariff rate arbitrage*.[9] To protect against tariff rate arbitrage, FTA members usually establish **rules of origin**, or ROOs. As outlined by Krishna (2009), ROOs can be defined using four criteria. The first of these is the amount of *domestic content* of the good, measured either in terms of value added or in direct, physical terms. The second is in terms of a *change in tariff heading* (CTH), whereby the good must move from one tariff category to another during a production process in an FTA member country. The third is in terms of *specified processes* (or tasks), which outline the actual production processes that must take place within the FTA.[10] The fourth approach is in terms of *substantial transformation*, a loosely defined term that can vary from one instance to another.

In many respects, FTAs are defined by their ROOs, and an understanding of them is therefore a key part of understanding any particular FTA. Further, empirical evidence suggests that they have significant impacts.[11] The case of automobile ROOs in the North American Free Trade Agreement is considered in the accompanying box.

NAFTA Automobile ROOs

Under the North American Free Trade Agreement, exporters must fill out a NAFTA Certificate of Origin (CO) based on NAFTA ROOs. In general, the origination of a product is defined in terms of *substantial transformation*, and substantial

[9] As noted by Tarr (2009), CUs do not need rules of origin because goods from outside the CU enter any CU member under the same tariff regime. This is one advantage of a CU over an FTA.

[10] Clearly, this can be very close to the CTH approach. Krishna (2009: 980) notes: "The difference between this and the CTH criterion is only that the latter is based on some commonly used description such as the tariff code, whereas the specified process definition is defined in terms of production processes specific to each industry."

[11] For the case of NAFTA, see Anson et al. (2005).

NAFTA Automobile ROOs (cont.)

transformation is, in turn, defined in terms of a *change in tariff heading*. This requirement can be relaxed, however, under a *de minimis rule* if non-originating materials make up less than 7 percent of the total value of the product. There is also the alternative of demonstrating sufficiently high *regional value content* (RVC). RVC, in turn, can be defined in two ways: in terms of transactions value or in terms of net cost. Even this superficial view of the NAFTA ROOs indicates that they are not a model of simplicity.

Automobiles have special provisions for a NAFTA CO. Here, the RVC must be calculated using the net cost method. The NAFTA automobile RVC calculation includes the *value of non-originating materials* (VNM), and this, in turn, is calculated using one of two sets of tracing rules for materials used in the manufacturing process, one for "heavy-duty" goods (engines and transmissions) and another for "light-duty" goods. Heavy-duty goods are required to include the total value of *all* non-originating materials in the VNM. Light-duty goods, on the other hand, need only include the value of non-originating materials specified on a light-duty tracing list.

The preparation of NAFTA CO is complicated in general, which is why Friedman (2003) advises: "It is imperative that producers and exporters asked to complete a NAFTA CO understand and properly apply the NAFTA Rules of Origin before certifying merchandise or relying on a CO from a supplier.… Consequently, advice concerning a specific circumstance should come from a qualified customs attorney." Exporters or producers of an automotive product needs to be particularly concerned that they have adequately addressed the complicated ROOs governing this kind of trade in North America.

In 2018 the NAFTA automobile ROOs were renegotiated at the insistence of the US government, increasing the automobile RVC from 62.5 percent to 75 percent. There is now also a requirement to have 40 percent of auto components made by workers earning at least US$16 per hour.

Sources: The Economist (2018a; 2018b), Friedman (2003), and Trade Information Center, US Department of Commerce.

The Economic Effects of Preferential Trade Agreements

What are the economic effects of PTAs? Trade economist Jacob Viner (1950) first addressed this question in a famous book entitled *The Customs Union Issue*. Viner distinguishes between the concepts of **trade creation** and **trade diversion** in PTAs.

Trade creation occurs when the formation of a PTA leads to a switching of imports from a high-cost source to a low-cost source. Trade diversion occurs when imports switch from a low-cost source to a high-cost source. As we will see, trade creation tends to improve welfare, whereas trade diversion tends to worsen welfare. Let us summarize this distinction in a box.

> ***Trade creation*** Switching of imports from a high-cost source to a low-cost source. Improves welfare.
>
> ***Trade diversion*** Switching of imports from a low-cost source to a high cost source. Tends to worsen welfare.

We are going to illustrate the concepts of trade creation and trade diversion using the absolute advantage model we developed in Chapter 2. We are going to consider two countries that are members of a PTA, Brazil (B) and Argentina (A). We are also going to refer to a third country, El Salvador (S), which is an excluded non-member. A PTA that involves *trade creation* is presented in Figure 9.1. In this figure, we take the perspective of Brazil. S^B is Brazil's supply curve of some good, and D^B is Brazil's demand curve for the same good. Brazil can import the good from Argentina at price P^A and from El Salvador at price P^S. The crucial point here is that Argentina is the lower-cost producer in comparison to El Salvador.

Before the PTA, Brazil has in place a specific (per unit) tariff of T on imports from *both* Argentina and El Salvador. Since $P^A + T < P^s + T$, Brazil imports the good from Argentina, and the initial import level is Z^B. Once Brazil joins the PTA with Argentina, the tariff is removed on imports from Argentina. Clearly, $P^A < P^S + T$, so the good continues to be imported from Argentina. Imports expand from Z^B to Z^B_{PTA}, however, as the price falls from $P^A + T$ to P^A.

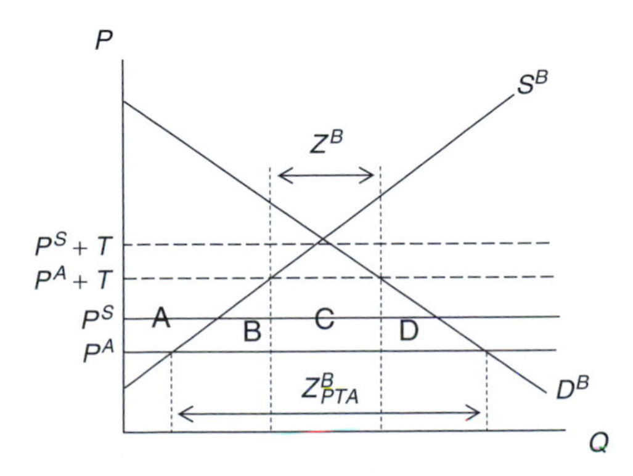

Figure 9.1 A trade-creating PTA between Brazil and Argentina
Note: Areas *A*, *B*, *C*, and *D* extend vertically between P^A and $P^A + T$.

As a result of the PTA with Argentina, consumer surplus in Brazil increases in Figure 9.1 by area $A+B+C+D$. Producer surplus falls by A, and government tariff revenue falls by C.[12] The net increase in welfare due to trade creation is $B+D$. Let us summarize this.

Consumer surplus: $A+B+C+D$.
Producer surplus: $-A$
Government revenue: $-C$
Net welfare: $B+D$

The switch in "imports" in the trade-creating PTA described in Figure 9.1 is from a high-cost source, namely Brazil itself, to a low-cost source, Argentina, and takes place in the movement down the Brazilian supply curve. This trade-creating switch is what generates the increase in welfare in Brazil.

A PTA that involves *trade diversion* is presented in Figure 9.2. In this figure, and in contrast to Figure 9.1, El Salvador is now the lower-cost producer in comparison to Argentina–that is, $P^S < P^A$. Since $P^S + T < P^A + T$, before the PTA Brazil imports the good from El Salvador, and the initial import level is Z^B. Once Brazil joins a PTA with Argentina, however, $P^A < P^S + T$, so Brazil switches to Argentina as an import supplier. Imports expand to Z^B_{PTA} as the domestic price falls from $P^S + T$ to P^A, but El Salvador loses its exports to the Brazilian market.

As a result of the PTA with Argentina, consumer surplus in Brazil increases by area $A+B+C+D$ in Figure 9.2. Producer surplus falls by A, and government revenue falls by $C+E$. The net increase in welfare is therefore $B+D-E$.

Let us summarize this.

Consumer surplus: $A+B+C+D$
Producer surplus: $-A$
Government revenue: $-C-E$
Net welfare: $B+D-E$

Whether the net welfare effect in Figure 9.2 is a positive or negative value depends on the relative sizes of $B+D$ and E. Area $B+D$ represents the trade-creating effects of switching "imports" from the higher-cost source of Brazil to the lower-cost source of Argentina. Area E represents the trade-diverting effects of switching imports from the lower-cost source of El Salvador to the higher-cost source of Argentina, however. If the trade-diverting effects outweigh the trade-creating effects (if $E > B+D$), then the PTA will *reduce* welfare in Brazil.

[12] Recall that the concepts of consumer and producer surplus were discussed in Appendix 2.1; please refer to this appendix if you need to.

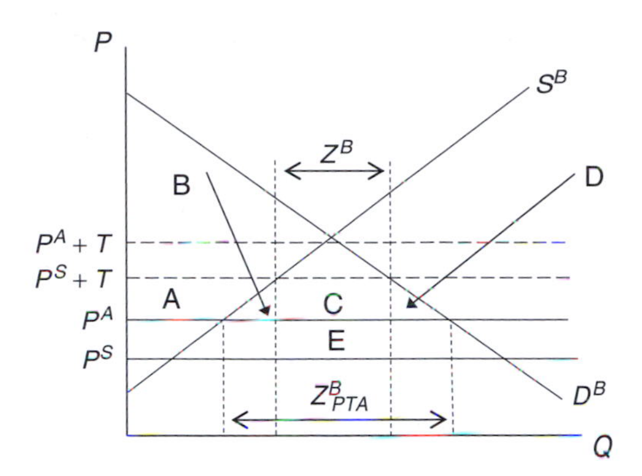

Figure 9.2 A trade-diverting PTA between Brazil and Argentina
Note: Areas *A*, *B*, *C*, and *D* extend vertically between P^A and $P^S + T$.

What should you take from the preceding discussion of trade creation and trade diversion? Let us summarize it in a box.

> PTAs can be either welfare-improving or welfare-worsening. Therefore, whether a specific PTA is welfare-improving or welfare-worsening is something that must be assessed on a *case-by-case* basis, based on evidence on the relative strengths of trade creation and trade diversion.

As a consequence of the above, assessments of PTAs are often made using more sophisticated and numerical versions of Figures 9.1 and 9.2. In other words, trade economists are often called upon to mathematically model the effects of PTAs.[13] If you are involved with the assessment of PTAs in any way, you might need to interpret the results of such modeling exercises. Each of the chapters in Part I of this book have contributed to your ability to do so.

The European Union

The European Union is the current name for a set of agreements between 28 (at the time of this writing) European countries in the realms of economics, foreign and security policies, and justice and home affairs. The evolution of the European Union is summarized in Table 9.3. Its roots extend back to the Marshall

[13] For the important case of the North American Free Trade Agreement, see the relevant chapters of Francois and Shiells (1997). This was one of the first instances when mathematical models played an important role in the actual policy deliberations surrounding a proposed PTA.

Table 9.3 The evolution of the European Union

Year	Initiative	Treaty	Members added
1951	European Coal and Steel Community	Treaty of Paris	Belgium France Germany Italy Luxembourg Netherlands
1958	European Economic Community	Treaty of Rome	
1965	Institutional reform	Brussels Treaty	
1973	Enlargement		Denmark Ireland United Kingdom
1981	Enlargement		Greece
1986	Institutional reform	Single European Act	
1986	Enlargement		Portugal Spain
1992	European Union	Treaty on European Union (TEU), or the Maastricht Treaty	
1995	Enlargement		Austria Finland Sweden
1997	Institutional reform	Treaty of Amsterdam	
1999	European Monetary Union		United Kingdom, Sweden, and Denmark not included
2001	Institutional reform	Treaty of Nice	
2002	Common EMU currency: the euro		United Kingdom, Sweden, and Denmark not included
2004	Enlargement		Cyprus Czech Republic Estonia Hungary Latvia Lithuania Malta Poland Slovakia Slovenia

Table 9.3 (cont.)

Year	Initiative	Treaty	Members added
2007	Enlargement		Bulgaria Romania
2007	EU constitution	Lisbon Treaty	
2013	Enlargement		Croatia
2016	Brexit vote	United Kingdom votes to eventually leave the EU	

Sources: Dinan (2010) and europa.eu.

Plan, under which the United States aided in the reconstruction of Europe after World War II and promoted the liberalization of trade and payments between the European countries in its zone of influence. These liberalization processes were facilitated by the Organisation for European Economic Co-operation and the European Payments Union.[14] In 1951 the Treaty of Paris was signed, leading to the formation of the European Coal and Steel Community (ECSC) between Belgium, France, Germany, Italy, Luxembourg, and the Netherlands, countries that became known as "the Six." The purpose of the ECSC was to liberalize trade and promote competition in the steel and coal sectors of the Western European economy.

In 1957 the Treaty of Rome was signed. This led to the formation of the European Economic Community (EEC) in 1958. The ultimate goal of the EEC was the creation of a common market. Initially, however, the EEC was a movement towards an FTA in a decade-long transitional period. The EEC took the step to becoming a CU in 1968 with the introduction of a common external tariff. Between 1973 and 1986 its membership increased from six to 12 countries. The year 1992 marked the *official* completion of a common market, in which barriers to labor and physical capital were to be removed (the *actual* completion of a common market will always be a work in progress). With the signing of the Maastricht Treaty in that year the EEC was joined by initiatives in the areas of foreign and security policy and justice and home affairs under what became known as the European Union. Austria, Finland, and Sweden joined the European Union in 1995, bringing the membership to 15. An ambitious enlargement in 2004 added ten more countries as EU members, and enlargements in 2007 and 2013 brought the total membership to 28.[15]

Beginning in 2002 the European Union ventured beyond a common market to a monetary union, with the launch of the euro. This was a bold move but one

---

[14] The Organisation for European Economic Co-operation later became the Paris-based Organisation for Economic Co-operation and Development (OECD).

[15] At the time of this writing, candidate countries included Croatia, Macedonia, and Turkey.

that has proved to be difficult to manage effectively. We take up these important developments in Chapter 21 on monetary unions.

Currently, a pressing issue facing the European Union is "Brexit," the decision via referendum in 2016 for the United Kingdom to eventually *leave* the union. Political forces calling for such a move had been present in the United Kingdom for some time, but there was a hope that these had been mollified by negotiations that took place in 2015 and early 2016 to reach a "new settlement" for the country within the European Union. The new settlement primarily addressed intra-EU migration issues and was an attempt by the then prime minister, David Cameron, to placate growing opposition to the European Union within the United Kingdom. It did not work, and the country voted to "leave" the union.

Ongoing negotiations for Brexit between the United Kingdom and the European Union are exceedingly complex. The trade policies of the United Kingdom as a member were those of the European Union. It now faces the daunting task of negotiating new arrangements with the European Union itself, as well as with all existing EU PTAs. Without such arrangements, UK exports will inevitably face most favored nation tariffs in EU markets rather than being granted free entry. Waking up to this reality in 2017, the United Kingdom proposed a transitionary customs union until a final arrangement could be worked out. In 2018 UK discussions turned on whether to pursue a "soft Brexit," permanently staying in the customs union, or a "hard Brexit," leaving it.[16] The year 2019 bought more Brexit-related political turmoil.

What about the impact of the European Union on trade? In an early round of research, some economists (e.g. Hufbauer, 1990; Lawrence, 1991; and Sapir, 1992) argued that trade creation dominated trade diversion in the EC and EU. Winters (1993) expresses a much more cautious view, noting that, despite the common external tariff of the European Union CU, non-tariff measures (e.g. quotas) had increased in sectors such as motor vehicles, VCRs, and footwear. He also notes that EU subsidies had increased in sectors such as aircraft, steel, shipbuilding, and agriculture. An intermediate view was offered by Tsoukalis (1997), who points to overall trade creation in manufactured goods and overall trade diversion in agricultural goods. The latter has been largely the result of the Common Agricultural Policy (CAP), which has protected EEC/EU agriculture from foreign competition and has involved the heavy use of export subsidies. Protection levels for EU agriculture under the CAP remain high, although the WTO Agreement on Agriculture, discussed in Chapter 8, introduced a modicum of discipline.[17]

---

[16] See *The Economist* (2017b; 2018c; 2018d). A separate and controversial issue is the border between Northern Ireland (part of the United Kingdom) and the Republic of Ireland (part of the European Union).

[17] The EU CAP also had implications for the failed Doha Round. See, for example, Reinert (2007).

A second round of research was provided by De Santis and Vicarelli (2007) and Gil, Llorca, and Martíniz-Serrano (2008). De Santis and Vicarelli (2007) examined the European Union's trade patterns between 1960 and 2000, as well as its network of PTAs with non-members. These authors find significant trade creation between EU members but only limited trade diversion because of the expanding set of external PTAs. Gil, Llorca, and Martíniz-Serrano (2008) focus on trade creation (but not trade diversion). These researchers carefully examined the evolution of the EU's trading relationships and trade flows over the years 1950 to 2004, accounting for the expansion of members. They conclude that each successive enlargement increased trade and that the deepening of the regional integration scheme from an FTA to a CU and, further, to a common market and monetary union also had a positive effect on trade. Because this study did not account for trade diversion, it is not a welfare analysis, as in Figures 9.1 and 9.2, but it is significant nonetheless.

Where the European Union is lagging is in *trade in services*, discussed in Chapter 1. As noted by *The Economist* (2019), services now account for nearly three-quarters of EU GDP and nearly all net employment growth. Liberalizing trade in services within the European Union requires harmonization of the regulation of services across EU members. Progress in this endeavor has long been stalled, however. Particularly in the age of digital services, this is a serious limitation.

As previously mentioned, in 2002 the European Union moved boldly in the direction of a monetary union. For this reason, the attention of trade economists turned to the effects of the European Monetary Union (EMU) on trade flows. This represents too large a body of research to summarize here. Suffice it to say that, although there has been substantial debate over the actual size of the impact of the EMU on intra-EMU trade, it has indeed been positive.[18]

At the time of this writing, the European Union is in a period of crisis—or, more accurately, a set of crises. Dinan (2017), for example, lists these as the Brexit crisis, the migration crisis, the Ukraine crisis, the euro crisis, and the political crisis.[19] Despite some real successes, then, the European Union is currently dealing with a number of simultaneous and serious challenges.

The North American Free Trade Agreement

In 1989 an FTA between Canada and the United States came into effect. Sometime thereafter the then Mexican president, Carlos Salinas de Gortari, approached a number of countries in Western Europe with the intent of convincing them to

[18] See, for example, Frankel (2010).

[19] The last of these refers to the retreat from democratic norms in some EU countries, namely Hungary and Poland.

enter into trade liberalization with Mexico. On his trip to Europe, he found these countries to be distracted with the movement to the European Union, described above. On a return flight from Europe, Salinas decided to pursue an FTA with the United States. In 1990 the then US president, George Bush, and Salinas announced their intention to begin negotiating an FTA. In 1991, however, they were joined by Canada to begin negotiations for a North American Free Trade Agreement involving all three countries. The agreement was signed in 1992 and took effect in 1994.[20] It was fully phased in by 2009. Unexpectedly, the US government insisted on a NAFTA renegotiation beginning in 2017.

The NAFTA agreement was ambitious. Along with trade in goods, it addressed financial services, transportation, telecommunications, foreign direct investment, intellectual property rights, government procurement, and dispute settlement. With regard to trade in goods, NAFTA liberalized trade in the highly protected automobile, textile, and clothing sectors, albeit with restrictive ROOs. In agriculture, NAFTA phased out tariffs over a ten-year period and transformed quotas into tariff rate quotas (see Appendix 7.2), which were phased out over ten- to fifteen-year periods. Foreign direct investment was liberalized, though not at first in the energy sector.[21] NAFTA also provided significant intellectual property protection in a manner similar to the TRIPs Agreement, discussed in Chapter 8.

During the discussions and political deliberations surrounding the NAFTA negotiations, issues of trade and the environment and trade and labor rose quickly to the surface. Mathematical models of these issues are discussed in the accompanying box. Institutionally, however, NAFTA was innovative in that it responded to these concerns with the North American Agreement on Environmental Cooperation (NAAEC) and the North American Agreement on Labor Cooperation (NAALC), sometimes referred to as the NAFTA "side agreements."

What does research on NAFTA tell us about its effects? Evidence suggests that the trade effects of NAFTA were overwhelmingly positive.[22] In addition, FDI into Mexico did indeed increase in response to NAFTA.[23] Despite arguments to the contrary, NAFTA's impacts on job losses in the United States have been *small* relative to overall employment trends in that country.[24] The NAFTA ROOs substantially limit market access for Mexico in all but textiles and clothing,[25] and the agreement

---

[20] Since then, Mexico and the European Union have signed an FTA.

[21] Despite the fact that NAFTA involves the removal of barriers to FDI, it is not a common market since it does not allow for the free movement of *labor* within North America. On Mexico's initial reluctance to liberalize its energy sector, see Ramirez (2006) and Puyana (2006).

[22] See, for example, Caliendo and Parro (2015).

[23] See, for example, Cuevas, Messmacher, and Werner (2005).

[24] See Hufbauer and Schott (2005).

[25] See Anson et al. (2005).

has had detrimental impacts on Mexico's corn producers.[26] Despite the ROOs, however, automobile trade (both parts and finished automobiles) within North America has expanded rapidly.

NAFTA, Wages, and Industrial Pollution

The issues of trade and wages in general and of North–South trade and wages in particular have recently received a great deal of attention by economists and public policy analysts. Most of the discussion has taken place in terms of the Heckscher–Ohlin model of international trade and its associated Stolper–Samuelson theorem, discussed in Chapters 4 and 6. Reinert and Roland-Holst (1998) set out to address this issue in the context of the North American Free Trade Agreement.

These researchers constructed a 26-sector model of the North American economy, including Canada, the United States, and Mexico. They simulated the effects of expanding trade that would take place under NAFTA on five labor categories: professional and managerial; sales and clerical; agricultural; craft; and operators and laborers. In a number of different simulations under different labor supply assumptions, they find that real wages in the United States *increased* for all five types of workers. There was no downward pressure on wages in the United States, even for blue-collar workers.

As suggested by Ruffin (1999) in another study, and as discussed in Chapter 5, these results reflect the presence of a great deal of *intra*-industry trade between the United States and Mexico, which the Reinert and Roland-Holst model captures. In most sectors, trade expanded in *both* directions between these two countries, something that is not possible in the strict Heckscher–Ohlin framework of *inter*-industry trade.

In 2000 the North American Commission for Environmental Cooperation (CEC) sponsored the First North American Symposium on Understanding the Linkages between Trade and Environment. In one contribution to this symposium, Reinert and Roland-Holst (2001) set out to assess the impacts of trade liberalization under NAFTA on industrial pollution in Canada, the United States, and Mexico. They used the same model of the North American economy described above, focusing on the manufacturing sectors in the model and utilizing pollutant data from the Industrial Pollution Projection System of the World Bank.

[26] See Ramirez (2003). Martin and Sirkeci (2017: 325) note: "When NAFTA went into effect in 1994, about 30 percent of Mexicans were employed in agriculture, and corn was the major crop of over half of Mexico's farmers. Iowa, which accounted for about 20 percent of US-produced corn, produced twice as much corn as Mexico, and at about half the price." This is partly attributable to the heavy subsidization of corn in the United States.

NAFTA, Wages, and Industrial Pollution (cont.)

Reinert and Roland-Holst find that the most serious environmental consequences of NAFTA occurred in the base metals sector. In terms of magnitude, the greatest impacts were in the United States and Canada, and this was the case for most of the pollutants considered. As alleged in the debate over NAFTA and the environment mentioned above, the Mexican petroleum sector was a significant source of industrial pollution, particularly in the case of air pollution. For specific pollutants in specific countries, the transportation equipment sector and the chemicals sector were also important sources of industrial pollution.

Modeling results such as the above alert policy-makers to likely labor market and pollution effects of PTAs and can be repeated for any new PTAs that come under negotiation. In this manner, trade policy models can inform trade policy formation.

Sources: Reinert and Roland-Holst (1998; 2001) and Ruffin (1999).

Truck transportation services were a sticking point in NAFTA. Full access to the US trucking market was to have been granted by 2000, and a NAFTA arbitration panel ruled in Mexico's favor on this in 2001. Even the US Supreme Court weighed in on the issue in favor of Mexico in 2004. But the US Congress removed funding for even a successful pilot project in 2009, and Mexico consequently imposed retaliatory tariffs. This issue was finally resolved in 2011.

Another sticking point has been migration. Despite hopes that NAFTA would decrease migration from Mexico to the United States, this has not been the case. Hopes for development and environmental improvements along the US–Mexican border have also been disappointed, on account of the lack of funding for the North American Development Bank. Mexican (and Central American) migrants have increasingly become a political issue in the United States, particularly in the presidency of Donald Trump, beginning in 2017.

2017 was also the year that the Trump administration demanded a *renegotiation* of NAFTA, with a focus on tightening rules of origin and weakening dispute settlement procedures. As discussed in the box above, the largest change in 2018 was in the NAFTA automobile ROOs. It is fair to say that most trade economists take a dim view of these renegotiations.[27]

[27] *The Economist* (2017a) writes: "NAFTA is not the failure [US President] Trump claims it is. Trade in goods among its three partners has more than trebled since it took effect in 1994; 14% of world trade in goods takes place under its rules. Cross-border supply chains have made American firms more competitive. The manufacturing jobs it has created in Mexico have slowed migration to the United States."

Mercosur

Mercosur, or the Common Market of the South, is a PTA between Argentina, Brazil, Paraguay, Uruguay, and (at times) Venezuela. Mercosur was launched in 1991 with the Treaty of Asunción, named after the capital city of Paraguay. Venezuela's membership has been problematic, with it joining in 2006 and being suspended in 2016. Bolivia is in the process of becoming a Mercosur member, having signed an accession protocol in 2012. Associate members include Chile, Colombia, Ecuador, Guyana, Peru, and Suriname. The name "Mercosur" is somewhat misleading, because it suggests that the PTA is an actual common market, with the free movement of labor and physical capital (see Table 9.2). This is not the case, however. Mercosur entered into force in 1995 as an FTA and officially became a customs union in 2006. Free movement of labor and physical capital is a long way off.[28]

Evidence suggests that the trade impacts of Mercosur have been moderately positive.[29] Evidence on FDI is harder to come by. Mercosur has also been troubled by two asymmetries. First, Argentina and Brazil dwarf Paraguay and Uruguay in economic size. Consequently, the smaller members find themselves somewhat sidelined from the core relationship between Argentina and Brazil. Second, for a number of years there was a fundamental macroeconomic asymmetry between Argentina and Brazil. After its crisis of 1998 the Brazilian real became a freely floating currency, while, until its crisis in 2002, the Argentine peso was rigidly pegged to the US dollar under a currency board arrangement (see Chapter 18). These asymmetries caused a great deal of friction between Argentina and Brazil and complicated the functioning of Mercosur.[30]

Finally, there is an intriguing possibility of an EU–Mercosur FTA, which was the subject of negotiations from 2010 to 2012 and 2016 to 2019. These negotiations actually failed in 2018 but were restarted a few months later. Success is unclear at the time of this writing, with any real progress not foreseen until 2020 at the earliest.[31]

---

[28] Politically, Mercosur is indeed an achievement. Its two main members, Brazil and Argentina, were estranged rivals as recently as the mid-1980s. Consider Reid (2002: 4): "Until 1985, apart from a couple of border encounters, only three Brazilian presidents had ever visited Argentina, and only two Argentine rulers had made the trip the other way. The two countries' railway networks had been built to different gauges. As recently as the 1970s, Argentina and Brazil were engaged in a nuclear arms race."

[29] See the gravity model analysis of García, Pabsdorf, and Herrera (2013).

[30] A conflict began in 2006 between Argentina and Uruguay over the issue of Uruguay's intent to site paper mills on the Uruguay River between the two countries. Despite adjudication of this issue by the International Court of Justice in The Hague in 2007, the issue was not resolved until 2010.

[31] See Reuters (2019).

The FTAA

At the end of 1994 the governments of 34 countries in the Western Hemisphere met at the First Summit of the Americas. They agreed to pursue a Free Trade Area of the Americas (FTAA), with the goal of concluding such an agreement by 2005. Negotiations concerning the FTAA were launched at the Second Summit of the Americas, in 1998.[32] A draft agreement was concluded by 2002. If it had been successful, the FTAA would have represented the largest free trade area in the world at that time, in terms of both market size and territory.

Beginning in 2002 the United States began to implement increased protection of its steel sector and increased subsidies for its agricultural sector. Within Latin America these measures were seen as unfortunate, and they called into question the spirit of the FTAA process. The Brazilian government was particularly concerned about US steel protection. Having at one time attempted to move up the FTAA negotiations deadline to the end of 2003, the United States eventually agreed to keep the original 2005 deadline. This deadline was missed.

The 2004 Summit of the Americas, which took place in Monterrey, Mexico, proved unable to solve the remaining issues. The most significant disagreement was between the United States and Brazil. The United States had insisted that issues related to agricultural subsidies and anti-dumping measures be excluded from the FTAA negotiations, to be pursued only in the ongoing *multilateral* trade negotiations taking place as part of the (ultimately failed) Doha Round, discussed in Chapter 8. Brazil objected to these stipulations, as well as to the US insistence that the FTAA negotiations include issues of government procurement and intellectual property.[33]

The Fifth Summit of the Americas took place in 2005 in Mar del Plata, Argentina. It was hosted by President Néstor Kirchner, who formed an alliance with Venezuela's Hugo Chávez. The political conflict that took place at this meeting between Argentina and Venezuela, on the one side, and the United States, on the other, brought the FTAA process to a complete halt. There has been no serious discussion about reviving it.

---

[32] Nine negotiating groups were formed, in the following areas: (1) market access, (2) investment, (3) services, (4) government procurement, (5) dispute settlement, (6) agriculture, (7) intellectual property rights, (8) subsidies, anti-dumping, and countervailing duties, and (9) competition policy.

[33] Rivas-Campo and Juk Benke (2003: 669) note: "Given the US position...to encourage global instead of regional liberalization in agriculture, Latin American countries have underlined the minimal gains that an FTAA without agricultural liberalization would signify for developing and agriculture-dependent countries." They also say (670): "As long as the US remains reluctant to eliminate agricultural subsidies, Latin American countries may also be unwilling to favor substantial agricultural liberalization in the region."

ASEAN and AFTA

PTAs have been proliferating in the Asia-Pacific region since the late 1990s. At the center of this proliferation is the Association of Southeast Asian Nations, or ASEAN. ASEAN was formed in 1967 and currently includes ten countries: Brunei, Cambodia, Indonesia, Laos, Malaysia, Myanmar, the Philippines, Singapore, Thailand, and Vietnam. Since the late 1970s it has turned its attention from political cooperation to economic integration.[34] In 1992 the first six members of ASEAN (ASEAN-6) formed the ASEAN Free Trade Area (AFTA), but this PTA now includes all ten members.

The AFTA is an attempt to reduce intra-PTA tariffs and non-tariff measures. This is done using what AFTA terms the Common Effective Preferential Tariff (CEPT). The CEPT is a means through which AFTA is in the process of reducing all intra-PTA tariffs to the 0 to 5 percent ad valorem range. ROOs are of course utilized to determine ASEAN origination. Efforts are under way to liberalize investment within ASEAN as well.

ASEAN has linked AFTA to other countries in the region. For example, in the wake of the Asian financial crisis of 1997, ASEAN formed a relationship with the East Asian countries China, Japan, and South Korea. This became known as the ASEAN+3. ASEAN+3 initially focused on financial issues, but there has been talk of this regional partnership evolving into a PTA. This was overshadowed by a number of "ASEAN+1" agreements, including ASEAN–China (2002), ASEAN–Japan (2002), ASEAN–India (2002), and ASEAN–Republic of Korea (2009). In 2009 there was also concluded an ASEAN–Australia–New Zealand Free Trade Area (AANZFTA).[35]

In 2015 ASEAN moved beyond AFTA to begin to take steps towards an ASEAN Economic Community (AEC). The aim is to further reduce intra-ASEAN tariffs, facilitate trade, move further into services liberation, attract more FDI, and integrate infrastructure. Most assessments of the AEC suggest that there will be difficulties in achieving the stated goals.[36]

The trade impacts of ASEAN have been positive. Initially, AFTA's major trading partners were outside ASEAN. As Cabalu and Alfonso (2007) note, this helped to suppress trade diversion effects. Although ASEAN's trade with the rest of the world continued to grow, so did intra-ASEAN trade. Approximately one-fourth on ASEAN trade is now within the PTA, and an increasing amount of this trade is vertical intra-industry trade (described in Chapter 5).[37] There is also an increasing

[34] See Feridhanusetyawan (2005) and Tongzon (2009).

[35] These dates refer to the first official statements of intent, not of implementation.

[36] See Menon and Melendez (2017).

[37] See Kawai and Naknoi (2017).

amount of FDI inflows into AFTA countries, particularly from the European Union, Japan, particular ASEAN countries (Singapore, Malaysia, and Indonesia), and the United States.[38] In these respects, the AFTA project of ASEAN can be seen as a success.

The Trans-Pacific Partnership

The Trans-Pacific Partnership (TPP) was to be an FTA between 12 Pacific Rim countries: Australia, Brunei, Canada, Chile, Japan, Malaysia, Mexico, New Zealand, Peru, Singapore, the United States, and Vietnam. Conceived in 2011 and signed in 2016, it was also the signature trade agreement of the administration of Barack Obama in the United States. The TPP was a recognition of increasing economic ties between Pacific Rim countries, ties that had been developing for decades.[39] It is important to understand that the TPP agreement went way beyond standard trade issues, to include environmental issues, investor–state dispute settlement (ISDS), labor standards, and regulatory cooperation. It was nothing if not ambitious.[40]

After the transition from the Obama administration to the Trump administration in the United States, and reflecting the anti-trade objectives of the latter, the United States pulled out of the TPP. Indeed, this decision was one of the very first taken by the new US administration. This left 11 remaining countries constituting the TPP. Signed in 2018 and formally known as the Comprehensive and Progressive Agreement for Trans-Pacific Partnership, the CP-TPP, or TPP-11, still has high hopes as a PTA covering half a billion people. It is a modified TPP that changes some original TPP language in areas of US interests (e.g. intellectual property).

Regionalism and Multilateralism

Because of their discriminatory nature, the presence of PTAs in the world trading system sits uneasily with principles of multilateralism. As we stated in the introduction, regionalism and multilateralism represent two alternative trade policy

[38] Again, see Kawai and Naknoi (2017).

[39] For a view from the 1990s, see Gehlhar, Hertel, and Martin (1994).

[40] For a view from 2015, towards the end of negotiations, see Fergusson, McMinimy, and Williams (2015). These authors state: "As a leading trade policy initiative of the Obama Administration, the TPP serves several strategic goals. It is a manifestation of the Administration's 'rebalance' to the Asia-Pacific, and if concluded may serve to shape the economic architecture of the region. It has the potential to harmonize existing agreements with the U.S. FTA partners, attract new participants and establish regional rules on new policy issues facing the global economy—possibly providing impetus to future multilateral liberalization under the WTO."

options available to the countries of the world, with "forum shopping" taking place between them. In the 1950s and 1960s there had been what is now called the "first wave" of PTAs in LMICs, particularly in Latin America. This was often in conjunction with protectionist policies against the rest of the world, again particularly in Latin America.[41] In the 1980s there began what is now called the "second wave" of PTAs, when the numbers began to increase substantially. In a sense, this second wave has never ended. The question on many observers' minds is whether this second wave of PTAs complements the multilateral framework or works at cross-purposes to it.

The (lengthy) policy discussions on the role of PTAs in the world trading system often address whether they are more appropriately described as "building blocks" or "stumbling blocks" to multilateral trade liberalization.[42] As building blocks, PTAs could evolve as ever-expanding systems that bring more and more countries into postures of trade liberalization. For example, Ethier (1998; 2001) saw the second wave of PTAs as a "new regionalism" or an "open regionalism," in contrast with the first wave. By this he means that PTAs were taking place alongside unilateral and multilateral trade liberalization, as well as increasing amounts of FDI. Another example was Baldwin (2006), who envisions PTAs evolving into a form of "multilateralized regionalism." As stumbling blocks, however, PTA negotiations can take energy and focus away from multilateral trade negotiations. As Bhagwati (1993: 30) stated many years ago, "The taking to two roads can affect adversely the travel down one."

There is also concern with regard to the overlapping and complex nature of PTAs and their ROOs. This has taken the form of what Bhagwati (1993) has famously termed the "spaghetti bowl" of PTAs (also called a "noodle bowl" in Asia). On this point, Bhagwati, Greenaway, and Panagariya (1998) warn of a movement towards "numerous and crisscrossing [PTAs] and innumerable applicable tariff rates depending on arbitrarily-determined and often a multiplicity of sources of origin" (1139).[43] This issue has only become more relevant over time.

More positively, the perspective of international political economy suggests that trading blocs and customs unions (and their increased levels of trade and FDI) can have a role in reducing international conflict, including military conflict—a

[41] In the Latin American case, see Bulmer-Thomas (2014: chap. 9).

[42] This terminology was first introduced by Bhagwati (1993).

[43] Take, for example, the case of Mexico. As discussed above, Mexico is a member of NAFTA, but it is also (at the time of this writing) a member of the following PTAs: Mexico–Chile, Mexico–Costa Rica, Mexico–European Union, Mexico–European Free Trade Area, Mexico–Guatemala, Mexico–Honduras, Mexico–Israel, Mexico–Japan, and Mexico–Nicaragua. Mexico is connected to the United States via NAFTA, and the Central American countries in this list are connected to the United States via the Central American Free Trade Agreement. Simplicity this is not.

clear benefit.[44] There are also repeated calls for attempts to better leverage PTAs as building blocks to strengthened multilateralism, on the grounds that trading blocs and customs unions are "here to stay." Economists, social scientists, and policy-makers will no doubt debate these issues for some time to come. What is clear, though, is that proper oversight of these arrangements at the level of the WTO is a *necessary condition* for a positive relationship between PTAs and the multilateral trading system. As discussed above, however, *this oversight is missing.*

The WTO could go further and tighten its requirements on the external protection of FTAs and CUs. To understand why this could be important, take a new look at the trade-diverting PTA between Brazil and Argentina as depicted in Figure 9.2. Suppose that the tariff on imports from El Salvador had been eliminated, along with the tariff on imports from Argentina. If this were the case, Brazil would continue to import from El Salvador, there would be no trade diversion, and welfare would unambiguously increase. This fact has led some analysts to argue that external tariffs ought to be reduced in a CU or FTA in order to mitigate against trade diversion. Analysts similarly call for common external tariffs in CUs to be set to the *lowest* of the pre-CU tariffs of the members.[45]

These considerations indicate that, although it is possible to *lessen* the tensions between regionalism and multilateralism, it is not possible to *eliminate* them. As stated at the beginning of this chapter, "when multilateralism falters, regionalism picks up the pace." It is the responsibility of all WTO members, but especially the larger WTO members, to ensure that multilateralism does not falter. The failed Doha Round, discussed in Chapter 8, suggests that this responsibility has not been taken seriously enough.

GATS-Plus and TRIPS-Plus

In Chapter 8, we considered the General Agreement on Trade in Services and the Agreement on Trade Related Aspects of Intellectual Property Rights. As it turns out, these were not the last word on services and intellectual property agreements. Since the Marrakesh Agreement, further services and intellectual property rights agreements have taken place within PTAs. These are known as GATS-Plus and TRIPS-Plus agreements.

As seen in Table 9.1, 160 PTAs have been notified under GATS Article V, indicating some level of agreement in services trade. In many cases, the type of

---

[44] See, for example, Mansfield and Pevehouse (2000).

[45] See McMillan (1993), Bhagwati (1993), and Serra et al. (1997).

liberalization taking place in PTAs is the locking in of previous unilateral regulatory liberalization that has taken place since GATS took effect in 1995. It is important to keep in mind that these lock-ins are *preferential* and therefore can violate MFN and NT non-discrimination principles. Much of the activity has been in Mode 1 (cross-border trade) and Mode 3 (commercial presence or FDI), with commitments that exceeded those initially made in the failed Doha Round. The PTA commitments also have taken place across the full range of service sectors.[46] For these reasons, a full appreciation of services trade development requires analysts to delve into the realm of PTAs.

Along with GATS-Plus agreements, there are TRIPS-Plus agreements that are part of PTAs.[47] NAFTA, for example, contains an intellectual property chapter that is more stringent than TRIPS itself. This is not unusual. Approximately one-half of the PTAs signed since 2000 have TRIPS-Plus agreements. Indeed, Forsyth (2017: 84) notes that, "worldwide, FTAs are being used by powerful states in the global North (high-income countries) as ways of ratcheting-up intellectual property standards." Because intellectual property protection does not necessarily exhibit the welfare gains of standard trade liberalization, these TRIPS-Plus agreements can be a cause for concern. In addition, TRIPS-Plus agreements can impose *enforcement costs* on LMICs that are not in a good position to absorb them.[48] For these reasons, TRIPS-Plus agreements need to be treated with a good deal of caution.

Conclusion

The GATT and WTO have allowed for exceptions to the basic non-discrimination principle in the case of four avenues to PTAs: FTAs, CUs, enabling clause arrangements, and GATS arrangements. These and other PTAs have been part of the world trading system for decades, and all evidence points to their continued presence. The evolution of PTAs in Europe, the Americas, and Asia are

[46] See, for example, Sauvé and Shingal (2011). These authors also give a list of the types of GATS-Plus commitments being made: "The value of services output; the number of service suppliers; the amount of foreign equity permitted; the type of legal structure required for market entry purposes; the technical standards, licensing, and qualification requirements applied; as well as the conditions of eligibility for service sector subsidies" (954).

[47] As pointed out by Drahos (2001), this can also be true of bilateral investment treaties (BITs) (to be discussed in Chapter 12).

[48] For example, Lindstrom (2009: 944) concludes that TRIPS-Plus enforcement requirements "place an immense resource burden on developing countries that lack well-established legal systems."

some prominent examples. PTAs may improve or worsen welfare depending on the balance between their trade creation and trade diversion effects. Trade policy faces the significant challenge of incorporating the preferential predilections of the WTO's member countries into a general multilateral evolution of world trade. This challenge can be met only by WTO oversight of active PTAs. Unfortunately, this important ingredient is missing.

Review Exercises

1. What distinguishes a customs union from a free trade area? What distinguishes a common market from a customs union?
2. What is the difference between trade creation and trade diversion? Can you provide an example of each?
3. Do you support regionalism and PTAs as a legitimate trade policy option? Why or why not?
4. We mentioned above that the size of Brazil's tariff against El Salvador affects the amount of trade diversion that occurs in a PTA. Use a version of Figure 9.2 to demonstrate that the lower is T against El Salvador, the more likely it is that the PTA will improve welfare. Show that, if the T on imports from El Salvador were eliminated, the PTA would unambiguously improve welfare.
5. Pay a visit to the WTO's website on regionalism. From www.wto.org, follow the link to "Trade Issues" and, from there, to "Regionalism." Spend some time perusing the WTO's materials on this issue.

FURTHER READING AND WEB RESOURCES

An early and important analysis of PTAs can be found in de Melo and Panagariya (1993a; 1993b). A more recent source on regional integration more broadly and its links to development is Schiff and Winters (2003). For a view from the perspective of the WTO, see Crawford and Fiorentino (2005) and Acharya (2016), and, for "rules of thumb" in evaluating PTAs, see Harrison, Rutherford, and Tarr (2003). An important overview of the European Union can be found in Dinan (2010). For NAFTA, see Hufbauer and Schott (2005). For a critical review of Mercosur, see Malamud (2005). For a concise introduction to the FTAA, see Feinberg (2009). Readers who want to delve deeper into issues of the role of ASEAN and AFTA in Asian PTAs can consult Francois and Wignaraja (2008).

The WTO maintains a Regional Trade Agreements Information System (RTA-IS). To access this, go to www.wto.org and select: "Trade Topics" ⇒ "Regional Trade Agreements" ⇒ "RTA Database." The European Union's website can be found at europa.eu. The NAFTA Secretariat's home page is www.nafta-sec-alena.org. The official Mercosur website is at www.mercosur.int, and the FTAA website is at www.alca-ftaa.org. Finally, the ASEAN Free Trade Area website is at www.aseansec.org.

REFERENCES

Acharya, R. (2016) *Regional Trade Agreements and the Multilateral Trading System*, World Trade Organization.

Anson, J., O. Cadot, A. Estevadeordal, J. de Melo, A. Suwa-Eisenmann, and B. Tumurchudur (2005) Rules of Origin in North–South Preferential Trading Arrangements with an Application to NAFTA," *Review of International Economics*, 13:3, 501–17.

Baldwin, R. (2006) "Multilateralising Regionalism: Spaghetti Bowls as Building Blocks on the Path to Global Free Trade," *World Economy* 29:2, 1451–518.

Bhagwati, J. (1993) "Regionalism and Multilateralism: An Overview," in J. de Melo and A. Panagariya (eds.), *New Dimensions in Regional Integration*, Cambridge University Press, 22–51.

Bhagwati, J., D. Greenaway, and A. Panagariya (1998) "Trading Preferentially: Theory and Policy," *The Economic Journal*, 108:449, 1128–48.

Bulmer-Thomas, V. (2014) *The Economic History of Latin America since Independence*, Cambridge University Press.

Cabalu, H., and C. Alfonso (2007) "Does AFTA Create or Divert Trade?," *Global Economy Journal*, 7:4, Article 6, https://doi.org/10.2202/1524-5861.1315.

Caliendo, L., and F. Parro (2015) "Estimates of the Trade and Welfare Effects of NAFTA," *Review of Economic Studies*, 82:1, 1–44.

Crawford, J.-A., and R. V. Fiorentino (2005) *The Changing Landscape of Regional Trade Agreements*, World Trade Organization.

Cuevas, A., M. Messmacher, and A. Werner (2005) "Foreign Direct Investment in Mexico since the Approval of NAFTA," *World Bank Economic Review*, 19:3, 473–88.

De Melo, J., and A. Panagariya (eds.) (1993a) *New Dimensions in Regional Integration*, Cambridge University Press.

De Melo J., and A. Panagariya (1993b) "Introduction," in J. de Melo and A. Panagariya (eds.), *New Dimensions in Regional Integration*, Cambridge University Press, 3–21.

De Santis, R., and C. Vicarelli (2007) "The 'Deeper' and the 'Wider' EU Strategies of Trade Integration: An Empirical Evaluation of EU Common Commercial Policy Effects," *Global Economy Journal*, 7:4, Article 4, https://doi.org/10.2202/1524-5861.1255.

Dinan, D. (2010) *Ever Closer Union: An Introduction to European Integration*, Lynne Rienner.

Dinan, D (2017) "Governance and Institutions: The Insidious Effect of Chronic Crisis," *Journal of Common Market Studies*, 55:S1, 73–87.

Drahos, P. (2001) "BITS and BIPS: Bilateralism in Intellectual Property," *Journal of World Intellectual Property*, 4:6, 791–808.

The Economist (2017a) "Reshape or Shatter: The Pitfalls of Renegotiating NAFTA," February 11.

The Economist (2017b) "Britain and the European Union: Reality Starts to Dawn," August 19.

The Economist (2018a) "An Axle to Grind: Cars Block the Road to a Renegotiated NAFTA," February 1.

The Economist (2018b) "Trade Negotiations: Puzzle Pieces," June 2.

The Economist (2018c) "Britain and the EU: Softer Is Better," June 16.

The Economist (2018d) "Mugged by Reality," October 27.

The Economist (2019) "Briefing: The Single Market," September 14.

Ethier, W. J. (1998) "The New Regionalism," *Economic Journal*, 108:449, 1149–61.

Ethier, W. J. (2001) "The New Regionalism in the Americas: A Theoretical Framework," *North American Journal of Economics and Finance*, 12:2, 159–72.

Feinberg, F. (2009) "Free Trade Area of the Americas," in K. A. Reinert, R. S. Rajan, A. J. Glass, and L. S. Davis (eds.), *Princeton Encyclopedia of the World Economy*, Princeton University Press, 505–8.

Fergusson, I. F., M. A. McMinimy, and B. R. Williams (2015) "The Trans-Pacific Partnership (TPP): Negotiations and Issues for Congress," Report R42694, Congressional Research Service.

Feridhanusetyawan, T. (2005) "Preferential Trade Agreements in the Asia-Pacific Region," Working Paper 05/149, IMF.

Forsyth, M. (2017) "Intellectual Property," in K. A. Reinert (ed.), *Handbook of Globalisation and Development*, Edward Elgar, 83–99.

Francois, J. F., and C. R. Shiells (1997) *Modeling Trade Policy: Applied General Equilibrium Assessments of North American Free Trade*, Cambridge University Press.

Francois, J. F., and G. Wignaraja (2008) "Economic Implications of Asian Integration," *Global Economy Journal*, 8:3, Article 1, https://doi.org/10.2202/1524-5861.1332.

Frankel, J. (2010) "The Estimated Trade Effects of the Euro: Why Are They Below Those from Historical Monetary Unions among Smaller Countries?," in A. Alesina and F. Giavazzi (eds.), *Europe and the Euro*, University of Chicago Press, 169–212.

Friedman, L. M. (2003) "NAFTA Rules of Origin," Barnes Richardson Global Trade Law, www.barnesrichardson.com.

García, E. C., M. N. Pabsdorf, and E. G. Herrera (2013) "The Gravity Model Analysis: An Application on Mercosur Trade Flows," *Journal of Economic Policy Reform*, 16:4, 336–48.

GATT Secretariat (1994) *The Results of the Uruguay Round of Multilateral Trade Negotiations: The Legal Text*, GATT Secretariat.

Gehlhar, M. J., T. W. Hertel, and W. Martin (1994) "Economic Growth and the Changing Structure of Trade and Production in the Pacific Rim," *American Journal of Agricultural Economics*, 76:5, 1101–10.

Gil, S., R. Llorca, and J. A. Martíniz-Serrano (2008) "Assessing the Enlargement and Deepening of the European Union," *World Economy*, 31:9, 1253–72.

Harrison, G. W., T. F. Rutherford, and D. G. Tarr (2003) "Rules of Thumb for Evaluating Preferential Trading Arrangements: Evidence from CGE Assessments," *Cuadernos de Economia*, 40:121, 460–8

Hufbauer, G. C. (ed.) (1990) *Europe 1992: An American Perspective*, Brookings Institution.

Hufbauer, G. C., and J. J. Schott (2005) *NAFTA Revisited: Achievements and Challenges*, Institute for International Economics.

Kawai, M., and K. Naknoi (2017) "ASEAN's Trade and Foreign Direct Investment: Long-Term Challenges for Economic Integration," *Singapore Economic Review*, 62:3, 643–80.

Krishna, K. (2009) "Rules of Origin," in K. A. Reinert, R. S. Rajan, A. J. Glass, and L. S. Davis (eds.), *Princeton Encyclopedia of the World Economy*, Princeton University Press, 980–2.

Lawrence, R. (1991) "Emerging Regional Agreements: Building Blocks or Stumbling Blocks?," in R. O'Brien (ed.), *Finance and the International Economy*, Oxford University Press, 23–35.

Lindstrom, B. (2009) "Scaling Back TRIPS-Plus: An Analysis of Intellectual Property Provisions in Trade Agreements and Implications for Asia and the Pacific," *New York University Journal of International Law and Politics*, 42, 917–80.

McMillan, J. (1993) "Does Regional Integration Foster Open Trade? Economic Theory and GATT's Article XXIV," in K. Anderson and R. Blackhurst (eds.), *Regional Integration and the Global Trading System*, Harvester Wheatsheaf, 292–310.

Malamud, A. (2005) "Mercosur Turns 15: Between Rising Rhetoric and Declining Achievement," *Cambridge Review of International Affairs*, 18:3, 421–36.

Mansfield, E. O., and J. C. Pevehouse (2000) "Trade Blocs, Trade Flows, and International Conflict," *International Organization*, 54:4, 775–808.

Martin, P., and I. Sirkeci (2017) "Recruitment, Remittances, and Returns," in K. A. Reinert (ed.), *Handbook of Globalisation and Development*, Edward Elgar, 312–30.

Matsushita, M., T. J. Schoenbaum, P. C. Mavroidis, and M. Hahn (2015) *The World Trade Organization: Law, Practice, and Policy*, Oxford University Press.

Menon, J., and A. C. Melendez (2017) "Realizing an ASEAN Economic Community: Progress and Remaining Challenge," *Singapore Economic Review*, 62:3, 681–702.

Puyana, A. (2006) "Mexican Oil Policy and Energy Security within NAFTA," *International Journal of Political Economy*, 35:2, 72–97.

Ramirez, M. D. (2003) "Mexico under NAFTA: A Critical Assessment," *Quarterly Review of Economics and Finance*, 43:5, 863–92.

Ramirez, M. D. (2006) "Is Foreign Direct Investment Beneficial for Mexico? An Empirical Analysis," *World Development*, 43:5, 863–92.

Reid, M. (2002) "Mercosur: A Critical Overview," unpublished paper for Chatham House.

Reinert, K. A. (2007) "The European Union, the Doha Round, and Asia," *Asia Europe Journal*, 5:3, 317–30.

Reinert, K. A., and D. W. Roland-Holst (1998) "North–South Trade and Occupational Wages: Some Evidence from North America," *Review of International Economics*, 6:1, 74–89.

Reinert, K. A., and D. W. Roland-Holst (2001) "NAFTA and Industrial Pollution: Some General Equilibrium Estimates," *Journal of Economic Integration*, 16:2, 165–79.

Reuters (2019) "EU–Mercosur Trade Deal Could Be Ready by Late 2000 in Best Case," August 28.

Rivas-Campo, J. A., and R. T. Juk Benke (2003) "FTAA Negotiations: Short Overview," *Journal of International Economic Law*, 6:3, 661–94.

Ruffin, R. J. (1999) "The Nature and Significance of Intra-Industry Trade," *Federal Reserve Bank of Dallas Economic and Financial Review*, 1999:4, 2–9.

Sapir, A. (1992) "Regional Integration in Europe," *Economic Journal*, 102:415, 1491–506.

Sauvé, P., and A. Shingal (2011) "Reflections on the Preferential Liberalization of Services Trade," *Journal of World Trade*, 45:5, 953–63.

Schiff, M., and L. A. Winters (2003) *Regional Integration and Development*, World Bank.

Serra, J., G. Aguilar, J. Córdoba, G. Grossman, C. Hills, J. Jackson, J. Katz, P. Noyola, and M. Wilson (1997) *Reflections on Regionalism: Report of the Study Group on International Trade*, Carnegie Endowment for International Peace.

Tarr, D. G. (2009) "Customs Unions," in K. A. Reinert, R. S. Rajan, A. J. Glass, and L. S. Davis (eds.), *Princeton Encyclopedia of the World Economy*, Princeton University Press, 256–9.

Tongzon, J. L. (2009) "Association of Southeast Asian Nations," in K. A. Reinert, R. S. Rajan, A. J. Glass, and L. S. Davis (eds.), *Princeton Encyclopedia of the World Economy*, Princeton University Press, 87–9.

Tsoukalis, L. (1997) *The New European Economy Revisited*, Oxford University Press.

Viner, J. (1950) *The Customs Union Issue*, Carnegie Endowment for International Peace.

Winters, L. A. (1993) "The European Community: A Case of Successful Integration?," in J. de Melo and A. Panagariya (eds.), *New Dimensions in Regional Integration*, Cambridge University Press, 202–28.

PART II
International Production

10 Multinational Enterprises and Foreign Direct Investment

In Chapters 3 and 4, we discussed the motorcycle market in Vietnam. We saw that the considerations of comparative advantage suggested that Japan would export motorcycles to the Vietnamese market while importing rice. Indeed, beginning in the 1990s exports of Japanese motorcycles to Vietnam began to increase significantly. The companies involved were Honda, Suzuki, and Yamaha, but the favorite motorcycle in Vietnam at that time was Honda. Indeed, Tiep (2007: 302) notes: "For a long period of time, Honda had become a common name for every motorcycle. Whenever someone saw a motorcycle, he called it 'Honda.'" In 1997, however, Honda began to produce motorcycles *in Vietnam itself*. This is not a possibility that we considered in Chapters 3 and 4. In those chapters, we implicitly assumed that there was only one means by which Japanese motorcycle manufactures could serve the Vietnamese market, namely exporting. In practice, however, other means are available. As we begin to examine these other means, we move from the exclusive realm of trade to that of **international production**, the subject of Part II of this book. We also shift our analytical focus from *countries* to *firms*.

As we will see, exports are one possibility in a menu of options by which a firm can serve a foreign market. Another broad option is **contracting** a foreign firm to carry out production in that country. A third broad option is **foreign direct investment**. FDI involves the holding of at least 10 percent of the shares in a foreign productive enterprise, considered to be a threshold indicating management influence. In this chapter, we will evaluate these three types of **foreign market entry**: exporting, contracting, and FDI. We will identify a set of *motivations* for international production and consider the entry mode choice decision. Then we will consider patterns of FDI in the global economy from the perspectives of both flows and stocks. Finally, we will consider a few specific aspects of FDI and multinational enterprises, namely MNE organizational design, the home base, joint ventures, and research and development.

Foreign Market Entry

A fundamental aspect of the globalization of business is that firms need to decide about foreign market entry: how they will place their products in foreign markets. As it turns out, there is a *menu* of ways in which firms can do this. This menu of options is presented in Table 10.1. As indicated in this table, there are *three broad categories* of entry: exporting, contractual, and investment.

Table 10.1 The foreign market entry menu

Category	Mode	Characteristics
Domestic	None	The home-country firm is a purely domestic firm relying solely on its home market for sales.
Exporting	Indirect exporting	The home-country firm relies on another firm, known as a sales agent or trading company, to complete the export transaction.
Exporting	Direct exporting	The home-country firm takes on the export transaction itself.
Contractual	Subcontracting	The home-country firm contracts with a foreign firm to produce a product to certain specifications (materials, processes, and quality). Also known as outsourcing and contract manufacturing.
Contractual	Licensing	The home-country firm licenses a foreign firm to allow it to use the home-country firm's production process (including logos, trade-marks, designs, and branding) in the foreign country.
Contractual	Franchising	The home-country firm licenses a foreign firm to allow it to use the home-country firm's production process in the foreign country but exerts more control over production and marketing to ensure consistency across foreign markets. The home-country firm also provides assistance to the foreign firm to ensure this consistency.
Investment	Joint venture (JV)	The home-country firm establishes a separate firm in the foreign country that is jointly owned with a foreign-country firm.
Investment	Mergers and acquisitions (M&As)	The home-country firm buys part (merger) or all (acquisition) of the shares of an already existing production facility in the foreign country.
Investment	Greenfield investment	The home-country firm establishes a brand new production facility in the foreign country that it fully owns.

Source: Based on Hill (2009) and Root (1998).

We begin considering a purely *domestic*, home-country firm. The entire sales of this firm are within its home-country base. What kind of foreign market entry strategy does this type of firm have? None at all. This is actually not at all unusual. In many countries, only a small fraction of firms thinks of foreign market entry even by the standard process of exporting.[1] But let us consider what happens when they do consider such options.

Exporting

How can the home-country firm begin its exporting activity? As suggested in Table 10.1, there are two basic approaches. If the firm has little experience with and knowledge of international trade, it might first enter foreign markets in an *indirect exporting* mode. Here it relies on another firm, known as a sales agent or trading company, to complete the export transaction.[2] This indirect mode of exporting can give the firm some limited experience with foreign market entry. Alternatively, given this experience, it can begin to make a commitment to a *direct exporting* mode. In this case, the firm undertakes the export transaction itself, namely the research, marketing, finance, and logistics requirements of the trade transaction. Despite these extra costs, there might be offsetting advantage for the firm in being able to develop and manage its own foreign market entry strategy.

Contractual

It is possible that our firm might grow dissatisfied with the exporting mode and wish to actually *produce* abroad. The firm might be motivated by the perceived need to engage in some final product finishing, service, or sales to address local demand conditions in an export market. Or it might simply need to engage in some trade-related services itself in that country.[3] Lack of experience in global production might make it wary of carrying out production itself in the foreign market, however. This would lead the firm to the *contractual* modes of foreign market

---

[1] As Bernard et al. (2007) emphasize, the extra costs of exporting to foreign markets can confine exporting activity to a relatively small set of firms. For example, even within the tradable industries of the United States, only 15 percent of firms export.

[2] Hill (2009: 403) notes: "Today's trading companies provide market contacts, trade expertise, commercial financing, foreign distribution, and quality control for traded goods. They vary considerably in size and in sophistication from small, independent operations...to...general trading companies."

[3] As Dunning and Lundan (2008: 217) state, "Where a market has to be created for a product, where the product needs to be adapted to the requirements of the local buyers, where multiple products are being marketed and there are net benefits to coordinating the sales of these products, or where an efficient after-sales usage, repair and maintenance service is a key ingredient of the product's appeal, a firm may decide that the risk that a foreign sales agent will not adequately meet its needs is likely to outweigh any setting up cost of marketing and distributing facilities from the start."

entry listed in Table 10.1. The key characteristic of contractual entry modes is that the relationships involved are arm's-length market-based relationships, not ones of ownership.

We can distinguish between at least three types of contractual foreign market entry. These are *subcontracting*, *licensing*, and *franchising*. The simplest of these is subcontracting, also known as foreign outsourcing and contract manufacturing.[4] Here the home-country firm contracts with a foreign firm to produce a product to certain specifications (materials, processes, and quality). This form of international production, though not new, has become increasingly important over time. Indeed, it is so significant in some sectors (e.g. clothing and electronics) that there are now contract manufacturing organizations (CMOs) that have evolved to facilitate the activity.

Consider the case of the Japanese firm Uniqlo, one of the world's largest clothing retailers. Its international production occurs via contract manufacturing relationships with approximately 70 other Asian firms, mostly in China. These relationships are managed by Uniqlo's international production management division. Interestingly, the contract manufacturers are not exclusive to Uniqlo. They supply other firms as well. So Uniqlo is a clothing company that does not produce any clothing itself. The core of the firm focuses on R&D (materials development), design, marketing, and retailing.[5]

In the licensing case, the home-country firm sells a license to a foreign firm to allow it to use the home-country firm's production process. This could include use of logos, trademarks, designs, and branding. In return, the foreign firm would pay royalties to the home-country firm for the license rights. In some cases, technology features prominently in decisions with regard to licensing. This is because, given the nature of the firm, the resulting licensing agreement is largely about licensed technology. This puts the firm in the realm of what is known as *technology licensing agreements*, on which a great deal of research has taken place. The key issue with technology licensing agreements is that there is always a danger that the home-country firm might lose aspects of the licensed technology to the foreign firm. We will return to this issue below.[6]

In the franchising case, the home-country firm licenses a foreign firm to allow it to use the home-country firm's production process in the foreign country but

---

[4] There is an important terminological point here. *Offshoring* generally refers to moving production to a foreign country but *retaining ownership*, and therefore belongs in the *investment* mode. *Outsourcing* or *foreign outsourcing* refers to moving production to a foreign country but *relinquishing ownership* through a contractual relationship, and therefore belongs in the *contract* mode. See Feenstra and Jensen (2009). In practice, not everyone is careful with these terms.

[5] For an analysis of contracting relationships in the Uniqlo case, see Usui, Kotabe, and Murray (2017).

[6] For a thorough review of technology licensing issues, see Caves (2007: chap. 7).

exerts more control over production and marketing to ensure consistency across foreign markets. The home-country firm also provides assistance to the foreign firm to ensure this consistency. Franchising arrangements are more common in service and retail firms than in manufacturing, and many of us are familiar with this type of mode through international hotel and restaurant chains.

Investment

Contracting is not the only way to produce abroad. The home-country firm can also engage in foreign direct investment, and thereby become a multinational enterprise. As listed in Table 10.1, there are three modes of FDI to consider. These are *joint venture*, *mergers and acquisitions*, and *greenfield investment*. In a JV, the home-country firm establishes a separate firm in the foreign country that is jointly owned with a foreign-country firm. Sometimes a JV is required by a foreign host country, while in other instances a home-country firm will enter into a JV willingly in order to tap into the local assets of the foreign partner. These local assets might include local market knowledge, existing production facilities, and knowledge of the local regulatory environment. We will consider JVs in more detail below.

The second way of engaging in FDI is through M&As. Here the home-country firm buys part (merger) or all (acquisition) of the shares of an already existing production facility in the foreign country. As has been pointed out by many observers, M&As have been the most common means of FDI. For example, Dicken (2007: 116) states that the M&A vehicle "offers the attraction of an already functioning business compared with the more difficult, and possibly more risky, method of starting a firm from scratch in an unfamiliar environment." Interestingly, though, cross-border M&A activity is somewhat volatile and characterized by waves.

The third means of engaging in FDI is through greenfield investment: starting a subsidiary from scratch. Here the home-country firm establishes a brand new production facility in the foreign country that it *fully owns*. This is, clearly, the investment option that requires the most commitment on part of the home-country firm but one that offers this firm the most control over the foreign-based production facility.[7]

In the case of Honda in Vietnam, it hoped to move from a direct exporting mode of foreign market entry to a greenfield investment mode with a wholly owned factory. The Vietnamese government prevented Honda from pursuing this strategy, however, and required that it enter the market as a JV with a Vietnamese firm. As

---

[7] Whereas, in the past, M&As were the most common form of FDI, greenfield investment is now the dominant FDI mode. See, for example, Anyanwu (2017).

a result, Honda Vietnam is only 70 percent owned by Honda. The Vietnam Engine and Agricultural Machinery Corporation (VEAM) owns the remaining 30 percent. This JV was established in 1997 outside Hanoi, producing the Super Dream motorcycle. It began producing the Future motorcycle in 1999 and the Wave Alpha motorcycle in 2001. It now produces a large array of motorcycle brands, as well as some automobiles.

An important insight to be gained from Table 10.1 is that achieving market entry involves the firm incurring various sorts of *costs*. This insight is largely left out of the trade framework of Part I of this book. It is partly for this reason that the field of international production is often cast in terms of what is known as *transactions costs*. This perspective emphasizes the empirical reality that foreign market entry is *not free*.[8]

A final point with regard to international production is something that we mentioned in Chapter 1, namely the extent to which it is supported by information and communication technology. Other than in services, this is known as **flexible manufacturing**. Consider, for example, this description of flexible manufacturing by Dicken (2007: 96, emphasis in original):

> The key to production flexibility in today's world lies in the use of *information technologies* in machines and operations. These permit more sophisticated control over the production process. With the increasing sophistication of automated processes and, especially, the new flexibility of electronically controlled technology, far-reaching changes in the process of production need not necessarily be associated with increased scale of production. Indeed, one of the major results of the new electronic and computer-aided production technology is that it permits rapid switching from one part of a production process to another and allows...the tailoring of production to the requirements of individual customers.

This is one of the many ways that ICT supports the processes of economic globalization.[9]

Motivations for International Production

Now that we have a sense of the means by which firms engage in international production, the next step is to say something about the *motivations* for these activities. Two central motivations that have emerged from international business research are *resource seeking* and *market seeking*. We consider each in turn.

---

[8] See, for example, Zhao, Luo, and Suh (2004).

[9] For more on this, see Baldwin (2016: chap. 3).

A primary motivation for international production is **resource seeking**. Here, the home-country firm is trying to gain access to certain resources in a foreign country. The resources involved could be natural resources, such as minerals or timber, as well as human resources, such as inexpensive or specially trained labor. Despite the continued relevance of resource seeking as a motivation for international production, the gradual shift over time away from resource-seeking international production is one of the most important aspects of the history of MNEs. In the current era, therefore, the use of a simple mental model in which MNEs locate production solely on the basis of wage considerations is incomplete. Indeed, in high-technology sectors, firms are often seeking expensive, highly trained labor markets in costly cities.[10]

A second, growing reason for international production is **market seeking**. A number of considerations can be active here. First, international production might be necessary to adapt and tailor products to local needs. Second, international production might be required to effectively deliver a product, as is the case for many financial services. Third, international production might be required for a firm supplying intermediate products to another firm opening up operations in a foreign country. For example, Japanese auto parts firms often follow Japanese auto companies to Europe and the United States. Finally, firms may simply locate where they expect demand to grow in the future. This certainly has been the case in China, where, despite losses, many foreign firms maintain at least small operations.[11]

Along with the two central motivations for international production, resource seeking and market seeking, there are two subsidiary motivations. One of these is **efficiency seeking**. As expressed by Dunning and Lundan (2008: 72), the concern here "is to rationalize the structure of established resource-based or market-seeking investment in such a way that the investing company can gain from the common governance of geographically dispersed activities." These efficiencies may stem from economies of scale, economies of scope, or a concept we will discuss in the next chapter called *firm-level economies*. The efficiency-seeking motivation is most important for large, mature MNEs with a great deal of international experience.

The next subsidiary motivation is **strategic asset seeking**. This motivation can be quite important for M&As in the current era but can also be difficult to

---

[10] This point has been made by Moretti (2012).

[11] A deputy chairman of a Malaysian conglomerate stated, "You cannot not be there" (*The Economist*, 1997). The reason for this statement was the anticipated growth of the market. With the perspective of more than another decade's experience, however, it became clear that the lure of the Chinese market disappointed many firms. See *The Economist* (2009), which notes: "Corruption, protectionism and red tape hamper foreigners in all fields" (73).

comprehend. Strategic-asset-seeking behavior tends to be part of the *strategic game* between competitors in oligopolistic sectors. Dunning and Lundan (2008: 73) describe a number of illustrative alternatives:[12]

> One company may acquire or engage in a collaborative alliance with another to thwart a competitor from so doing. Another might merge with one of its foreign rivals to strengthen their joint capabilities *vis à vis* a more powerful rival. A third might acquire a group of suppliers to corner the market for a particular raw material. A fourth might seek to gain access over distribution outlets to better promote its own brand of products. A fifth might buy out a firm producing a complementary range of goods or services so it can offer its customers a more diversified range of products. A sixth might join forces with a local firm in the belief that it is in a better position to secure contracts from the host government, which are denied to its exporting competitors.

It is important to appreciate that these four motivations are *not exclusive* of each other. More than one may be relevant for a given MNE.

Entry Mode Choice

As we have seen in the above discussion, Table 10.1 identifies exporting, contractual, and investment as three categories of foreign market entry mode choice. What prompts a firm to choose one category over another? It turns out that the answer to this question is not as straightforward as we might wish. Both international economists and international business researchers would like to be able to effectively capture all the relevant factors affecting firms' foreign market entry decision-making process—that is, they would like to accurately explain and predict firms' choices between the entry possibilities of Table 10.1. As it turns out, however, a fully satisfying explanation for this process has proved to be elusive. Instead, we have to make do with a *set of possible explanations*, each with its own relevance.

From a purely economic point of view, we can begin with the observation that a firm will choose the entry mode that will provide it with the greatest risk-adjusted or expected return on the entry investment.[13] Although this statement in itself is

---

[12] To take one example, in the 1990s the US-based MNE Kodak established a film sales affiliate in Japan called Nagase. As noted by Baron (1997), its motivation was to *attack the profit sanctuary* of the Japanese film company Fujifilm. For Kodak, Nagase was a strategic asset. Along with explaining some types of FDI, strategic-asset-seeking behavior also helps to explain some *non*-FDI activities of MNEs, especially strategic alliances, which do not involve the exchange of equity.

[13] We will make a similar statement about the purely economic point of view on the migration decision in Chapter 13.

accurate, it is not entirely helpful, because it does not specify the types or magnitudes of risks involved nor how returns would differ between the mode choices. Consequently, we need to take a slightly more applied approach, and there are a few of these we can consider.

The first approach to foreign market entry is the *sequential approach*, and it focuses on the firm's learning process.[14] The foreign market itself as well as the entry process are largely unknown to the purely domestic home-country firm at the top of Table 10.1. This firm develops its understanding of the environment and proceeds by slowly moving down Table 10.1 in a sequential or evolutionary process, from indirect exporting to greenfield FDI. This approach makes some sense and captures some important features of the firm's decision-making process: learning is indeed important. Its limitation is that not all firms abide by it. Instead, they sometimes jump into foreign market entry modes farther down Table 10.1 rather than moving sequentially.[15]

Why might that be so? An answer can be found in a second approach to foreign market entry, namely the **firm-specific asset approach**. The term "firm-specific assets" refers to *tangible* and *intangible* resources that the firm owns and that contribute to its competitiveness over time. It might be a patent on particular technology, or it might be a corporate product brand. It could even be some aspect of corporate culture that allows a firm to be more productive. Whatever the asset's form, its presence is the result of the firm incurring costs to acquire it, and it provides the firm with value in enhancing its competitiveness.

It is worth noting that, among all the different types of firm-specific assets that can exist, **knowledge capital** can play a particularly important role. Of course, some knowledge is also embedded in individuals rather than firms, in the form of human capital, but a lot of knowledge is embedded in firms themselves. Indeed, one of the well-known models of FDI behavior is known as the *knowledge capital model*.[16] The presence of knowledge capital as an important firm-specific asset leads to the issue of **dissemination risk**. Dissemination risk refers to the possibility of a foreign firm obtaining knowledge capital of the home-country firm and

---

[14] It is also sometimes called the *evolutionary approach*.

[15] For example, Fima and Rugman (1996) examined the Upjohn pharmaceuticals company, and find that "Upjohn [used] multiple entry modes at the same time. This [provided] flexibility in an industry which is very dependent on political factors and is often dictated to by changes in host-government regulations" (211). Some firms also emerge with international scope right from the beginning. On this phenomenon of being "born global," see Gabrielsson et al. (2008).

[16] For an accessible review, see Urban (2009). For the larger role of knowledge capital in modern economies, see Haskel and Westlake (2017).

exploiting it for its own commercial advantage. This risk is especially prevalent in the licensing mode of entry.[17]

Given the possibility of dissemination risk for knowledge-intensive firms, FDI can be a favored means of entry. It also requires a greater degree of resource commitment on the part of the potential MNE, however. The way in which issues of control, resource commitment, and dissemination risk affect the choice of foreign market entry mode can be appreciated using Table 10.2. Suppose a firm's most important concern was the degree of control over the production and marketing process. This would draw the firm towards an investment mode of foreign market entry based on a subsidiary obtained either through M&A or greenfield investment. Alternatively, if a firm were concerned only with limiting resource commitment to low levels, it would consider either trade or contractual modes of foreign market entry. Finally, if a firm were solely concerned with maintaining a low degree of dissemination risk, then either trade or investment via a subsidiary would be the preferred mode of entry. In most instances, firms have more than one primary concern, so the entry strategy is less than clear-cut.

Because of the role of dissemination risk in pushing firms towards adopting FDI as a market entry process, a robust correlation emerges between knowledge intensity and FDI. In fact, one of the most common predictors of FDI in any particular sector is its research and development spending. Recall from Chapter 1 that MNEs account for approximately three-fourths of worldwide civilian R&D. This is

Table 10.2 Factors influencing choice of foreign market entry mode

Mode	Degree of control	Level of resource commitment	Degree of dissemination risk
Trade	Low	Low	Low
Contractual	Low	Low	High
Investment: joint venture	Medium	Medium	Medium
Investment: M&A or greenfield	High	High	Low

Source: Adapted from Hill, Hwang, and Kim (1990)

[17] For example, Hill, Hwang, and Kim (1990: 119) state: "Unfortunately, if a (firm) grants a license to a foreign enterprise to use firm-specific know-how to manufacture or market a product, it runs the risk of the licensee, or an employee of the licensee, disseminating that know-how, or using it for purposes other than those originally intended. For example, RCA once licensed its color TV technology to a number of Japanese companies. The Japanese companies quickly assimilated RCA's technology and then used it to enter the US market."

not by chance. Indeed, as has been emphasized by Caves (2007), the relationship between MNEs and knowledge intensity is two-way. MNEs are most likely to form in knowledge-intensive sectors, but, once they do form, the network of subsidiaries in different countries helps the MNE to absorb and deploy new ideas more effectively than domestic firms. Consequently, MNEs find themselves at the center of global innovation. We will return to this issue below.

Patterns of FDI

Now that we understand the relationship of FDI to global production more generally, as well as the motivations for it, let us consider some patterns of FDI in the global economy. First recall Figure 1.3 from Chapter 1 on nominal FDI inflows to low-, middle-, and high-income countries. In examining that figure, we noted that the 1990s were characterized by a large surge of FDI inflows, mostly into high-income countries and partly reflecting an upturn in mergers and acquisitions activity. We also noted that the middle-income countries of the world are hosting a growing amount of FDI but that FDI inflows into low-income countries are very low and stagnant.

Let us now complement Figure 1.3 by breaking down nominal FDI inflows by region instead of income level. This is done in Figure 10.1, which takes a long view in terms of years. This allows us to see that something significant changed in the mid-1980s, namely that FDI inflows began to increase above the historical levels in the case of Europe and Central Asia and East Asia and the Pacific. The

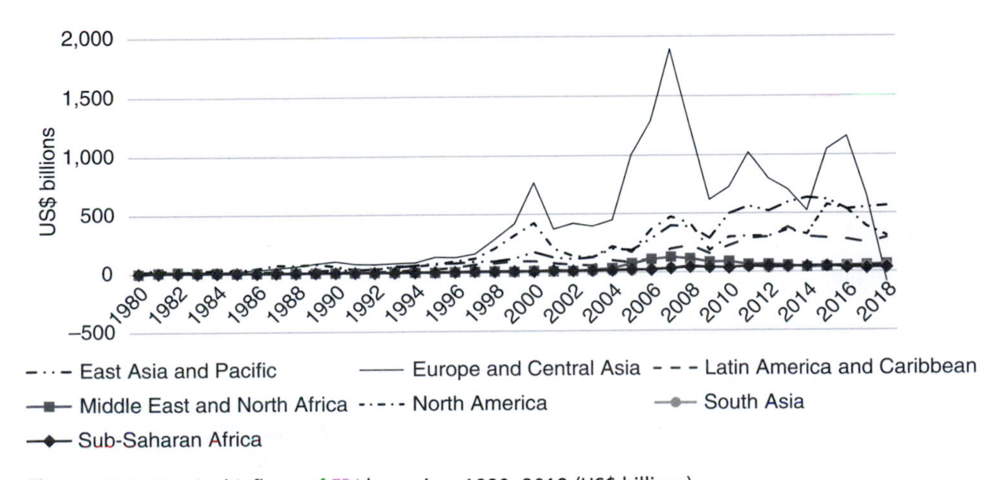

Figure 10.1 Nominal inflows of FDI by region, 1980–2018 (US$ billions)
Source: World Bank, World Development Indicators.

same thing happened in the case of Latin America and the Caribbean in the 1990s, to be followed by the Middle East and North Africa in the 2000s. South Asia and sub-Saharan Africa have not seen much FDI inflows at all by global standards. Also note that there can be some *volatility* to regional FDI inflows, most notably the collapse of the inflows to Europe and Central Asia during the 2008 global financial crisis.

Next let us shift the focus from annual flows to accumulated *stocks* of FDI.[18] We do this from two perspectives: outward stocks and inward stocks. Table 10.3 provides data on the leading *sources* of world FDI from the perspective of the owned, outward stocks. In 1980 the United States dominated global FDI, accounting for over 40 percent of total outward FDI stocks. This position in global outward stocks quickly declined to between 22 and 25 percent, depending on the decade. The United Kingdom, another historical source of much global FDI, experienced a similar decline. Germany, France, and Japan have held somewhat steady as sources of FDI over the decades considered in Table 10.3. An interesting, new development is the emergence of low- and middle-income countries as sources of FDI, up from only 3 percent in 1980 to over 20 percent in 2017. China accounted for 5 percent of this in 2017.[19] A further example, from South Africa, is given in the accompanying box.

Table 10.3 Leading sources of world FDI, 1980–2017 (percentage of global outward stocks)

Source	1980	1990	2000	2010	2017
United States	43	24	22	23	25
United Kingdom	16	13	15	8	5
Germany	8	8	9	7	5
France	4	6	7	6	5
Japan	4	11	5	4	5
China	0	0	0	2	5
Brazil	0	2	1	1	1
All developing	3	8	14	15	22

Sources: UNCTAD, *World Investment Reports*, various years.

[18] The distinction between flows and stocks is fundamental in economics. A flow is an amount per unit of time, whereas a stock is an amount in existence at a point in time. For example, your wage or salary is a flow, while your wealth (positive or negative) is a stock.

[19] Initially, this trend was known as the "rise of Third World multinationals," after Heenan and Keegan (1979). This trend initially reflected the fact that developing countries began to relax restrictions on FDI capital outflows.

SAB and the Emergence of a South African MNE

Many of us think of South Africa in terms of the transition from the apartheid regime. For beer drinkers worldwide, however, South Africa is an important country as the home base of an MNE in the brewing sector. Castle Breweries was founded in South Africa in 1895. It was listed as South Africa Breweries (SAB) on the Johannesburg Stock Exchange in 1897 and the London Stock Exchange a year later. In 1925 it acquired a stake in the British Schweppes beverage company. In 1964 it was granted the first license by the Irish brewery Guinness to produce outside Ireland.

SAB's foreign market entry process began in earnest in the 1990s. In 1993 it acquired breweries in Tanzania (Tanzania Breweries) and Hungary (Dreher). Further acquisitions were made in other African countries, as well as in Poland (Lech), Romania (Vultural, Ursus, and Pitber), Slovakia (Pivovar), Russia (Kaluga), the Czech Republic (Pilsner Urquell and Radegast), and China. In 2002, to the astonishment of beer drinkers in the United States, it acquired Miller brewers and became SABMiller. Further acquisitions followed in Italy (Birra Peroni) and Ukraine (Sarmat). For 2007 it ranked as the 78th largest non-financial MNE by foreign assets with a transnationality index of nearly 80 percent.

Drawing on a long-standing philanthropic tradition, in recent years the company has become quite active in HIV/AIDS and hunger in its South African home base. Consequently, both in commercial and human terms, SAB has made its mark in the global brewing industry.

Sources: sabmiller.com, *The Economist* (1995; 2006).

The others side of these trends can be seen in Table 10.4 on leading *destinations* of global FDI. Here, too, the United States plays an important role, currently with 25 percent of global inward *stocks*. The United Kingdom and China are also important destinations, currently each hosting 5 percent of global FDI. LMICs have played a relatively constant role hosting FDI, with approximately one-third of global inward stocks. Since LMICs appear significantly in both Tables 10.3 and 10.4, they are sometimes both the sources and the destinations of FDI, a phenomenon known as South–South FDI.[20] Measuring the actual extent of South–South FDI is imprecise, but all indications are that it is growing. It would be growing even more rapidly were it not for the remaining restrictions in LMICs on FDI capital flows.[21]

[20] See, for example, Gold et al. (2017). These authors note that South–South FDI can be helpful for both employment growth and technology transfer in the destination country.

[21] See *The Economist* (2018). We take up capital flows in some detail in Chapter 15.

Which are the current main players in the world of MNEs? We can get a sense of this by looking at the top 25 non-financial MNEs as measured by foreign assets in Table 10.5. Each MNE is assessed both by foreign assets and UNCTAD's transnationality index, or TNI. The TNI is an average of three ratios expressed in percentage terms: foreign assets to total assets, foreign sales to total sales, and foreign employment to total employment. We see here that this group of firms is dominated by firms from Western Europe, the United States, and Japan. Prominent sectors are mining, petroleum, food and beverages, motor vehicles, telecommunications, and utilities.

Table 10.4 Leading destinations of world FDI, 1980–2017 (percentage of global inward stocks)

Destination	1980	1990	2000	2010	2017
United States	16	20	22	17	25
United Kingdom	12	10	8	5	5
Germany	7	6	5	5	3
France	5	5	5	3	3
Japan	1	1	1	1	1
China	0	1	3	3	5
Brazil	3	2	2	3	2
All developing	26	27	30	30	33

Sources: UNCTAD, *World Investment Reports*, various years.

Table 10.5 The world's 25 largest non-financial MNEs, 2016

MNE	Home country	Sector	Total foreign assets (US$ billions)	Transnationality Index (TNI, percent)
Royal Dutch Shell	United Kingdom	Mining, quarrying, and petroleum	350	74.3
Toyota Motor Corporation	Japan	Motor vehicles	304	60.2
British Petroleum	United Kingdom	Petroleum refining and related	235	74.9
Total	France	Petroleum refining and related	233	80.9
Anheuser-Busch InBev	Belgium	Food and beverages	208	82.1
Volkswagen	Germany	Motor vehicles	197	60.3

Table 10.5 (cont.)

MNE	Home country	Sector	Total foreign assets (US$ billions)	Transnationality Index (TNI, percent)
Chevron	United States	Petroleum refining and related	189	57.9
General Electric	United States	Industrial and commercial machinery	179	56.8
Exxon	United States	Petroleum	166	52.1
Softbank	Japan	Telecommunications	146	62.5
Vodafone Group	United Kingdom	Telecommunication	144	81.4
Daimler	Germany	Motor vehicles	139	59.6
Honda	Japan	Motor vehicles	130	77.6
Apple	United States	Computer equipment	127	47.9
BHP Billiton	Australia	Mining, quarrying, and petroleum	119	79.1
Nissan	Japan	Motor vehicles	117	70.1
Siemens	Germany	Industrial and commercial machinery	115	65.9
Enel	Italy	Electricity, gas, and water	111	55.3
CK Hutchison Holdings	Hong Kong	Retail trade	110	84.5
Mitsubishi	Japan	Motor vehicles	108	62.4
Glencore Xstrata	Switzerland	Mining, quarrying, and petroleum	107	74.9
Telefonica	Spain	Telecommunications	107	78.5
Eni	Italy	Petroleum refining and related	106	58.2
Nestle	Switzerland	Food and beverages	106	92.5
BMW	Germany	Motor vehicles	106	56.1

Note: UNCTAD calculates the TNI using three ratio measures: foreign assets to total assets, foreign sales to total sales, and foreign employment to total employment.

Source: UNCTAD (2017).

MNE Organizational Design

As we will discuss further in Chapter 11 on global **value chains**, MNEs face the twofold decision as to what *tasks* in which *countries* to include within their corporate boundaries. Consequently, MNE management involves the consideration of how to organize the MNE itself. As it turns out, the issue of MNE design is not straightforward. Before the process of foreign market entry (domestic firms in Table 10.1), the firm might consist of *functional divisions* (management, finance, research and development, production, sales) all reporting to the head office or chief executive. This is shown in Table 10.6 as the single-product, single-country firm. With foreign market entry via FDI, the question arises as to what functions to locate abroad: just production and sales, or more? Initially, it might be just production and sales occurring in a *foreign division*, but, as foreign operations develop and mature, there is a tendency to locate a greater number of corporate functions abroad. The MNE moves beyond the "Single product, few countries" row of Table 10.6.

As global presence increases, pressures build on the foreign division. It has more countries and functions to look after, and, eventually, something needs to give way. As noted by Caves (2007: 79), "A single international division is seldom used if the firm makes 40 percent or more of its sales abroad." One option that is generically associated with single-product, multi-country MNEs is that of *country/regional divisions*, whereby each country or region covered by the MNE has its own division responsible for all functions. Another option that is generically associated with multi-product but few-country MNEs is that of *product divisions*, whereby each of the firm's products has its own corporate division for global production and sales. The most complicated but relevant generic case is that of the multi-product, multi-country MNE. Here, a standard approach is that of *matrix management*, whereby there are both product and country/regional dimensions to reporting lines.[22]

Table 10.6 Generic types of MNE organizational design

MNE characteristics	MNE intra-firm design
Single product, single country	Functional divisions
Single product, few countries	Single, foreign division
Single product, multi-country	Country/regional divisions
Multi-product, few countries	Product divisions
Multi-product, multi-country	Mixed structure based on matrix management or "heterarchy"

[22] The problems of matrix management are summarized by Dunning and Lundan (2008: 248), who state that, "because it is made for a more intensive network of intra-firm communication, the matrix structure created its own organizational challenges, notably those that arose from ambiguities over the locus of management responsibility, and a conflict of goals and strategies of the members of the network."

If we generalize a little from the generic types of organizational design listed in Table 10.6, we can identify *two general tendencies*. First, the narrower the range of its products, the more likely the MNE is to adopt a country/region divisional structure. Second, the wider the range of its products, the more likely the MNE is to adopt a product divisional structure.[23] These are rather limited statements, and the truth of the matter is that there is no complete set of principles that can guide MNE organizational design. Consequently, a last option has emerged that is also mentioned at the bottom of Table 10.6: that of *heterarchy*. Heterarchy involves information sharing and informal ways of circumventing the limitations of formal organizational design. This approach involves a number of different elements, including subsidiary differentiation, the use of multiple methods of coordination, including intra-firm social networks, and the creative use of human resource development.[24]

The End of Corporate Imperialism?

Prahalad and Lieberthal (2008) emphasize the growing importance of a few large, emerging markets to MNEs' long-term corporate strategy. The countries they have in mind are the likes of Brazil, China, India, and Indonesia. They warn against what they term the "imperialist mind-set" of many MNE executives, in which these large emerging markets are just seen as an extension of their operations in their Western home bases. Instead, these researchers emphasize that the bulk of the household markets in these economies have relatively low incomes, and that this has an impact on the preferences of the households. In addition, local responsiveness needs to consider relationships to suppliers, distribution system design, and the political environments. In the view of Prahalad and Lieberthal, MNEs need to rethink their approach to product design, distribution system, supplier relationships, and personnel policies.

One area of challenge is the role of MNEs' expatriate managers. For example, Prahalad and Lieberthal (2008: 30) state: "In the early stages of market development, expatriates are the conduits for information flow between the multinational's corporate office and the local operation. But while headquarters staffs usually recognize the importance of sending information to the local operation, they tend to be less aware that information must also be received from the other direction." Lines of communication can be very complicated. Reporting on an

[23] See Dunning and Lundan (2008: chap. 8).

[24] This shift of thinking had many sources, but one important one was the work of Bartlett and Ghoshal (2002).

The End of Corporate Imperialism? (cont.)

expatriate MNE representative in China, these researchers state that, "as the head of his company's China effort, he has to coordinate with the company's regional headquarters in Japan, report to international headquarters in Europe, and maintain close contact with corporate headquarters in North America" (37–8). This is the practical difficulty of "heterarchy."

These management issues become all the more acute as the emerging markets themselves are no longer just destinations for innovations occurring in the corporate headquarters but sources of innovation in themselves. The authors emphasize that "the imperialist assumption that innovation comes from the center will gradually fade away and die" (45). Product development innovations will start to flow from the periphery to the center instead. Prahalad and Lieberthal warn that "success in the big emerging markets will surely change the shape of the modern multinational as we know it today" (43).

The Economist (2010) takes this argument one stage further, stating that developing countries "are reinventing systems of production and distribution, and they are experimenting with entirely new business models. All the elements of modern business, from supply-chain management to recruitment and retention, are being re-jigged or reinvented in one emerging market or another." Western MNEs should take note.

Sources: Prahalad and Lieberthal (2008) and *The Economist* (2010).

The Home Base

In very rare instances, MNEs are "born global," with operations distributed across countries.[25] But, in the vast majority of cases, MNEs start in one country or another in what is known as the **home base**. In many cases, home bases account for nearly one-half of total MNE operations and sales, so the home base is often much more than a convenient address. Let us consider this further.

The home base of an MNE is almost always the location of its *corporate headquarters*.[26] Although the role of headquarters can vary from one MNE to another, there are a few generalizations we can make about them. There is a tendency for certain functions in the MNE to be centralized within the headquarters in the home base. These functions include finance, corporate control, and R&D. Production,

[25] See Gabrielsson et al. (2008).

[26] For a review of corporate headquarters, see Young et al. (2000).

marketing and sales, on the other hand, tend to be disbursed outwards towards subsidiaries.

International business research has also explored the role of the home base in supporting MNE competitiveness. It is possible for these home bases to support the firm-specific assets that drive MNEs into international production. There is even the possibility that large groups of related firms, even competitors, will locate in a particular place in the form of a **cluster**.[27] This can occur because all the firms in a cluster want to draw from particular resources or factors, particularly certain types of human capital, but perhaps also infrastructure and local research institutions. They also want to share in knowledge.[28] One example of this is the biotech industry, with its clusters in Boston/Cambridge, the San Francisco Bay Area, and San Diego, all of which developed to access certain types of human capital.[29] One way of thinking about home base clusters is in terms of the economic concept of *agglomeration economies*, which suggests that there can be a set of positive externalities accruing to a set of firms that co-locate in a particular urban area.[30]

Sometimes these considerations can even cause an MNE to effectively *change its home base*. Ericsson is a Swedish telecommunications MNE that had its formal home base in Stockholm. But it has been increasing its presence in the San Francisco Bay Area, with an increasing number of facilities there. In 2014 Ericsson's chief human resources officer and senior vice president said: "Ericsson's expansion in Silicon Valley has grown in tandem with the region's increasing gravitational pull on the technology sector. Our company has a growing need for software engineers and employees with a technology savvy skill set who can partner, create, learn, sustain and innovate; helping us move toward what Ericsson calls the Networked Society." This senior vice president subsequently relocated to the Bay Area.[31]

---

[27] This is the argument made, for example, by Porter (1990: 1), who asks the question: "Why are firms based in a particular nation able to create and sustain competitive advantage against the world's best competitors in a particular field?" Malmberg, Sölvell, and Zander (1996) define a spatial cluster as "a set of interlinked firms/activities that exist in the same local and regional milieu, defined as to encompass economic, social, cultural and institutional factors" (91).

[28] As emphasized by Kogut and Zander (1992), much productive knowledge cannot be codified into explicit forms. Rather, this *tacit knowledge* must be communicated via a social process of face-to-face interaction over a relatively long period of time.

[29] See, for example, Zucker, Darby, and Armstrong (2002).

[30] Baldwin (2016: 187) states that "technically, when the spatial concentration of economic activity creates forces that encourage further spatial concentration, we call these agglomeration forces." For example, Moretti (2012: 124, emphasis in original) states: "As it turns out, in the world of innovation, productivity and creativity can outweigh labor and real estate costs. [There can be] three important competitive advantages [to a] location, which economists refer to collectively as the *forces of agglomeration*: thick labor markets (that is, places where there is a good choice of skilled workers trained in a specific field), the presence of specialized service providers, and, most important, knowledge spillovers."

[31] See www.ericsson.com/en/press-releases/2014/5/ericsson-to-grow-silicon-valley-presence-with-new-campus.

The role of the home base in MNE operations is something that corporate strategists and international business researchers will be exploring for a long time. It is an important part of the ways that MNEs function in and impact the global economy via patterns of international production.

Joint Ventures

Table 10.1 listed three types of FDI, namely joint ventures, mergers and acquisitions, and greenfield, noting that M&As have been the most common type. It is worthwhile to spend some time examining JVs, because they pose a set of challenges not generally encountered in M&A and greenfield FDI. Recall that, in a JV, the home-country firm establishes a separate firm in the foreign country that is jointly owned with a foreign-country firm. Sometimes this is simply because the host-country government requires this to be the case. Other times the firms involved find that they have complementary "firm-specific assets" that they would like to combine.[32] JVs also occur in large, resource extraction FDI projects when both firms are interested in risk sharing and achieving large-scale economies.

Despite advantages in some circumstances, JVs are notoriously unstable and relatively short-lived.[33] This is because of the difficulty of managing two firms together, clashes of organizational culture, and clashes of national culture. This is probably why Hill (2009) reports that successful JVs usually involve up to two years of preliminary negotiations in the areas of technology transfer, asset valuation, divisions of management responsibility, financial policy, and strategic objectives. Ironically, cultural distance is one additional reason why JVs are considered in the first place. The home-country firm might not feel confident enough to execute an M&A when cultural differences loom large and therefore opt for a JV to lessen resource exposure and engage in cultural learning. Indeed, the JV irony is even larger than that. They tend to form because of differences between the firms involved, but these very differences make them difficult to manage. A classic case of JV mishaps is considered in the box on Beijing Jeep.

---

[32] Raff (2009) summarizes this very well: "A joint venture is a mechanism for combining complementary assets owned by separate firms. These assets can be tangible, such as machinery and equipment, or intangible, such as technological know-how, production or marketing skills, brand names, and market-specific information" (714). A more extensive consideration can be found in Choi and Beamish (2004).

[33] Evidence on this goes far back, but one example is Park and Ungson (1997). For an early and important analysis of JVs, see Kogut (1988).

Beijing Jeep

In 1983 the American Motors Corporation (AMC) formed a *joint venture* with the Beijing Auto Works (BAW) to build a Chinese version of the Jeep. The joint venture was called the Beijing Jeep Company, Ltd., and it involved both AMC and BAW owning large shares of the company's equity. The negotiations leading up to the joint venture took years to complete, but the resulting agreement was "the first major manufacturing joint venture set up after China opened its doors to foreign investment" (Mann, 1997: 25). The most important consideration on the part of AMC in entering into the joint venture was the large and growing market for automobiles in China. As Mann explains, "Even those companies hoping to cut their production costs by manufacturing in China…were interested mainly because of the possibility of selling their output there. You could find cheap labor elsewhere in the world, but you couldn't find a billion consumers anywhere else" (53).

The Chinese have a saying: *Tong chuang yi meng*. It means "Same bed, different dreams." There was a large measure of this in the AMC/BAW relationship. Cultural conflict, financial difficulties, and opposing business interests plagued the operation from the start. To the disappointment of the Chinese, the Beijing Jeep Company actually did *not* make a Chinese version of the Jeep. Instead, it assembled American Jeep Cherokees from imported kits. To the disappointment of the Americans, finding the foreign exchange (US dollars) to pay for these kits was a serious problem. The Americans thought the Chinese workers were lazy; the Chinese had great difficulty respecting American executives who used foul language.

The Beijing Jeep Company is still operating, but in a new form. Chrysler bought AMC in 1987. In 1995, two decades after the start of the joint venture, a Chrysler executive commented: "Our Beijing Jeep is starting to be a halfway decent little company, but there are going to be lots of ups and down in China." Many different firms that have invested in China would probably concur with that last observation. As of 2005 the firm became known as the Beijing Benz-DaimlerChrysler Automotive Company. *Business Week* commented in 2007 on this new company, saying: "It's been a long road for Chrysler in China, and an equally challenging path lies before the company. But after years of wandering aimlessly in the Middle Kingdom, we can say the company has finally chosen a new direction and is moving with a renewed sense of purpose." Despite that upbeat assessment, Chrysler and Daimler Benz parted ways in 2007, with Chrysler being bought by Fiat. At present the China-based company is known simply as Beijing Benz and focuses on producing Mercedes brand automobiles.

Sources: Mann (1997) and Dunne (2007).

Research and Development

MNEs are central to research and development activities globally. For example, the 2017 European Union Industrial R&D Investment Scorecard reported that the R&D activities of the top 100 companies ranked by R&D expenditures accounted for more than half the total.[34] This shows that private R&D is *highly concentrated* among firms. It is also concentrated geographically, with the United States having accounted for approximately 40 percent of the total, the European Union with approximately 25 percent, Japan approximately 15 percent, and China less than 10 percent (but increasing rapidly).

Let us consider some specific firms from Table 10.5. Royal Dutch Shell spent approximately US$1 billion on R&D in 2016.[35] But that falls below the top automakers, with Volkswagen and Toyota spending approximately US$12 billion and US$9 billion, respectively, in that year. The computer equipment MNE Apple spent approximately US$8 billion, and the machinery manufacturer Siemens spent approximately US$5 billion.[36] What do these R&D levels compare to? The highest 2016 R&D expenditures by companies stood at approximately US$12 billion, by Amazon, Alphabet (Google), Intel, Samsung, Volkswagen, and Microsoft, with only Volkswagen having appeared in Table 10.5. This clearly shows that the top MNEs are also among the top firms in terms of R&D.

Let us also get a sense of scale at the country level. We do this in Figure 10.2, by combining four MNEs from Table 10.5 (Volkswagen, Toyota, Apple, and Siemens) with four countries (the Netherlands, Mexico, Denmark, and Chile). What we see here is that the R&D expenditures of MNEs can be on the *same order of magnitude* as some important countries. Given these magnitudes, where MNEs choose to locate their R&D is no small matter.

The way in which MNEs configure R&D within their GVCs matters enormously to global technological capabilities. There is a *tendency* to centralize R&D functions in the home-base country, or even in the corporate headquarters.[37] There is also movement towards locating particular aspects of R&D outside the home base, however. One factor behind this change has been the improvement in ICT discussed in Chapter 1, which allows for a more effective distribution of R&D across countries. A second reason was identified in the box above on the "end of

---

[34] See http://iri.jrc.ec.europa.eu/home/.

[35] See www.shell.com/energy-and-innovation/overcoming-technology-challenges/innovation-through-research-and-development.html.

[36] See www.strategyand.pwc.com/innovation1000#GlobalKeyFindingsTabs2.

[37] For example, some time ago UNCTAD (2005: 121) reported: "R&D is among the least internationalized segments of the [MNE's] value chain; production, marketing and other functions have moved abroad much more quickly."

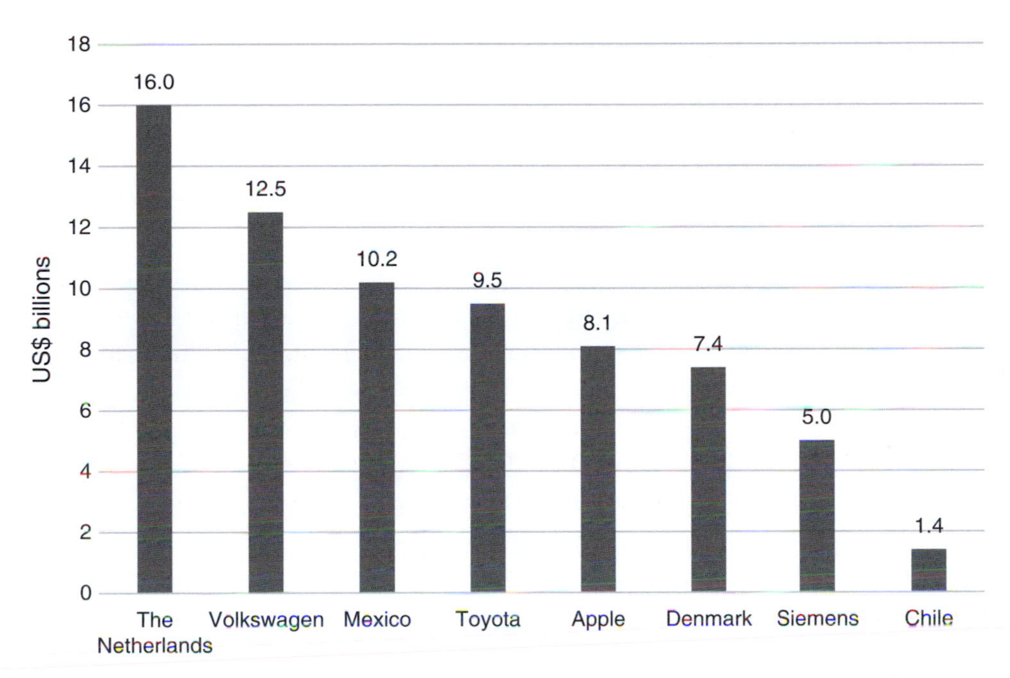

Figure 10.2 R&D expenditures of selected MNEs and countries, 2016 (US$ billions)
Sources: www.strategyand.pwc.com/innovation1000#GlobalKeyFindingsTabs2 and https://data.oecd.org/rd/gross-domestic-spending-on-r-d.htm.

corporate imperialism," namely the rise of emerging markets and the need to better tailor products to these markets.

A third reason, however, might be the most fundamental of all. As we have seen in Table 10.5, the list of largest MNEs in the world is dominated by firms from Western Europe, the United States, and Japan. But the talent and creativity for effective R&D is no longer confined to these three areas. To name just two countries, China and India have emerged as sources of scientific and engineering talent.[38] MNEs that want to tap into this talent can either recruit it by bringing it to their home bases and other R&D sites (the high-skilled migration possibility we will discuss in Chapter 13) or begin to relocate their R&D. Many MNEs have chosen to relocate some aspects of their R&D.

For example, Jaruzelski, Staack, and Chwalik (2017) report that "more and more companies look for talent outside their headquarters country and set up R&D centers close to their target markets. They have grown skilled at managing these distributed elements and are connecting them to a strong central R&D organization

[38] See, for example, Yusuf, Nabeshima, and Perkins (2006). As reported by Khurana (2006: 50), "Both China and India offer dramatic cost advantages of 30–60 percent, even after accounting for training and coordination costs."

while maintaining fluidity throughout the network." This new pattern of R&D is often in the form of *regional or support R&D facilities* that they link together in coordinated networks. These often focus on more applied research (the "D" in R&D), with basic research (the "R" in R&D) remaining in the home base.[39] The potential role of intellectual property in these changes is discussed in the accompanying box.

TRIPS and International Production

In Chapter 8, we considered the World Trade Organization's Agreement on Trade-Related Intellectual Property Rights (TRIPS) and noted that this was a new and powerful area of operation for the WTO. In this chapter, we have considered the three general modes of market entry (exporting, contractual, and FDI) and noted that the choice was influenced by dissemination risk and the role of firm-specific assets. One key type of firm-specific asset is *intellectual property*, so the question arises as to whether increased intellectual property protection might have an impact on the mode of international production.

There are many ambiguities involved in this issue, but one thing is clear: to the extent that increased protection of intellectual property occurs under the TRIPS with recourse to WTO dispute settlement, dissemination risk should decrease. As dissemination risk decreases, we should see a switch from FDI to contractual modes of entry, particularly that of licensing. We can say that TRIPS had a *switching effect* on international production.

In addition to the switching effect, there might also be a *volume effect*. In other words, increased intellectual property protection might increase the overall amount of international production through all modes: exporting, contractual, and FDI. In the case of exports, evidence suggests that stronger enforcement of intellectual property rights does lead to increased exporting overall. Two caveats to this result appear, however. The result is strongest for middle-income export destinations, for which the threat of dissemination risk is greater. In addition, the result is less strong for high-technology exports, for which FDI and licensing appear to be preferred modes of foreign market entry.

In the case of contracting, there also seems to be a volume effect that reinforces the switching effect. It is possible that this can have a positive impact on

[39] See, for example, Caves (2007: chap. 7) and the many references therein. In the words of Dicken (2007), the purpose of support laboratories is to "adapt parent company technology to the local market and to provide technical backup" (144), and *The Economist* (2010: 4) writes that "the world's biggest multinationals are becoming increasingly happy to do their research and development in emerging markets."

TRIPS and International Production (cont.)

technology transfer in the case of technology licenses, but this particular possibility needs further investigation and case studies.

For volume effects in the case of FDI, the results are more mixed. Intellectual property protection does seem to matter for FDI flows to middle-income countries, but less so for low-income countries. As Fink and Maskus (2005: 7) put it: "A poor country hoping to attract inward FDI would be better advised to improve its overall investment climate and business infrastructure than to strengthen its patent regime sharply, an action that would have little effect on its own."

Given the ongoing controversies regarding TRIPS, subsequent research on its impact on FDI was keenly awaited. Indeed, to cite just a few studies, there does seem to be evidence of increased intellectual property rights protection of FDI inflows in Asia in general (Hsu and Tiao, 2015), China in particular (Awokuse and Yin, 2010), and LMICs in general (Zhang and Yang, 2016). There is thus continuing evidence that TRIPS might play a significant role in promoting FDI.

Sources: Awokuse and Yin (2010), and Maskus (2005), Hsu and Tiao (2015), Nicholson (2007), and Zhang and Yang (2016).

Finally, there is an emerging concern about the role of increased nationalism on the trajectory of R&D among MNEs. Because the recent MNE innovation model relies on economic globalization of various types (if only in the form of high-skilled migration—to be discussed in Chapter 13), current interruptions to economic globalization (some of which are directly focused on migration) can compromise R&D efforts. For example, based on a survey of many MNEs, Jaruzelski, Staack and Chwalik (2017) conclude:

> Economic nationalism is motivated by a range of intentions, many of which continue to be debated. But it has an unanticipated consequence that has received less attention to date: as many politicians and policymakers in the world's major economic powers look inward, the realm of innovation has been thrown into uncertainty. The global innovation model long embraced by leading multinationals, one based on the free flow of information, money, and talent across borders, is at risk. The policies inspired by economic nationalism may prove self-defeating, in part by disrupting R&D activities for the new products and services that will generate the jobs, growth, and wealth of the future.

It is not clear that current proponents of economic nationalism are sufficiently aware of these negative impacts.

Conclusion

International trade is only one possible mode of foreign market entry. The other modes of contracting and investment take us into the realm of international production. The choice between trade, contracting, and investment depends on balancing considerations of control, resource commitment, and dissemination risk. The motivations for international production include resource seeking, market seeking, efficiency seeking, and strategic asset seeking.

In at least two important ways, our discussion in this chapter is very much incomplete. Being motivated to engage in international production does not mean that a firm can actually be *successful* in doing so. Indeed, a home-country firm faces *additional costs* in operating in a foreign country compared to foreign-country firms. For this reason, a home-country firm operating in a foreign country must have command over some sort of scarce resource that gives it an advantage over foreign firms. This is one issue we will take up in Chapter 11. Additionally, there can be tensions between host countries and MNEs. We take up this issue in Chapter 12.

In this chapter, we have made a significant change of perspective from *countries* to *firms*. This is a natural perspective for corporate strategists and international business researchers, but it is one that came somewhat late for economists, particularly trade economists. The reason for the shift was the significant changes in patterns of globalization that have taken place in the last few decades (since about 1990). For example, Baldwin (2016: 12) states: “With firms mixing and matching different nations’ sources of competitiveness, nations are no longer the only natural unit of analysis. Increasingly, the boundaries of competitiveness are controlled by firms who run international production networks.” Baldwin calls this pattern of competitiveness the “new globalization.” Indeed, he suggests that the new globalization applies competitive pressure even below the level of firms, to the level of *tasks*. This, he suggests, is “globalization with a finer degree of resolution” (169). We will begin to better understand these aspects of globalization in Chapter 11.

Review Exercises

1. Why should a firm move beyond trading relationships into international production? What is its motivation for doing so?
2. Suppose a firm’s competitiveness was based on its proprietary knowledge, perhaps in the form of a patent on a product or process. What can you say about its considerations with regard to foreign market entry?
3. In what ways have advances in information and communication technology made international production more common?

4. For each of the four motivations for international production, please provide an example. The more specific your example, the better.
5. Please use an internet search to identify a joint venture that is currently in operation. Can you gain some insight into the motivation for this JV?

FURTHER READING AND WEB RESOURCES

A recent review of foreign market entry is given in Hill (2009: chap. 9). One of the very first works on MNEs in international economics was Hymer (1976). Dunning and Lundan (2008: chap. 6) offer a very useful review of the historical rise of international production and multinational enterprises. Interesting books that place international production within the broader context of a changing world economy are Dicken (2007) and Baldwin (2016). Doremus et al. (1998) also offer a useful, thematically arranged bibliography, and Caves (2007) provides an economic analysis of MNEs. A review of the political economy of FDI is also given in Walter and Sen (2009: chap. 6). For a view of FDI and development, see Anyanwu (2017).

The United Nations Conference on Trade and Development publishes an annual *World Investment Report*. This is a good place to turn for data on and discussion of FDI in the world economy. The website is www.unctad.org, and the *World Investment Report* is at www.unctad.org/wir.

REFERENCES

Anyanwu, J. C. (2017) "Foreign Direct Investment," in K. A. Reinert (ed.), *Handbook of Globalisation and Development*, Edward Elgar, 131–52.

Awokuse, T. O., and H. Yin (2010) "Intellectual Property Rights Protection and the Surge of FDI in China," *Journal of Comparative Economics*, 38:2, 217–24.

Baldwin, R. (2016) *The Great Convergence: Information Technology and the New Globalization*, Harvard University Press.

Baron, D. P. (1997) "Integrated Strategy, Trade Policy, and Global Competition," *California Management Review*, 39:2, 145–69.

Bartlett, C. A., and S. Ghoshal (2002) *Managing across Borders: The Transnational Solution*, Harvard Business School Press.

Bernard, A. B., J. B. Jenson, S. J. Redding, and P. K. Schott (2007) "Firms in International Trade," *Journal of Economic Perspectives*, 21:3, 105–30.

Caves, R. E. (2007) *Multinational Enterprise and Economics Analysis*, Cambridge University Press.

Choi, C.-B., and P. W. Beamish (2004) "Split Management Control and International Joint Venture Performance," *Journal of International Business Studies*, 35:3, 201–15.

Dicken, P. (2007) *Global Shift: Mapping the Changing Contours of the World Economy*, Guilford.

Doremus, P. N., W. W. Keller, L. W. Pauly, and S. Reich (1998) *The Myth of the Global Corporation*, Princeton University Press.

Dunne, T. (2007) "Can Chrysler Rebound in China?," *Business Week*, November 2.

Dunning, J. H., and S. M. Lundan (2008) *Multinational Enterprises and the Global Economy*, Edward Elgar.

The Economist (1995) "Lion of Africa, Brewer to the People," September 9.

The Economist (1997) "The China Syndrome," June 21.

The Economist (2006) "South African Business: Going Global," July 15.

The Economist (2009) "Impenetrable: Selling Foreign Goods in China," October 17.

The Economist (2010) "The World Turned Upside Down," April 17.

The Economist (2018) "Going South: South–South Investment Is Rising Sharply," February 8.

Feenstra, R. C., and J. B. Jensen (2009) "Outsourcing/Offshoring," in K. A. Reinert, R. S. Rajan, A. J. Glass, and L. S. Davis (eds.), *The Princeton Encyclopedia of the World Economy*, Princeton University Press, 881–7.

Fima, E., and A. M. Rugman (1996) "A Test of Internalization Theory and Internationalization Theory: The Upjohn Company," *Management International Review*, 36:3, 199–213.

Gabrielsson, M., V. H. M. Kirpalani, P. Dimitratos, C. A. Solberg, and A. Zucchella (2008) "Born Globals: Propositions to Help Advance the Theory," *International Business Review*, 17:4, 385–401.

Gold, R., H. Görg, A. Hanley, and A. Seric (2017) "South–South FDI: Is It Really Different?," *Review of World Economics*, 153:4, 657–73.

Haskel, J., and S. Westlake (2017) *Capitalism without Capital: The Rise of the Intangible Economy*, Princeton University Press.

Heenan, D. A., and W. J. Keegan (1979) "The Rise of Third World Multinationals," *Harvard Business Review*, 57:1, 101–9.

Hill, C. W. L., P. Hwang, and W. C. Kim (1990) "An Eclectic Theory of the Choice of International Entry Mode," *Strategic Management Journal*, 11:2, 117–28.

Hill, J. S. (2009) *International Business: Managing Globalization*, Sage.

Hsu, J., and Y.-E. Tiao (2015) "Patent Rights Protection and Foreign Direct Investment in Asian Countries," *Economic Modelling*, 44, 1–6.

Hymer, S. H. (1976) *The International Operations of National Firms: A Study of Direct Foreign Investment*, MIT Press.

Jaruzelski, B., V. Staack and R. Chwalik (2017) "Will Stronger Borders Weaken Innovation?," *Strategy+Business*, 89, 1–16, www.strategy-business.com/feature/Will-Stronger-Borders-Weaken-Innovation.

Khurana, A. (2006) "Strategies for Global R&D," *Research Technology Management*, 49:2, 48–57.

Kogut, B. (1988) "Joint Ventures: Theoretical and Empirical Perspectives," *Strategic Management Journal*, 9:4, 319–32.

Kogut, B., and U. Zander (1992) "Knowledge of the Firm, Combinative Capabilities, and the Replication of Technology," *Organizational Science*, 3:3, 383–97.

Malmberg, A., Ö. Sölvell, and I. Zander (1996) "Spatial Clustering, Local Accumulation of Knowledge and Firm Competitiveness," *Geografiska Annaler*, 76B:2, 85–97.

Mann, J. (1997) *Beijing Jeep*, Westview Press.

Moretti, E. (2012) *The New Geography of Jobs*, Houghton Mifflin Harcourt.

Nicholson, M. W. (2007) "The Impact of Industry Characteristics and IPR Policy on Foreign Direct Investment," *Review of World Economics*, 143:1, 27–54.

Park, S. H., and G. R. Ungson (1997) "The Effect of National Culture, Organizational Complementarity, and Economic Motivation on Joint Venture Dissolution," *Academy of Management Journal*, 40:2, 279–307.

Porter, M. E. (1990) *The Competitive Advantage of Nations*, Free Press.

Prahalad, C. K., and K. Liberthal (2008) *The End of Corporate Imperialism*, Harvard Business Press.

Raff, H. (2009) "Joint Ventures," in K. A. Reinert, R. S. Rajan, A. J. Glass, and L. S. Davis (eds.), *The Princeton Encyclopedia of the World Economy*, Princeton University Press, 714–17.

Root, F. R. (1998) *Entry Strategy for International Markets*, Jossey-Bass.

Tiep, N. D. (2007) "The Honda Motorcycle Business in the Vietnamese Emerging Market," *International Journal of Emerging Markets*, 2:3, 298–309.

United Nations Conference on Trade and Development (2005) *World Investment Report 2005: Transnational Corporations and the Internationalization of R&D*, UNCTAD.

United Nations Conference on Trade and Development (2017) *World Investment Report 2017: Investment and the Digital Economy*, UNCTAD.

Urban, D. M. (2009) "Knowledge-Capital Model of the Multinational Enterprise," in K. A. Reinert, R. S. Rajan, A. J. Glass, and L. S. Davis (eds.), *The Princeton Encyclopedia of the World Economy*, Princeton University Press, 719–23.

Usui, T., M. Kotabe, and J. Y. Murray (2017) "A Dynamic Process of Building Global Supply Chain Competence by New Ventures: The Case of Uniqlo," *Journal of International Marketing*, 25:3, 1–20.

Walter, A., and G. Sen (2009) *Analyzing the Global Political Economy*, Princeton University Press.

Young, D., M. Goold, G. Blanc, R. Bühner, D. Collis, J. Eppink, T. Kagono, and C. Jiménez Seminario (2000) *Corporate Headquarters: An International Analysis of Their Roles and Staffing*, Pearson.

Yusuf, S., K. Nabeshima, and D. H. Perkins (2006) "China and India Reshape Industrial Geography," in S. Yusuf and L. A. Winters (eds.), *Dancing with the Giants: China, India and the Global Economy*, World Bank, 35–66.

Zhang, H., and X. Yang (2016) "Trade-Related Aspects of Intellectual Property Rights and the Upsurge in Foreign Direct Investment in Developing Countries," *Economic Analysis and Policy*, 50, 91–9.

Zhao, H., Y. Luo, and T. Suh (2004) "Transaction Cost Determinants and Ownership Entry Mode Choice: A Meta-Analytical Review," *Journal of International Business Studies*, 35:6, 524–44.

Zucker, L. G., M. R. Darby, and J. S. Armstrong (2002) "Commercializing Knowledge: University Science, Knowledge Capture, and Firm Performance in Biotechnology," *Management Science*, 48:1, 138–53.

11 Global Value Chains

As we saw in Chapter 1, one of the great drivers of economic globalization has been information and communication technology. At the center of ICT, in turn, we find the *semiconductor*. Semiconductors are the various devices and integrated circuits made using silicon that control the flow of electrical signals. These devices are included in personal computers, communications equipment (including mobile phones), audiovisual equipment, automobiles, and many other types of modern machinery. The manufacturing of semiconductors is a global industry, but one broken up into discrete *tasks* connected by a number of possible organizational forms, including contracting and foreign direct investment. The latter, as we will see, can involve intra-firm trade.[1]

In this chapter, we will introduce the basic frameworks of the **value chain**, as well as the **global value chain**.[2] We will use these frameworks to understand key concepts related to the FDI process, namely **firm-specific assets** and **internalization**. These will help us to further understand FDI and intra-firm trade. We will relate the internalization process to the standard cost analysis of microeconomics. We will introduce an integrative framework to understand GVCs in terms of task, location, and mode (TLM). Finally, we will consider the allocation of value added within GVCs and the implications of GVCs for trade policy.

GVCs are a central aspect not just of international production but also of economic globalization more broadly. Having a sense of them and their dynamics is therefore very important. The objective of this chapter is to give you this basic understanding.

Tasks and Value Chains

A clear understanding of international production within GVCs begins with an appreciation of *tasks*. Traditional trade theory, as considered in Part I of this book, is largely focused on sectors of production. In recent years, however, it has been

[1] Recall from Chapter 1 that approximately one-third of world trade takes place *within* MNEs in the form of intra-firm trade.

[2] Global value chains are also known as global production networks (GPNs). The GVC and GPN terms are, essentially, interchangeable.

recognized among trade theorists that the "action" of the global production and trading system has dropped down to a lower, more detailed level of economic activity.[3] These are tasks. Consider, for example, the following quote from Grossman and Rossi-Hansberg (2008: 1978):

> The nature of international trade is changing. For centuries, trade mostly entailed an exchange of goods. Now it increasingly involves bits of value being added in many different locations, or what might be called trade in tasks. Revolutionary advances in transportation and communications technology have weakened the link between labor specialization and geographic concentration, making it increasingly viable to separate tasks in time and space. When instructions can be delivered instantaneously, components and unfinished goods can be moved quickly and cheaply, and the output of many tasks can be conveyed electronically, firms can take advantage of factor cost disparities in different countries without sacrificing the gains from specialization.

Tasks in international production have a certain logic to them: they generally have an *order*, in that they follow one another in *stages* of production. The collection of these task stages is what international business researchers call a *value chain*. A value chain is a series of value-added processes (tasks) required for the production of any good or service. It proceeds in steps, from beginning or *upstream* tasks to subsequent *downstream* tasks. For example, the semiconductor value chain is very complex, but we can simplify it by considering the following four tasks.[4]

1. *Research, development and design* leading up to the details of the physical circuitry of the chip to be placed on the silicon.
2. *Fabrication* (or just *fab*, in semiconductor jargon) in an advanced manufacturing process in which circuitry layouts are etched onto silicon wafers containing many dies. This step also requires sophisticated equipment and materials.[5] Plants engaged in fabrication are known as *foundries*.
3. *Assembly and testing*, in which the dies are cut from wafers and mounted or packaged into a functioning device with wire contacts and insulation.
4. *Final incorporation*, in which the semiconductor is incorporated into the final piece of equipment, such as a personal computer or mobile phone.

These four stages are represented in Figure 11.1 as a semiconductor value chain, a particular case of a manufacturing value chain.[6] Not represented in Figure 11.1,

[3] This relates to what Baldwin (2016: 165) refers to as globalization at a "finer degree of resolution."

[4] *The Economist* (2018d) presents a similar set of tasks.

[5] On the role of Japanese firms in providing this equipment, see *The Economist* (2009).

[6] Wang and Chiu (2014: 60) also characterize the semiconductor industry as follows: "This manufacturing industry is characterized by long manufacturing lead times, increasingly short product life cycles, complicated manufacturing processes, and substantial capital investments."

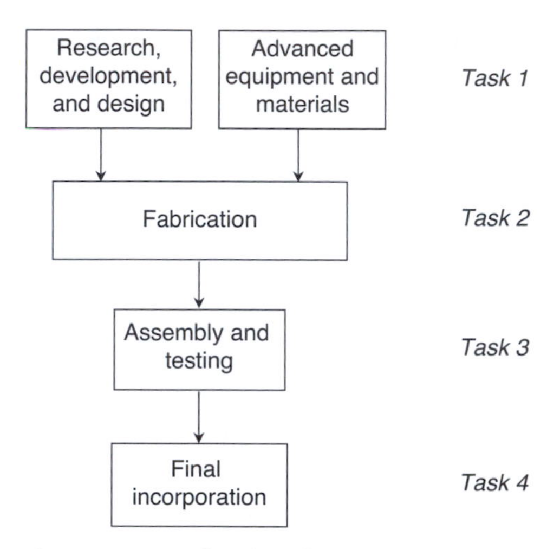

Figure 11.1 A value chain for semiconductors

however, are numerous supporting *producer services*, such as accounting, transportation and logistics, legal services, human resource management, and the like. Producer services are therefore an integral part of value chains in manufacturing. Indeed, sometimes the arrows in Figure 11.1 are referred to as service linkages.[7] Outside manufacturing, there are also pure-service value chains.

It is not necessary for a firm to be active across all the stages of semiconductor manufacturing depicted in Figure 11.1. The *task scope* of a firm in the industry is the result of a firm's *decision-making* regarding which tasks to perform. Consider the case of perhaps the most famous semiconductor firm of them all, Intel. Intel is involved in the first three stages of the value chain: research, development, and design; fabrication; and assembly and testing. It is not involved in final incorporation, leaving that task to other firms. For example, one of its biggest customers is Dell, which incorporates Intel's semiconductors into its personal computers. Having chosen to operate in the first three tasks of the semiconductor value chain, however, Intel is known as an *integrated device manufacturer*, or IDM.

Other semiconductor firms approach the value chain differently. For example, some firms, such as the US-based Nvidia, operate only in the first task of research, development, and design, contracting out fabrication and assembly. These firms are known as *fabless* semiconductor companies. Usually the companies

[7] See, for example, Lodefalk (2015). Chanda (2017: 45) states: "Manufacturing firms today are buying and producing more services than ever before. 'Servicification' of manufacturing refers to the fact that services are becoming important as both inputs and outputs for manufacturing." Low (2013: 63) refers to services, and particularly producer services, as "the glue that holds supply chains together and ensures that they function in a fluid manner." He also states (76) that their role in GVCs is "often underestimated and poorly understood."

to which they contract out fabrication are fabrication-only companies, known as *pure-play foundries*. The most famous of these is the Taiwan Semiconductor Manufacturing Company (TSMC), which makes most of Nvidia's semiconductors. TSMC is part of a much larger semiconductor industry in Taiwan, described in the accompanying box.

The Semiconductor Industry in Taiwan

Taiwan is sometimes called the "Silicon Valley of the East." In contrast to most other country cases, the semiconductor industry in Taiwan is characterized by vertical disintegration of the value chain rather than by vertical integration—that is, by a movement away from IDMs. But, as it turns out, Taiwanese firms hold *leading positions* in *all* the tasks or stages along the semiconductor value chain. Along with vertical disintegration, each stage is characterized by something we discussed in Chapter 10, namely clusters, and this has supported agglomeration economies for the industry. Taiwanese firms are also moving into semiconductor applications in photovoltaics and LED lighting.

Wang and Chiu (2014) describe the evolution of the semiconductor industry in Taiwan as having relied on a "fast follower" approach, and this effort has been supported by the Taiwanese government. The entity involved in this effort has been the Industrial Technology Research Institute (ITRI), established in 1973. The early activities of the ITRI involved something we also mentioned in Chapter 10: licensing—or, more precisely, technology licensing. The ITRI signed an agreement with the then existing US-based electronics company RCA to license two semiconductor process technologies. More generally, the Taiwanese semiconductor industry has benefited from government financial subsidies, human capital development, and government procurement.

Perhaps the most famous firm in Taiwan's semiconductor industry is the Taiwan Semiconductor Manufacturing Company, founded in 1987. This firm is a dedicated or pure-play foundry that engages only the fabrication task. As such, it is now the world's third largest semiconductor manufacturer, behind Intel and Samsung. Beyond technological prowess, its success involves entering into partnerships with its customers and pledging to never compete against them.

East Asia as a whole is an iconic example of success in manufacturing development. The case of Taiwan's semiconductor industry is a key example of this success, and is therefore worth studying in some detail.

Sources: Wang and Chiu (2014) and www.investopedia.com.

From Value Chains to Global Value Chains

The semiconductor firm could in principle be a purely domestic firm. If that were the case, the task decision would be the only value chain decision it needed to make. There is a big, wide world out there, however, because value chains can be distributed *across countries*. This brings to the firm a *location decision* related to foreign market entry. When value chains are linked together across countries in potential buyer–supplier or ownership relationships, they become known as *global value chains*. An example of this is given in Figure 11.2. Here we have only two countries, the United States and Costa Rica. In reality, of course, the GVC for semiconductors spans *many countries* around the world (particularly those of the Pacific Basin but also those in Europe), but we want to keep things as simple as possible here.[8] Figure 11.2 alerts us to the fact that the semiconductor production decision is multiple, including the decisions as to what part of the value chain to take on and in which countries to do so. Thus, there are both *task* and *location* decisions to consider.

There is another way to look at the GVC decision-making process. This is in terms of the distinction between what is known as the horizontal and vertical dimensions of GVCs. Movements up and down the value chains of Figure 11.2, whether in the United States or Costa Rica, are *vertical* movements. Movements from one country to another–from the United States to Costa Rica, for example–are *horizontal* movements. Further, movements up a value chain, from subsequent to previous tasks, are *backward vertical* movements, and movements down a value

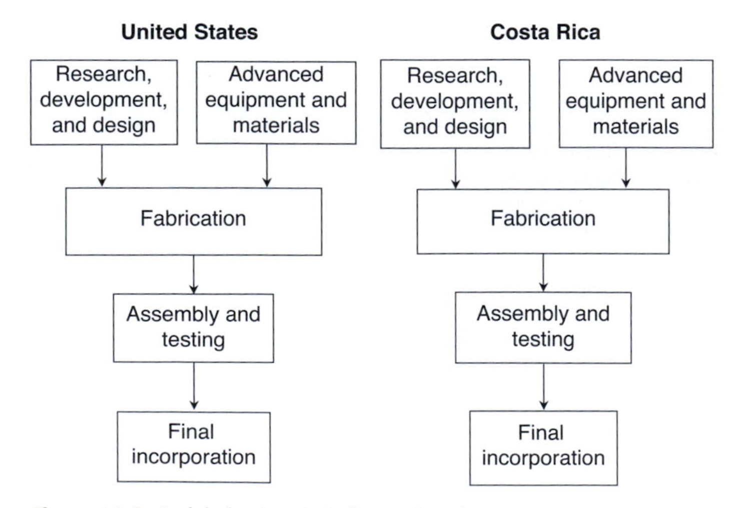

Figure 11.2 A global value chain for semiconductors

[8] For an excellent review of the GVC in semiconductors, see Dicken (2007: chap. 11).

chain, from previous to subsequent tasks, are *forward vertical* movements. We will return to these distinctions when we take up the concept of internalization below, but for now we can see that the GVC decision that firms face involves both the vertical (task) and horizontal (location) dimensions.

Firm-Specific Assets and Internalization

As is clear from the above discussion, firms can, and do, take more than one approach to the semiconductor GVC. Our next task is to try to understand *why* one approach might prevail over another in a particular instance. We will do this using Intel as an example. As mentioned above, Intel is an *integrated device manufacturer*. It maintains fabrication plants in the United States, its home base. It also has assembly and testing plants in a few other countries, including in Costa Rica from 1997 to 2014. We can therefore view its simplified GVC as in Figure 11.3. The dashed lines indicate potential areas where Intel has chosen not to operate, namely research, development, design, and fabrication in Costa Rica and final incorporation everywhere. The semiconductors assembled in Costa Rica from 1997 to 2014 were for *export* and, at its peak, composed approximately 20 percent of Costa Rica's exports.

How can we explain the GVC configuration in Figure 11.3? To begin, suppose that Intel has a demonstrated competitive ability in research, development, and design in the United States and is successfully operating as a "fabless" semiconductor firm. What might explain this competitive success? Corporate strategists typically point to the role of something we discussed in Chapter 10, namely

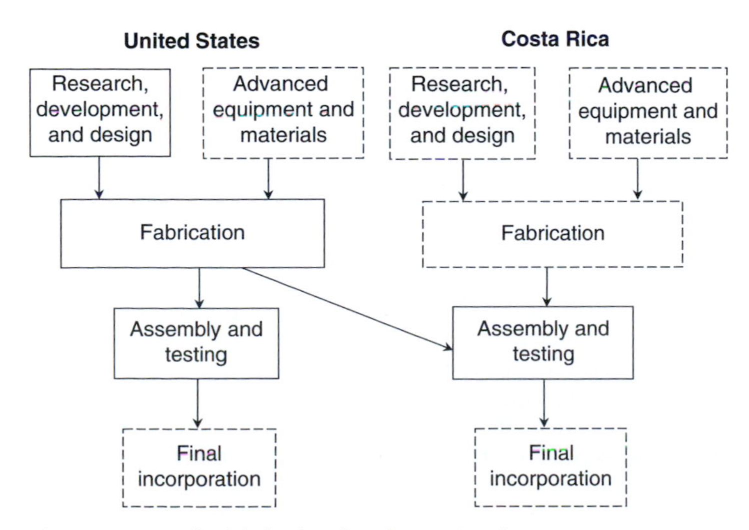

Figure 11.3 Intel's global value chain for semiconductors

firm-specific assets. These can either be *tangible*, such as access to silicon and other advanced materials, or *intangible*, such as specialized knowledge, patented products or processes, organizational abilities, or even brand distinctiveness and loyalty ("Intel inside").[9]

Intel might begin to consider a move down the value chain in the United States to fabrication. Why might it do so? One answer, typically given by corporate strategists analyzing this kind of forward vertical integration, is that Intel might experience an *efficiency gain* by spreading the costs incurred in acquiring its firm-specific assets (both tangible and intangible) over more value chain stages. These efficiency gains are known as **firm-level economies.**[10] Given the vast amount of firm-specific assets in the form of intellectual property that Intel possesses, this explanation appears to be relevant to this specific case.

The concept of firm-level economies is very helpful. It is not, in general, sufficient to explain the above integration process, however. Why? Because Intel always had the option (discussed in Chapter 10) of *licensing* its firm-specific assets to other fabrication producers. In other words, Intel could draw up a contract to rent its firm-specific assets to a fabrication firm for a specific time period in return for an agreed-upon payment. Indeed, in at least one specific instance, Intel has done just that, using TSMC as a pure-play foundry. Therefore, part of the explanation for forward or backward integration must answer the question: why did Intel choose *not* to exercise the licensing option in Costa Rica for assembly and testing from 1997 to 2014? Or, to state it another way: why did Intel choose not to engage in a market transaction for its assets but, rather, to *internalize* this asset market within itself?

Corporate strategists suggest that a firm's decision to internalize the firm-specific asset market reflects a kind of *market failure*.[11] In other words, for a number of reasons, it has difficulty in selling its firm-specific assets in a contractual arrangement. This explanation can be relevant for all sorts of firm-specific assets, but has been shown to be particularly relevant for the case of intangible assets. In the case of tangible assets, Intel or any other firm might be reluctant to incur the *dissemination risk* we discussed in Chapter 10. In the case of intangible assets such as management practices or reputation, firms might find that the assets are

[9] Caves (2007: chap. 1) provides a description of the role of intangible assets in MNEs. See also Toubal (2009). *The Economist* (2018c) notes that US-based firms "derive 80% of their market value from intangible assets such as patents and brands, as opposed to physical ones.... At the biggest 50 multinationals, 65% of foreign profits come from IP-intensive business such as tech and drugs." So *knowledge capital* is a critical firm-specific asset.

[10] The concept of firm-level economies is discussed by Markusen (1995). They are similar to the microeconomic concept of declining average fixed costs.

[11] This insight is part of what is known as transaction cost economics, and has its root in the work of Williamson (1975) on what is known as the boundary of the firm.

inseparable from the firm's human resources or organization. How do you license reputation? Such market failures are what sometimes lead firms with competitive success in one task of a value chain to internalize an adjacent task via forward or backward vertical integration. It could certainly be of relevance to Intel and its many firm-specific assets.[12]

The concepts of firm-specific assets, firm-level economies, and internalization help us to explain why Intel operates as an IDM across the first three tasks of the semiconductor value chain in the United States. But what of the relationship of this value chain to the one in Costa Rica illustrated in Figure 11.3? Let us consider this next.

Intra-Firm Trade

In 1996, to the surprise of many observers, Intel decided to locate an assembly and testing plant in Costa Rica for its Pentium processor. The significance of this decision for Costa Rica can be appreciated by the fact that, at the time, the sales of Intel were twice that of Costa Rica's GDP. The strategic thinking that motivated Intel to engage in this expansion of its GVC included a search for a relatively low-cost but technically savvy and highly trainable workforce.[13] Whatever the strategic reasons, however, we know from Chapter 10 that Intel could have *contracted* for the assembly and testing processes. It decided against this, opting instead for greenfield FDI (see Table 10.1). As we discussed above, contracting in the presence of dissemination risk and intangible firm-specific assets can be difficult.

There is another point worth emphasizing here. If an MNE decides to engage in FDI in a foreign country, it can be at a disadvantage in that it is operating in a foreign country (e.g. Intel in Costa Rica or Starbucks in China). The home-country MNE will have to incur the additional costs of operating its business internationally, including increased transportation, communication, and coordination costs. Therefore, if the home-country MNE is indeed able to successfully engage in

---

[12] Some of these considerations that are relevant to the Intel case are listed by Clausing (2009: 707): "For example, there may be a need to control the quality of the product, accompanied by difficulties in the formation of contracts at arm's length to ensure the reputation of the firm. Also, proprietary firm-specific knowledge can make it difficult to appropriate the gains from production via licensing, as it is difficult to charge the appropriate fee for knowledge without revealing the knowledge itself, thus lowering the incentive to pay for it."

[13] See Multilateral Investment Guarantee Agency (2006). Costa Rica had been promoted for some time by the Coalición Costarricense de Initiativas para el Desarrollo (CINDE), which first approached Intel in 1993.

business in the foreign country, there must be an extra "something" that the firm possesses to offset these additional costs. This is just the firm-specific assets we have been mentioning in this chapter.[14]

With the GVC of Figure 11.3 established, we can observe a pattern of *intra-firm trade*. As we see in that figure, Intel exports fabricated dies from its home base to its subsidiary in Costa Rica. This is not an arm's-length, market-based transaction that takes place at world prices. Rather, it is a trade transaction *within Intel itself* at a price set by it. This is not a rare occurrence. As noted by Taglioni and Winkler (2016: 9), "a significant share of GVC trade is intra-firm." For example, Antràs (2015) estimates that approximately one-half of the exports of the United States are intra-firm.

The FDI depicted in Figure 11.3 is known as *forward vertical* FDI, since the FDI links fabrication in the United States to the next stage in the value chain, assembly and testing in Costa Rica. If, instead, Intel had sourced dies in Costa Rica for assembly and testing in the United States (not likely), this would have been a case of *backward vertical* FDI. Finally, if Intel had engaged only in assembly and testing in both the United States and Costa Rica without any intra-firm trade, this would have been an example of *horizontal* FDI.

Recall that, in Chapter 5, we made an important distinction between *inter-industry* trade and *intra-industry* trade. We now have also distinguished between *inter-firm* trade and *intra-firm* trade. Things are becoming a little complicated! To help you sort all this out, please consult Table 11.1. This table characterizes international trade along two dimensions: industry and firm. Along the industry dimension (rows), it distinguishes between *inter-industry* and *intra-industry*. Along the firm dimension (columns), it distinguished between *inter-firm* and *intra-firm*. This gives us four cells in the table.

Table 11.1 Industry and firm dimensions of trade

Industry dimension	Firm dimension	
	Inter-firm	*Intra-firm*
Inter-industry	Trade that takes place between two different industries and two different firms.	Trade that takes place between two different industries and within a single firm.
Intra-industry	Trade that takes place within a single industry and between two different firms.	Trade that takes place within a single industry and within a single firm.

[14] This insight was originally due to Hymer (1976), who, it can be argued, originated the modern, firm-based analysis of the MNE.

Down the *inter-firm* column of Table 11.1 we have the types of trade considered in Chapters 2 to 5 of Part I of this book—that is, *inter-firm* trade either between or within industries. Down the *intra-firm* column of the table we have the types of trade considered in this chapter—that is, *intra-firm* trade either between or within industries. Consider Figure 11.3. Given an industry classification of "computer products," the trade depicted there would be *intra-firm* and *intra-industry*. If we distinguish between "semiconductor fabrication" and "semiconductor assembly and testing" as two separate industries, however, the trade depicted there would be *intra-firm* and *inter-industry*. This gives you an appreciation of how the degree of detail in industry classification determines the extent of *inter-industry* and *intra-industry* trade.[15]

The tools of value chains and GVCs allow us to understand how FDI and intra-firm trade arise. Given the large amount of intra-firm trade taking place in the world economy, this is an important insight.

A Cost View of Internalization

The above discussion considered a number of issues that relate to firm decision-making with regard to GVCs. What we have seen is that GVC decisions are *threefold*, involving the decisions as to what part of the value chain to take on (task), in which countries to do so (location), and how to engage (mode). As it turns out, some standard economic analysis can help in GVC decision-making as to mode. Recall from your microeconomics course that, when considering the costs of a firm, we can distinguish between fixed and variable costs. Suppose that a home-country firm faces a fixed cost of setting up a production facility in country j of FP_j. Suppose also that the firm faces a *smaller* fixed cost of establishing a contractual relationship with a firm from country j of FC_j. There are also variable costs associated with these two options: VP_j and VC_j. Suppose that the variable costs of international production are *smaller* than the variable costs of international contracting because of the firm-specific assets that give it an advantage over the potential contracting partner. In other words, the firm itself knows how to make its product more easily than other firms.

These considerations lead us to Figure 11.4. Here, the solid $FP_j + VP_j$ line begins at the vertical axis intercept equal to the fixed cost of production and increases from there with a slope equal to the variable costs of production. The solid $FC_j + VC_j$ line begins at a lower vertical axis intercept equal to the lower fixed cost of contracting and increases from there with a slope equal to the variable

[15] Recall Table 5.2 in Appendix 5.1.

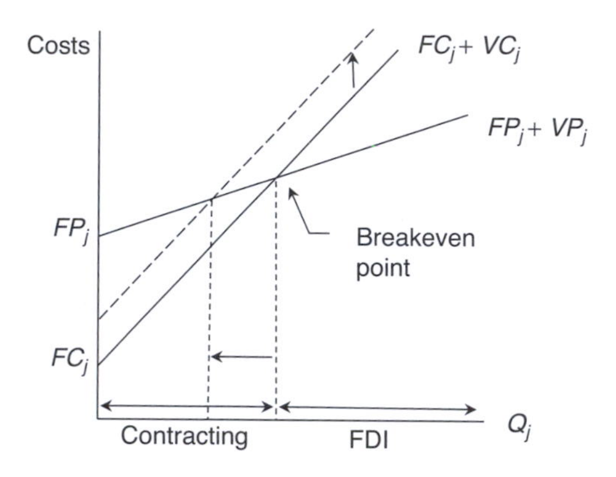

Figure 11.4 A cost analysis of production and contracting

costs of contracting. The two solid lines intersect at a "breakeven point" that establishes a boundary between quantities at which it would be better for the firm to engage in contracting and quantities at which it would be better for the firm to engage in production or FDI. This analysis is useful, because it allows us to see that the contracting/production decision might be related to the volume of output the firm has in mind.

The dissemination risk involved in contracting can be included in this diagram in a simplified way. It increases the fixed cost of contracting and moves the solid "Contracting" line upwards to the dashed line. This moves the breakeven point to the left and reduces the range of quantities at which contracting is to be preferred.

Inter-Firm Relationships

Let us again recall that a firm's decision-making with regard to GVCs has three aspects: what part of the value chain to take on (task), in which countries to do so (location), and how to engage (mode). When the mode chosen is contracting, the issue of *inter-firm relationships* arises. Within this issue, an important consideration is that of vertical connections to supplying firms. Here, Gereffi, Humphrey, and Sturgeon (2005) emphasize that some of the considerations of Chapter 10 that lead MNEs with firm-specific assets (and, in particular, intangible assets) to pursue FDI modes of foreign market entry (rather than contractual modes) can be overcome in certain kinds of relationships that we might describe as *contractual-plus*. Contractual-plus arrangements consist of "repeated transactions, reputation, and social norms that are embedded in particular geographic locations or social groups" (81). These features can help overcome the difficulties of the contractual mode in the presence of intangible assets and dissemination risk.

These researchers go on to distinguish between four types of relationships between an MNE and its suppliers: market, modular, relational, and captive.[16] The *market model* consists of standard contractual relationships, but these can be augmented by trust and normality developed through repeated transactions. The *modular model* occurs when the product and production process in question are standard and generic, and the suppliers are coalesced around specific breakpoints in GVCs. We saw this in the semiconductor case with "fabless" semiconductor firms contracting with pure-play foundries, but this situation usually occurs in sectors that are less technologically advanced, such as clothing and footwear.[17] In the *relational model*, MNE–supplier interactions are more complex, described by Gereffi, Humphrey, and Sturgeon as "mutual dependence." This can be associated with ethnic ties or geographic proximity. Finally, in the *captive model*, we find an asymmetric relationship in which the MNE is dominant over its suppliers.

To generalize a little, the more a GVC is producer-driven rather than buyer-driven, the farther the GVC tends to move towards the relational and captive models. The example usually cited to support this observation is the case of Toyota and its suppliers.[18]

What is clear from this brief discussion is that MNE management, in both its intra-firm design and inter-firm relationship components, is a relatively complex and difficult task. There is *no single approach* that can be grasped as the "answer" to multinational management. Rather, there is an ongoing learning process that takes place, with varying degrees of success, within the historical trajectories of MNEs. This is what makes global corporate strategy such an interesting and dynamic field.

Tying Things Together: The TLM Framework

Let us pause for a moment to tie things together a little. We do this by using an informal framework of task, location, and mode (TLM). As previously mentioned, a firm's decision-making regarding GVCs has three aspects:

- task: what part of the value chain to engage in
- location: in which countries to do so
- mode: *how* to engage

---

[16] See also Ruigrok and van Tulder (1995: chaps. 4 & 5) for a political economy view of buyer–supplier relationships.

[17] Some researchers refer to this as the "Lego" or "turnkey" model of MNE–supplier relationship. See Dicken (2007: chap. 5).

[18] Ruigrok and van Tulder (1995: 114) note that "Toyotism can be described as a system of constructed (structural) dependencies within networks" and that "under Toyotism signing a contract will mark the beginning of extensive bargaining."

Let us briefly review these aspects of GVCs in terms of the TLM framework.

The *task* scope of a firm within a GVC is the result of a firm's decision-making regarding which tasks to *engage* in the network. By the term "engage" we mean to either perform themselves or contract for the tasks in some way. This is the first strategic decision facing any firm thinking about international production. The decision involves deciding how to deploy its tangible and intangible firm-specific assets. As we discussed above, by deploying these assets over a larger range of tasks, the firm can realize cost advantages through firm-level economies. Alternatively, the firm can husband its firm-specific assets and engage the task less directly through contractual relationships of various kinds, including contractual-plus relationships. Either way, it needs to decide on a set of tasks.

Having identified the tasks that it will engage in, a second strategic decision awaits the firm. This is the *location* of the tasks to be engaged in. The firm needs to decide which tasks will be performed in which countries. In doing this, the firm weighs what has been called the *location advantages* of countries and cities.[19] These location advantages can include input costs, transportation costs, import restraints, foreign government promotional policies, and access to foreign consumers. They often closely relate to the first two motivations for international production discussed in Chapter 10: resource seeking and market seeking.

Having a sense of tasks and location, the firm needs to decide on a *mode*. Recall for a moment Table 10.1 from the previous chapter. This table identified a set of modes of international production. Although the key decision is contracting versus FDI, as seen in Table 10.1, there are more detailed decisions to be made within these two categories. The result is a GVC potentially composed of both ownership relationships (and, potentially, intra-firm trade) and contracting relationships. Importantly, firms can choose different modes in different locations. Uniformity is not required.

The way we have described TLM here suggests a sequential decision-making process, but firms think about the process in a *holistic* way. Each possible GVC design is a combination of task, location, and mode. Therefore, what the firm actually does is to assess and compare a large number of possible TLM combinations. This is no easy task. Further, once a GVC has been designed, firms often *redesign* them in response to new conditions. As mentioned above, Intel's decision to locate assembly and testing in Costa Rica lasted only from 1997 to 2014. In 2014 Intel decided to close this operation.[20] Currently, Intel has an R&D and services center based in Costa Rica.[21] As if the TLM decision-making were not enough, firms are coming under increasing scrutiny to address *environmental* and *labor standard* issues within GVCs. This important subject is considered in the accompanying box.

---

[19] On location advantages, see Dunning (1988) and Dunning and Lundan (2008).

[20] For an informative discussion of both the causes and effects of this decision, see Aguilera (2014).

[21] See www.intel.com/content/www/us/en/corporate-responsibility/intel-in-costa-rica.html.

There is nothing sacrosanct about the TLM framework. It is just a handy way of beginning to think about GVCs in an organized fashion. Next let us consider the important issue of how value added is distributed across GVCs.

Labor and Environmental Issues within GVCs

In recent years attention has focused on labor and environmental issues within GVCs. These issues jumped onto the global scene in the case of Nike in the early 1990s, with a number of high-profile labor abuses and environmental issues among its contract manufacturers. Initially Nike took a defensive position, arguing that it was not responsible for labor conditions in its contract manufacturing facilities, since the workers involved were not Nike employees. By the late 1990s, however, Nike had established a Nike Code of Conduct for its contract manufacturers. It has engaged its suppliers in training and developed a staff of compliance specialists. Nike recognized that its responsibility extended upstream in its GVC, not just in FDI modes but in contractual modes as well.

A second case is Apple's production of iPhones in China. This has involved *both* contracting *and* FDI within GVCs. Apple contracts production in China to Foxconn, while Foxconn, based in Taiwan, engages in FDI in China. Beginning in 2006, labor and environmental issues in Foxconn contract manufacturing facilities were raised. After what Clark and Boersma (2017: 119) term "a public relations nightmare," which included worker suicides and exposure to hazardous chemicals, Apple followed Nike and instituted an Apple Code of Conduct for its suppliers and began to use independent auditors. Nevertheless, Clark and Boersma conclude in their study that there are still "human and employment rights abuses in the Apple supply chain" (125) and that "Foxconn makes symbolic efforts, while circumstances on the factory floor have changed little" (126).

Efforts to address these sorts of problems are often cast in terms of GVC "governance." By "governance," for example, Boström et al. (2015: 2) refer to "regulation and coordination of activities by public and private institutions through a variety of formal and informal instruments. Instruments of governance may include policies and guidelines, rules or laws, norms, standards, monitoring and verification procedures, financial and other incentives, the exercise of authority and so on." These authors note that the geographical distance involved in GVCs makes their environmental and social impacts difficult for final consumers to appreciate and respond to. Of necessity, GVC governance involves standards and codes of conduct of some kind, but auditing compliance is not always straightforward.

With regard to *labor standards*, there are a number of ongoing efforts. These include the Better Work Program, co-sponsored by the International Labour

Labor and Environmental Issues within GVCs (cont.)

Organization (ILO) and the International Finance Corporation (a part of the World Bank Group). The Better Work Program (https://betterwork.org) is focused on the clothing sector across approximately 1,600 factories in Bangladesh, Cambodia, Haiti, Indonesia, Jordan, Nicaragua, and Vietnam. In the words of Elliott (2017: 193), the Better Work Program "aims to reassure brand-name firms that sweatshop scandals in their supply chains are less likely to occur if factories participate in the program."

There is also the United Nations Global Compact, which Debebe (2017: 479) describes as a "network-based organization" between UN agencies (www.unglobalcompact.org). The Global Compact endorses ten principles covering human rights, labor, the environment, and anti-corruption activities. It now works with nearly 10,000 companies to ensure these principles are abided by, including throughout GVCs.

In the environmental realm, there is the Restriction of Hazardous Substances (RoHS) directive for the electronics industry (www.rohsguide.com), which develops standards for the handling of ten hazardous substances, including lead, mercury, and cadmium. There is also the Responsible Minerals Assurance Process (RMAP), which focuses on minerals sourcing in supply chains (wwwresponsiblemineralsinitiative.org). The RMAP relies on third-party audits and involves over 350 companies.

The issues of labor and environmental standards in GVCs will become increasingly important over time, and GVC governance will continue to be an active area of policy formation across many organizational entities.

Sources: Boström et al. (2015), Clark and Boersma (2017), Debebe (2017), Elliott (2017) and Locke, Qin, and Brause (2007).

Value Added in GVCs

Given the complexity of GVCs, it is natural to ask where most of their *value added* is to be found.[22] For example, this was analyzed some time ago by Ali-Yrkkö et al. (2011) in the case of the Nokia N95 smartphone. These authors find that, even after this phone was assembled "offshore" in China, most of the value added,

[22] Using the basic microeconomic concept of producer surplus (see Appendix 2.1), Dedrick, Kraemer, and Linden (2010: 83) state: "Value capture within the supply chain can be thought of as a two-level process: (i) the determination of producer surplus and (ii) the division of that surplus among the supply chain partners."

about one-half, was retained in Europe. Why? Because "value capture–the ultimate variable of interest for both business and countries–is considerably less dispersed than tasks within a supply chain" (264). More specifically, value added was concentrated in less tangible aspects of the value chain, such as technology and software licenses, design, advertising and marketing, and distribution (wholesale and retail). The actual assembly of the smartphone captured only 2 percent of the value added![23] As shown by Dedrick, Kraemer, and Linden (2010), something similar happens in the GVC for the Apple iPod. More generally, *The Economist* (2018b) suggests that Apple, along with its semiconductor chip suppliers, captures more than 90 percent of the profits in its extensive GVC.

Observations such as these were generalized into a visual depiction by Stan Shih, the founder and CEO of Acer, a Taiwanese electrical technology MNE. Shih proposed what was to become known as the "smile curve." This curve is depicted in Figure 11.5, and plots tasks or stages of production in a GVC along the horizontal axis and value added on the vertical axis. The smile curve suggests that the greatest value added is to be found in upstream tasks such as R&D, branding, and design, as well as in downstream tasks such as distribution, marketing, and after-sales service. The smallest amount of value added is to be found in the manufacturing or assembly stage of the GVC.

Why does the smile curve matter? Popular opinion in high-income countries mistakenly focuses on manufacturing and assembly as the great hope for

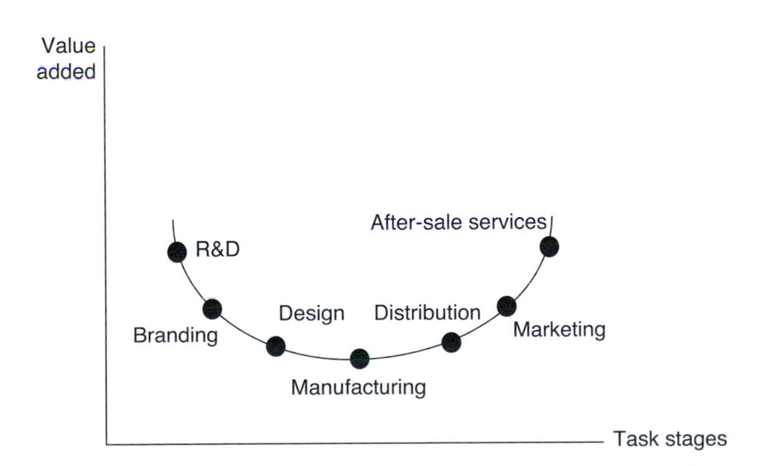

Figure 11.5 The smile curve of GVCs
Source: Gupta (2017).

[23] These authors also echo Lodefalk (2015) and Chanda (2017) regarding the relationship between manufacturing and services. They state: "The recorded value added by manufacturing has a significant service component; most services need supporting physical infrastructure and complementing goods. The distinction between manufacturing and services is immaterial and should perhaps be laid to rest completely" (273–4).

economic revival. This is often contained in the lament "We don't make anything anymore!" Although it is true that much of the "making" has moved to low- and middle-income countries, this is not necessarily a bad thing from a value added and profit point of view. As stated by Moretti (2012: 69), "More assembly jobs in China and more customer assistance jobs in India ultimately mean more R&D jobs in America as well as more jobs for the professionals–advertisers, designers, analysts, accountants–who cluster around high-tech companies." Further, Moretti suggests that all the "innovation" jobs, as he calls them, at the ends of the smile curve have significant multiplier effects for local services–multiplier effects that are about three times those of traditional manufacturing.

Kimura (2013) presents similar results for Japan, noting:

> Many people in Japan, both capitalists and labor, believe that globalization of Japanese firms, *particularly in the context of production networks* in East Asia, has been good for the Japanese economy. If a firm sets up a proper international division of labor..., it can actually enlarge its domestic operation and even increase employment (375, emphasis added).

For these reasons, paying attention to the *ends* of the smile curve matters a great deal, both in the North American and East Asian contexts.[24]

Trade in Value Added

The above considerations of value added began in the international business research arena but quickly caught the eye of trade policy researchers. These researchers noticed an important difference between *gross trade* and *trade in value added.* Let us consider a simple example in Figure 11.6. This figure considers trade in the intermediate good cloth and the final good clothing. China exports US$50 of clothing in gross terms to Vietnam. Vietnam uses this cloth as an intermediate input to produce clothing, adding US$50 of value added in the process. Vietnam exports the clothing to the United States at a gross export value of US$100. From a gross export value perspective, the total exports in this process are US$50 for China and US$100 for Vietnam, for a total of US$150.

The net or value-added perspective is different. Vietnam's gross exports are US$100, but its value-added exports are only US$50. The total value-added exports are only U$100. There is also a difference from the US import perspective

[24] Baldwin (2016: chap. 5) suggests that the smile curve is becoming increasingly U-shaped or deeper over time. Indeed, Baldwin finds example of "smirk curves" that are more V-shaped than U-shaped. These changes have a great deal of impact on countries trying to leverage GVCs for development, something we will return to in Chapter 12.

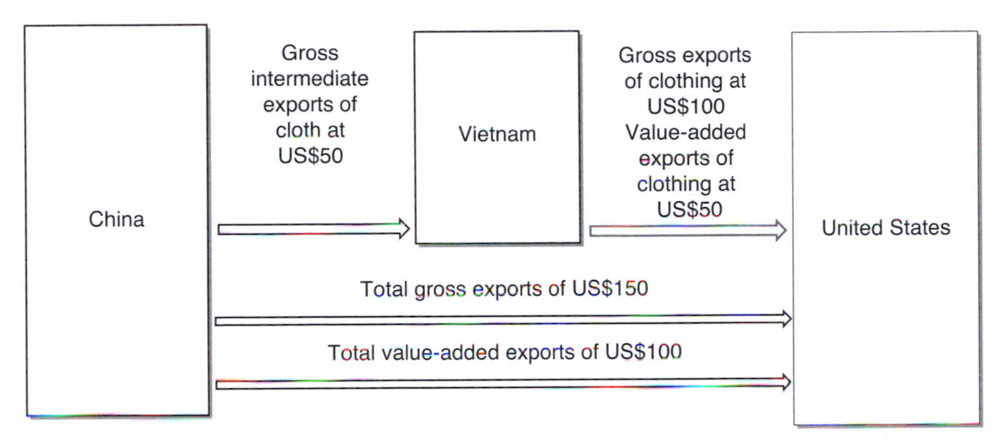

Figure 11.6 A simple example of trade in value added

regarding its bilateral trade with Vietnam. The official gross imports of the United States from Vietnam are US$100, but its value-added imports from Vietnam are only US$50.

There are many ways in which the trade in value added perspective offers insights into both trade itself and trade-and-development processes.[25] We will mention just a few of these. First, policy-makers and politicians often focus on gross bilateral trade imbalances (deficits) as signs of "unfair" trade. This is misleading, however, because a significant portion of the "unfairness" is actually attributable to the foreign exporter's intermediate imports. As stated by Ahmad (2013: 89, emphasis added), "As pressure for rebalancing increases in the context of persistent deficits, there is a risk of protectionist responses that target countries at the *end* of global value chains on the basis of an inaccurate perception of the origin of trade imbalances." So, when politicians cry "unfair trade" based on gross bilateral trade statistics, we need to be very careful.

Second, trade in value added reveals a different perspective on trade in services. We mentioned in Chapter 1 that a standard statistic is that services trade accounts for one-fifth of total global trade. This refers to global gross trade. From a net value-added trade perspective, however, trade in services is larger than this: somewhere around two-fifths of the total. Trade in services is even more important than is often appreciated.

Third, the trade in value added perspective can help us better understand trade-and-development policies and processes in ways that reflect the realities of GVCs. This is well described by Ahmad (2013: 87): "Better understanding how much domestic value-added is generated by the export of a good or service in a country is crucial for development strategies and industrial policies." Trade

[25] See Ahmad (2013: 87–90), for example.

policies consequently need to be cognizant of value added along with gross exports.

One ongoing effort to better consider trade from the value added perspective is a joint initiative between the OECD and the WTO. The Trade in Value Added (TiVA) initiative involves developing a set of indicators over time for a set of over 60 countries and 34 sectors.[26] Some of the subjects included in the indicators are:

- domestic and foreign value-added content of gross exports by exporting industry
- services content of gross exports by exporting industry, by type of service and value-added origin
- participation in GVCs via intermediate imports embodied in exports and domestic value added in partners' exports
- bilateral trade relationships based on flows of value added embodied in domestic final demand

These types of indicators will give trade policy analysts a better sense of the actual flows of value added between the countries of the world rather than just the gross values of trade.[27] We can get a small sense of this by looking at Figure 11.7. This figure uses the TiVA data to calculate domestic value added in total exports as a percentage of total exports for a sample of countries for 2011. In the table, the

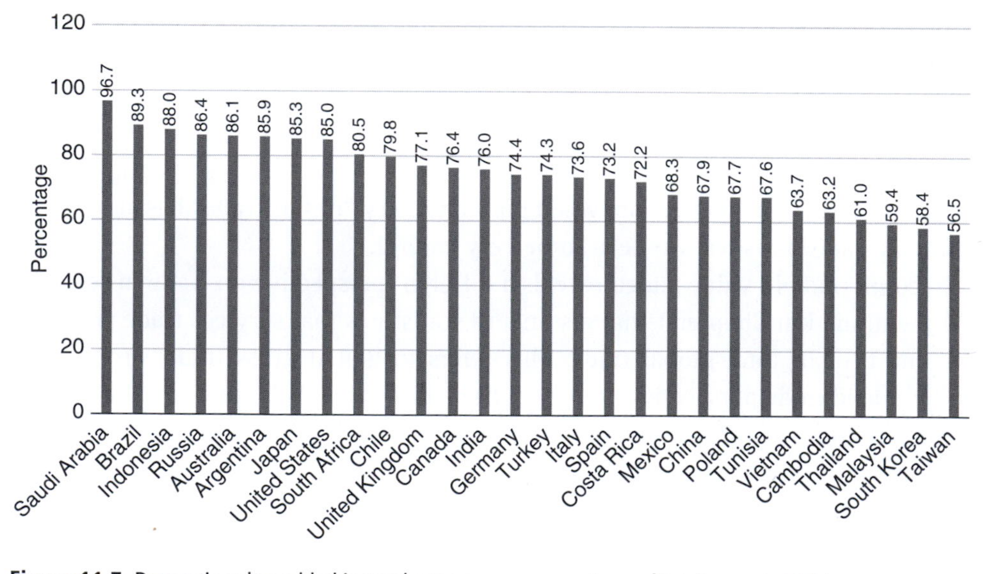

Figure 11.7 Domestic value added in total exports as a percentage of total exports, 2011
Source: Organisation for Economic Co-operation and Development.

[26] See www.oecd.org/industry/ind/measuring-trade-in-value-added.htm.

[27] Taglioni and Winkler (2016: 11) state: "The development of value-added trade data represents a fundamental step toward understanding GVC trade."

percentage ranges from approximately 97 percent to approximately 57 percent. High percentages indicate that exports draw largely from domestic resources. So, for example, Saudi Arabia exports mostly petroleum extracted domestically, so its domestic value added in total exports as a percentage of total exports is the highest in Figure 11.7. Countries that engage in a lot of assembly that relies on imported intermediate inputs (e.g. China, Cambodia, and Vietnam) have correspondingly low domestic value added in total exports as a percentage of total exports. In this way, the operations of GVCs are reflected in the trade data. The TiVA database is therefore an important new information source for trade economists.

Trade Policy and Global Value Chains

The evolution of GVCs has some significant implications for trade policy. Trade policy analysts, if not the general public, are beginning to appreciate the impacts of trade policies on GVCs.[28] Protection in a world of GVCs can look very different from protection in a world of pure final goods. This has been pointed out by Krugman (2018), for example. In referring to the increased tariffs of the US government during the Trump administration, the bulk of which were on intermediate and capital goods, he states that the Trump administration imagined

> that the world still looks the way it did in the 1960s, when trade was overwhelmingly in final goods like wheat and cars. In that world, putting a tariff on imported cars would cause consumers to switch to domestic cars, adding auto industry jobs, end of story (except for the foreign retaliation). In the modern world economy, however, a large part of trade is in intermediate goods – not cars but car parts. Put a tariff on car parts, and even the first-round effect on jobs is uncertain: maybe domestic parts producers will add workers, but you've raised costs and reduced competitiveness for downstream producers, who will shrink their operations.

These issues came to the fore in 2018, as the Trump administration began to apply tariffs against imports from China (and China retaliated). China is a significant participant in GVCs. *The Economist* (2018a) addresses the question of how US firms would react to the increased costs of imported intermediate goods from their suppliers. It states the following:

> For many companies, switching may be easier said than done. Around half of the products threatened with tariffs are intermediate goods, used by companies to make other

[28] See, for example Bown (2018), who examines the use of non-tariff measures (specifically anti-dumping and countervailing duties, as well as safeguards) on imports of intermediate goods in the Group of 20.

> stuff.... Yet given how customized intermediate goods can be, importers may struggle to find a ready alternative. Supply chains can be complex beasts, requiring each component to be checked and tested. According to the [US] Census Bureau, around a quarter of American imports from China come from a "related party," which could include an affiliate, a subsidiary or a parent company. Where two companies are embedded in a supply chain or part of the same company, dodging duties may require moving premises.

What is clear from these considerations is that officials with responsibilities for international trade policies need to keep GVCs firmly in mind. They should try to avoid building "walls inside factories" with protective measures that disrupt GVCs.

Conclusion

Global value chains are a central feature of international production and, more generally, of modern patterns of globalization. They are an integral part of firm strategy in the global economy. As we have seen, firms offset the extra costs of doing business internationally through their tangible or intangible assets, which provide ownership advantages to them and generate firm-level economies. Firms choose to operate abroad because various foreign countries offer location advantages to them, and they choose between contractual modes and investment modes based on circumstances. When investment modes are chosen, patterns of intra-firm trade can emerge. Indeed, approximately one-third of world trade is intra-firm trade, taking place within MNEs. Some of these issues can be examined using cost analysis, but the full set of issues can be appreciated through the informal TLM framework.

Measures of trade that reflect the realities of GVCs are beginning to arise. Trade in value added data can help to better inform trade policies so that they avoid disrupting GVCs. This is a new and exciting area for trade policy analysis and helps researchers to understand where along GVCs value added is actually located.

Review Exercises

1. Choose any production process that might be of interest to you. Both merchandise and services are appropriate. As best you can, draw a value chain for this production process, illustrating a relevant set of tasks.
2. Next, for this production process, choose two countries. Place the value chains for these two countries side by side in a GVC. Show how FDI in the second country by a firm based in the first country can be depicted for the cases of horizontal FDI, backward vertical FDI, and forward vertical FDI.

3. Make a list of as many firm-specific assets as you can think of, both tangible and intangible.
4. Recreate your own version of Figure 11.6 using an example that interests you. As best you can, draw distinctions between gross trade and value-added trade.
5. Using an internet search, find an example of FDI or international contracting. Do some further research to describe the FDI or contracting in terms of the TLM framework.

FURTHER READING AND WEB RESOURCES

For very useful reviews of the global semiconductor industry, see Dibiaggio (2007), Dicken (2007: chap. 11), and Macher, Mowery, and Simcoe (2002). For a concise review of intra-firm trade, see Clausing (2009). For reviews of value chains and GVCs, respectively, see McIvor (2005: chap. 5), Coe, Dicken, and Hess (2008), Gupta (2017), and Gereffi (2018). For a more general discussion relating the material of this chapter to broader trends in economic globalization, see Baldwin (2016: chaps. 3 & 5). An excellent introduction to global corporate strategy is Verbeke (2009). A global political economy view of some of the issues discussed in this chapter can be found in Walter and Sen (2009: chap. 6).

The United Nations Conference on Trade and Development is an organization that has dedicated itself to the analysis of FDI and its role in economic development. Its website is www.unctad.org. Of particular interest is its annual *World Investment Report*, which is highlighted at www.unctad.org/wir. The World Trade Organization has recently released statistical profiles of GVCs, which can be found at www.wto.org/english/res_e/statis_e/miwi_e/countryprofiles_e.htm. The WTO/OECD TiVA data can be found at www.oecd.org/industry/ind/measuring-trade-in-value-added.htm.

REFERENCES

Aguilera, R. (2014) "Costa Rica: Life after Intel," *Huffington Post*, May 1.

Ahmad, N. (2013) "Estimating Trade in Value Added: Why and How?," in D. K. Elms and P. Low (eds.), *Global Value Chains in a Changing World*, World Trade Organization, 85–108.

Ali-Yrkkö, J., P. Rouvinen, T. Seppälä, and P. Ylä-Anttila (2011) "Who Captures Value in Global Supply Chains? Case Nokia N95 Smartphone," *Journal of Industry, Competition and Trade*, 11:3, 263–78.

Antràs, P. (2015) *Global Production: Firms, Contracts and Trade Structure*, Princeton University Press.

Baldwin, R. (2016) *The Great Convergence: Information Technology and the New Globalization*, Harvard University Press.

Boström, M., A. M. Jönsson, S. Lockie, A. P. J. Mol, and P. Oosterveer (2015) "Sustainable and Responsible Supply Chain Governance: Challenges and Opportunities," *Journal of Cleaner Production*, 107, 1–7.

Bown, C. (2018) "Trade Policy toward Supply Chains after the Great Recession," *IMF Economic Review*, 66:3, 602–16.

Caves, R. E. (2007) *Multinational Enterprise and Economics Analysis*, Cambridge University Press.

Chanda, R. (2017) "Trade in Services," in K. A. Reinert (ed.), *Handbook of Globalisation and Development*, Edward Elgar, 36–58.

Clark, T., and M. Boersma (2017) "The Governance of Global Value Chains: Unresolved Human Rights, Environmental and Ethical Dilemmas in the Apple Supply Chain," *Journal of Business Ethics*, 143:1, 111–31.

Clausing, K. A. (2009) "Intrafirm Trade," in K. A. Reinert, R. S. Rajan, A. J. Glass, and L. S. Davis (eds.), *The Princeton Encyclopedia of the World Economy*, Princeton University Press, 706–8.

Coe, N. M., P. Dicken, and M. Hess (2008) "Global Production Networks: Realizing the Potential," *Journal of Economic Geography*, 8:3, 271–95.

Debebe, G. (2017) "Global Organizations," in K. A. Reinert (ed.), *Handbook of Globalisation and Development*, Edward Elgar, 463–84.

Dedrick, J., K. L. Kraemer, and G. Linden (2010) "Who Profits from Innovation in Global Value Chains: A Study of the iPod and Notebook PCs," *Industrial and Corporate Change*, 19:1, 81–116.

Dibiaggio, L. (2007) "Design Complexity, Vertical Disintegration and Knowledge Organization in the Semiconductor Industry," *Industrial and Corporate Change*, 16:2, 239–67.

Dicken, P. (2007) *Global Shift: Mapping the Changing Contours of the World Economy*, Guilford.

Dunning, J. H. (1988) *Explaining International Production*, Unwin Hyman.

Dunning, J. H., and S. M. Lundan (2008) *Multinational Enterprises and the Global Economy*, Edward Elgar.

The Economist (2009) "Briefing: Japan's Technology Champions," November 7.

The Economist (2018a) "Tariffs: Who Pays?," September 8.

The Economist (2018b) "iSupply," September 8.

The Economist (2018c) "An Empire of the Mind," September 15.

The Economist (2018d) "The Chips Are Down," December 1.

Elliott, K. A. (2017) "Labor Standards," in K. A. Reinert (ed.), *Handbook of Globalisation and Development*, Edward Elgar, 183–97.

Gereffi, G. (2018) *Global Value Chains and Development: Redefining the Contours of 21st Century Capitalism*, Cambridge University Press.

Gereffi, G., J. Humphrey, and T. Sturgeon (2005) "The Governance of Global Value Chains," *Review of International Political Economy*, 12:1, 78–104.

Grossman, G., and E. Rossi-Hansberg (2008) "Trading Tasks: A Simple Theory of Offshoring," *American Economic Review*, 98:5, 1978–97.

Gupta, P. (2017) "Global Production Networks," in K. A. Reinert (ed.), *Handbook of Globalisation and Development*, Edward Elgar, 153–68.

Hymer, S. H. (1976) *The International Operations of National Firms: A Study of Direct Foreign Investment*, MIT Press.

Kimura, F. (2013) "How Have Production Networks Changed Development Strategies in East Asia?," in D. K. Elms and P. Low (eds.), *Global Value Chains in a Changing World*, World Trade Organization, 361–83.

Krugman, P. (2018) "How to Lose a Trade War," *New York Times*, July 7.

Locke, R. M., F. Qin, and A. Brause (2007) "Does Monitoring Improve Labor Standards? Lessons from Nike," *Industrial and Labor Relations Review*, 61:1, 3–31.

Lodefalk, M. (2015) "Servicification of Manufacturing Firms Makes Divides in Trade Policy-Making Antiquated," Working Paper 2015:1, Örebro University School of Business.

Low, P. (2013) "The Role of Services in Global Value Chains," in D. K. Elms and P. Low (eds.), *Global Value Chains in a Changing World*, World Trade Organization, 61–81.

Macher, J. T., D. C. Mowery, and T. S. Simcoe (2002) "E-Business and Disintegration of the Semiconductor Industry Value Chain," *Industry and Innovation*, 9:3, 155–81.

McIvor, R. (2005) *The Outsourcing Process: Strategies for Evaluation and Management*, Cambridge University Press.

Markusen, J. R. (1995) "The Boundaries of Multinational Enterprise and the Theory of International Trade," *Journal of Economic Perspectives*, 9:2, 169–89.

Moretti, E. (2012) *The New Geography of Jobs*, Houghton Mifflin Harcourt.

Multilateral Investment Guarantee Agency (2006) *The Impact of Intel in Costa Rica*, World Bank.

Ruigrok, W., and R. van Tulder (1995) *The Logic of International Restructuring*, Routledge.

Taglioni, D., and D. Winkler (2016) *Making Global Value Chains Work for Development*, World Bank.

Toubal, F. (2009) "Intangible Assets," in K. A. Reinert, R. S. Rajan, A. J. Glass, and L. S. Davis (eds.), *The Princeton Encyclopedia of the World Economy*, Princeton University Press, 638–40.

Verbeke, A. (2009) *International Business Strategy: Rethinking the Foundations of Global Corporate Success*, Cambridge University Press.

Walter, A., and G. Sen (2009) *Analyzing the Global Political Economy*, Princeton University Press.

Wang, C.-T., and C.-S. Chiu (2014) "Competitive Strategies for Taiwan's Semiconductor Industry in a New World Economy," *Technology in Society*, 36, 60–73.

Williamson, O. E. (1975) *Markets and Hierarchies*, Free Press.

12 Engaging International Production

Many years ago I attended a conference on the economies of Latin America that took place just outside the city of San José in Costa Rica. Before the conference began I took a long walk through the neighborhoods surrounding the conference hotel. As I walked, I passed the offices and factory gates of many foreign corporations that were operating in the area. During the conference I spoke to a representative of the Costa Rican government. With some passion, she said, "Foreign firms are buying our companies! We are losing ownership of our economy!" When it comes to such inward flows of foreign direct investment, the citizens of many countries have had similar reactions.

Similar concerns exist with the evolution of global value chains. Recall from Chapter 11 that Kimura (2013) reports that, in general, Japanese citizens are relatively sanguine about the evolution of Japanese GVCs. Such an attitude is not universal, however. Citizens of various countries express concern about the "offshoring" of jobs via GVCs, as well as the potential for labor abuses. Therefore, the FDI and GVC aspects of international production can both raise concerns.

Despite these concerns, however, an increasing number of countries are engaged in both FDI and GVCs. In the case of FDI, for example, Anyanwu (2017: 132) notes that "FDI can play an important role in the development efforts of developing nations." In the case of GVCs, Taglioni and Winkler (2016: 9) suggest that "the new characteristic of GVCs from a development perspective is that factories in [low- and middle-income countries] have become full-fledged participants in international production networks, and this fact can present important development prospects."

In truth, ambiguities concerning international production are ever-present, with pros and cons both being relevant. For this reason, engaging and leveraging international production in both its FDI and GVC aspects is not straightforward. The best policy responses to these important aspects of economic globalization are not fully established. Therefore, the purpose of this chapter is to provide an overview of these issues in as balanced a manner as possible.

We begin in the following section by considering how countries become desired destinations for international production and the role of institutions in this process. Next, we characterize the benefits and costs of hosting MNEs from a development perspective. We then describe the various policy stances that a host country can adopt towards inward FDI and consider FDI's benefits and costs. We also consider different policy stances towards FDI. Next, we turn to the question of GVCs and how countries and firms can gain access to them. We then consider the important issue of linkages between MNEs and host-country firms. Finally, we take up the issue of the global institutional framework governing international production.

Attracting International Production

Recall from Figure 1.3 in Chapter 1 that FDI inflows are concentrated in high-income countries, with substantially smaller flows going to middle-income countries and almost no flows at all going to low-income countries. For example, in 2018 low-income countries received only 1 percent of total global FDI inflows, and middle-income countries received approximately 25 percent of these inflows. These patterns raise a question, namely what makes low- or middle-income countries attractive to multinational enterprises as a potential destination for international production in the form of FDI? A similar question could be asked regarding MNEs contracting in LMICs.

We know from Chapter 11 and our discussion of the task, location, and mode framework that *location advantages* matter for MNE choices. So we can rephrase our question in terms of what types of *location advantages* matter for developing countries to be able to attract international production.[1] These could include domestic or adjacent markets for market-seeking FDI or particular types of resources for resource-seeking FDI. We also need to recognize, as emphasized by Caves (2007: chap. 9), that there are three distinct patterns of FDI in LMICs: natural resource or resource-based FDI (e.g. petroleum, mining, rubber), domestic-market-serving FDI, and export processing. The case of natural resource FDI is relatively straightforward: the MNE wants access to the resource and the host-country government needs to manage this so as to share in the income for the benefit of the country.[2]

The cases of domestic-market-serving and export-processing FDI require a bit more investigation, and it is here that *institutional issues* appear as a relevant factor.[3] As it turns out, these considerations can also be relevant for FDI inflows and contracting possibilities. To summarize, a significant number of new studies

[1] On location advantages, see also Dunning (1988) and Dunning and Lundan (2008).

[2] There can be perennial issues of corruption and mismanagement associated with natural resource rents, however. On the management of natural resource rents, see Caves (2007: chap. 4).

[3] We will discuss the role of institutions in growth and development processes in Chapter 22 on growth in the open economy.

have demonstrated that *institutional quality* has a positive effect on FDI inflows.[4] Having reviewed this literature for LMICs, Anyanwu (2017: 149), for example, concludes the following:[5]

> To attract increased FDI to the developing economies, high priority should be given to improvements in governance systems and human capital development. Efforts should be made to improve the efficiency and effectiveness of public institutions, while increasing investment in human capital to generate the skills required in a competitive global environment. In addition, governments should respect private property rights, allow the rule of law to prevail and be accountable for their actions, as well as improve the legal, judicial, regulatory and infrastructure environment.

Another means through which countries can attempt to increase FDI inflows is through *bilateral investment treaties* (BITs) or *regional investment treaties* (RITs). Sometimes these are jointly known as *international investment agreements* (IIAs). BITs are defined by the United Nations Conference on Trade and Development as "agreements between two countries for the reciprocal encouragement, promotion and protection of investments in each other's territories by companies based in either country."[6] BITs have grown rapidly over time, from approximately 400 in 1990 to approximately 2,950 in 2018.[7] RITs are generally part of free trade areas or customs unions, discussed in Chapter 9.

The use of BITs and RITs is a way for a host country to signal to MNEs from signatory countries that they are committed to maintaining an institutional and legal environment favorable to MNE operations–a means of enhancing location advantages. These arrangements are occasionally criticized for being *too favorable* to MNEs, but are widely used nevertheless. Further, available evidence seems to suggest that BITS do indeed increase FDI flows.[8]

---

[4] Globerman and Shapiro (2002) find that a measure of good governance matters for FDI inflows, and this result has been confirmed by Buchanan, Le, and Rishi (2012). The same is true of democracy, as studied by Li and Resnick (2003). Many institutional indicators were used in a sophisticated statistical analysis by Bénassy-Quéré, Coupet, and Mayer (2007), who also find that institutional quality supports FDI inflows. Additionally, measures of corruption are *negatively* related to FDI inflows, as shown by Zhao, Kim, and Du (2003) and others. These sorts of results were also confirmed for FDI-deprived sub-Saharan Africa by Asiedu (2006) and Asamoah, Adjasi, and Alhassan (2016).

[5] There is another dimension of institutional quality that often proves to be important regarding FDI and GVCs, namely *intellectual property protection*. We discussed this in a box in Chapter 10.

[6] UNCTAD also reports: "Treaties typically cover the following areas: scope and definition of investment, admission and establishment, national treatment, most-favored-nation treatment, fair and equitable treatment, compensation in the event of expropriation or damage to the investment, guarantees of free transfers of funds, and dispute settlement mechanisms, both state–state and investor–state" (unctad.org).

[7] See http://investmentpolicyhub.unctad.org/IIA. UNCTAD notes there that, in 2018, of the approximately 2,950 BITS in existence, only about 2,360 were "in force."

[8] See, for example, Falvey and Foster-McGregor (2018).

Benefits and Costs

Suppose for a moment that you are a policy-maker responsible for policy towards MNEs and FDI. It might be helpful to you to have some sense of *both* the benefits *and* costs that FDI can entail. We are going to discuss the benefits and costs with the help of Table 12.1. The items we will consider are: employment and wages, competition, education and training, technology, the balance of payments, health and the environment, and culture.

Employment and wages If a foreign firm engages in FDI in a host-country sector in which there is unemployment, it is possible for this FDI to increase the total

Table 12.1 The benefits and costs of inward FDI

Item	Benefits	Costs
Employment and wages	Generates direct and indirect increases in employment. Might offer higher wages.	Transfers jobs from home to foreign firms.
Competition	Promotes competition by increasing the number of firms in an industry.	Retards competition in cases in which the foreign firm has a large amount of market power.
Education and training	Improves the education and training of host-country workers.	Restricts education and training to expatriate employees. Discriminates against host-country workers.
Technology	Transfers technology from developed to developing countries.	Technology employed might not be appropriate for the host-country economy.
Balance of payments	Improves the import and export components of the current account. Improves the direct investment component of the capital/financial account.	Worsens the import component of the current account. Worsens the net factor receipt component of the capital/financial account.
Health and the environment	Employs new technology that is more environmentally sound. Increases incomes and thereby makes more resources available for the enforcement of existing environmental regulations.	Increases the amount of pollution and subjects workers to unsafe workplaces.
Culture	Introduces progressive aspect of business culture in the areas of organizational development and human resource management.	Increases dominance of urban and Western culture over rural and non-Western culture.

Sources: Adapted from Dunning and Lundan (2008) and Hill (2009).

number of jobs in that sector. This is a positive employment effect and constitutes a benefit of FDI. Such *direct* employment benefits can be supplemented by *indirect* employment benefits, when local firms supply the foreign MNE with intermediate products (something we will discuss below). It is also possible, in cases of acquisition, for a simple transfer of jobs from local to foreign firms to occur with no net increase in employment. Depending on one's point of view, this might be interpreted as a cost of FDI. In addition to employment effects, there is accumulating evidence that MNEs often offer higher wages than domestic firms.[9]

Competition If a foreign firm engages in FDI in a home-country sector characterized by imperfect competition, it is possible for the FDI to increase competition in the sector. As you learned in introductory microeconomics, an increase in competition tends to lower prices and increase quantities supplied through the erosion of market power. Since this benefits consumers, this positive competition effect constitutes a benefit of FDI. On the other hand, in cases when the foreign MNE possesses a large amount of market power itself compared to the host-country firms, FDI could *worsen* competition, and this would be a cost of FDI.

Education and Training As we will discuss in Chapter 22, the accumulation of human capital via education and training is a crucial component of economic growth and development. It is possible for foreign MNEs to provide education and training to host-country workers that were not available from domestic firms.[10] This provides benefits to the host-country economy. It is equally possible, however, for the foreign MNE to restrict education and training to its own transplanted employees, and to even discriminate against host-country workers. Such discrimination would constitute a cost of FDI to the host country. Dunning and Lundan (2008) summarize the empirical evidence on the education and training issue, reporting that "the accumulated evidence suggests that, while the amount and character of training varies considerably between firms, as a general rule it is fairly narrowly focused on the specific needs of the investing enterprises, rather than on the wider economic and social goals of the countries in which they operate" (445). For this reason, although MNEs probably do make a significant contribution, the overall human resource trajectory of a country remains the responsibility of the country government.[11]

---

[9] For example, this has been found in Mexico (Feenstra and Hanson, 1997), a set of African countries (te Velde and Morrissey, 2003), Indonesia (Sjöholm and Lipsey, 2006), and Hungary (Earle, Telegdy, and Antal, 2017).

[10] Dunning and Lundan (2008: chap. 13) include this possibility as one of the intangible assets of MNEs. They state: "One of the key...advantages which MNEs enjoy...is their ability to train and upgrade human resources, and to motivate their employees. They derive this advantage, in part at least, from their access to different labor market institutions and to their cross-border experiences in human resource management" (444).

[11] See, for example, Kheng, Sun, and Anwar (2017).

Technology Many LMICs lack access to the technologies available in high-income countries, and acquiring this technology is a key component of the development process.[12] Recall from Chapter 1 that MNEs account for approximately three-fourths of worldwide civilian research and development. Consequently, hosting MNEs is one way to gain access to that technology. There are two problems, however. First, MNEs will employ the technology that most suits *their* strategic needs, and these can differ from the development needs of the host country. For example, foreign MNEs might employ processes that are much more capital-intensive than would be desired on the basis of host-country employment considerations. Caves' (2007: chap. 9) relatively extensive review suggests that, although some MNEs adapt their technologies to local environments, this adaptation is not widespread or more than minimal.

Second, as we discussed in Chapter 10, MNEs tend to concentrate their R&D in their home bases, limiting potential technology transfer. That said, there are movements away from this traditional pattern of innovation in MNEs with the emergence of regional laboratories focused on the development aspect of R&D, if not applied research. For this reason, it is still valid to consider MNEs as *potential* sources of technology in some cases.

There is a presumption in much of the literature on FDI that MNEs provide positive "spillovers" in the form of technology upgrading to domestic firms in the countries. This line of thinking goes back to Caves (1974), who tested this possibility for Canada and Australia. The evidence of *generalized* technology spillovers is mixed, however. A sample of evidence from LMICs is provided in Table 12.2. As can be seen in the table, many studies do find evidence of positive spillovers. As noted by Caves (2007: 221, emphasis added), however, "demonstrated spillovers occur so as to suggest domestic firms must possess *substantial competence* before they can sup up spilled technology." This has led to an exploration of domestic preconditions (particularly human capital) that can make positive spillovers more likely.[13]

Balance of Payments We will not consider the balance of payments accounts until Chapter 14 (Table 14.2), so, at this juncture, we are not yet familiar with balance of payments terminology. To make things simple, we can note that the direct impact

---

[12] For example, Dunning and Lundan (2008: 340) state: "It is widely accepted that the ability to create, acquire, learn how to use and effectively deploy technological capacity is one of the key ingredients of economic success in virtually all societies. It is also acknowledged that, together with institutional reform, advances in product, production, information and organizational technology have accounted for much of the economic growth of nations over the past century."

[13] This general conclusion was also reached by Dunning and Lundan (2008: chap. 16). These authors state that, "while the...evidence strongly suggests that the benefits from linkages and spillovers should not be underestimated, the...evidence confirms that their benefit to the economy as a whole cannot be assumed as a matter of course" (605). Indeed, in an extensive review of the research literature, Iršová and Havránek (2012) find technological spillovers to be, on average, nonexistent—or, in their words, "zero."

Table 12.2 A sample of studies on the potential spillover effects of FDI

Study	Country	Findings
Aitken and Harrison (1999)	Venezuela	Two effects of FDI on local firms. First, a positive relationship between foreign equity and performance in plants with fewer than 50 workers. Second, negative spillovers from market-stealing effects. On net, evidence of only a small impact of FDI on plant productivity.
Anwar and Nguyen (2014)	Vietnam	Positive spillovers do exist but vary significantly by region and can be zero in some regions.
Arnold and Javorcik (2009)	Indonesia	Evidence of positive spillovers thanks to acquisition and restructuring of domestic firms. Foreign ownership leads to higher productivity and share of skilled workers.
Blalock and Gertler (2008)	Indonesia	Evidence of positive spillovers thanks to technology transfer to local suppliers and positive externality from these suppliers to other downstream buyers.
Blomström (1986)	Mexico	Evidence of positive spillovers thanks to increased competition.
Blomström and Persson (1983)	Mexico	Evidence of positive spillovers associated with increased technological efficiency.
Blomström and Sjöholm (1999)	Indonesia	Evidence of positive spillovers thanks to increased competition being restricted to non-exporting local firms.
Fauzel, Seetanah, and Sannasee (2015)	Mauritius	Evidence of positive spillovers, especially in the long run. In the short run the effects are very small.
Haddad and Harrison (1993)	Morocco	Although the dispersion of productivity levels is narrower in sectors with more foreign firms, no evidence of positive spillovers.
Kohpaiboon (2006)	Thailand	Foreign firms can either positively or negatively affect the productivity of local firms, depending on the trade regime.
Kokko (1994)	Mexico	Potential positive spillovers are negatively related to productivity gaps between MNEs and domestic firm and differ between industries.
Kokko, Tansini, and Zejan (1996)	Uruguay	Little evidence of positive spillovers, with only a small effect when the technology gap between local and foreign firms is small.
Kugler (2006)	Colombia	Evidence of spillovers to local upstream suppliers through diffusion of generic upstream suppliers.
Liang (2017)	China	Domestic firms with high absorptive capacity benefit from foreign suppliers but not from foreign customers.
Liu (2002)	China	Evidence of positive spillover effect on domestic sectors through technology transfers.
Marin and Bell (2006)	Argentina	Evidence of positive spillovers conditional on activity of MNE subsidiaries. Spillover effects depend on the local knowledge creation of subsidiaries.
Wei and Liu (2006)	China	Evidence of positive spillovers.

of an FDI inflow is a positive one in the direct investment component of the capital/financial account of the balance of payments. The capital/financial account of the balance of payments records transactions that involve the exchange of assets, as in the case of FDI. After the FDI takes place, the MNE involved can begin to repatriate its profits back to the home base. This would cause a negative entry in the net income component of current account. The current account of the balance of payments records transactions that do not involve the exchange of assets.

If the good produced by the MNE is sold domestically and replaces previously imported goods, the FDI will have the effect of making the goods and services trade balance component of the current account more positive (less negative). The MNE might import a significant amount of intermediate products, however, and this would tend to make the goods and services trade balance component of the current account less positive (more negative). Finally, if the MNE exports the good it produces, this would tend to make the goods and services trade balance component of the current account more positive (less negative). Clearly, the net effect of all these balance of payments influences would need to be evaluated on a case-by-case basis.

Health and the Environment Recently a great deal attention has been focused on the impacts of MNEs on health and the environment. This relates to something known as the **pollution haven hypothesis**, the notion that MNEs locate environmentally damaging production in countries with lax environmental standards. The evidence to date suggests two things.[14] First, it is difficult to detect an *overall* pattern of FDI consistent with the pollution haven hypothesis. This is because there are so many other factors at play in FDI decisions.[15] Second, it is clear that there are *individual cases* of pollution haven behavior, however. For example, in resource extractive industries, certain (not all) MNEs have been grossly negligent. The accompanying box presents a brief discussion of the petroleum industry in the Ecuadorian Amazon region. A similar story applies to the petroleum industry in Nigeria, discussed in Chapter 1.

The Petroleum Industry in the Ecuadorian Amazon

In the 1960s Ecuador opened itself up to oil exploration, and in 1967 the US MNE Texaco discovered the first commercially viable oil reserve in the Amazon region. Along with its local partner, Petroecuador, Texaco began to pump oil in 1972. Texaco was active in this manner until 1992, when its contract with Petroecuador expired. Thereafter its operations were taken over by Petroecuador itself. Other

[14] For reviews, see Dunning and Lundan (2008: chap. 10) and Copeland (2009).

[15] See, however, Bokpin (2017) on FDI in Africa.

The Petroleum Industry in the Ecuadorian Amazon (cont.)

US-based MNEs operating in this region during the 1970s and 1980s included Occidental Petroleum, ARCO, Unocal, Conoco, and Mobil. In 1993 Ecuador and the United States signed a bilateral investment treaty.

Texaco's operations included 350 wells and 1,000 open waste pits. Estimates vary, but approximately 19 billion gallons of oil were spilled, along with the release of toxic wastewater. Epidemiological studies also vary as to the health effects of these spills, but there have been allegations of substantial impacts in the areas of cancers, birth defects, and spontaneous abortions. There were also large-scale dislocations of indigenous peoples as a result of the oil exploration and pumping operations. For example, Kane (1996: 157) reports:

> While I was in Toñampare a valve in an oil well near the Napo [River] broke, or was left open, and for two days and a night raw crude streamed into the river – at least 21,000 gallons and perhaps as many as 80,000, creating a slick that stretched from bank to bank for forty miles. Ecuador's downstream neighbors, Peru and Brazil, declared states of emergency, but Petroecuador shrugged off the problem.... Three weeks later the pipeline itself burst, in the Andean foothills that rise beyond the west bank of the Napo, and spilled another 32,000 gallons into the watershed.

Initially the growing wrath of Ecuadorian environmentalists and indigenous peoples of Ecuador was directed against Texaco, resulting in the now famous Aguinda vs. Texaco class action lawsuit of 1993. Texaco agreed to engage in some amount of environmental mitigation as a result of this lawsuit, but this was seen as too small a response. Texaco was acquired by Chevron in 2001, and Chevron consequently inherited this lawsuit. It was not uncommon for Chevron's attorneys to enter court in Ecuador accompanied by armed guards given the level of anger against them.

In 2009 a Chevron spokesperson stated that the firm would "fight the case until hell freezes over and then fight it on the ice." In 2011, however, Chevron was hit by a US$12 billion judgment in a class action lawsuit brought by Ecuadorian citizens. This was overturned in 2018 by the Permanent Court of Arbitration (PCA) in The Hague. Ecuador plans to appeal this finding, questioning the authority of the PCA. The case offers a sad, cautionary tale of the potential environmental impacts of some MNEs, as well as a testament to the potential complexities of international disputes involving MNEs.

Sources: Kane (1996), Kelsh, Morimoto, and Lau (2009), McAteer and Pulver (2009), Nagarkatti and McWilliams (2018), and Navarro (2018).

Culture MNEs serve as conduits of their home countries' national and business cultures. They also sometimes introduce new goods with cultural content into host countries. These activities can further the dominance of urban and "Western" culture over rural and "non-Western" culture, and, in some LMIC host countries, exacerbate already existing tensions between these cultural/regional poles. In the case of resource extraction activities, FDI can result in the dislocation of indigenous peoples, as in the Ecuadorian case discussed in the box. In these ways, FDI can impose significant cultural costs on host countries. More positively, however, MNEs can introduce progressive elements of business culture into their host countries. These might include new practices in the areas of organizational development and human resource management.

One would hope that, by assessing each of the items in Table 12.1, we could make a *general statement* about the degree to which FDI supports the process of international economic development. It appears, however, that this is *not the case*. Even some of the best minds that have focused on the issue do not agree on the matter. Consider the following. Rodrik (1999) is relatively *pessimistic* about the role of FDI in development, stating: "Absent hard evidence to the contrary, one dollar worth of FDI is worth no more (and no less) than a dollar of any other kind of investment" (37). UNCTAD (1999) offers a somewhat *less pessimistic* view: "The role of FDI in countries' processes and efforts to meet development objectives can differ greatly across countries, depending on the nature of the economy and the government" (29). A somewhat *more enthusiastic* view is offered by Moran (1998: 153): "The direct and indirect benefits from well-constructed FDI projects are substantially greater than commonly assumed, but they do not come easily."

Can FDI generate net benefits for host countries? Yes. Does it *always* do so? No. The role that FDI plays in international economic development needs to be assessed on a case-by-case basis, with close attention being paid to the country characteristics, the firm characteristics and strategy, and the national policy environment. Once these features have been carefully accounted for, we can begin to assess the benefits and costs of the FDI project under consideration. In general, countries should be looking to FDI to help them in their development, but they need to do so with some care and consideration.[16]

Policy Stances

Historically, there have been very different policy stances by national governments towards FDI. For example, Anyanwu (2017) makes a distinction between a *nationalist approach* and a *traditional economic approach* towards FDI. He describes the nationalist approach as follows:

[16] Goldin and Reinert (2012: chap. 4) make the same general argument.

> The nationalist approach argues that FDI damages host economies through the suppression of domestic entrepreneurship, importation of unsuitable technology and unsuitable products, the extension of oligopolistic practices such as unnecessary product differentiation, heavy advertising or excessive profit-taking, and the worsening of income distribution by a self-perpetuating process, which simultaneously reinforces high-income elites and provides them with expensive consumer goods (133).

Anyanwu describes the traditional economic approach as follows:

> The traditional economic approach...argues that FDI is a net addition to investible resources in host countries, and as such raises their rates of growth. According to this school of thought, FDI introduces products and markets, creates taste, meets needs and brings about a desirable growth pattern. It is also conducive both to total world welfare and to the welfare of each individual country (133).

It is fair to say that, historically, the traditional economic approach is on the rise. This evolution of policy should not blind us to the costs and benefits approach we have just described, however. Indeed, any policy-maker with responsibilities for FDI would want to minimize the costs and maximize the benefits of the FDI.[17]

What about the actual policies towards FDI? These can be grouped into **ownership requirements** and **performance requirements**. Ownership requirements limit the degree of foreign ownership of a subsidiary. These can be absolute, as in the case of foreign firms being excluded from certain sectors on national security grounds. For example, until recent years Mexico did this with its petroleum sector. Alternatively, they may simply limit foreign ownership to a maximum specified amount. For example, China once limited foreign enterprises to joint ventures with Chinese firms in which the foreign firm can own a maximum of 50 percent of the venture.[18]

Performance requirements place controls on the *behavior* of the foreign firm in a number of areas. For example, a host country might require that the MNE maintain a minimum level of locally sourced intermediate inputs. This is known as a *local content requirement*. Other performance requirements can include stipulations in the areas of training, technology transfer, exports, local research and development, and the hiring of local managers. These matters are usually settled in negotiations

[17] In the case of Intel's 1997–2014 investment in Costa Rica, discussed in Chapter 11, most of the items in Table 12.1 were benefits rather than costs. Intel was generating new employment and bringing new technology. It went so far as to assist the Costa Rican government in the education and training of future Intel workers. Its exports would generate foreign exchange. One significant potential cost, however, was in the environmental category, in the form of toxic industrial waste. The solution to this problem was to re-export this waste back to the United States to be processed by US companies.

[18] Recall the example of Beijing Jeep in Chapter 10.

between the host-country government and the foreign MNE. Historically, most East Asian countries used performance requirements focused on local content and export performance.[19] Many LMICs have significantly relaxed their performance requirements over time, however.

Many of the above requirements are also known as **trade-related investment measures** (TRIMs), and are listed in Table 12.3. The Marrakesh Agreement on

Table 12.3 Types of trade-related investment measures

Measure	Explanation	Comment
Local content requirement	Requires that a certain amount of local input be used in production.	Prohibited by TRIMs
Trade balancing requirement	Requires that imports be a certain proportion of exports.	Prohibited by TRIMs
Foreign exchange balancing requirement	Requires that use of foreign exchange for importing be a certain proportion of exports and the foreign exchange brought into the host country by the firm.	Prohibited by TRIMs
Domestic sales requirement	Requires that a proportion of output be sold locally.	Prohibited by TRIMs
Manufacturing requirement	Requires that certain products be manufactured locally.	
Manufacturing restriction	Prohibits the manufacturing of certain products in the host country.	
Export performance requirement	Requires that a certain share of output be exported.	Prohibited or discouraged by many BITs and RITs
Exchange restriction	Limits a firm's access to foreign exchange.	
Technology transfer requirement	Requires that certain technologies be transferred or that certain R&D functions be performed locally.	Prohibited or discouraged by many BITs and RITs
Licensing requirement	Requires that the foreign firm license certain technologies to local firms.	
Remittance restriction	Limits the right of the foreign firm to repatriate profits.	
Local equity requirement	Restricts the amount of a firm's equity that can be held by local investors.	Prohibited or discouraged by many BITs and RITs

Sources: Low and Subramanian (1996) and UNCTAD (2003).

[19] See, for example, Hill (1990).

Trade in Goods (see Chapter 8) included an Agreement on TRIMs, which prohibits some types of TRIMs in the case of goods. These include domestic content, trade balancing, foreign exchange balancing, and domestic sales requirements. Export performance requirements were *not* prohibited. Investment-related policies in services are covered under the General Agreement on Trade in Services (again, see Chapter 8). Some international economic policy experts are now calling for policies that would go beyond TRIMs, to require the abandonment of all policies that discriminate between domestic and foreign firms. Others are critical of the Agreement on TRIMs itself.[20]

Some countries also offer potential MNEs *location incentives* in the form of tax breaks. These policies often take the form of "customs-free zones," in which tax rates have been lowered. This was the case, for example, for Intel in Costa Rica. It is not clear, however, that these policies are worthwhile in attracting FDI. They can result in excessive bidding wars between host countries and simply become transfers to the MNEs involved.[21] Indeed, there is some evidence that, rather than subsidizing FDI through tax incentives, efforts need to be made to understand how to best *tax* MNEs instead of subsidizing them.[22]

Entering Global Value Chains

As we discussed in Chapter 11, global value chains have become an increasingly important aspect of international production. Consider the following from Foss, Mudambi, and Murtinu (2019):

> Empirical analyses of the location choices of MNEs suggest that they increasingly disaggregate their global value chains into fine-sliced activities. These activities are often placed in or sourced from very different locations before the final value proposition is orchestrated through reaggregation. While this gives rise to substantial management challenges, the ongoing trend towards fine-slicing global value chains suggests that specialization and location advantages dominate the increased costs of managing complex contractual and other corporate arrangements across borders.

The question facing many countries is *how* to enter into GVCs in this new, complex world.[23] The first thing to recognize here, as we emphasized in Chapter 11, is

[20] See, for example, Lee (2016: chap. 5).

[21] See Hoekman and Saggi (2000) and Foss, Mudambi, and Murtinu (2019).

[22] See Foss, Mudambi, and Murtinu (2019).

[23] Baldwin (2016: 271) actually puts the question more broadly: "How can policy ensure that global value chain participation benefits the domestic economy as a whole through more and better paid jobs, better living conditions, superior training, infrastructure, and the like?"

that GVCs are all about *tasks*. So, potentially entering GVCs is about what Taglioni and Winkler (2016: 147) call a "task-based development strategy." These researchers point out that there are two approaches to a task-based development strategy: attracting FDI and facilitating domestic firms' access to GVCs. Let us briefly consider the second of these strategies.

There are a number of entry points for a domestic firm into GVCs. These include: supplying intermediate inputs (e.g. parts) to a foreign subsidiary operating in the firm's home country, supplying intermediate inputs to foreign firms abroad, and becoming a final assembler for foreign firms (contract manufacturing). Taglioni and Winkler (2016) correctly point out that identifying which tasks a firm might have competitive advantages in is *not easy*. The least risky approach is to build on existing capabilities, but it is also possible to use the revealed comparative advantage measure (discussed in Chapter 4) applied to the trade in value added data (discussed in Chapter 11). There is also the possibility of identifying incipient clusters (discussed in Chapter 10) as indicators of task potential.

A country also needs to be cognizant of *resource endowments* when judging where to try to enter GVCs. As stated by Taglioni and Winkler (2016: 150):

> In the absence of market failures..., tasks tend to depend on the know-how (quantity and quality of workers) and capital stock (including technology) available to perform them. If only a fraction of the workforce is highly skilled, launching into tasks that depend primarily on skilled workers does not make sense for a country. The goal is to choose tasks that create the largest domestic value added given the labor and capital endowments in the home country.

In other words, some of the insights from the Heckscher–Ohlin model of Chapter 4 are relevant.

Finally, as emphasized by Baldwin (2016: chap. 9), the choice of tasks needs to be informed by the country's geographic *location*. Despite the way that advances in transportation and ICT have "shrunk" the world, distance still matters. In some cases, countries need to look to *regional* GVCs as appropriate entry points.[24]

One policy stance towards hosting GVCs is to set up an **export processing zone**, or EPZ. An EPZ is an area of the host country in which MNEs can locate and in which they enjoy, in return for exporting most or the whole of their output, favorable treatment in the areas of infrastructure, taxation, tariffs on imported intermediate goods, and labor costs. Caves (2007: 261) notes that EPZs "are simply

---

[24] For example, Gereffi and Sturgeon (2013: 343) note: "In East Asia, China benefits from close economic ties with many of its East Asian neighbors that facilitate imports of materials and components that go into China's manufactured export products."

a device for bundling together many concessions" on the part of a host country. EPZs have been a popular policy device and have been used in many countries around the world.[25] Their number has increased rapidly, from fewer than 100 in 1975 to approximately 3,000 in 2000, and then to approximately 4,000 in 2015.[26] In most cases, EPZs involve relatively labor-intensive, "light" manufacturing such as textiles, clothing, footwear, and electronics.

It seems clear that EPZs are indeed trade-promoting (see, for example, Yücer and Siroën, 2017). The more important question, however, is how EPZs perform in cost–benefit analyses. The answer to this question is: "Not always too well." In many cases, the costs outweigh the benefits.[27] For this and other reasons, Engman, Onodera, and Pinali (2007) suggest that EPZs are "suboptimal" and cannot replace more general reforms and investments that would increase a country's location advantages.

A final issue with EPZs is that they tend to have an "enclave" characteristic, lacking linkages to the rest of the economy. In other words, few domestic firms supply intermediate inputs to the EPZ. As stated by Taglioni and Winkler (2016: 162), "Most studies find that the backward linkages from firms in EPZs are minimal, with domestic orders remaining very low and technology spillovers rare." We will further consider the issue of linkages in the following section.

Like other modes of participation in the global economy, GVC participation is not without *risks*. Being embedded inside a GVC exposes a country and its participating firms to commercial shocks, both upstream (supply-side shocks), in the form of potential intermediate product supply interruptions, and downstream (demand-side shocks), in the form of demand volatility. This reflects the fact that, if there is a lead firm in the GVC, that firm will have the interest and ability to shift the impacts of shocks to other firms within the GVC. The adjustment within GVCs to shocks of various kinds reflects (in complex ways) the relational aspects of contracting relationships discussed in Chapter 10: market, modular, relational, and captive.[28] As stated in that chapter, the more a GVC is producer-driven rather than buyer-driven, the farther the GVC tends to move towards the relational and captive models.

The main takeaway from a consideration of GVCs from a development process perspective is that, as emphasized by many researchers, it affords the possibility that countries can become part of GVCs without having to build entire value chains from scratch domestically. The possibility of specializing in a particular

---

[25] See Schrank (2001) and Singa Boyenge (2007).

[26] See Singa Boyenge (2007) and UNCTAD (2015).

[27] See, for example, Johansson and Nilsson (1997), Schrank (2001), Jayanthakumaran (2003), Jenkins (2006), Engman, Onodera, and Pinali (2007), and Quaicoe, Aboagye, and Bokpin (2017).

[28] See Gereffi, Humphrey, and Sturgeon (2005) and Ruigrok and van Tulder (1995: chaps. 4 & 5).

task and developing a potential cluster of firms around that task is much more feasible than constructing a whole value chain. This is a new possibility in the modern world economy that was not previously available.[29]

Promoting Linkages

In a world of GVCs, MNEs decide what part of the GVC to undertake themselves and what part to leave to other firms in buyer or supplier relationships. It is possible for MNEs to leave some parts of the upstream components of the GVC to other firms, choosing to buy from *local firms* in the country in which they are located. This is known as **backward linkages** to domestic suppliers.

Historically, and as just mentioned, backward linkages have been *weak*.[30] This has been of concern to LMICs, because the increased use of local firms as sources of intermediate product would increase their levels of employment and support their technological development. The increased role of MNEs in an economy and the increased participation in GVCs without significant backward linkages results in what are termed "enclaves" with little connection to the rest of the economy and little contribution beyond direct employment effects. Traditionally, the means to avoid enclave FDI was via local content requirements, discussed above, but these are no longer allowed for WTO members.

Some new thinking in the area of facilitating backward linkages suggests that local content requirements should be replaced by attempts to support local suppliers in their efforts to secure contracts with foreign MNEs. For example, Taglioni and Winkler (2016: 163) state: "A key difference between GVC-led and other avenues of development is that GVCs require government coordination at the micro level." If a foreign MNE can be *induced* to source inputs locally rather than by importing them, the host country can gain a number of important benefits.

1. Employment can increase, since the sourced inputs are new production.
2. The balance of payments (Chapter 14) can improve, since the inputs will no longer be imported.

---

[29] For example, Gereffi and Sturgeon (2013: 354) state the following: "Policies that promote linkages to GVCs have very different aims from traditional industrial policies that intend to build fully blown, vertically integrated domestic industries. Policies can target specialized niches in GVCs. These can be higher-value niches suited to existing capabilities. They can also be generic capabilities that can be pooled across foreign investors. Either of these can serve both domestic or export markets."

[30] For example, some time ago Battat, Frank, and Shen (1996) reported that US MNEs operating for export assembly in northern Mexico (known as *maquiladoras*) sourced only 2 percent of their inputs from Mexican firms. More recently, in the Costa Rican case, Jenkins (2006) demonstrates a reluctance of textile, clothing, and electronics MNEs to form backward linkages within that country.

3. Production technologies can be better adapted to local conditions.
4. The tangible and intangible assets we discussed in Chapter 10 can potentially be passed from the foreign MNE to the local suppliers.
5. Local suppliers can coalesce into a spatial cluster that supports agglomeration economies in the form of innovation and upgrading.[31]

The key policy question for developing countries is how to foster backward linkages between foreign MNEs and potential local suppliers. The linkage promotion process involves many players, including the government, foreign MNEs, local suppliers, professional organizations, commercial organizations, and academic institutions. The key role of the government is one of *coordination*, attempting to bridge the "information gaps" between the players. This is what Taglioni and Winkler (2016) refer to as "light-handed industrial policy." This can be done in a number of different ways.[32]

1. In the realm of *information*, attempts can be made to provide a matching service between MNEs and local suppliers in the form of linkage promotion forums and online directories.
2. In the realm of *technology*, efforts can be made to provide support in standards formation, materials testing, and patent registration. In addition, foreign MNEs can be invited to be involved in programs designed to upgrade local suppliers' technological capabilities.
3. In the realm of *human resource development*, efforts can be made to provide technical training and managerial training.
4. In the realm of *finance*, obstacles to access on the part of small firms can be removed.
5. In the realm of *infrastructure*, attempt can be made to ensure that customs, ports, and logistics operate effectively so that intermediate products can enter easily and be processed for re-export.

---

[31] This last potential benefit is emphasized by Battat, Frank, and Shen (1996: 5): "Rapid changes in design and technology have made it necessary to make more frequent modifications of inputs at all stages of production. In such cases, subcontracting based on a long-term consultative or networked relationship becomes more desirable.... The ability of the supplier to react quickly to the manufacturer's changing design and production needs has often become an even more crucial factor than price. This form of backward linkage...makes the relationship between suppliers of inputs and the company purchasing the inputs more stable than the relationship between suppliers of off-the-shelf goods and the purchasers of such goods. This stability, in turn, helps suppliers to make better planning and technological decisions."

[32] See Battat, Frank, and Shen (1996), Dunning and Lundan (2008: chap. 16), Taglioni and Winkler (2016: chap. 8), and UNCTAD (2001).

Efforts in these and other areas are typically coordinated by a lead agency. The Irish case, including its National Linkage Programme, is discussed in the accompanying box. Fortunately, in recent years some MNEs themselves have developed an interest in forging backward linkages in some countries. For example, Intel, Toyota, and Volvo have developed programs for suppliers in some countries.[33] In some circumstances, then, host-country governments and MNEs can work together to support backward linkages.

Lessons from FDI in Ireland

An acquaintance of mine, who grew up in Ireland in the 1970s, told me that, as a child and teenager, he had one major ambition: to emigrate. Even as of the mid-1980s Ireland was recognized as a fairly poor country and was plagued with a number of serious difficulties: declining employment, high levels of emigration, and rapidly rising levels of debt. In the 1960s and 1970s, though, Ireland began a process of selectively attracting MNEs through tax holidays. During this time the country also entered the European Community (see Chapter 9).

Policy towards MNEs grew even stronger in the 1980s, when a number of government agencies and business incentive programs were created to attract MNEs into particular industrial clusters (such as electronics, chemicals, and pharmaceuticals), including in high-technology sectors. These policies proved to be successful, and by the mid-1990s over 1,000 foreign-based companies had established manufacturing facilities in the country. Included in these efforts was an EPZ strategy in the form of the Shannon Free Trade Zone (FTZ), which met with great success. Indeed, Buckley and Ruane (2006: 1611) note that "Ireland is unusual in the extent to which it has consistently promoted export-platform inward investment into the manufacturing sector for over four decades." By the mid-2000s MNEs accounted for approximately one-half of manufacturing employment in the country.

The government did not neglect the service sector, however. The positive outcome of the Shannon FTZ inspired the creation of the International Financial Services Centre (IFSC) in Dublin in 1987. The establishment of the IFSC was an attempt at urban renewal, involving a dockside site in the heart of Dublin being converted into an attractive business center. It attracted hundreds of

[33] For the case of Japanese MNEs in Thailand, see Moran (2001). On the Volvo case, see Ivarsson and Alvstam (2005).

Lessons from FDI in Ireland (cont.)

financial services firms. In coordinating efforts to support the IFSC, the Industrial Development Authority of Ireland (IDA Ireland) played a key role. The government also supported the IFSC with a state-of-the-art telecommunications network and an educated workforce. World Bank data from that time demonstrated that Ireland spent a larger portion of its GDP on education (over 6 percent) than most other EU countries. Further, these educational efforts were tailored to emerging clusters, whether in manufacturing or services.

Ireland's economic growth rates during the 1990s were often on a par with those of East Asia, and in 1998 Ireland was one of the 11 countries of the European Union selected for inclusion in the European Monetary Union (EMU). Success in hosting MNEs contributed significantly to these positive changes in the Irish economy. Emigration was no longer the prime goal of young, talented Irish citizens. As we will discuss in Chapter 20, however, a real estate boom and bust contributed to a banking crisis during the period from 2007 to 2009, severely compromising the Irish development model. Nevertheless, Ireland's recovery from the crisis was driven by FDI. Recent investors include LinkedIn, Google, Facebook, and Apple. For this reason, the decades-old FDI and development policy of Ireland still holds some lessons for other countries.

Sources: Buckley and Ruane (2006), *The Economist* (2018), and World Bank (1999).

Governing International Production

Institutions governing international trade and international finance exist in the form of the World Trade Organization and the International Monetary Fund, but no such counterpart exists in the realm of international production. Instead, by default, there has evolved a piecemeal and incomplete approach to governing international production. Let us consider just a few aspects of this approach.

A key player in the attempted governing of international production has been the Organisation for Economic Co-operation and Development. The OECD has been active in this realm for some time.[34] In 1995 OECD ministers announced their intent to develop a Multilateral Agreement on Investment, or MAI. The purpose of the agreement was to liberalize the cross-border flows of foreign direct investment.

[34] OECD-sponsored agreements include the 1961 Code of Liberalization of Capital Movements and the 1976 Declaration of International Investment and Multinational Enterprises. In 1991 the OECD tried to develop a comprehensive set of investment rules, but it failed.

It would have required host countries to apply "national treatment" (see Chapter 8) to all foreign firms. This would prevent host countries from implementing both the ownership and performance requirements discussed earlier in this chapter. The OECD consisted at that time of fewer than thirty, mostly high-income countries, however, and was therefore unrepresentative of WTO membership.[35] Consequently, the MAI failed to gain enough traction within the WTO membership.

With the failure of the OECD's MAI, it was essentially left to the WTO to consider any further multilateral governance frameworks. There was also the possibility that, if WTO members proved unable to agree on a new investment framework, one could be developed as a plurilateral agreement, which only a subset of members would sign.[36] Although a working group on the issue was established at the 1996 WTO Ministerial Conference in Singapore, it was not possible to establish a negotiating group. Since then work on this issue has been confined to the working group.[37]

With regard to the social governance of international production, there have been calls (see, for example, Goldin and Reinert, 2012: chap. 8) for *de minimus* binding constraints on MNE behavior. It is fair to say that this is not on the active international agenda. One non-binding "soft law" effort has been the OECD's Guidelines for Multinational Enterprises. These guidelines were developed in 1976 and revised in 2000 and 2011. By mid-2019 they had been adopted by 48 countries (36 OECD countries and 12 non-OECD countries). In the 2011 revision there are 15 OECD guidelines.[38] They partially address concerns regarding human rights, local capacity building, labor relations, health and the environment, corporate governance, and science and technology. Further, a "risk-based due diligence approach" is applied to responsible value chain management. The OECD guidelines thereby extend beyond the actions of MNEs themselves to their suppliers and business partners.

One perennial issue of MNE behavior and governance is that of **transfer pricing**, and this is considered in the accompanying box.

---

[35] *The Economist* (1998: 81) reported at that time: "Few developing countries seemed prepared to sign something they did not help to shape. Instead, the governments of developing countries increasingly see MAI as an exercise in neo-colonialism, designed to give rich-world investors the upper hand."

[36] The Marrakesh Agreement establishing the WTO contains an Annex 4 of plurilateral agreements to which members are not required to adhere. For example, Graham (1996: 104) writes: "All of the nations that would sign an OECD agreement would presumably also sign such a plurilateral agreement, and some nations not party to the OECD agreement might sign on as well. In such a case, a plurilateral WTO agreement would definitely be preferable to an OECD-only agreement."

[37] In a detailed review of this issue, Hoekman and Saggi (2000) find no compelling reason for further negotiations in this area. See also www.wto.org/english/tratop_e/invest_e/invest_e.htm.

[38] See http://mneguidelines.oecd.org and Reinert, Reinert, and Debebe (2016).

Transfer Pricing

There is a common practice among MNEs that can, in some circumstances, be detrimental to the countries hosting them. This practice is known as *transfer pricing*. Transfer pricing problems arise from the fact that MNEs are global corporations, whereas tax systems are locally defined. MNEs can therefore adjust the *internal* pricing of their intra-firm trade to shift the declared profits of subsidiaries to low-tax countries. The goal is to maximize the post-tax profits of the firm.

Consider, for example, a vertically integrated MNE producing copper. Perhaps this MNE mines the copper in an African country and engages in some elementary processing of the ore in that country. The ore is then exported and is further processed in the MNE's home country, an example of intra-firm trade (discussed in Chapter 11). The price of the partially processed ore exported out of the African country is therefore an *intra*-firm price. Consequently, the firm can pay an artificially low price for the copper ore in the country, reducing its profits and tax obligations there. Given the administrative and enforcement resources, the African country could require the firm to pay world prices for the ore, but resources in many African countries are very scarce. The MNE also has the option of artificially inflating its costs in the African country. This is as simple as sending employees from the home base to the African country for a holiday and then recording the expenses as a cost.

The solution to the transfer pricing problem is multifaceted. Dunning and Lundan (2008 : 633) note that, although unilateral policy options exist, "because there is competition for MNE activity between home and host countries, and between different host countries, the opportunities for MNEs to play one nation against another are enhanced without the establishment of supra-national institutions and harmonized inter-governmental action towards [transfer pricing]." Options include: international guidelines and codes of conduct; the international standardization of invoicing and customs procedures; global tax harmonization; negotiating and concluding international conventions; and the establishment of international arbitration procedures. For many LMICs, however, resources may need to be provided for them to effectively combat transfer pricing abuses.

Sources: Bartelsman and Beetsma (2003), Dunning and Lundan (2008: chap. 17), and Grubert and Mutti (1991).

The governance of international production will continue to be an area of policy deliberation, with a number of piecemeal and overlapping efforts in place. This policy area also overlaps with private efforts in *corporate social responsibility*. But we are far from the types of governance systems that exist in the realm of trade and finance.

Conclusion

Imagine yourself as a government official with responsibilities related to international production. What do you take from this chapter? Most importantly, you understand that inward FDI into your country can *both* provide benefits *and* impose costs. These benefits and costs occur in the areas of employment, competition, education and training, technology, the balance of payments, health and the environment, and culture. There are also means to make it more likely for your domestic firms to join GVCs. Within the limits of the TRIMs Agreement, you can potentially manage the FDI process through ownership and performance requirements. A more effective means of maximizing the benefits of inward FDI and GVC participation, however, might be through facilitating linkages between domestic suppliers and foreign MNEs in long-term relationships.

The institutional structure governing international production is not well developed. Despite efforts on the part of the OECD to resolve this issue, it is really the WTO that could potentially provide the best hope for a multilateral or plurilateral agreement on investment. In the meantime, however, the governance of international production is a piecemeal effort, with the OECD Guidelines for Multinational Enterprises playing a growing but incomplete role.

Review Exercises

1. What institutional elements do you think would make it more likely for an MNE to locate in a particular country?
2. Table 12.1 lists a set of benefits and costs of hosting foreign MNEs in the areas of employment, competition, education and training, technology, the balance of payments, health and the environment, and culture. Are there any additional benefits and costs that you think are important? Are there additional considerations that a host government should address before hosting foreign MNEs?
3. The Agreement on Trade-Related Investment Measures (TRIMs) of the Marrakesh Agreement requires WTO members to phase out local content requirements. Do you think this is a good idea? Why or why not?
4. Should there be multilateral agreements either constraining the behavior of governments towards MNEs or constraining the behavior of the MNEs themselves?
5. In what ways can the *task-based* participation in GVCs be considered a "game changer" relative to old-style, *sector-based* economic activities?

FURTHER READING AND WEB RESOURCES

An encyclopedic coverage of the material addressed in this chapter can be found in Dunning and Lundan (2008: Part III), and a more concise coverage is given Caves (2007: chap. 9). For GVCs, see Gereffi (2018), Gereffi and Sturgeon (2013), and Taglioni and Winkler (2016). The OECD maintains a web site at www.oecd.org; it provides materials on its activities in the area of international investment. The United Nations Conference on Trade and Development publishes an annual *World Investment Report*. This is a good place to turn for data on and discussion of FDI in the world economy. Its website is www.unctad.org, and the *World Investment Report* is at www.unctad.org/wir.

REFERENCES

Aitken, B. J., and A. E. Harrison (1999) "Do Domestic Firms Benefit from Direct Foreign Investment?," *American Economic Review*, 89:3, 605–18.

Anwar, S., and L. P. Nguyen (2014) "Is Foreign Direct Investment Productive? A Case Study of the Regions of Vietnam," *Journal of Business Research*, 64:7, 1376–87.

Anyanwu, J. C. (2017) "Foreign Direct Investment," in K. A. Reinert (ed.), *Handbook of Globalisation and Development*, Edward Elgar, 131–52.

Arnold, J. M., and B. S. Javorcik (2009) "Gifted Kids or Pushy Parents? Foreign Direct Investment and Plant Productivity in Indonesia," *Journal of International Economics*, 79:1, 42–53.

Asamoah, M. E., C. K. D. Adjasi, and A. L. Alhassan (2016) "Macroeconomic Uncertainty, Foreign Direct Investment and Institutional Quality: Evidence from Sub-Saharan Africa," *Economic Systems*, 40:4, 612–21.

Asiedu, E. (2006) "Foreign Direct Investment in Africa: The Role of Natural Resources, Market Size, Government Policy, Institutions and Political Instability," *The World Economy*, 29:1, 63–77.

Baldwin, R. (2016) *The Great Convergence: Information Technology and the New Globalization*, Harvard University Press.

Bartelsman, E. J., and R. M. W. J. Beetsma (2003) "Why Pay More? Corporate Tax Avoidance through Transfer Pricing in OECD Countries," *Journal of Public Economics*, 87:9–10, 2225–52.

Battat, J., I. Frank, and X. Shen (1996) *Suppliers to Multinationals: Linkage Programs to Strengthen Local Companies in Developing Countries*, Foreign Investment Advisory Service, World Bank.

Bénassy-Quéré, A., M. Coupet, and T. Mayer (2007) "Institutional Determinants of Foreign Direct Investment," *World Economy*, 30:5, 764–82.

Blalock, G., and P. J. Gertler (2008) "Welfare Gains from Foreign Direct Investment through Technology Transfer to Local Suppliers," *Journal of International Economics*, 74:2, 402–21.

Blomström, M. (1986) "Foreign Investment and Productive Efficiency: The Case of Mexico," *Journal of Industrial Economics*, 35:1, 97–110.

Blomström, M., and H. Persson (1983) "Foreign Investment and Spillover Efficiency in an Underdeveloped Economy: Evidence from the Mexican Manufacturing Industry," *World Development*, 11:6, 493–501.

Blomström, M., and F. Sjöholm (1999) "Technology Transfer and Spillovers: Does Local Participation with Multinationals Matter?," *European Economic Review*, 43:4/6, 915–23.

Bokpin, G. A. (2017) "Foreign Direct Investment and Environmental Sustainability in Africa," *Research in International Business and Finance*, 39:A, 239–47.

Buchanan, B. G., Q. V. Le, and M. Rishi (2012) "Foreign Direct Investment and Institutional Quality: Some Empirical Evidence," *International Review of Financial Analysis*, 21, 81–9.

Buckley, P. J., and F. Ruane (2006) "Foreign Direct Investment in Ireland: Policy Implications for Emerging Economies," *World Economy*, 29:11, 1611–28.

Caves, R. E. (1974) "Multinational Firms, Competition, and Productivity in Host-Country Markets," *Economica*, 41:162, 176–93.

Caves, R. S. (2007) *Multinational Enterprises and Economic Analysis*, Cambridge University Press.

Copeland, B. R. (2009) "Pollution Haven Hypothesis," in K. A. Reinert, R. S. Rajan, A. J. Glass, and L. S. Davis (eds.), *The Princeton Encyclopedia of the World Economy*, Princeton University Press, 924–9.

Dunning, J. H. (1988) *Explaining International Production*, Unwin Hyman.

Dunning, J. H., and S. M. Lundan (2008) *Multinational Enterprises and the Global Economy*, Edward Elgar.

Earle, J., Á. Telegdy, and G. Antal (2017) "Foreign Ownership and Wages: Evidence from Hungary, 1986–2008," *ILR Review*, 71:2, 458–91.

The Economist (1998) "The Sinking of the MAI," March 14.

The Economist (2018) "Ireland's Economy: On Firmer Foundations," December 15.

Engman, M., O. Onodera, and E. Pinali (2007) "Export Processing Zones: Past and Future Role in Trade and Development," Trade Policy Paper 53, OECD.

Falvey, R., and N. Foster-McGregor (2018) "North–South Foreign Direct Investment and Bilateral Investment Treaties," *World Economy*, 41:1, 2–28.

Fauzel, S., B. Seetanah, and R. V. Sannasee (2015) "Productivity Spillovers of FDI in the Manufacturing Sector of Mauritius: Evidence from a Dynamic Framework," *Journal of Developing Areas*, 49:2, 295–316.

Feenstra, R. C., and G. H. Hanson (1997) "Foreign Direct Investment and Relative Wages: Evidence from Mexico's Maquiladoras," *Journal of International Economics*, 42:3/4, 371–93.

Fink, C., and K. E. Maskus (2005) "Why We Study Intellectual Property Rights and What We Have Learned," in C. Fink and K. E. Maskus (eds.), *Intellectual Property and Development: Lessons from Recent Economic Research*, World Bank, 1–15.

Foss, N. J., R. Mudambi, and S. Murtinu (2019) "Taxing the Multinational Enterprise: On the Forced Redesign of Global Value Chains and Other Inefficiencies," *Journal of International Business Studies*, 50:9, 1644–55.

Gereffi, G. (2018) *Global Value Chains and Development: Redefining the Contours of 21st Century Capitalism*, Cambridge University Press.

Gereffi, G., J. Humphrey and T. Sturgeon (2005) "The Governance of Global Value Chains," *Review of International Political Economy*, 12:1, 78–104.

Gereffi, G., and T. Sturgeon (2013) "Global Value Chain-Oriented Industrial Policy: The Role of Emerging Economies," in D. K. Elms and P. Low (eds.), *Global Value Chains in a Changing World*, World Trade Organization, 329–60.

Globerman, S., and D. Shapiro (2002) "Global Foreign Direct Investment Flows: The Role of Government Infrastructure," *World Development*, 30:11, 1899–919.

Goldin, I., and K. A. Reinert (2012) *Globalization for Development: Meeting New Challenges*, Oxford University Press.

Graham, E. M. (1996) *Global Corporations and National Governments*, Institute for International Economics.

Grubert, H., and J. Mutti (1991) "Taxes, Tariffs and Transfer Pricing in Multinational Corporate Decision Making," *Review of Economics and Statistics*, 73:2, 285–93.

Haddad, M., and A. Harrison (1993) "Are There Positive Spillovers from Direct Foreign Investment? Evidence from Panel Data for Morocco," *Journal of Development Economics*, 42:1, 51–74.

Hill, C. W. L. (2009) *International Business: Competing in the Global Marketplace*, Irwin McGraw-Hill.

Hill, H. (1990) "Foreign Investment and East Asian Economic Development," *Asian-Pacific Economic Literature*, 4:2, 21–58.

Hoekman, B., and K. Saggi (2000) "Assessing the Case for Extending WTO Disciplines on Investment-Related Policies," *Journal of Economic Integration*, 15:4, 629–53.

Iršová, Z., and T. Havránek (2012) "Determinants of Horizontal Spillovers from FDI: Evidence from a Large Meta-Analysis," *World Development*, 42:1, 1–15.

Ivarsson, I., and C. G. Alvstam (2005) "Technology Transfer from TNCs to Local Suppliers in Developing Countries: A Study of AB Volvo's Truck and Bus Plants in Brazil, China, India, and Mexico," *World Development*, 33:3, 1325–44.

Jayanthakumaran, K. (2003) "Benefit-Cost Appraisals of Export Processing Zones: A Survey of the Literature," *Development Policy Review*, 21:1, 51–65.

Jenkins, M. (2006) "Sourcing Patterns of Firms in Export Processing Zones (EPZs): An Empirical Analysis of Firm-Level Determinants," *Journal of Business Research*, 59:3, 331–4.

Johansson, H., and L. Nilsson (1997) "Export Processing Zones as Catalysts," *World Development*, 25:12, 2115–28.

Kane, J. (1996) *Savages*, Vintage.

Kelsh, M. A., L. Morimoto, and E. Lau (2009) "Cancer Mortality and Oil Production in the Amazon Region of Ecuador, 1990–2005," *International Archive of Occupational and Environmental Health*, 82:3, 381–95.

Kheng, V., S. Sun, and S. Anwar (2017) "Foreign Direct Investment and Human Capital in Developing Countries: A Panel Data Approach," *Economic Change and Restructuring*, 50:4, 341–65.

Kimura, F. (2013) "How Have Production Networks Changed Development Strategies in East Asia?," in D. K. Elms and P. Low (eds.), *Global Value Chains in a Changing World*, World Trade Organization, 361–83.

Kohpaiboon, A. (2006) "Foreign Direct Investment and Technology Spillovers: A Cross-Industry Analysis of Thai Manufacturing," *World Development*, 34:3, 541–56.

Kokko, A. (1994) "Technology, Market Characteristics, and Spillovers," *Journal of Development Economics*, 43:2, 279–93.

Kokko, A., R. Tansini, and M. C. Zejan (1996) "Local Technological Capability and Productivity Spillovers from FDI in the Uruguayan Manufacturing Sector," *Journal of Development Studies*, 32:4, 602–11.

Kugler, M. (2006) "Spillovers from Foreign Direct Investment: Within or between Industries?," *Journal of Development Economics*, 80:2, 444–77.

Lee, Y. S. (2016) *Reclaiming Development in the World Trading System*, Cambridge University Press.

Li, Q., and A. Resnick (2003) "Reversal of Fortunes: Democratic Institutions and Foreign Direct Inflows to Developing Countries," *International Organization*, 57:1, 175–211.

Liang, F. H. (2017) "Does Foreign Direct Investment Improve the Productivity of Domestic Firms? Technology Spillovers, Industry Linkages, and Firm Capabilities," *Research Policy*, 46:1, 138–59.

Liu, Z. (2002) "Foreign Direct Investment and Technology Spillover: Evidence from China," *Journal of Comparative Economics*, 30:3, 579–602.

Low, P., and A. Subramanian (1996) "Beyond TRIMs: A Case for Multilateral Action on Investment Rules and Competition Policy?," in W. Martin and L. A. Winters (eds.), *The Uruguay Round and the Developing Countries*, Cambridge University Press, 380–408.

McAteer, E., and S. Pulver (2009) "The Corporate Boomerang: Shareholder Transnational Advocacy Networks Targeting Oil Companies in the Ecuadorian Amazon," *Global Environmental Politics*, 9:1, 1–30.

Marin, A., and M. Bell (2006) "Technology Spillovers from Foreign Direct Investment (FDI): The Active Role of MNC Subsidiaries in Argentina in the 1990s," *Journal of Development Studies*, 42:4, 678–97.

Moran, T. H. (1998) *Foreign Direct Investment and Development*, Institute for International Economics.

Moran, T. H. (2001) *Parental Supervision: The New Paradigm for Foreign Direct Investment and Development*, Institute for International Economics.

Nagarkatti, K., and G. McWilliams (2018) "International Tribunal Rules in Favor of Chevron in Ecuador Case," Reuters, September 8.

Navarro, G. C. B. (2018) "A Comparative Analysis of International Enforcement Procedures in the Chevron Case," Research Paper 2018-08, Max Planck Institute for Comparative Public Law and International Law.

Quaicoe, A., A. Q. Q. Aboagye, and G. A. Bokpin (2017) "Assessing the Impact of Export Processing Zones on Economic Growth in Ghana," *Research in International Business and Finance*, 42, 1150–63.

Reinert, K. A., O. T. Reinert, and G. Debebe (2016) "The New OECD Guidelines for Multinational Enterprises: Better but Not Good Enough," *Development in Practice*, 26:6, 816–23.

Rodrik, D. (1999) *The New Global Economy and Developing Countries: Making Openness Work*, Overseas Development Council.

Ruigrok, W., and R. van Tulder (1995) *The Logic of International Restructuring*, Routledge.

Schrank, A. (2001) "Export Processing Zones: Free Market Islands or Bridges to Structural Transformation?," *Development Policy Review*, 19:2, 223–42.

Singa Boyenge, J.-P. (2007) "ILO Database on Export Processing Zones," Working Paper 251, International Labour Office.

Sjöholm, F., and R. E. Lipsey (2006) "Foreign Firms and Indonesian Manufacturing Wages: An Analysis with Panel Data," *Economic Development and Cultural Change*, 55:1, 201–21.

Taglioni, D., and D. Winkler (2016) *Making Global Value Chains Work for Development*, World Bank.

Te Velde, D. W., and O. Morrissey (2003) "Do Workers in Africa Get a Wage Premium If Employed in Firms Owned by Foreigners?," *Journal of African Economies*, 12:1, 41–73.

United Nations Conference on Trade and Development (1999) *World Investment Report 1999: Foreign Direct Investment and the Challenge of Development*, UNCTAD.

United Nations Conference on Trade and Development (2001) *World Investment Report 2001: Promoting Linkages*, UNCTAD.

United Nations Conference on Trade and Development (2003) *Foreign Direct Investment and Performance Requirements: New Evidence from Selected Countries*, UNCTAD.

United Nations Conference on Trade and Development (2015) *Enhancing the Contribution of Export Processing Zones to the Sustainable Development Goals*, UNCTAD.

Wei, Y., and X. Liu (2006) "Productivity Spillovers from R&D, Exports and FDI in China's Manufacturing Sector," *Journal of International Business Studies*, 37:4, 544–57.

World Bank (1999) *World Development Report 1998/99: Knowledge for Development*, Oxford University Press.

Yücer, A., and J.-M. Siroën (2017) "Trade Performance of Export Processing Zones," *World Economy*, 40:5, 1012–38.

Zhao, J. H., S. H. Kim, and J. Du (2003) "The Impact of Corruption and Transparency on Foreign Direct Investment: An Empirical Analysis," *Management International Review*, 43:1, 41–62.

13 Migration

As described in Chapters 10 through 12, international production occurs when firms either form contractual relationships across national borders or engage in foreign direct investment. But there is a *third means* by which international production can take place, namely the *movement of people* across national borders in the form of temporary or permanent **migration**. At the time of this writing this mode of international production involves approximately 260 million migrants, or approximately 3.5 percent of the world's population (United Nations, 2017). Expectations are that the absolute number of migrants will continue to increase over time.[1] As such, migration is an important component of the world economy. Indeed, it is sometimes known as the "third pillar" of globalization, behind international trade and international finance, albeit a pillar for which there has been *much less* liberalization than the other two.

As we discussed in Chapter 1, the world economy has experienced significant liberalization of trade, foreign direct investment, and financial flows. These are the processes that have characterized economic globalization. This is not the case with labor, however. As barriers to the movements of goods, services, direct investment, and finance transactions have fallen over time, barriers to the movement of people have largely remained in place, or even *increased*. This has caused some international economists (for example, Pritchett, 2006) to refer to "everything but labor" globalization.[2] That said, some specific *types* of labor flows have significantly increased over time, high-skilled and low-skilled workers alike depending on the case in question.

We begin our consideration of migration by considering types of migration. We then consider the migration decision in its economic aspects. We take up

[1] Milanovic (2016: 150) notes that 10 percent of the world's population (at least 750 million people) would *like to* migrate. Why? Because "a lot of our income depends on where we live. Just by being born in the United States rather than in Congo, a person would multiply her income by 93 times" (133).

[2] The study of migration as a part of globalization is also less prominent than other aspects of globalization. For example, Omelaniuk (2017: 289) states: "In the migration context, globalization is discussed from several angles: the increasingly globalized nature of migration, the impact of globalization on migration and migration as a force of globalization. All angles are under-researched, inconclusive and open to debate."

high-skilled and low-skilled migration and then turn to the issues of remittances and migration policy.

Types of Migration

There are many *types* of international migration, with different degrees of relevance to the issue of international production. To take one possible categorization, and drawing on Beath, Goldin, and Reinert (2009), we can distinguish between the following different types of international migration:

- *Permanent high-skilled migration* involves permanent residence and is sometimes granted in countries such as Australia, New Zealand, Canada, the United States, and the European Union. It is granted to high-skilled migrants, often at the urging of hiring corporations, including multinational enterprises. Leading source countries include China and India.
- *Temporary high-skilled migration* is similar in motivation to permanent high-skilled migration but can be more politically palatable in some cases, when there is political resistance to granting permanent residence or when the need itself is temporary.
- *Temporary low-skilled migration* is more important in volume than temporary high-skilled migration. Temporary low-skilled migration includes migrant workers in the areas of manual labor (including agricultural labor), construction, and domestic services.
- *Family migration* allows permanent residence to the families of those who have already gained residence. Beath, Goldin, and Reinert (2009: 766) note that "family migration is among the largest channels of migration and represents a disproportionate share of flows from low- and middle-income countries (LMICs) to high-income countries."
- *Asylum seekers and refugees.* Asylum seekers are granted certain rights by the 1951 Geneva Convention, addressing persons with well-founded fears of persecution. Refugees are those who flee to neighboring countries to escape war, famine, or environmental catastrophes. They become the responsibility of the United Nations High Commissioner for Refugees (UNHCR).[3]
- *Irregular/undocumented migration* involves both voluntary and non-voluntary (trafficked) illegal migrants. In some regions (such as North America and parts of Africa) these flows can be quite significant.

---

[3] Although not germane to this chapter, an important development has been the increase in the number of "forcefully displaced" persons, including refugees, to just under 70 million in 2017 (UNHCR, 2018). Approximately 40 million of these were internally displaced, approximately 25 million were refugees, and approximately 3 million were asylum seekers.

- *Visa-free migration* relates to our discussion in Chapter 9 of common markets, in that it involves the free movement of both labor and capital. The European Union is a prime example of visa-free migration, but this arrangement also exists between Australia and New Zealand, for example.

Each of these types of migration is important from political, human rights, and public policy perspectives, but not all of them are relevant to international production. In this chapter, we will focus on high-skilled and low-skilled migration. These are the two that have the most relevance from an economic point of view. The accompanying box considers the phenomenon of irregular or undocumented migration. But, before we take on specific types of migration, we need to consider the migration decision itself.

Irregular Migration

Irregular or illegal migration is said to occur when non-citizens enter into a country to reside and/or work without official documentation and authorization. Rough estimates suggest that between 10 and 15 percent of all migrants are irregular, and they include workers, family members, and rejected asylum seekers. Other terms used to describe irregular migrants include "illegal" and "undocumented." Some researchers working from a human rights perspective are critical of the very concept of human beings as "illegal" or even "irregular," however (e.g. Dauvergne, 2008).

Irregular migration occurs through different pathways. These include both remaining in a country longer than permitted and working illegally. The pathways to a destination country can include *smuggling* and *human trafficking*. Smuggling of irregular migrants is done at the will of the migrant, and there are large networks of organizations that participate in these activities. Human trafficking occurs *against* the will of the migrant, involves the threat of violence, and can also involve long-term exploitation in destination countries, including sexual exploitation and forced labor.

Irregular migration in the form of working illegally is an economic phenomenon. In many countries, the demand for and supply of irregular migrants are both large, and labor markets therefore respond. Castles et al. (2012: 119) even note: "Some employers actually prefer irregular migrants, because they lack rights, cannot complain to authorities or trade unions, and are therefore easily exploitable."

Consider the case of the United States. Although estimates vary, as of 2018 the United States hosted approximately 11 million irregular ("illegal," in US parlance) migrants, approximately 8 million of whom were in the workforce. This

Irregular Migration (cont.)

represented *5 percent* of the US workforce, including about one-half of the country's farmworkers and 15 percent of its construction workers. Given this demand for irregular labor in the US economy, the phenomenon is not going to disappear. If these workers were somehow removed from the US economy, this would constitute a supply-side shock of very large magnitude.

Irregular migration is also a development issue. Although legal migration has potentially positive development impacts, through remittances and return migration, these positive impacts can be suppressed when migration is irregular. Many of the policy discussions taking place regarding irregular migration have to do with trying to increase the likelihood of it having positive development impacts. This involves improving the human rights prospects of irregular migrants, the prevention of trafficking, moving irregular migrants to legal status, and facilitating return or "circular" migration. This is part of the ongoing agenda of the Global Forum on Migration and Development, for example.

Irregular migration is also a political issue. A country's ability to manage who enters it is seen as part of its national sovereignty. As stated by Castles et al. (2012: 144), however, irregular migration is also "an almost universal phenomenon." Balancing national sovereignty with the ubiquitous presence of irregular migration requires a hard look at the realities of irregular migration and a willingness to explore new avenues to begin to regularize this aspect of globalization.

Sources: Castles et al. (2012), Dauvergne (2008), López, Bialik, and Radford (2018), Omelaniuk (2017), von Koppenfels (2017), and https://gfmd.org.

The Migration Decision

Just as we need to know what considerations are involved for firms in the foreign market entry decision (Chapter 10), so we need to know what motivates migrants in their decision-making. We will focus on the economic decision-making of potential migrants, understanding that, in some cases (such as refugees, considered above), non-economic issues might be more potent. In focusing on the economic decision-making of migration, we will identify a set of factors that influence the decision-making process.[4] To set the stage, consider the following summary from de Haas (2007: 832):

[4] There is a subtle point that we will gloss over here. We will assume that the decision-making locus of migration is the *individual* migrant. As noted by some migration researchers, however (such as Stark and Bloom, 1985), the *family* can be the real locus of migration decisions.

> In reality, migration is a selective process. The poorest tend to migrate less than those who are slightly better off. This seems particularly true for relatively costly and risky international migration.... Labor migrants generally do not flee from misery but move deliberately in the expectation of finding a better or more stable livelihood, and of improving their social and economic status. Moreover, in order to migrate, people need the human, financial and social resources as well as the aspiration to do so.

Let us see how we might capture these considerations analytically by identifying *five factors* that influence the migration decisions of potential migrants from Morocco (M) to the European Union (EU). These factors are: relative wages, youth population growth, financial resources, education levels, and migrant networks. We consider each of these factors in turn, using Figure 13.1. The first factor (relative wages) and the following four factors (youth population growth, financial resources, education levels, and migrant networks) affect Figure 13.1 differently. Relative wages will be a "movement along" factor, while the other four will be "shift" factors.[5]

Relative wages One central variable that influences migration is relative wages (rw), particularly relative unskilled wages, and we measure the wage in the European Union relative to that in Morocco as $rw = w_{EU}/w_M$. The larger this relative wage measure, the greater the number of Moroccans who would like to emigrate to the European Union. As rw increases or decreases, there is a movement along (up or down) an "emigration supply" (ES) curve in Figure 13.1. For example, an increase of the relative wage from rw_1 to rw_2 will increase the desired emigration from E_1 to E_2.

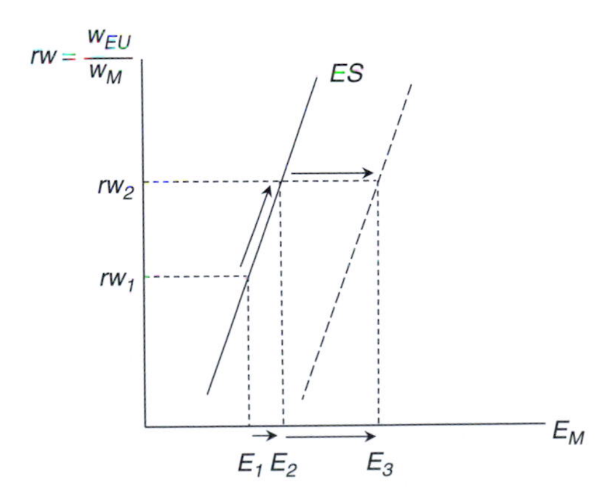

Figure 13.1 The migration decision

[5] This is similar to "movement along" and "shift" factors affecting the demand and supply curves of Chapter 2 on absolute advantage.

Despite the importance of the relative wage as a factor in the migration decision, other factors can be equally relevant. Indeed, Hatton and Williamson (2009: 17) emphasize that wage gaps between countries "will not by themselves explain emigration." The other four factors in our list each have the effect of *shifting* the *ES* curve in Figure 13.1.

Youth population growth Population grown in Morocco will increase the number of individuals who are considering emigrating from Morocco to the European Union. Particularly important here is growth of the *youth* population. The young are more prone to be risk takers, and, since the net benefits of migration can take a long time to accrue to the individual migrant, the young are more likely to have the years ahead of them for net benefits to become positive. The age structure of populations can therefore influence the migration decision. An increase in the youth population will have the effect of shifting the *ES* curve in Figure 13.1 to the right.

Financial resources The cost of emigration can be substantial, and include not just the direct costs of (legally or illegally) traveling from one country to another but also the opportunity costs of leaving the home country, with its family and friends, and the risks involved in settling in a new country. A consequence of these costs is that, despite the desire to migrate, many poor people cannot finance migration. Reflecting this, there is a tendency for the *ES* curve of Figure 13.1 to move to the right as per capita GDP rises from low- to middle-income levels and the ability of potential migrants to finance the move consequently increases. This is why de Haas (2007: 832) states, as above: "The poorest tend to migrate less than those who are slightly better off."

Education levels An increase in education levels in Morocco will have the effect of increasing the aspirations of Moroccans and make them more aware of economic and social possibilities abroad. Increased education also allows Moroccans to better absorb and process information flows from the European Union in order to assess opportunities there. Increased education levels have the effect of shifting the *ES* curve in Figure 13.1 to the right.

Migrant networks Beath, Goldin, and Reinert (2009: 770) note that "the willingness of people to migrate will increase with the quantity and quality of information that is available." The information in question is that related to the destination country. The potential migrant in Morocco needs to know something about the economic and social environment in the European Union. In many cases, this information is provided by preceding migrants. Migrant networks are conduits of information back to potential migrants in origin countries. As migrant networks develop, the quality of information flows increases and the *ES* curve of Figure 13.1, again, shifts to the right.

Historical evidence suggests that shifts of the *ES* curve in Figure 13.1 can be more significant than movements along the curve.[6] What is more, the four shift

---

[6] See Hatton and Williamson (2009).

factors can work together as origin countries develop. Suppose we turn the clock back a little, to a time when per capita GDP in Morocco was much lower than it is today. As GDP per capita increases from this initial low level, education levels and youth population both increase. The increases in GDP per capita, youth population, and education levels shift the *ES* curve to the right. As the first Moroccan migrants succeed in establishing lives in the European Union, good-quality information flows increase and the *ES* curve shifts even farther to the right.

The approximate correlation of all these four shift factors in time can lead to a phenomenon known as the *migration hump*.[7] A highly stylized migration hump is presented in Figure 13.2. This figure shows that, as GDP per capita increases from low to medium levels, emigration increases. As GDP per capita increases further, from medium to high levels, economic opportunities expand in Morocco relative to the European Union, youth population begins to shrink in Morocco, and emigration decreases.[8] It is for these reasons that some observers (such as de Haas, 2007) see the migration hump as simply a part of the socio-economic development process in source countries.

What is the significance of the migration hump for understanding global migration patterns? First, it alerts us to the fact that, barring political or ecological impetus, relatively little international migration occurs from low-income countries. Rather, most of it is from middle-income countries. Second, the migration flows that occur near the peak of the migration hump can *persist* for some time (perhaps a decade or two) as source countries move through the middle-income range of GDP per capita. Third, as pointed out by de Haas (2007), economic development

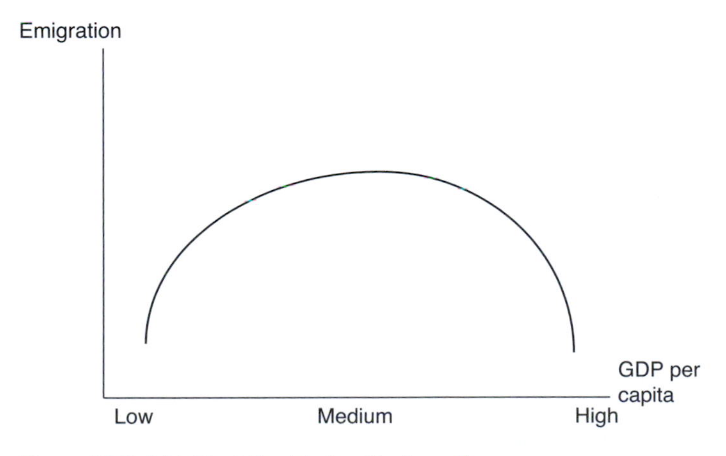

Figure 13.2 A highly stylized "migration hump"

[7] See, for example, Zelinsky (1971), Martin and Taylor (1996), and Olesen (2002).

[8] The sharp-eyed reader will begin to see a link here to the idea of a *demographic transition* in development and population studies.

from relatively low levels of GDP per capita can *increase* rather than decrease outward migration flows, in contrast to some claims. Globalization in some forms might support the development of low-income countries, but this development can spur outward migration.

High-Skilled Migration

High-skilled migration is a central subject in economic globalization. It is the way that countries and firms access human capital from all corners of the globe. It is not something for which high-quality data are available, however. There are different approaches to defining "high-skilled," including education (tertiary level), occupation, sector of employment, and income. Data on each of these are incomplete.[9] More importantly, different approaches to defining "high-skilled" provide different results. As stated by Kone and Özden (2017: 356, emphasis added), "There is a relatively *small overlap* of the sets of highly skilled migrants if we are to use different criteria...to measure the skill levels." Further, when using tertiary education as an indicator of skill, data on *where* the tertiary education was received (country of origin versus country of destination) are not always available. This issue further limits the quality of information.

Despite these informational challenges, some patterns of high-skilled migration are discernible. First, the most important destination of high-skilled migrants is the set of countries that form the Organisation for Economic Co-operation and Development. More specifically, approximately three-fourths of the *stock* of high-skilled migrants reside in OECD destination countries (Kone and Özden, 2017). Within the OECD, high-skilled migrants are further concentrated within English-speaking countries, particularly the United States, Canada, and Australia.[10]

Second, high-skilled migration is *increasing* over time. The increase in demand for high-skilled migrants appears to be related to skills-biased technological change in high-income destination countries, which is, in turn, related to the information and communication technology advances we discussed in Chapter 1. There is increasing evidence that the demand for high-skilled migrants will not abate.[11]

---

[9] This was pointed out some time ago by Hart (2006), but, for a more comprehensive study of the issue, see Parsons et al. (2014).

[10] In the case of Australia, *The Economist* (2018a: 11) reports: "Some 29% of its inhabitants were born in another country – twice the proportion of the United States. Half of Australians are either immigrants themselves or children of immigrants.... In Australia both main parties argue that admitting lots of skilled immigrants is essential to the health of the economy."

[11] Bauer and Kunze (2004) note that the rising relative wage for high-skilled workers indicates that, despite the rise of high-skilled migration, there is an increasing demand for these kinds of workers. For example, the *Financial Times* (2010) reports that, even after the US manufacturing sector shed more than 2 million jobs between 2008 and 2010, skilled shortages were acute.

Third, although destinations for high-skilled migrants are concentrated in the OECD, origin countries are widely dispersed. As stated by Kone and Özden (2017: 353), "As opposed to destination countries, we see that emigration is less concentrated and a non-negligible share of the tertiary educated people emigrate abroad from almost every country." This can pose some challenges for origin countries, which we will discuss below.

Evidence presented by Bauer and Kunze (2004) and Kerr, Kerr, and Lincoln (2015) suggests that the types of firms that hire high-skilled migrants tend to be larger firms that are more internationalized via foreign ownership and exports. Further, it is not always domestic firms demanding skilled migrants in a country, but foreign firms as well. For example, Indian MNEs operating in the United States hire high-skilled migrants in that country. There is also evidence that high-skilled migration supports the innovation of firms hiring them.[12] It is for this reason that large innovative firms tend to be supportive of high-skilled migration.[13]

Despite the keen interest of large and globalized firms in hiring high-skilled migrants, they face somewhat volatile policy regimes. For example, in the case of the United States, the H1-B visa supports high-skilled immigration. The baseline quota is only 65,000, however. This jumped up to 115,000 in 1999 and 2000, and then to 195,000 in 2001, 2002, and 2003. Then it was abruptly decreased back to 65,000 in 2004, at which level it has stayed ever since. Declining receptivity to high-skilled migrants in the United States appears to have made some of them consider other destinations.[14] In another case, in 2012 the United Kingdom ended its popular, post-study work visa for foreign students.

Both by definition and in practice, high-skilled migrants remove their human capital from their countries of origin. This phenomenon is known as the **brain drain**. The term "brain drain" was first used by the British Royal Society to describe the loss of British human capital to Canada and the United States during the 1950s and 1960s. Today the term primarily applies to the loss of human capital in LMICs as a result of the migration of citizens to foreign destination countries.[15]

From an economic theory point of view, brain drain has a couple of different components. First, there is a recognized positive externality associated with human

---

[12] High-skilled immigrants tend to file for more patents than their domestic counterparts. See, for example, Hunt and Gauthier-Loiselle (2010). In addition, Moretti (2012: 242) reports that, in the case of the United States, "immigrants are almost 30 percent more likely than non-immigrants to start a business."

[13] See Kerr, Kerr, and Lincoln (2015) and reference therein.

[14] See *The Economist* (2010a; 2018b).

[15] As stated by the OECD (2005: 129), "Emigration of highly skilled workers may adversely affect small countries by preventing them reaching a critical mass of human resources, which would be necessary to foster long-term economic development." See also Gibson and McKenzie (2011).

capital accumulation.[16] When a high-skilled migrant leaves an LMIC, this externality can evaporate. Second, the human capital accumulated in a high-skilled citizen is the end result of at least some public expenditure. The hoped-for return on the human capital investment is captured by high-skilled migration destination countries that did not make the investment. This is recognized as an important public finance issue. Third, there is another public finance issue at work. When high-skilled migrants leave, their future tax payments leave with them.[17]

There is also the somewhat counterintuitive possibility of a **brain gain**. The brain gain hypothesis relates to the possibility that the presence of emigration opportunities increases the incentive for human capital accumulation in origin countries and, thereby, can contribute to an *increase* in total human capital.[18] There are actually a number of *conditions* that must hold for the brain gain hypothesis to be a reality. These are well described by Hart (2009: 136, emphasis added):

> First, many emigrants must receive substantially higher returns on their education and skills than they would have done had they stayed home. Second, these gains must be perceived by individuals in the sending countries who have the interest and potential to acquire more education and skills, thereby inducing a demand for them. Third, domestic institutions must be able to respond effectively to this demand. Fourth, some of those who have been induced to acquire more education and skills, and thus add to their human capital stock, by the prospects of emigration, must be *unable* to emigrate. Finally, this group must be able to put their newly gained education and skills to good use at home.

Clearly, the brain gain hypotheses is an empirical issue, and somewhat difficult to sort out in general. It remains a *possibility*, to be assessed on a case-by-case basis.

When brain drain takes the form of doctors and nurses, it is known as **medical brain drain**. It is clear that, in this case, the brain gain hypothesis is not relevant. For example, Kone and Özden (2017: 362) conclude that the required supply response "is unlikely to be the case for publicly funded medical schools in sub-Saharan Africa," the very place where the issue is most acute. Medical brain drain is therefore a significant development issue, particularly for lower-income countries with HIV/AIDS and other health crises.[19]

Finally, there is the issue of **brain waste**, or what is sometimes referred to as "occupational downgrading," when a high-skilled immigrant ends up in a job that

---

[16] In the realm of international economics, this insight goes back to Bhagwati and Hamada (1974), but it is actually a widely noted idea.

[17] For a well-known study of the Indian case, see Desai et al. (2009).

[18] This idea was first introduced by Stark, Helmenstein, and Prskawetz (1997).

[19] Approaches to deal with the difficult issue of brain drain in terms of health professionals are discussed in Martineau, Decker, and Bundred (2004). See also Bhargava and Docquier (2008).

is actually less skilled that what he or she is qualified for.[20] This can reflect the quality of education in the country of origin, as well as selection processes in the country of destination. The evidence suggests that this is indeed a relevant phenomenon.

In addition, there is the process of *return migration*, whereby high-skilled workers bring newly acquired know-how and entrepreneurial skills back to their countries of origin. This process was first recognized by Saxenian (2002), who emphasizes the role of Chinese and Indian return migrants in developing high-technology clusters in Taiwan, China, and India. She regards these "transnational communities" as players in their own right in the world economy, global actors along with MNEs and national governments.[21] Return migration flows have potential consequences for brain drain. There is a hope that the phenomenon of brain drain can evolve into *brain circulation*, in which expatriates from LMICs return either temporarily or permanently to contribute to what might be called "intellectual remittances." For example, Saxenian (2005: 36) describes some of these return migrants as follows:

> When foreign-educated venture capitalists invest in their home countries, they transfer first-hand knowledge of the financial institutions of the new economy to peripheral regions. These individuals, often among the earliest returnees, also typically serve as advisers to domestic policymakers who are anxious to promote technology growth. As experienced engineers and managers return home, either temporarily or permanently, they bring worldviews and identities that grow out of their shared professional and educational experiences. These cross-regional technical communities have the potential to jump-start local entrepreneurship.

As shown by Docquier and Lodigiani (2010), these return migrants can even have a subsequent positive effect on inflows of FDI. The return migration and subsequent enterprise development act as a signal to foreign MNEs that conditions are ripe for FDI by enhancing the location advantages we discussed in Chapter 11. To the extent that these reverse high-skilled flows can assist in the development of home countries, they are to be welcomed and encouraged.

Low-Skilled Migration

Although high-skilled migration might be the more interesting subject from a technological perspective, more migrants fall into the category of **low-skilled migration**. There is no standard definition of low-skilled migration, which is

[20] See Mattoo, Neagu, and Özden (2008) and Debebe (2009).

[21] Saxenian (2002) also explores the role of these "technical communities" in the development of global value chains, discussed in Chapters 11 and 12.

defined either in terms of the education of the worker or in terms of the qualities of the job performed. As noted by Goldin and Reinert (2012: 169), "Low-skilled migrants are diverse in origin, destination, and function, but they typically arrive under a short-term, low-cost service contract (or illegally) and are expected to return home at the end of it."

There are fundamental economic forces at play in low-skilled migration, forces that show no signs of abating. The supply side of low-skilled migration can be roughly described using our discussion of Figure 13.1 above. But there are also interesting characteristics of the demand side in destination countries. The first of these relates to demographic trends in some destination countries, namely declining fertility rates below "replacement" levels and therefore declining native populations (as in Japan and some EU countries). This is sometimes referred to as the "birth dearth."[22] The evolving birth dearth can cause an increase in demand for migrants.

A second fundamental demand-side characteristic involves what Pritchett (2006) refers to as "productivity-resistant," "low-skill," "hard-core," "non-tradable services." It has long been recognized that some types of services are resistant to productivity growth. This has been associated with the work of William Baumol, and is known as the "Baumol effect" or "cost disease."[23] In an example often mentioned, it is difficult to increase the productivity of haircuts. This is also true of other low-skilled services, and these are often non-tradable services. The persistence of these kinds of services in the structures of modern economies, as well as their non-tradable nature, ensures that there will always be increasing demand for migrants to perform them. As Pritchett notes (35), "Although the future belongs to greater and greater levels of technology, information revolution, and capital–labor substitution, the future of employment belongs to haircuts." That might be an exaggeration, but it is one that makes a point.

These two demand-side characteristics, combined with the supply-side changes discussed above, ensure that low-skilled migration is an important component of the modern world economy. We can get a graphical sense of these changes using Figure 13.3. This figure combines the emigration supply (*ES*) line of Figure 13.1 with an immigration demand (*ID*) line. For reasons we have discussed here, both lines can shift to the right over time. As they do, low-skilled emigration from Morocco to the European Union increases. As this graph is drawn, the relative unskilled wage remains the same, but it could either increase or decrease.

---

[22] One important exception to this is the United States, also a key low-skilled migration destination. On the birth dearth in Japan, see *The Economist* (2010b; 2018a). On Germany, see Dempsey (2011).

[23] This goes back to Baumol (1967).

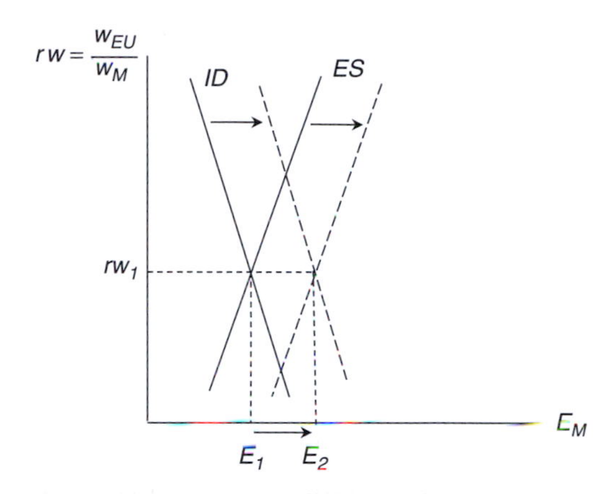

Figure 13.3 The market for low-skilled migration

Low-skilled migration is subject to a great deal of *political opposition*. This opposition to low-skilled migration often focuses on three alleged problems: identity, wage pressure, and fiscal burden. Let us consider each in turn.

The *identity* issue falls under the category of *culture*, discussed in Chapter 1. There is an allegation that "they" are not like "us." There is also a question of assimilation or integration into the host country. As noted by the World Bank (2018: 25), "Low-skilled or undocumented immigrants face some of the greatest barriers to assimilation and integration." Language acquisition helps to overcome these hurdles. In the case of irregular low-skilled migrants, a path to legal status of some kind also helps. The identity issue in destination countries has increasingly manifested itself in a rise in ethno-nationalism, discussed in Chapter 1.

The *wage pressure* argument is that influxes of low-skilled migrants place downward pressure on local wages. From the point of view of basic economic theory, this is a distinct possibility. Labor economists and international economists alike have extensively examined this issue, and the resulting research literature is vast. As it turns out, Figure 13.3 is insufficient to properly assess this issue, because it does not distinguish between low-skilled and high-skilled labor in the destination country. Research on the "wage issue" thus uses a different framework, shown in Figure 13.4.

Figure 13.4 considers the destination labor market as a whole rather than just the market for migrants.[24] It also distinguishes between low-skilled and high-skilled workers in the destination country by employing ratios.[25] So the wage on the vertical axis is the relative wage of low-skilled workers to high-skilled workers

[24] This figure draws on World Bank (2018: chap. 3).

[25] This approach goes back to Katz and Murphy (1992).

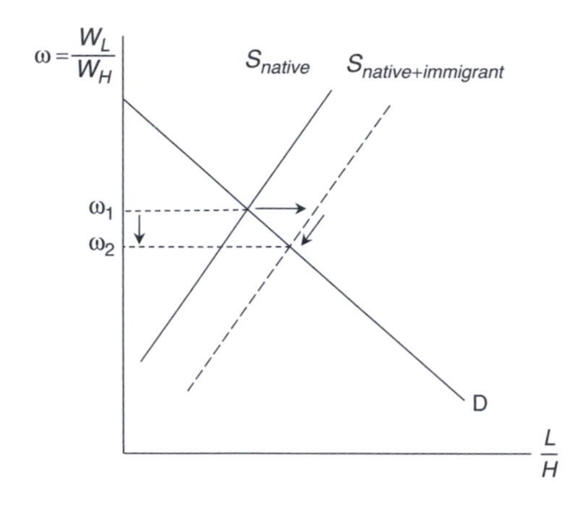

Figure 13.4 The impact of low-skilled migration on the destination labor market

in the destination country, $\omega = {}^{w_L}\!/_{w_H}$. On the horizontal axis is the ratio of low-skilled to high-skilled workers in the destination country, ${}^{L}\!/_{H}$. The demand curve is the *relative* demand for low-skilled workers, and the supply curve is the *relative* supply of low-skilled workers.

For simplicity, we begin with the labor market consisting of just native workers, with the supply curve S_{native} and the relative wage at ω_1. We then allow for some amount of low-skilled immigration, which shifts the supply curve to the right to $S_{native+immigrant}$. As expected from the supply and demand logic, the relative wage of unskilled workers *falls* in Figure 13.4, to ω_2. The question is: how much does it fall *in practice*?

There is a diligent group of researchers assessing the size of the fall in the relative wage in Figure 13.4. The technical details of the research are too intricate to describe here. Perhaps the best way to summarize the results is as follows: low-skilled immigrants can suppress local wages but do so by small amounts.[26] There are two reasons for this. First, immigrants turn out to be *imperfect substitutes* for native workers.[27] Second, native workers reduce their supply by moving to different labor markets. As stated by the World Bank (2018: 149), "They can change jobs, toccupations, sectors, or cities or exit the labor market altogether." This is shown in Figure 13.4 by the downward movement along the new supply curve.

To get back to the political considerations, those observers who claim that low-skilled immigrants have no impact on wages and those who claim that the impacts

[26] See, for example, Borjas (2003), Card (2005), Ottaviano and Peri (2012), and World Bank (2018: chap. 3).

[27] This is a little like the imperfect substitutes model of trade described in Appendix 7.1, but for labor markets rather than markets for goods and services.

are large (both groups exist) are probably both wrong. The impacts are there, but they are not dramatic.

With regard to *fiscal burden*, there is also a lot of misinformation, with a typical argument being made that immigrants are a "burden" on national governments. This is no doubt true in the case of large-scale refugee flows (such as Syrian refugees in Jordan and Lebanon), but what about the general case? Evidence comes from the OECD (2013), which estimates the net fiscal impacts of immigrants in European OECD countries, Australia, Canada, and the United States. As an average across this set of destination countries, the estimated net fiscal impact was *zero*, but in some specific countries it was *small*. So, again, political concerns need to be tempered with evidence.

Migration Gone Wrong: The Morecambe Bay Cockle Tragedy

In February 2004 35 Chinese migrants (both men and women) were working in Morecambe Bay in the United Kingdom, collecting cockles. The workers were irregular unskilled migrants, most from the Fujian province of China. Many of them had migrated with the financial help of family and village members, with the hopes that they would send remittances back home. Most of the workers paid criminal "snakehead" gangs in order to migrate to the United Kingdom. Consequently, their work in the country was overseen by a "gang-master."

Morecambe Bay is notorious for its swift tides and quicksand. Tragically, the Chinese migrants were cut off from the shore by a rising tide. They tried to place a distress call with the words "sinking water," but the language barrier meant that this was not successful. Twenty-three of the cockle gatherers drowned. Realizing the danger he was in, one migrant, Guo Bin Long, was able to use his mobile phone to call his wife in China. He said to her, "I am in great danger. I am up to my chest in water. Maybe I am going to die." He did, as did most of his fellow unskilled workers.

While this terrible human drama was taking place, the gang-master was safe in his car. He later threatened the surviving workers to force them to lie about the circumstances of the disaster. Nevertheless, he was arrested and eventually found guilty of manslaughter.

Here we have a small piece of globalization in which Guo Bin Long was financed by his village to the extent that he was equipped with a mobile phone, utilizing advanced ICT to communicate with his wife in China. At that level, globalization was operating with sophistication. Nevertheless, Guo Bin Long was working under conditions that, though perhaps not "forced," were desperate. At that level, globalization was acting in tragic form. As a survivor reported, "We

Migration Gone Wrong: The Morecambe Bay Cockle Tragedy (cont.)

worked in conditions of hell; we had rotten food, rotten accommodation, and worked in very cold conditions and dark, risking our lives trying to make a living in this country."

This tragedy of migration became immortalized in a 2006 British film, *Ghosts*. One newspaper described the film as a "harsh, in-your-face movie that should have audiences worrying that something must be done about the issue it raises" (*The Guardian*, 2007). Advocates for low-skilled and irregular migrants worldwide would agree.

Sources: Olson (2008) and *The Guardian* (2007).

Remittances

When migrants begin working in foreign countries, they do not abandon all ties to their home country. Particularly in an era of calling cards and electronic money transfers, maintaining ties with family and friends in one's home country is easier now than in past decades. One part of maintaining ties with the home country involves migrants sending money back to family members in the form of what is known as **remittances**. These flows have become increasingly important in the world economy.[28]

Data on remittance flows going back to 1971 are presented in Figure 13.5. As is clear from these data, remittance flows have increased dramatically since the mid-1990s. What is also clear is that most of the increase in remittances has been to middle-income countries.[29] In some countries and regions, remittance inflows now exceed FDI inflows. Total remittances in 2018 were approximately US$625 billion, with over US$450 billion being received by middle-income countries but less than US$30 billion being received by low-income countries. Just by way of comparison, official development assistance (ODA) in 2018 was approximately US$150 billion.

As emphasized by *The Economist* (2009) and others, remittances can have significant and positive impacts in developing countries by directly transferring

[28] Pozo (2009: 963–4) notes: "Previously, little effort was expended to measure and analyze [remittance] flows because they were thought to be small in magnitude and of little significance for most countries. Evidence to the contrary has motivated policymakers and others to pay closer attention to the measurement, determinants, and impact of remittances."

[29] This parallels the increase in FDI flows to middle-income countries we discussed in Chapter 1. See Figure 1.2 of that chapter.

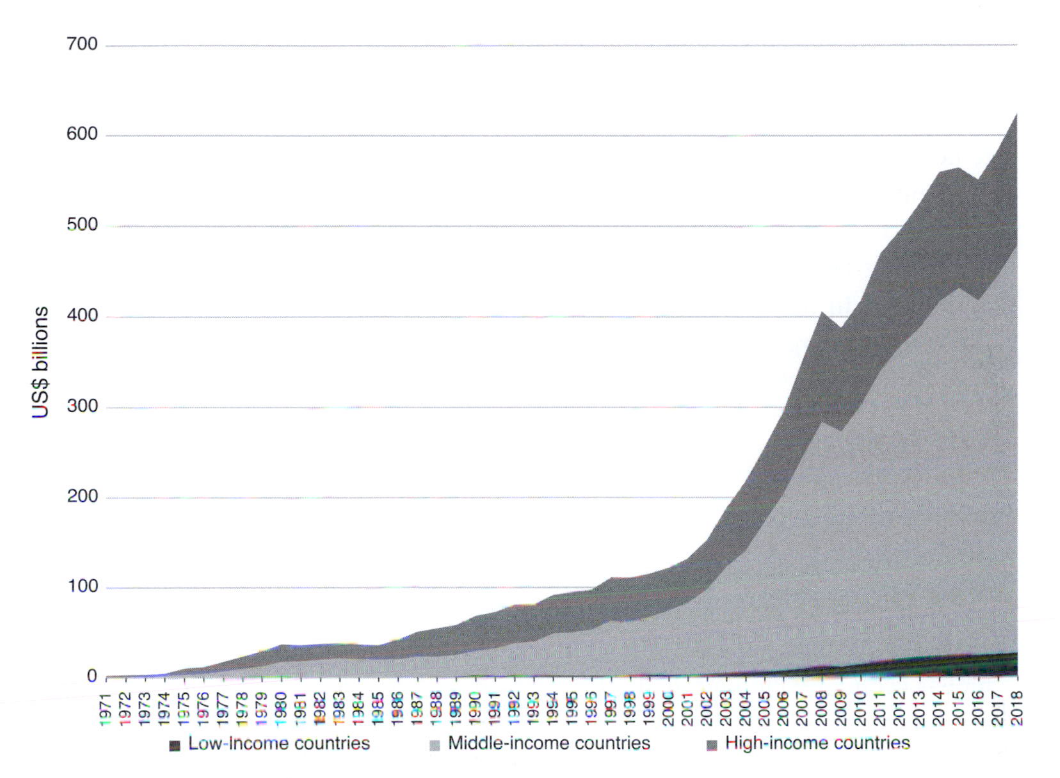

Figure 13.5 Remittance inflows, 1971–2018
Source: World Bank, World Development Indicators.

income more efficiently than foreign aid. They seem to positively contribute to growth (see, for example, Chowdhury, 2016). Further, they are also relatively stable in aggregate. You can see in Figure 13.5 that remittances held up during the 2008 global financial crisis and subsequent recession. That was not the case for trade, foreign direct investment, or other private capital flows. It is for this reason that Sirkeci, Cohen, and Ratha (2012: 3) state that "remittances remain one of the less volatile sources of foreign exchange earnings for developing countries."

The positive role that remittances (and, therefore, international production via migration) can play in source countries seems to be related to something we considered at the beginning of this chapter, namely migrant networks. For example, Woodruff and Zenteno (2007) provide evidence that migrant networks between the United States and Mexico have helped channel remittance flows to microenterprise development in Mexico, and the Mexican government has tried to leverage remittances for infrastructure improvements (Orozco and Rouse, 2012). Similar efforts have taken place in El Salvador. There is also evidence that remittances can act as a risk management strategy for poor households in LMICs through income source diversification and can contribute to human capital investments in some cases, offsetting to some extent brain drain effects.[30] Further, Dadush and Falcau (2009: 2) note that "the availability of foreign exchange through remittances increases the food security of drought-prone countries and enables countries to import medicines and other technologies."

Remittance flows are therefore a potentially positive result of international production based on migration. They are not international production per se, but harnessing them for development outcomes shows a great deal of promise. This is one area in which international production and international development can interact with largely happy outcomes.

Migration Policy

Migration poses a policy dilemma. At the macro level, increases in migration have been shown to potentially provide a very large increase in economic welfare. For example, in a review of the research literature, Goldin and Reinert (2012: 161) conclude that "a small increase in migration would produce a much greater boon to the global economy and developing countries than free trade and development assistance combined." That is a significant reality. The dilemma of migration appears in the distribution of costs, however. As summarized by Goldin and Reinert (2012: 161):

> While most of the benefits of migration are dispersed and generalized, the burden of bearing the costs falls narrowly and unevenly on particular people, sectors, and localities. The costs of migration are often short run, while the full benefits of increased mobility appear only in the medium or long run. In this respect, the issues raised by increasing migration resemble the long-standing debate over free trade: the economic benefits are distributed and not necessarily tangible, whereas the costs are highly visible and localized.

As a result of this reality, country governments and international organizations need to consider how to promote the benefits of increased migration while mitigating the unevenly distributed costs. The growing political opposition to migration in many countries suggests that this has not been done well.

We can break up this discussion into recommended policies at the national level and ongoing efforts at the multilateral level. The World Bank (2018) has put forward a number of recommendations for national-level policies. These include the following.

- Designing migration policies with the realities of labor markets in mind.
- Aiding native workers in their adjustments to immigration, for example via relocation assistance.[31]

---

[30] See Maimbo and Ratha (2005).

[31] Moretti (2012: chap. 5) makes the same suggestion in the form of mobility vouchers.

- Especially in the case of high-skilled migration, moving from a "quota" system to a "tax" system via visa fees and additional income taxes.[32]
- Promoting work permits and a path to permanent residency to long-term-employed migrants.
- Investing in the education of migrants' children to promote adjustment.
- For high-skilled migrants, promote and expand demand-driven schemes, such as the H-1B visa system in the United States.

These are a set of ideas to be used as a starting point for national policies towards international migration. The World Bank (2018) also notes, however, that migration policy "would greatly benefit from international cooperation" (35). But here we encounter yet another issue. Unlike in the realms of international trade (the World Trade Organization), international finance (the International Monetary Fund), and international development (the World Bank), there is no multilateral organization for migration policy.

In most cases, the policy locus of international migration policy is the nation state based on the principle of *sovereignty*. In contrast to the "pro-market" orientations of policy regimes in trade, finance, and development policy, intervention and coercion are the order of the day in migration policy.[33] There are international governance mechanisms applying to refugees, in the form of the 1951 Geneva Convention and a few International Labour Organization conventions. There is also the International Organization for Migration (IOM), which provides for intergovernmental coordination in some areas related to migration policy. But, by and large, it is sovereignty that rules in migration policy.

Beginning in 2001 the Berne Initiative involved extensive consultations on the possibility of developing non-binding guidelines for best practices in migration policy. The Berne Initiative was followed by the Global Commission on International Migration (GCIM), established in 2003 by the UN secretary-general. In 2005 the GCIM suggested that greater multilateral coordination of migration policies would be a good idea. The GCIM was followed by the United Nations High-Level Dialogue (HLD) on International Migration and Development, in 2006.[34] The HLD was quickly followed later the same year by the International Labour Organization's

---

[32] This is analogous to tariffs being more market-friendly than import quotas, as discussed in Chapter 7.

[33] Pritchett (2006: 63) is very frank here: "People with guns apply force to prevent people from crossing borders. People with guns force people to leave if discovered in a country without permission. The fact that this coercive force is (usually) exercised with domestic political legitimacy, restraint, or even prudence in rich countries should not mask the fact that it is coercion." See also *The Economist* (2008).

[34] As assessed by Martin, Martin, and Cross (2007), the HLD was an important event for furthering multilateral communication on migration issues, but it did not translate into specific action items for the increased global governance of migration.

Multilateral Framework on Labor Migration, which takes a human rights approach to non-binding principles.

Some observers (such as Bhagwati, 2003; Goldin and Reinert, 2012: chap. 8) have suggested that such a multilateral organization would be a good idea. One area for renewed multilateral cooperation in trade-related migration policy is Mode 4 of the World Trade Organization's General Agreement on Trade in Services, discussed in the accompanying box.

GATS Mode 4: The Temporary Movement of Natural Persons

Recall from Chapter 8 that the WTO's General Agreement on Trade in Services defines trade in services in four ways: cross-border trade (Mode 1); movement of consumers (Mode 2); commercial presence or FDI (Mode 3); and movement of natural persons (Mode 4). The movement of natural persons involves a temporary non-commercial presence by individuals to supply any sort of service in another country. Although there exists a protocol under the GATS for Mode 4 service delivery, this is largely to address the transfer of personnel within MNEs to support FDI. In other words, it is designed to benefit high-income countries rather than LMICs and high-skilled migrants rather than low-skilled migrants.

There have been calls to establish a multilateral system to identify individuals seeking temporary Mode 4 migration, providing national security clearance to them, and granting *multi-entry* GATS visas to them. This would be a step towards harnessing temporary migration for development and would require a new GATS protocol dedicated to the issue. As Winters et al. (2003) demonstrate, the gains for LMICs from an increase of only 3 percent in their temporary labor quotas would exceed the value of total aid flows and be similar to the expected benefits from the Doha Round of trade negotiations. Most of the benefits to LMICs would come from increased access by unskilled workers to jobs in high-income countries.

Given these development benefits, it is interesting that Mode 4 migration was not an active part of the Doha Round and constitutes only about 1 percent of total services trade. As noted by Zaman (2016: 392), high-income countries mounted pressure "to liberalize more services of their own interests such as financial, telecommunication, medical and high-tech services," while they maintained "high restrictions on the liberalization of the movement of natural persons and manual labor-intensive services," where LMICs have comparative advantages.

This appears to be another example of an "everything but labor" approach to international economic liberalization. It is a bit of an irony, however, since, as previously mentioned in this chapter, a number of "birth dearth" high-income

GATS Mode 4: The Temporary Movement of Natural Persons (cont.)

countries are going to need increasing amounts of immigrants to perform labor intensive services. But, without progress on Mode 4, these demands continue to be met through irregular migration, including trafficking.

Based on poverty and development considerations, Zaman (2016: 403) identifies "an urgent necessity to take fruitful steps for liberalizing Mode 4, which is clearly linked to illegal migration attempts and economic development of poor communities of the world." There have been many such calls for action since the birth of the WTO, but no response to date.

Sources: Bhatnagar (2009), Goldin and Reinert (2012), Winters et al. (2003), and Zaman (2016).

Not everyone is convinced that multilateral approaches to migration policy are the best. For example, Pritchett (2006) explicitly states that, given political realities, migration policy advances can best be achieved *bilaterally*. He states: "In the end, domestic politics will dictate that each country have control over who may or may not enter its borders, and that this will not be part of any general international or multilateral binding commitment.... Pushing for multilateral agreements along the lines of the WTO is unlikely to be successful" (121).

This might well be true, but it does not rule out the pursuit of limited, basic principles at the multilateral level. For example, the IOM oversees an International Dialogue on Migration, which it describes as "an opportunity for governments, inter-governmental and non-governmental organizations and other stakeholders to discuss migration policy issues, in order to explore and study policy issues of common interest and cooperate in addressing them." It also sponsors the Global Forum on Migration and Development. Efforts such as these can move forward dialogue and cooperation at both the bilateral and multilateral levels.

Conclusion

Migration is an important component of globalization in general and international production in particular. It is one area of globalization that has experienced less liberalization than others, however. Migration comes in a relatively large number of varieties, with important political, human rights, and public policy considerations. In the area in which migration is most relevant to international production, Martin and Sirkeci (2017: 328) note that "economically motivated migration is usually a journey of hope." This journey of hope includes both low-skilled and high-skilled varieties and has significant influences on global patterns of international production. It also has development implications, positive in the case of remittances and negative in the case of brain drain. Migration policy is an evolving, complex, and crucial area of global public policy that will be near the top of national and, to a lesser extent, global policy agendas for the foreseeable future.

Review Exercises

1. Do you know any migrants? To what extent and how does their experience fit into the discussion of this chapter? To what extent and how does it differ?
2. Can you identify *reasons* why the liberalization of the trade, FDI, and finance components of economic globalization have proceeded much more rapidly than that of the labor migration component?
3. We discussed the political economy of trade policy in Chapter 6. Can you identify any insights from that chapter that could be used in thinking about the political economy of migration policy?
4. Can you identify any benefits from relaxing sovereignty in favor of the multilateral policy coordination of migration?
5. Pick a country of interest. A large country might be easier. Conduct an internet search to describe this country's migration policy in as much detail as possible.

FURTHER READING AND WEB RESOURCES

Overviews of migration issues can be found in Goldin, Cameron, and Balarajan (2011), de Haas (2007), Omelaniuk (2017), Kone and Özden (2017), Martin and Sirkeci (2017), and World Bank (2018). For considerations of migration from a development perspective, see Pritchett (2006), Özden and Schiff (2007), and Goldin and Reinert (2012: chap. 6). A review of remittances can be found in Maimbo and Ratha (2005). For a concise review of migration policy, see Martin (2009) and Dadush and Falcau (2009). For a striking story about Mexican migrants in the United States, see *The Economist* (2010c).

A multilateral organization dedicated to migration issues is the International Organization for Migration (www.iom.int). See also the International Migration Institute at Oxford (www.imi.ox.ac.uk) and the Institute for the Study of International Migration (ISIM: http://isim.georgetown.edu). The IOM and the ISIM jointly publish the *International Migration Journal*. The Global Forum on Migration and Development can be found here: https://gfmd.org/.

REFERENCES

Bauer, T. K., and A. Kunze (2004) "The Demand for High-Skilled Workers and Immigration Policy," *Brussels Economic Review*, 47:1, 1–19.

Baumol, W. J. (1967) "Macroeconomics of Unbalanced Growth: The Anatomy of Urban Crisis," *American Economic Review*, 42:3, 415–26.

Beath, A. L., I. Goldin, and K. A. Reinert (2009) "International Migration," in K. A. Reinert, R. S. Rajan, A. J. Glass, and L. S. Davis (eds.), *The Princeton Encyclopedia of the World Economy*, Princeton University Press, 764–70.

Bhagwati, J. (2003) "The World Needs a New Body to Monitor Migration," *Financial Times*, October 24.

Bhagwati, J., and K. Hamada (1974) "The Brain Drain, International Integration of Markets for Professionals and Unemployment: A Theoretical Analysis," *Journal of Development Economics*, 1:1, 19–42.

Bhargava, A., and F. Docquier (2008) "HIV Pandemic, Medical Brain Drain, and Economic Development in Sub-Saharan Africa," *World Bank Economic Review*, 22:2, 345–66.

Bhatnagar, P. (2009) "Temporary Movement of Natural Persons," in K. A. Reinert, R. S. Rajan, A. J. Glass, and L. S. Davis (eds.), *The Princeton Encyclopedia of the World Economy*, Princeton University Press, 1081–4.

Borjas, G. J. (2003) "The Labor Demand Curve Is Downward Sloping: Reexamining the Impact of Immigration on the Labor Market," *Quarterly Journal of Economics*, 118:4, 1335–74.

Card, D. (2005) "Is the New Immigration Really So Bad?," *Economic Journal*, 115:507, 300–23.

Castles, S., M. A. Cubas, C. Kim, and D. Ozkul (2012) "Irregular Migration: Causes, Patterns, and Strategies," in I. Omelaniuk (ed.), *Global Perspectives on Migration and Development*, Springer, 117–51.

Chowdhury, M. (2016) "Financial Development, Remittances and Economic Growth: Evidence Using a Dynamic Panel Estimation," *Margin: Journal of Applied Economic Research*, 10:1, 35–54.

Dadush, U., and L. Falcau (2009) "Migrants and the Global Financial Crisis," Policy Brief 83, Carnegie Endowment for International Peace.

Dauvergne, C. (2008) *Making People Illegal: What Globalization Means for Migration and Law*, Cambridge University Press.

De Haas, H. (2007) "Turning the Tide? Why Development Will Not Stop Migration," *Development and Change*, 38:5, 819–41.

Debebe, G. (2009) "Brain Waste," in K. A. Reinert, R. S. Rajan, A. J. Glass, and L. S. Davis (eds.), *The Princeton Encyclopedia of the World Economy*, Princeton University Press, 138–41.

Dempsey, J. (2011) "As Germany Booms, It Faces a Shortage of Workers," *New York Times*, February 4.

Desai, M. A., D. Kapur, J. McHale, and K. Rogers (2009) "The Fiscal Impact of High-Skilled Emigration Flows of Indians to the US," *Journal of Development Economics*, 88:1, 32–44.

Docquier, F., and E. Lodigiani (2010) "Skilled Migration and Business Networks," *Open Economies Review*, 21:4, 565–88.

The Economist (2008) "Migration: A Turning Tide?," June 28.

The Economist (2009) "Migration and Development: The Aid Workers Who Really Help," October 10.

The Economist (2010a) "Skilled Immigration: Green Card Blues," October 20.

The Economist (2010b) "Into the Unknown: A Special Report on Japan," November 20.

The Economist (2010c) "Fields of Tears," December 18.

The Economist (2018a) "Ageing in Japan: Demographic Warrior," November 17.

The Economist (2018b) "Technology Centres: Migrating Nerds," December 22.

Financial Times (2010) "US Manufacturers Face Skills Shortages," February 28.

Gibson, J., and D. McKenzie (2011) "Eight Questions about the Brain Drain," *Journal of Economic Perspectives*, 25:3, 107–28.

Goldin, I., G. Cameron, and M. Balarajan (2011) *Exceptional People: How Migration Shaped Our World and Will Define Our Future*, Princeton University Press.

Goldin, I., and K. A. Reinert (2012) *Globalization for Development: Meeting New Challenges*, Oxford University Press.

The Guardian (2007) "Ghosts," January 14.

Hart, D. M. (2006) "Managing the Global Talent Pool: Sovereignty, Treaty, and Intergovernmental Networks," *Technology in Society*, 28:4, 421–34.

Hart, D. M. (2009) "Brain Gain," in K. A. Reinert, R. S. Rajan, A. J. Glass, and L. S. Davis (eds.), *The Princeton Encyclopedia of the World Economy*, Princeton University Press, 136–8.

Hatton, T. J., and J. G. Williamson (2009) "Emigration in the Long Run: Evidence from Two Global Centuries," *Asian-Pacific Economic Literature*, 23:2, 17–28.

Hunt, J., and M. Gauthier-Loiselle (2010) "How Much Does Immigration Boost Innovation?," *American Economic Journal: Macroeconomics*, 2:2, 31–56.

Katz, L. F., and K. M. Murphy (1992) "Changes in Relative Wages, 1963–1987: Supply and Demand Factors," *Quarterly Journal of Economics*, 107:1, 35–78.

Kerr, S. P., W. R. Kerr, and W. F. Lincoln (2015) "Firms and the Economics of Skilled Immigration," *Innovation Policy and the Economy*, 15, 115–52.

Kone, Z. L., and Ç. Özden (2017) "Brain Drain, Gain and Circulation," in K. A. Reinert (ed.), *Handbook of Globalisation and Development*, Edward Elgar, 349–69.

López, G., K. Bialik, and J. Radford (2018) "Key Findings about US Immigrants," Pew Research Center, September 14, www.pewresearch.org/fact-tank/2018/09/14/key-findings-about-u-s-immigrants.

Maimbo, S. M., and D. Ratha (eds.) (2005) *Remittances: Development Impacts and Future Prospects*, World Bank.

Martin, P. (2009) "Migration Governance," in K. A. Reinert, R. S. Rajan, A. J. Glass, and L. S. Davis (eds.), *The Princeton Encyclopedia of the World Economy*, Princeton University Press, 770–5.

Martin, P., S. Martin, and S. Cross (2007) "High-Level Dialogue on Migration and Development," *International Migration*, 41:1, 7–25.

Martin, P., and I. Sirkeci (2017) "Recruitment, Remittances, and Returns," in K. A. Reinert (ed.), *Handbook of Globalisation and Development*, Edward Elgar, 312–30.

Martin, P., and J. E. Taylor (1996) "The Anatomy of a Migration Hump," in J. E. Taylor (ed.), *Development Strategy, Employment, and Migration: Insights from Models*, OECD, 43–62.

Martineau, T., K. Decker, and P. Bundred (2004) "Brain Drain of Health Professionals: From Rhetoric to Responsible Action," *Health Policy*, 70:1, 1–10.

Mattoo, A., I. C. Neagu, and Ç. Özden (2008) "Brain Waste? Educated Immigrants in the US Labor Market," *Journal of Development Economics*, 87:2, 255–69.

Milanovic, B. (2016) *Global Inequality: A New Approach for the Age of Globalization*, Harvard University Press.

Moretti, E. (2012) *The New Geography of Jobs*, Houghton Mifflin Harcourt.

Olesen, H. (2002) "Migration, Return and Development," *International Migration*, 40:5, 125–50.

Olsen, H. H. (2008) "The Snake from Fujian Province to Morecambe Bay: An Analysis of the Problem of Human Trafficking in Sweated Labor," *European Journal of Crime, Criminal Law and Criminal Justice*, 16:1, 1–37.

Omelaniuk, I. (2017) "Migration," in K. A. Reinert (ed.), *Handbook of Globalisation and Development*, Edward Elgar, 289–311.

Organisation for Economic Co-operation and Development (2005) *Trends in International Migration, 2004*, OECD.

Organisation for Economic Co-operation and Development (2013) *International Migration Outlook 2013*, OECD.

Orozco, M., and R. Rouse (2012) "Migrant Hometown Associations and Opportunities for Development: A Global Perspective," in J. DeFilippis and S. Saegert (eds.), *The Community Development Reader*, Routledge, 280–5.

Ottaviano, G. I., and G. Peri (2012) "Rethinking the Effect of Immigration on Wages," *Journal of the European Economic Association*, 10:1, 152–97.

Özden, Ç., and M. Schiff (eds.) (2007) *International Migration, Economic Development and Policy*, World Bank.

Parsons, C. R., S. Rohon, F. Samani, and L. Wettach (2014) "Conceptualising International High-Skilled Migration," Working Paper 104, International Migration Institute, Oxford University.

Pozo, S. (2009) "Remittances," in K. A. Reinert, R. S. Rajan, A. J. Glass, and L. S. Davis (eds.), *The Princeton Encyclopedia of the World Economy*, Princeton University Press, 963–8.

Pritchett, L. (2006) *Let Their People Come: Breaking the Gridlock on Global Labor Mobility*, Center for Global Development.

Saxenian, A. (2002) "Transnational Communities and the Evolution of Global Production Networks," *Industry and Innovation*, 9:3, 183–202.

Saxenian, A. (2005) "From Brain Drain to Brain Circulation: Transnational Communities and Regional Upgrading in India and China," *Studies in Comparative International Development*, 40:2, 35–61.

Sirkeci, I., J. H. Cohen, and D. Ratha (2012) "Introduction: Remittance Flows and Practices during the Crisis," in I. Sirkeci, J. H. Cohen, and D. Ratha (eds.), *Remittances during the Global Financial Crisis and Beyond*, World Bank, 1–12.

Stark, O., and D. E. Bloom (1985) "The New Economics of Labor Migration," *American Economic Review*, 75:2, 173–8.

Stark, O., C. Helmenstein, and A. Prskawetz (1997) "A Brain Gain with a Brain Drain," *Economic Letters*, 55:2, 227–34.

United Nations (2017) *International Migration Report, 2017*, United Nations.

United Nations High Commissioner for Refugees (2018) *Global Report 2017*, UNHCR.

Von Koppenfels, A. K. (2017) "Human Trafficking," in K. A. Reinert (ed.), *Handbook of Globalisation and Development*, Edward Elgar, 331–48.

Winters, L. A., T. L. Walmsley, Z. K Wang, and R. Grynberg (2003) "Liberalizing the Temporary Movement of Natural Persons: An Agenda for the Development Round," *The World Economy*, 26:8, 1137–61.

Woodruff, C., and R. Zenteno (2007) "Migration Networks and Microenterprise in Mexico," *Journal of Development Economics*, 82:2, 509–28.

World Bank (2018) *Moving for Prosperity: Global Migration and Labor Markets*, World Bank.

Zaman, K. (2016) "Blocking the Trade in Mode 4 Services and Its Impact on the Ongoing Refugee Crisis and Migrant Trafficking," *Manchester Journal of International Economic Law*, 13:3, 389–406.

Zelinsky, W. (1971) "The Hypothesis of Mobility Transition," *Geographical Review*, 61:2, 219–49.

PART III
International Finance

14 Accounting Frameworks

In this chapter, we will begin to develop your understanding of our third realm of the world economy, *international finance*. Recall from Chapter 1 that, whereas "international trade" refers to the exchange of goods and services between the countries of the world economy, "international finance" refers to the exchange of **assets** between these countries. Recall also that the global exchange of assets in the world economy is between 60 and 100 times larger than the exchange of goods and services. This is one central reason why international finance is such an important subject.

There is a basic principle in economics that can be informally stated as "things add up." In the realm of international economics, this principle is a very important one. If you forget it, you can find yourself making claims that are simply *incorrect*. Many otherwise knowledgeable individuals do this. If you remember the principle and know how to use it, you will have a powerful tool in your hands for analyzing economies and their relationships to the larger world economy. Consideration of the way "things add up" takes us into the realm of economic accounting, the subject of this chapter. We will take a simple approach to the accounting issue, but the insights you will gain will be crucial to your understanding of the world economy.

We will begin with a consideration of **open-economy accounts**, taking as our starting point the **circular flow diagram**. Next, we will consider the **balance of payments** as a more detailed look at one important relationship in the open-economy accounts, namely the interactions of an economy with the rest of the world. For the interested reader, we consider the subject of *accounting matrices* in Appendix 14.1. Appendix 14.2 presents a simple *open-economy macroeconomic model.*

Open-Economy Accounts

In your introductory economics course, it is very likely that you came across a graphical description of an economy called the *circular flow diagram*. We are going to use this diagram to initiate our analysis of open-economy accounts. We want to view an economy as being aggregated into *one giant sector*. To make things more concrete, let us take the example of Mexico. To begin, we treat the Mexican

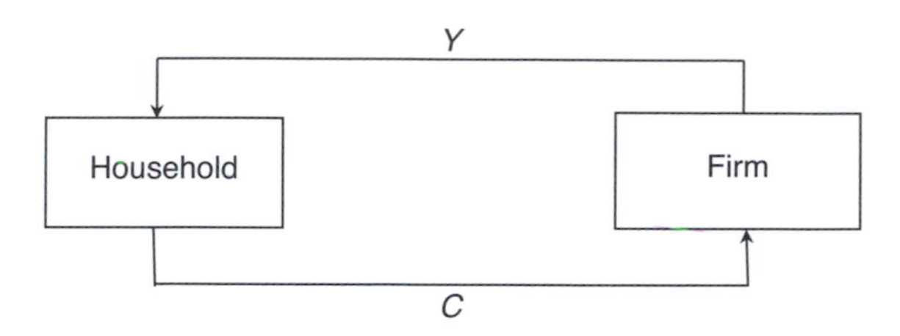

Figure 14.1 A circular flow diagram for a simple closed economy

economy as being composed of two accounts: a Firm account and a Household account. The relationships between these two accounts are summarized as a circular flow diagram of a *simple closed economy* in Figure 14.1. The term "simple" refers to the absence of capital (savings/investment) and government considerations, while the term "closed" refers to the absence of any trade and financial interactions with the rest of the world economy.

In Figure 14.1, the production process of the Firm generates income that accrues to the Household. This income is denoted as Y and consists of wages, salaries, and payments for the use of property assets. Given the simple assumptions of this chapter, Y is also equal to both the nominal **gross domestic product** (GDP) and the nominal **gross national income** (GNI) of Mexico.[1] The consumption process of the household generates consumption expenditures that accrue to the Firm. This consumption is denoted as C in the figure.

Figure 14.1 corresponds to the circular flow diagrams found in introductory textbooks, but it is exceedingly simple and begs for more realism. For our purposes in this chapter, we need to add *three new accounts*. The first we will call Capital, and this account acts as a financial intermediary in the savings/investment process. These financial intermediaries are composed of institutions such as banks, mutual funds, and brokers, which receive funds from savers and use these funds to make loans or buy assets, thereby placing the funds in the hands of investors. The term "capital" used here does not refer to physical capital such as machinery and buildings. Instead, it refers to *income not consumed*, which is available for use in investment. The second new account is Government, and the third is Rest of the World. The Rest of the World account captures the interactions of the Mexican economy with the other countries of the world.

Including these three new institutions results in a circular flow diagram for an *open economy with government, savings, and investment*. This is illustrated in Figure 14.2. As in Figure 14.1, the production process of the Firm generates income

[1] Differences between GDP and GNI arise in practice because of the presence of international factor payments, including remittances (considered in Chapter 13) and repatriated profits of multinational enterprises. We discuss these items when we consider the balance of payments below. Their relationships to GDP and GNI are presented in Appendix 14.3.

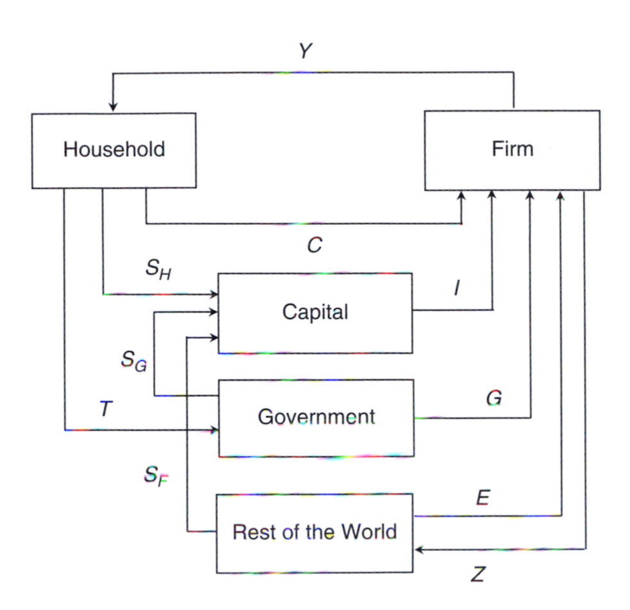

Figure 14.2 An open economy with government, savings, and investment

that accrues to the Household. Now, however, the Household has three types of expenditures. The first of these is consumption of goods and services, C. The second expenditure type is household savings, which is denoted S_H. Through the work of financial intermediaries, Household savings accrues as income to the Capital account. The third expenditure is taxes paid to Government and is denoted T.[2]

Government makes two alternative expenditures: government spending (denoted G) and government savings (denoted S_G). In many cases, government savings are negative (a government deficit), and the flow is reversed, from Capital to Government. You can treat these cases as a negative S_F. Finally, Capital has a single expenditure, I, which consists of funds provided to firms for investment purposes.

The Rest of the World interacts with the Mexican economy in three ways. First, the Rest of the World makes an expenditure that accrues to the Firm account in the form of its purchases of Mexico's exports. We denote these total exports as E. Second, the Rest of the World receives income in the form of Mexico's purchases of imports. We denote these total imports as Z. Finally, the Rest of the World makes an expenditure that accrues to Capital in the form of **foreign savings**, denoted S_F.

To begin your understanding of the open economy, we are going to focus on the Capital and Rest of the World accounts of Figure 14.2. Let us consider the Capital account first. The Capital account has a single expenditure, depicted by an arrow leaving the Capital box in Figure 14.2. This is the expenditure on domestic

[2] To simplify matters for ourselves, we ignore corporate taxes.

investment. The Capital account also has three types of receipts, depicted by arrows entering the Capital box. These are all savings flows, namely household, government, and foreign savings. The first two of these, household and government savings, together give us *domestic savings*. In the introduction to this chapter, we stated that a basic principle of economics is that "things add up." The application of this principle here is that expenditures must equal receipts for the Capital account.[3] Expressing this as an equation gives us

$$I = (S_H + S_G) + S_F \tag{14.1a}$$

In words:

$$\text{Domestic investment} = \text{Domestic savings} + \text{Foreign savings} \tag{14.1b}$$

It will be helpful to rearrange this equation by subtracting domestic savings from both sides. This gives us

$$I - (S_H + S_G) = S_F \tag{14.2a}$$

Or:

$$\text{Domestic investment} - \text{Domestic savings} = \text{Foreign savings} \tag{14.2b}$$

The fact that "things add up" for the Capital account implies that *any gap between domestic investment and domestic savings is made up for by an inflow of foreign savings*. We will discuss this further in just a moment.

Next, let us turn our attention to the Rest of the World account. This account has two expenditures, depicted by arrows leaving the Rest of the World box in Figure 14.2. These expenditures are Mexico's exports and foreign savings. The Rest of the World account also has a single receipt, in the form of Mexico's imports, depicted by an arrow entering the Rest of the World box. The equation expressing the equality between expenditures and receipts for the Rest of the World account is

$$E + S_F = Z \tag{14.3a}$$

Or, in words:

$$\text{Exports} + \text{Foreign savings} = \text{Imports} \tag{14.3b}$$

In this and subsequent chapters, we want to place foreign savings (S_F) on equal footing with the two sources of domestic savings (S_H and S_G). We therefore solve Equation 14.3a for S_F, to obtain

$$S_F = Z - E \tag{14.4a}$$

---

[3] For example, Reinert and Roland-Holst (1997: 95) state: "Economic accounting is based on a fundamental principle of economics: For every income or receipt there is a corresponding expenditure or outlay."

Or:

$$\text{Foreign savings} = \text{Trade deficit} \tag{14.4b}$$

The fact that "things add up" for the Rest of the World account implies that *any gap between imports and exports (any trade deficit) has a counterpart in an inflow of foreign savings*. We will discuss this further below.[4]

Take a look at the Capital account in Equation 14.2a and the Rest of the World account in Equation 14.4a. Notice that both these equations have foreign savings on one side. This means that we can combine them into a single relationship, which we will call the **fundamental accounting equation** for open economies. This equation is

$$I - (S_H + S_G) = S_F = Z - E \tag{14.5a}$$

Or:

$$\text{Domestic investment} - \text{Domestic savings} = \text{Foreign savings} = \text{Trade deficit} \tag{14.5b}$$

The fundamental accounting equation is also written in a different form, obtained by multiplying it by the number −1. This form is

$$(S_H + S_G) - I = -S_F = E - Z \tag{14.6a}$$

Or:

$$\text{Domestic savings} - \text{Domestic investment} = \text{Foreign investment} = \text{Trade surplus} \tag{14.6b}$$

In Equations 14.6a and 14.6b, foreign investment ($-S_F$) refers to Mexico's *capital outflows*—that is, its investment in foreign countries. It is just the reverse of foreign savings (S_F) being capital inflows.

Depending on the source, you might find the fundamental accounting equations expressed in either Equation 14.5a/14.5b form or Equation 14.6a/14.6b form. They communicate the same important accounting insight, which we will repeat in the following box for emphasis:

Fundamental Accounting Equations

Domestic investment – Domestic savings = Foreign savings = Trade deficit

Domestic savings – Domestic investment = Foreign investment = Trade surplus

[4] As we will see in the next section of the chapter, on the balance of payments, the trade deficit will correspond to the current account of the balance of payments, while foreign savings will correspond to the capital/financial account of the balance of payments.

What do the fundamental accounting equations tell us? Let us study them very carefully, with the help of Table 14.1. There are *two cases* to consider, one for each equation. First, suppose that Mexico's domestic investment exceeds its domestic savings. This case is explained by the first equation in the box. The shortfall in domestic savings is made up for by a positive inflow of foreign savings. Then, according to the first equation, there must be a *trade deficit*. Does this make sense? A trade deficit means that the Mexican economy is importing more goods and services in value terms than it is exporting. Therefore, Mexico must sell something else other than goods and services to the rest of the world to make up the difference. This "something else" turns out to be *assets*: government and corporate bonds, corporate equities, and even real estate. The purchase of Mexican assets by the Rest of the World is the very thing that generates the inflow of foreign savings into Mexico. The first equation therefore *makes sense*.

Next, suppose that Mexico's domestic savings exceeds its domestic investment. This case is explained by the second equation in the box. An excess of domestic savings generates a positive outflow of foreign investment by Mexico. Then, according to the second equation, there must be a *trade surplus*. Does this make sense? A trade surplus means that the Mexican economy is exporting more goods and services in value terms than it is importing. Therefore, Mexico must buy something else other than goods and services from the rest of the world to make up the difference. That "something else" again is *assets*. The purchase of foreign assets by

Table 14.1 Domestic savings, domestic investment, foreign savings, and the trade balance

Domestic investment and domestic savings	Foreign savings	Trade balance	Explanation
Domestic investment exceeds domestic savings	Foreign savings is positive	Trade deficit	Domestic savings is too small to finance domestic investment. Therefore, the country requires an inflow of foreign savings to make up the difference. This inflow of foreign savings finances the trade deficit.
Domestic savings exceeds domestic investment	Foreign savings is negative or foreign investment is positive.	Trade surplus	Domestic savings exceeds the requirements of domestic investment. Therefore, the country lends the difference to the rest of the world. This outflow of foreign investment generates a trade surplus.

Mexico generates the outflow of foreign investment to the Rest of the World. The second equation also makes sense.[5]

It is often the case that the accounts of this section are expressed in the form of *accounting matrices*. This possibility is considered in Appendix 14.1. In addition, the accounts can be utilized in a basic *open-economy macroeconomic model*, and this is described in Appendix 14.2.

The field of international finance is concerned with the *international* aspects of economies as aggregate entities. Therefore, a focus is often placed on the Rest of the World account Equation 14.4a/14.4b above, in the form of a more detailed set of accounts known as the balance of payments accounts. We take up these important accounts next.

Balance of Payments Accounts

The balance of payments accounts of any country focus exclusively on the relationship of the country with the rest of the world. Recall from the previous section that the open-economy accounts were divided into five sub-accounts, namely Firm, Household, Capital, Government, and Rest of the World. The purpose of the balance of payments accounts is to examine in more detail the final, Rest of the World account, almost like holding up a magnifying glass to it. This examination is in its own style of accounting, however, with a terminology that is not entirely consistent with the open-economy accounts discussed above. Consequently, the balance of payments accounts sometimes require a little patience on the part of the user.

We are going to begin our discussion of the balance of payments accounts by considering a simplified summary accounts for Mexico in 2017. This is presented in Table 14.2. The balance of payments in this table has *five parts*, each with a heading in italics. These parts are the **current account**, the **capital/financial account**, official reserve transactions, errors and omissions, and the overall balance. The current account of the balance of payments records transactions that create earnings and generate expenditures between Mexico and the rest of the world. These *do not* involve the exchange of assets. The capital/financial account of the balance of payments records transactions between Mexico and the rest of the world that *do* involve the exchange of assets. The official reserve transactions also involve the exchange of assets between Mexico and the rest of the world, but

[5] Some time ago, Krugman (1996: ix) wrote of "the disturbingly difficult ideas of people who know how to read national accounts or understand that the trade balance is also the difference between savings and investment." You are now one of these people.

Table 14.2 Mexican simplified balance of payments, 2017 (US$ billions)

Item	Gross	Net	Major balance
Current account			
1. Goods exports	409.8		
2. Goods imports	−420.8		
3. Goods trade balance		−11.0	
4. Service exports	27.6		
5. Service imports	−37.5		
6. Goods and services trade balance		−20.9	
7. Net income (primary income)		−28.3	
8. Net transfers (secondary income)		30.5	
9. Current account balance			−18.7
Capital/financial account			
10. Direct investment (FDI)		26.9	
11. Portfolio investment		8.2	
12. Other investment		−8.0	
13. Capital/financial account balance, net of official reserves balance			27.1
Official reserve transactions			
14. Official reserves balance			4.8
Errors and omissions			
15. Errors and omissions			−13.2
Overall balance			
16. Overall balance			0

Sources: data.imf.org and banxico.org.mx.

these are governmental (central bank and treasury) transactions rather than the private transactions of the capital/financial account. Finally, there are, inevitably, errors and omissions.[6]

[6] High (2009: 102) notes: "Although balance of payments accounts are constructed using sophisticated accounting principles..., a country's cross-border transactions are not measured with the accuracy of a corporation's accounts. Balance of payments figures are statistically estimated based on sampling data gathered by government agencies.... Although these agencies do their utmost to provide reliable estimates, of necessity the accounts contain errors; the statistical estimates are based on data that are incomplete and otherwise imperfect."

The starting point for understanding the balance of payments is to recognize that the overall balance must be zero. This is another example of the principle that "things add up." Consequently, we can think of the balance of payments in the following terms:

$$\text{Current account} + \text{Capital/financial account} + \text{Official reserve transactions} + \text{Errors and omissions} = 0 \quad (14.7)$$

Now let us consider the balance of payments accounts of Table 14.2 in some detail. As we just mentioned, the first section of the balance of payments is known as the *current account* and includes items 1 through 9. Some of these items are reported in gross terms, some in net terms, and one as a major balance.[7] We will consider them one at a time. Item 1 is Mexico's total goods exports. It is reported in gross terms at a 2017 value of US$409.8 billion. Similarly, item 2 is Mexico's total goods imports, reported in gross terms at a value of –US$420.8 billion. You can see here that goods exports, generating a receipt for Mexico, have a positive value, while goods imports, generating a payment for Mexico, have a negative value. The net of these two items is known as the *goods trade balance* and is reported in net terms as –US$11.0 billion.[8]

Services trade is reported separately in items 4 and 5 of the balance of payments in Table 14.2. Service exports are reported in gross terms in item 4 as US$27.6 billion, and service imports are reported in gross terms in item 5 as –US$37.5 billion. Again, we see that service exports, generating a receipt for Mexico, have a positive value, while service imports, generating a payment for Mexico, have a negative value. Item 6 gives our second net balance, namely the *goods and services trade balance* of –US$20.9 billion. This value corresponds to the $(E - Z)$ value in the open-economy accounts considered above. It is a much better focus point than the goods trade balance.

Items 7 and 8 in Table 14.2 are *new* items that we have not yet encountered. Furthermore, they are the two items that cause a difference between the goods and services trade balance and the current account balance. Item 7 is *net income* (also known as *primary income*). It requires a little explanation. Residents of Mexico, either households or firms, own factors of production located in the rest of the world. In other words, a Mexican firm might own a factory in a foreign country. This firm receives income or profits from this factory during the year in question, and this is income receipts or income credits. Alternatively, residents of

[7] Items reported in *gross* terms record the inflow or outflow separately. Items reported in *net* terms record the *difference* between the inflow and the outflow.

[8] There is a tendency for politicians to focus on the goods trade balance to the exclusion of trade in services. This downplaying of trade in services is not a useful habit. As we emphasized in Chapter 1, trade consists of both goods trade and services trade.

foreign countries own factors of production located in Mexico, and they receive payments from Mexico. From Mexico's point of view, these are income payments or income debits. Item 7 of Table 14.2 records the *net* of income receipts and income payments. Income payments exceed income receipts, and net income is –US$28.3 billion.

Item 8 is *net transfers* (also known as *secondary income*) and includes foreign aid, foreign remittances (discussed in Chapter 13), and international pension flows. For Mexico in 2017, inward transfers exceeded outward transfers by US$30.5 billion, and it is this net figure that is entered into the balance of payments.

The sum of the net items 6 through 8 composes the *current account balance* and is entered into the accounts as a major balance in item 9 of Table 14.2. In 2017 Mexico had a current account *deficit* of US$18.7 billion. This was equivalent to less than 2 percent of GDP, which is quite modest by global standards. Since the accounts between Mexico and the rest of the world must balance ("things add up," once again), there must have been other transactions in the balance of payments offsetting the current account deficit.

As mentioned above, whereas the current account records earnings and expenditure transactions that *do not* involve the exchange of assets, the *capital/financial account* has the distinguishing feature of consisting of transactions that *do* involve the exchange of assets.[9] The type of asset exchanged and who exchanges them determine the capital/financial account item in which a transaction is recorded.[10] Let us take a look in Table 14.2.

Item 10 in Table 14.2 is **direct investment**, which is just the foreign direct investment we discussed in previous chapters. As we discussed in Chapter 1, the assets involved in direct investment contain an element of management influence reflected in shares amounting to at least 10 percent of the enterprise in question. In the case of Mexico in 2017, there was a net inward flow of direct investment of US$26.9 billion.

The second capital account item is *portfolio investment*. Portfolio investment includes government bonds of various maturities, corporate equities, and corporate

---

[9] The International Monetary Fund breaks up this *account* into separate capital and financial accounts, but we do not do that here. The financial account is where the actual capital flows are recorded and is therefore more important in most cases. The capital account includes other items, such as revaluation, and, for most countries, is quite small. In the past the entire capital/financial account was known as the "capital account." This has caused some confusion with some individuals and textbooks still using "capital account" under its old meaning. In the words of one observer on this, "Sigh." See http://faculty.washington.edu/danby/bls324/macro/categories.html.

[10] The IMF also now takes a different approach to the sign of the entries in the capital/financial account from what we do here (and they did in the past). For the IMF, positive entries are for lending (selling assets) and negative entries are for borrowing (buying assets). We do not follow this practice here, but, if you are using IMF capital/financial account data, please be careful of this.

bonds. Unlike direct investment, portfolio investment does *not* involve an element of management influence.[11] As we see in item 11 in Table 14.2, in the case of Mexico in 2017 there was a net inward flow of portfolio investment of US$8.2 billion.

The third capital/financial account item is *other investment*. This includes commercial bank lending and other residual items. As we see in item 12 of Table 14.2, in the case of Mexico in 2017 there was a net outward flow with an entry of –US$8.0 billion.[12]

The sum of the net items 10 through 12 composes the *capital/financial account balance* and is entered into the accounts as a major balance in item 13 of Table 14.2. In 2017 Mexico had a capital/financial account *surplus* of US$27.1 billion, more than offsetting the current account deficit of US$8.4 billion. This value corresponds most closely to the S_F value in the open-economy accounts considered above.

The third component of the balance of payments accounts is *official reserve transactions*, reported in net terms as a major balance in Table 14.2. It is an item that did not appear in the open-economy accounts relationship of the balance of payments equation above. The **official reserves balance** is recorded as item 14, at a value of US$4.8 billion in 2017. The official reserves balance reflects the actions of the world's *treasuries and central banks*. Central banks need to hold reserves of foreign exchange. They hold these in the form of other countries' government bonds and in accounts at foreign central banks. Transactions on the official reserves balance occur in four instances.

- When Mexico's central bank sells foreign exchange holdings, this generates an inward flow of funds and income or receipts on Mexico's official reserves balance (positive entries).
- When Mexico's central bank buys foreign exchange holdings, this generates outlays or expenditures on the official reserves balance (negative entries).
- When foreign central banks sell their reserves of Mexico's currency, this generates an outward flow of funds and an outlay or expenditure on Mexico's official reserves balance (negative entries).
- Finally, when foreign central banks buy reserves of Mexico's currency, this generates an income or receipts on Mexico's official reserves balance (positive entries).

---

[11] Portfolio investment can be broken down further into *long-term capital* and *short-term capital*. This distinction is important, because short-term capital is more volatile than long-term capital. For example, a long time ago *The Economist* (2002: 64) noted: "The volatility of portfolio finance – its tendency to pour in when investors are confident, and flee just as suddenly – is the main reason for growing scepticism about the whole process of foreign borrowing by emerging market economies." For a detailed discussion of this, see Goldin and Reinert (2005).

[12] Along with short-term components of portfolio investment, commercial bank lending recorded in other investment can be quite volatile. Again, see Goldin and Reinert (2005).

Looking at these four possibilities, we can see that there is a negative relationship between flows of official reserve transactions and the stock of reserves. Inflows on the official reserve transactions are associated with reductions in reserves, and outflows on the official reserve transactions are associated with increases in reserves.

Let us take stock of our balances up to this point: the current account balance is –US$18.7 billion; the capital/financial account balance is US$27.1 billion; and the official reserves balance is US$4.8 billion. Adding these three balances gives us US$13.2 billion. The balance of payments accounts address this kind of difference through the *errors and omissions* entry. This (rather large) entry, item 15 in Table 14.2 of –US$13.2 billion, ensures that the overall balance of payments in item 16 is indeed zero. "Things add up."

Analyzing the Balance of Payments Accounts

With this understanding of the balance of payments accounts in hand, we can now turn to how we might use the accounts in a more analytical fashion. As we saw in Equation 14.7 above, the sum of the current account, the capital/financial account, official reserve transactions and errors and omissions must be zero. Analytically, we often ignore errors and omissions in order to gain some insights. This gives us:

$$\text{Current account} + \text{Capital/financial account} + \text{Official reserve transactions} = 0 \quad (14.7a)$$

This is the analytical application of "things add up" for the balance of payments accounts. We have also seen that the current account contains the trade balance and the capital account contains foreign savings. So, Equation 14.7a is similar to Equations 14.5 and 14.6 of our open-economy macroeconomic accounts. It is more inclusive than those accounts, however, and also allows for official reserve transactions.

What does Equation 14.7a tell us? There are many ways of going about describing this, but perhaps the easiest is to recognize that, if two of the items in Equation 14.7a have the same sign (positive or negative), then the third must have the opposite sign (negative or positive). To be more specific, we can state the following.

- If the current and capital/financial accounts are both positive (negative), then official reserve transactions must be negative (positive).
- If the current and official reserve transaction accounts are both positive (negative), then the capital/financial account must by negative (positive).
- If the capital/financial and official reserve transaction accounts are both positive (negative), then the current account must be negative (positive).

Let us examine two cases of this with reference to the *first* of these bullet points. Suppose that the current and capital/financial accounts are both positive. Roughly, this means that Mexico is selling more goods, services, and assets in the private realm to the rest of the world than it is buying. The official reserve transactions must make up for the difference. The central bank must buy additional assets to generate an offsetting expenditure with a negative entry and bring the overall balance of payments back to zero. The buying of additional assets increases the stock of total reserves.

Alternatively, suppose that the current and capital/financial accounts are both negative. Roughly, this means that Mexico is buying more goods, services, and assets in the private realm from the rest of the world than it is selling. Again, the official transactions must make up for the difference. The central bank must sell additional assets to generate an offsetting receipt with a positive entry and bring the overall balance of payments back to zero. The selling of additional assets decreases (or "draws down") the stock of total reserves.

These considerations lead to another view of Equation 14.7a as follows:

$$\text{Current account} + \text{Capital/financial account} = \text{Change in official reserves} \quad (14.7\text{b})$$

Another way to look at Equation 14.7a/14.7b is in terms of financing current account deficits. This often has relevance to countries in deficit positions and is a focal point for many types of analysis. Perhaps Mexico has a negative goods and services trade balance that is not offset by income and transfer receipts. Consequently, there is a current account deficit. Perhaps, however, the capital/financial account, even with a positive balance, is insufficient to finance the current account deficit. The central bank must step in to sell assets and generate additional receipts. This entails drawing down foreign exchange reserves. There is a limit to central banks' abilities to do this, however, because foreign exchange reserves cannot fall below zero. This is why, in some instances, a current account deficit with an insufficient capital account surplus draws so much attention: it can precipitate a crisis.

The balance of payments accounts are thus an important *diagnostic tool* for international economists.[13] They help to identify patterns of relationships of the country in question with the rest of the world that might not be sustainable. For example, in the case just described, an international economist might begin considering potential corrective measures. The current account deficit, for example, may need to be suppressed through increases in government

[13] James (1996: 124) states that "analyzing the origins of balance of payments problems [can] provide a tool for diagnosing more wide-ranging economic difficulties. The balance of payments [acts] as a fever thermometer."

tax revenues that allow an increase in government savings. As stated by Obstfeld (2012: 478), "Large and persistent current account imbalances can be an indicator of trouble ahead...and therefore deserve close monitoring by policymakers."[14]

Global Imbalances

The discussion in this chapter on open-economy and balance of payments accounts helps to provide a window onto a central aspect of the current world economy. There is a tradition in international economics that suggests that it is natural for high-income countries to have capital/financial account deficits or outflows and for most low- and middle-income countries to have capital/financial account surpluses or inflows. As a result, LMICs would receive net inflows of capital that would yield relatively high rates of return, the capital being supplied from high-income countries where rates of return are relatively low. This reflects the fact that, at early stages of development, the need for capital in LMICs is high, while domestic saving is low. As development proceeds, the need for capital slowly declines, while domestic saving slowly increases.[15]

Let us examine whether this proposition holds in the current world economy. We do this from the high-income country perspective first, considering the United States. Figure 14.3 plots the current and capital/financial account balances of the US balance of payments from 1990 to 2016. As you can see in this figure, the United States has run a persistent current account deficit over this time period. This has had its counterpart in a capital/financial account surplus, or borrowing from abroad, that reached a peak of nearly US$800 billion in 2006.[16] This was the result of a deficit of domestic savings (both household and government), wars in Afghanistan and Iraq, and government tax cuts. Rather than being a source of capital for the developing world, the United States became a *capital sink*.

---

[14] One important reason for this is that inflows of private capital on the capital/financial account can contribute to "credit booms," which can, in turn, lead to financial instability. We take up capital flows in Chapter 15.

[15] This theoretical framework predicting net capital flows from the "developed" to the "developing" world is *highly idealized*, with intervening factors inhibiting the idealized flows. These include political risk, default risk, differences in levels of human capital and technology, and differences in institutional quality. These points have been emphasized by Lucas (1990).

[16] *The Economist* (2005: 24) reports that "the growing imbalances are weakening America's economy, not only because of the extra foreign debt the country has taken on, but because of the domestic toll of being the world's consumer of last resort. America is saving too little and not investing enough in productive assets, especially in the export sector."

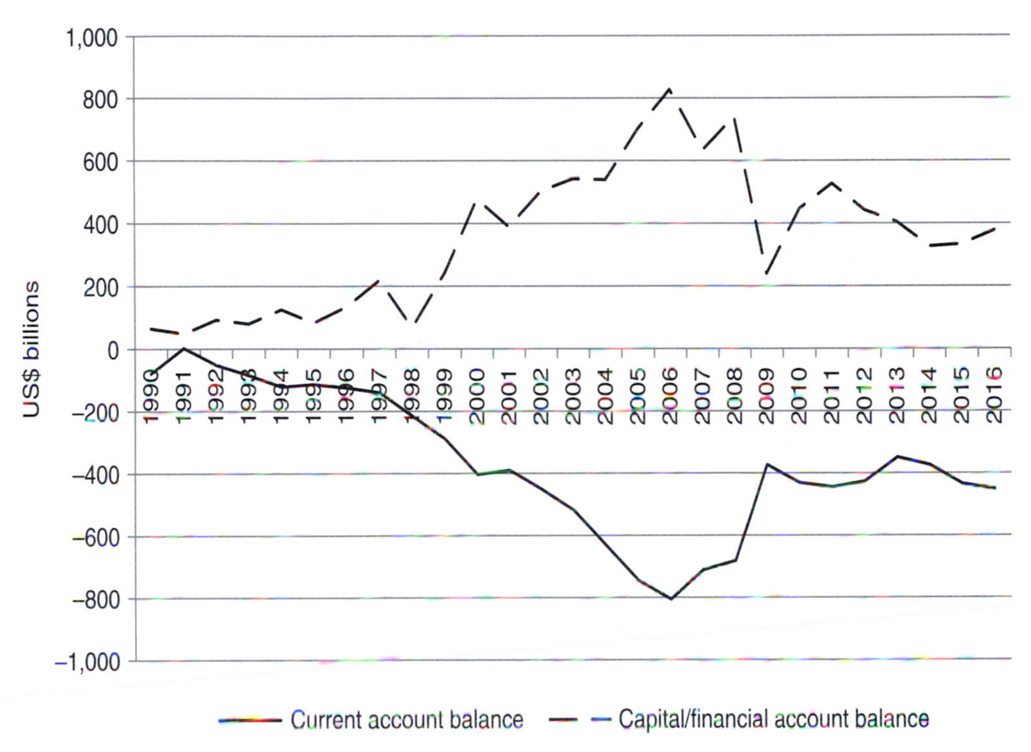

Figure 14.3 US current and capital/financial account balances, 1990–2016 (US$ billions)
Source: US Bureau of Economic Analysis.

Figure 14.4 repeats Figure 14.3 for the case of China from 1990 to 2016. It paints a very different picture. Both the current and capital/financial accounts were in relative balance until the mid-1990s. At that point in time the current account moved into slight surplus, while the capital/financial account moved into slight deficit. These accounts returned to balance in 1999 and 2000, but a new episode began in 2001. The current account moved into surplus, and the capital/financial account moved into deficit. These imbalances reached over US$400 billion in 2007, after which they declined. What we observe here is the *lending* by China to the rest of the world (including the United States). The indications are that this situation might soon be reversed, however.[17]

So here we have an interesting paradox in the modern world economy. Economic intuition suggests that high-income countries will be sources of capital

[17] *The Economist* (2005: 4) reports: "Between 2000 and 2004, China's national savings rate rose by an extraordinary 12 percentage points to 50% of GDP." At the time of this writing China's foreign exchange reserve holdings have reached approximately US$2.5 trillion. As reported in *The Economist* (2019), however, China's current account surplus might soon *disappear*, reversing a primary feature of the world economy. *The Economist* (2019) notes that "the shift from lender to borrower will create a knock-on effect, gradually forcing it to attract more foreign capital and liberalize its financial system."

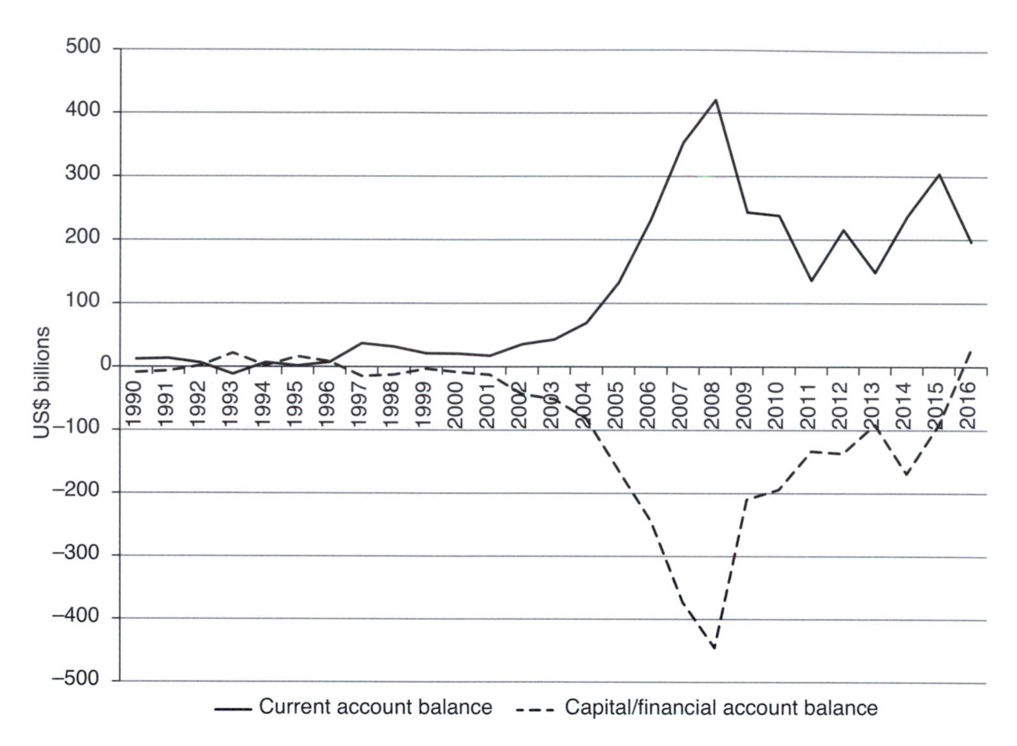

Figure 14.4 China's current and capital/financial account balances, 1990–2016 (US$ billions)
Source: IMF, *International Financial Statistics.*

and LMICs will be capital destinations. But simple analysis of the US and Chinese balance of payments accounts shows that this has definitely not been the case. In fact, there have been large *global imbalances* in savings and investment flows, imbalances that *The Economist* (2005) refers to as the "great thrift shift."[18] These seem to have been coincident with the advance of financial globalization that was well under way by 1990.[19] The financial globalization made it more likely that expanded asset transactions could take place between countries, leading to global imbalances.

Global imbalances can appear at the regional level as well. Figure 14.5 considers the case of Europe. After the year 2000 Germany began to be characterized by large and growing current account surpluses. At the same time, other European countries developed significant current account deficits. These deficits peaked around the time of the 2008 global financial crisis and played a role in them. With the passing of time these imbalances disappeared, though Germany's current

[18] On the link between global balances and an open trade regime, see Wolf (2008).

[19] This point is emphasized by Mendoza, Quadrini and Ríos-Rull (2009), who also point to the differences ("heterogeneity") of financial markets across countries.

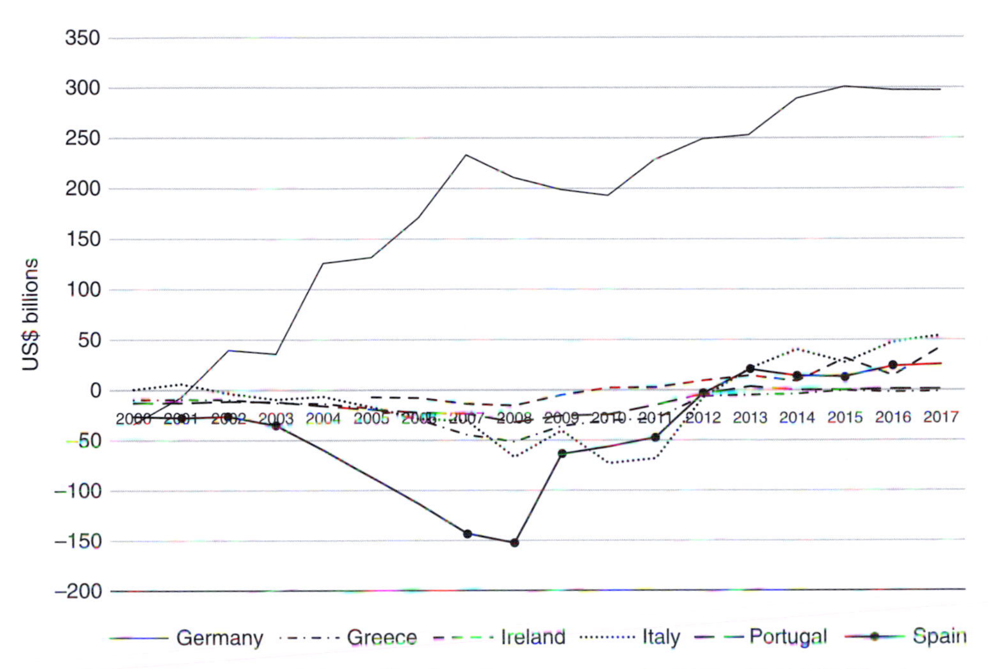

Figure 14.5 Current account balances for selected European countries, 2000–2017 (US$ billions)
Source: IMF, *International Financial Statistics.*

account surplus remains high. We will return to this case in Chapter 20, on crises and responses.

Conclusion

Chapter 1 discussed three realms of the world economy: international trade (the exchange of goods and services), international production (foreign direct investment), and international finance (the exchange of assets). In this chapter, we have used accounting schemes to develop linkages between these three realms. These linkages were present in the open-economy accounts as well as in the balance of payments accounts. The key insight is that current account deficits and surpluses have a counterpart in capital/financial account surpluses and deficits, respectively.

The trade balance is one major component of the current account. Foreign savings in the form of direct and portfolio investment is one major component of the capital/financial account. The open-economy and balance of payments accounts can both be used as diagnostic tools for the assessment of the sustainability of current economic conditions in the country in question. They can also be used to analyze imbalances of savings between the countries of the world.

Review Exercises

1. This book considers three elements of economic globalization: international trade, international production, and international finance. Looking back on this chapter, please identify where in the open-economy accounts and balance of payments accounts connections appear between these three realms.
2. Looking at the open-economy circular flow diagram of Figure 14.2, please explain how an increase in government expenditures, G, without any increase in tax revenues, T, would tend to impact the trade balance. You will need to use one of the fundamental equations to answer this question.
3. Repeat the exercise of Question 2 for an increase in household consumption, C, without any increase in income, Y.
4. Consider the global imbalances issue discussed in this chapter. Given your understanding of the issue, try to suggest policies that might address it. You are just at the beginning of your exploration of international finance, but try to be as detailed as you can in your policy suggestions.
5. Using the open-economy macroeconomic model of Appendix 14.2, graphically analyze an increase in either tax revenues or the entire $S_H(Y)$ relationship. To do this, use a diagram like that of Figures 14.6 and 14.7.

FURTHER READING AND WEB RESOURCES

A concise reviews of balance of payments accounts can be found in Cumby and Levich (1992) and High (2009). A much more thorough and complete introduction is available in the International Monetary Fund's latest *Balance of Payments and International Investment Position Manual* (BPM6: IMF, 2009). At nearly 400 pages, this document will go a long way to answering detailed questions about balance of payments accounts, and it is available online at www.imf.org/external/pubs/ft/bop/2007/pdf/bpm6.pdf. For a recent blog entry on global imbalances by Maurice Obstfeld, see https://blogs.imf.org/2018/07/24/addressing-global-imbalances-requires-cooperation.

Both open-economy accounts and balance of payments data are available from the IMF's monthly publication *International Financial Statistics* (IFS). Most important is the annual *Yearbook* in this series. The IFS is also available in an online version, which many libraries have subscribed to. It is not user-friendly, but nevertheless is an important source for standardized data. See the website of the International Monetary Fund at www.imf.org.

REFERENCES

Cumby, R., and R. Levich (1992) "Balance of Payments," in P. Newman, M. Milgate, and J. Eatwell (eds.), *The New Palgrave Dictionary of Money and Finance*, vol. 1, Macmillan, 113–20.

Dornbusch, R. (1988) *Open Economy Macroeconomics*, Basic Books,.

The Economist (2002) "Special Report: The IMF," September 28.

The Economist (2005) "The Great Thrift Shift," September 24.

The Economist (2019) "China's Balance of Payments: The Big Flip," March 16.

Goldin, I., and K. A. Reinert (2005) "Capital Flows and Development: A Survey," *Journal of International Trade and Economic Development*, 14:4, 453–81.

High, J. (2009) "Balance of Payments," in K. A. Reinert, R. S. Rajan, A. J. Glass, and L. S. Davis (eds.), *The Princeton Encyclopedia of the World Economy*, Princeton University Press, 102–7.

International Monetary Fund (2009) *Balance of Payments and International Investment Position Manual*, IMF.

James, H. (1996) *International Monetary Cooperation since Bretton Woods*, Oxford University Press.

Keynes, J. M. (1936) *The General Theory of Employment, Interest and Money*, Harcourt Brace.

Krugman, P. (1996) *Pop Internationalism*, MIT Press.

Lucas, R. E. (1990) "Why Doesn't Capital Flow from Rich to Poor Countries?," *American Economic Review*, 80:2, 92–6.

Mendoza, E. G., V. Quadrini, and J. V. Ríos-Rull (2009) "Financial Integration, Financial Development, and Global Imbalances," *Journal of Political Economy*, 117:3, 371–416.

Obstfeld, M. (2012) "Financial Flows, Financial Crises, and Global Imbalances," *Journal of International Money and Finance*, 31:3, 469–80.

Reinert, K. A., and D. W. Roland-Holst (1997) "Social Accounting Matrices," in J. F. Francois and K. A. Reinert (eds.), *Applied Methods for Trade Policy Analysis*, Cambridge University Press, 94–121.

Wolf, M. (2008) "Global Imbalances Threaten the Survival of Liberal Trade," *Financial Times*, December 2.

Appendix 14.1: Accounting Matrices

In many instances, international and development economists arrange open-economy accounts in the form of *an accounting matrix*.[20] This process begins with Figure 14.2 above. In setting up accounting matrices, we need to abide by four rules: (1) the number of accounts composes the dimensions of the square matrix; (2) expenditures or payments are recorded down the columns of the matrix; (3) receipts or incomes are recorded across the rows of the matrix; and (4) the row and column sums of the matrix are equal. Since Figure 14.2 has five accounts, it translates into a matrix with five rows and columns. Such a matrix is presented in Table 14.3.

[20] See, for example, Reinert and Roland-Holst (1997). They advocate the accounting matrix approach, arguing that "it represents a comprehensive and consistent framework for developing databases for rigorous economic methods" and that "it helps in the reconciliation of the numerous data sources to complete the detailed picture of economywide activity" (117).

Table 14.3 An open-economy accounting matrix

	Firm	Household	Capital	Government	Rest of the World
Firm		C	I	G	E
Household	Y				
Capital		S_H		S_G	S_F
Government		T			
Rest of the World	Z				

To fill in Table 14.3, we can either record expenditures down columns or receipts across rows. Let us record expenditures down columns, leaving it to you to check that recording receipts across rows gives us the same result. The Firm has two expenditures: income, Y, accruing to the Household, and imports, Z, accruing to the Rest of the World. We record these down the first column. The Household has three expenditures: consumption, C, accruing to the Firm; household savings, S_H, accruing to Capital; and taxes, T, accruing to the Government. We record these down the second column. Capital has a single expenditure, I, accruing to the Firm, and we record this in the third column. The Government has two expenditures: government spending, G, accruing to the Firm, and government savings, S_G, accruing to Capital. We record these down the fourth column. Finally, the Rest of the World has two expenditures: exports, E, accruing to the Firm, and foreign savings, S_F, accruing to Capital. We record these down the fifth column.

We can gain insights into open economies by applying the fourth rule of accounting matrices to Table 14.3. The rule states that the row and column sums of the accounting matrix are equal. Applying this rule gives us the following set of accounting identity equations:

$$Y + Z = C + I + G + E \tag{14.8}$$

$$C + S_H + T = Y \tag{14.9}$$

$$I = S_H + S_G + S_F \tag{14.10}$$

$$G + S_G = T \tag{14.11}$$

$$E + S_F = Z \tag{14.12}$$

Equation 14.8 can be rearranged to give the standard national income equation from introductory macroeconomics:

$$Y = C + I + G + (E - Z) \tag{14.13}$$

Equations 14.10 and 14.12 can be rearranged to give the fundamental accounting equation discussed earlier in this chapter:

$$I - (S_H + S_G) = S_F = Z - E \tag{14.5a}$$

Or:

$$(S_H + S_G) - I = -S_F = E - Z \tag{14.6a}$$

The accounting matrix of Table 14.3 contains all the information on open-economy macroeconomics accounts in a succinct form. We will next consider how to move from the open-economy accounts of Equations 14.8 to 14.12 to a simple, open-economy, macroeconomic model.

Appendix 14.2: An Open-Economy Model

An open-economy model can be derived from the accounting equations of this chapter.[21] We begin with Equation 14.6a. Combining this with the government income/expenditure identity in Equation 14.11 gives us

$$S_H + T - G - I = E - Z \tag{14.14}$$

Keynesian thinking in macroeconomics suggests that household savings (S_H) increase with the level of income (Y).[22] Experience also shows that imports (Z) increase with the level of income. We will denote these responses in functional form as $S_H(Y)$ and $Z(Y)$, with both S_H and Z responding positively to Y. If these two relationships are linear, and the other variables in this equation are independent of income (that is, exogenous), we have the lines depicted in Figure 14.6.

Figure 14.6 depicts a situation in which the trade balance is initially zero. Suppose that, from this initial position, there is an *increase in export demand.* This shifts the $E - Z(Y)$ curve upwards by the amount of the increase in export demand from point A to point B. At point B, however, the trade surplus exceeds the net of domestic savings over domestic investment. The only way for the fundamental accounting equation to be restored is via an increase in Y. As Y increases, both S_H and Z increase. The former increases the net of domestic savings over domestic investment (a movement from A to C), while the latter reduces the trade surplus

[21] See Dornbusch (1988: chap. 3).

[22] This goes back to Keynes (1936), who states: "The fundamental psychological law...is that men are disposed, as a rule and on the average, to increase their consumption as their income increases, *but not by as much as the increase in their income*" (96, emphasis added).

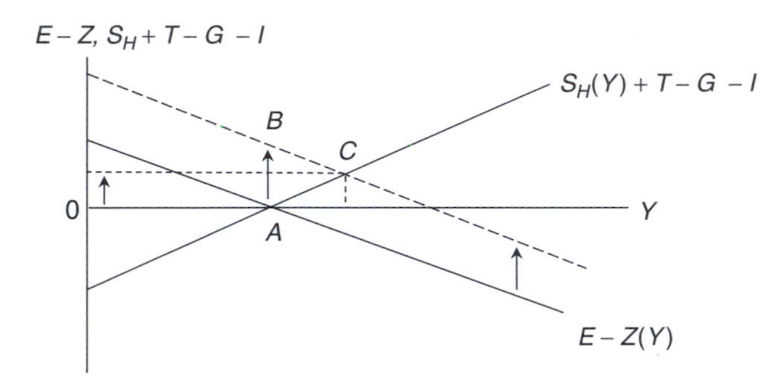

Figure 14.6 An open-economy macroeconomic model and an increase in export demand

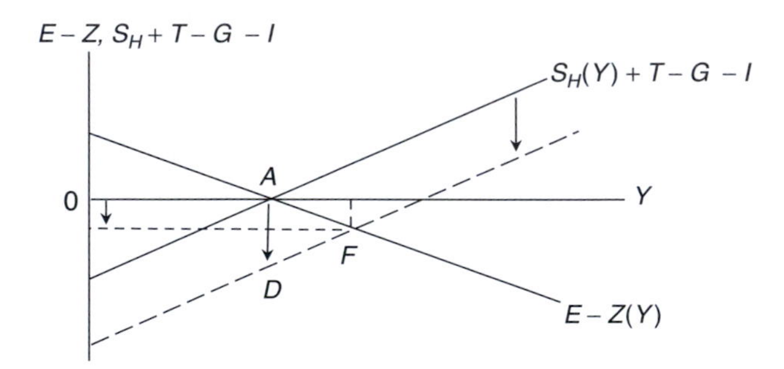

Figure 14.7 An increase in government spending or investment

(a movement from B to C). The fundamental accounting equation and macroeconomic equilibrium are restored at point C.[23]

Next, consider Figure 14.7. We begin at the same initial equilibrium as in Figure 14.6, at point A. Suppose that, from this initial position, there is an *increase in government spending or investment*. This shifts the $S_H(Y)+T-G-I$ curve downwards by the amount of the increase in government spending or investment from point A to point D. At point D, however, the net of domestic savings over domestic investment (now negative) is below the trade surplus (still at zero). The only way for the fundamental accounting equation to be restored is via an increase in Y. As Y increases, both S_H and Z increase. The former increases the net of domestic savings over domestic investment (a movement from D to F), while the latter reduces the trade surplus (a movement from A to F). The fundamental accounting equation and macroeconomic equilibrium are restored at point F, characterized by a trade deficit.[24]

Finally, we can have *an increase either tax revenues or the entire $S_H(Y)$ relationship*. This shifts the $S_H(Y)+T-G-I$ curve upwards rather than downwards, as in Figure 14.7, and is left as an exercise for the reader (see Review Exercise 5 above).

[23] As emphasized by Dornbusch (1988), the trade surplus at point C is smaller than it was at B.

[24] Governments cannot use a fiscal stimulus in an open economy without moving the economy into a trade deficit. This is one of the limitations on domestic policy independence placed by globalization.

There is one important point about Figures 14.6 and 14.7. What is being captured in these two diagrams is, in macroeconomics terms, *aggregate demand* independent of aggregate supply. In other words, these diagrams represent a Keynesian theory of aggregate demand, which would need to be combined with a representation of aggregate supply to provide a complete picture of the macroeconomy in question.

Appendix 14.3: Gross Domestic Product and Gross National Income

There is an important distinction between gross domestic product and gross national income.[25] GDP is defined as the value of goods and services produced within a country's borders. We will call this country "Home" and call its GDP Y^H_{GDP}. The distinction between GDP and GNI begins with the "Home" country's *factor payments*. This is the income from property in "Home" owned by foreign citizens and wages paid to foreign laborers working in "Home." We will call the "Home" country's factor payments Y^H_{HF}. But the opposite flow is given by *factor income*. This is income from property in foreign countries owned by "Home" citizens and wages from "Home" workers in foreign countries. We will call the "Home" country's factor income Y^H_{FH}.

The difference between factor income and factor payments gives **net factor income**, as follows:

$$\text{"Home" country's } \textit{net factor income} = Y^H_{FH} - Y^H_{HF} \quad (14.15)$$

This is what is recorded in item 7 of the balance of payments in Table 14.2.

We can then state the relationship between the "Home" country's GDP and GNI as follows:

$$\text{"Home" country's } \textit{gross national income} = Y^H_{GNI} = Y^H_{GDP} + (Y^H_{FH} - Y^H_{HF}) \quad (14.16)$$

In countries hosting multinational enterprises that are repatriating a lot of profits, Y^H_{HF} is large, and consequently $Y^H_{GDP} > Y^H_{GNI}$. But, in countries with many citizens working abroad, Y^H_{FH} is large, and consequently $Y^H_{GNI} > Y^H_{GDP}$. The bottom line of these distinctions, however, is that GNI is a better measure of the income and purchasing power of the citizens of a country than GDP.[26] That said, researchers often rely on GDP because it fits neatly into growth models, such as those we will discuss in Chapter 22.

---

[25] The term for *gross national income* used to be *gross national product*, or GNP. The World Bank changed this terminology, however, and we follow that convention here.

[26] A further adjustment for transfers (e.g. aid and remittances) converts GNI into gross national disposable income (GNDI).

15 Global Capital Flows

In the realm of international finance, and in the process of financial globalization, global **capital flows** loom large. It would not be an exaggeration to say that, without global capital flows, the subject of international finance would hardly exist. In this chapter, we will consider four main types of capital flows: foreign direct investment, equity investment, bond finance, and commercial bank lending. These appear in different parts of the capital/financial account of the balance of payments, discussed in Chapter 14. They are also *different* from one another in both their behavior and their economic impacts. The purpose of this chapter is to help you to understand these differences, as well as their implications.

This chapter will introduce you to each of the four capital flows and then consider them one at a time. You will be introduced to their content and properties, as well as the varying degrees of hope and concern that accompany each of them. We will then consider the question of *net* versus *gross* capital flows. Here, what might seem like a simple technical issue turns out to be quite important from both analytical and policy viewpoints. Next, we consider the broad *determinants* of global capital flows. We will end the chapter by considering arguments for capital account liberalization, as well as arguments for **capital controls**.

Capital flows have emerged as a central research topic in international economics.[1] In her review of the subject, Guichard (2017: 1–2) states the following:

> There is now a wide consensus that these flows can bring both good and bad. On the one hand, they support long-term growth through better international allocation of saving and investment; when taking the form of foreign direct investments, they can also induce technology and management improvements; and, when taking the form of portfolio investments, they can enhance transparency and corporate governance by exposing recipients to international investors. On the other hand, they complicate macroeconomic management of recipient countries, increase financial vulnerabilities, and can lead to financial crises and sudden stops with negative implications for growth.

The purpose of this chapter is to introduce you to this uneven landscape and give you a sense of the research results and policy discussions relevant to it. Let us begin with the types of capital flows.

---

[1] For brief introductions, see Cavoli and Rajan (2009), Guichard (2017), and Pagliari and Hannon (2017).

Types of Capital Flows

We will consider the four types of global capital flows with the help of Table 15.1. This figure lists the capital flow type, explanations of each type, the location in the balance of payments capital/financial account (Table 14.2 in Chapter 14), and a brief description of its characteristics, leaving detailed characteristics to subsequent sections of the chapter.

We begin with foreign direct investment. As we have discussed in detail in Chapters 10 through 12, FDI is the acquisition of shares by a firm in a foreign-based enterprise that exceeds a threshold of 10 percent. This ownership threshold implies managerial influence and participation in the foreign enterprise. As we have also discussed, FDI is at the center of international production and, along with contracting of various kinds, is intimately involved in evolving patterns of global value chains.

Equity portfolio investment is similar to FDI in that it involves the ownership of shares in foreign countries. It differs from FDI, however, in that the share

Table 15.1 Types of capital flows

Capital flow type	Explanation	Location in balance of payments	Characteristics
Foreign direct investment	Shares held in a foreign enterprise of at least 10 percent, indicating managerial influence.	Item 10 in Table 14.2, "direct investment."	Because it is for productive purposes, FDI tends to be the least volatile of all capital flows. It plays a key role in international production and global value chains.
Equity portfolio investment	Shares held in a foreign enterprise of less than 10 percent, indicating indirect or portfolio interest rather than managerial influence.	Part of item 11 in Table 14.2, "portfolio investment."	Because it is motivated by portfolio considerations, equity investment tends to have a shorter time horizon than FDI. Consequently, it can be more volatile.
Portfolio bond finance	The purchase of debt instruments in the form of either corporate (private debt) or government bonds (public debt).	Part of item 11 in Table 14.2, "portfolio investment."	Also motivated by portfolio considerations. In the case of central government debt, is part of what is known as "sovereign debt."
Commercial bank lending	Another form of debt but without a generally tradable asset.	Item 12 in Table 14.2, "other investment."	Large inflows are often leading indicators of financial crises.

holdings are too small to imply managerial influence and participation in the foreign enterprise (below 10 percent). It is thus *indirect* investment, rather than direct investment. Because equity portfolio investment is undertaken for portfolio reasons rather than managerial reasons, the behavior of investors can be quite different from how it is with FDI. To generalize, equity portfolio investment tends to be motivated by shorter time horizons than FDI.

Bond finance or *debt issuance* is a second kind of portfolio activity. In a bond finance transaction, firms (private debt) or the government (public debt) in a country issue bonds to foreign investors. These bonds can be issued in either the domestic currency or in foreign currencies and can involve different kinds of default risks. Bond finance has much in common with equity investment being held in international portfolios, so it is therefore part of portfolio investment.

For the sake of completeness, let us pause here for just a moment on equity investment and bond finance. Table 14.2 in Chapter 14 presented the balance of payments accounts. Item 11 in that table was called "portfolio investment." We now see that this part of the capital/financial account has *two different subcomponents*: equity investment and bond finance. Sometimes it is just fine to consider it in aggregate as portfolio investment–but *not always*. Sometimes it is important to look *within* portfolio investment and consider its subcomponents individually. We will get a better sense of why this is the case as we move through the rest of the chapter.

Commercial bank lending is another form of debt. Unlike bond finance, it does not in general involve a *tradable* asset. Commercial bank loans can be short-term or long-term, can be made with fixed or flexible interest rates, and can take the form of interbank loans. A single bank or a syndicate of banks can be involved in a particular loan package. Historically, commercial bank lending has played a role in a number of financial crises. In the balance of payments, commercial bank lending is known as "other investment."

With a sense of the four types of capital flows, and their relationship to the balance of payments, let us now consider them one by one.

Foreign Direct Investment

At this point in the textbook, FDI needs no introduction. We defined it in Chapter 1 and examined it in some detail in Chapters 10 through 12. For completeness sake, let us take another look at Figure 1.3, here reproduced as Figure 15.1. When we first looked at this figure, we noted the following. The 1990s were characterized by a large surge of FDI inflows, mostly into high-income countries and partly reflecting an upturn in mergers and acquisitions activity. Middle-income countries are

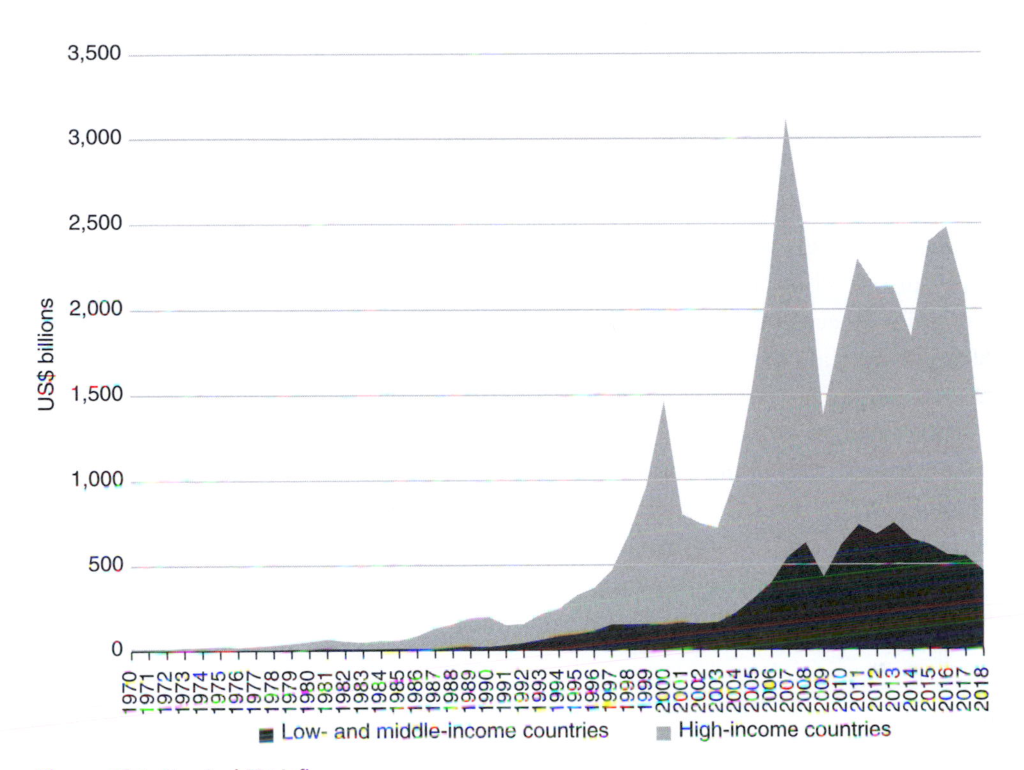

Figure 15.1 Nominal FDI inflows
Source: World Bank, World Development Indicators.

hosting a growing amount of FDI, however. FDI inflows into low-income countries are very low and stagnant, with these countries being largely excluded from this facet of economic globalization. As a result of the financial crisis and global recession, total FDI flows decreased substantially in 2008 and 2009. They subsequently recovered to approximately US$2 trillion, a value that had been reached in the mid-2000s in the previous FDI upturn.

FDI is a critical capital flow that has implications in the realms of international trade, international production, international finance, and international development. In general, it is considered the "safest" type of capital flow. For example, for low- and middle-income countries, Pagliari and Hannon (2017) find that FDI was significantly less volatile than the other three types of capital flows.[2] In Chapter 13, however, we did point out the need for a cost–benefit approach to FDI flows to avoid downside risks, particularly from a development standpoint.

[2] This is a subtle point, but Pagliari and Hannon (2017) also find that the low volatility of FDI for LMICs is itself more constant than other forms of capital flows—that is, its volatility characteristics do not change much over time.

Equity Portfolio Investment

Equity investment is a new concept to this chapter and an important global capital flow. Figure 15.2 gives us the history on equity portfolio investment into low- and middle-income countries and high-income countries. It is perhaps no surprise that inflows into high-income countries tend to be much larger than into LMICs.[3] The series also tend to be "spikey," indicating a certain degree of volatility. Indeed, on a couple of occasions, net inflows became negative, particularly in the case of the global financial crisis (GFC) of 2008. This spikey characteristic is known as equity market *volatility*.

There are some long-standing arguments as to why equity inflows could be useful from an economic viewpoint. Many years ago, for example, Rousseau and Wachtel (2000) identified a few mechanisms by which equity flows could support economic growth. Equity inflows can supplement domestic savings as a source of capital and be part of a movement away from short-term finance (e.g. bank lending) to long-term finance. They can help to provide both an informational

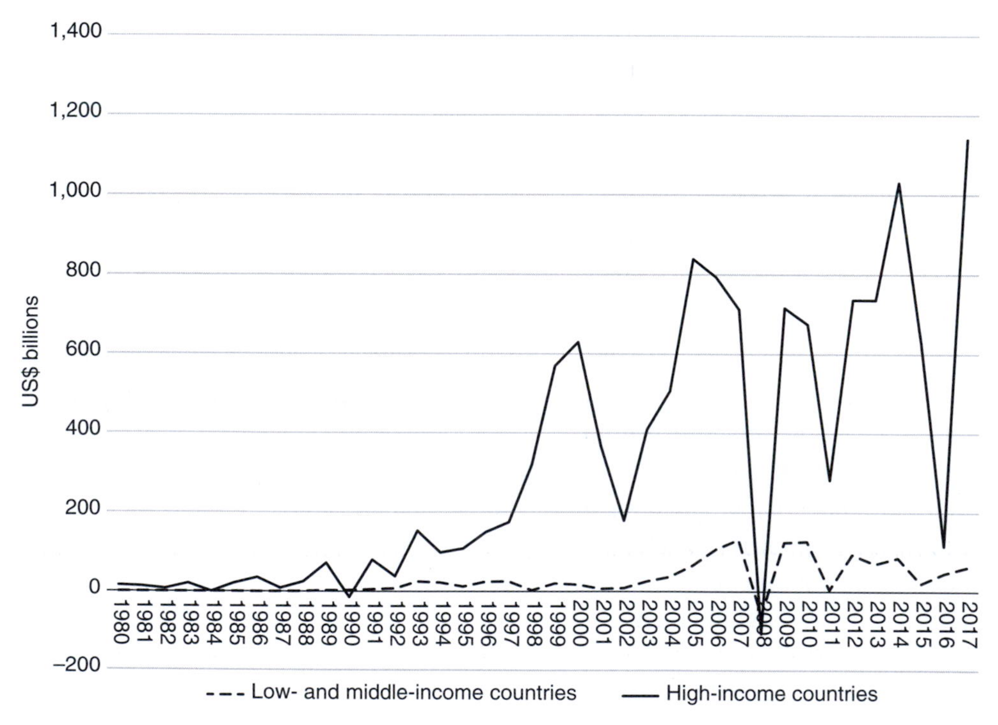

Figure 15.2 Net equity inflows (US$ billions)
Source: World Bank, World Development Indicators

[3] Equity investment into low-income countries is *very small* compared to that into middle-income countries.

mechanism on the performance of firms and an incentive mechanism for firm managers.[4] There is also evidence, however, that, when equity markets exist in LMICs, their market capitalization (percentage of GDP) tends to be significantly lower than in high-income countries, limiting these positive effects. "Emerging market" equity markets also tend to have fewer listed firms, less liquidity, and more volatility.[5]

Although the results are somewhat mixed, it would appear prudent to approach the international liberalization of equity markets with some caution. As stated by Kodongo and Ojah (2017: 208), "Many studies have found a link between stock market liberalization and potentially disruptive volatility, of prices and cash flows, and contagion in emerging stock markets." Building up the legal and institutional foundation of domestic equity markets before opening up this element of the capital account appears to be wise. This will help to ensure that the potential positive effects of global equity flows will be realized.

Bond Finance

Whether in its government or corporate form, bond finance involves the international exchange of *debt* instruments. There is an important difference, however, between bond finance and the alternative form of debt, commercial bank lending, namely *transferability*. As stated by Rethel and Hardie (2017: 218):

> What distinguishes bond debt from the other major form of debt provided by the formal financial system, bank loans, is that bonds are easily transferable. Through bonds, a loan is broken up into smaller denominations and claims are usually marketable, meaning that they can be sold and bought in a secondary market. As a consequence, an intrinsic feature of bonds is that they are typically more liquid...than traditional bank loans."

There is one way in which bank loans and bonds can be connected, however. This is through a process known as "securitization." The securitization process takes loans of certain varieties (e.g. mortgages or consumer loans), pools them, and then sells them in small pieces in the form of bonds.[6] Theoretically, the securitization process is an effective means of distributing risks across financial institutions

---

[4] At about the same time, however, the World Bank (2001: 173) issued the following cautionary note for LMICs: "There is no clear theoretical presumption as to whether local stock prices will be more or less volatile after integration into the world market. Integration should insulate the prices from shocks that affect the nonmarket wealth or savings behavior of local investors, but could expose them more to fluctuations in world asset prices and to shifts in external investor preferences."

[5] See, for example, Kodongo and Ojah (2017). On volatility, see Blitz, Pang, and van Vliet (2013). On illiquidity, see Amihud et al. (2015).

[6] Without going into details here, the resulting asset classes can include asset-backed securities, mortgage-backed securities, collateralized debt obligations, and asset-backed commercial paper.

and countries. In practice, however, it can increase or concentrate some types of risk, as it did in the 2008 GFC.[7]

One fact that has been emphasized for quite some time is that, in the case of firm bankruptcies, debt is usually given priority over equity. There is also the phenomenon of debt service payments being tax-deductible in many countries. There is, therefore, an expressed concern that this shifts priority away from equity sales to corporate bond financing. Recently there has been the observation that corporate debt inflows into the subset of LMICs known as emerging market economies (EMEs) has increased substantially, and that much of this corporate debt is denominated in foreign currencies.[8] So this concern is still relevant.

There is ample evidence over a very long time period that bond finance is relatively volatile and potentially destabilizing. Figure 15.3 provides data on inflows of bond finance (along with commercial bank lending) into LMICs. Like equity

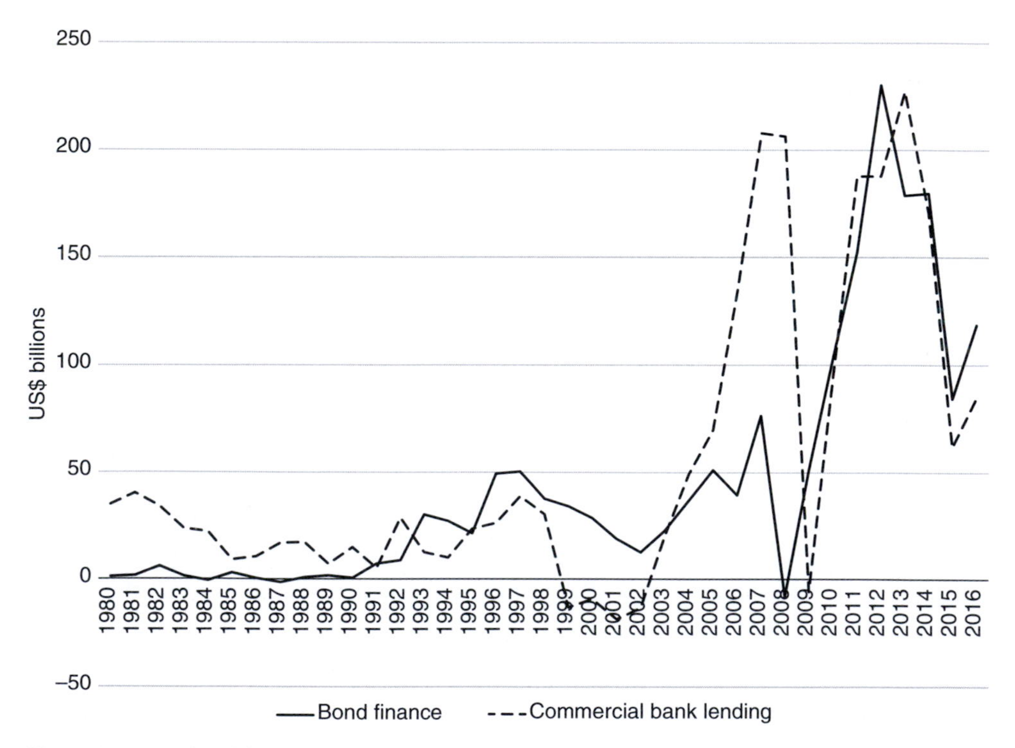

Figure 15.3 Net bond finance and commercial bank lending inflows to low- and middle-income countries, 1980–2016 (US$ billions)
Source: World Bank, World Development Indicators.

[7] See, for example, Acharya and Schnabl (2010). The relevant risks here are known as "tail risks": negative events that happen very infrequently (in the tails of probability distributions) but that can have significant detrimental impacts.

[8] There is more than one list of EMEs, but they tend to include 20 to 25 specific LMICs. EME is not a term endorsed by this textbook, but it is one that is frequently used. See *The Economist* (2017).

flows, this tends to be relatively "spikey," especially during but even *after* the GFC. For example, bond finance inflows into LMICs fell by more than 60 percent between 2012 and 2015. This volatility calls into question the extent to which bond finance can be relied upon for long-term development finance.

To be more specific, there is also evidence that debt flows (both bond finance and commercial bank lending) are potentially more destabilizing than equity flows.[9] There is a tendency to group equity investment and bond finance together into portfolio investment. Breaking out equity investment and bond finance seems to be important, however, given their different behaviors. For example, for LMICs, Pagliari and Hannon (2017) find bond finance to be significantly more volatile than equity investment.[10] So, this is one instance in which analysts should take the step to disaggregate capital flow data to an appropriate degree. Within bond finance, there is also a need to distinguish between private or corporate bond finance and government bond finance. The latter is part of what is known as sovereign debt, described in the accompanying box.

Sovereign Debt

Sovereign debt is the debt of central governments, represented by its total outstanding bond issues. It has two components, *internal* sovereign debt and *external* sovereign debt. Internal debt is accumulated when a central government issues bonds to its own citizens, and external debt is accumulated when it issues bonds for foreign entities. So net inflows of bond finance through sales of central government bonds increase total external debt. For many countries with shallow domestic bond markets, much sovereign debt is also external sovereign debt.

We need to keep in mind that *corporations* also issue bonds that are bought by foreign entities. The total external debt of a country therefore has two components: external sovereign debt and external corporate debt. The latter is sometimes referred to as "corporate debt exposure." As external corporate debt increases over time, this distinction is becoming increasingly important.

The assessment of the *riskiness* of sovereign debt is often taken on by private entities, such as Standard and Poor's sovereign ratings. Sovereign debt issued in domestic currencies is considered to be safer than that issued in foreign currencies. Sovereign debt is not risk-free, as evidence by episodes of sovereign default. Recent cases of default include Greece, Ukraine, and Venezuela. These events are often relatively dramatic, with negative welfare impacts for citizens.

Sources: The Economist (2014) and www.spratings.com/en_US/governments.

[9] See, for example, Eichengreen (2016), Ghosh and Qureshi (2016), and Langedijk et al. (2015).

[10] Pagliari and Hannon (2017) also find that the high volatility of bond finance for LMICs is itself less constant than FDI and equity investment–that is, its volatility characteristics change more over time.

There is also an issue in terms of the *currency* in which bonds are issued. For many countries (including their corporations and governments), issuing bonds in domestic currencies is not possible given the risk concerns among market participants. This difficulty has been called "original sin" by Eichengreen, Hausman and Panizza (2005), a term that has stuck. These authors argue that the currency composition of bond issues, particularly the need to issue bonds in foreign currencies, has implications for the stability of capital flows and for overall macroeconomic stability. In particular, debt in the form of foreign-currency-denominated bonds will increase in value if a country's currency weakens, making it even more difficult to pay off. We will return to this issue in subsequent chapters.

Commercial Bank Lending

As previously stated, commercial bank lending is a form of debt that does not involve a tradable asset such as bond finance. It appears as "other investment" in the balance of payments, a label that tends to hide its connection to the banking sector. Examining commercial bank lending as a capital flow is important, because the banking sector is widely recognized as a special and important type of financial intermediary, one that is often characterized by crises of one sort or another. For example, many years ago Dobson and Hufbauer (2001: 47) noted that "bank lending may be more prone to run than portfolio capital, because banks themselves are highly leveraged, and they are relying on the borrower's balance sheet to ensure repayment." Similarly, Reinhart and Rogoff (2009: 141) note that "banking crises have long impacted rich and poor countries alike."

Inflows of commercial bank lending into LMICS were illustrated in Figure 15.3, along with bond finance. We noted that bond finance was "spikey," but this is even more the case for commercial bank lending. For example, commercial bank lending turned negative for four years beginning in 1999 and spiked up higher than bond finance just before the GFC. After the GFC it collapsed, just like bond finance. The large volatility of commercial bank lending has been verified for LMICs by Pagliari and Hannon (2017).[11] Further, Reinhart and Rogoff (2009: 155) note "the striking correspondence between freer capital mobility and the incidence of banking crises."[12] Given the volatility of commercial bank lending and

[11] In addition, recall that there is also evidence that debt flows (both bond finance and commercial bank lending) are potentially more destabilizing than equity flows. See, for example, Ghosh and Qureshi (2016).

[12] These authors state (155): "Periods of high international capital mobility have repeatedly produced international banking crises, not only famously, as they did in the 1990s, but historically."

the association of banks with crises, capital flows in the form of commercial bank lending are worth careful observation by analysts.

Net versus Gross Flows

Since the GFC of 2008 researchers have become attuned to an important distinction between *net* and *gross* capital flows. For example, in her review of global capital flows, Guichard (2017: 3) states that "one of the key lessons from the GFC has been 'decoupling' between gross and net flows." The basic insight here is that, even with small net balances, there can be large gross flows and that the distinction between the two is increasingly important.

We can get a sense of this using Figure 15.4. As seen in the top of this figure in the current account, Brazil has a deficit in its relationship with the rest of the world. This deficit is equal to the distance from the "Rest of the world" box to the vertical dotted line. As discussed in Chapter 14, this requires net inflows on the capital account, and two different possibilities are represented. In the first case ("Capital account I"), Brazil has capital inflows, represented by the arrow coming out of the "Rest of the world" box, but no capital outflows. In the second case ("Capital account II"), Brazil has much larger capital inflows and also has capital outflows. The net inflow is exactly the same as in the "Capital account I" case, but the gross flows are much larger and in both directions.

There is ample evidence that the distinction made in Figure 15.4 is a relevant one. As stated by Eichengreen (2016: 29) in an important review, "Gross flows are large relative to net flows, and the gap has been widening," This is true for both high-income and middle-income countries. Why does this matter? The main insight from research on global capital flows is that the "Capital account I" and "Capital account II" cases in Figure 15.4 can be *fundamentally different* from each other. To put it simply, the "Capital account II" case can be riskier.

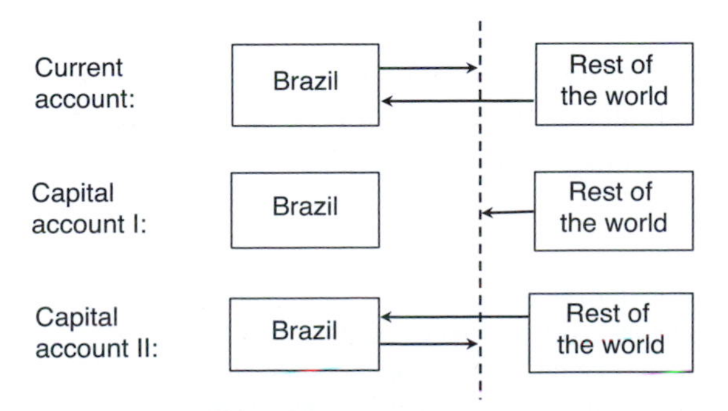

Figure 15.4 Net versus gross flows
Source: Adapted from Obstfeld (2012: 471, fig. 1).

Given the above, there is an emerging recognition that simply focusing on current account imbalances as a device to assess emerging risks is incomplete. As stated by Guichard (2017: 4, emphasis in original), for example, "Current accounts have likely become a less relevant predictor of crisis than in past decades and their monitoring needs to be complemented by a monitoring of *gross* international financial flows and positions."[13] One focus area here is gross flows in the form of commercial bank lending.

The distinction between net and gross capital flows is related to a concept we developed in Part I of this book on international trade, namely **intra-industry trade**. Recall that intra-industry trade is characterized by both imports and exports in a sector, with the goods or services involved differentiated in some way. Similarly, large gross capital flows (such as in "Capital account II" in Figure 15.4) are characterized by a two-way exchange of differentiated assets. So, large gross asset flows can be considered as potentially a form of "intra-industry" trade, but in differentiated assets rather than differentiated goods and services.

Recall also from Appendix 5.1 that there is a means of measuring the extent of intra-industry trade known as the Grubel–Lloyd index. This measure was given in Equation 5.1 of that appendix. As it happens, researchers in the field of international finance (e.g. Obstfeld, 2012) have used the same index on global capital flows. The results show that these capital flow Grubel–Lloyd indices are high (e.g. between 50 and 90, depending on the set of countries considered) and are increasing over time. This is another piece of evidence supporting the distinction between net and gross capital flows.

Determinants of Capital Flows

The literature on global capital flows generally groups flow determinants into "push factors" and "pull factors" that operate at the country level.[14] Push factors are reasons for capital to leave origin countries, while pull factors are reasons for capital to enter destination countries. The purpose of this analytical exercise is to judge the relative strength of these two sets of factors. Unfortunately, we will not be able to develop a complete picture of push and pull factors here. The subject is

---

[13] See also Obstfeld (2012) and Borio and Disyatat (2015). Borio and Disyatat comment (3) that: "Current accounts have been asked to tell us more than they can about several key macroeconomic magnitudes – about the volume and direction of capital flows; about how economic activity is financed; about the role countries play in financial intermediation, lending and borrowing; and about the risks of financial instability and the mechanisms involved."

[14] The distinction between push and pull factors goes back to Fernández-Arias (1996).

Table 15.2 Factors affecting global capital flows

Push/pull	Factor	Explanation
Push	Global risk aversion	Increases in global risk aversion negatively affect equity investment, bond finance, and commercial bank lending. They do not seem to affect FDI flows.
Push	High-income country interest rates	Lower interest rates in high-income countries give incentives to investors to look for higher interest rates elsewhere. This effect is strongest for equity investment and bond finance but does not affect FDI flows.
Push	High-income country output growth	High-income country output growth increases flows of equity investment and bond finance.
Pull	Domestic output growth	Domestic output growth in destination countries positively affects all four types of capital flows.
Pull	Asset return indicators	Asset returns in destination countries attract commercial banking and bond finance inflows.
Pull	Country risk indicators	Increased country risk in destination countries negatively affects all four types of capital flow.

Sources: Adapted from Koepke (2019) but also Guichard (2017) and Pagliari and Hannon (2017).

simply too complex.[15] But we can give a simplified sense of the two sets of factors using Table 15.2.

Let us begin with push factors. The first important factor is *global risk aversion.* Evidence reviewed by Koepke (2019) suggests that increases in global risk aversion negatively affect equity investment, bond finance, and commercial bank lending. Changes in global risk aversion do not seem to affect FDI flows, however. The considerations discussed in Part II of this book dominate those decisions. The second push factor is *high-income country interest rates.* Lower interest rates in high-income countries give incentives to investors to look for higher interest rates elsewhere. This effect is strongest for equity investment and bond finance but does not affect FDI flows. The third push factor is *high-income country output growth*, which increases flows of equity investment and bond finance to other destination countries.

Turning to pull factors, the most important one is *domestic output growth* in destination countries. Koepke (2019: 520) states that "domestic output growth is the determinant that is most consistently found to show a strong and statistically

[15] For example, Koepke (2019: 518) notes that "the drivers of capital flows...vary across components (like portfolio flows, FDI, and banking flows), differ between institutional and retail investors, and depend on the currency denomination and maturity of instruments, among other factors." "Other factors" include time and countries.

robust relationship with the four types of capital flows." The second pull factor is *asset return indicators* in destination countries. Higher asset returns in destination countries attract commercial banking and bond finance inflows. The third pull factor is *country risk indicators* in destination countries, increases in which tend to negatively affect all four types of capital flow.[16]

In the research on the determinants of capital flows, the distinction between net and gross capital flows becomes relevant. Most of the research now focuses on gross flows as indicators of the degree of this form of economic globalization.[17] So it is best to envision the factors identified in Table 15.2 as operating on gross capital flows, with the net capital flows being determined in the process. Further, as discussed in the accompanying box, capital flows are not fully a process of their own but are related to other dimensions of economic globalization, particularly migration.

Capital Flows and Migration

There is a tendency to view the processes of economic globalization in isolation from one another. This has been shown to be a limited view, however. In the case of capital flows, there is evidence that they are affected by other globalization processes, particularly migration. For example, Kugler and Rapoport (2007) find that *skilled* migration (discussed in Chapter 13) from an origin to a destination country tends to cause FDI flows from the migrant destination country to the migrant origin country. In other words, skilled migration and FDI can be *complements*. The reason for this is that the migration flows tend to increase information flows and reduce transaction costs. Ma and Pozo (2012) find a similar result for the specific case of FDI in the banking sector.

Interestingly, in a subsequent study, Kugler, Levintal, and Rapoport (2018) find that a similar result exists for commercial bank lending and for bond finance, particularly long-term bonds. Their argument, again, is that skilled migration flows tend to increase information flows and reduce transaction costs. In their words (149), "Migrants create or integrate into international business or financial networks, thereby enhancing financial transactions between their home and host countries." Sometimes looking at the relationships *between* dimensions of economic globalization produces results.

Sources: Kugler and Rapoport (2007), Kugler, Levintal, and Rapoport (2018) and Ma and Pozo (2012).

[16] Here, Koepke (2019: 520) notes that "the evidence is not as robust and there are some exceptions for those country risk measures that reflect increasing financing needs."

[17] See, for example, Broner et al. (2013), who emphasize the large and volatile nature of gross capital flow.

Capital Account Liberalization

There is a standard "free-market" argument for the increased liberalization or opening of capital accounts. In simple terms, the argument is that the global freeing of capital markets will lead to an allocatively efficient distribution of capital between countries and to an overall decrease in the cost of capital. This, in turn, will tend to increase growth rates for the countries involved.[18] This argument was one part of a general policy posture taken by the International Monetary Fund and World Bank, which we can visualize in simple form as follows.[19]

Economic liberalization → Growth → Poverty reduction

The apogee of this policy position came in 1997, when a committee of the IMF recommended that the full liberalization or "convertibility" of capital/financial accounts be made an explicit objective of the IMF, to be enshrined in an amended Articles of Agreement. Historically, this was a radical proposal.[20] The IMF's deputy managing director, Stanley Fischer, defended the proposal. Fischer (1998: 2) cited two arguments in support of capital account liberalization. First, he claimed, "it is an inevitable step on the path of development." Second, he claimed (2–3) that "free capital movements facilitate an efficient allocation of savings and help channel resources into their most productive uses, thus increasing economic growth and welfare." In the end, neither of these claims stood the test of time.

Months after this proposal was made a financial crisis in Asia developed (the Asian financial crisis, to be discussed in Chapter 20). Further, some prominent international economists began to argue *against* the proposal.[21] In the view of these economists, excessive borrowing within the short-term portfolio component of the capital account was a contributing factor to financial crises. In addition, they noted that financial capital is too prone to panics and manias to be trusted. Finally, they suggested that controls on the capital account do not always adversely affect the growth and development of countries with the controls (an example being the People's Republic of China).

---

[18] For example, Kodongo and Ojah (2017: 203) state: "Policies that encourage capital account opening were, at inception, encouraged based on the argument that they would work, through increased cross-border capital flows, to lower the cost of capital for domestic corporations by increasing the domestic supply of funds relative to domestic demand for funds." See also Obstfeld (1998).

[19] For a well-known example of this general argument, see World Bank (2002).

[20] The liberalization of current accounts had always been an objective of the IMF and World Bank, but never the liberalization of capital/financial accounts. For a more complete history, see Epstein (2017).

[21] See, for example, Bhagwati (1998), Eichengreen (1999), and Rodrik (1998).

Given the Asian financial crisis, and arguments against full capital/financial account liberalization, the proposed amendment to the IMF Articles of Agreement was dropped. After the 2008 GFC, and to the surprise of many, the IMF revisited **capital controls** and gave them an endorsement (Ostry et al., 2010; 2011). The 2010 IMF study suggests that market-friendly capital controls can help countries cope with surges of capital inflows, which can end in sudden stops and contribute to macroeconomic instability and financial crises. Consequently, the 1997 position of the IMF on capital flows is now a thing of the past.[22] Let us consider this new position on capital controls.

Capital Controls

Concerns regarding global capital flows (particularly gross flows) have led to policy discussions on potential ways to restrict their mobility. These measures are known as capital controls, but also as capital account regulations (CARs) and capital flow (management) measures (CFMs). "CFM" is the term most used by the International Monetary Fund, but CARs also receive a good deal of use. Here, however, we will use the term "capital controls."

Capital controls have a long history, which we will not go into here.[23] It is now recognized that they can take many forms. Some of the relevant dimensions involved are inflows versus outflows, different asset classes, residents versus non-residents, and quantitative versus qualitative. To take an example, a country might impose a quantitative 2 percent tax on inflows of equity purchases by non-residents. You might recognize in this example a relationship to the ad valorem tax on imports discussed in Chapter 7, and you would not be far off in this recognition. We will come back to this point shortly.

The purpose of capital controls is to address the volatile nature of gross capital flows, the pattern of large inflows of short-term, portfolio capital that is later followed by a reversal in the form of *capital flight*. As previously mentioned, these volatile gross capital flows make macroeconomic management difficult and can contribute to financial crises.[24] The hope is that capital controls can address

---

[22] Even Stanley Fischer modified his views. Fischer (2000) states: "That is not to say...that countries should open their accounts prematurely: rather they need to ensure that their economies and the financial systems are sufficiently strong; and they may particularly want to avail themselves for some time of controls on short-term capital flows."

[23] The most thorough of these can be found in Eichengreen (2008).

[24] Korinek (2011: 524) states: "The destabilizing pattern of international capital flows in economies that have liberalized their capital markets have imposed severe welfare costs and hence are of grave concern for policymakers and societies at large." Korinek draws an explicit connection to negative externalities in the form of environmental pollution, suggesting that global capital flows can "pollute" economies (particularly LMICs) with financial fragility.

these issues.[25] One way of thinking about this issue is in terms of *externalities*. As argued by Jeanne and Korinek (2010) and Korinek (2011), the potential negative macroeconomic effects of global capital flows can be viewed as a type of negative externality, and standard microeconomic theory suggests that taxing activities with significant negative externalities can be an appropriate policy response.[26]

But can capital controls be effective? The answer has been debated for some time now, and the tentative answer appears to be "*yes*, but not *always* and *everywhere*." One recent review of many studies by Magud, Reinhart, and Rogoff (2018) concludes that capital controls were by and large effective in altering the *composition* of capital flows towards more long-term flows. This is a significant conclusion. The ability to shift the composition of capital flows in this manner is their primary purpose. Also noting the evident effectiveness of capital controls in this regard, Ostry et al. (2011: 565) state that "capital controls may be a valuable addition to the toolkit for dealing with financial-stability risks, where the objective is not so much to reduce the volume of inflows as to make them less risky (including by altering their composition)."

What do we take from this discussion of capital controls? First, there is a range of different policy instrument involved. Some are more onerous and operate like quotas, while others are less intrusive and operate more like tariffs. The latter are to be preferred over the former as being more market-friendly. Moreover, opposition to market-friendly tariff-like capital controls might be misplaced. Most ardent "free traders" want to see a multilateral world of tariffs set at perhaps 5 percent, not necessarily a world of zero tariffs. Perhaps a similar world of capital controls would still be one that allowed for the effective global movement of capital.[27]

Second, different policies can be designed for different types of capital flows. Even opponents of full capital account liberalization acknowledge that controls on direct and long-term portfolio investment should be minimal. Their concern is with short-term assets used primarily for speculative purposes. If market-friendly capital controls are to be applied, they will address the latter category of capital flows and not the former. One way of doing this is with variable deposit requirements, discussed in the accompanying box.

---

[25] Epstein (2017: 277) states that "capital account regulations can promote financial stability through their ability to reduce currency flight, fragility and/or contagion risks, thereby reducing the potential for financial crises and attendant economic and social devastation." We address contagion risks in Chapter 20.

[26] This goes back to the work of Arthur Pigou (1932), and is therefore known as a Pigovian tax.

[27] So, for example, Eichengreen (1999: 13, emphasis added) concludes that "cautious steps in the direction of capital-account liberalization…should *not* extend to the removal of taxes on capital inflows."

Variable Deposit Requirements

Perhaps the most well-known example of a market-friendly capital control is the variable deposit requirement (VDR), also known as the unremunerated reserve requirement (URR). First introduced by Australia in 1972, VDRs require that specified types of foreign borrowing be accompanied by a portion of the borrowed amount being deposited in an interest-free account with the central bank for a specified time period. As emphasized by Bhinda et al. (1999), VDRs are flexible in multiple dimensions: the type of borrowing, the applied percentage, the deposit period, and their application to new versus existing transactions. Each of these dimensions can be modified over time in response to changing conditions.

Our discussion in this chapter suggests that the most risky type of foreign borrowing is commercial bank lending. So, for example, Eichengreen (1999: 117) argues that "banks borrowing abroad should be required to put up additional noninterest-bearing reserves with the central bank." This is a type of VDR that can help to prevent commercial bank over-borrowing.

The most well-known application of a VDR was Chile's *encaje*. The word *encaje* in Spanish has a few meanings, one of which is "reserve" in the financial sense. In 1991 the newly independent central bank of Chile introduced a requirement that 20 percent of specified capital inflows would be required to be deposited into non-interest-bearing deposits with the bank for a period of one year. It was explicitly designed to penalize short-term capital inflows over long-term capital inflows. The *encaje* rate was increased to 30 percent in 1992 and was in place through 2001.

There have been many studies of the effectiveness of the *encaje*, and there are mixed results. But there does seem to be evidence that this VDR caused a substitution away from short-term to long-term debt, which was indeed its main objective. A review of these studies by Carrière-Swallow and García-Silva (2013: 23) concludes that "there is also evidence that the measure had some impact on reducing net short-term inflows and shifting the debt profile towards longer maturities, but that this impact was relatively small."

Our purpose here is to simply draw attention to the VDR or URR policy option as a flexible and market-friendly version of capital controls now recognized as potentially appropriate by the IMF. Set at relatively low rates, it has the potential to be a "tariff" on capital inflows that could replace less market-friendly regulations, which would be more like a "quota." How VDRs would function in particular circumstances is a matter that would need to be studied carefully. Such experiments have taken place in Colombia, Malaysia, and Thailand, for example. Their evaluation is an ongoing project.

Sources: Bhinda et al. (1999) and Carrière-Swallow and García-Silva (2013).

Balance of Payments Revisited

Let us finish this chapter by going back for a moment to the previous chapter on accounting frameworks. We saw there that, if domestic savings are too small to finance domestic investment, a country requires an inflow of foreign savings to make up the difference This inflow of foreign savings finances the trade deficit and shows up as positive entries (asset sales) in the capital/financial account. We now see that these positive entries include net inflows of foreign direct investment, equity investment, bond finance, and commercial bank lending. They do not *all* have to be positive net inflows, but the sum of them needs to be.

Alternatively, if domestic savings exceed the requirements of domestic investment, the country lends the difference to the rest of the world. This outflow of foreign investment generates a trade surplus and shows up as negative entries (asset purchases) in the capital/financial account. We now see that these negative entries include net outflows of FDI, equity investment, bond finance, and commercial bank lending. They do not *all* have to be negative net inflows, but the sum of them needs to be.

Capital flows are therefore central to the balance of payments of each country. As previously discussed, however, despite the fact that the balance of payments records *net* flows, *gross* flows matter in their own right.

Conclusion

Capital flows are an integral part of the global economy and the processes of economic globalization. They come in four forms, namely foreign direct investment, equity investment, bond finance, and commercial bank lending. These capital flow varieties differ from one another in both their behavior and their economic impacts. Therefore, an important task of international economic analysis is to examine each of them separately rather than just as aggregate "capital flows." It is also important to distinguish between the *net* capital flows reported in the balance of payments and *gross* flows. International economists have learned the hard way that ignoring gross flows can hide impending issues.

In a review of "neoliberal" economic policy, a group of IMF economists touch on global capital flows, stating the following (Ostry, Loungani, and Furceri, 2016: 40):

> In sum, the benefits of some policies that are an important part of the neoliberal agenda appear to have been somewhat overplayed. In the case of financial openness, some capital flows, such as foreign direct investment, do appear to confer the benefits claimed for them. But for others, particularly short-term capital flows, the benefits to growth are difficult to reap, whereas the risks, in terms of greater volatility and increased risk of crisis, loom large.

It is notable that international economists representing an institution that has been pushing market-based reforms for decades now offer us this *cautionary view* of global capital flows, including a potential role for market-friendly capital controls. The cautionary approach is the one taken in this chapter.

Review Exercises

1. Carefully distinguish, first, equity investment from FDI and, second, bond finance from commercial bank lending.
2. We have stated that an increasing amount of attention is being paid to the distinction between net and gross capital flows. Please carefully explain *why* this distinction is so important.
3. From a "free-market" perspective, why would we expect benefits from the general liberalization of global capital flows? Are there any other considerations that might limit the desirability of a "free-market" approach to global capital flows?
4. What are the main objectives of ongoing experiments with capital controls? Please be as specific as you can.

FURTHER READING AND WEB RESOURCES

Accessible introductions to the subject of capital flows can be found in Cavoli and Rajan (2009), Goldin and Reinert (2005), Goldin and Reinert (2012: chap. 4), and Guichard (2017). For equity and bond markets, respectively, see Kodongo and Ojah (2017) and Rethel and Hardie (2017). On the importance of the distinction between net and gross capital flows, see Obstfeld (2012). For a review of capital controls, see Epstein (2017). The original IMF reconsideration of capital controls can be found here: www.imf.org/external/pubs/ft/spn/2010/spn1004.pdf.

REFERENCES

Acharya, V. V., and P. Schnabl (2010) "Do Global Banks Spread Global Imbalances? Asset-Backed Commercial Paper during the Financial Crisis of 2007–2009," *IMF Economic Review*, 58:1, 37–73.

Amihud, Y., A. Hameed, W. Kang, and H. Zhang (2015) "The Illiquidity Premium: International Evidence," *Journal of Financial Economics*, 17:2, 350–68.

Bhagwati, J. (1998) "The Capital Myth: The Difference between Trade in Widgets and Dollars," *Foreign Affairs*, 77:3, 7–12.

Bhinda, N., S. Griffith-Jones, J. Leape, and M. Martin (1999) *Private Capital Flows to Africa*, Fondad.

Blitz, D., J. Pang, and P. van Vliet (2013) "The Volatility Effect in Emerging Markets," *Emerging Markets Review*, 16, 31–45.

Borio, C., and P. Disyatat (2015) "Capital Flows and the Current Account: Taking Finance (More) Seriously," Working Paper 525, Bank for International Settlements.

Broner, F., T. Didier, A. Erce, and S. L. Smuckler (2013) "Gross Capital Flows: Dynamics and Crises," *Journal of Monetary Economics*, 60:1, 113–33.

Carrière-Swallow, Y., and P. García-Silva (2013) "Capital Account Policies in Chile: Macro-Financial Considerations along the Path to Liberalization," Working Paper 13/107, IMF.

Cavoli, T., and R. S. Rajan (2009) "Capital Mobility," in K. A. Reinert, R. S. Rajan, A. J. Glass, and L. S. Davis (eds.), *The Princeton Encyclopedia of the World Economy*, Princeton University Press, 163–6.

Dobson, W., and G. C. Hufbauer (2001) *World Capital Markets: Challenge to the G-10*, Institute for International Economics.

The Economist (2014) "Sovereign Defaults: Empty Vaults," October 11.

The Economist (2017) "What's in a Name? Defining Emerging Markets," October 7.

Eichengreen, B. (1999) *Toward a New Financial Architecture: A Practical Post-Asia Agenda*, Institute for International Economics.

Eichengreen, B. (2008) *Globalizing Capital: A History of the International Monetary System*, Princeton University Press.

Eichengreen, B. (2016) "The Global Monetary Order," in *The Future of the International Monetary and Financial Architecture*, European Central Bank, 21–63.

Eichengreen, B., R. Hausman, and U. Panizza (2005) "The Pain of Original Sin," in B. Eichengreen and R. Hausman (eds.), *Other People's Money: Debt Denomination and Financial Instability in Emerging Market Economies*, University of Chicago Press, 13–47.

Epstein, G. (2017) "Capital Controls," in K. A. Reinert (ed.), *Handbook of Globalisation and Development*, Edward Elgar, 272–86.

Fernández-Arias, E. (1996) "The New Wave of Private Capital Inflows: Push or Pull?," *Journal of Development Economics*, 48:2, 389–418.

Fischer, S. (1998) "Capital-Account Liberalization and the Role of the IMF," *Princeton Essays in International Finance*, 207, 1–10.

Fischer, S. (2000) "Managing the International Monetary System," address to the International Law Association biennial conference, London, July 26, www.imf.org/en/News/Articles/2015/09/28/04/53/sp072600.

Ghosh, A. R., and M. S. Qureshi (2016) "Capital Inflow Surges and Consequences," Working Paper 585, Asian Development Bank.

Goldin, I., and K. A. Reinert (2005) "Capital Flows and Development: A Survey," *Journal of International Trade and Development*, 14:4, 453–81.

Goldin, I., and K. A. Reinert (2012) *Globalization for Development: Meeting New Challenges*, Oxford University Press.

Guichard, S. (2017) "10 Years after the Global Financial Crisis: What Have We Learnt about International Capital Flows?," *Journal of International Commerce, Economics and Policy*, 8:3, 1–30.

Jeanne, O., and A. Korinek (2010) "Excessive Volatility in Capital Flows: A Pigouvian Taxation Approach," *American Economic Review Papers and Proceedings*, 100:2, 403–7.

Kodongo, O., and K. Ojah (2017) "Equity Markets," in K. A. Reinert (ed.), *Handbook of Globalisation and Development*, Edward Elgar, 201–17.

Koepke, R. (2019) "What Drives Capital Flows to Emerging Markets? A Survey of the Empirical Literature," *Journal of Economic Surveys*, 33:2, 516–40.

Korinek, A. (2011) "The New Economics of Prudential Capital Controls: A Research Agenda," *IMF Economic Review*, 59:3, 523–61.

Kugler, M., and H. Rapoport (2007) "International Labor and Capital Flows: Complements or Substitutes?," *Economic Letters*, 94:2, 155–62.

Kugler, M., O. Levintal, and H. Rapoport (2018) "Migration and Cross-Border Financial Flows," *World Bank Economic Review*, 32:1, 148–62.

Langedijk, S., G. Nicodème, A. Pagano, and A. Rossi (2015) "Debt Bias in Corporate Income Taxation and the Costs of Banking Crises," Discussion Paper 10616, Centre for Economic Policy Research.

Ma, R., and S. Pozo (2012) "International Labor Migration and Foreign Bank Penetration in Developing Economies," *Journal of International Commerce, Economics and Policy*, 3:1, 1–17.

Magud, N. E., C. M. Reinhart, and K. S. Rogoff (2018) "Capital Controls: Myth and Reality," *Annals of Economics and Finance*, 19:1, 1–47.

Obstfeld, M. (1998) "The Global Capital Market: Benefactor or Menace?," *Journal of Economic Perspectives*, 12:4, 9–30.

Obstfeld, M. (2012) "Financial Flows, Financial Crises, and Global Imbalances," *Journal of International Money and Finance*, 31:3, 469–80.

Ostry, J. D., A. R. Ghosh, M. Chamon, and M. S. Qureshi (2011) "Capital Controls: When and Why?," *IMF Economic Review*, 59:3, 562–80.

Ostry, J. D., A. R. Ghosh, K. Habermeier, M. Chamon, M. S. Qureshi, and D. B. S. Reinhardt (2010) "Capital Inflows: The Role of Controls," Staff Position Note 10/04, IMF.

Ostry, J. D., P. Loungani, and D. Furceri (2016) "Neoliberalism: Oversold?," *Finance and Development*, 53:2, 38–41.

Pagliari, M. A., and S. A. Hannon (2017) "The Volatility of Capital Flows in Emerging Markets: Measures and Determinants," Working Paper 17/41, IMF.

Pigou, A. C. (1932) *The Economics of Welfare*, Macmillan.

Reinhart, C. M., and K. S. Rogoff (2009) *This Time Is Different: Eight Centuries of Financial Folly*, Princeton University Press.

Rethel, L., and I. Hardie (2017) "Bond Markets," in K. A. Reinert (ed.), *Handbook of Globalisation and Development*, Edward Elgar, 218–33.

Rodrik, D. (1998) "Who Needs Capital-Account Convertibility?," *Princeton Essays in International Finance*, 207, 55–65.

Rousseau, P. L., and P. Wachtel (2000) "Equity Markets and Growth: Cross-Country Evidence on Timing and Outcomes, 1980–1995," *Journal of Banking and Finance*, 24:12, 1933–57.

World Bank (2001) *Finance for Growth: Policy Choices in a Volatile World*, World Bank.

World Bank (2002) *Globalization, Growth, and Poverty: Building an Inclusive World Economy*, World Bank.

16 Exchange Rates and Purchasing Power Parity

For US companies with large trade and investment exposures to Western Europe, the year 2000 was a very difficult time. During that year the euro fell in value from just under US$1.00 to approximately US$0.80. US-based firms such as Compaq, IBM, Intel, Polaroid, Microsoft, Baxter International, Heinz, Caterpillar, Dow Chemical, DuPont, and TRW all suffered as a result. Why? Their euro sales were worth less in dollar terms, and dollar terms mattered given their US home base. A Wall Street analyst estimated that the fall of the euro in 2000 shaved 3 percent off total Standard and Poor 500 operating profits in the third quarter alone. The president of TRW lamented, "If I could report in euros, we would be having a bang-up year."[1] Unfortunately, this was not possible.

In 2003 the euro increased in value. This was good news for US-based firms selling in the euro area, but bad news for EU-based firms selling in the United States and reporting profits in euros. Volkswagen, for example, attributed a €1 billion fall in profits to the strengthened euro.[2] One way or another, changing exchange rates affect firms engaged in international production.

Exchange rates matter, and they matter in multiple ways to many different participants in the world economy. Much of this section of the book on international finance will be directly or indirectly concerned with exchange rates. Indeed, this and the next two chapters will be exclusively devoted to developing your understanding of exchange rates. In this chapter, we will begin with two important exchange rate definitions. These are the **nominal exchange rate** and the **real exchange rate**. Next, we will develop a first model of exchange rate determination: the **purchasing power parity model** (PPP model). Having developed this model, we will relate it to our definition of the real exchange rate.

We will then turn to the relationship of exchange rates and trade flows. Finally, we will consider the difference between **spot rates** and **forward rates** and how this difference can, at times, be used by firms to hedge **exchange rate exposure**. The real exchange rate definition and the purchasing power parity model utilize the notion of the overall **price level** in an economy. For those who are not familiar with this idea, price levels are discussed in Appendix 16.1. Appendix 16.2

---

[1] See Tully (2000) and McMurray (2000).

[2] See *The Economist* (2004a).

considers an extension of the PPP model in the form of the **monetary approach to exchange rate determination**.

As you conclude this chapter, you will understand one model of exchange rates: the PPP model. As you will see, this model has validity in helping to predict the *long-run* trends in nominal exchange rates. We will also need a model to help predict *short-run* trends in nominal exchange rates. This will be the central task of Chapters 17 and 18.

The Nominal Exchange Rate

We are going to place our discussion of exchange rates within a particular context in order to make the concepts more concrete. Exchange rates are defined in terms of a *home* and a *foreign* country. In this chapter, we will usually take Mexico as our home country and the United States as our foreign country.[3] Our first exchange rate definition is the **nominal exchange rate**. The nominal exchange rate is the home-country currency price of a foreign currency. It is expressed as the number of units of the local or home currency that are required to buy a unit of the foreign currency. The Mexican currency is the *Mexican peso*, which we will express simply as the *peso*. The US currency is the *US dollar*, which we will express simply as the *dollar*. Therefore, Mexico's nominal exchange rate is defined as

$$e = \frac{pesos}{dollar} \tag{16.1}$$

which is in the form of

$$e = \frac{home\ currency}{foreign\ currency} \tag{16.2}$$

As implied in these equations, we will be using the symbol e to denote the nominal exchange rate. Nominal exchange rates for a sample of countries are presented in Table 16.1 for February 2016 and for one year earlier.

Let us examine the nominal exchange rate a little more closely. Suppose that, for some reason, e were to increase. What would this mean for the value of the peso? The increase in e implies that it takes *more* pesos to purchase a dollar. This, in turn, implies that the value of the peso has *fallen* (the peso *depreciates*). The opposite is the case when e falls. When e falls, it takes *fewer* pesos to buy a dollar, and this implies that the value of the peso has *increased* (the peso *appreciates*). Since these relationships are very important, we will put them in a box for you to remember.

---

[3] Readers in the United States, please be careful here. The United States is the *foreign* country.

$e \uparrow \Rightarrow$ value of the home currency (peso) *falls*, or *depreciates*
$e \downarrow \Rightarrow$ value of the home currency (peso) *rises*, or *appreciates*

Table 16.1 Nominal exchange rates, February 17, 2016 (per US dollar)

Country or region	Currency	Nominal exchange rate	Nominal exchange rate 1 year earlier
Argentina	Peso	14.9	8.68
Brazil	Real	3.98	2.83
Canada	Dollar	1.37	1.24
Chile	Peso	701	621
China	Yuan	6.53	6.26
Eurozone	Euro	0.90	0.88
Indonesia	Rupiah	13,510	12,770
Japan	Yen	114	119
Mexico	Peso	18.4	14.9
Pakistan	Rupee	105	102
Russia	Ruble	75.3	63.2
South Africa	Rand	15.5	11.7
Thailand	Baht	35.6	32.6
Turkey	Lira	2.95	2.45
United Kingdom	Pound	0.70	0.65

Source: www.economist.com.

Let us consider a couple of the exchange rates in Table 16.1. Between February 2015 and February 2016, for example, the exchange rate of the Japanese yen to the US dollar decreased from 119 to 114 yen per US dollar. This means that it took fewer yen to buy a US dollar in 2016 than in 2015. Consequently, the value of the yen *increased*. Consider next the Russian ruble. Between February 2015 and February 2016 the ruble price of the US dollar increased from 63.2 to 75.3. It took more rubles to buy a US dollar in 2016 than in 2015, so the value of the ruble *decreased*.

As you can see in the above box and the examples of the Japanese yen and Russian ruble, e and the value of the peso are *inversely* related. For this reason, e is often graphed as its *inverse*, which is equal to the *value* of the peso or home currency. This inverted scale is presented in Figure 16.1. In this figure, a movement

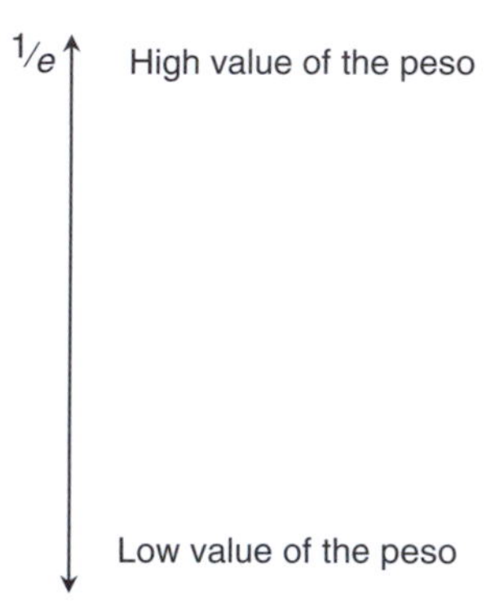

Figure 16.1 The value of the peso scale

up the scale indicates a fall in e and a rise in the value of the peso. A movement down the scale indicates a rise in e and a fall in the value of the peso. Make sure you are comfortable with this inverse scale before continuing with the remainder of the chapter.

It is important to emphasize that the definition of the nominal exchange rate depends on the choice of the home country. Consider another example. If Japan is our home country, we might be interested in the $yen/euro$ nominal exchange rate. But if the Eurozone is our home country, we would instead consider the $euro/yen$ nominal exchange rate. For this reason, we always need to *pause for a moment* to make sure we express the nominal exchange rate in the correct way and to ensure that we understand how our research sources are expressing it. Otherwise, we can make some significant mistakes.

As a final example of a nominal exchange rate, let us maintain Japan as our home country but consider the $yen/dollar$ rate. This is plotted for the years 1960 to 2016 in Figure 16.2. As you see in this figure, for the period of time from 1960 to 1970 the nominal rate did not move at all. In fact, it was *fixed* at 360 yen per dollar for this decade.[4] Beginning in 1971 the exchange rate became flexible, and began to decline as the yen strengthened against the US dollar or the dollar weakened against the yen. There were periods of volatility within a general strengthening of the yen up until the 1990s. Then the volatility took place within a range of approximately 100 to 130 yen per dollar through 2009. This was followed by a strengthening of the yen through 2011, a weakening to 2014, and then the slight strengthening between 2015 and 2016 described above.

Our discussion of exchange rates so far has been in terms of two currencies at a time. In most cases, however, a country has significant economic relationships with

[4] We will consider the difference between fixed and flexible exchange rates in detail in Chapters 17 and 18.

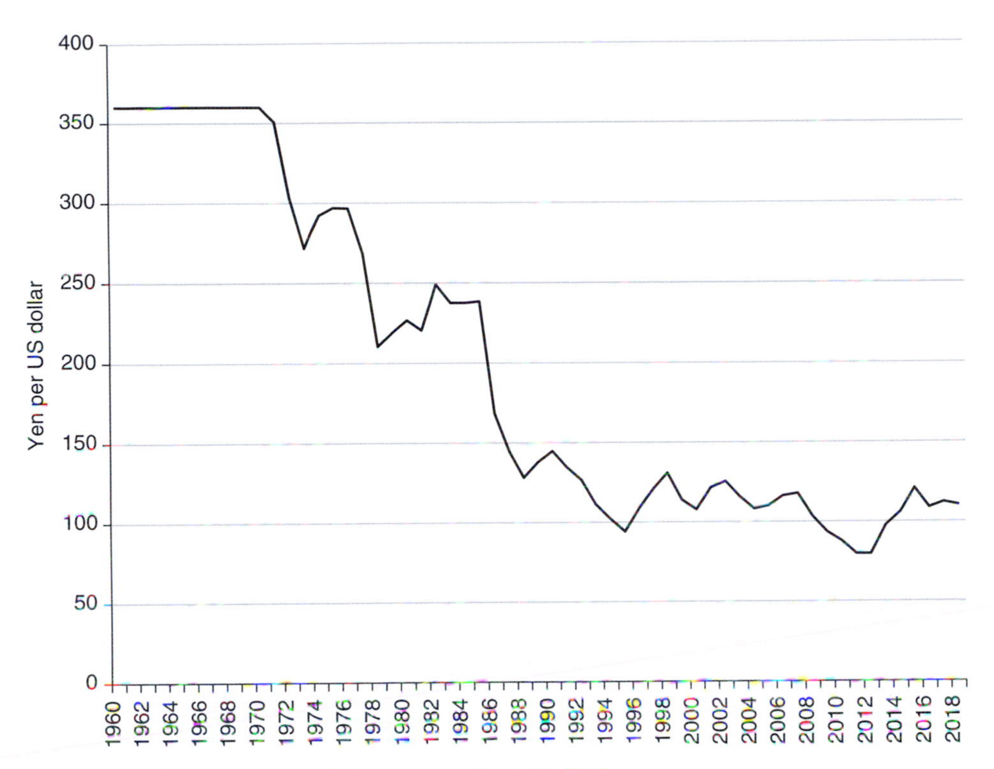

Figure 16.2 The yen/dollar nominal exchange rate, 1960–2016
Source: World Bank, World Development Indicators.

more than one foreign country, so more than one nominal exchange rate becomes relevant. This leads us to consider the **effective exchange rate.**[5] To understand this, let us turn back to Mexico and its relationships to the United States and the European Union. Mexico's effective exchange rate (e^{eff}) would be

$$e^{eff} = a_{US}e_{dollar} + a_{EU}e_{euro} \tag{16.3}$$

Here, e_{dollar} and e_{euro} are the $^{peso}/_{dollar}$ and the $^{peso}/_{euro}$ nominal exchange rates, respectively. The terms a_{US} and a_{EU} are *weights* that sum to one and determine how much the two nominal exchange rates affect e^{eff} as they change in value. The standard means of determining the weights in Equation 16.3 is via bilateral trade volumes, typically measured as the sum of imports and exports to the United States and the European Union, respectively, as a proportion of Mexico's total imports and exports. Recognizing the increasing role of financial relationships in the world economy, however, there has been increased consideration given to asset-related determination of the weights. But the key thing for you to understand is that the effective

[5] The origin of the effective exchange rate is Black (1976) but see also Chin (2009).

exchange rate is a means of generalizing the two-country nominal exchange rate for Mexico—or any other country—across its relevant partner countries.

As it turns out, the nominal exchange rate is not the only type of exchange rate that we need to understand in international economics. Just as important is the real exchange rate. Let us consider it next.

The Real Exchange Rate

Along with the nominal exchange rate, it is also important to understand a second exchange rate definition, namely the **real exchange rate.**[6] Recall that the nominal exchange rate measures the relative price of two countries' currencies. Another way to state this is that it measures the rate at which two countries' *currencies* trade against each other. In contrast, the real exchange rate measures the rate at which two countries' *goods and services* trade against each other. Let us distinguish the real exchange rate from the nominal exchange rate in a second box.

> ***Nominal exchange rate*** The rate at which two countries' *currencies* trade against each other.
>
> ***Real exchange rate*** The rate at which two countries' *goods and services* trade against each other.

The real exchange rate makes use of the **price levels** in the two countries under consideration. P^M is the overall price level in Mexico (the home country), and P^{US} is the overall price level in the United States (the foreign country). These can be thought of as the averages of all the prices in the two countries. If you are not familiar with the concept of price levels, please see Appendix 16.1 before continuing with the remainder of this section. If you are already familiar with the price level concept, please continue.

The real exchange rate definition, denoted re, is as follows:

$$re = e \times \frac{P^{US}}{P^M} \tag{16.4}$$

which is in the form of

$$re = e \times \frac{P^{foreign}}{P^{home}} \tag{16.5}$$

[6] Ouyang and Rajan (2013: 844) call the real exchange rate "one of the most important price variables in macroeconomics."

We have stated that *re* measures the rate at which the two countries' goods and services trade against each other. More specifically, it measures the amount of Mexican goods and services that trade against US goods and services. A formal demonstration of this is provided in Appendix 16.1. Here, we will show intuitively that this definition makes sense, dropping the term "services" for simplicity. We do so with the help of Table 16.2.

Suppose that the price level in the United States (P^{US}) rises. It now takes more Mexican goods to purchase US goods. Therefore, there has been a *fall* in the *real* value of the peso. Alternatively, suppose that the price level in Mexico (P^{M}) rises. It now takes fewer Mexican goods to purchase US goods. Therefore, there has been a *rise* in the *real* value of the peso. Finally, suppose that the nominal exchange rate (e) increases. It now takes more Mexican pesos to buy a US dollar and, therefore, more Mexican goods to buy US goods. There has been a *fall* in the *real* value of the peso. These are the changes presented in Table 16.2.

Given a long-term move in exchange rate arrangements in the world economy towards more flexibility in nominal exchange rates, one can generalize that changes in these nominal exchange rates tend to explain more of changes in real exchange rates than do changes in price levels. Further, because many nominal exchange rates are rather volatile, so too are real exchange rates.[7]

Table 16.2 Changes in the real exchange rate

Change	Intuition	Effect in "*re*" equation
P^{US} increases	US goods increase in price. Therefore, it takes more Mexican goods to buy a unit of US goods. The real value of the peso has fallen.	Since it is in the numerator, the increase in P^{US} increases the value of *re*.
P^{M} increases	Mexican goods increase in price. Therefore, it takes fewer Mexican goods to buy a unit of US goods. The real value of the peso has risen.	Since it is in the denominator, the increase in P^{M} decreases the value of *re*.
e increases	It takes more Mexican pesos to buy US dollars. The real value of the peso has fallen.	The increase in e increases the value of *re*.

[7] See Popper (2009), for example. But, for a more recent study, see Ouyang and Rajan (2013).

Finally, just as there is an effective exchange rate for the nominal exchange rate, so there is a **real effective exchange rate** (REER) for the real exchange rate. This multi-country measure would be

$$re^{eff} = a_{US} re_{dollar} + a_{EU} re_{euro} \tag{16.6}$$

Here, the real exchange rates of the peso against the US dollar and the euro are weighted, as in Equation 16.3. The REER gives a measure of the rate at which Mexico's goods and services trade against relevant partners. As such, it is a very important measure in international finance.

We now have an understanding of both nominal and real exchange rates. Public and private analysts keep track of both these types of exchange rates for countries of interest because they provide different perspectives on the exchange of goods, services, and assets between the countries of the world economy.

Purchasing Power Parity

Closely related to the definition of the real exchange rate is a model of exchange rate determination known as **purchasing power parity**. The PPP approach to exchange rates begins with the hypothesis that *the nominal exchange rate will adjust so that the purchasing power of a currency will be the same in every country.* This hypothesis is also worth putting in a box.

> ***PPP hypothesis*** The nominal exchange rate will adjust so that the purchasing power of a currency will be the same in every country.

Let us explore the implications of this hypothesis. The purchasing power of a currency in a given country is inversely related to the price level in that country. For example, the purchasing power of the peso in Mexico can be expressed as $1/P^M$. The higher the price level in Mexico, the lower the purchasing power of the peso there. The purchasing power of the peso in the United States is a bit more complicated. First, we need the rate at which a peso can be exchanged into dollars. This is $1/e$. Second, we need the purchasing power of a dollar in the United States. This is $1/P^{US}$. Putting these together, we have the purchasing power of a peso in the United States as $\left(1/e\right) \times \left(1/P^{US}\right)$. Now, we can state the PPP hypothesis as follows:

$$\frac{1}{P^M} = \frac{1}{e} \times \frac{1}{P^{US}} \tag{16.7}$$

This equation can be rearranged to give us[8]

$$e = \frac{P^M}{P^{US}} \tag{16.8}$$

which is in the form of

$$e = \frac{P^{home}}{P^{foreign}} \tag{16.9}$$

What do Equations 16.8 and 16.9 mean? Suppose that the price level in Mexico, P^M in the numerator, were to increase. According to the PPP model, e would therefore increase. The value of the peso would consequently move down the scale in Figure 16.1. Alternatively, suppose that the price level in the United States, P^{US} in the denominator, were to increase. According to the PPP model, e would decrease. In this case, the value of the peso would move up the scale in Figure 16.1. In this way, the nominal value of the peso adjusts to changes in its real purchasing power in the two countries. Although this makes a great deal of sense, the restrictiveness of the PPP model can be seen when we re-express it in a third equation. We obtain this equation by multiplying both sides of the Equation 16.8 by $\left(P^{US}/P^M\right)$. This gives us

$$e\frac{P^{US}}{P^M} = 1 \tag{16.10}$$

If we compare Equation 16.10 of the PPP model with Equations 16.4 and 16.5 of the real exchange rate, we can see here that the PPP model is a *special case* of the real exchange rate. More specifically, the PPP theory implies that the real exchange rate is *fixed at unity*–that is, there will not be any change in the real exchange rate. It turns out that real exchange rates *do* change, a humorous case of which is presented in the box below. If the PPP theory implies that real exchange rates do not change, and yet we observe real exchange rates varying in the real world, there must be important elements of the real world that the PPP theory ignores. In fact, some important elements come readily to mind.

Underlying the PPP idea is the assumption that all goods entering into the price levels of both countries are internationally *traded*. It is the traded nature of all the goods in the price levels of both countries that contributes to the strong relationship between price levels and nominal exchange rates expressed in the

---

[8] This equation is known as the "absolute version" of PPP. The "relative version" used in most empirical studies can be stated as $\%\Delta e = \%\Delta P^M - \%\Delta P^{US}$. In this equation, Δ stands for "change in." This equation relates the percentage change in the nominal exchange rate to the inflation rate difference between the home and foreign country. See, for example, Froot and Rogoff (1996) and Sarno and Taylor (2002: chap. 3).

PPP equations. In fact, however, many goods are *non-traded*. For example, a large part of most economies consists of locally supplied services, such as many kinds of cleaning, repairs, and food preparation. These services are not typically traded. As stated by *The Economist* (2019), "A Chinese lawyer is not qualified to execute wills in Berlin and Texan dentists cannot drill in Manila." The presence of these **non-traded goods** weakens the PPP relationship.[9] So does the fact that, as discussed in Chapter 1, currency trading is dominated by asset considerations rather than trade considerations.

The Big Mac Index

In 1986 *The Economist* began to publish an annual test of the PPP theory of exchange rates based on an unusual measure of price levels around the world. This "Big Mac index" measures price levels using just one good, the McDonald's Big Mac hamburger. *The Economist* (2007) describes its efforts as follows: "The Big Mac index is based on the theory of purchasing power parity (PPP), according to which exchange rates should adjust to equalize the price of a basket of goods and services around the world. Our basket is a burger: a McDonald's Big Mac." Calculations of this index for 2015 are given in the table below.

The Economist first measures the local-currency price of Big Macs. These are given in the second column of the table. Next, *The Economist* converts these local currency prices into US dollar terms using nominal exchange rates, given in the fourth column. These US dollar prices are given in the third column. Dividing each of these US dollar prices by US$4.79 (the US price of a Big Mac) gives the implied PPP of the dollar, presented in the fifth column. Comparing this to the purchasing power parities gives the degree of overvaluation or undervaluation of the currency according to the Big Mac index. *The Economist* (2015) states: "If the local cost of a Big Mac converted into dollars is above US$4.79 (its price in America), a currency is dear; if it is below the benchmark, it is cheap."

Should we take the Big Mac index seriously? *The Economist* (2000) gleefully notes that "several academic studies have concluded that the Big Mac index is surprisingly accurate in tracking exchange rates over the long term." One of these studies is Ong (1997), and a more recent study is Pakko and Pollard (2003). But the Big Mac index is not without its criticisms. For example, Mazumder (2016) calls for it to be replaced by an iPad index.

---

[9] As Schnabl (2001: 37) states: "The more traded, or fewer non-traded goods, are included in the price index, the better the approximation of exchange rates by PPP would be."

The Big Mac Index (cont.)

Country	Big Mac prices: In local currency	Big Mac prices: In US dollars	Nominal exchange rate used	Implied PPP	Over- (+) or under- (–) valuation (%)
United States	$4.79	4.79	–	–	–
Switzerland	SFr 6.5	6.82	0.95	1.36	+42.38
Denmark	DK34.59	5.08	6.81	7.22	+6.05
Canada	C$5.85	4.94	1.18	1.22	+3.13
United Kingdom	£2.89	4.51	0.64	0.60	–5.85
Brazil	Real 13.5	4.28	3.15	2.82	–10.65
Eurozone	€3.7	4.05	0.91	0.77	–15.45
Turkey	Lire 10.25	3.87	2.65	2.14	–19.21
South Korea	Won 4,300	3.76	1,143.62	897.70	–21.50
Philippines	Peso 163	3.61	45.15	34.03	–24.63
Chile	Peso 2,100	3.27	642.20	438.41	–31.73
Thailand	Bhat 108	3.17	34.07	22.55	–33.82
Mexico	Peso 49	3.11	15.76	10.23	–35.07
Argentina	Peso 28	3.07	9.12	5.85	–35.91
Japan	¥370	2.99	123.75	77.24	–37.58
China	Yuan 17	2.74	6.20	3.55	–42.80
Indonesia	Rupiah 30,500	2.29	13,318.79	6,367.43	–52.19
South Africa	Rand 26	2.09	12.44	5.43	–56.37
Russia	Ruble 107	1.88	56.91	22.34	–60.75

Note: These exchange rates may differ from those of Table 16.1.

There is one more serious issue embedded in the Big Mac index, and that is the case of China, shown to have an undervalued currency by over 40 percent in the above table. Given concerns over the bilateral trade deficit of the United States with China, this sort of information can have political implications. It is important to keep in mind, though, the issue of non-tradable goods mentioned above. As noted by Yang (2004), the estimated undervaluation would be less if the non-tradable sector in China were better accounted for in the Big Mac index. This point has also been made by Parsley and Wei (2007).

Sources: The Economist (2000; 2004b; 2007; 2009; 2015), Ong (1997), Mazumder (2016), Pakko and Pollard (2003), Parsley and Wei (2007), and Yang (2004).

Does this imply that the PPP theory is useless? No. It is best to use the following interpretation. The real exchange rate equation captures reality at any point in time; the PPP relationship never holds exactly. The PPP equation does give us a sense, however, of a *long-term tendency* towards which nominal exchange rates move *absent other changes.*[10] And, indeed, these PPP equations are in the backs of the minds of currency traders. Before exchange rates have the chance to move fully towards the PPP relationship, however, other changes invariably intervene. This necessitates alternative models of exchange rate determination more appropriate for the *short term*, which we consider in Chapters 17 and 18.

Exchange Rates and Trade Flows

Changes in e, and therefore in the value of the peso, have an impact on trade flows that it is important for you to understand. To see this, we are going to consider the case of Mexico's imports and exports. World prices (P^W) are typically in US dollar terms, and Mexican prices (P^M) are in peso terms. The relationship between the Mexican peso and world dollar prices of Mexico's import (Z) goods can be expressed as

$$P_Z^M = e \times P_Z^W \tag{16.11}$$

P_Z^W is in dollar terms. Multiplying it by e gives us P_Z^M in peso terms. Now, suppose that e were to increase (the value of the peso falls). This movement down the scale in Figure 16.1 increases the peso price of the imported good in Mexico. Following the "law of demand," import demand consequently decreases.[11] Next, suppose e were to decrease (the value of the peso rises). This movement up the scale in Figure 16.1 decreases the peso price of the imported good in Mexico. Import demand consequently increases.

Next, consider the case of Mexico's exports. The relationship between the peso and dollar prices of Mexico's exported (E) goods can be expressed as

$$P_E^M = e \times P_E^W \tag{16.12}$$

In this equation, P_E^M is the price of Mexican export goods. For a given P_E^M, if e were to increase (the value of the peso falls), P_E^W will fall to maintain equality. The

---

[10] For example, Sarno and Taylor (2002: 87) conclude: "The main conclusion emerging from the recent literature on testing the validity of the PPP hypothesis appears to be that PPP might be viewed as a valid long-run international parity condition when applied to bilateral exchange rates among major industrialized countries." Similarly, Lothian (2016: 20) concludes that, "as a long-run proposition, PPP is indeed a very useful approximation."

[11] This is similar to the way that an increase in the world price of rice would decrease Japan's rice imports in Figure 2.4 in Chapter 2.

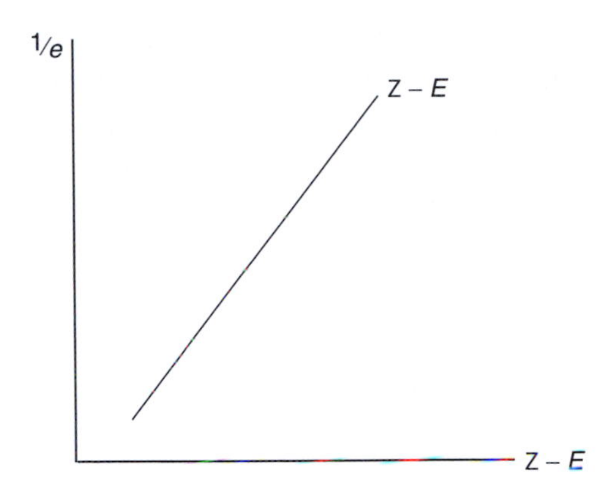

Figure 16.3 The value of the peso and Mexico's trade deficit

movement down the inverse scale in Figure 16.1 will consequently cause a fall in the world price of Mexico's exports. This increases foreign demand for Mexico's goods, and Mexico's exports consequently increase.[12] Next, suppose that e were to decrease (the value of the peso rises). This movement up the inverse scale in Figure 16.1 increases the world price of Mexico's exports, and export demand will consequently decrease.[13]

What we have seen here is that, as the nominal exchange rate increases or the value of the peso falls, imports decrease and exports increase. We can represent these relationships as one between the value of the peso and the *trade deficit*, $Z - E$. This is done in Figure 16.3. As you can see, there is a *positive* relationship between the value of the peso and the trade deficit. We will use this relationship in the remaining chapters of this section of the book on international finance.[14]

Hedging and Foreign Exchange Derivatives

In Part I of this book, we considered the possibility of firms entering foreign markets via exports. In Part II of this book, on international production, we considered the possibility of firms entering foreign markets via contracting and foreign direct investment. If the sales from any of these market entry strategies are

---

[12] Alternatively, P_E^W can be thought of as the price of Mexican exports in dollar terms. Multiplying it by e gives us P_E^M in peso terms. Now, suppose that e were to increase (the value of the peso falls). This increases the peso price of the export good in Mexico, and export supply in Mexico consequently increases, because Mexican firms now have more of an incentive in peso terms to export. This is similar to the way an increase in the world price of rice would increase Vietnam's exports in Figure 2.4 in Chapter 2.

[13] For a discussion of this process as it affected Mexican exporters in the past, see Malkin (2011).

[14] The graph in Figure 16.3 is not necessarily linear. We draw it that way for simplicity's sake.

not denominated in the currencies of the firms' home-base countries, issues of **exchange rate exposure** arise. For example, in the introduction to this chapter we mentioned the impact of a fall in the value of the euro on the dollar value of US-based firms' revenues and the rise of the value of the euro on the euro value of EU-based firms' revenues. Let us take a closer look at this exposure problem.

Suppose that the €/US$ exchange rate is currently at a value of 1.00. Suppose also that a US firm is expecting euro revenues of €1.0 million. Given the current exchange rate, known as a **spot rate**, the US firm might be expecting dollar revenues of US$1.0 million. Suppose, however, that the euro weakens, and the spot rate moves to $e = 1.25$ (a dollar value of the euro of $0.80). It now takes more euros to purchase a dollar, and the dollar revenues shrink to $800,000. Is there anything the firm can do to overcome this exposure? Possibly, yes; and this brings us to the issue of hedging and foreign exchange derivatives.

The most reliable source of data on foreign exchange derivatives is the Bank for International Settlements (BIS). The BIS distinguishes three categories of foreign exchange derivatives: forwards and foreign exchange swaps, currency swaps, and options. These categories, with forwards and foreign exchange swaps broken out, are defined in Table 16.3. The important thing to notice about each derivative type in this table is that there is a *time element* involved, an expectation about the future that involves some degree of uncertainty.

Data from the Bank for International Settlements on the composition of foreign exchange derivatives are presented in Figure 16.4 for 2017. As you can see in this figure, most derivatives consist of forwards and foreign exchange swaps, with currency swaps and options playing smaller roles. For the most part, this holds true over time.

Foreign exchange derivatives are financial instruments that have the effect of "locking in" a forward exchange rate. How can they play a role in hedging

Table 16.3 Foreign exchange derivatives

Derivative type	Explanation
Forward contracts	Two parties agree on a foreign exchange transaction to take place at a specified future date.
Foreign exchange swaps	Two parties exchange currencies for a specified length of time, after which the currency exchange is reversed.
Currency swaps	Two parties exchange interest payments in different currencies for a specified period of time and then exchange principals at a specified maturity date.
Options	A party purchases the right to exchange one currency for another at a specified future date and at a specified rate.

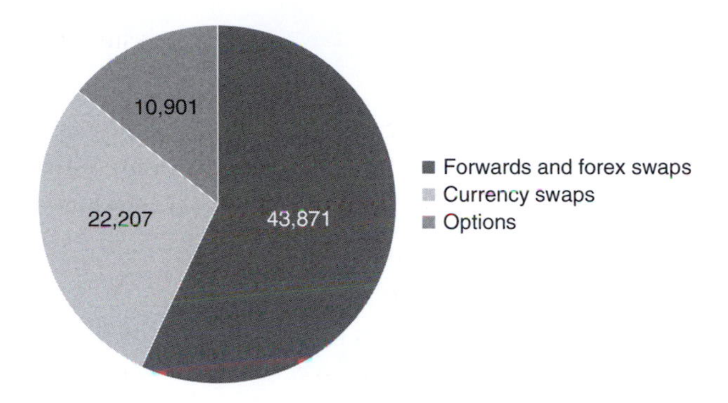

Figure 16.4 Foreign exchange derivatives, 2017 (US$ billions)
Note: "Forex" = "foreign exchange."
Source: Bank for International Settlements.

exchange rate exposure? Let us get a sense of this by looking at the most fundamental derivative, the **forward rate**. Forward rates are the rates of current contracts for "forward" transactions in currencies, usually for one, three, or six months in the future. If the forward rate of the euro (€/US$) is the same as the spot rate, the euro is said to be "flat." If the forward rate of the euro is above the spot rate, the euro is said to be at a "forward discount." Finally, if the forward rate of the euro is below the spot rate, the euro is said to be at a "forward premium."

Suppose now that we again begin with the exchange rate (€/US$) being currently at a value of 1.00 and that a US firm is expecting euro revenues of €1.0 million in six months' time. Suppose also, though, that the euro is at a six-month forward discount of 1.11. The US firm could take out a forward contract and, at that future time, convert the euro revenue into $900,900 of dollar revenue. Would this be a smart move? If the firm knew with certainty that the future spot rate were to be 1.25, as in the above example, it certainly would be. With the forward contract, the firm would earn $900,900 rather than $800,000. If the future spot rate were actually to be below 1.11, though, it would not. The firm could have earned more than $900,900 without the forward contract.

As becomes apparent even in this simple example, hedging exchange rate exposure requires that firms have *expectations* or *forecasts* of future spot rates that they can compare to forward rates. Such forecasts range from the simple (e.g. those based on PPP projections, discussed in this chapter) to the complex (e.g. multivariate econometric analysis) and can be either performed in house or contracted out to a forecasting service. Whatever the approach taken to exchange rate exposure, it is an ever-present problem for those firms engaging in foreign market entry, and forms a key link between the realms of international finance and international production.

Conclusion

The nominal exchange rate is the relative price of two currencies, and is expressed as the number of units of a home currency required to buy a unit of a foreign currency. Another way of stating this is that the nominal exchange rate measures the rate at which the two countries' *currencies* trade against each other. In contrast, the real exchange rate measures the rate at which two countries' *goods and services* trade against each other. The real exchange rate uses the price levels of home and foreign countries to adjust the nominal exchange rate.

The purchasing power parity model of exchange rate determination begins with the idea that *the nominal exchange rate will adjust so that the purchasing power of a currency will be the same in every country.* The PPP model is a restricted version of the real exchange rate definition, and applies only in the long run. An extension of the PPP model into the monetary approach to exchange rates is given in Appendix 16.2.

Home-country imports have a direct or positive relationship with the value of its currency. Home-country exports, on the other hand, have an inverse or negative relationship with the value of the currency. Consequently, a country's trade deficit has a direct or positive relationship with the value of the currency. In these ways, the realms of international trade and international finance are linked.

Review Exercises

1. Use supply and demand diagrams such as those we used in Chapter 2 to demonstrate why the relationships between the value of the peso and imports and exports illustrated in Figure 16.3 make sense. In doing so, keep in mind that $P_Z^M = e \times P_Z^W$ and $P_E^M = e \times P_E^W$.
2. Explain the *intuition* of how each of the following changes affect the real exchange rate, re: a fall in P^M, a fall in P^{US}, and a fall in e. In each case, describe the impact of the change on the rate at which Mexican goods trade against US goods.
3. Use the PPP model of exchange rate determination to predict the impact on the nominal exchange rate of the following changes: a fall in P^M and a fall in P^{US}.
4. As shown in Table 16.1, the spot nominal exchange rate for the Canadian dollar was 1.37 in February 2016. What happened to the value of the Canadian dollar during the previous year? What would have to be true of the forward rate for the Canadian dollar to be at a forward premium? A forward discount?

FURTHER READING AND WEB RESOURCES

A good source for the material of this chapter at a slightly more advanced level is Melvin and Norrbin (2017). More advanced treatments are in Hallwood and MacDonald (2000) and Sarno and Taylor (2002). For a review of the real exchange rate, see Popper (2009), and, for a review of effective exchange rates, see Chin (2009). For reviews of the PPP model, see Dornbusch (1992), Froot and Rogoff (1996), and Cheung (2009). A discussion of *The Economist* Big Mac Index is given in Pakko and Pollard (2003). Cox (2008) provides a similar application of PPP analysis to the video game market, and Mazumder (2016) does the same for iPads.

Exchange rate data are available from the International Monetary Fund's monthly publication *International Financial Statistics*. Most important is the annual *Yearbook* in this series. The IFS is also available in an online version, which many libraries have subscribed to. It is not user-friendly, but nevertheless is an important source for standardized data. See the website of the International Monetary Fund: imf.org/en/Data. Note that some of the IMF data are provided in a more user-friendly format by the World Bank, at databank.worldbank.org.

REFERENCES

Black, S. W. (1976) "Multilateral and Bilateral Measures of Effective Exchange Rates in a World Model of Traded Goods," *Journal of Political Economy*, 84:3, 615–22.

Cheung, Y.-W. (2009) "Purchasing Power Parity," in K. A. Reinert, R. S. Rajan, A. J. Glass, and L. S. Davis (eds.), *The Princeton Encyclopedia of the World Economy*, Princeton University Press, 942–5.

Chin, M. (2009) "Effective Exchange Rates," in K. A. Reinert, R. S. Rajan, A. J. Glass, and L. S. Davis (eds.), *The Princeton Encyclopedia of the World Economy*, Princeton University Press, 337–9.

Cox, J. (2008) "Purchasing Power Parity and Cultural Convergence: Evidence from the Global Video Games Market," *Journal of Cultural Economics*, 32:3, 201–14.

De Long, J. B. (2000) "The Triumph of Monetarism?," *Journal of Economic Perspectives*, 14:1, 83–94.

Dornbusch, R. (1992) "Purchasing Power Parity," in D. Newman, M. Milgate, and J. Eatwell (eds.), *The New Palgrave Dictionary of Money and Finance*, Macmillan, 236–44.

The Economist (2000) "Big Mac Currencies," April 29.

The Economist (2004a) "Currency Hedging," February 21.

The Economist (2004b) "The Starbuck's Index: Burgers or Beans?," January 15.

The Economist (2007) "The Big Mac Index," February 1.

The Economist (2009) "Big Mac Index," February 4.

The Economist (2015) "The Big Mac Index," July 18.

The Economist (2019) "Briefing: Slowbalisation," January 26.

Froot, K. A., and K. Rogoff (1996) "Perspectives on PPP and Long-Run Real Exchange Rates," in G. M. Grossman and K. Rogoff (eds.), *Handbook of International Economics*, vol. 3, North Holland, 1647–88.

Hallwood, C. P., and R. MacDonald (2000) *International Money and Finance*, Wiley-Blackwell.
Johnson, H. (1972) "The Monetary Approach to Balance-of-Payments Theory," *Journal of Financial and Quantitative Analysis*, 7:2, 1555–72.
Lothian, J. R. (2016) "Purchasing Power Parity and the Behavior of Prices and Nominal Exchange Rates across Exchange Rate Regimes," *Journal of International Money and Finance*, 69, 5–21.
McMurray, S. (2000) "The Lost Art of Hedging," *Institutional Investor*, 34:12, 63–9.
Malkin, E. (2011) "Peso's Rise Pressuring Mexican Exporters," *New York Times*, February 8.
Mazumder, S. (2016) "iPad Purchasing Parity: Farewell to the Big Mac Index," *Economics Bulletin*, 36:4, 2128–36.
Melvin, M., and S. Norrbin (2017) *International Money and Finance*, Academic Press.
Ong, L. L. (1997) "Burgernomics: The Economics of the Big Mac Standard," *Journal of International Money and Finance*, 16:6, 865–78.
Ouyang, A. Y., and R. S. Rajan (2013) "Real Exchange Rate Fluctuations and the Relative Importance of Nontradables," *Journal of International Money and Finance*, 32, 844–55.
Pakko, M. R., and P. S. Pollard (2003) "Burgernomics: A Big Mac™ Guide to Purchasing Power Parity," *Federal Reserve of St Louis Review*, 85:6, 9–27.
Parsley, D. C., and S.-J. Wei (2007) "A Prism into the PPP Puzzles: The Micro-Foundations of Big Mac Real Exchange Rates," *Economic Journal*, 117:523, 1336–56.
Popper, H. (2009) "Real Exchange Rate," in K. A. Reinert, R. S. Rajan, A. J. Glass, and L. S. Davis (eds.), *The Princeton Encyclopedia of the World Economy*, Princeton University Press, 955–7.
Rapach, D. E., and M. E. Wohar (2002) "Testing the Monetary Model of Exchange Rate Determination: New Evidence from a Century of Data," *Journal of International Economics*, 58:2, 359–85.
Sarno, L., and M. P. Taylor (2002) *The Economics of Exchange Rates*, Cambridge University Press.
Schnabl, G. (2001) "Purchasing Power Parity and the Yen/Dollar Exchange Rate," *The World Economy*, 24:1, 31–50.
Tully, K. (2000) "Feeling Over-Exposed," *Corporate Finance*, 194, 47.
Yang, J. (2004) "Nontradables and the Valuation of the RMB: An Evaluation of the Big Mac Index," *China Economic Review*, 15:3, 353–9.

Appendix 16.1: Price Levels and the PPP Model

In this chapter, we use the concept of price levels in the definition of the real exchange rate and in the purchasing power parity model of exchange rate determination. The purpose of this appendix is to introduce you to the concept of price levels. We are going to do this with reference to a macroeconomic variable defined in Chapter 14, namely income, or Y. Recall that, given the simple assumptions of

Chapter 14, Y is equal to both the nominal gross domestic product and the nominal gross national income.

Now, suppose that we observed this flow in two years, year 1 and year 2. Suppose also that $Y_2 > Y_1$, or that total nominal income/output is greater in year 2 than in year 1. From this fact, can we conclude that a greater *quantity* of goods and services is produced in this economy in year 2 than in year 1? No, we cannot. It may be that $Y_2 > Y_1$ simply reflects increases in *prices* between year 1 and year 2. The problem we face here is to separate the increase in Y into the part due to an increase in the number of goods and services and the part due to an increase in the prices of goods and services.

In practice, the division of Y into price and quantity components is accomplished through a slightly complex application of *index numbers*. For our purposes here, however, we are going to take a simpler approach. Let us assume that only *one type* of good or service is produced in the economy. Its price is P. Let a lower-case y represent the total *quantity* of this good produced in the economy. Whereas Y is known as the *nominal* output or income, y is known as the *real* output or income. The relationship between nominal and real output or income is given by $Y = P \times y$. The price level, P, can therefore be calculated as the ratio of nominal to real output or income: $P = Y/y$. This measure of the price level is known as the **GDP price deflator**. This is the price level measure used in this chapter.

The real exchange rate equation, involving price levels from two countries, is

$$re = e \times \frac{P^{US}}{P^{M}}$$

To see that this equation actually measures the rate at which Mexico's goods and services trade against US goods and services, we can rewrite it as follows:

$$re = \frac{pesos}{dollar} \times \frac{\dfrac{dollars}{US\ goods}}{\dfrac{pesos}{Mexican\ goods}}$$

Next, let us rewrite the above equation as follows:

$$re = \frac{pesos}{dollar} \times \frac{dollars}{US\ goods} \times \frac{Mexican\ goods}{pesos} = \frac{Mexican\ goods}{US\ goods} \tag{16.13}$$

As you can see in this last equation, the real exchange rate indeed represents the rate at which Mexican goods trade against US goods.

Appendix 16.2: The Monetary Approach to Exchange Rate Determination

There is an approach to monetary theory known as *monetarism.*[15] At the center of this approach we find the *quantity theory of money*, expressed as the *equation of exchange*:

$$MV = Py \tag{16.14}$$

In this equation, M is the money stock, V is the velocity of money, P is the overall price level of the economy, measured here as the GDP deflator defined in Appendix 16.1, and y is real output or GDP, also defined in Appendix 16.1.

Equation 16.14 is an economic *identity* that always holds true as a definition. Monetarist thinking adds two assumptions to this equation. The first assumption is that the velocity of money is stable. In other words, any changes taking place in V take place very slowly over time.[16] The second assumption is that, in the long run, y is determined by the *supply side* of the economy, especially the availability of factors of production and the operation of these factor markets. Given these two assumptions, any changes in the stock of money will translate into changes in the price level in the long run. Deviations in this relationship would be attributable to incremental changes in real output or velocity.

This long-run monetarist relationship can be combined with the long-run PPP relationship of Equation 16.8 (repeated here) to form the monetary approach to balance of payments:[17]

$$e = \frac{P^M}{P^{US}} \tag{16.8}$$

First, we solve the equation of exchange in Equation 16.14 for the price level, once for Mexico and a second time for the United States:

$$P = \frac{MV}{y} \tag{16.15}$$

Substituting these into the real exchange rate equation, we get

$$e = \frac{\dfrac{M^M V^M}{y^M}}{\dfrac{M^{US} V^{US}}{y^{US}}} = \left(\frac{M^M}{M^{US}}\right)\left(\frac{y^{US}}{y^M}\right)\left(\frac{V^M}{V^{US}}\right) \tag{16.16}$$

[15] The monetarist paradigm has a *very long* intellectual history. For a review, see De Long (2000).

[16] Empirically, this assumption has proved to not always hold, and constitutes a weak spot of monetarist theory.

[17] This approach goes back to Johnson (1972).

Equation 16.16 represents the **monetary approach to exchange rate determination**. Here, the nominal exchange rate is determined primarily by the money stock ratio, secondarily by the real output ratio, and finally by the velocity ratio.[18] Since PPP has validity only in the long run, the monetary approach to exchange rate determination also can have validity only in the long run. There is some evidence for this.[19] The approach can also be helpful in understanding exchange rates during periods of hyperinflation when the home-country money stock and price level are increasing very rapidly.

---

[18] This is the absolute version of the monetary approach to exchange rate determination. The relative approach would be $\%\Delta e = (\%\Delta M^{M} - \%\Delta M^{US}) + (\%\Delta y^{US} - \%\Delta y^{M})$ on the assumption that velocity is stable (not a good assumption). In this equation, Δ stands for "change in."

[19] See, for example, Rapach and Wohar (2002). Sarno and Taylor (2002: 137, emphasis in original) state: "One finding which does...seem to have some validity, is that the monetary model does resurface in a number of empirical studies as a *long-run* equilibrium condition.... This finding itself is not, of course, completely robust, but it occurs with sufficient regularity in the empirical literature as to suggest that we may be observing the emergence of a stylized fact."

17 Flexible Exchange Rates

Years ago a student was in my office complaining about increases in tuition payments. Naively, I said, "But tuition did not increase very much this past year." The student responded: "In Canadian dollars it has!" My mistake. More recently a Pakistani student had the same issue, as that country's rupee devalued against the US dollar. The forces of supply and demand in currency markets determine the exchange rates of the Canadian dollar and the Pakistani rupee to the US dollar (the nominal rates). This is true for all currencies that are allowed to move in response to market forces. These market-based movements are what characterize a **flexible or floating exchange rate regime**.

What makes a flexible exchange rate move one way or another? In this chapter, we will help you answer this question by developing models of how the *nominal* exchange rate is determined in currency markets. To begin, we will consider a simple supply-and-demand model of the peso or home-country currency. We will then begin to link exchange rates to the balance of payments accounts. We will do this in two stages. First, we will consider a *trade-based* model in which the nominal exchange rate is determined by currency transactions arising from imports and exports. Second, we will extend this model to account for the exchange of *assets*.

The second, **assets-based approach** to exchange rate determination is a more modern and sophisticated model of exchange rate determination. It will give you a picture of how the current and capital accounts interact in determining the value of currencies. In doing this, we will also develop one of the most important frameworks in international finance: the **interest rate parity condition**.

In Chapter 16, we also developed the **purchasing power parity model** of exchange rate determination. Recall that this model was best interpreted as a model applying to the *long run*. The models we develop in this chapter, however, are best applied in the *short run* to describe the week-to-week or month-to-month movements in flexible exchange rates between the countries of the world.

Let us begin with our simple model of nominal exchange rate determination.

A Simple Model of Exchange Rate Determination

Currencies are traded in markets, and, like all markets, currency markets respond to the forces of supply and demand. Since exchange rates function as prices in currency markets, our first look at exchange rate determination will be a simple supply-and-demand model. This is illustrated in Figure 17.1, describing the *peso market.*[1] The value of the peso is on the vertical axis, and the quantity of pesos transacted is on the horizontal axis. The supply curve has the usual positive slope, and the demand curve has the usual downward slope.

Where do the supply and demand for pesos originate? We can think about this using the balance of payments table (Table 14.2) from Chapter 14. Any positive transaction or inflow on the balance of payments for Mexico generates a demand for pesos. Any negative transaction or outflow generates a supply of pesos. In this way, the balance of payments is linked to currency markets.

We need to specify the way in which the exchange rate adjusts. In this chapter, we are considering the case of a *flexible exchange rate regime*. This is the case when e can vary in response to excess supply of or excess demand for pesos. In the case of flexible exchange rates, we also need to introduce some terminology for changes in e. These definitions are given in Table 17.1. As shown in this table, under a flexible exchange rate regime, an increase in e or a fall in the value of the peso is called a **depreciation** of the peso. A decrease in e or a rise in the value of the peso is called an **appreciation** of the peso.[2]

Table 17.1 Exchange rate terminology

Case	e	Value of peso	Term
Flexible e	↑	↓	Depreciation
Flexible e	↓	↑	Appreciation

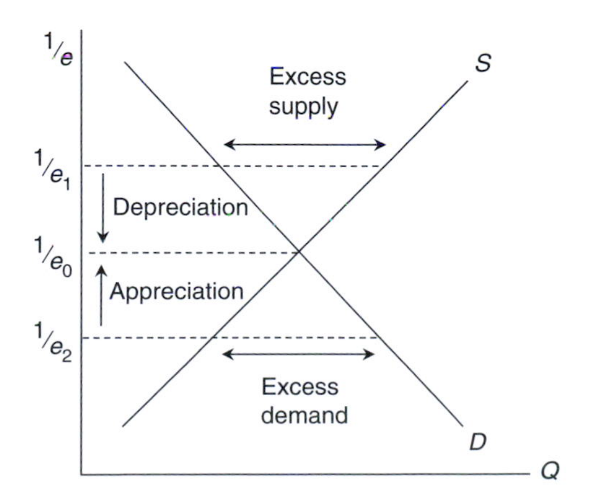

Figure 17.1 The peso market

[1] *The Economist* (2016) notes that the Mexican peso market "is very liquid and trades round the clock offshore."

[2] We will consider alternative exchange rate regimes in Chapter 18, where we will expand Table 17.1.

Under our assumption of a flexible exchange rate regime, let us consider three alternative values of the peso in Figure 17.1. The first of these is $1/e_1$. At $1/e_1$, we can see that the quantity of pesos supplied exceeds the quantity demanded. In other words, there is an *excess supply* of pesos. The presence of an excess supply of pesos has the effect of reducing the value of the peso, or causing a *depreciation* of the peso. As the peso depreciates, the quantity of pesos supplied falls, and the quantity demanded rises. These effects (working within the balance of payments) move the peso market towards equilibrium.

Next, consider $1/e_2$. At $1/e_2$, we can see that the quantity of pesos demanded exceeds the quantity supplied. In other words, there is an *excess demand* for pesos. The presence of an excess demand for pesos has the effect of increasing the value of the peso, or causing an *appreciation* of the peso. As the peso appreciates, the quantity of pesos supplied increases, and the quantity demanded decreases. These effects (again, working within the balance of payments) move the peso market towards equilibrium.

Finally, consider $1/e_0$. Here the demand for and supply of pesos are the same. For this reason, $1/e_0$ is the *equilibrium* value of the peso, and e_0 is the *equilibrium nominal exchange rate*. As in any other market, the adjustment of the value of the peso brings the peso market into equilibrium.

Figure 17.1 is a very simple model of nominal exchange rate determination. International economists have more sophisticated models of this process, however, that explicitly link adjustments in the value of currencies to adjustments in the balance of payments. We will next consider two of these models: a trade-based model and an assets-based model. We begin with the trade-based model.

A Trade-Based Model

In Chapter 14, we used the circular flow diagram to develop open-economy accounts. In doing this, we came up with an important relationship, namely

$$\text{Foreign savings} = \text{Trade deficit} \tag{17.1}$$

This relationship was one version of the **fundamental accounting equations** developed in that chapter.

To develop more sophisticated models of exchange rate determination, we are going to rewrite the relationship of Equation 17.1 in terms of symbols introduced in Figure 14.2 of Chapter 14. These were S_F (foreign savings), Z (imports), and E (exports). The rewritten relationship is

$$S_F = (Z - E) \tag{17.2}$$

We are going to use this relationship to create a model of nominal exchange rate determination, beginning in this section with a *trade-based model.* In building our model, we will maintain Mexico as our *home* country and the United States as our *foreign* country.

S_F is foreign savings. This is savings supplied by US residents who buy Mexican assets. Consequently, we can consider S_F to be a *demand for pesos* (or supply of dollars) by the United States. In our trade-based model, this demand for pesos is invariant with respect to the value of the peso. This gives us the *perfectly inelastic* demand for pesos curve represented in Figure 17.2.[3]

$Z - E$ is the trade deficit. The trade deficit is a net demand for US goods by Mexico. We can therefore consider $Z - E$ to be a *supply of pesos* (or demand for dollars) by Mexico. Before examining this supply side of the peso market, let us summarize in a box what we have stated here for you to remember.

> S_F (foreign savings) ⇔ *demand* for pesos (supply of dollars)
>
> $Z - E$ (trade deficit) ⇔ *supply* of pesos (demand for dollars)

In Chapter 16, we showed that Z has a positive relationship to the value of the peso and that E has a negative relationship to the value of the peso. Since Z and E have positive and negative relationships, respectively, to the value of the peso,

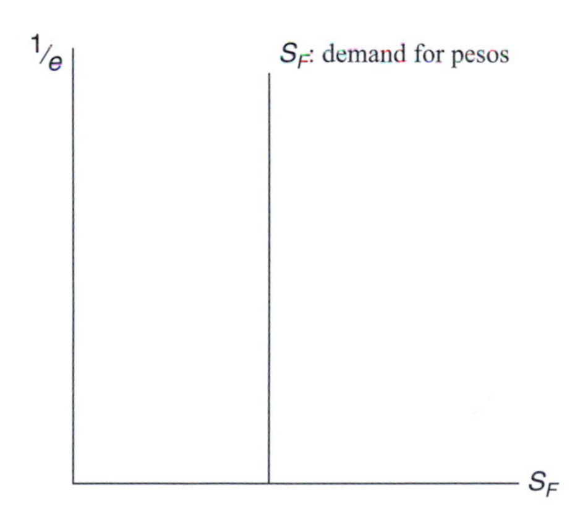

Figure 17.2 The demand for pesos

[3] Recall from introductory microeconomics that elasticities are ratios of percentage changes between two economic variables. The term "perfectly inelastic" means that the value of the elasticity is zero–that is, there is no response of one economic variable to another. In this case, the percentage change in S_F is zero no matter what the percentage change in $\frac{1}{e}$ happens to be.

$Z - E$ has a positive relationship to the value of the peso. As the value of the peso increases, the trade deficit expands. This upward-sloping supply of pesos line is represented in Figure 17.3. As you can see, there is a *positive* relationship between the value of the peso and the trade deficit, and therefore between the value of the peso and the supply of pesos.

If we put Figure 17.2 and Figure 17.3 together, we can establish the equilibrium value of the peso and nominal exchange rate as we did in Figure 17.1. This is shown in Figure 17.4. Just as in Figure 17.1, $1/e_0$ is the equilibrium value of the peso, and e_0 is the equilibrium nominal exchange rate.

We can use the trade-based model of Figure 17.4 to analyze one aspect of increased global financial integration, namely the possibility of *capital inflows*, discussed in Chapter 15. We do this in Figure 17.5. Here we begin in equilibrium in the market for pesos, with an initial equilibrium value of the peso of $1/e_0$. From this initial equilibrium an inflow of capital in the form of foreign savings shifts the S_F curve to the right. At the equilibrium value of the peso, $1/e_0$, the demand for

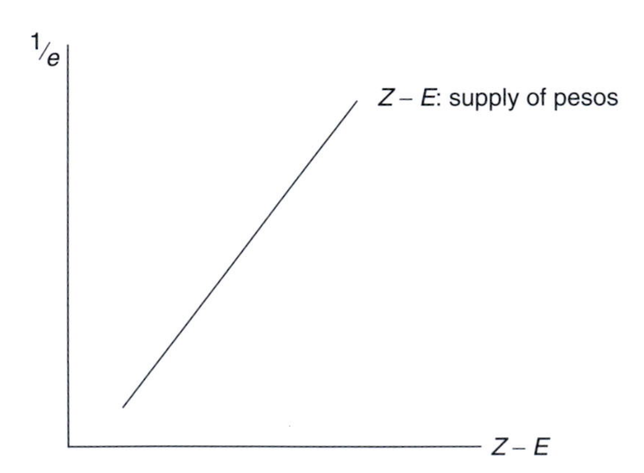

Figure 17.3 The supply of pesos

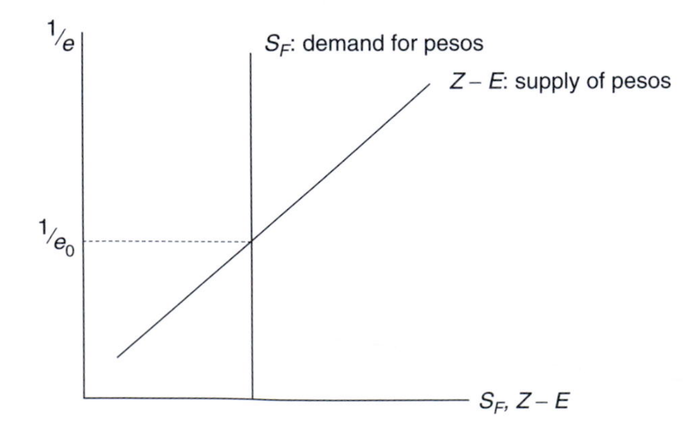

Figure 17.4 The peso market

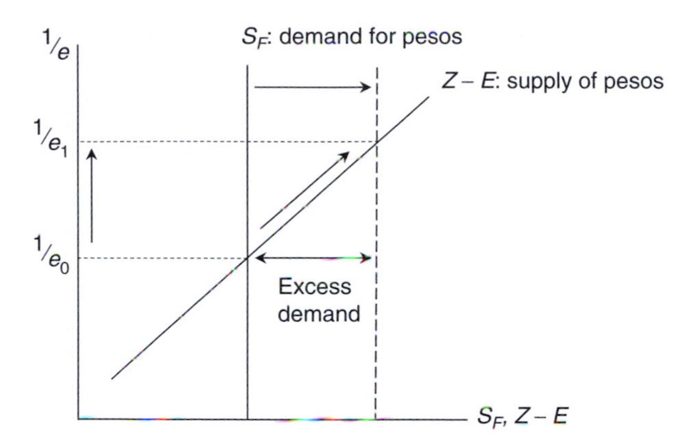

Figure 17.5 Capital inflows and the peso market

pesos represented by S_F exceeds the supply of pesos represented by $Z - E$. Given this excess demand for pesos, the value of the peso will begin to increase towards $1/e_1$. In other words, there will be an *appreciation* of the peso. As this occurs, the trade deficit will expand along the $Z - E$ line, and the supply of pesos will therefore increase to meet the demand at $1/e_1$.

Of course, this process can (and does) go in reverse. We could just as easily examine capital *outflows* in Figure 17.5 to see how they contribute to a *depreciation* of the peso. The analysis of both capital inflows and outflows helps us to understand the relationship between capital flows discussed in Chapter 15 and nominal exchange rates.

This model of exchange rate determination is *trade-based* in the sense that only trade flows respond to a change in the value of the peso. Consequently, balance of payments adjustment happens only in the current account. In the next section, we will allow foreign savings in the capital account to adjust to changes in the value of the peso, leading us to an *assets-based* model. Theory is not everything, however. For a view from a trading desk, see the accompanying box.

Theory and Practice

Professor Richard Lyons, former dean of the Haas School of Business at the University of California, Berkeley, is an expert on exchange rate theory. He was in for a surprise when he was invited by a friend to experience currency trading first-hand:

> A friend of mine who trades spot foreign exchange for a large bank invited me to spend a few days at his side. At the time I considered myself an expert, having

Theory and Practice (cont.)

written my thesis on exchange rates. I thought I had a handle on how it worked. I thought wrong. As I sat there my friend traded furiously, all day long, racking up over $1 billion in trades each day ($US). This was a world where the standard trade was $10 million, and a $1 million trade was a "skinny one." Despite my belief that exchange rates depend on macroeconomics, only rarely was news of this type his primary concern. Most of the time he was reading tea leaves that were, at least to me, not so clear. The pace was furious—a quote every 5 or 10 seconds, a trade every minute or two, and continual decisions about what position to hold. Needless to say, there was little time for chat. It was clear my understanding was incomplete when he looked over, in the midst of his fury, and asked me "What should I do?" I laughed. Nervously.

Source: Lyons (2001).

An Assets-Based Model

The **assets** approach to exchange rate determination views foreign currency transactions as arising from the buying and selling of foreign-currency-denominated *assets* rather than just from trade flows.[4] In other words, it focuses on foreign savings rather than on the trade deficit in the $S_F = Z - E$ relationship. To introduce this approach into our model, pretend that you are a *Mexican investor*, deciding upon the allocation of your wealth portfolio between two assets: a peso-denominated asset and a dollar-denominated asset. To make things simple, we will take both assets to be open-ended mutual funds with fixed domestic-currency prices.[5] As with all investors, you will allocate your portfolio with an eye to the *rates of return* of the alternative assets. Let us consider each asset in turn.

In the case of *peso-denominated assets*, the return you obtain is simply the interest rate. We will denote this rate of interest as r_M. Thus, *the total expected return on the peso-denominated asset*, R_M^e, is simply

$$R_M^e = r_M \tag{17.3}$$

[4] The assets approach to exchange rate determination is sometimes referred to as the *portfolio balance model* (see Sarno and Taylor, 2002: chap. 4). Early sources on this model are Branson and Henderson (1985) and Isard (1995: chap. 6). Engel (2016) provides a reconsideration of the model from the point of view of liquidity effects.

[5] Because additional shares of open-ended mutual funds are issued upon demand, their supply curves are horizontal. Changes in demand therefore do not affect their prices. Readers in the United States, please be careful. You are pretending to be a Mexican investor, not a US investor.

Since you are a Mexican investor, *dollar-denominated assets* are a bit more complicated. There are two things you must consider. The first is the interest payment on the dollar-denominated assets. We will denote this rate of interest r_{US}. The second consideration is the exchange rate. To see this, suppose that the initial exchange rate is $e_1 = 1.0$. Suppose also that, at this exchange rate, you purchase a dollar-denominated asset worth \$1,000. This asset is worth 1,000 pesos. Now suppose that the peso depreciates, so that the new exchange rate is $e_2 = 1.1$. With this change, the \$1,000 asset has increased in value to 1,100 pesos. Depreciation of the peso causes the foreign asset's value to increase in peso terms. You have experienced a **capital gain** in peso terms. This, along with interest payments, is what investors (including you) are looking for.

At any point in time, the nominal exchange rate is at a value e. In addition, at any point in time, you have your *expectation* of what the exchange rate will be in the future. We will denote this *expected exchange rate* as e^e. Therefore, your *expected rate of depreciation of the peso* is given by

$$\frac{(e^e - e)}{e}$$

Finally, your expected total rate of return on dollar-denominated assets is the sum of the interest rate and the expected rate of depreciation of the peso. We will denote this *total expected rate of return on dollar-denominated assets* as R^e_{US}. This is given as follows:

$$R^e_{US} = r_{US} + \frac{(e^e - e)}{e} \tag{17.4}$$

This relationship tells us that your total expected rate of return on dollar-denominated assets is composed of the interest rate plus the expected rate of depreciation of the peso.

We now have expressions for your total expected return on both peso- and dollar-denominated assets. Next, we need to think about how you will allocate your portfolio between these two asset types. To help us along, we are going to consider three alternative possibilities.

The first possibility is that $R^e_M > R^e_{US}$. In other words, the expected total rate of return on peso-denominated assets exceeds the expected total rate of return on dollar-denominated assets. What will you do in this case? Since peso-denominated assets offer a higher expected rate of return, you will *reallocate* your portfolio towards these assets, selling dollars and buying pesos in the process.

The second possibility is that $R^e_M < R^e_{US}$. In other words, the expected total rate of return on dollar-denominated assets exceeds the expected total rate of return on peso-denominated assets. In this case, you will reallocate your portfolio towards dollar-denominated assets, buying dollars and selling pesos in the process.

The third possibility is that $R_M^e = R_{US}^e$. In this case, there is no reason or incentive for you to reallocate your portfolio. You would gain nothing by doing so. Time to relax!

As we have just seen, whenever R_M^e and R_{US}^e are not equal, there will be reason for you to reallocate your portfolio between dollar-denominated and peso-denominated assets. These reallocations cause the buying of one currency and the selling of another. *Equilibrium* in the foreign exchange market, in the sense that there is no reason for you (or any other investors) to reallocate your portfolio, requires that $R_M^e = R_{US}^e$. This requires that Equations 17.3 and 17.4 be equal to one another:

$$r_M = r_{US} + \frac{(e^e - e)}{e} \tag{17.5}$$

This equation is known as the **interest rate parity condition.**[6] It states that equilibrium in the foreign exchange market requires that the interest rate on peso deposits equals the interest rate on dollar deposits plus the expected rate of peso depreciation. Since it is one of the most important relationships in international finance, we are going to put it in a box for you to remember.[7]

Interest Rate Parity Condition

$r_M = r_{US} + \frac{(e^e - e)}{e}$ Mexico/United States

$r_H = r_F + \frac{(e^e - e)}{e}$ Home/foreign

We are now going to incorporate the interest rate parity condition into a new version of Figure 17.4 of the peso market. We begin by focusing on the role of the value of the peso in the interest rate parity condition. Suppose that, initially, we are in equilibrium, so that $R_M^e = R_{US}^e$. Next, suppose the value of the

---

[6] Technically, this condition is known as the *uncovered interest parity condition*, or UIP. The term "uncovered" refers to the fact that it assumes that investors are not making use of forward exchange markets. When investors do make use of these forward markets, the *covered interest parity condition* (CIP) comes into play. We consider the difference further in a box below.

[7] In practice, violations of the interest parity condition can arise in the form of what is known as the *carry trade*. Here, a currency trader borrows in a low-interest-rate country to purchase foreign exchange in a high-interest-rate country, hoping to earn returns *above* that described by the interest rate parity condition. See, for example, *The Economist* (2009) and Adams (2009).

peso increases or e falls. *For a given expected future exchange rate* (e^e), the total expected rate of return on the dollar-denominated asset, R^e_{US}, increases because, as e falls, $\left(e^e - e\right)/e$ increases in value. Since now $R^e_{US} > R^e_M$, you (along with other investors) will sell peso-denominated assets and buy dollar-denominated assets. S_F, the asset-based demand for pesos, consequently declines. Therefore, we have shown that, *for a given* e^e, as e falls (and $1/e$ rises), S_F falls. This gives us the *downward-sloping* demand curve for pesos presented in Figure 17.6.

To understand the adjustment process in this expanded view of the peso market, let us again consider three alternative values of the peso. The first of these is $1/e_1$. At $1/e_1$, we can see that the supply of pesos exceeds the demand for pesos. Given this surplus or excess supply of pesos, the value of the peso falls. The fall in the value of the peso (rise in e) causes two types of balance of payments adjustment.

1. In the current account, the trade deficit falls as Z decreases and E increases. This decreases the supply of pesos.
2. Foreign savings, or S_F, rise as the expected rate of depreciation of the peso and, therefore, the expected total rate of return on dollar-denominated assets fall. Investors move into peso-denominated assets, and this increases the demand for pesos.[8]

A combination of changes in the current account and changes in the capital account brings the peso market towards equilibrium.

Next, consider the value of the peso $1/e_2$. At $1/e_2$, we can see that the demand for pesos exceeds the supply of pesos. Given this shortage or excess demand for pesos, the value of the peso rises. The rise in the value of the peso (fall in e) does two things.

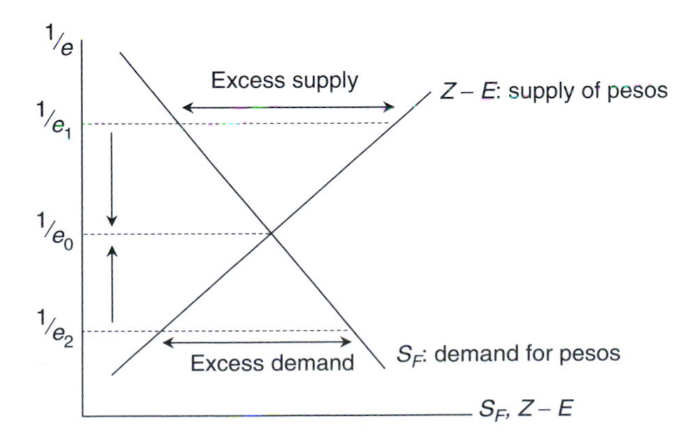

Figure 17.6 An assets-based view of the peso market

[8] It is important to remember that this effect is *for a given* e^e.

1. The trade deficit rises as Z increases and E decreases. This increases the supply of pesos.
2. Foreign savings, or S_F, fall as the expected rate of depreciation of the peso and, therefore, the expected total rate of return on dollar-denominated assets rise. Investors move out of peso-denominated assets into dollar-denominated assets, and this decreases the demand for pesos.[9]

Again, a combination of changes in the current account and changes in the capital account bring the peso market towards equilibrium.

Finally, at e_0, the demand for and supply of pesos are equal, and the peso market is in equilibrium.

Recall from Chapter 1 that the volume of foreign exchange transactions vastly exceeds the volume of trade transactions. This points to the weakness of the trade-based model of exchange rate determination and to the relative strength of the assets-based approach. This fact is effectively described by Montiel (2011: 442):

> The important fact is that...the demand for foreign exchange and supply of foreign exchange that arise from the buying and selling of financial assets is [*sic*] much larger than the demand that arises from the buying of goods and services. The implication of this situation is that for the exchange market to be in equilibrium, agents have to be willing to hold the existing composition of their portfolios between assets dominated in foreign exchange and assets dominated in domestic currency. The nominal exchange rate must adjust to make it so. This means that at a given moment in time, the nominal exchange rate has to be consistent with equilibrium in the international market for financial assets.

We have shown that this is true, but we still have some distance to go to fully appreciate the assets-based model of exchange rate determination. An important, remaining issue is the role of *changes in interest rates* and *shifts of expectations* in the model. We next turn to these interesting and important factors.

Interest Rates, Expectations, and Exchange Rates

To appreciate the role of interest rates and expectations in the determination of flexible exchange rates, we need to go back to the interest rate parity condition of Equation 17.5. Note that, in this equation, an increase in r_M increases the total expected rate of return on peso-denominated assets, and that an increase in r_{US} increases the total expected rate of return on dollar-denominated assets. Both these changes will impact the peso market. To understand how this occurs, we

[9] Again, it is important to remember that this effect is for a given e^e.

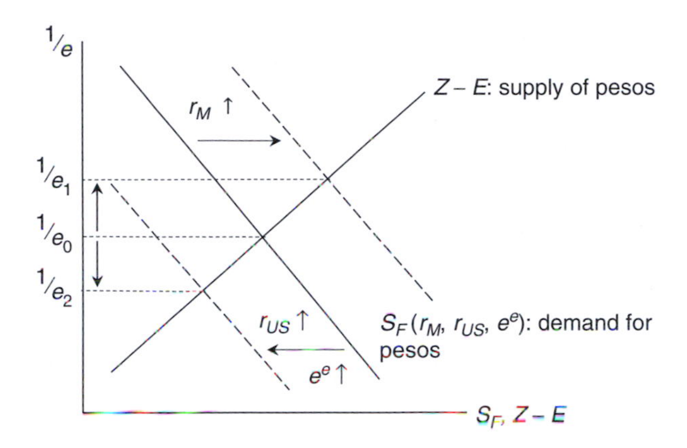

Figure 17.7 Interest rates and the peso market

need to recognize the role of r_M and r_{US} as variables that *shift the demand for peso curve*. This is done in Figure 17.7.[10]

We begin in equilibrium in Figure 17.7, with the value of the peso equal to $1/e_0$. From this initial equilibrium, suppose that r_M increases. This increases the total expected rate of return on peso-denominated assets. Consequently, there is an *increase in demand for pesos*, which shifts the demand curve to the right and raises the value of the peso to $1/e_1$. This is an interest-rate-caused capital inflow that expands the trade deficit via the exchange rate. More generally, an increase in the Mexican (home-country) interest rate causes an appreciation of the Mexican (home-country) currency in a flexible exchange rate regime.

Next, suppose that r_{US} increases. This increases the total expected rate of return on dollar-denominated assets. Consequently, there is a *decrease in demand for pesos*, which shifts the demand curve to the left and lowers the value of the peso to $1/e_2$. This is an interest-rate-caused capital outflow that contracts the trade deficit via the exchange rate. More generally, an increase in the US (foreign-country) interest rate causes a depreciation of the Mexican (home-country) currency in a flexible exchange rate regime.[11] For a more complete discussion of monetary policies and their link to exchange rates via interest rates, see Appendix 17.1.

[10] As a general principal, when a relevant explanatory variable is not on the axis of a graph, changes in that variable *shift* the graph. This was true, for example, of non-price variables affecting supply and demand in Chapter 2 on absolute advantage, as well as the non-relative-wage variables affecting emigration supply and immigration demand in Chapter 13.

[11] These are not just theoretical results. When the United States Federal Reserve Bank began increasing interest rates in 2013 (known as the "taper"), capital began to leave a number of low- and middle-income countries (known as the "taper tantrum"). Consider this from 2018: "As the United States Federal Reserve...steadily lifts interest rates,...investors have been pulling money out of riskier, developing countries and entrusting it to safer, more established economies like the United States" (Goodman, 2018).

A final remaining issue in the assets-based model of exchange rate determination is a *change in expectations*. The interest rate parity condition involves expectations about future exchange rates. These expectations are formed in the minds of investors and are therefore *subjective*. Suppose, for example, that the expected future exchange rate, e^e, were to increase in the minds of investors. Let us consider the effect of this change in Figure 17.7. Just like an increase in r_{US}, this would increase the total expected rate of return on dollar-denominated assets. Consequently, there is a decrease in demand for pesos, which shifts the demand curve to the left and lowers the value of the peso to $1/e_2$. This is an expectations-caused capital outflow that contracts the trade deficit via the exchange rate. More generally, an increase in the expected future exchange rate for Mexico's (the home country's) currency causes a depreciation of Mexico's (the home country's) currency in a flexible exchange rate regime.

An important point here is that, in some circumstances, expectations can change *rapidly*. Furthermore, they can do so in response to non-economic (e.g. political) events. As we will discuss further in Chapter 20 on crises, changes in expectations can be *self-fulfilling* in foreign exchange markets. This causes a certain amount of instability, a continual difficulty for countries around the world. We mentioned in Chapter 16 that much of the volatility in real exchange rates is because of volatility in nominal exchange rates. In turn, much of the volatility in nominal (and therefore real) exchange rates is attributable to changes in expectations.[12]

The above insights concerning interest rates and expectations are very important for your understanding of how currency markets operate in flexible exchange rate regimes. For this reason, we summarize them in Table 17.2. So that you might generalize these insights, this table is in terms of home and foreign countries

Table 17.2 Changes in currency markets

Change	Effect on foreign savings curve	Effect on value of home currency	Term
Increase in home-country interest rate	Shifts to right	Increases	Appreciation
Increase in foreign-country interest rate	Shifts to left	Decreases	Depreciation
Increase in expected future home-country exchange rate	Shifts to left	Decreases	Depreciation

[12] For example, Montiel (2011: 442) states: "Expectations about the future have an important effect on the prices of financial assets, and because these expectations tend to be volatile, this transmits the volatility to the prices of the financial assets, among them the nominal exchange rate."

rather than in terms of Mexico and the United States. Please take a close look at this table. The accompanying box on types of interest rate parity conditions also considers the empirical role of expectations in the interest parity condition.

Covered versus Uncovered Interest Rate Parity

The interest rate parity condition introduced in this chapter is one of the most important relationships in international finance. In practice, this relationship comes in two varieties: *uncovered interest rate parity* and *covered interest rate parity*. The variety we have been working with in this chapter is the UIP. In terms of home/foreign countries, we express it as

$$r_H = r_F + \frac{(e^e - e)}{e}$$

In other words, the home-country interest rate equals the foreign-country interest rate plus the rate of depreciation of the home-country currency.

CIP is expressed in terms of something we discussed in Chapter 16, namely the **forward rate**. The CIP is expressed as

$$r_H = r_F + \frac{(e^f - e)}{e}$$

where e^f is the forward rate of the home-country currency, and the expression $(e^f - e)/e$ is the *forward discount rate*.

In actual practice, forward rate traders do make use of interest rates and spot exchange rates in the transactions on forward markets. Consequently, CIP is considered to hold nearly exactly. The question is whether the UIP relationship also holds, and investigations into this issue typically compare expected and forward rates. If UIP is to hold, expected rates should be very close to forward rates. There is evidence that this is the case at time horizons of longer than one year but also that it depends on the level of uncertainty in financial markets. Deviations of expected and forward rates are sometimes interpreted in terms of *risk discounts* and *risk premia* (depending on the direction) in the UIP relationship, reflecting the extra returns demanded by investors when holding assets denominated in a particular currency. These deviations can be relatively large in time horizons as short as a month.

Sources: Chinn (2006; 2009), Du, Tepper, and Verdelhan (2018), Ismailov and Rossi (2018) and Sarno and Taylor (2002).

Conclusion

The purchasing power parity model of exchange rate determination that we considered in Chapter 16 applies only in the long run. In order to understand the short-run behavior of nominal exchange rates, we have the simple, trade-based, and assets-based models. The trade-based model focuses on the response of $(Z - E)$ to changes in the nominal exchange rate, whereas the assets-based model focuses on the response of *both* $(Z - E)$ *and* S_F to changes in the nominal exchange rate. The assets-based model is expressed as the interest rate parity condition. Expected future exchange rates play an important role in this condition, and, hence, in the determination of nominal exchange rates. This can make flexible exchange rates volatile in practice. We take up alternatives to flexible exchange rates in Chapter 18.

Review Exercises

1. As we will discuss in some detail in Chapter 21, in 1999 the European Union introduced a common currency known as the *euro*. Take the European Union as your home country and the United States as your foreign country. In this case, $e = {}^{euros}\!/_{dollar}$. Set up the equivalent of Figure 17.6 to show the determination of e. Next, use three additional diagrams to show the impacts on e of the following changes: a fall in the euro interest rate; a fall in the dollar interest rate; and a fall in the expected value of the exchange rate (e^e). In each case, *explain the intuition of your result.*
2. In this and the previous chapter, we discussed the links between trade flows and the nominal exchange rate. All other things constant, what would an *increase* in a home country's interest rate tend to do to its exports, imports, and trade deficit? Explain the intuition of your answer.
3. In this and the previous chapter, we discussed the links between trade flows and the nominal exchange rate. All other things constant, what would a *decrease* in a home country's interest rate tend to do to its exports, imports, and trade deficit? Explain the intuition of your answer.
4. For Appendix 17.1 readers only. For the euro example of Question 1 above, set up the equivalent of Figure 17.10. Next, show the impacts in this figure of a contractionary monetary policy in the European Union and a contractionary monetary policy in the United States. In each case, *explain the intuition of your results.*

FURTHER READING AND WEB RESOURCES

An introduction to exchange rate economics can be found in Isard (1995), and a more advanced treatment can be found in Sarno and Taylor (2002). The assets approach to exchange rate determination was discussed in Branson and Henderson (1985), in Isard (1995: chap. 6), and in Chinn (2009). Monetary theory, taken up in Appendix 17.1, was, effectively, reviewed many years ago by Harris (1981). Finally, an important source in international macroeconomics is Montiel (2011).

Exchange rate data are available from the International Monetary Fund's monthly publication *International Financial Statistics*. Most important is the annual *Yearbook* in this series. The IFS is also available in an online version, which many libraries have subscribed to. It is not user-friendly, but nevertheless is an important source for standardized data. See the IMF website: imf.org/en/Data. Note that some of the IMF data are provided in a more user-friendly format by the World Bank, at databank.worldbank.org.

REFERENCES

Adams, C. (2009) "Carry Trade," in K. A. Reinert, R. S. Rajan, A. J. Glass, and L. S. Davis (eds.), *The Princeton Encyclopedia of the World Economy*, Princeton University Press, 166–9.

Branson, W. H., and D. W. Henderson (1985) "The Specification and Influence of Asset Markets," in R. Jones and P. B. Kenen (eds.), *Handbook of International Economics*, North-Holland, 749–805.

Chinn, M. D. (2006) "The (Partial) Rehabilitation of Interest Parity: Longer Horizons, Alternative Explanations and Emerging Markets," *Journal of International Money and Finance*, 25:1, 7–21.

Chinn, M. D. (2009) "Interest Parity Conditions," in K. A. Reinert, R. S. Rajan, A. J. Glass, and L. S. Davis (eds.), *The Princeton Encyclopedia of the World Economy*, Princeton University Press, 649–53.

Du, W., A. Tepper, and A. Verdelhan (2018) "Deviations from Covered Interest Rate Parity," *Journal of Finance*, 73:3, 915–57.

The Economist (2009) "Buttonwood: Bucking the Trend," April 30.

The Economist (2016) "The Return of an Old Enemy," March 12.

Engel, C. (2016) "Exchange Rates, Interest Rates, and the Risk Premium," *American Economic Review*, 106:2, 436–74.

Froyen, R. T. (2013) *Macroeconomics: Theories and Policies*, Pearson.

Goodman, P. S. (2018) "Investors Are in Retreat and the Poorest Countries Are Paying for It," *New York Times*, December 20.

Harris, L. (1981) *Monetary Theory*, McGraw-Hill.

Isard, P. (1995) *Exchange Rate Economics*, Cambridge University Press.

Ismailov, A., and B. Rossi (2018) "Uncertainty and Deviations from Uncovered Interest Rate Parity," *Journal of International Money and Finance*, 88, 242–59.

Keynes, J. M. (1936) *The General Theory of Employment, Interest and Money*, Harcourt, Brace.

Lyons, R. K. (2001) *The Microstructure Approach to Exchange Rates*, MIT Press.
Montiel, P. J. (2011) *Macroeconomics in Emerging Markets*, Cambridge University Press.
Sarno, L., and M. P. Taylor (2002) *The Economics of Exchange Rates*, Cambridge University Press.
Skidelsky, R. (1992) *John Maynard Keynes: The Economist as Savior 1920–1937*, Macmillan.
Skidelsky, R. (2009) *Keynes: The Return of the Master*, Public Affairs.

Appendix 17.1: Monetary Policies and the Nominal Exchange Rate

Some readers of this book will be familiar with the macroeconomic topic of *monetary policies* from a course on macroeconomics. If this is the case for you, you will be able to extend our analysis of this chapter to an understanding of the link between monetary policies, interest rates, and exchange rates. This is the purpose of this appendix.

In December 1935 the British economist John Maynard Keynes finished writing his *General Theory of Employment, Interest and Money* (see Keynes, 1936). Among other things, this book proposed a new theory of **money demand** that we will utilize here.[13] Keynes' theory of money demand will help you understand where the interest rates in the interest parity condition come from and, then, to understand the impact of monetary policies on exchange rates.

To begin, we need to define some notation. M^D denotes money demand in the country in question. This is the amount of money households want to hold at any particular time. M^S denotes **money supply** in the country in question, and this value is determined by the monetary authority (central bank or treasury) of the country. We need to ask ourselves why households want to hold money. One obvious reason is that they hold money in order to conduct the economic transactions of everyday life. Keynes and other economists hypothesized that these transaction demands for money would increase as the income of the economy increased. As in Chapter 15, we will denote this income as Y. M^D is related *positively* to Y.

That is not the whole story, however. Like all economic decisions, holding money has *opportunity costs* associated with it. When a household holds money, it forgoes the *interest* it could be earning if the money were put into an interest-bearing deposit. Unlike his predecessors, Keynes hypothesized that M^D would therefore be

[13] An excellent overview of monetary theory can be found in Harris (1981). Harris discusses Keynes' contribution to money demand theory in chapter 9 of his book. As Skidelsky (1992: chap. 14) notes, this theory was first developed in lectures Keynes gave in the autumn of 1933. See also Skidelsky (2009: chap. 6) and Froyen (2013: chap. 6).

negatively related to the interest rate. The higher the interest rate, the more households would economize on money holdings, and the less money they would hold.

We want to summarize the above considerations in a *money demand function*. This function is as follows:

$$M^D = L(Y,r) \tag{17.6}$$

Money demand in Equation 17.6 is a function of income and the interest rate. The function itself is usually denoted with L for *liquidity*. To be in possession of money is to be financially liquid. As we described above, theory tells us that $\Delta M^D/\Delta Y$ is positive, while $\Delta M^D/\Delta r$ is negative.[14] Money demand is positively related to income but negatively related to the interest rate.

As we mentioned above, we will assume that the money supply, M^S, is set by the central bank or treasury of the country in question. Although the money supply process is not this straightforward in the real world, we will ignore any complications here in order to focus on our primary objective in this chapter: exchange rate determination.[15] We want to bring money demand and money supply into a single diagram. This diagram has money on the horizontal axis and the interest rate on the vertical axis, and is depicted in Figure 17.8.

The money supply does not vary with the rate of interest. Therefore, the M^S curve is vertical. Money demand varies inversely with the rate of interest. This gives the negative slope to the M^D curve in the diagram. The position of the M^D curve–that is, how far to the left or right it is lies in the diagram–depends on the level of

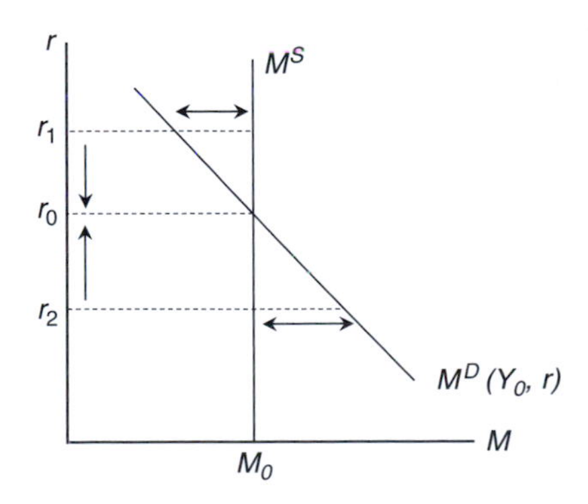

Figure 17.8 The money market

[14] As elsewhere in this book, "Δ" denotes "change in."

[15] It is often the case that, instead of targeting M^S as suggested in our diagrams, monetary authorities target an interest rate. For example, the US Federal Reserve often targets an overnight bank rate. However, in achieving the target interest rate, the monetary authority usually conducts open market operations (the buying or selling of government debt), which has the effect of changing the money supply as indicated in our diagrams. For more on the approach used here, see Chapter 6 of Froyen (2013).

income. The M^D curve in Figure 17.8 has been drawn for an initial income level, Y_0. Given this income level and the initial money supply, $M^S = M_0$, the interest rate is r_0.

If the interest rate were to be above r_0 at r_1, there would be *excess supply* of money. This would put downward pressure on the interest rate. As the interest rate falls, the opportunity cost of holding money would also fall, increasing money demand to meet money supply. If the interest rate were to be below r_0 at r_2, there would be *excess demand* for money. This would put upward pressure on the interest rate. As the interest rate rises, the opportunity cost of holding money would also rise, decreasing money demand to meet money supply.

Figure 17.8 gives us a description of the equilibrium in the money market. Let us try to determine whether it provides any intuitive explanations of the link between monetary policy and the interest rate. Suppose that the central bank of the country decides to engage in an *expansionary monetary policy* by increasing M^S. This change is depicted in Figure 17.9. The increase in the money supply shifts the M^S curve to the right. At the original interest rate, r_0, money supply exceeds money demand. The excess supply of money puts downward pressure on the interest rate. As the interest rate falls, the opportunity cost of holding money falls, and the demand for money increases. The economy moves to a new equilibrium in the money market at a lower interest rate, r_1, and a higher quantity of money, M_1. As we observe in the real world, an expansionary monetary policy is associated with a lower interest rate. Similarly, a contractionary monetary policy is associated with a decrease in the money supply and an increase in the interest rate.

In this chapter, we developed a model of exchange rate determination that viewed currency markets being affected by assets allocations (Figures 17.6 and 17.7). In this model, interest rates in Mexico and the United States played primary roles in determining the nominal exchange rate. In this appendix, we have developed a model of interest rate determination based on the money market of the economy. We next want to bring all the elements together to understand how

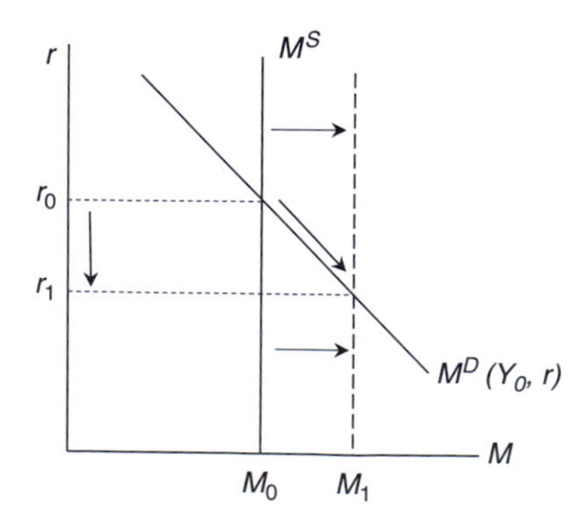

Figure 17.9 An expansionary monetary policy

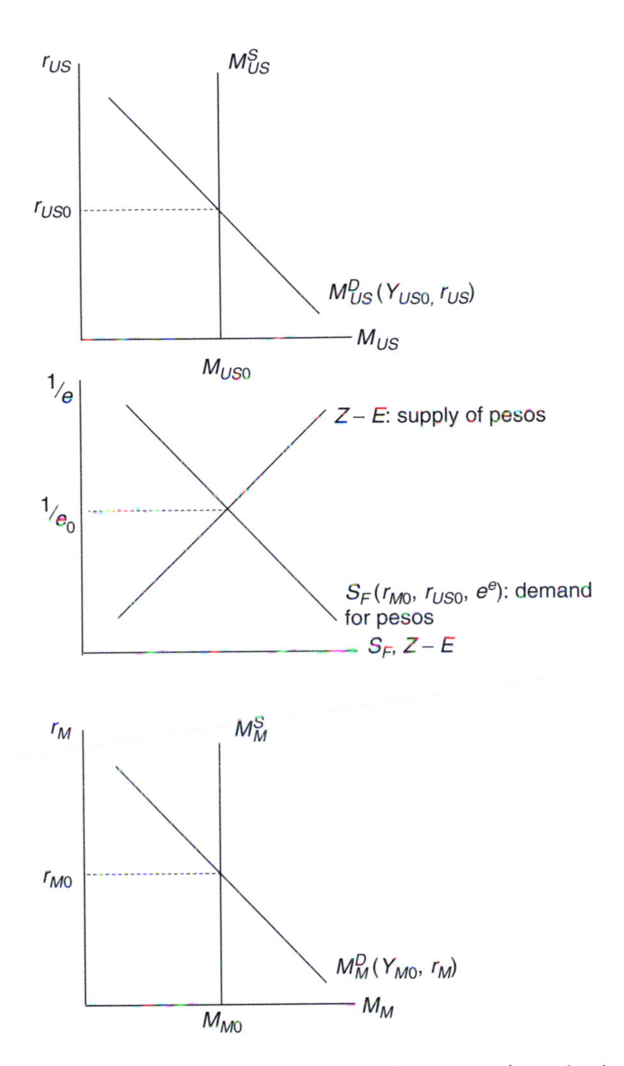

Figure 17.10 Money markets and exchange rate determination

monetary policy affects exchange rates. To do this, we are going to combine Figure 17.6 with two versions of Figure 17.8, one for the Mexican money market and a second for the US money market. This is done in Figure 17.10.

The top diagram in Figure 17.10 depicts the equilibrium in the US money market, which determines the interest rate on the dollar. The bottom diagram of Figure 17.10 depicts the equilibrium in the Mexican money market, which determines the interest rate on the peso. The dollar interest rate, r_{US}, the peso interest rate, r_M, and the expected rate of peso depreciation, e^e, all help to determine the position of the line for demand for the peso in the middle diagram. These three diagrams together give us a sense that *monetary policies help to determine exchange rates*. Our next task is to use the three diagrams in Figure 17.10 to analyze the impacts of changes

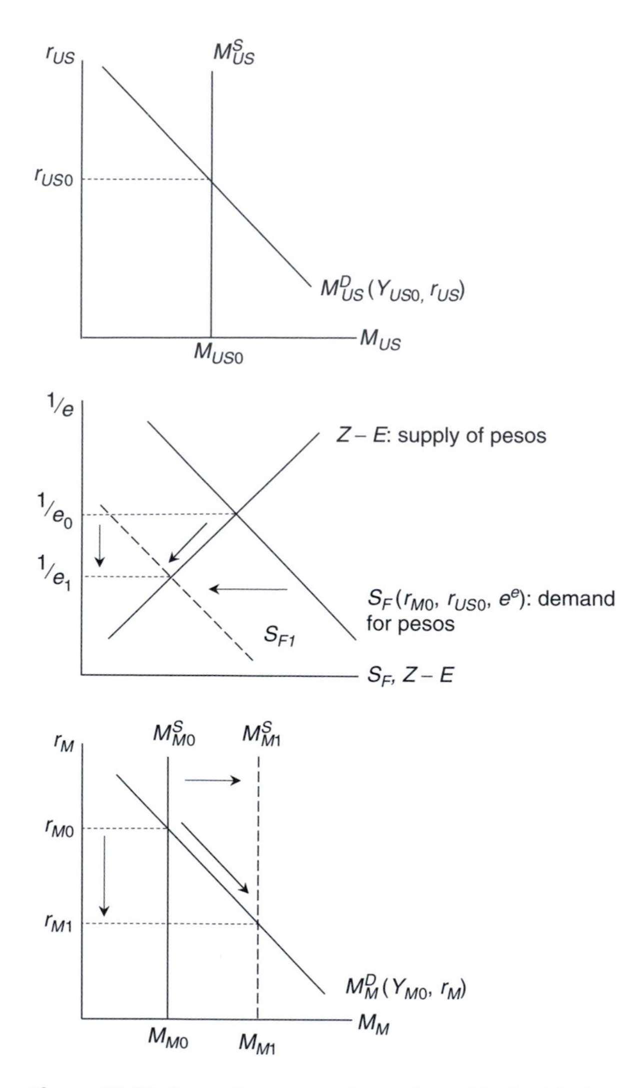

Figure 17.11 Expansionary monetary policy in Mexico (the home country)

in monetary policies on the value of the peso. To begin this exploration, we are going to consider an expansionary monetary policy in Mexico. We will then turn to an expansionary monetary policy in the United States.

The case of *expansionary monetary policy in Mexico* is presented in Figure 17.11. In the Mexican money market diagram, the increase in the money supply causes an excess supply of pesos at the initial interest rate. In order to clear the peso market, the interest rate falls to r_{M1}, increasing the demand for pesos to equal the increased supply. The lower interest rate on pesos means that the expected total rate of return on peso-denominated assets is now less than the expected total rate of return on dollar-denominated assets. Investors sell pesos and buy dollars, which

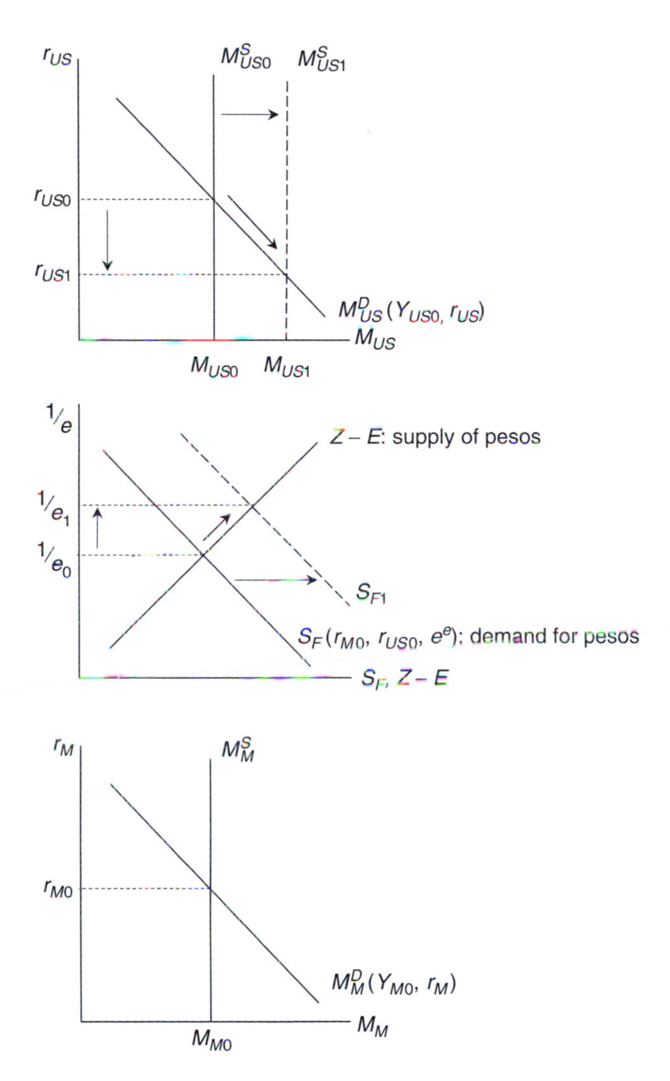

Figure 17.12 Expansionary monetary policy in the United States (the foreign country)

causes the line for the demand for pesos, S_F, to move to the left, to S_{F1}. As a result of this decrease in the demand for pesos, the value of the peso falls. In other words, there is a *depreciation* of the Mexican peso.

The case of *expansionary monetary policy in the United States* is presented in Figure 17.12. In the US money market diagram, the increase in the money supply causes an excess supply of dollars at the initial interest rate. In order to clear the dollar market, the interest rate falls to r_{US1}, increasing the demand for dollars to equal the increased supply. The lower interest rate on dollars means that the expected total rate of return on dollar-denominated assets is now less than the expected total rate of return on peso-denominated assets. Investors sell dollars and buy pesos, which causes the line for the demand for pesos, S_F to move to the right, to S_{F1}. As a result of this increase in the demand for pesos, the value of the peso rises. In other words, there is an *appreciation* of the Mexican peso.

As we have shown here, monetary policies affect interest rates and exchange rates. In Chapter 16, we saw that exchange rates affect trade flows. Monetary policies, then, can affect trade flows. Take the case of an expansionary monetary policy in Mexico, the home country. An increase in the money supply in the home country causes a depreciation of the home-country currency, the peso. This involves a movement down the value of the peso scale. This will tend to cause the trade deficit to contract or the trade surplus to expand.

On the other hand, an expansionary monetary policy tends to encourage investment because of the lower cost of capital that is implied by the lower domestic interest rate. Any increase in investment would appear as the downward shift of the $S_H(Y)+T-G-I$ line in Figure 14.6 of Chapter 14. As was shown there, this tends to *increase* the trade deficit. The impact of monetary policy on the trade balance, then, depends on the relative strengths of the exchange rate and investment effects.

18 Fixed Exchange Rates

In Chapter 17, we analyzed the case of flexible exchange rates. But not all exchange rates are flexible. Consider the case of Poland. In 1990 Poland had a fixed exchange rate, with the złoty pegged to the US dollar. Inadequate foreign reserves forced a change, however. In 1991 the Polish government set up a crawling peg, but expanded the peg to include a "basket" or collection of currencies, including the US dollar. The crawling peg involved a monthly devaluation against the currency basket at a rate of 1.8 percent. This too proved unworkable at times, and larger devaluations were required in 1992 and 1993. In 1995 the Polish government changed the crawling *peg* to a crawling *band* against the currency basket of ±7.0 percent. This band was widened to ±10.0 percent, and then to ±12.5 percent in 1998. In 1999 the currency basket was changed to reflect the introduction of the European Union's euro. Finally, in 2000, the złoty began to float.[1]

We will not get too far in understanding such complicated exchange rate histories without understanding *non-flexible* exchange rate regimes, including fixed exchange rates. Developing such an understanding is the purpose of this chapter. We will begin by defining a number of alternative exchange rate regimes, placing them on a continuum between "fixed" and "flexible." Next, we will focus on the case of fixed exchange rates and examine the various ways that balance of payments adjustment can occur under this regime. We then consider the role of interest rates and credibility in maintaining fixed exchange rate regimes. Finally, we will consider what has come to be known as the **impossible trinity** in the field of international finance. Appendix 18.1 discusses monetary policies under fixed exchange rate regimes. As such, it follows on Appendix 17.1.

Alternative Exchange Rate Regimes

The models of exchange rate determination we developed in Chapter 17 assume that the nominal exchange rate is perfectly flexible. In reality, however, there is a *menu* of exchange rate arrangements from which a country can choose. The

[1] See Kokoszczyński (2001). With the floating regime, the National Bank of Poland now pursues what is known as an "inflation targeting" regime.

menu is analyzed by the International Monetary Fund in its *Annual Report on Exchange Arrangements and Exchange Restrictions* (AREAER).[2] A recent version is presented in Table 18.1.[3] As you can see in this table, in 2017 69 countries pursued

Table 18.1 De facto exchange rate arrangements, 2017

Category	Arrangement	Description	Number of countries
Floating	Flexible (clean) float	The exchange rate is market-determined.	31
Floating	Managed (dirty) float	The exchange rate is primarily market-determined, but the country's monetary authority intervenes in the currency market to influence the movements of the exchange rate.	38
Residual	Other managed arrangements	Volatile currency market conditions prevent the use of any clearly defined exchange rate arrangement.	18
Soft peg	Crawling bands	The country's monetary authority intervenes to maintain the exchange rate in a band around a central rate, and these bands are periodically adjusted.	1
Soft peg	Crawling pegs	The exchange rate is fixed in value to another currency or to a "basket" of other currencies but is adjusted periodically by small amounts.	13
Soft peg	Stabilized arrangement	The exchange rate is officially fixed in value to another currency or to a "basket" of other currencies but actual practice might deviate from this.	24
Hard peg	Fixed or conventional peg	The exchange rate is fixed in value to another currency or to a "basket" of other currencies.	43
Hard peg	Currency board	The exchange rate is fixed in value to another currency, and the domestic currency is fully backed by reserves of this foreign currency.	11
Hard peg	No separate legal tender	The legal tender of the country is a currency of another country.	13

Source: www.imf.org.

[2] For a background paper on the current classification system, see Habermeier et al. (2009).

[3] Levy-Yeyati and Sturzenegger (2005) distinguish the de jure exchange rate regimes reported to the International Monetary Fund from de facto regimes uses in practice. For some countries, these diverge in significant ways. Table 18.1 reports the de facto regimes determined by the IMF. Husain, Mody, and Rogoff (2005) caution that de facto classifications can vary widely depending on the methodology used, so the classification of Table 18.1 might not be definitive.

a **floating** exchange rate regime, whereby the value of the nominal exchange rate floats, allowing it to be determined by the play of market forces.[4] Thirty-eight countries pursued "soft pegs." These include **managed floating regimes**, in which the monetary authority may have intervened by buying and/or selling its currency to influence the nominal exchange rate in some way; **crawling bands**, in which the monetary authorities intervened to maintain the nominal exchange rate in a band around a central rate, these bands being periodically adjusted; and **crawling pegs**, in which the nominal exchange rate was fixed in value to another currency or to a "basket" or collection of other currencies, but adjusted periodically by small amounts.

Sixty-seven countries pursued "hard pegs," including **fixed exchange rates**, in which monetary authorities adopted a policy goal of keeping the nominal exchange rate at a fixed value in terms of another currency or in terms of a "basket" of other currencies.[5] These include an extreme form of fixed exchange rate known as a **currency board**. Here, the monetary authority is required to fully back up the domestic currency with reserves of the foreign currency to which the domestic currency is pegged. Hard pegs also include countries that went even a step further and maintained no independent currency whatsoever. Finally, there is a residual category of "other managed arrangements," in which volatile currency market conditions prevent the use of a clearly defined exchange rate arrangement.

One issue that has arisen in the analysis of exchange rate regimes is their *durability* or ability to persist over time without a necessary change or transition to another regime. The regime characterization of Table 18.1 is a snapshot in time. A more thorough analysis based on a more sophisticated conception of regime change (that due to Reinhart and Rogoff, 2004) for the 1975–2001 time period is presented in Table 18.2. The average durability of all regimes across all countries is just over 11 years. We see in this table that, for all countries, pegged exchange rates were quite durable, with an average duration of 23 years. But, for emerging markets," the average durability of pegs was only eight years, a significant difference.[6] As can also be seen in this table, free floats were very durable in "advanced" countries but much less so in "developing" and "emerging" countries, because of problems with volatility.

The overall conclusion we can take from Table 18.2 is that there is probably no "one size fits all" exchange rate regime that works for all countries in the

---

[4] Whereas pure floats are referred to as "clean" floats, managed floats are known as "dirty" floats.

[5] A peg against a currency basket or a "basket peg" uses a weighted average of a collection of other important currencies as the pegged value. This was the case in the Polish example given in the introduction.

[6] Emerging markets are a subset of low- and middle-income countries that have experienced higher rates of growth and have access to international capital flows. See *The Economist* (2017).

Table 18.2 The durability of exchange rate regimes, 1975–2001 (years)

Countries	All regimes	Pegs	Intermediate	Floats
All countries	11.4	23.2	18.4	14.3
Advanced countries	19.4	46.0	26.8	88.0
Emerging markets	8.6	8.4	16.5	11.0
Developing	10.7	27.3	16.2	5.5

Sources: Husain, Mody, and Rogoff (2005), based on Reinhart and Rogoff (2004).

world economy. Indeed, as has been pointed out by many observers (e.g. Montiel, 2011: chap. 19), the durability of exchange rate regimes can depend on other "fundamentals," such as low inflation, prudential financial regulation, and capital account policies. Nevertheless, the choice of exchange rate regime is a very important decision for a country. In this chapter, we will try to get of sense of why this is so by contrasting the case of fixed or pegged rates with the flexible rates we discussed in Chapter 17. In doing so, we will get a sense of both the strengths and weaknesses of fixed exchange rate regimes.[7]

A Simple Model of Fixed Exchange Rates

In Chapter 17, we introduced a *simple model* of exchange rates in Figure 17.1 to examine the case of flexible exchange rates. We will now use this model to consider the case of fixed exchange rates. As in Chapter 17, Mexico will be our home country, and the United States will be our foreign country. The currency market we consider is, again, the peso market.

Before beginning, we need to establish some terminology and, in so doing, expand Table 17.1. This is done in Table 18.3. The first two rows of Table 18.3 repeat the flexible exchange rate terminology of Chapter 17. The third and fourth rows introduce new terminology for the fixed exchange rate regime. Let us consider them one at a time. Under a fixed exchange rate regime, when the Mexican government raises e and thereby decreases the value of the peso, there is said to be a **devaluation** of the peso. This contrasts with a market-driven upward movement in e under a flexible exchange rate regime, known as a **depreciation**. Under a

[7] A thorough empirical investigation into exchange rate regime choice can be found in Levy-Yeyati, Sturzenegger, and Reggio (2010). These researchers consider both economic and political determinants. One interesting result in their research is that, "whereas financial integration tends to foster flexible regimes among industrialized countries..., it increases the propensity to peg among non-industrialized countries" (660).

Table 18.3 Exchange rate terminology revisited

Case	Nominal exchange rate	Value of peso	Term
Flexible *e*	↑	↓	Depreciation
Flexible *e*	↓	↑	Appreciation
Fixed *e*	↑	↓	Devaluation
Fixed *e*	↓	↑	Revaluation

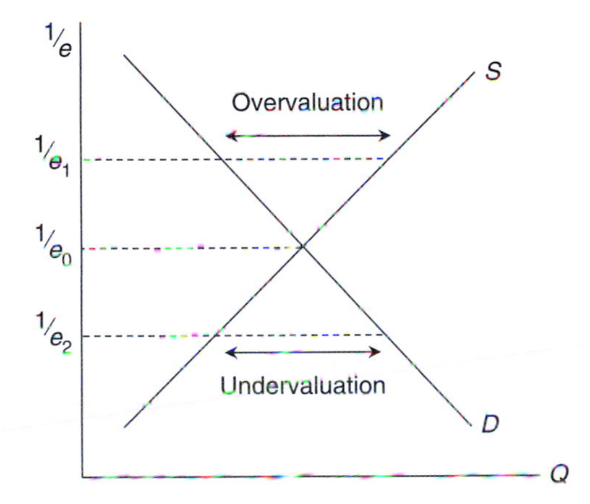

Figure 18.1 The peso market

fixed exchange rate regime, when the Mexican government lowers e and thereby increases the value of the peso, there is said to be a **revaluation** of the peso. This contrasts with a market-driven downward movement in e under a flexible exchange rate regime, known as an **appreciation**. In practice, devaluations are much more common than revaluations.

Now let us look at Figure 18.1. Suppose that the nominal exchange rate is fixed at e_1 and the value of the peso is therefore fixed at $1/e_1$. At $1/e_1$, we can see that the quantity of pesos supplied exceeds the quantity demanded. In other words, there is an *excess supply* of pesos. In a fixed exchange rate regime, this situation is known as an **overvaluation** of the peso. Recall from Chapter 17 that, under a flexible exchange rate regime, the presence of an excess supply of pesos has the effect of reducing the value of the peso or causing a *depreciation* of the peso. Under a fixed exchange rate regime, however, this type of adjustment could occur only if there were a government-instituted *devaluation* of the peso.

Next, suppose that the exchange rate is fixed at e_2 and the value of the peso is therefore fixed at $1/e_2$. At $1/e_2$, we can see that the quantity of pesos demanded exceeds the quantity supplied. In other words, there is an *excess demand* for pesos.

In a fixed exchange rate regime, this situation is known as an **undervaluation** of the peso. Under a flexible exchange rate regime, the presence of an excess demand for pesos has the effect of increasing the value of the peso or causing an *appreciation* of the peso. Under a fixed exchange rate regime, however, this could occur only if there were a government-instituted *revaluation* of the peso.

Finally, if the exchange rate is fixed at e_0 and the value of the peso is therefore fixed at $1/e_0$, there is neither overvaluation nor undervaluation of the peso. The fixed nominal exchange rate and the equilibrium exchange rate are the same.

There are further issues behind fixed exchange rates that we need to explore. For example, we need to understand how an overvaluation or an undervaluation of the peso can be maintained. We can begin to develop this understanding by considering the assets-based model of exchange rate determination we developed in Chapter 17.

An Assets-Based Model of Fixed Exchange Rates

Recall that the assets-based model of Chapter 17 helped us to understand how the balance of payments was involved in exchange rate adjustment in a flexible exchange rate regime. We now want to understand how the balance of payments can be involved in the *lack* of exchange rate adjustment in a fixed exchange rate regime. For your convenience, our balance of payments table of Chapter 14 is reproduced here as Table 18.3. We will refer to the balance of payments in the discussion that follows.

Our assets-based model is presented in Figure 18.2. This diagram represents the peso market as we developed it in Chapter 17. Suppose that e_0 represents the equilibrium exchange rate under a flexible exchange rate regime. This is where the supply of pesos given by the trade deficit $Z - E$ equals the demand for pesos given

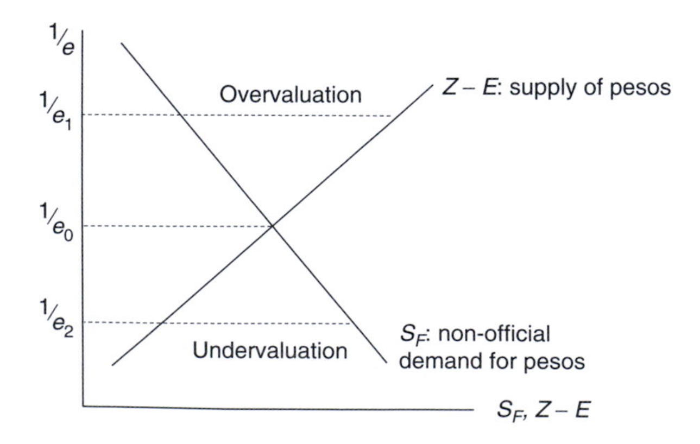

Figure 18.2 The peso market in the assets-based model

by foreign savings, S_F.[8] In terms of the balance of payments accounts of Table 18.4, the supply of pesos is the negative of item 6, the goods and services trade balance. It excludes net income (item 7) and net transfers (item 8). The demand for pesos relates to item 13, the capital/financial account balance. The demand for pesos illustrated in Figure 18.2 is therefore the *non-official* capital account balance. This excludes the actions of central banks (item 14), which we will discuss below.

Table 18.4 Mexican simplified balance of payments, 2017 (US$ billions)

Item	Gross	Net	Major balance
Current account			
1. Goods exports	409.8		
2. Goods imports	-420.8		
3. Goods trade balance		-11.0	
4. Service exports	27.6		
5. Service imports	-37.5		
6. Goods and services trade balance		-20.9	
7. Net income (primary income)		-28.3	
8. Net transfers (secondary income)		30.5	
9. Current account balance			-18.7
Capital/financial account			
10. Direct investment (FDI)		26.9	
11. Portfolio investment		8.2	
12. Other investment		-8.0	
13. Capital/financial account balance, net of official reserves balance			27.1
Official reserve transactions			
14. Official reserves balance			4.8
Errors and omissions			
15. Errors and omissions			-13.2
Overall balance			
16. Overall balance			0

Sources: data.imf.org and banxico.org.mx.

[8] As mentioned in Chapter 16, trade surpluses can be handled in this diagram by the placement of the zero value towards the middle of the horizontal axis rather than at the left endpoint.

Suppose that the Mexican government chooses to fix the exchange rate at e_1. The value of the peso, $1/e_1$, is therefore above the equilibrium value of the peso, $1/e_0$. This overvaluation of the peso implies an excess supply of pesos or an excess demand for dollars. How can this be sustained? There must be some additional demand for pesos or supply of dollars. As we see in Table 18.3, this can come from three sources: positive net income (item 7), positive net transfers (item 8), and positive net official reserve transactions (item 14).[9] Let us examine the last of these in some detail. If e is fixed at e_1, there is an excess non-official supply of pesos or demand for dollars. Mexico's central bank can address this by selling its holdings of dollars (buying pesos). In this process of *drawing down foreign reserves*, the central bank helps to eliminate the excess supply of pesos or demand for dollars. It is for this reason that we often find countries with overvalued currencies drawing down their foreign reserves. We will explore the limits of this process in Chapter 20 on crises.

Next, suppose that the Mexican government chose to fix the exchange rate at e_2. The value of the peso, $1/e_2$, is therefore below the equilibrium value of the peso, $1/e_0$. This undervaluation of the peso implies an excess demand for pesos or an excess supply of dollars. This situation can be sustained via some additional supply of pesos or demand for dollars. As we see in Table 18.3, this can come from: negative net income (item 7), negative net transfers (item 8), and negative net official reserve transactions (item 14). Again, it is worthwhile to examine the last of these in some detail. Mexico's central bank can address the excess demand for pesos or supply of dollars by buying dollars (selling pesos). In this process of *building up foreign reserves*, the central bank helps to eliminate the excess demand for pesos or supply of dollars.[10] The case of China is described in the accompanying box.

The conclusion we reach here, which coincides with experience, is that central banks in countries with overvalued currencies tend to draw down foreign exchange reserves, while central banks in countries with overvalued currencies tend to build up foreign reserves. Let us summarize this in a box for you to remember.

> Overvaluation ⇒ Excess supply of pesos (demand for dollars) ⇒ Central bank draws down foreign reserves
>
> Undervaluation ⇒ Excess demand for pesos (supply of dollars) ⇒ Central bank builds up foreign reserves

---

[9] It is helpful to view positive entries in the balance of payments as (net) demands for pesos or supply of dollars. Here we ignore errors and omissions. Note also the inflows of foreign aid in item 8 can help to sustain the overvalued domestic currency.

[10] Some development economists have argued that it is a good idea to maintain a slightly *undervalued* currency in order to keep trade deficits at manageable levels, to more generally overcome market failures in tradable sectors, and to accumulate foreign reserves for future emergencies. See Rodrik (2008) and Frieden (2017). As noted by Frieden, however, other countries can object to this strategy.

Is China's Currency Undervalued?

Although its specific character has changed over time (conventional peg versus crawling peg), China can be thought of as having pursued a fixed exchange rate regime. Prior to 2016 this peg was set in terms of the US dollar, but since 2016 there were signs that the peg has shifted to a basket of currencies with a bit more flexibility (the confusingly known "basket band crawl").

In Chapter 14, we noted that China experienced a dramatic expansion of its current account surplus to approximately US$400 billion in 2007, which subsequently declined to approximately US$200 billion in 2016. During this process China accumulated some US$2.5 trillion of foreign reserves as of 2010, which later expanded to over US$3.0 trillion. As we have seen in this chapter, these are the sorts of things we associate with an undervalued currency. This has not gone unnoticed. As stated by Frieden (2017: 34), "For over 15 years, many US manufacturers have complained the renminbi is kept artificially weak by the Chinese government, giving Chinese manufacturers an artificial advantage in US and other markets."

But has the renminbi (RMB) been undervalued? A great deal of research and policy discussion has gone into this question. Makin (2007), for example, attributes RMB undervaluation not only to China's trade surplus but also to the trade deficit of the United States. More controversially, Nobel laureate Paul Krugman (2010) calls for the United States to impose a 25 percent surcharge (tariff) an all imports from China. Estimates of the extent of China's undervaluation have varied widely, from 20 percent by Goldstein and Lardy (2009) to 30 percent by Subramanian (2010).

There has been agreement, however, that the RMB was undervalued through at least 2015, leading the United States to occasionally threaten to declare China a "currency manipulator." Therefore, the question of the transition process for the Chinese economy towards an equilibrium exchange rate became an important issue. Movements to a basket peg and some increased flexibility beginning in 2016 seemed to have helped in this regard.

Sources: Frieden (2017), Goldstein and Lardy (2009), Krugman (2010), Makin (2007), Mertens and Shultz (2017), and Subramanian (2010).

Interest Rates and Exchange Rates

There is another approach to maintaining fixed exchange rates, by affecting the *equilibrium* rate e_0. This approach is best analyzed using the **interest rate parity condition** from Chapter 17:

$$r_M = r_{US} + \frac{\left(e^e - e\right)}{e} \tag{18.1}$$

Suppose that the Mexican government successfully ensures that a *fixed* rate e_3 is an equilibrium rate. What must be the relationship between e_3 and e^e? A moment of thought tells us that, if e_3 is both a *fixed* and an *equilibrium* rate, then e_3 *must equal* e^e. This causes a change in our interest rate parity condition. Since $e^e = e$, $(e^e - e)$ is zero, and therefore

$$r_M = r_{US} \tag{18.2}$$

This relationship tells us that, for the Mexican government to maintain a fixed equilibrium exchange rate, it must ensure that its interest rate equals that in the United States. Another way of looking at this is shown in Figure 18.3. By increasing or decreasing r_M into equality with r_{US}, the Mexican government can move the S_F line to the left or right until the equilibrium e and e_3 are identical.

How does this work? Suppose that initially $r_M = r_{US}$, and this allows for a fixed exchange rate e_3. Next, suppose that the US government *increases* r_{US} so that $r_M < r_{US}$. This shifts the demand for pesos line to the left. In order to maintain the fixed e_3, the Mexican government will need to increase r_M, moving the demand for pesos line back to its original position. Similarly, if, from the initial equilibrium, the US government were to *decrease* r_{US} so that $r_M > r_{US}$, this would shift the demand for peso line to the right. Here, in order to maintain the fixed e_3, the Mexican government will need to decrease r_M, moving the demand for peso line back to its original position.[11]

In a less technical analysis of exchange rates, Frieden (2017) reaches this same conclusion. He states (35):

> Imagine that Mexico fixes its exchange rate against the dollar. If interest rates in the United States are three percent, then they have to be three percent in Mexico. If interest

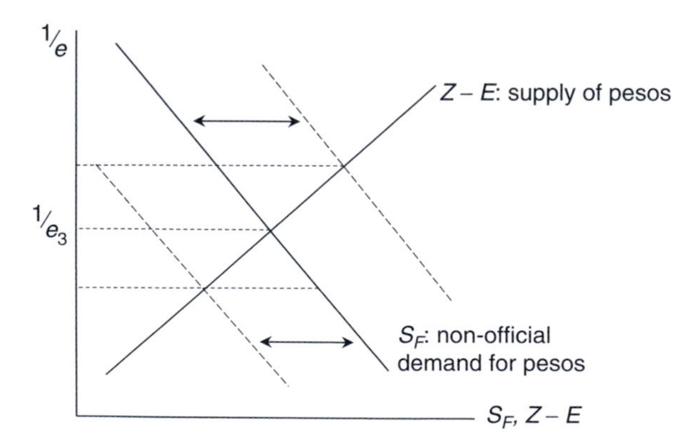

Figure 18.3 An equilibrium fixed exchange rate

[11] For the role of monetary policies in this process, please see Appendix 18.1.

rates in Mexico were lower, money would flood out of Mexico to get the higher interest rates in the United States; if interest rates in Mexico were higher, money would flood into Mexico. Either way, the Mexican interest rate would be driven back to the US rate. This means that whatever interest rate is set by the US central bank, the Federal Reserve, will have to be the policy rate for Mexico as well.

We have gained an important insight here into the operation of fixed exchange rate regimes. Let us summarize it in a box for you to remember.

> If a home country wants to maintain an *equilibrium* fixed exchange rate, it must set its interest rate equal to that prevailing in the foreign country whose currency serves as a peg for the home-country currency.

The real world is a complex place, and, in practice, fixed exchange rates are maintained with combinations of net income receipts, net transfers, official reserve transactions, and interest rates. In other words, in practice, *both* Figure 18.2 and Figure 18.3 are relevant. We discuss this for the case of Brazil's exchange rate crisis in 1998/99 in the accompanying box. One principle is always operable, however. The farther a fixed exchange rate is from the equilibrium exchange rate, the more difficult it is to maintain for an extended period of time. This principle brings us to the issue of the *credibility* of fixed exchange rates.

Defending the Brazilian Real, 1998/99

In October 1998 Brazilian citizens reelected Fernando Henrique Cardoso to a second term as president. In the months preceding the election, however, Brazilian monetary authorities had been engaged in an intense struggle with international investors to maintain a crawling peg of the Brazilian real against the US dollar. By September 1998 interest rates had reached 40 percent. Despite this strong measure, however, foreign reserves had been drawn down from nearly US$75 billion to US$50 billion. Brazil began to talk to the International Monetary Fund about a support package to maintain investor confidence in the face of a fiscal deficit equivalent to almost 8 percent of GDP and a current account deficit of approximately 4 percent of GDP.

Shortly after taking office, and in close consultation with the IMF, Cardoso's economic team drew up a package of budget cuts and tax increases. In November an official agreement with the IMF worth US$41.5 billion was announced, and Cardoso's government denied that it would abandon the crawling peg. In

Defending the Brazilian Real, 1998/99 (cont.)

December the government also denied that it would abandon its central bank president, Gustavo Franco, whose job it was to defend the real.

In mid-January 1999 Gustavo Franco resigned, and the real was devalued. Two days later the real was allowed to float. It very quickly lost almost a third of its value.

Sources: The Economist (1998a; 1998b; 1998c)

The Role of Credibility

Our discussion of interest rates and fixed exchange rates has been based on the expected rate of depreciation being zero in Equation 18.2. In Chapter 17, however, we noted that expectations regarding the future exchange rate can be *volatile* and subject to a host of economic and political events. For example, if a fixed exchange rate comes under pressure from an incipient fall in demand (shift of S_F to the left), this pressure must be alleviated via an increase in the home-country interest rate. There are two difficulties here, however. First, increases in interest rates are *recessionary*, in that they suppress domestic investment. Second, increases in interest rates can potentially play havoc in fragile domestic financial systems. This point is summarized by Montiel (2011: 453):

> The currency should be in a strong position to resist speculative attack, and the currency peg should be sustainable.... when the real exchange rate is not misaligned..., the financial sector is strong, the public sector does not have a large stock of domestic currency debt, and the economy is growing rapidly. Alternatively, if the currency appears to be overvalued, the domestic financial sector is weak, the public sector's solvency is precarious, and it has a large stock of short-term domestic debt, and/or the economy is in recession, the prospects for a successful speculative attack would tend to be strong.

The reason for this is that investors know what the potentially negative impacts of an interest rate can be, and this information feeds back into expectations. If investors begin to question the willingness and ability of the home-country government to defend the fixed peg with interest rate increases, the expected rate of depreciation again becomes positive and the peg is no longer credible. This process operates in some of the crises we will consider in Chapter 20 and contributes to the lack of durability of pegs in emerging markets that we saw in Table 18.2.

The Impossible Trinity

Our discussions in this chapter lead up to a concept in international finance that has received a lot of attention lately. It is known as the **impossible trinity.**[12] The impossible trinity recognizes that, in the realm of international finance, countries would ideally like to pursue *three desired objectives* (the trinity).

1. *Monetary independence*, or the ability to conduct an independent monetary policy with an eye to stabilizing domestic macroeconomic policy.
2. *Exchange rate stability*, or the ability to avoid destabilizing volatility in the nominal exchange rate.
3. *Capital mobility*, or the ability to take advantage of flows on the direct and portfolio capital accounts from foreign savings.

As it turns out, however, countries must sacrifice one of the above desired objectives in order to achieve the other two. The impossible trinity, illustrated in Figure 18.4, helps to explain why this is the case. We will develop your understanding of this figure in three steps.

First, suppose a country wants to maintain both capital mobility and exchange rate stability. These two objectives appear as italicized terms in Figure 18.4 associated with the bottom and right-hand sides of the triangle. Arrows from these two terms converge in the lower right-hand corner of the triangle on the policy regime of a fixed exchange rate. This indicates that the only way to maintain both capital mobility and exchange rate stability is to pursue a fixed exchange rate

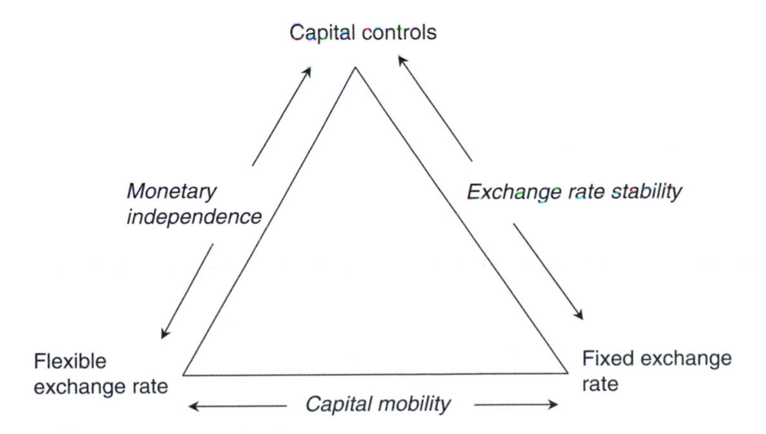

Figure 18.4 The impossible trinity

[12] It also goes by the name of the "policy trilemma." The term "trilemma" is not one you will find in a dictionary. The term "dilemma" refers to a necessary choice between *two* undesirable alternatives. The term "trilemma," then, refers to a necessary choice between *three* undesirable alternatives, in the form of lost desirable policies.

regime. The desired objective that the country must *give up* is the one on the side of the triangle opposite the fixed exchange rate corner, namely monetary independence. As you have seen above in this chapter, if a country wants to maintain its fixed exchange rate as an equilibrium rate, it must adjust its interest rate to that in the country to which its currency is pegged. Since, as is discussed further in Appendix 18.1, interest rates are set via monetary policy, *in maintaining capital mobility and exchange rate stability the country must sacrifice its independent monetary policy.*

Second, suppose a country wants to maintain both capital mobility and monetary independence. These two objectives appear as italicized terms in Figure 18.4 associated with the bottom and left-hand sides of the triangle. Arrows from these two terms converge in the lower left-hand corner of the triangle on the policy regime of a flexible exchange rate. This indicates that the only way to maintain both capital mobility and monetary independence is to allow the currency to float. The desired objective that the country must *give up* is the one on the side of the triangle opposite the flexible exchange rate corner, namely exchange rate stability. As we discussed in Chapter 17, changes in foreign interest rates and in expectations will, in the face of a given monetary policy in the country, alter the flexible nominal exchange rate. Since, in practice, such movements in flexible exchange rates can be large, we see that *in maintaining capital mobility and monetary independence the country must sacrifice exchange rate stability.*[13]

We should mention here that there are possible *intermediate positions* between these first two cases. With capital mobility, a country can in practice achieve a mix of some monetary independence and some exchange rate stability through the use of the intermediate regimes of managed floats, crawling bands, and crawling pegs described in Table 18.1. What these countries *cannot* achieve is *both* full monetary independence *and* full exchange rate stability.[14]

Third, suppose a country wants to maintain both monetary independence and exchange rate stability. These two objectives appear as italicized terms in Figure 18.4 associated with the left-hand and right-hand sides of the triangle. Arrows from these two terms converge at the apex of the triangle on the policy regime of capital controls. This indicates that the only way to maintain both monetary independence and exchange rate stability is to restrict transactions on the capital account of the balance of payments, in order to suppress portfolio behavior in the capital/financial account. The desired objective that the country must *give up* is the one on the side of the triangle opposite the capital control

---

[13] But see Calvo and Mishkin (2003) on the challenges of building monetary policy credibility even in flexible exchange rate regimes. The market-friendly capital controls discussed in Chapter 15 can play a role here.

[14] The role of these intermediate regimes is emphasized by Frankel (1999).

corner, namely capital mobility. In order to *maintain monetary independence and exchange rate stability the country must sacrifice capital mobility.*

Economic analysis often helps to highlight trade-offs between alternatives. Here we have highlighted some central trade-offs between policies facing each country in the world economy. As with economic trade-offs in general, there are *opportunity costs* with any choice. In the realm of international finance, countries must give up one desired objective (monetary independence, exchange rate stability, or capital mobility) to attain the other two. To assume otherwise in policy deliberations is wishful thinking.

Currency Boards

Exchange rate volatility and episodes of inflation in low- and middle-income countries have led some observers to suggest the use of **currency boards** to stabilize exchange rates.[15] Currency boards are a fixed exchange rate regime with two additional characteristics: First, the fixed rate is presented as an *inviolable commitment* with legal backing in domestic legislation. Second, the central bank serving as the currency board fully backs up its base money (cash and commercial bank reserves) with foreign reserves and stands ready to exchange the domestic currency and the foreign currency in response to any request. As seen in Table 18.1, 11 countries utilized currency boards in 2017.[16] The most well-known case of a (failed) currency board was Argentina, which introduced a currency board to help stabilize the country's economy after a period of hyperinflation in the late 1980s.

Currency boards are effective ways to establish sound currencies and to limit excessive money creation that can fuel **inflation**. It is not clear, however, how useful currency boards are in the *long run*, except perhaps for the world's smallest and most open economies. In the case of Argentina, a larger and less open economy, the currency board was introduced as part of the Plan Convertibilidad, or Convertibility Plan, in 1991, which also included a set of fiscal and structural reforms. One assessment of the currency board arrangement through 1996 used the term "miracle" and hailed it as "the most successful program in the last half-century" (Kiguel and Nogués, 1998: 143). Indeed, between 1991 and 1995 annual inflation fell from 170 percent to 0 percent. A dangerous process of **deflation**

---

[15] See Enoch and Gulde (1998) and Ghosh, Gulde, and Wolf (2000). Steve Hanke of the libertarian Cato Institute is a perennial advocate of currency boards.

[16] The 11 countries were: Antigua and Barbuda, Bosnia and Herzegovina, Brunei Darussalam, Bulgaria, Djibouti, Dominica, Grenada, Hong Kong, St Kitts and Nevis, St Lucia, and St Vincent and the Grenadines.

began to occur in 1998, however, and, without an independent monetary policy, the Argentine government was helpless to address it.

Argentina's real troubles began in mid-2001, when it was required to significantly increase interest rates on its Treasury bills in order to attract investors. By early 2002 the situation had become dire. Despite ongoing talks with the IMF and limits on cash withdrawals within the country, all eyes began to focus on the country's US$135 billion public debt, and speculation grew that a devaluation was imminent. Indeed, the debt default came quickly in 2002, and the government began to prepare for a devaluation. Initially the government attempted a 30 percent devaluation, adjusting the peg from 1.0 to 1.4 pesos per US dollar. By mid-2002, however, it had reached nearly 4.0 to the dollar, later appreciating back to approximately 3.5 to the dollar. Because most debt in the country was denominated in US dollars, devaluation immediately increased the peso value of the debt. In the aftermath of the currency board's demise, GDP shrank by more in percentage terms than in the United States during the Great Depression, and poverty exploded.

Given this history, it seems that the usefulness of currency boards is *not universal* but *limited* to certain small and very open economies. In terms of the impossible trinity, these boards constitute an unusual commitment to remain in the lower right-hand corner of Figure 18.3 and to forsake any possibility of an independent monetary policy.[17]

A Role for Fixed Rates?

From a basic economic perspective, policy arguments in favor of fixed exchange rates appear to be strange. We have shown that fixed rates require countries to give up their independent monetary policy. More fundamentally, however, fixing a price runs counter to most of the logic of basic economics, in which prices are supposed to move in response to changing conditions. Is there any reason to view fixed exchange rates as a potentially fruitful policy?

One *potential* reason is macroeconomic management. If countries experience high rates of inflation, perhaps even hyperinflation (e.g. Zimbabwe and Venezuela), it might be a good idea to take away their independent monetary policy and place them in a hard peg/currency board straitjacket. Although this argument is sometimes made, floating exchange rates have many positive characteristics in their

[17] For further discussion of the Argentine case, see Corden (2002: chap. 11). Montiel (2011: 439) notes that advocates of currency boards argue that they "impose macroeconomic discipline, thereby enhancing the credibility of inflation objectives." Montiel reviews the arguments in favor of currency boards, and concludes (439) that "none of these arguments is fully convincing."

favor. They can facilitate balance of payments adjustment through real exchange rate flexibility (e.g. Gervais, Schembri, and Suchanek, 2016), make countries less susceptible to crises (e.g. Ghosh, Ostry, and Qureshi, 2015), and help countries weather macroeconomic shocks that occur abroad (e.g. Corsetti, Kuester, and Müller, 2017). Each of these effects is important.

Despite these advantages of flexible exchange rates, fixed exchange rates have been and continue to be a chosen regime for many countries. As we will see in Chapter 19, historically, fixed exchange rates have been something of a norm. In Chapter 21 we will also see that some countries (such as most of those in Europe) choose to band together into a **monetary union**, whereby the exchange rate is fixed by the adoption of a single currency (such as the euro). That said, in Chapter 20 we will also highlight the role of fixed exchange rates in balance of payments crises. It is an unfortunate fact of international economic policy that the choice of exchange rate regime, and therefore the position of countries in the impossible trinity of Figure 18.4, is not straightforward.

Conclusion

Although Chapter 17 considered the case of freely floating or flexible exchange rates, this is only one possible exchange rate regime. Other alternatives include managed floating, crawling pegs, adjustable pegs, fixed exchange rates, and currency boards. The current chapter has focused on fixed exchange rates, with a quick look at currency boards.

Governments can maintain *overvalued* exchange rates through positive net income receipts, positive net transfers, and positive net official reserve transactions (drawing down foreign reserves). These provide the requisite extra demand for the home-country currency. Alternatively, governments can raise the domestic interest rate to increase the equilibrium value of the currency so that it is no longer overvalued. An overvalued exchange rate is not always sustainable. The home-country central bank can run out of foreign reserves to sell. We take up the complications of such situations in Chapter 20, on crises.

Governments can maintain *undervalued* exchange rates through negative net income receipts, negative net transfers, and negative net official reserve transactions (building up foreign reserves). These provide the requisite extra supply for the currency. Alternatively, the government can lower the domestic interest rate to decrease the equilibrium value of the currency so that it is no longer undervalued.

Every country faces the impossible trinity, in which it must sacrifice one desired objective (monetary independence, exchange rate stability, or capital mobility) to attain the other two. This reality puts significant constraints on possible policies available to countries to address the (often stormy) realities of international finance.

Review Exercises

1. Until January 2002 the Argentine peso was pegged on a one-to-one basis against the US dollar in an arrangement known as a *currency board.* Suppose that, to begin with, this exchange rate is an equilibrium rate. Next, using a diagram such as Figure 18.3, show how Argentina can respond to a decrease in the interest rate on the US dollar.
2. Suppose that a country has a fixed exchange rate and that, over the past few years, it has been quickly accumulating foreign reserves. What does this tell you about the value of the pegged currency? Why?
3. Given what you have read in this book up to this point, can you say anything about the desirability of the three policy regime corners in the impossible trinity diagram of Figure 18.4? Please explain your reasoning.
4. For Appendix 18.1 readers only. For the example in the first exercise above, set up the equivalent of Figure 18.5. Next, show the actions required on the part of the Mexican monetary authority in response to: a decrease in income in Mexico; a decrease in income in the United States; and a contractionary monetary policy in the United States. In each case, *explain the intuition of your results.*

FURTHER READING AND WEB RESOURCES

On the classification of exchange rate regimes, see Corden (2002), Reinhart and Rogoff (2004), and Habermeier et al. (2009). A thorough review of the process of maintaining a fixed exchange rate regime is given in Montiel (2011: chap. 19). On the impossible trinity, see Siklos (2009), and, on currency boards, see Slavov (2009). For sources on the political economy of fixed exchange rate regimes, see Obstfeld and Rogoff (1995), Garber and Svensson (1996), Calvo and Mishkin (2003), and Levy-Yeyati, Sturzenegger, and Reggio (2010).

Exchange rate data are available from International Monetary Fund's monthly publication *International Financial Statistics.* Most important is the annual *Yearbook* in this series. The IFS is also available in an online version, which many libraries have subscribed to. It is not user-friendly, but nevertheless is an important source for standardized data. See the IMF website: imf.org/en/Data. Note that some of the IMF data are provided in a more user-friendly format by the World Bank, at databank.worldbank.org.

For the IMF's *Annual Report on Exchange Arrangements and Exchange Restrictions,* first go to imf.org/en/Publications. Use the drop-down menu for "Series" and choose the AREAER.

REFERENCES

Bernanke, B. S., and F. S. Mishkin (1997) "Inflation Targeting: A New Framework for Monetary Policy?," *Journal of Economic Perspectives,* 11:2, 97–116.

Calvo, G. A., and F. S. Mishkin (2003) "The Mirage of Exchange Rate Regimes for Emerging Market Countries," *Journal of Economic Perspectives,* 17:4, 99–118.

Corden. W. M. (2002) *Too Sensational: On the Choice of Exchange Rate Regimes*, MIT Press.

Corsetti, G., K. Kuester, and G. J. Müller (2017) "Fixed on Flexible: Rethinking Exchange Rate Regimes after the Great Recession," *IMF Economic Review*, 65:3, 586–632.

The Economist (1998a) "Can Cardoso Use Financial Chaos to Reform Brazil?," September 26.

The Economist (1998b) "Cracking the Brazil Nuts," October 31.

The Economist (1998c) "Brazilian Jitters," December 19.

The Economist (2017) What's in a Name? Defining Emerging Markets," October 7.

Enoch, C., and A.-M. Gulde (1998) "Are Currency Boards a Cure for All Monetary Problems?," *Finance and Development*, 35:4, 40–3.

Frankel, J. A. (1999) "No Single Currency Regime Is Right for All Countries or At All Times," *Princeton Essays in International Finance*, 215, 1–38.

Frieden, J. (2017) "Currency Politics in the Developing World," *Harvard International Review*, 38:2, 33–5.

Friedman, M. (1953) "The Case for Flexible Exchange Rates," in *Essays in Positive Economics*, University of Chicago Press, 157–203.

Garber, P. M., and L. E. O. Svensson (1996) "The Operation and Collapse of Fixed Exchange Rate Regimes," in G. M. Grossman and K. S. Rogoff (eds.), *Handbook of International Economics*, vol. 3, North-Holland, 1865–1911.

Gervais, O., L. Schembri, and L. Suchanek (2016) "Current Account Dynamics, Real Exchange Rate Adjustment, and the Exchange Rate Regime in Emerging-Market Economies," *Journal of Development Economics*, 119, 86–99.

Ghosh, A. R., A.-M. Gulde, and H. Wolf (2000) "Currency Boards: More Than a Quick Fix?," *Economic Policy*, 31, 269–321.

Ghosh, A. R., J. D. Ostry, and M. S. Qureshi (2015) "Exchange Rate Management and Crisis Susceptibility: A Reassessment," *IMF Economic Review*, 63:1, 238–76.

Goldstein, M., and N. Lardy (2009) "The Future of China's Exchange Rate Policy," Policy Analysis in International Economics 97, Peterson Institute of International Economics.

Habermeier, K., A. Kokenyne, R. Veyrune, and H. Aderson (2009) "Revised System for the Classification of Exchange Rate Arrangements," Working Paper 09/211, IMF.

Husain, A. M., A. Mody, and K. S. Rogoff (2005) "Exchange Rate Regime Durability and Performance in Developing versus Advanced Economies," *Journal of Monetary Economics*, 52:1, 35–64.

Kiguel, M., and J. J. Nogués (1998) "Restoring Growth and Price Stability in Argentina: Do Policies Make Miracles?," in H. Costin and H. Vanolli (eds.), *Economic Reform in Latin America*, Dryden, 125–44.

Kokoszczyński, R. (2001) "From Fixed to Floating: Other Country Experiences: The Case of Poland," paper presented at the IMF seminar "Exchange Rate Regimes: Hard Peg or Free Floating?," Washington, DC, March 19.

Krugman, P. (2010) "Taking On China," *New York Times*, March 15.

Levy-Yeyati, E., and F. Sturzenegger (2005) "Classifying Exchange Rate Regimes: Deeds vs. Words," *European Economic Review*, 49:6, 1603–35.

Levy-Yeyati, E., F. Sturzenegger, and I. Reggio (2010) "On the Endogeneity of Exchange Rate Regimes," *European Economic Review*, 54:5, 659–77.

Makin, A. J. (2007) "Does China's Huge External Surplus Imply an Undervalued Renminbi?," *China and World Economy*, 15:3, 89–102.

Mertens, T. M., and P. Shultz (2017) "China's Exchange Rate Policies and US Financial Markets," Economic Letter 2017–28, Federal Reserve Bank of San Francisco.

Montiel, P. J. (2011) *Macroeconomics in Emerging Markets*, Cambridge University Press.

Obstfeld, M., and K. S. Rogoff (1995) "The Mirage of Fixed Exchange Rates," *Journal of Economic Perspectives*, 9:4, 73–96.

Reinhart, C. M., and K. S. Rogoff (2004) "The Modern History of Exchange Rate Arrangements: A Reinterpretation," *Quarterly Journal of Economics*, 119:1, 1–48.

Rodrik, D. (2008) "The Real Exchange Rate and Economic Growth," *Brookings Papers on Economic Activity*, 39:2, 365–412.

Siklos, P. (2009) "Impossible Trinity," in K. A. Reinert, R. S. Rajan, A. J. Glass, and L. S. Davis (eds.), *The Princeton Encyclopedia of the World Economy*, Princeton University Press, 619–22.

Slavov, S. (2009) "Currency Board Arrangement," in K. A. Reinert, R. S. Rajan, A. J. Glass, and L. S. Davis (eds.), *The Princeton Encyclopedia of the World Economy*, Princeton University Press, 240–3.

Subramanian, A. (2010) "New PPP-Based Estimates of Renminbi Undervaluation and Policy Implications," Policy Brief 10–8, Peterson Institute for International Economics.

Appendix 18.1: Monetary Policies and Fixed Exchange Rates

As mentioned in Appendix 17.1, some readers of this book will be familiar with monetary policies from a course on macroeconomics. If this is the case for you, the present appendix will explain to you the monetary consequences of fixed exchange rate regimes. We begin with a collection of diagrams presented in Appendix 17.1. This collection of diagrams is presented in Figure 18.5. The top diagram of this figure depicts equilibrium in the US money market and determines the interest rate on the dollar. The bottom diagram depicts equilibrium in the Mexican money market and determines the interest rate on the peso. The middle diagram depicts the peso market, e_0 being an equilibrium fixed exchange rate. As discussed in this chapter, an equilibrium fixed exchange rate requires $r_M = r_{US}$. Let us examine some implications of this requirement.

First, let us suppose that income in Mexico (Y_M) increased. What would be the implication of this? An increase in income in Mexico would tend to increase the demand for pesos. This would shift the Mexican money demand curve in Figure 18.5 to the right, which, in turn, would tend to increase r_M. This would shift the demand for pesos line to the right in the center diagram, increasing the value of the peso. In order to prevent this peso appreciation, the Mexican central bank would need to increase the supply of pesos, selling them in the peso market. This will shift the M_M^S curve to the right until r_M falls back to its original level and e is maintained at e_0.

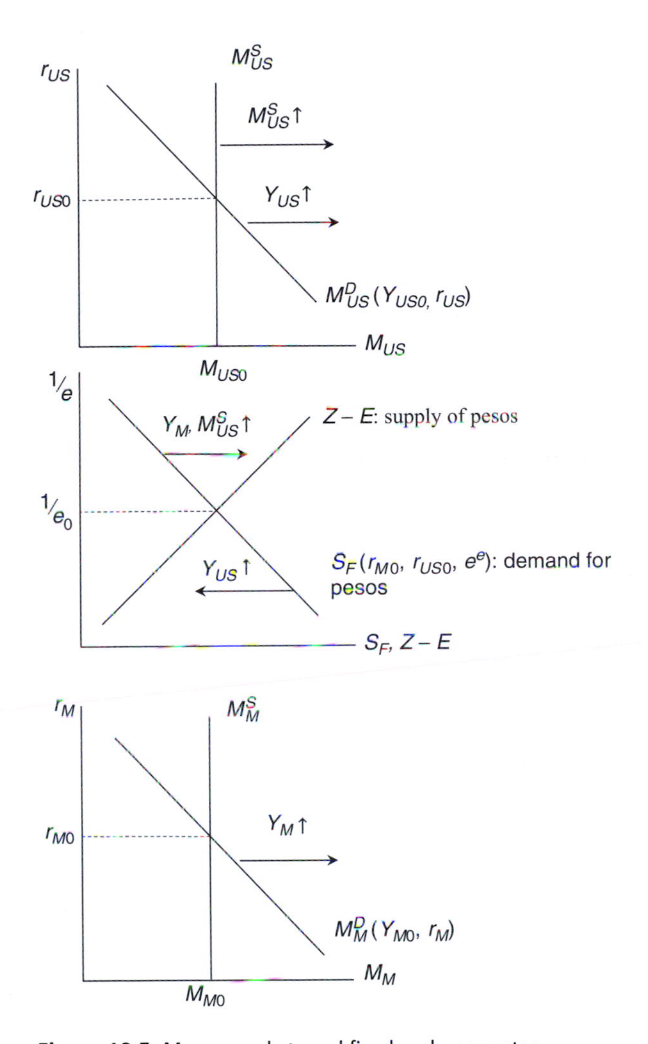

Figure 18.5 Money markets and fixed exchange rates

Second, let us suppose that income in the United States (Y_{US}) increased. What would be the implication of this change? An increase in income in the United States would tend to increase the demand for US dollars. This would shift the US money demand curve in Figure 18.5 to the right, which, in turn, would tend to increase r_{US}. This would shift the demand for pesos line to the left in the center diagram, decreasing the value of the peso. In order to prevent this depreciation, the central bank would need to decrease the supply of pesos, buying them in the peso market. This will shift the M_M^S curve to the left until r_M increases to match the increase in r_{US}. This is the only way to maintain e at e_0.

Finally, let us consider an increase in money supply in the United States. An increase in M_{US}^S would decrease r_{US}. Just like the increase in Mexican income, this would lead to an increase in the value of the peso. In order to prevent this appreciation, the Mexican central bank would need to increase the supply of pesos, selling them in the peso market. This will shift the M_M^S curve to the right until r_M falls enough to meet the fall in r_{US}. This policy response will maintain e at e_0.

In each of the above three cases, the Mexican government must stand ready to buy and sell pesos at e_0 to meet any excess supply or demand for pesos and, thereby, maintain the fixed exchange rate. M_M^S is used to ensure that the exchange rate is fixed. Importantly, then, under a fixed exchange rate regime, a country cannot pursue monetary policy independently of the rest of the world, such as with an eye to stabilizing its own macroeconomy. Instead, the monetary policy is committed to keeping the exchange rate fixed. This was *not* the case under the flexible or floating exchange rate policy. Under a flexible exchange rate regime, a country can pursue an independent monetary policy, but it gives up control of the exchange rate. Another way of expressing this is simply to say that *a country can control its interest rate or its exchange rate, but not both.* An integrated international financial system makes controlling both the interest rate and the exchange rate impossible.[18]

[18] This is one reason why some monetarists, such as Milton Friedman, supported the use of flexible exchange rate regimes rather than fixed exchange rate regimes. See Friedman (1953). In more recent decades it has been recognized that a flexible exchange rate regime can leave room for inflation-targeting monetary policy. See Bernanke and Mishkin (1997).

19 The International Monetary System

In the history of global financial arrangements, the year 1941 stands as a turning point. In September of that year the British economist John Maynard Keynes spent "several days of peace writing a heavy memorandum on post-war international currency plans."[1] The result was a proposal for an International Clearing Union (ICU), an idea subsequently taken up by the British Treasury. Three months later, and across the Atlantic, US Treasury official Harry Dexter White wrote a proposal for an International Stabilization Fund (ISF), subsequently embraced wholeheartedly by US Treasury secretary Henry Morgenthau. These two proposals, known as the Keynes Plan and the White Plan, respectively, competed for prominence in the international deliberations over how to reconstitute the institutions of international finance after the end of World War II.

The Keynes Plan and White Plan were taken up at the Bretton Woods Conference in 1944, with the White Plan gaining prominence. The result was the creation of the **International Monetary Fund** (IMF) and the International Bank for Reconstruction and Development (part of the **World Bank** Group). Neither Keynes nor White would live out the decade, both dying of heart attacks while the Fund and Bank were being established.[2]

In Chapter 8, you were introduced to the institutions of international trade embodied in the World Trade Organization. This chapter will introduce you to the international monetary system, including the IMF. The purpose of this chapter is to familiarize you with the basic "rules of the game" in international finance. We begin with a brief history of international monetary arrangements during the twentieth century. This will allow you to place the IMF in the context of recent financial history. Next we will turn to the actual operations of the IMF and the political economy of IMF lending. Finally, we will make a preliminary assessment of the IMF and its role in the world economy. We will take up the controversial role of the IMF in recent financial crises in Chapter 20.

---

[1] Skidelsky (2000: 202–3).

[2] On Keynes' contributions during this period, see Skidelsky (2000). On White, see Skidelsky (2000: chap. 7) and Boughton (1998).

Some Monetary History

Throughout the twentieth century the countries of the world struggled with various arrangements for the conduct of international finance. None of these arrangements proved satisfactory. Over time, international economic policy-makers attempted to set up one system after another, and, in each case, they were overtaken by events. In retrospect, we can see that the international financial system had a dynamic of its own, one much stronger than the institutional scaffolding temporarily built around it. As the 2008 global financial crisis reminded us, this is also no doubt true today. In this section of the chapter, we will briefly review some main events to give you an appreciation of the evolutionary power of international finance and to place the IMF in the context of this dynamic.

The Gold Standards

The decades from 1870 to 1914 were characterized by a highly integrated world economy that was supported by an international financial arrangement known as the **gold standard**. Under the gold standard, each country defined the value of its currency in terms of gold. Most countries also held gold as official reserves. Since the value of each currency was defined in terms of gold, the rates of exchange between the currencies were *fixed*. Thus, the gold standard was one type of fixed exchange rate system.[3] When World War I began, in 1914, the countries involved in that conflict suspended the convertibility of their currencies into gold.[4] After the war there was an attempt to resurrect the gold standard. Success in this endeavor was to prove elusive.

The new gold standard began in 1922 as a result of an economic conference held in Genoa, Italy. It was *different* from the pre-war gold standard, however. There was a gold shortage at the time, and, to address this problem, countries that were not important financial centers did not hold gold reserves. Instead, they held gold-convertible currencies, a practice utilized by a number of countries before the war. For this reason, the new gold standard was known as the **gold exchange standard**.

One goal of the gold exchange standard was to set major rates at their pre-war levels. The most important exchange rate was that of the British pound.

---

[3] As students of the history of economic thought know, the operation of the gold standard was first described by Hume (1924 [1752]). A more modern treatment can be found in McClosky and Zecher (1976). For a complete historical assessment, see Eichengreen (1992).

[4] Eichengreen (2015: 17) notes: "With the outbreak of the World War, government embargoed gold exports. Buying gold where it was cheap and selling it where it was dear had been the mechanism through which exchange rates were held stable. With the embargoes, which effectively suspended gold market transactions, currencies began fluctuating against one another."

Unfortunately, inflation in the United Kingdom had been higher than in the United States, so the pre-war exchange rate was no longer an *equilibrium* real rate. In 1925, and with the support of the US Federal Reserve, it was set to gold at the *overvalued* pre-war rate of US$4.86 per pound.[5] This caused balance of payments problems and market expectations of devaluation. To use the term introduced in Chapter 18, the gold exchange standard lacked *credibility*. At a system-wide level, each major rate was set to gold, ignoring the implied rates between the various currencies. As is often the case, the politics of the day prevailed over economic common sense.

The gold exchange standard thus consisted of a set of *center* countries tied to gold and a set of *periphery* countries holding the center-country currencies as reserves. By 1930 nearly all the countries of the world had joined. The design of the system held within it a significant *incentive problem* for the periphery countries, however. Suppose a periphery country expected that the foreign currency it held as reserves was going to be devalued against gold. It would be in the interest of this country to *sell* its reserves *before* the devaluation took place, so as to preserve the value of its total reserves. This, in turn, would put even greater pressure on the value of the center currency.

As mentioned above, the British pound was set at an overvalued rate. In 1931 there was a run on the pound, and this forced Britain to cut the pound's tie to gold. As the 1930s continued, a system of separate currency areas evolved, and there was a combination of both fixed and floating rates. Austria and Germany left the gold standard system in 1931, the United States in 1933, and France in 1936.

Many other countries subsequently cut their ties to gold. By 1937 no countries remained on the gold exchange standard. Therefore, the gold exchange standard was not an overall success. Some international economists (most notably Eichengreen, 1992) have even seen it as a major contributor to the Great Depression.[6] During the unraveling of the system, countries engaged in a game of

---

[5] Keynes opposed this policy strenuously, famously calling the gold standard a "barbarous relic." In the same essay (1963 [1923]: 211–12), he stated: "[Since] I feel no confidence that an old-fashioned gold standard will even give us the modicum of stability that it used to give, I reject the policy of restoring the gold standard on pre-war lines." His observations were to prove prescient.

[6] Eichengreen (1992: xi) states: "The gold standard of the 1920s set the stage for the Depression of the 1930s by heightening the fragility of the international financial system. The gold standard was the mechanism transmitting the destabilizing impulse from the United States to the rest of the world. The gold standard magnified that initial destabilizing shock. It was the principal obstacle to offsetting action. It was the binding constraint preventing policymakers from averting the failure of banks and containing the spread of financial panic." Eichengreen (2015: 13) also notes: "Freeing themselves from the gold standard...enabled countries to regain control of their destinies. It allowed them to print money where money was scarce. It allowed them to support their banking systems. It allowed them to take other steps to end the Depression."

competitive devaluation, each trying to gain greater export competitiveness over other countries. This breakdown in international economic cooperation helped to fuel the rise of nationalism that eventually erupted in World War II.

The Bretton Woods System

During World War II the United States and Britain began to plan for the post-war economic system. As mentioned above, in the United States the planning occurred at the US Treasury under the direction of Harry Dexter White, while John Maynard Keynes took the lead at the British Treasury.[7] These individuals understood the contribution of the previous breakdown in the international economic system to the war, and they hoped to avoid the same mistakes that were made after World War I. In addition, however, White and Keynes were fighting for the *relative positions* of the countries they represented. In this competition, White and the US Treasury had the upper hand, and White largely got his way during the 1944 Bretton Woods Conference.

The conference produced a plan for a new international financial system, which became known as the **Bretton Woods system**. The essence of the system was an **adjustable gold peg**.[8] Under the Bretton Woods system, the US dollar was to be pegged to gold at US$35 per ounce. The other countries of the world were to peg to the US dollar or directly to gold. This placed the dollar at the center of the new international financial system, a role envisaged by White and the US Treasury. The currency pegs were to remain fixed except under conditions that were termed "fundamental disequilibrium," a concept that was never carefully defined.

Views of the Bretton Woods Conference

The Bretton Woods Conference of July 1944 was unusual in the breadth of its international representation and the scope of its work. The name of the conference derived from the New Hampshire resort where it took place. The 730 delegates from 45 countries were housed at the Mount Washington Hotel from July 1 to 22, with the British and US delegations having begun work on June 23. Here are a few views of this extraordinary gathering.

---

[7] James (1996: 33) reports: "Already weeks after the outbreak of war in 1939, Keynes was sending memoranda to President Roosevelt that included suggestions on how the postwar reconstruction of Europe might be handled better than after 1918."

[8] Keynes and the British government had advocated flexible rates, and White and the US government had advocated fixed rates. The adjustable peg was the compromise between these two positions. See, for example, Eichengreen (2008: chap. 4).

Views of the Bretton Woods Conference (cont.)

Financial historian Harold James (1996: 53–4) writes: "The Bretton Woods conference wove consensus, harmony, and agreement as if under a magician's spell.... The participants met almost around the clock in overcrowded and acoustically unsuitable hotel rooms. Gradually exhaustion set in. Keynes wrote: 'We have all of us worked every minute of our waking hours practically without intermission for what is now four weeks.... At one moment Harry White told me that at last even he was all in, not having been in bed for more than five hours a night for four consecutive weeks.' On July 19, 1944, Keynes collapsed with a mild heart attack."

Keynes' biographer, Robert Skidelsky (2000: 348), writes: "At Bretton Woods, the problems of peace were discussed in the shadow of war about to end. It was a war, moreover, which the Soviet Union was doing most to win, and this was reflected in the number of honorary posts its delegates were assigned. It was the first time Keynes had encountered the Commissars *en masse* since his visits to the Soviet Union in the late 1920s. He used the opportunity to try to persuade them to send the Bolshoi Ballet over to Covent Garden the following year. The Foreign Office took up the idea, but nothing came of it. There would be no Russian ballet in London till 1956. The reason, it turned out, was that the Russians had a well-founded fear of defections."

And, finally, Keynes' wife, Lydia Keynes (née Lapakova), a former Russian ballerina herself, writes (Skidelsky, 2000: 347): "The taps run all day, the windows do not close or open, the pipes mend and unmend and no one can get anywhere."

Sources: James (1996) and Skidelsky (2000).

The Bretton Woods system came into being in 1946. Like the gold exchange standard, it contained the seeds of its own demise. Problems became apparent even by the end of the 1940s, in the form of the growing non-official balance of payments deficits of the United States. These deficits reflected official reserve transactions in support of expanding global dollar reserves.[9] Although the Bretton Woods agreements allowed par values to be defined either in gold or dollar terms, in practice the dollar became the central measure of value. Consequently, the adjustable gold peg became a de facto dollar standard.

---

[9] These official sales of dollars by the United States to the central banks of the world (a US official reserve surplus) had its counterpart in a deficit on the sum of the US current and non-official capital accounts. See Chapter 14, especially Equation 14.7a.

The problems with the Bretton Woods system were recognized by Robert Triffin (1960) in the form of what became known as the **Triffin dilemma**. The Triffin dilemma can be conceived of as a contradiction between the requirements of international *liquidity* and those of international *confidence*. With the dollar being the centerpiece of the system, international liquidity required a continual increase in the holdings of dollars as reserve assets. As dollar holdings of central banks expanded relative to US official holdings of gold, however, international confidence would suffer. Could the United States back up an ever-expanding supply of dollars with a relatively constant amount of gold holdings? "No," said Triffin. The requirements of international liquidity would compromise the requirements of international confidence, and a crisis was inevitable. This process is represented in Figure 19.1.

The first sign of trouble occurred in 1960, when the London gold market price rose above US$35 to US$40 an ounce. At this time there were calls for a change in the gold–dollar parity, but in early 1961 the newly elected administration of President Kennedy pledged to maintain the US$35 per ounce convertibility. The United States and other European countries set up a *gold pool*, in which their central banks would buy and sell gold to support the US$35 price. Nevertheless, at the 1964 annual IMF meeting in Tokyo representatives began to talk publicly about potential reforms in the international financial system, and in 1965 the US Treasury announced that it was ready to join in these discussions. Further, the adamant stance of the Kennedy administration gave way (after Kennedy's assassination) to a somewhat more flexible posture in the administration of President Johnson. Meanwhile, the British pound was under pressure to devalue against the dollar, and, as it happened, the pound was devalued in late 1967.

After the devaluation of the pound, President Johnson issued a statement recommitting the United States to the US$35 per ounce gold price. In early 1968, however, the rush began. The London gold market was closed in mid-March, and central bank officials from around the world met at the Federal Reserve Board in Washington, DC. At this meeting, a two-tiered system was constructed. Official foreign exchange transactions were to be conducted at the old rate of US$35 per ounce. The rate in the London gold market, however, was allowed to float freely.

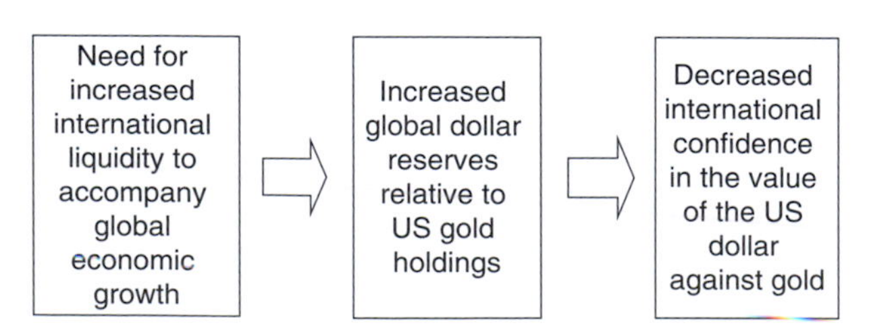

Figure 19.1 The Triffin dilemma

The London price reached a high of US$43 in 1969 and then returned to US$35 in 1970. The Triffin dilemma was temporarily avoided.[10]

The Triffin dilemma soon reasserted itself, though. In early 1970 Canada let its dollar begin to float. Germany and a few other European countries joined Canada in 1971. In August 1971 the US president, Richard Nixon, closed the US government "gold window," effectively suspending the convertibility of the US dollar into gold. With this announcement, the Bretton Woods adjustable peg system came to an end. This date remains a milestone in international financial history. What followed was a period of experimentation, often referred to as the "non-system," that continues to the present day.

The Non-System

In late 1971 a two-day conference began in Washington, DC, that came to be known as the **Smithsonian Conference**. At this conference, several countries revalued their currencies against the dollar, and the gold price was raised to US$38 per ounce. Canada maintained its floating rate. The fact that it took the August closing of the gold window, a period of managed floating, and an international conference to introduce a small amount of adjustment into the adjustable peg system speaks to the failure of the Bretton Woods agreement as an effective system.

In fact, the Smithsonian Conference largely *ignored* the entire adjustment question and the Triffin dilemma, and this quickly became apparent. In early 1973 the United States announced a second devaluation of the dollar against gold, to US$42. Within a short while the Japanese yen, the Swiss franc, the Italian lira, the British pound, the Canadian dollar, the German mark, the French franc, the Dutch guilder, the Belgian franc, and the Danish krone were all floating. The members of the IMF found themselves in violation of the Bretton Woods Articles of Agreement. The international financial system had crossed a threshold, though this was not fully appreciated at the time.[11]

During 1974 and 1975 the countries of the world went through nearly continuous consultation and disagreement in the process of accommodating their thinking to the new reality of floating rates.[12] The French government, in particular, was skeptical of the long-term viability of the floating regime, whereas the US government appeared reconciled to it. In late 1975 the heads of state or

---

[10] Eichengreen (2008: 127) writes: "The array of devices to which the Kennedy and Johnson administrations resorted became positively embarrassing. They acknowledged the severity of the dollar problem while displaying a willingness to address only the symptoms, not the causes. Dealing with the causes required reforming the international system in a way that diminished the dollar's reserve-currency role, something the United States was still unwilling to contemplate."

[11] For example, Solomon (1977: 267) notes: "The move to generalized floating in...1973 was widely regarded as a temporary departure from normality." It was decidedly not temporary.

[12] See Solomon (1977) for a book-length discussion of these years.

heads of government of the United States, France, Germany, the United Kingdom, Italy, and Japan met at the Château de Rambouillet, outside Paris. In a declaration, these leaders proposed an amendment to the IMF's Articles of Agreement, restricting allowable exchange rate arrangements to: (1) currencies fixed to anything *other than gold*; (2) cooperative arrangements for managed values between countries; and (3) floating. In early 1976 the IMF's Articles of Agreement were indeed amended to reflect the Rambouillet Declaration, institutionalizing what had, in fact, already occurred. The monetary "non-system" had come into being.

The Operation of the IMF

The IMF is an international financial organization comprised, at the time of this writing, of 189 member countries. Its purposes, as stipulated in its Articles of Agreement, are:

1. to promote international monetary cooperation
2. to facilitate the expansion of international trade
3. to promote exchange stability and a multilateral system of payments
4. to make temporary financial resources available to members under "adequate safeguards"
5. to reduce the duration and degree of international payments imbalances

The administrative structure of the IMF includes a board of governors (the primary decision-making body), an executive board (handling day-to-day business), and a managing director (traditionally a European) who chairs the executive board and conducts the IMF's business.[13] There are also a set of deputy managing directors.[14]

The IMF can be thought of as a sort of *global credit union*, in which member-country shares are determined by a *quota system*. Members' quotas are their *paid subscriptions* to the IMF and roughly reflect their relative sizes in the world economy.[15] The higher a member's quota, the more it can borrow, and the greater its voting power.[16] A sense of quota allocations can be seen in Figure 19.2.

---

[13] The president of the World Bank is traditionally a US citizen.

[14] For more details, see www.imf.org/external/np/obp/orgcht.htm/external/np/obp/orgcht.htm.

[15] Quotas are calculated as a weighted average of gross domestic product, economic openness, economic variability, and foreign reserves. They are paid in terms of a special IMF currency known as special drawing rights (SDRs), other members' currencies, and countries' own currencies.

[16] Major decisions (including changing the way quotas are determined) require an 85 percent majority. Some observers argue that this gives the United States an effective veto power in these cases. The same can be said about the European Union if its member countries vote as a block.

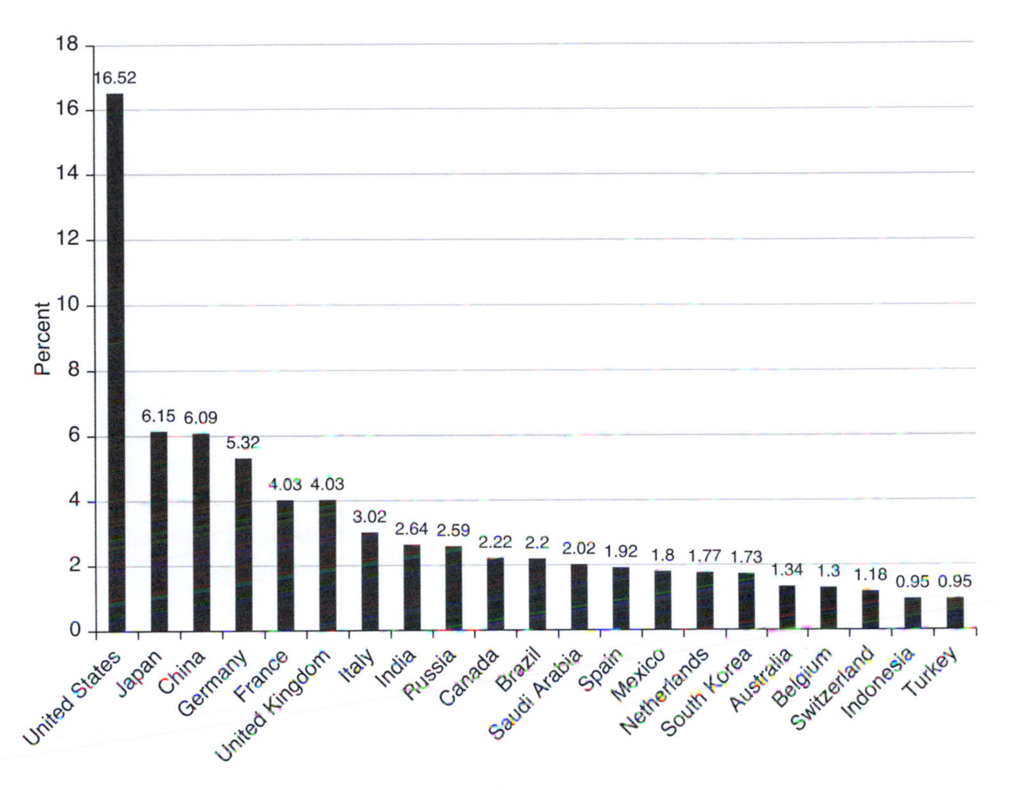

Figure 19.2 IMF quotas, 2019 (percentage shares above 0.90)
Source: www.imf.org.

In times of difficulty, an IMF member country gains access to the Fund's resources through a somewhat complex borrowing process. In the IMF's own words, its lending "aims to give countries breathing room to implement adjustment policies in an orderly manner, which will restore conditions for a stable economy and sustainable growth."[17] In many cases, however, it is not always that simple.

The IMF provides resources for adjustment through various "lending instruments," summarized in Table 19.1. Historically, the most important of these instruments have been Stand-By Arrangements (SBAs), whose purpose is to "give breathing room" in the case of *short-term* balance of payments difficulties. For low-income members, the equivalent instrument is the Standby Credit Facility (SCF). In the case of *medium-term* issues, the SBA equivalent is the Extended Fund Facility (EFF), and, for low-income members, the Extended Credit Facility (ECF). There are other instruments as well, presented in Table 19.1, particularly for rapid financing in the face of emergencies.

[17] See www.imf.org/en/About/Factsheets/IMF-Lending.

Table 19.1 IMF lending instruments

Category	Name	Purpose
Standard	Stand-By Arrangement (SBA)	The standard IMF credit facility for *short-term* balance of payments adjustment in *middle-income* countries.
Special non-concessional	Extended Fund Facility (EFF)	For balance of payments adjustment for *medium-term* balance of payments adjustment in *middle-income* countries.
Special non-concessional	Flexible Credit Line (FCL)	For balance of payments adjustment in periods of heightened risk for *middle-income* countries with strong fundamentals.
Special non-concessional	Rapid Financing Instrument (RFI)	For rapid assistance to *middle-income* countries with urgent needs in cases such as commodity price shocks, natural disasters, and conflict.
Special concessional	Standby Credit Facility (SCF)	Equivalent to the SBA but for *short-term* balance of payments adjustment in *low-income* countries on *concessional* terms.
Special concessional	Extended Credit Facility (ECF)	Equivalent to the EFF but for *medium-term* balance of payments adjustment in *low-income* countries on *concessional* terms.
Special concessional	Rapid Credit Facility (RCF)	For rapid assistance to *low-income* countries with urgent needs in cases such as commodity price shocks, natural disasters, and conflict.

Source: www.imf.org.

Under normal circumstances, the amount of resources an IMF member can access is determined by its quota amount. Through a complex process involving lending "tranches," a member can borrow up to 145 percent of its quota annually and 435 percent cumulatively. We shall see, however, that, in recent years, this limit has been exceeded. Further, nothing comes for free, and a country requesting access to IMF resources has to sign a *letter of intent* committing itself to a certain set of *policy changes*. These policy changes are known as *conditionalities*, and are described in the accompanying box. More generally, "policy conditionality," or just **conditionality**, is a central feature of both IMF and World Bank lending. Whether a country meets the conditionalities of a lending arrangement is determined by a process of IMF *monitoring*.

In historical perspective, the above lending arrangements reflect the dominance achieved by the White Plan over the Keynes Plan at the Bretton Woods Conference. The Keynes Plan had an ingenious feature in that it penalized both creditors and debtors symmetrically. This spread international adjustment responsibilities between countries with balance of payments surpluses *and* countries with balance of payments deficits *alike*. This feature was not adopted in the final agreements, global adjustment being the responsibility of the deficit countries.[18] As evidenced by the Keynes Plan, this structure is not the only possible one, but it is the one the world has lived with since the Bretton Woods Conference.

This discussion has focused on the disbursement of IMF resources, but where do the resources come from? The first and most traditional source of IMF resources is the quotas themselves. Additionally, the IMF can sell small portions of its large holdings of gold. More importantly, the IMF has standing bilateral and multilateral borrowing arrangements. The multilateral borrowing arrangements are more significant and are in the form of the General Arrangements to Borrow (GAB) and the New Arrangements to Borrow (NAB). These arrangements were significantly increased by major players in 2009 to set the Fund's total resources to US$750 billion. There have been ongoing long-term discussions to increase this further to US$1 trillion.[19]

IMF Conditionality

As previously stated, access to IMF resources for balance of payments adjustment requires signing on to policy conditionality. Among international economists, there is disagreement as to *what* and *how many* conditions should be attached to IMF lending. Before the Asian financial crisis, discussed in Chapter 20, the IMF tended to impose many conditions. After that crisis there was a decision to use a more focused approach. A 2015 SBA with Ukraine included a condition to "strengthen the rule of law," however—an institutional element that can take a very long time to achieve.

In theory, conditionality is supposed to be an expression of a country's "ownership" of the requisite policy changes. But, if the country really "owns" them, there would be no need to impose conditionality. And, if there is a need to impose conditionality, then the country does not own them. This confusion was identified by Drazen (2002) and Eichengreen and Woods (2015), and exists to this day.

[18] See, for example, Buira (1995).

[19] See *Financial Times* (2010).

IMF Conditionality (cont.)

But what of the conditions themselves? They can take different forms, including prior actions, quantitative performance criteria (QPCs), and structural benchmarks. Prior actions consist of measures the borrowing country agrees to *before* loan approval. According to Copelovitch (2010: 18), "Prior actions are intended as a signal to the IMF and private markets that a borrower has made a firm 'upfront' or *ex ante* commitment to reforming its economic policies and resolving its financial problems."

QPCs are measurable conditions that need to be met before an approved amount of credit is actually disbursed. According to the IMF, QPCs can include "macroeconomic variables under the control of the authorities, such as some monetary and credit aggregates, international reserves, fiscal balances, or external borrowing." The number and type of QPCs imposed by the IMF have varied widely over time.

Finally, structural benchmarks are less quantifiable measures that the IMF considers to be "critical to achieve program goals." These can address financial sector operations, public financial management, the privatization of state-owned enterprises, and any other policy realms deemed important by IMF staff.

In recent years the IMF has suggested that it has cut back on conditionality requirements. Although this seems to have been the case in the years leading up to the 2008 GFC, that trend was subsequently reversed. IMF conditionality is still very much part of global financial policy, perhaps because the diversity of development trajectories among the world's economies has held back a fundamental rethinking of the content of conditionality.

The economic and political analysis of the extent and qualities of IMF conditionality is an ongoing enterprise, and is part of the analysis of the political economy of IMF lending discussed below. They continue to be controversial.

Sources: Copelovitch (2010), Drazen (2002), Eichengreen and Woods (2015), Güven (2012), International Monetary Fund (2010), and Kentikelenis, Stubbs, and King (2016).

A History of IMF Operations

In its initial years the IMF was nearly irrelevant, being pushed aside by the United States' own programs for post-war European reconstruction via the European Recovery Program and the Organisation for European Economic Co-operation (see accompanying box). The IMF did play an advisory role to a series of European devaluations, beginning in 1949, in the face of "fundamental disequilibria."

Nevertheless, the *Financial Times* described the IMF in early 1956 as a "white elephant." The claim proved to be ill-timed. The Suez crisis of that year forced Britain to draw on its reserve and first credit tranches; Japan drew on its reserve tranche in 1957; and from late 1956 through 1958 the IMF was involved in the policies that led to the convertibility of both the British pound and the French franc. These successes were followed by a general increase in quotas of 50 percent in 1959. During these few years SBAs (described above) were made with many other countries, including many low- and middle-income countries. The IMF had become an active institution with an increased membership as a result of decolonization.

Limited Liquidity in the Early Years

One of the important functions of the IMF envisioned by its Bretton Woods originators was the provision of global liquidity. The Keynes Plan envisaged US$23 billion in total "drawing rights." The White Plan proposed total drawing rights of only US$5 billion, however. The resulting Articles of Agreement total set drawing rights at US$8.8 billion. By the time the IMF opened for business, in 1947, postwar Europe's combined trade deficit was US$7.5 billion. As noted by Walter and Sen (2009: 117), "By late 1947 it had become clear that the IMF's total resources were wholly inadequate." Given the size of Europe's deficit in relationship to the IMF's resources, the United States had to step in to fill the gap. Through 1951 and in response to the emerging Cold War, it provided US$13 billion in Marshall Plan aid to Europe, thus significantly supplementing IMF resources. Despite this infusion of liquidity, which amounted to more than four times the total drawing rights of Europe, a number of European currencies had to be devalued in 1949.

Sources: Eichengreen (2008) and Walter and Sen (2009).

As described above, the Bretton Woods system was one in which the US dollar played the role of major reserve asset for member countries. We also described the difficulty of this arrangement, which first erupted on the London gold market in 1960. This "dollar problem," embodied in the Triffin dilemma (Figure 19.1), did not escape the notice of the IMF. Concerned about the United States' ability to defend the dollar and other major industrialized countries' abilities to maintain their parities, the IMF introduced the above-mentioned GAB in 1962.

By 1965, facing the Triffin dilemma, the United States was in a position such that it faced two unappealing options: reducing the world supply of dollars, to enhance international confidence but reduce international liquidity; or expanding the world supply of dollars, to enhance international liquidity but reduce international confidence. Other countries (particularly France) were objecting to the central role of the United States altogether. But where was the world to turn for a reserve asset? Back to gold? Between the 1964 and 1968 annual meetings of the IMF, discussions took place between major players, and the result was the creation of an entirely new reserve asset to supplement both gold and the dollar. This reserve asset was known as a **special drawing right**, or SDR.

The SDR was "the first international currency to be created in the manner of a national paper currency—purely through a series of legal obligations to accept it on the part of members of the system" (James, 1996: 171), in the way envisioned by the Keynes Plan. It came into being in 1969. Ironically, given its intended use to supplement gold and the dollar, its value was set in terms of gold at a value identical to the dollar (US$35 per ounce). In 1971, when the United States broke the gold–dollar link, the SDR was redefined in terms of a basket of five currencies: the US dollar, the British pound, the West German mark, the Japanese yen, and the French franc. It is currently defined in terms of the US dollar, the British pound, the Japanese yen, and the euro and comprises the unit of account of the IMF.

Oil Shocks, Crises, and Adjustment

The oil price increases of 1973/74 caused substantial balance of payments difficulties for many countries of the world, and, in response, the IMF established special oil facilities. Using these, the IMF acted as an intermediary, borrowing the funds from oil-producing countries and lending them to oil-importing countries. Despite the presence of these facilities, the bulk of oil-producing-country revenues were "recycled" to other countries by the *commercial* banking system. Recycled petrodollars allowed oil-importing countries to avoid IMF conditionality. Further, the commercial loans were often at negative real (inflation-adjusted) interest rates, and were thus very attractive to borrowing countries.

Beginning in 1976 the IMF began to sound warnings about the sustainability of LMIC borrowing from the commercial banking system. Banks reacted with hostility to these warnings, arguing that the Fund had no place interfering with private transactions. As we shall see below, however, the Fund proved prescient on this issue.

The 1980s began with a significant increase in real interest rates and a significant decline in non-oil commodity prices. This increased the cost of borrowing and reduced export revenues. In 1982 the IMF calculated that US banking system outstanding loans to Latin America represented approximately 100 percent of total bank capital: the IMF's concern in the latter half of the 1970s about the sustainability of LMIC borrowing had been justified. In 1982, in the face of capital flight, Mexico announced that it would stop servicing its foreign-currency debt and nationalized its banking system.[20] Negotiations took place between the Mexican government, the IMF, the US Federal Reserve Bank, and an Advisory Committee of New York banks. An agreement was established that involved the New York banks lending *additional* funds to Mexico. The New York banks complied under threat of additional regulation to address their inability to assess country risk.

The year 1982 also found debt crises beginning in Argentina and Brazil.[21] These and the Mexican crisis were addressed by the IMF via a number SBAs and other special facilities throughout the 1980s, many of which fell apart and had to be renegotiated. As in the Mexican case, the New York banks had to be cajoled into releasing more funds. More systematically, in 1986 and 1987 the IMF introduced new borrowing facilities, which raised the total credit ceiling for member countries to 250 percent of quota.

Despite these efforts, international commercial banks began to withdraw credit from many LMICs. The debt crisis became global. Within a few years of the outbreak of the crises the phenomenon of *net capital outflows* appeared. The resulting capital/financial account deficits had their counterparts in current account surpluses: the LMICs were using trade surpluses to finance debt repayment. Poverty increased substantially, and many LMICs, particularly in Latin America and Africa, entered what came to be known as the *lost decade*. It also began a new policy era for the IMF and World Bank, known as the **Washington Consensus**, and discussed in the accompanying box.

The Washington Consensus

In 1990 John Williamson of the Institute for International Economics (now the Peterson Institute for International Economics) introduced a new term into the international economic policy lexicon. The new term was "Washington Consensus." At the time, he was referring to the "lowest common denominator" of policy advice being offered by the World Bank and the IMF. According to Williamson, this common denominator consisted of ten policy components:

1. fiscal discipline

---

[20] The lack of foresight of the financial sector with regard to this event was noted by Krugman (1999: 41, emphasis in original): "As late as July 1982 the yield on Mexican bonds was slightly *less* than that on those of presumably safe borrowers like the World Bank, indicating that investors regarded the risk that Mexico would fail to pay on time as negligible."

[21] In the case of Argentina, the crisis ensued from an overvalued exchange rate, used as a "nominal anchor" to curb inflationary expenditures. In Brazil, rates of devaluation did not keep up with rates of inflation, causing an overvalued real exchange rate.

The Washington Consensus (cont.)

2. a redirection of government expenditures to primary health care, primary education, and infrastructure
3. tax reform
4. financial and interest rate liberalization
5. competitive exchange rates
6. trade liberalization
7. liberalization of foreign direct investment
8. privatization
9. deregulation
10. secure property rights

Since 1990 the term "Washington Consensus" has taken on a slightly different meaning. It has come to stand for "market fundamentalism," "neoliberal obsession," or "global laissez-faire." It has also become the target of many participants in the anti-globalization movement, as well as of many in the global non-governmental organization (NGO) community. Interestingly, Williamson himself is in disagreement with "market fundamentalism," stating (2000: 357): "I would not subscribe to the view that such policies offer an effective agenda for reducing poverty." What, then, is Williamson's position?

First, Williamson has repudiated the financial and interest rate liberalization component included in the above list, recognizing that such liberalization can contribute to financial instability. Second, Williamson is opposed to the across-the-board liberalization of capital accounts. Third, Williamson opposes both the purely flexible exchange rate regimes and currency boards (discussed in Chapter 18), both (intriguingly) often advocated by supporters of "market fundamentalism." Instead, he supports exchange rate target zones.

Fourth, regarding the components of privatization and deregulation, his policy proposals are rather nuanced. He favors privatization only if it is carried out in a manner that prevents the transfer of formerly state-owned enterprises to a narrow group of elites, and is in favor of many types of government regulation. He calls only for the deregulation of entry and exit barriers, not the "roll-back of the state" called for by many market fundamentalists.

As time went on, Washington Consensus thinking began to move into what were known as "second-generation reforms." Although the lists here varied, Rodrik (2007) identifies ten further elements: corporate governance, anti-corruption policies, flexible labor markets, adherence to World Trade Organization disciplines (discussed in Chapter 8), adherence to international financial codes and standards,

The Washington Consensus (cont.)

capital account liberalization (discussed in Chapter 15), non-intermediate exchange rate regimes (fixed or floating but not adjustable), independent central banks, social safety nets, and targeted poverty reduction. Thus, with the addition of these second-generation reforms, the to-do list for World Bank borrowers tended to double in size.

To put it mildly, doubts about the Washington Consensus quickly arose (e.g. Naím, 2000). It would be fair to say that many development economists (and some international economists) found it to be *lacking as a development strategy*. Even among international economists, there is disagreement about its appropriateness as a guide to effective policy. This became apparent when some countries such as China, Vietnam, and Bangladesh began to achieve substantial poverty reduction without having ticked off many of the boxes on the Washington Consensus list. For example, one World Bank official commented to me some years ago, "Our two new stars [China and Vietnam] are both communist dictatorships." That is something for Washington Consensus advocates to ponder.

Sources: Naím (2000), Rodrik (2007), and Williamson (1990; 2000).

Starting in the 1990s, private capital began to flow into LMICs in the form of foreign direct investment, portfolio investment, and commercial bank lending. The lost decade remained lost, however. Furthermore, a number of highly indebted countries began to show increasing levels of unpaid IMF obligations. In 1992 a Third Amendment to the Articles of Agreement allowed for the suspension of voting rights in the face of large unpaid obligations. This was hardly a sign of a well-functioning system of international adjustment.

Mexico underwent a second crisis in late 1994 and early 1995 (to be discussed in Chapter 20). In this instance, the IMF became involved after the US Treasury made its own commitments. There were controversies within the executive board with regard to the IMF loan package, the largest to that date, but the United States was able to apply pressure to push the package through.[22] Then, in 1997, crises struck a number of Asian countries, most notably Thailand, Indonesia, South Korea, and Malaysia (also to be discussed in Chapter 20). In each of these cases, sharp depreciations of the currencies resulted. In the cases of Thailand, Indonesia, and South Korea, the IMF played substantial and controversial roles in addressing

[22] See the detailed analysis of this in Copelovitch (2010: chap. 4).

the crises. During the Asian financial crisis, questions were raised about the appropriateness of the IMF's response and its advocacy of liberalizing capital accounts in the run-up to the crisis (discussed in Chapter 15).[23]

The Russian economy was also hit by a crisis in 1998, and the IMF responded. This was in the wake of "Western" economic and financial support (including from the IMF after Russia became a full member in 1992) that went back to the late 1980s. The purpose of this support had been to facilitate the transition in Russia from a communist system to a market democracy (a fool's errand, in the light of subsequent decades). The IMF had begun large-scale lending in 1992 to support Russia through an earlier crisis and to support the "reformers" in the new government that had formed in 1991.

The year 1995 found the IMF providing one of its largest loans ever to support the Russian economy. Although 1997 initially appeared to be a positive one for the Russian economy, oil prices and government revenues began to fall, the Asian crisis hit, and the government's debt service responsibilities began to exceed its resources. Foreign reserves began to fall precipitously, and the IMF was required to provide another large package, drawing on the GAB for the first time since 1978. That was not enough, and a full-fledged banking and currency crisis ensued, with a significant devaluation of the ruble.[24]

In 1998 the IMF also put together a package to support the Brazilian currency, the real, in order to attempt to prevent the Asian and Russian crises from spreading to Latin America. Despite these arrangements, Brazil was forced to devalue the real in 1999 (see box in Chapter 18). In 2001 a currency board crisis in Argentina occurred despite IMF involvement, which resulted in an economic catastrophe for the country (discussed in Chapter 18). Although the IMF was initially skeptical of this exchange rate regime, it later became involved in supporting it. Some observers (such as Eichengreen, 2008) suggested that the IMF should have been more active in helping Argentina plot an exit strategy from this exchange rate arrangement rather than attempting to support it.[25]

---

[23] The IMF first deputy managing director at that time, Stanley Fischer, was a particularly emphatic advocate of capital account liberalization, but he was forced to curtail his advocacy after the Asian crisis. For the advocacy position, see Fischer (1998). For an empirical analysis, see Joyce and Noy (2008).

[24] See Gaidar (1997). The IMF's role in Russia came under severe criticism. For example, Gould-Davies and Woods (1999: 19) conclude that "the Fund failed on two counts: both in the narrower and immediate aim to stabilize, and in the long-term goal of fostering the right conditions for reform in Russia."

[25] Eichengreen (2008: 207) writes: "The IMF's failure to push harder for modification of this rigid currency regime is harder to justify. The Fund had seen hard pegs come to grief in other countries. Unlike [other] cases..., it had programs with Argentina throughout this period. It was in continuous contact with the authorities and possessed detailed knowledge of their problems.... But it failed to push for a change in the regime while there was still time."

The IMF in Ethiopia

In 1996 the IMF announced a new, three-year loan to Ethiopia under its Enhanced Structural Adjustment Facility (ESAF). As part of this package, objectives were set for the period from 1997 to 1999 in the areas of real GDP growth, the inflation rate, the current account deficit, and gross official foreign reserves. The second tranche of the loan was never delivered. According to the IMF, "the midterm review...could not be completed." Behind the scenes, however, conflicts were brewing between the Ethiopian government and the IMF. According to Wade (2001) and Nobel laureate Joseph Stiglitz (2001), one major issue was the early repayment of a US bank loan for aircraft brought to supply Ethiopian Airlines, a successful state-owned enterprise. The government lent Ethiopian Airlines the money to repay the loan. According to Stiglitz (2001: 30), "The transaction made perfect sense. In spite of the solid nature of its collateral (an airplane), Ethiopia was paying a far higher interest rate on its loan than it was receiving on its reserves."

Both the IMF and the US Treasury objected to the nature of the loan repayment. Additionally, according to Wade (2001), the IMF began to insist that Ethiopia begin to liberalize its capital account despite the fact that the IMF's Articles of Agreement do not give it jurisdiction in this area. The Ethiopian government refused, and the IMF canceled the release of the second tranche of the 1997 ESAF. In late 1997 the Ethiopian government contacted Stiglitz, then chief economist at the World Bank. Stiglitz visited Ethiopia, as did the then World Bank president, James Wolfenson, who, in turn, raised Ethiopia's case with the then IMF managing director, Michel Camdessus. As a consequence of these communications, a new ESAF was concluded in 1998.

In response to consultations with Ethiopia, the IMF expressed support for the government's economic management in 1999, but the ESAF was not extended that year. According to Wade (2001: 73), IMF officials "saw themselves as having lost the argument the previous year due to the (illegitimate) intervention of the World Bank. They thought that the government had been let off the hook, and now they were going to bring it to heel by not agreeing to continue Ethiopia's ESAP [Enhanced Structural Adjustment Program] status, even though the conditions had been fulfilled."

A new program was negotiated in 2000 under the Poverty Reduction and Growth Facility (PRGF), but it was delayed until March 2001. In 2002 the IMF called Ethiopia's performance "commendable," and released a second tranche. The 2002 loan was followed by disagreements between the Ethiopian government and the Fund over the privatization of state-owned enterprises, however.

The IMF in Ethiopia (cont.)

Ethiopia and the IMF continued their entanglements and disagreements. Echoing a long-standing criticism of IMF conditionality, for example, concern was raised over the government expenditure limits imposed in these recent loans (e.g. Molina 2009), particularly given the significant poverty prevalent in the country.

Sources: IMF, Stiglitz (2001), Wade (2001), and Molina (2009).

Recent Events

The early 2000s found the IMF sinking into irrelevance. As can be seen in Figure 19.3, the number of new arrangements the IMF concluded held fairly steady between 1990 and 2003. It then began to decline precipitously, to only eight in 2008. This was due to booming private capital markets and the buildup of foreign exchange reserves in some Asian countries, notably China and South Korea. This proved difficult for the IMF, because its operating budget depends on the charges it places on loans.[26] The 2008 GFC gave renewed life to the IMF, however. As can be seen in Figure 19.3, new IMF arrangements finally recovered substantially in 2009 thanks to the GFC. Interestingly, a number of these loans were to European countries (Belarus, Iceland, Hungary, Latvia, Romania, and Ukraine) rather than to traditional LMICs. In the face of the crisis, the IMF changed its posture on capital controls.[27]

As noted by Eichengreen and Woods (2015), the IMF failed to foresee a number of crises (which we will discuss in Chapter 20). These include the US sub-prime mortgage crises of 2007, which morphed into the GFC of 2008; subsequent banking crises in Ireland and Iceland; and a sovereign debt crisis in Greece. Indeed, the IMF was caught unawares by the GFC. The 2007 *World Economic Outlook* (IMF, 2007a), the flagship publication of the IMF, states (xv): "Notwithstanding the recent bout of financial volatility, the world economy still looks well set for robust growth in 2007 and 2008." This proved *not* to be the case! A 2006 Financial System Stability Assessment Report on Ireland states that "the financial system seems well placed to absorb the impact of a downturn in house prices or growth more generally" (IMF, 2006: 5). Wrong again.

[26] See IMF (2007b: 36, fig. 3.1), which shows that the IMF's outstanding loans fell nearly tenfold between 2003 and 2007. Kentikelenis, Stubbs, and King (2016: 544) report: "In the mid-2000s, demand for its services was at historic lows, resulting in staff layoffs and widespread doubts about its future."

[27] We considered the capital control issue in Chapter 15. After the GFC the World Bank also increased its lending.

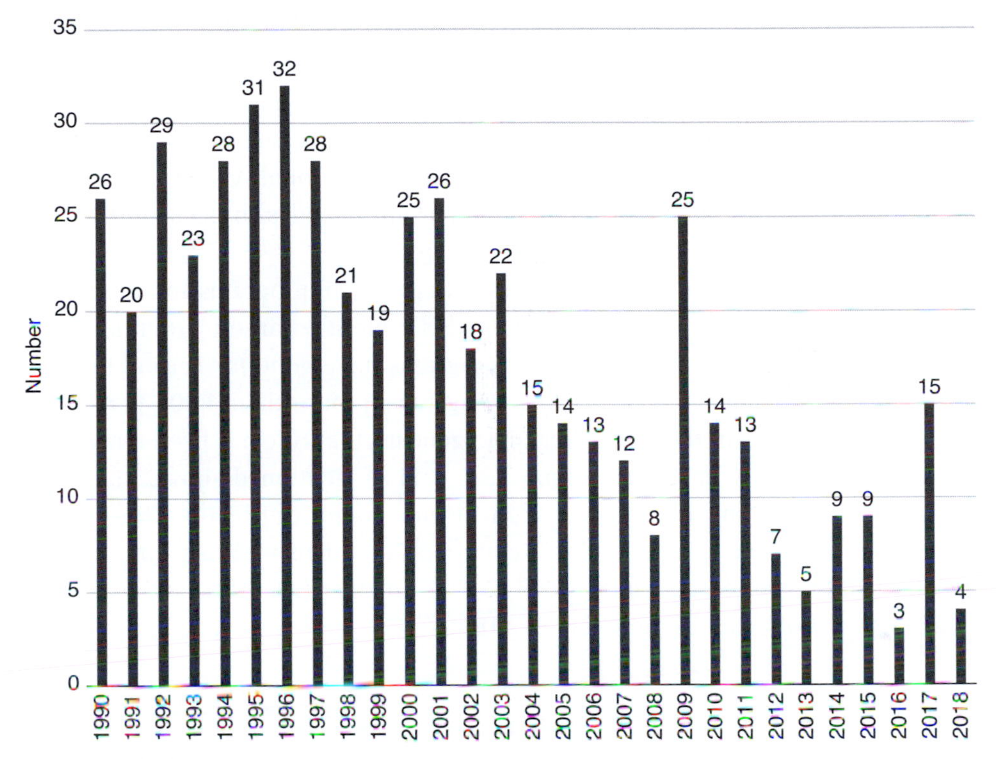

Figure 19.3 New arrangements approved, 1990–2018
Source: IMF Annual Reports.

In the case of Greece's sovereign debt crisis, it appears that the IMF waited too long to suggest the option of debt restructuring. As noted by Eichengreen and Woods (2015: 43, emphasis added), "The Fund's decision not to insist on a Greek debt restructuring in 2010 is a widely cited example of what *not* to do." The macroeconomic fundamentals of Greece had been poor beginning in 2001 with its accession to the European Monetary Union, and the crisis had reached a critical phase by mid-2008. Although, in 2010, the IMF was arguing that Greece's debt was sustainable, by 2012 restructuring had become inevitable. In the event, the restructuring that took place was one of the largest in history, calling into question the IMF's judgment.[28]

The year 2008 was also significant for the IMF in that its members agreed to institute a significant quota reform, resulting in the quotas reported in Figure 19.2. This quota reform involved the following elements: a new formula for calculating

[28] See, for example, Arghyrou and Tsoukalas (2011) and Zettelmeyer, Trebesch, and Gulati (2013). Even the IMF (2013: 28) admits that "an upfront debt restructuring would have been better for Greece."

quotas; an additional "ad hoc" quota increases to selected countries that were "underrepresented" in the new quota formula; increasing the number of "basic votes" for low-income countries; and a decision to review quotas at a minimum of every five years. The new quota formula is a weighted average of GDP, economic openness, economic variability, and the level of international reserves. The entire quota reform package is one of the most important changes to occur at the IMF in some time.[29]

Given the above, let us take a look at the largest IMF programs to date. These are listed in Table 19.2. As you can see in this table, the largest programs have been in recent years. Further, the largest programs have gone *far beyond* the formal 435 percent of quota limit on borrowing (up to more than 3,000 percent of quota). It seems that, in the face of real emergencies, that rule has been repeatedly transgressed. It is also apparent in Table 19.2, and as mentioned above, that some of the largest programs have been to high-income countries (Ireland, Greece, and Portugal) rather than to LMICs. Some countries have had multiple large agreements, including Argentina (2000, 2003, 2018), Brazil (1998, 2001, 2002), Turkey (1999, 2002, 2005), and Ukraine (2008, 2010).

Table 19.2 The largest IMF programs, ranked by percentage of quota

Country	Year	Size (US$ billions 2009)	Percentage of quota	Percentage of GDP
Greece	2010	39.1	3,212	13.7
Argentina	2018	57.0	3,083	11.0
Ireland	2010	29.3	2,322	14.2
Portugal	2011	36.3	2,306	15.8
Greece	2012	34.7	2,159	14.7
South Korea	1997	27.3	1,938	3.8
Turkey	1999	25.7	1,560	8.2
Turkey	2002	19.5	1,330	7.1
Romania	2009	17.6	1,111	10.7
Hungary	2008	16.8	1,015	10.8
Brazil	2002	41.7	902	7.0

[29] That said, it is not clear that the 2008 quota reform package addressed the critiques of Bird and Rowlands (2006), who point out that the quotas try to address too many functions at once: resource availability, access to resources, SDR distribution, and voting rights. They state (169–70): "It is difficult to see how current problems can be overcome by simply modifying existing quota formulas. As currently constituted, quotas are being asked to do too much. One instrument will not achieve all the targets that it has been set."

Table 19.2 (cont.)

Country	Year	Size (US$ billions 2009)	Percentage of quota	Percentage of GDP
Ukraine	2008	17.5	802	9.7
Argentina	2000	27.3	800	6.5
Ukraine	2010	15.1	729	11.2
Pakistan	2008	11.5	700	6.7
Turkey	2005	10.7	691	2.0
Mexico	1995	24.3	688	5.3
Indonesia	1997	14.7	557	5.3
Brazil	1998	17.9	480	1.7
Argentina	2003	14.5	424	8.0
Brazil	2001	18.5	400	2.8
Russia	1996	25.0	306	4.9
India	1981	12.1	291	3.0
United Kingdom	1977	11.1	120	1.5

Sources: Adapted from Reinhart and Trebesch (2016) and imf.org.

The Political Economy of IMF Lending

The original conception of IMF lending was quite simple. A country (typically a LMIC) develops balance of payments problems and is forced to approach the IMF for resources. It reluctantly proceeds through the lending process described in this chapter and takes on the associated conditionality conditions required by the IMF. The two relevant variables in the relationship between the member country and the IMF are the value of loans (L) and the number and strength of conditions (C). The member country was conceived of as wanting L to be high and C to be low. The negotiations proceed between the member country and the IMF in the space described in Figure 19.4. Figure 19.4 distinguishes between a "hard bargaining" line on the part of the IMF and a "soft bargaining" line. The former involves a lower level of L for a given level of C.

As Bird and Rowlands (2003) emphasize, seeking loans (L) from the IMF is a political decision on the part of a member country. As emphasized by Joyce (2006) and Bird (2008), member-country governments are continually weighing the perceived (marginal) benefits and costs of being involved in an IMF program. A standard story assumes that a member country would like to be as far as possible to the left of either of these IMF bargaining positions–that is, they would prefer points along the vertical dashed line A than along the vertical dashed line B. This

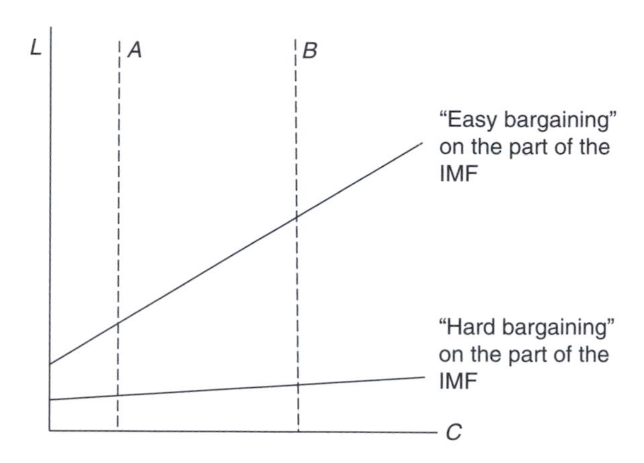

Figure 19.4 IMF lending
Source: Vreeland (2003).

is because there is a sovereignty cost to any level of conditionality (C). There also can be threshold effects, in that, once a member country pays the sovereignty cost of an initial IMF loan and program, it is more likely to do so again.[30]

Subsequent thinking and evidence provided by Vreeland (2003) and Bird and Rowlands (2003) suggests that conditionality impacts might not be fully explained by sovereignty cost considerations. Instead, some member-country governments might actually be interested in some significant amount of conditionality in order to push through reforms in the face of domestic political opposition. These country governments use IMF conditionality as a way of shifting the blame for unpopular reforms outside the country, to the "blue suits" of the IMF bureaucrats. In other words, country governments might prefer points along the vertical dashed line B than along A. Some of these considerations are explained by Bird and Rowlands (2003: 1260) as follows:

> Do governments turn to the IMF in an attempt to import the superior reputation of the IMF for economic management? Are they trying to improve the credibility of policy reform by tying themselves into a Fund supported program, the signing of which signals a commitment to reform? [...] However, it may be unrealistic to view governments as being unified. They may be fragmented and represent fragile coalitions. This creates the possibility that one part of the government may seek to involve the IMF in order to strengthen its hand. Fund involvement may be sought in order to "tip the balance" in favor of economic reform.

Importantly, perceived benefits and costs on the part of a member country can change significantly over time in response to a host of factors. Sometimes these

[30] One way of thinking of this is that the sovereignty cost involves a significant fixed (as opposed to variable) component.

changes will occur in the middle of a loan program and lead a country to fail to meet agreed-to conditionality packages and seek additional tranches or programs. These "implementation failures" are often attributed to a "lack of political will" or "lack of ownership." But behind these failed cases are cost–benefit calculations on the part of the member countries involved, and these are subject to political and economic analysis.[31]

These sorts of considerations give us some insight into the demand side of IMF loans, but what about the supply side? What determines whether the Fund will adopt the "easy bargaining" or "hard bargaining" positions in Figure 19.4? The work of Copelovitch (2010) suggests that one determining factor here is the size and composition of international capital flows. For example, he suggests that, in countries with strong ties to private capital sources such as commercial banks in the G-5 countries (the United States, Japan, Germany, the United Kingdom, and France), the IMF tends to adopt an easier bargaining position with a larger L for a given C. In addition, when borrowing is in the form of bond finance as opposed to commercial bank lending or is by private borrowers (firms) rather than the central government, the staff of the IMF tend to promote larger loan size in order to overcome the collective action problems inherent in the potentially large number of bond holders.[32]

The importance of these insights is that IMF operations are not fully economic in character. For this reason, there is room for political scientists and other policy analysts outside economics to make a contribution to our understanding of the IMF.

An Assessment

As seen in Chapter 8, the World Trade Organization embodies the institutional structure of the global *trading* system. In a similar way, the IMF embodies the institutional structure of the global *financial* system. What can we make of these latter global financial institutions?

In Chapter 18, we considered the impossible trinity (Figure 18.4). This concept identified three objectives that countries desire in the realm of international finance, namely monetary independence, exchange rate stability, and capital mobility. In principal, only two of these three objectives are attainable at the same

[31] See, for example, Joyce (2006) and Bird (2008). Joyce (2006: 358) notes: "Blaming incomplete completion on a lack of political resolve misses the reasons for its absence."

[32] In these cases, "the Fund staff will...propose larger loans with more extensive conditionality, in an attempt to alleviate international creditors' concerns about a country's future ability to service its debt, and to convince them to 'bail in' rather than 'bail out' in response to an IMF loan" (Copelovitch, 2010: 289).

time. Given the history we considered in the present chapter, we can view the gold standard as a period of time in which monetary independence was sacrificed for exchange rate stability and capital mobility. The Bretton Woods system, on the other hand, was one in which there was an attempt to sacrifice capital mobility to achieve exchange rate stability and monetary independence. Eichengreen (2008) strongly defends the view that this change was necessitated by the expansion of democratic processes and interest representation, which demanded an expanded agenda for domestic monetary policy beyond maintaining exchange rate stability. This system did not work in the face of increasing capital mobility, however.

The IMF was originally designed to support the Bretton Woods system. It was therefore conceived of in an era of hoped-for limited capital mobility. John Maynard Keynes and Harry Dexter White could not have anticipated the extent to which a resurgent momentum in international finance would weaken the role of capital controls in the system. With the end of the Bretton Woods era in 1971, the IMF needed to reinvent itself. It did so as a multilateral development institution (along with the World Bank), as well as a lender to emerging economies in crisis. Its lending shifted towards LMICs and its involvement in what is called **structural adjustment** increased substantially. It has played that role to the present time

Aspects of the international financial system are often assessed from the point of view of their contributions to providing *liquidity* and *adjustment*. In the realm of liquidity, the IMF never had the resources necessary to make a substantial contribution. In his initial Bretton Woods proposal, Keynes envisioned a global central bank with an international currency, the *bancor*. This central bank would be responsible for regulating the expansion of international liquidity. This vision was never to come to fruition, and it still seems a long way off.

In the realm of adjustment, as previously mentioned, Keynes' original Bretton Woods proposal distributed this requirement across deficit and surplus countries. This proposal was also discarded, and adjustment became solely the responsibility of deficit countries. Furthermore, as Dell (1981) emphasized a long time ago, deficit countries have been required to adjust *no matter what the source of the deficit*. Oil shocks, commodity price declines, and rapid and unforeseen changes in interest rates, all of which occur through no fault of the deficit (often LMIC) countries, become events requiring conditionality and structural adjustment. At times these requirements have appeared to violate the purposes of the IMF developed at Bretton Woods: to promote "the development of productive resources" and to achieve balance of payments adjustment "without resorting to measures destructive of national and international prosperity."[33]

[33] See also Dell (1983) on this era of conditionality.

Reform of the existing IMF framework could involve two things: (1) reconstituting it more along the lines of a world central bank, reaffirming the role of the SDR as a reserve asset, and giving the IMF independent responsibility for regulating world liquidity through dramatically expanded quotas and SDR management; and (2) redesigning adjustment mechanisms to spread responsibility over deficit and surplus countries. These changes are radical and would require a complete redrafting of the IMF's Articles of Agreement.[34]

Conclusion

During the twentieth century the countries of the world struggled with three major transitions in financial arrangements: from a gold standard to a gold exchange standard; from a gold exchange standard to an adjustable gold peg (the Bretton Woods system); and from an adjustable gold peg to the current "non-system," whereby the IMF attempts to stabilize a whole host of currency arrangements. The IMF has played a central, but imperfect, role in managing the non-system. In a review of the IMF, Eichengreen and Woods (2015: 29) conclude that "there is an important role for the IMF to solve information, commitment, and coordination problems with significant implications for the stability of national economies and the international monetary and financial system." Very few observers (outside the IMF itself) are satisfied with the way it has played its role, but, to put it colloquially, "it's all we got."[35]

The IMF's lending operations described in this chapter have been crucial in helping countries cope with balance of payments problems, but they have also been very controversial, regarding both the appropriateness of conditionality and their effectiveness. The critical argument is that the IMF should adjust its conditionality packages in response to different national conditions and to systematic critiques. It has only just begun to do this.[36]

We mentioned in Chapter 1 that data on international trade and international finance indicate that international finance is of an order of magnitude larger than trade. Despite its imperfect character, the IMF is a major player in the international finance realm, attempting to contribute to liquidity, adjustment, and stabilization. Having come back from the brink of irrelevance in 2009, the IMF has quickly re-established its relevance (and controversy) within the crisis-prone global financial system.

---

[34] For proposals along these lines (as well as others), see Eichengreen (2010).

[35] Copelovitch (2010: 4) notes that "virtually no one in today's global economy is happy with the IMF, and almost everyone has a proposal for how it should be reformed."

[36] See Kentikelenis, Stubbs, and King (2016).

Review Exercises

1. How did the gold exchange standard differ from the gold standard? How did the adjustable gold peg (Bretton Woods) system differ from the gold exchange standard?
2. Why are monetary arrangements since Bretton Woods referred to as a "non-system"?
3. What is your reaction to the different visions of the Keynes Plan and the White Plan? If you had been a participant at the Bretton Woods Conference, which would you have supported?
4. Would you be in favor of expanding the role of the SDR to make it an international currency along the lines of Keynes' *bancor*? Why or why not?
5. Choose an IMF member in which you have a special interest. Spend a little time perusing the "Country Information" section of the IMF website at www.imf.org by clicking the "Country" tab along the top of the home page.
6. For the ten elements of the Washington Consensus (box above) and the ten elements of the "second-generation reforms," give your own assessment of their appropriateness as policies.

FURTHER READING AND WEB RESOURCES

For a concise introduction to the IMF, see Joyce (2009). An excellent and more extensive source is Copelovitch (2010). On the political economy of the global monetary system, see Walter and Sen (2009: chaps. 4 & 5). On the political economy of IMF lending, see Vreeland (2003), Copelovitch (2010), and Kentikelenis, Stubbs, and King (2016). On alleged intellectual bias within the IMF, see Chwieroth (2007).

The reader with an interest in the material of this chapter would do well by consulting the concise and insightful books by Eichengreen (2008; 2015). A longer but now somewhat dated treatment can be found in James (1996). Solomon (1977) is also a very worthwhile insider's account of the Bretton Woods system, and Skidelsky's (2000) biography of Keynes is also an important look at the period of history that gave birth to the IMF.

REFERENCES

Arghyrou, M. G., and J. D. Tsoukalas (2011) "The Greek Debt Crisis: Likely Causes, Mechanism and Outcomes," *World Economy*, 34:2, 173–91.

Bird, G. (2008) "The Implementation of IMF Programs: A Conceptual Framework," *Review of International Organizations*, 3:1, 41–64.

Bird, G., and D. Rowlands (2003) "Political Economy Influences within the Life-Cycle of IMF Programs," *World Economy*, 26:9, 1255–78.

Bird, G., and D. Rowlands (2006) "IMF Quotas: Constructing an International Organization Using Inferior Building Blocks," *Review of International Organizations*, 1:2, 153–71.

Boughton, J. M. (1998) "Harry Dexter White and the International Monetary Fund," *Finance and Development*, 35:3, 39–41.

Buira, A. (1995) "Reflections on the International Monetary System," *Princeton Essays in International Finance*, 195, 1–41.

Chwieroth, J. M. (2007) "Testing and Measuring the Role of Ideas: The Case of Neoliberalism in the International Monetary Fund," *International Studies Quarterly*, 51:1, 5–30.

Copelovitch, M. S. (2010) *The International Monetary Fund in the Global Economy*, Cambridge University Press.

Dell, S. (1981) "On Being Grandmotherly: The Evolution of IMF Conditionality," *Princeton Essays in International Finance*, 144, 1–34.

Dell, S. (1983) "Stabilization: The Political Economy of Overkill," in J. Williamson (ed.), *IMF Conditionality*, Institute for International Economics, 17–45.

Drazen, A. (2002) "Conditionality and Ownership in IMF Lending: A Political Economy Approach," *IMF Staff Papers*, 49:S1, 36–67.

Eichengreen, B. (1992) *Golden Fetters: The Gold Standard and the Great Depression, 1919–1939*, Oxford University Press.

Eichengreen, B. (2008) *Globalizing Capital: A History of the International Monetary System*, Princeton University Press.

Eichengreen, B. (2010) "Out-of-the-Box Thoughts about the International Financial Architecture," *Journal of International Commerce, Economics and Policy*, 1:1, 1–20.

Eichengreen, B. (2015) *Hall of Mirrors: The Great Depression, the Great Recession, and the Uses – and Misuses – of History*, Oxford University Press.

Eichengreen, B., and N. Woods (2015) "The IMF's Unmet Challenges," *Journal of Economic Perspectives*, 30:1, 29–52.

Fischer, S. (1998) "Capital-Account Liberalization and the Role of the IMF," *Princeton Essays in International Finance*, 207, 1–10.

Financial Times (2010) "IMF Seeks $250bn to Boost Resources," July 18.

Gaidar, Y. (1997) "The IMF and Russia," *American Economic Review*, 87:2, 13–16.

Gould-Davies, N., and N. Woods (1999) "Russia and the IMF," *International Affairs*, 75:1, 1–21.

Güven, A. B. (2012) "The IMF, the World Bank, and the Global Economic Crisis: Exploring Paradigm Continuity," *Development and Change*, 43:4, 869–98.

Hume, D. (1924 [1752]) "On the Balance of Trade," in A. E. Monroe (ed.), *Early Economic Thought*, Dover, 323–38.

International Monetary Fund (2006) "Ireland: Financial System Stability Assessment Update," Country Report 06/292, IMF.

International Monetary Fund (2007a) *World Economic Outlook April 2007: Spillovers and Cycles in the Global Economy*, IMF.

International Monetary Fund (2007b) *Annual Report 2007: Making the Global Economy Work for All*, IMF.

International Monetary Fund (2010) "IMF Conditionality Factsheet," IMF.

International Monetary Fund (2013) "Greece: Ex Post Evaluation of Exceptional Access under the 2010 Stand-By Arrangement," Country Report 13/156, IMF.

James, H. (1996) *International Monetary Cooperation since Bretton Woods*, Oxford University Press.

Joyce, J. (2006) "Promises Made, Promises Broken: A Model of IMF Program Implementation," *Economics and Politics*, 18:3, 339–65.

Joyce, J. (2009) "International Monetary Fund," in K. A. Reinert, R. S. Rajan, A. J. Glass, and L. S. Davis (eds.), *The Princeton Encyclopedia of the World Economy*, Princeton University Press, 686–90.

Joyce, J., and I. Noy (2008) "The IMF and the Liberalization of Capital Flows," *Review of International Economics*, 16:3, 413–30.

Kentikelenis, A. E., T. H. Stubbs, and L. P. King (2016) "IMF Conditionality and Development Policy Space," *Review of International Political Economy*, 23:4, 543–82.

Keynes, J. M. (1963 [1923]) "Alternative Aims in Monetary Policy," in *Essays in Persuasion*, Norton, 186–212.

Krugman, P. (1999) *The Return of Depression Economics*, Norton.

McCloskey, D. N., and J. R. Zecher (1976) "How the Gold Standard Worked, 1880–1913," in J. A. Frenkel and H. G. Johnson (eds.), *The Monetary Approach to the Balance of Payments*, University of Toronto Press, 357–85.

Molina, N. (2009) "IMF Emergency Loans for Low-Income Countries," Policy Brief 48, Group of 24.

Naím, M. (2000) "Washington Consensus or Washington Confusion?," *Foreign Policy*, 118, 86–103.

Reinhart, C. M., and C. Trebesch (2016) "The International Monetary Fund: 70 Years of Reinvention," *Journal of Economic Perspectives*, 30:1, 3–28.

Rodrik, D. (2007) *One Economics, Many Recipes: Globalization, Institutions, and Economic Growth*, Princeton University Press.

Skidelsky, R. (2000) *John Maynard Keynes: Fighting for Freedom 1937–1946*, Viking.

Solomon, R. (1977) *The International Monetary System, 1945–1976*, Harper & Row.

Stiglitz, J. (2001) "Thanks for Nothing," *Atlantic Monthly*, 288:3, 36–40.

Triffin, R. (1960) *Gold and the Dollar Crisis: The Future of Convertibility*, Yale University Press.

Vreeland, J. R. (2003) *The IMF and Economic Development*, Cambridge University Press.

Wade, R. H. (2001) "Capital and Revenge: The IMF and Ethiopia," *Challenge*, 44:5, 67–75.

Walter, A., and G. Sen (2009) *Analyzing the Global Political Economy*, Princeton University Press.

Williamson, J. (1990) "What Washington Means by Policy Reform," in J. Williamson (ed.), *Latin American Adjustment: How Much Has Happened?*, Institute for International Economics, 5–38.

Williamson, J. (2000) "What Should the World Bank Think about the Washington Consensus?," *World Bank Research Observer*, 15:2, 251–64.

Zettelmeyer, J., C. Trebesch, and M. Gulati (2013) "Greek Debt Restructuring: An Autopsy," *Economic Policy*, 28:75, 513–63.

20 Crises and Responses

Mexico in 1994 and 1995. Thailand, Indonesia, the Philippines, Malaysia, and South Korea in 1997. Russia in 1998. Brazil in 1999. Argentina in 2001. The United States and a select few European countries beginning in 2007. These are examples of recurrent **crises** that have plagued the world economy. At the time, each of these crises was described by some as unexpected, but, as it turns out, there are good reasons to expect crises to occur with some regularity. Why? Unlike markets for most goods and services, financial markets are characterized by market "imperfections." Because of these imperfections, we cannot be assured of economic or allocative efficiency in markets for financial products.[1] Furthermore, these imperfections tend to make financial markets somewhat *unstable*, with "booms" of one kind or another being followed by "busts." The purpose of this chapter is to help you understand why this is so, and the role that financial market imperfections have played in crises.

We begin by considering different *types* of crises. These include hyperinflation, balance of payments and currency crises, asset price deflation, banking crises, external debt crises, and domestic debt crises. This is followed by a brief consideration of **contagion** and **systemic risk**. We then consider the analysis of "old-fashioned" balance of payments and currency crises. This is followed by a consideration of the more "high-tech" Asian crisis and the response of the International Monetary Fund. We take up the global financial crisis that began in 2007, and, finally, we discuss two proposals for addressing crises: prudential regulation, including the Basel standards; and **capital controls**. Having studied this chapter, you will be in a better position to assess much of the current debate on crises in the international financial system, an issue that will be with us for some time to come.

Types of Crises

It is often the case that the popular and financial presses use the word "crisis" or "financial crisis" without being more specific. This is somewhat unfortunate, because financial crises come in *different varieties*. Being more specific about

[1] The most fundamental imperfection in financial markets is *imperfect information*, particularly asymmetric information, whereby the parties to a financial transaction have different sets of information about factors relevant to the transaction. See Marks (2009) and Tirole (2017: chap. 11).

Table 20.1 Types of crises

Crisis type	Characteristics	Examples
Hyperinflation	A rapid increase in the overall price level of a country, typically defined to be 40 percent or higher on an annual basis.	Zimbabwe, 1998–2009 Venezuela, 2016–
Balance of payments and currency crises	A large devaluation or rapid depreciation in the value of a domestic currency in response to balance of payments difficulties.	Mexico, 1994–1995 Brazil, 1999
Asset price deflation	A sustained and large decline in the prices of financial assets.	Japan, 1990 United States, 2007–2009
Banking crises	The occurrence of bank runs and/or the merger, closure, or government takeover of banking institutions.	Argentina, 2001 Cyprus, 2012–2013
External debt crises	Sovereign default on debt obligations to *foreign* creditors or substantial restructuring of this debt.	Mexico, 1982 Greece, 2010–2015
Domestic debt crises	Sovereign default on debt obligations to *domestic* creditors or substantial restructuring of this debt.	Argentina, 1989

Sources: Eichengreen (1999) and Reinhart and Rogoff (2009).

these types of crises is an important first step to understanding them. A summary of crisis types is presented in Table 20.1 and includes hyperinflation, balance of payments and currency crises, asset price deflation, banking crises, external debt crises, and domestic debt crises. Importantly, these crisis types often occur in *combination* with each other rather than individually. Let us briefly consider each type.

Hyperinflation is a period of rapid increase in the price level of a country, typically defined to be 40 percent or more annually.[2] Periods of hyperinflation are associated with rapid expansions of money supply.[3] Consider Zimbabwe, for example. Inflation in Zimbabwe began to increase in 1998, reaching about 50 percent annually. In 2001 inflation reached 100 percent, and in 2006 it increased further, to 1,500 percent. From there, it increased even further, to billions in percentage terms

[2] Inflation is typically measured in terms of percentage increases in either the GDP price deflator or consumer prices (consumer price index).

[3] See Appendices 16.1 and 16.2 on the relationship between monetary stocks and price levels.

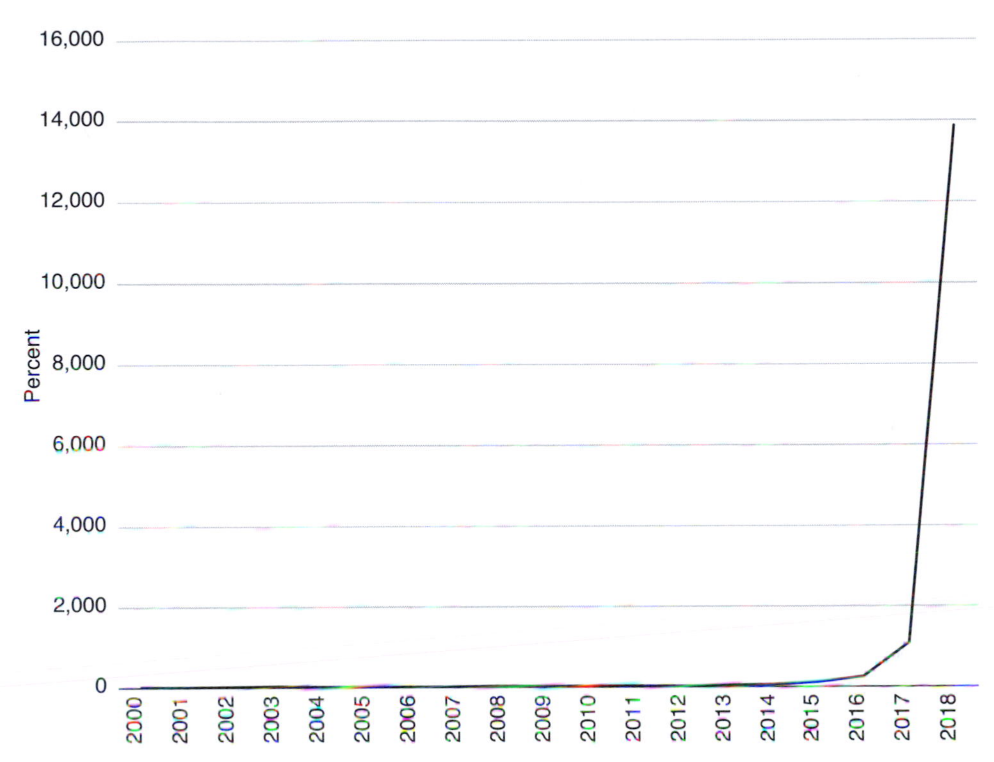

Figure 20.1 Inflation in Venezuela, 2000–2018 (percentage change in consumer prices)
Source: International Monetary Fund.

in 2008. In 2009, with the Zimbabwe dollar essentially worthless, the Zimbabwean government was forced to replace it with the US dollar.[4]

The more recent case of Venezuela is presented in Figure 20.1. Venezuela had experienced moderately high inflation for many years, but the price level began to increase significantly in 2013, rising at a year-on-year rate of over 40 percent, the technical threshold for hyperinflation. This was just the beginning, however. By 2015 inflation reached over 100 percent, by 2017 over 1,000 percent, and by 2018 over 10,000 percent. Estimates of inflation for 2019 vary widely but reach up to 1,000,000 percent. Economic life in Venezuela completely collapsed, with extreme food insecurity, emigration, and a generalized public health crisis.[5]

[4] See, for example, McIndo-Calder (2018). As described in Dugger (2010), this episode of hyperinflation forced Zimbabweans to turn to barter.

[5] López Glass (2019) reports: "In the Weimar Republic hyperinflation was largely the result of reparations: payment imposed on Germany after World War I. In Zimbabwe it was the result of Robert Mugabe's land reform policy and the drop in food production and foreign investment that followed. In Venezuela it has been the result of two decades of gross economic mismanagement, profligate public spending, government debt despite a historic oil windfall, and epic corruption. What was once the most prosperous country in the region is now a man-made disaster."

Although the economic policy tools to prevent episodes of hyperinflation have existed for some time (such as basic market principles and intelligent monetary policy), certain governments choose to ignore them. By doing so, they cause crises that have severe detrimental effects on the well-being of their citizens. As the Zimbabwe and Venezuela cases make clear, what should be a historic relic is still part of recent history.

Balance of payments and currency **crises** consist of large devaluations or rapid depreciations in the value of domestic currencies. We considered the case of the 1999 Brazilian devaluation in Chapter 18 and will consider the 1994/95 currency crash in Mexico below. As it turns out, periods of hyperinflation can contribute to currency crashes.[6] The reason for this is that, as significant degrees of inflation occur, asset owners move out of domestic-currency-denominated assets into foreign-currency-denominated assets in order to maintain the value of portfolios. This is a decrease in demand for the domestic currency relative to the foreign currency and puts downward pressure on the value of the domestic currency (upward pressure on the nominal exchange rate *e*, as defined in Chapter 16). Because the foreign currency involved is often the US dollar, this process is sometimes referred to as "dollarization." Reinhart and Rogoff (2009: chap. 12) show that, once dollarization sets in, it is difficult to reverse even after inflation rates have declined. This is a sort of *path dependence* in currency preferences that makes recovery from inflationary episodes difficult.

Asset price deflation involves a large and sustained decline in the prices of financial assets. This typically follows on an episode of large and sustained increases in asset prices, what is commonly referred to as **bubbles**. Formally, bubbles need to be defined in statistical terms, but their key characteristics are described by Vogel (2010: 16, emphasis added) as follows:[7]

> Generally, a bubble is considered to have developed when assets trade at prices that are far in excess of an estimate of the *fundamental value* of the asset, as determined from discounted expected future cash flows using current interest rates and typical long-run risk premiums associated with the asset class. Speculators, in such circumstances, are much more interested in profiting from trading in the asset than in its use or earnings capacity or true value.

The last significant episode of international asset price deflation took place between 2007 and 2009, and we will discuss this crisis in more detail below. A classic case of asset price deflation is that of Japan in 1990, however. Consider Figure 20.2. This shows the total values of equities and land in Japan between 1981 and 1992, land values being restricted to that of Tokyo. These both increased

---

[6] For empirical evidence of this, see Reinhart and Rogoff (2009: chap. 12).

[7] See also Tirole (2017: chap. 11).

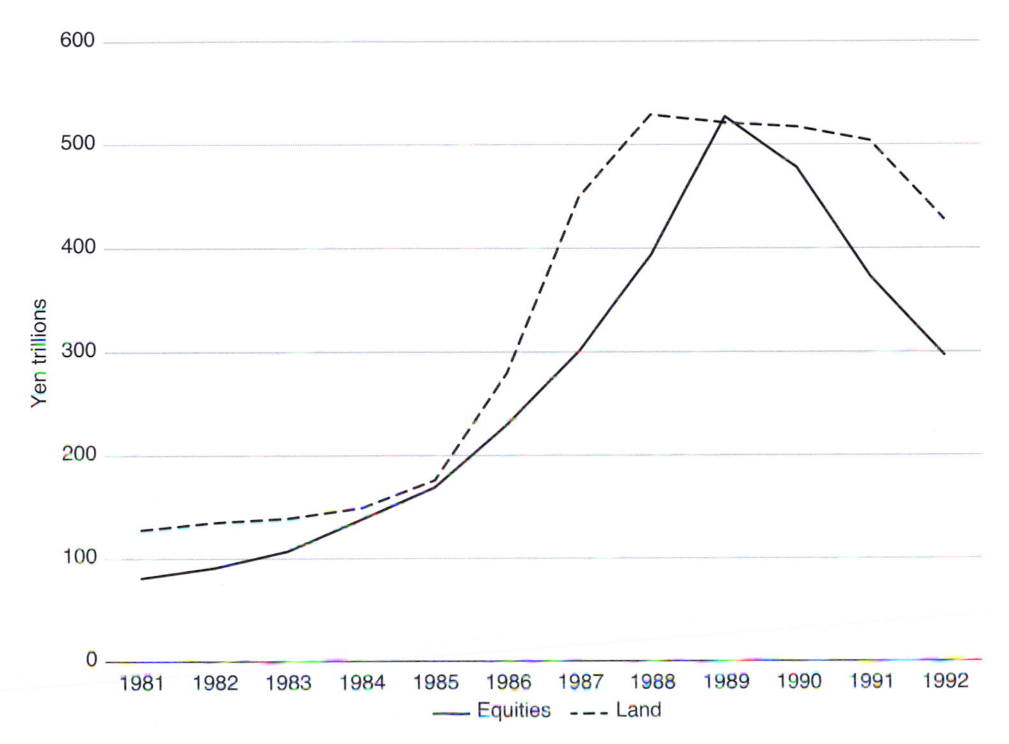

Figure 20.2 Asset prices in Japan, 1981–1992 (¥ trillions)
Note: The land value is only that of Tokyo.
Source: Noguchi (1994).

fivefold between 1981 and 1989. At the peak, the total land value of Japan (Tokyo plus the rest of the country) was estimated to be equivalent to 20 percent of global wealth and five times that of the land value in the United States (Stone and Ziemba, 1993). As of 1989 most observers expected values to keep increasing, but, as is evident from Figure 20.2, they quickly declined as the bubble burst. Japan subsequently spent two decades struggling to recover from the bursting of the 1989 bubble, the struggle involving slow growth and even *deflation* in terms of goods and services prices.[8]

Banking **crises** involve bank runs, mergers, closures, or government takeovers of banking institutions. As described by a number of observers in the accompanying box, the banking sector is a particularly fragile element of the global financial system.[9] This is because of what is known as *maturity transformation*, namely the

[8] Krugman (2010) writes: "In the 1990s, Japan conducted a dress rehearsal for the crisis that struck much of the world in 2008. Runaway banks fueled a bubble in land prices; when the bubble burst, these banks were severely weakened, as were the balance sheets of everyone who had borrowed in the belief that land prices would stay high. The result was protracted economic weakness."

[9] This insight goes back at least as far as Diamond and Dybvig (1983), but see also Bird and Rajan (2001).

role of banks in borrowing short-term funds but lending for the long term, and it makes the banking sector prone to bank runs. For example, as is well described by Reinhart and Rogoff (2009: 144):

> In normal times, banks hold liquid resources that are more than enough to handle any surges in deposit withdrawals. During a "run" on a bank, however, depositors lose confidence in the bank and withdraw en masse. As withdrawals mount, the bank is forced to liquidate assets under duress. Typically the prices received are "fire sale" prices, especially if the bank holds highly illiquid and idiosyncratic loans (such as those to local businesses about which it has better information than other investors). The problem of having to liquidate at fire sale prices can extend to a far broader range of assets during a systemic banking crisis.... Different banks often hold broadly similar portfolios of assets, and if all banks try to sell at once, the market can dry up completely. Assets that are relatively liquid during normal times can suddenly become highly illiquid just when the bank most needs them.

Views of the Banking Sector

Going back some time, many observers have noted the *fragility* of the banking system in the world economy. Here are a few examples. The World Bank (2001: 11) states: "If finance is fragile, banking is the most fragile part." Dobson and Hufbauer (2001: 47) note: "Bank lending may be more prone to runs than portfolio capital, because banks themselves are highly leveraged, and they are relying on the borrower's balance sheet to ensure repayment." Crook (2003) writes that "breakdowns in banking lie at the center of most financial crises. And banks are unusually effective at spreading financial distress, once it starts, from one place to another."

More recently, Kose et al. (2009: 38) state: "The procyclical and highly volatile nature of...short-term bank loans...can magnify the adverse impact of negative shocks on economic growth." Reinhart and Rogoff (2009: xxix) state that "the aftermath of systemic banking crises involves a protracted and pronounced contraction in economic activity and puts significant strains on government resources." These sorts of insights are summarized succinctly by Montiel (2011: 528), who states that "vulnerability to panic is inherent in banking."

These few quotations give a flavor of the potential volatility of the banking sector and why it needs to be treated with caution in both national and international policymaking. Prudential regulation of the banking system, discussed below, is a high priority in trying to make crises less likely.

Sources: Crook (2003), Dobson and Hufbauer (2001), Kose et al. (2009), Montiel (2011), Reinhart and Rogoff (2009), and World Bank (2001).

Research into the banking sector and its role in crises provides us with a number of insights.[10] First, banking crises are often set off by asset price deflation or the bursting of financial bubbles, capital inflow surges, and financial sector liberalization, all of which can work in tandem with one another.[11] For example, all of these ingredients seem to have contributed to the 2008 GFC. Second, historically, banking crises are *quite common* in countries at *all income levels*. They are not limited to low- and middle-income countries. Third, banking crises are usually followed by a *protracted downturn* in economic output and *substantial fiscal costs*. Recovery can consequently be difficult.

External debt crises involve sovereign *default* on debt obligations to foreign creditors or the substantial *restructuring* of this debt. The classic case of this was Mexico in 1982 discussed in Chapter 19. Recall from that chapter that the 1980s began with a significant increase in real interest rates and a significant decline in non-oil commodity prices. These increased borrowing costs and reduced export revenues for many LMICs, including Mexico. In 1982, in the face of substantial capital flight, the Mexican government announced that it would stop servicing its foreign-currency debt. Subsequently, both Argentina and Brazil entered into similar debt and balance of payments crises.

Research into external debt crises (e.g. Reinhart and Rogoff, 2009) suggests that (like banking crises) they tend to be set off by a previous period of large capital inflows. Recent debt default and debt restructuring have taken place in Africa (Côte d'Ivoire, 2000; Kenya, 2000; Nigeria, 2001 and 2004; Zimbabwe, 2000), Asia (Indonesia, 2000 and 2002; Myanmar, 2002), and Latin America (Argentina, 2001; Ecuador, 2008; Paraguay, 2003; Uruguay, 2003; Venezuela, 2004 and 2017), and even Europe (Greece and Portugal, 2010–2012; and Ukraine, 2016). Although these European crises just mentioned were recent, there were others going back to the 1970s.[12]

Domestic debt crises involve sovereign *default* on debt obligations to domestic creditors or substantial *restructuring* of this debt. As strongly emphasized by Reinhart and Rogoff (2009), this set of crises has not been sufficiently appreciated and studied. As it turns out, levels of *domestic* debt help to explain a significant portion of *external* debt defaults and inflation crises. National governments default on external debt to help support domestic debt restructuring. They also have historically turned to inflation to reduce the real (price-adjusted) value of

[10] See, for example, Goldstein, Kaminsky, and Reinhart (2000), Kaminsky, Reinhart, and Végh (2003), and Reinhart and Rogoff (2009).

[11] The role of financial liberalization in banking crises was pointed out many years ago by Diaz-Alejandro (1985), but see also Bird and Rajan (2001).

[12] Along with Reinhart and Rogoff (2009), see the less official but useful list at https://en.wikipedia.org/wiki/List_of_sovereign_debt_crises.

domestic debt obligations. As with banking crises and external debt crises, preceding inflows of capital are often a contributing factor.

We mentioned above that crises often occur in *combinations*. For example, Table 20.1 mentioned Argentina in 2001 as a case of a banking crisis, but much more was going on in that country. The banking crisis was accompanied by a currency crisis (discussed in Chapter 18), the Argentine government defaulted on both its domestic and foreign debt, and there was deflation of some types of asset prices. Thus, although they are useful for sorting out different crisis types, the rows of Table 20.1 should not be interpreted a set of isolated compartments. The real world of international finance is much more complicated than that.

Contagion and Systemic Risk

It is sometimes the case that crises that begin in one country spread to other countries. This is called **contagion**. As expressed by Kaminsky, Reinhart, and Végh (2003: 51), "Some financial events...trigger an immediate and startling adverse chain reaction among countries within a region and in some cases across regions." These contagion episodes are sometimes given special names. For example, the spread of the 1994/95 Mexican crisis to other countries in Latin America became known as the "tequila effect," and the spread of the 1997 crisis in Thailand to other countries in Asia became known as the "Asian flu." Contagion can make economic management even more difficult than it normally is.

The notion of a crisis "spreading" from one country to another is informal. More formally, we need to consider *what exactly is transmitted* across national boundaries. There are a variety of possibilities and differing opinions among specialists in international finance. Some common identifiers include shifts in expectations and confidence ("herding" or "informational cascades"), asset prices ("financial linkage"), and capital flight ("sudden stops"). Contagion does not always occur in episodes where we might most expect it. For example, Kaminsky, Reinhart, and Végh (2003) note the lack of contagion accompanying the 1999 devaluation of the Brazilian real, the 2001 demise of the Argentine currency board, and the 2001 devaluation of the Turkish lira. Brazil, Argentina, and Turkey are all very large and important emerging markets, so the lack of contagion in these cases was notable.

Kaminsky, Reinhart, and Végh (2003) identify three causal factors that contribute to episodes of contagion: sudden stops in capital inflows, surprise announcements to financial markets, and highly leveraged financial institutions. Further, Joyce and Nabar (2009) show that sudden stops interact with banking sectors to cause banking crises. It therefore appears that sudden stops, banking crises, and contagion can all be related to one another. More generally, as suggested by Kalemni-Ozcan, Papaioannou, and Perri (2013), international banking itself appears to transmit crises across national borders.[13] Country governments can help shield themselves from contagion through avoiding over-borrowing (which can accompany pro-cyclical fiscal policy in open capital markets), continuous information sharing, the prudential regulation of financial markets (especially banking), and market-friendly capital controls discussed in (Chapter 15).

At times, contagion spreads so rapidly and widely that it becomes *global*, affecting the entire world financial system. This is known as **systemic risk**. Unlike simple contagion, systemic risk is a rare event. It characterized the Great Depression of the 1930s, but it also characterized the GFC, which we will discuss below. Goldin and Vogel (2010) strongly suggest that there has been an increase in systemic risk as a result of the process of financial globalization.[14] They sound a note of alarm, stating (12): "Global finance is the best understood and most institutionally developed of the global governance regimes, yet these institutions failed to predict, prevent or understand the endemic systemic risks in the system, and they have yet to elicit the structural changes need to manage proactively future systemic risks." It is fair to say that the field of international finance is now sensitive to this issue and has developed means of measuring systemic risk threats.[15]

Analyzing Balance of Payments and Currency Crises

Some observers have made a distinction between "old-fashioned" and "high-tech" crises.[16] A standard balance of payments and currency crisis is an example of an "old-fashioned" crisis. These have their roots in overvalued fixed exchange rates and large current-account deficits. For example, in Chapters 18 and 19 we mentioned the possibility of a balance of payments crisis ensuing when the capital/financial account can no longer support a current account deficit. In this section, we want to return to our fixed exchange rate model of Chapter 18 to analyze the exchange rate dynamics behind such crises. As in Chapter 18, our home country is Mexico and our foreign country is the United States. The market for Mexican pesos is depicted in Figure 20.3. This diagram depicts an initial *equilibrium fixed exchange rate* at e_0, plotting the value of the peso ($\frac{1}{e}$) on the vertical axis, as in Chapters 16 to 18.[17]

---

[13] See also Dungey and Gajurel (2015), who distinguish between four types of contagion in the banking sector: systematic, idiosyncratic, shift, and volatility.

[14] For example, they note that, by 2007, global derivatives trading had increased to "16 times global equity market capitalization and 10 times global gross domestic product" (6).

[15] See, for example, Acharya et al. (2017), who develop a systemic expected shortfall (SES) measure of under-capitalization of financial institutions.

[16] See, for example, Eichengreen (1999: chap. 1).

[17] Mexico had adopted a fixed exchange rate regime in 1987, which lasted through 1994.

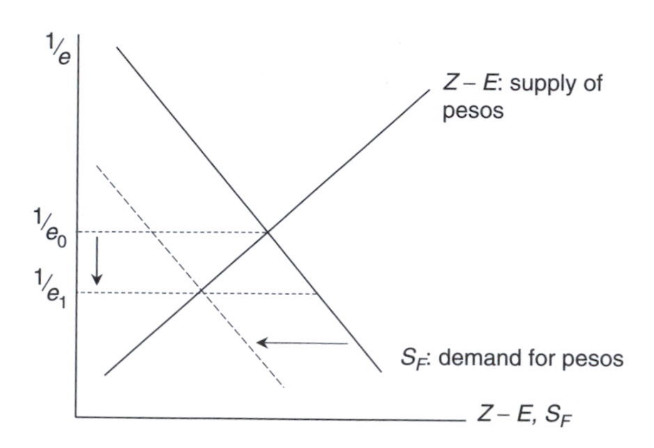

Figure 20.3 A balance of payments and currency crisis

In Figure 20.3, let us suppose that Mexico is initially successful in implementing an equilibrium exchange rate at e_0. Recall from Chapter 18 that this equilibrium exchange rate requires that $e^e = e_0$. In other words, the expected future exchange rate must equal the equilibrium rate. This, in turn, requires that the interest rate on the peso must equal the interest rate on the dollar, or $r_M = r_{US}$. Next, suppose that we find Mexico in a position of a *current account deficit.* This was the actual case for Mexico in the early 1990s (the current account deficit in Mexico was equivalent to 8 percent of GDP in 1994). As we know from Chapter 14, such a current account deficit is always financed by a *capital/financial account surplus.* In Mexico's case, in the early 1990s the capital/financial account surplus was primarily in the form of short-term portfolio investment, much of it denominated in *US dollars.* When a large trade deficit is financed by an inflow of short-term capital, trouble is in the air. That it was denominated in a foreign currency (US dollars) made the trouble worse, because any fall in the value of the home currency would inflate the domestic-currency value of the debt. Many domestic investors were aware of these problems and began to sell pesos during 1994.

Let us pretend that you are a Mexican investor. If you feel that the Mexican government will have to devalue the peso in order to suppress the trade deficit, then, in your mind, $e^e > e_0$. When this occurs, the interest rate parity condition comes back into play. If $r_M = r_{US}$ and $e^e > e_0$, then the following will be true:

$$r_M < r_{US} + \frac{(e^e - e)}{e} \qquad (20.1)$$

On the left-hand side of Inequality 20.1 is the expected total rate of return on peso-denominated assets. On the right-hand side is the expected total rate of return on dollar-denominated assets. Given that the expected total rate of return on dollar-denominated assets exceeds that of peso-denominated assets, you will adjust your portfolio, buying dollars and selling pesos. This is known as **capital flight**, and Mexican investors engaged in this type of portfolio reallocation during 1994.

This situation is depicted in Figure 20.3. The change in expectations shifts the demand for pesos line to the left. At the original exchange rate, e_0, the total expected return on dollar-denominated assets exceeds the total expected return on peso-denominated assets. The *equilibrium* value of the peso falls to $1/e_1$. In response to such changes, in late 1994 the Mexican government devalued the peso by 15 percent. Unfortunately, this proved to be too little and simply fueled speculation of further devaluations. The demand for pesos line in Figure 20.3 shifted further to the left, and Mexico was forced to let the peso float. Beginning in early 1995 international investors began a sudden and massive portfolio shift out of peso-denominated assets, sending the peso into a deep fall.[18]

The severity of the capital flight from Mexico caused some observers to question the functioning of the international financial system. As Woodall (1995: 18, emphasis added) put it at the time:

> There were many good reasons behind the run on the peso—political turbulence, a widening current-account deficit, a pre-election public spending spree and a lax monetary policy. But on their own they did not justify the scale of the capital outflow or of the depreciation of the peso; the markets simply *lost their heads.*

It is useful to summarize the above discussion with a second diagram, presented in Figure 20.4. Here we see that an overvalued exchange rate causes an increase in the current account deficit (capital/financial account surplus) and a fall in official reserve levels. At some point, expectations shift, causing capital flight. Eventually, and often despite strenuous denials, the government devalues the currency or shifts to floating.

The Mexican balance of payments crisis and currency crash should give us an appreciation of the delicacy of managing a fixed exchange rate regime. Although,

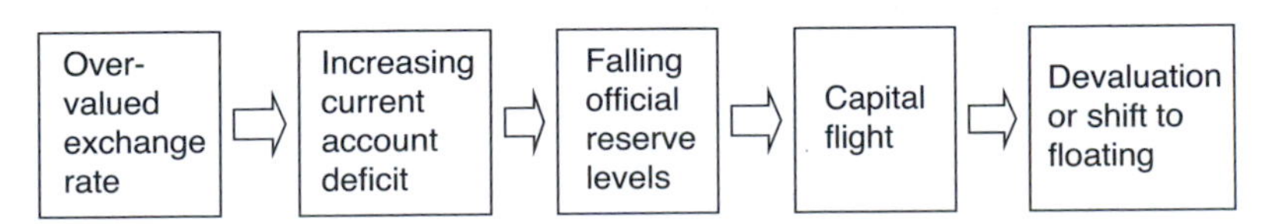

Figure 20.4 Balance of payments and currency crises

[18] A basic and well-known article on balance of payments crises is presented in Krugman (1979). For more on the Mexican crisis, see Calvo and Mendoza (1996). An excellent and concise review of economic models of crises is presented in Eichengreen (1999: appendix B).

at the time, the crisis was contained by swift action on the part of the US Treasury in supplying loans to Mexico, a similar set of crises began during the summer of 1997. This was the beginning of what now is known as the Asian crisis, which was more of a "high-tech" crisis than the Mexican one.

The Asian Crisis

Although "high-tech" crises typically include some elements of the balance of payments and currency crises described in Figures 20.3 and 20.4, they include some less concrete factors as well. High-tech crises combine current account deficits with weak financial sectors (especially in the banking system, as discussed above) and/or inappropriate capital/financial account liberalization.[19] The "high-tech" view of crises is summarized in Figure 20.5, and characterized the Asian crisis of 1997.

The Asian crisis began in Thailand, as described in the accompanying box. In some ways, the Thai crisis was similar to the Mexican crisis. It began with current account deficits amounting to the equivalent of nearly 8 percent of GDP under a fixed exchange rate regime. A devaluation of the baht took place in mid-1997. Again, the markets lost their heads. Although most analysts expected that the baht would fall by 15 to 20 percent in value against the dollar, it fell by more than 50 percent. Despite these standard aspects, and unlike the Mexican crisis, the

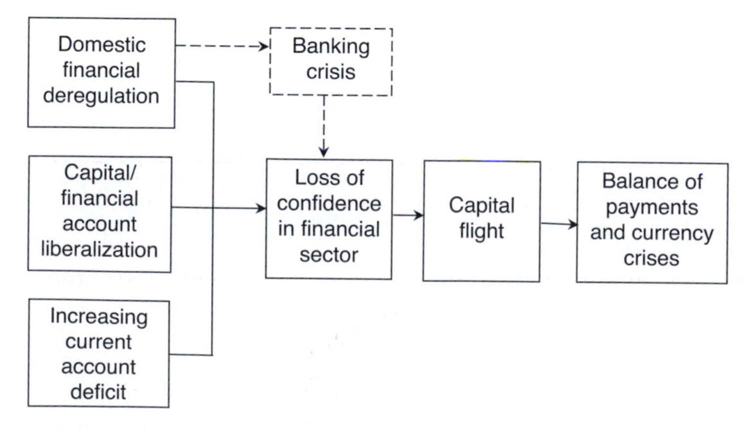

Figure 20.5 A "high-tech" balance of payments crisis
Note: The dashes around the banking crisis box suggest that this element might not always be present in a particular instance.

---

[19] For example, in the case of the Asian crisis, Stiglitz (2002: 113) states that it "was, first and foremost, a crisis of the financial system."

financial sector was at the heart of the Thai crisis. This fact is well summarized by Reynolds et al. (2002: 237):

> Briefly, the [Thai] crisis occurred when banks and financial companies...borrowed heavily on a short-term basis from banks in other countries (mainly in Japan and the United States) and made overly risky loans to finance the construction of commercial and residential units. When the demand for such units was not forthcoming as expected, a domino effect occurred: the real estate investors who borrowed defaulted, their lenders defaulted, and the banks were left with foreign-currency-denominated loans requiring payment. A subsequent foreign exchange crisis followed the collapse of the real estate market.

These characteristics are what led to the loss of confidence in the Asian financial sector. The general features of such high-tech crises are depicted in Figure 20.5. As seen in this figure, domestic financial deregulation, capital account liberalization, and increasing current account deficits combine to eventually and suddenly cause a loss of confidence. This loss of confidence, in turn, causes capital flight, and balance of payments and currency crises ensue. As stated by Reinhart and Rogoff (2009: xxxviiii), "Highly indebted governments, banks, or corporations can seem to be merrily rolling along for an extended period, when *bang!*—confidence collapses, lenders disappear, and a crisis hits." The speed at which this process can unfold often surprises even the most seasoned analyst.

The Baht Crisis

Until the summer of 1997 the Thai baht was pegged at 25 baht per US dollar. In June 1997 the baht came under pressure, and the Thai government attempted to support it through cooperative agreements with Asian central banks and controls on foreign exchange transactions. The government's foreign reserves were approaching exhaustion, however. In early July these strategies failed, and the government attempted to devalue the baht in the face of a speculative attack. This strategy also failed, and the baht began to float. The Thai government contacted the IMF for assistance at the end of July. In August 1997 the Thai government, under the prime minister, Chavalit Yongchaiyudh, accepted an IMF package worth $17 billion.

In October 1997 the Thai finance minister resigned, and in November Chavalit resigned. He was replaced by Chuan Leekpai. In December the government closed nearly 60 financial companies that were in very difficult financial conditions. The Thai economy, which had typically grown by over 8 percent a year, plunged into a recession. The stock market also plunged. By January 1998 the baht had fallen through the crucial barrier of 50 per US dollar, less than half the value of its previously pegged rate.

Sources: The Economist (1997) and Mydans (1997a; 1997b; 1998).

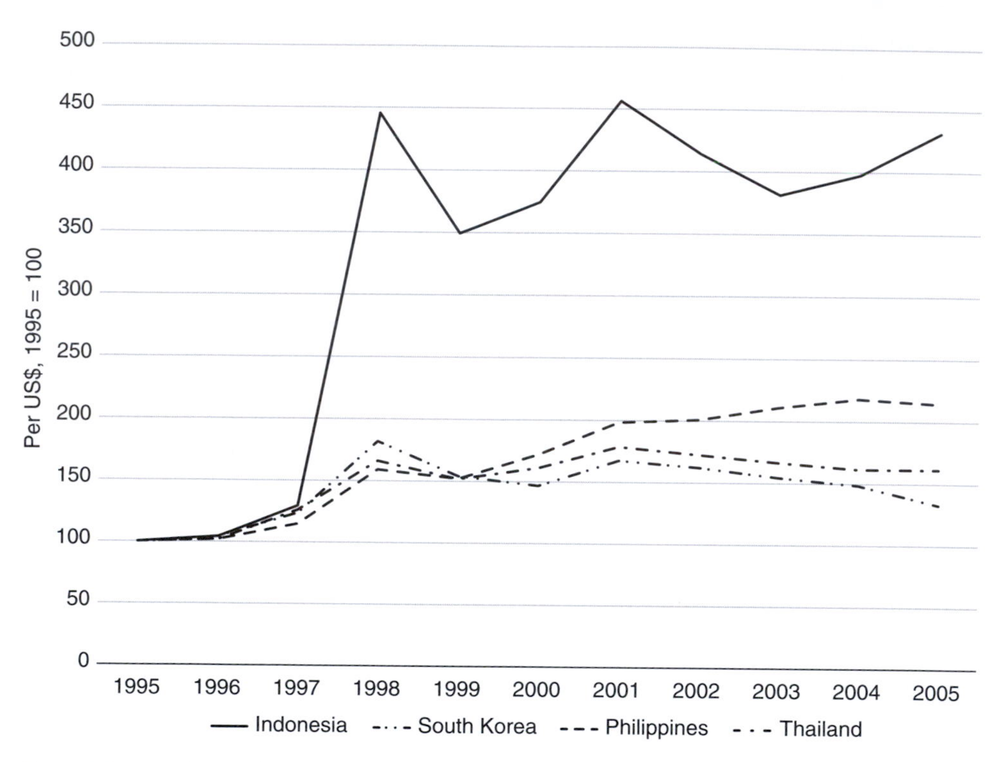

Figure 20.6 Nominal exchange rates of four Asian currencies, 1995–2005
Source: World Bank, World Development Indicators.

By the end of September 1999 the ensuing Asian crisis had spread to Malaysia and Indonesia. The Indonesian case was something of a surprise, because its current account deficit was less than 4 percent of GDP. From there, the crisis spread to the Philippines, Hong Kong, South Korea, and Taiwan. Only the Hong Kong dollar escaped devaluation.[20] Figure 20.6 plots the nominal exchange rates for four of these countries (Indonesia, South Korea, Philippines, and Thailand) for the years 1995 to 2005, normalized so that each exchange rate is 100 in 1995. You can see here that the largest decline in value occurred in Indonesia, where the nominal exchange rate increased by a factor of 4.5. The other three countries experienced increases in their nominal exchange rates of much smaller but still substantial amounts, of over 50 percent.

What were some of the "high-tech" features of the Asian financial crisis? Here is a partial list.[21]

[20] This Asian crisis was later followed by the Russian ruble crisis of 1998, the Brazilian real crisis of 1999, and the Argentine currency board crisis of 2001. We considered the Brazilian and Argentine crises in Chapter 18 and the Russian crisis in Chapter 19.

[21] For a fuller discussion, see Eichengreen (1999: appendix C).

1. Financial firms in the region (including banks) had significant exposures in real estate and equities, and both these markets had begun to deflate prior to the crisis. Thus, *asset price deflation* was part of the Asian crisis.
2. Capital accounts had been liberalized to allow firms (including banks) to take on short-term foreign debt, including debt denominated in foreign currencies.[22] In two countries (Thailand and South Korea), capital account liberalization began with short-term debt, rather than long-term debt and FDI, as is more prudent.
3. Banks were, in general, poorly regulated and supervised as the countries liberalized their financial markets and capital/financial accounts. Indeed, banks were a crucial component of government industrial policies, which, in some instances, supported systems of "crony" or "access" capitalism, rather than sound investment policies.[23]
4. Because of previous confidence in fixed exchange rates, firms (including banks) were not in the practice of hedging their foreign exchange exposures in the manner we described in Chapter 16. This led them to very vulnerable positions by the eve of the crisis. When the crisis finally hit, their attempts to secure foreign exchange put extra downward pressure on the value of domestic currencies.

These are some of the key aspects of the 1997 Asian crisis. As depicted in Figure 20.5, loss of confidence in the financial sectors of the countries involved was a central part of the evolution of the crisis, and the banking sector was a main culprit.

The IMF Response to the Asian and Brazilian Crises

The IMF response to the 1997 Asian crisis and the 1999 Brazilian crises became a point of serious contention and debate. The case of Indonesia is discussed in the accompanying box. In simple form, we can characterize the IMF's policies as consisting of three elements: interest rate increases, fiscal austerity, and structural reforms. The IMF required that the afflicted economies increase their interest rates dramatically. Why? As we saw in Chapters 17 and 18 in our discussion of the interest rate parity condition, an increase in the domestic interest rate tends to increase the equilibrium value of a country's currency. The trouble with this policy as applied in Asia and Brazil was that increases in domestic interest rates also

---

[22] "Between 1990 and 1996, roughly 50 percent of net private portfolio capital inflows into Thailand took the form of short-term borrowing. Sixty-two percent of net capital inflows in South Korea consisted of short-term borrowing in the three years 1994–97, compared with 37 percent in 1990–93" (Eichengreen, 1999: 156).

[23] See, for example, Wade (1998).

tended to suppress domestic investment and push debt-burdened firms (including banks) into default. This, in turn, fed into a sense of panic.[24] In the case of Brazil, the IMF insisted on interest rate increases after the real had been allowed to float despite the fact that its value had quickly stabilized. In doing so, it may have exacerbated the crisis.

As we discussed in Chapter 14, current account deficits can result from a lack of domestic savings ($S_H + S_G$, in terms of Figure 14.2). The IMF's fiscal austerity requirements were strategies to increase S_G. In the case of the Asian crisis, this strategy was probably misguided both economically and politically. The crises of Indonesia and other Asian countries were *not* the result of profligate governments. Rather, they generally involved excessive *private* borrowing. For this reason, some critics alleged that the IMF inappropriately applied rescue packages designed for previous crises in Latin America to Indonesia and Thailand.

Structural reforms refer to economic policy changes outside the fiscal and monetary realms. For example, the IMF required Indonesia to close 16 banks and dismantle monopolies. Some economists saw these structural reforms as misguided. For instance, Krugman (1999: 116) writes: "The sheer breadth of IMF demands, aside from raising suspicions that the United States was trying to use the crisis to impose its ideological vision on Asia, more or less guaranteed a prolonged period of wrangling between Asian governments and their rescuers, a period during which the crisis of confidence steadily worsened." In addition, the bank closures appear to have exacerbated depositor runs on other banks in a manner described above in this chapter.

Beyond these criticisms, however, a more fundamental point was at stake. In venturing into the realm of structural reforms, the IMF ventured beyond the scope of its past practices into what has traditionally been the purview of the World Bank. The IMF stood by its policies, however, and claimed that they contributed to the recovery of the countries involved.[25] This reflected the thinking of the Washington Consensus, discussed in Chapter 19.

The Indonesian Crisis

One day in January 1998 the IMF's managing director, Michel Camdessus, met with Indonesian President Suharto to review the details of an IMF bailout package for Indonesia. Among the conditions stipulated by the IMF was the dismantling of monopolies in cloves and palm oil owned by Suharto associates. Another

[24] Some prominent international economists (e.g. Jeffrey Sachs, Paul Krugman, and Joseph Stiglitz) considered that the increases in interest rates were a big mistake.

[25] See, for example, IMF (1999).

The Indonesian Crisis (cont.)

condition was that government food and energy subsidies be removed. As we discussed in Chapter 16, depreciation of a currency increases the domestic prices of traded goods such as food and energy. This, combined with attempts to remove subsidies and a very severe drought in Indonesia, drove up food and energy prices beyond the reach of millions of the Indonesian poor. Riots were the result, and these continued for nine months afterwards. Also contributing to this unrest was a widely distributed photograph of Camdessus hovering over Suharto with arms folded, an image that brought back bitter colonial memories.

Another component of the IMF's Indonesian program involved the closing of 16 insolvent banks. The IMF hoped that this move would restore confidence in the banking system. This was not the case. Critics alleged that the closing of these banks precipitated a banking panic. There was a run on remaining private banks as depositors withdrew funds and placed them in state-owned banks. The IMF's chief economist, Stanley Fischer, denied that the closing of the banks had this effect, however. In his view, "the main culprits were President Suharto's illness…, perceptions that the government would not carry out the program, and excessive creation of liquidity by the central bank" (Fischer, 1998).

As it turned out, after receiving US$3 billion from the IMF, Indonesia reneged on its commitments. Some observers claim that Suharto never intended to abide by the agreement and that the IMF was naïve not to have recognized this. In April 1998 a new agreement was reached between the IMF and the Suharto government, and this agreement allowed for a total of US$40 billion of IMF loans to Indonesia. As part of the conditionality principles of the IMF, however (discussed in Chapter 19), the funds were to be delivered in billion-dollar installments based on Indonesia's progress in keeping its commitments. Food and fuel subsidies were allowed to remain, though. In May 1998 continued rioting in Jakarta finally led to President Suharto stepping down, after 32 years as president.

Sources: Fischer (1998), Kristof (1998), and Sanger (1998).

The Global Financial Crisis

Not all crises originate in LMICs. Indeed, the work of Reinhart and Rogoff (2009) suggests that, historically, high-income countries are almost as likely as LMICs to experience crises of the sort described in Table 20.1. Further, the causes of crises in the high-income world are not much different from those in the LMICs: capital inflows, financial liberalization, asset price inflation, and over-borrowing. Beginning in mid-2007 the world economy began grappling with what became known as the global financial crisis. The causes of this crisis were located in the US economy, and included an unprecedented housing price bubble (nearly doubling in real terms in the decade up to 2007), huge inflows of capital (financing a current account deficit of over 6 percent of GDP), and a lack of prudential financial regulation (including overly sanguine chairmen of the US Federal Reserve Alan Greenspan and Ben Bernanke).[26] The government-led interventions to address the crisis were very large. Alessandri and Haldane (2011) report that, in the United States, the United Kingdom, and the euro area, these were of the order of US$14 trillion, or *one-fourth of global GDP*.

Regarding the housing market in the United States, there developed a *sub-prime* mortgage market that even included mortgages known by the acronyms NINA (no income, no asset) and NINJA (no income, no job or asset). Sub-prime mortgages became bundled and resold in the form of mortgage-backed securities (MBSs). Buyers of these securities were distributed around the world.[27] The fact that there was pure speculation in the market is described by Vogel (2010: 43–4):

> It was not unusual to see crowds and bidding frenzies whenever blocks of new housing units were opened for public sale. Many of these most aggressive buyers never intended to actually reside in the units; they were leveraged speculators taking advantage of easy credit and regulatory conditions and buying only with the intention of quickly flipping them to someone else at a higher price. For a number of years, this was a high-probability bet.

Members of the US-based investment banking sector (such as Bear Sterns, Citigroup, Lehman Brothers, and Merrill Lynch) took on a great deal of mortgage-related risk. Unfortunately, housing prices in the United States displayed a classic pattern of asset price deflation between 2005 and 2007. Exposed too, however, were select European banks. For example, the French bank BNP Paribas announced in August 2007 that it was overly exposed to sub-prime mortgage assets.[28] The Britain-based Northern Rock followed in September 2007 and ended

---

[26] There was a very strong *reluctance* on the part of the US Federal Reserve, particularly under Greenspan's chairmanship, to address the asset price bubble. In a now famous speech he gave to the Economic Club of New York in 2002, Greenspan (2002) stated: "If the bursting of an asset bubble creates economic dislocation, then preventing bubbles might seem an attractive goal. But whether incipient bubbles can be detected in real time and whether, once detected, they can be defused without inadvertently precipitating still greater adverse consequences for the economy remain in doubt." For an important counterpoint to this view, see Shiller (2016).

[27] In his analysis of MBS, Tirole (2017: 302) notes that "the issuer of a securitized bundle of loans loses its incentive to monitor the quality of the underlying loans, as it knows it will not suffer the consequences." For evidence of this, see Keys et al. (2010).

[28] In an important analytical history of the GFC, Eichengreen (2015: 176) states: "Not all financial crises have a definitive starting date, but this one clearly did. The 2007 crisis can be said to have erupted on August 9, the day of the BNP Paribas announcement. Realizing that if this land mine could have been hiding in BNP's financials it could be hiding anywhere, banks abruptly stopped lending to one another."

up in the hands of the Bank of England. In early 2008 there was a run on US-based Bear Stearns, which, with the help of the US Federal Reserve and Treasury, fell into the hands of JPMorgan Chase.[29] The US government also had to prop up its housing finance institutions Fannie Mae and Freddie Mac.[30]

Relatively quickly concerns began to be raised about Lehman Brothers, which, by most measures, was in more difficult straits than Bear Stearns had been.[31] As it turned out, nearly six months to the day after the Bear Stearns bailout, with its stock price in free fall and the US Federal Reserve and Treasury unable to assist, Lehman Brothers declared bankruptcy. This was the largest bankruptcy in US history, and the effects rippled through the global banking system.[32] Banks are tied to one another by an interbank or "overnight" lending system, and after the collapse of Lehman Brothers this critical system shut down completely.

Bear Stearns was rescued and then Lehman Brothers was allowed to fail. The next domino was the insurance giant AIG–or, more specifically, its UK-based arm, AIG Financial Products. The US Federal Reserve and Treasury decided to bail out AIG in a similar manner to how they had bailed out Bear Stearns. With many observers and participants wondering which financial firm was next, the US Congress passed the Troubled Asset Relief Program (TARP), which allowed the US Treasury to buy up compromised assets to prevent further deflation and take them off the books of financial firms.

We stated above that the GFC, like many other high-tech crises, involved capital inflows, financial liberalization, asset price inflation, and over-borrowing. Indeed, in their analysis of the GFC, Reinhart and Rogoff (2009: 212) state: "The US conceit that its financial and regulatory system could withstand massive capital inflows on a sustained basis without any problems arguably laid the foundations for the global financial crisis of the late 2000s.... Outsized financial market returns were in fact greatly exaggerated by capital inflows, just as would be the case in emerging markets." No country is immune from these financial storms. Indeed, as we will see in Chapter 21, Europe became the next locus of the GFC.

---

[29] In a now famous editorial, Wolf (2008) states: "Remember Friday March 14 2008: it was the day the dream of global free-market capitalism died. For three decades we have moved towards market-driven financial systems. By its decision to rescue Bear Stearns, the Federal Reserve, the institution responsible for monetary policy in the US, chief protagonist of free-market capitalism, declared this era over.... Deregulation has reached its limits."

[30] James (2009) is frank here, stating (108) that Fannie Mae and Freddie Mac "were placed under government 'conservatorship'–in effect, nationalized."

[31] Eichengreen (2015: 198) states: "There may have been a tendency...to assume that because Bear Stearns was rescued the same treatment would be extended to Lehman Brothers. But Lehman's problems ran deeper. It owned more toxic mortgages. It had more debt than Bear Stearns, in excess of $660 billion."

[32] See, for example, De Haas and van Horen (2012).

In our discussion of contagion above, we mentioned the notion of *systemic risk*, when a financial crisis spreads among a relatively large number of countries. The GFC was an example of a systemic crisis. At an International Monetary Fund meeting in October 2008, the then managing director, Dominique Strauss-Kahn, explicitly recognized this, stating (IMF, 2008: 1, emphasis added):

> The financial crisis that originated in the collapse of U.S. subprime mortgage market in August 2007 has deepened further and is now affecting many parts of the global financial system, including emerging markets. Intensifying solvency concerns about a number of the largest U.S.-based and European financial institutions have pushed the global financial system to the brink of *systemic meltdown*.

Contagion in the form of systemic risk was no longer a concept but, rather, a lived reality. This concentrated minds on how to prevent such episodes in the future.

Prudential Regulation and the Basel Standards

We stated in the introduction that, unlike markets for most goods and services, financial markets are characterized by "imperfections." Further, given the presence of these imperfections, we cannot be assured of economic or allocative efficiency in markets for financial products. The most fundamental imperfection in financial markets is *imperfect information*, particularly *asymmetric information*, when two parties to a financial transaction have different sets of information about factors relevant to the transaction.[33] Given these informational issues, there is a general recognition that financial systems, particularly banking systems, can benefit from *prudential regulation*.

The aim of prudential regulation is to help support the *solvency* of financial intermediaries and, thereby, to limit contagion and systemic risk. In principle, the prudential regulation agenda can be quite expansive. Consider, for example this list from Tirole (2017: 340):

> Protecting regulated institutions against the risk of contagion from the unregulated sector; increasing their levels of equity capital and putting greater emphasis on liquidity; making regulation more countercyclical; monitoring the pay structures of senior bank officers; allowing securitization, but supervising how it is used; monitoring the rating agencies.

---

[33] See Marks (2009) and Tirole (2017: chap. 11). In the case of the GFC, for example, Tirole states (327) that "the 2008 crisis is a textbook case for the theory of information and incentives taught in economics departments. At every link in the chain of transfers of risk, one of the parties had more information than the other (asymmetry of information), and this distorted the proper functioning of financial markets and their regulation."

In practice, much of the attention in prudential regulation is on *capital adequacy ratios* (CARs). CARs measure banks' available capital as a ratio of a risk-weighted measure of credit exposure. The regulation of CARs can be a purely domestic policy matter, but there has also been an international effort in this regard. Let us briefly consider this effort.

In 1974 the central bank heads of the Group of 10 (G-10) established the Basel Committee on Banking Supervision (BCBS).[34] The BCBS resides at the Bank for International Settlements and consists of representatives from central banks around the world. In 1988 the Committee introduced a banking CAR that became known as the Basel Capital Accord and, after some time, Basel I (see Table 20.2). Basel I set a minimum CAR of 8 percent, as well as a framework for measuring credit risk. It made a distinction between Tier I, or core banking capital, and Tier II, or supplementary capital. Tier I was to consist mostly of equity capital, whereas Tier II was to consist of reserves of various kinds.[35] The 8 percent CAR was measured across asset classes in a form of risk weighting.

A new set of standards went into effect in 2004 in the form of Basel II. Basel II specified requirements in terms of *three pillars*. These three pillars were: minimum capital requirements, supervisory review based on internal risk assessments, and disclosure for market discipline. Basel II recognized that different asset classes involve different levels of risk and developed complex procedures for taking these risk differences into account in the first pillar. This involved leaving the

Table 20.2 The Basel Accords

Stage	Year of Issue	Components
Basel I	1988	Proposed regulatory capital requirements of 8 percent and introduced two tiers of capital.
Basel II	2004	Introduced three pillars of bank regulation (minimum capital requirements, supervisory review, and disclosure for market discipline), as well as two tiers of capital. Effectively reduced the capital requirement and allowed asset measurements to be risk-adjusted by banks' internal models.
Basel III	Phased 2010–2017	Improved asset risk adjustment, increased capital requirements to 7 percent, and allowed for countercyclical capital requirements.

[34] The G-10 includes Belgium, Canada, France, Germany, Italy, Japan, the Netherlands, Sweden, Switzerland, the United Kingdom, and the United States.

[35] Attention to bank capital standards was and is an important issue. As documented by Alessandri and Haldane (2011), banking sector capital ratios in the United States and the United Kingdom fell by a factor of five in percentage terms during the twentieth century.

risk adjustment process to banks' own internal models (known as the internal ratings-based approach, or IRB). Many observers thought that Basel II was *far too flexible*, however, with increased weight given to the second and third pillars but not to the first pillar. *The Economist* (2004) quipped that "bank regulators...have ended up committing themselves to almost nothing" and that "the central bankers might as well have stayed at home."

As the GFC testified, Basel II was indeed insufficient. As noted by *The Economist* (2010), "The definition of Tier I capital was far too lax. Many of the equity-like instruments allowed were really debt. In effect, the fine print allowed banks' common equity, or 'core' Tier I, the purest and most flexible form of capital, to be as little as 2 percent of risk-adjusted assets." Further, the IRB process proved to be insufficient given banks' predilection for financial mischief.[36]

Having not succeeded in its mission, the BCBS began to try again, this time in the form of Basel III standards, phased in between 2010 and 2017. Under Basel III, Tier I capital was strictly limited to equity capital, the amount of this core capital was required to increase from 2 percent to 7 percent, and risk adjustment was less determined by banks' internal models. Immediately, some leading commentators questioned whether this was adequate. Indeed, Wolf (2010) dubbed the Basel III capital adequacy ratio as the "capital inadequacy ratio." He correctly pointed out that "this amount of equity is far below levels markets would impose if investors did not continue to expect governments to bail out creditors in a crisis." By some reckonings (e.g. *The Economist*, 2010), something on the order of 15 percent is necessary.

In early 2011 the BCBS set out specific standards for both Tier I and Tier II bank capital that, upon initial examination, seemed to strengthen standards significantly. Basel III has also allowed for CARs to have a countercyclical component, increasing in booms and decreasing in busts. More recently, special conditions for "globally systemically important banks" (GSIBs) have been introduced. The question is whether the incremental improvements pursued by the BCBS will prove to be sufficient to prevent further banking crises in the near future. Time will tell whether this is the case.[37]

Capital Controls

Recall that we considered the issue of capital controls in Chapter 15. We noted that capital controls are also referred to as capital account regulations (CARs) and capital flow (management) measures (CFMs). Recall also that capital controls can

[36] Given the failure of Basel II standards in the GFC, central banks resorted to their own "stress testing" of banks. See, for example, Wall (2014).

[37] See, for example, *The Economist* (2017b).

take many forms, some of which were discussed in Chapter 15. We stated that the purpose of capital controls is to address the volatile nature of gross capital flows, the pattern of large inflows of short-term portfolio capital that is later followed by a reversal in the form of *capital flight*. To the extent that such volatility contributes to crises, capital controls might play a role in crisis prevention.

The potential role of capital controls in crisis prevention has been recognized for a long time now. Wyplosz (1986) has shown how capital controls can help to prevent the "old-fashioned" balance of payments crises discussed above. There were also a number of evaluations of the role of capital controls in Malaysia and Thailand during the "high-tech" Asian financial crisis (e.g. Edison and Reinhart, 2001). There has been investigation as well of the implications of the GFC on how we think about capital controls (e.g. Gallagher, 2012), specifically whether in their market-friendly form they might have made it less severe. The case of Iceland is discussed in the accompanying box.

Capital Controls and the Iceland Crisis

The GFC reached many countries. One unexpected case was that of Iceland. The crisis was certainly of a "high-tech" nature and was located in the banking sector. In the run-up to the GFC the Icelandic banking sector had assets that were approximately ten times the GDP of the country. That certainly suggested a potential problem. As it turned out, the largest banks in Iceland (Glitnir, Landsbanki, and Kaupthing) had borrowed heavily abroad, much of the debt being denominated in foreign currencies. All three of these banks collapsed in 2008 and the Icelandic krona rapidly depreciated. Some banking executives were even imprisoned.

In order to prevent the krona from depreciating even farther and inflating the krona value of foreign-denominated debt, Iceland quickly put in place onerous capital controls on both firms and households, including pension funds. Interestingly, the government had the support of the IMF in this policy decision. Initially these were to be temporary, but they were removed only in 2017. The capital controls prevented capital from leaving the country and froze offshore krona holdings. When the controls on outflows were removed in 2017, they were replaced with a form of variable deposit requirement (VDR) on capital inflows, described in Chapter 15.

The question posed by the Iceland case is whether it might have been better to have used market-friendly capital controls on inflows *before* the crisis rather than onerous controls on capital outflows after the crisis.

Sources: Alderman (2017), Baldursson and Portes (2014), *The Economist* (2017a), and Eichengreen (2015).

As discussed in Chapter 15, in the wake of the GFC the IMF revisited capital controls and gave them an endorsement (Ostry et al., 2010). This study suggests that market-friendly capital controls can help countries cope with surges of capital inflows, which can end in sudden stops and contribute to the kinds of crises discussed in this chapter. It endorsed many of the observations concerning capital controls discussed in Chapter 15. For this reason, the role of capital controls in mitigating crises is worth continued attention.

Conclusion

Financial crises come in many varieties, but these are varieties that can occur together. Hyperinflation, balance of payments and currency crises, asset price deflation, bank crises, external debt crises, and domestic debt crises can combine in ways in which one crisis makes another more likely and more sustained. Balance of payments and currency crises can put pressure on any entity that holds foreign-currency-denominated debt, which consequently increases in domestic-currency value. If this includes banks, it can make a banking crisis more likely. If it includes the government, it can make default crises more likely. Balance of payments and currency crashes can worsen inflation by increasing the prices of trade goods, and asset price deflation can make banking crises more likely.

Fixed exchange rate regimes can be very fragile. In the face of large changes in the expected future exchange rate, a government can have a very difficult time supporting the fixed rate; at some point, it simply runs out of foreign reserves. "Old-fashioned" balance of payments crises can also occur as a result of capital flight. Weak financial (especially banking) systems add to the likelihood of "high-tech" crises, in which confidence in the financial system deteriorates. This is particularly true if the regulatory framework supporting the banking system is weak.

In response to the GFC, a new set of BCBS standards known as Basel III were developed in phased form between 2010 and 2017, a form of prudential regulation. The jury is still out on them. Market-friendly capital controls can also play a role, and they have been finally endorsed by the IMF. Better data on sovereign debt and asset prices can also help sound the alarm on future crises, but policy-makers need to act in response to unsustainable debt levels and asset price bubbles. Unfortunately, in the case of asset price bubbles, central banks have been loath to respond to curb their growth. Given this reluctance, the proposals of Reinhart and Rogoff (2009) and Eichengreen (2010) for an international financial regulatory organization (to replace the Basel Committee) are worth considering seriously.[38]

[38] Eichengreen (2010) has also proposed a Global Systemic Risk Facility, to attempt to address some of the concerns raised by Goldin and Vogel (2010).

Review Exercises

1. What is the key difference between "old-fashioned" and "high-tech" crises?
2. In Chapter 18 we addressed fixed exchange rates. Policies to maintain fixed exchange rates fell into two categories. First, there were policies to address the excess demand or supply of the home country (official reserve transactions). Second, there were policies to change the equilibrium exchange rate (interest rate changes). Please answer the following questions with regard to the use of these policies in balance of payments crises.
   a. In a balance of payments crisis, what kind of official reserve transactions will be made?
   b. What are the limits of the official reserve transactions approach to resolving balance of payments crises?
   c. In a balance of payments crisis, what kind of interest rate policies will be used?
   d. What are the limits of the interest rate approach to resolving balance of payments crises?
3. The argument in favor of current account convertibility (free trade) is that it leads to gains from trade. Are there any reasons you can think of why we might not be able to extend this argument to the financial transactions of the capital/financial account? Or, to put it differently, are there any ways that financial markets differ from merchandise and service markets?
4. Take the crisis varieties in Table 20.1 and try to list the ways in which one can contribute to another.
5. Suppose you were tasked with the responsibility of developing a set of *leading indicators* of crises. What would you include in this set and why?

FURTHER READING AND WEB RESOURCES

A short introduction to finance can be found in Tirole (2017: chap. 11). Readable and worthwhile reviews of crises can be found in Krugman (1999), Eichengreen (1999), Reinhart and Rogoff (2009), and Montiel (2011: chaps. 25–9). For a more advanced treatment, see Allen and Gale (2007), and, for the specific case of bubbles, see Vogel (2010). For a description of a more "sensible" way to conduct finance, see Bhidé (2010). The Alessandri and Haldane (2011) chapter is very much worth a read for a historical perspective on the 2007–2009 bailout of the global financial system. Excellent comparisons of the GFC to the Great Depression can be found in James (2009) and Eichengreen (2015). Also on the GFC, see Tirole (2017: chap. 12).

REFERENCES

Acharya, V. V., L. H. Pedersen, T. Philippon, and M. Richardson (2017) "Measuring Systemic Risk," *Review of Financial Studies*, 30:1, 2–47.

Alderman, L. (2017) "Iceland, Symbol of Financial Crisis, Finally Lifts Capital Controls," *New York Times*, March 14.

Alessandri, A., and A. Haldane (2011) "Banking on the State," in A. Demirgüç-Kunt, D. D. Evanoff, and G. G. Kaufman (eds.), *The International Financial Crisis: Have the Rules of Finance Changed?*, World Scientific, 169–95.

Allen, R., and D. Gale (2007) *Understanding Financial Crises*, Oxford University Press.

Baldursson, F. M., and R. Portes (2014) "Capital Controls and the Resolution of Failed Cross-Border Banks: The Case of Iceland," *Capital Markets Law Review*, 9:1, 40–54.

Bhidé, A. (2010) *A Call For Judgment: Sensible Finance for a Dynamic Economy*, Oxford University Press.

Bird, G., and R. S. Rajan (2001) "Banks, Financial Liberalization and Financial Crises in Emerging Markets," *World Economy*, 24:7, 889–910.

Calvo, G. A., and E. G. Mendoza (1996) "Mexico's Balance-of-Payments Crisis: A Chronicle of a Death Foretold," *Journal of International Economics*, 41:3/4, 235–64.

Crook, C. (2003) "A Cruel Sea of Capital: A Survey of Global Finance," *The Economist*, May 3.

De Haas, R., and N. van Horen (2012) "International Shock Transmission after the Lehman Brothers Collapse: Evidence from Syndicated Lending," *American Economic Review*, 102:3, 231–7.

Diamond, D., and P. H. Dybvig (1983) "Bank Runs, Deposit Insurance and Liquidity," *Journal of Political Economy*, 91:3, 401–19.

Diaz-Alejandro, C. (1985) "Goodbye Financial Repression, Hello Financial Crash," *Journal of Development Economics*, 19:1/2, 1–24.

Dobson, W., and G. C. Hufbauer (2001) *World Capital Markets: Challenges to the G-10*, Institute for International Economics.

Dugger, C. W. (2010) "Zimbabwe Health Care, Paid with Peanuts," *New York Times*, December 18.

Dungey, M., and D. Gajurel (2015) "Contagion and Banking Crises: International Evidence for 2007–2009," *Journal of Banking and Finance*, 60, 271–83.

The Economist (1997) "Lessons for Thailand, et al," July 12.

The Economist (2004) "Bank Capital Adequacy: Basel Light," July 3.

The Economist (2010) "Reforming Banking: Base Camp Basel," January 23.

The Economist (2017a) "The End of a Saga: Iceland Lifts Capital Controls," March 18.

The Economist (2017b) "Basel 3, an International Capital-Adequacy Standard, Is Unloved But Much Needed," May 4.

Edison, H. J., and C. M. Reinhart (2001) "Capital Controls during Financial Crises: The Cases of Malaysia and Thailand," in R. Glick, R. Moreno, and M. M. Spiegel (eds.), *Financial Crises in Emerging Markets*, Cambridge University Press, 427–56.

Eichengreen, B. (1999) *Toward a New Financial Architecture: A Practical Post-Asia Agenda*, Institute for International Economics.

Eichengreen, B. (2010) "Out-of-the-Box Thoughts about the International Financial Architecture," *Journal of International Commerce, Economics and Policy*, 1:1, 1–20.

Eichengreen, B. (2015) *Hall of Mirrors: The Great Depression, the Great Recession, and the Uses – and Misuses – of History*, Oxford University Press.

Fischer, S. (1998) "Lessons from a Crisis," *The Economist*, October 3.

Gallagher, K. (2012) "Regaining Control: Capital Controls and the Global Financial Crisis," in W. Grant and G. K. Wilson (eds.), *The Consequences of the Global Financial Crisis: The Rhetoric of Reform and Regulation*, Oxford University Press, 109–38.

Goldin, I., and T. Vogel (2010) "Global Governance and Systemic Risk in the 21st Century: Lessons from the Financial Crisis," *Global Policy*, 1:1, 4–15.

Goldstein, M., G. K. Kaminsky, and C. M. Reinhart (2000) *Assessing Financial Vulnerability*, Institute for International Economics.

Greenspan, A. (2002) "Issues for Monetary Policy," speech to the Economic Club of New York, December 19, www.federalreserve.gov/boarddocs/speeches/2002/20021219/default .htm.

International Monetary Fund (1999) "The IMF's Response to the Asian Crisis," IMF.

International Monetary Fund (2008) "Statement by Dominique Strauss-Kahn," IMF.

James, H. (2009) *The Creation and Destruction of Value: The Globalization Cycle*, Harvard University Press.

Joyce, J. P., and M. Nabar (2009) "Sudden Stops, Banking Crises and Investment Collapses in Emerging Markets," *Journal of Development Economics*, 90:2: 314–22.

Kalemni-Ozcan, S., E. Papaioannou, and F. Perri (2013) "Global Banks and Crisis Transmission," *Journal of International Economics*, 89:2, 495–510.

Kaminsky, G. L., C. M. Reinhart, and C. A. Végh (2003) "The Unholy Trinity of Financial Contagion," *Journal of Economic Perspectives*, 17:4, 51–74.

Keys, B. J., T. Mukherjee, A. Seru, and V. Vig (2010) "Did Securitization Lead to Lax Screening? Evidence from Subprime Loans," *Quarterly Journal of Economics*, 125:1, 307–62.

Kose, M. A., E. Prasad, K. Rogoff, and S.-J. Wei. (2009) "Financial Globalization: A Reappraisal," *IMF Staff Papers*, 56:1, 8–62.

Kristof, N. D. (1998) "Has the IMF Cured or Harmed Asia? Dispute Rages after Months of Crisis," *New York Times*, April 23.

Krugman, P. (1979) "A Model of Balance of Payments Crises," *Journal of Money, Credit and Banking*, 11:3, 311–25.

Krugman, P. (1999) *The Return of Depression Economics*, Norton.

Krugman, P. (2010) "Things Could Be Worse," *New York Times*, September 9.

López Glass, V. (2019) "Nothing Can Prepare You for Life with Hyperinflation," *New York Times*, February 12.

McIndo-Calder, T. (2018) "Hyperinflation in Zimbabwe: Money Demand, Seigniorage and Aid Shocks," *Applied Economics*, 50:15, 1659–75.

Marks, S. (2009) "Asymmetric Information," in K. A. Reinert, R. S. Rajan, A. J. Glass, and L. S. Davis (eds.), *The Princeton Encyclopedia of the World Economy*, Princeton University Press, 89–94.

Montiel, P. J. (2011) *Macroeconomics in Emerging Markets*, Cambridge University Press.

Mydans, S. (1997a) "Thai Prime Minister Falls Victim to Economic Crisis," *New York Times*, November 4.

Mydans, S. (1997b) "Economists Cheer Thailand's Tough Action on Ailing Finance Companies," *New York Times*, December 9.

Mydans, S. (1998) "Struggling Thailand Seeks Easier IMF Terms," *New York Times*, January 9.

Noguchi, Y. (1994) "The 'Bubble' and Economic Policies in the 1980s," *Journal of Japanese Studies*, 20:2, 291–329.

Ostry, J. D., A. R. Ghosh, K. Habermeier, M. Chamon, M. S. Qureshi, and D. B. S. Reinhardt (2010) "Capital Inflows: The Role of Controls," Staff Position Note 10/04, IMF.

Reinhart, C. M., and K. S. Rogoff (2009) *This Time Is Different: Eight Centuries of Financial Folly*, Princeton University Press.

Reynolds, S., R. Fowles, J. Gander, W. Kunaporntham, and S. Ratanakomut (2002) "Forecasting the Probability of Failure of Thailand's Financial Companies in the Asian Financial Crisis," *Economic Development and Cultural Change*, 51:1, 237–46.

Sanger, D. E. (1998) "IMF Role in World Economy Is Hotly Debated," *New York Times*, October 2.

Shiller, R. J. (2016) *Irrational Exuberance*, rev. 3rd edn., Princeton University Press.

Stiglitz, J. E. (2002) *Globalization and Its Discontents*, Norton.

Stone, D., and W. T. Ziemba (1993) "Land and Stock Prices in Japan," *Journal of Economic Perspectives*, 7:3, 149–65.

Tirole, J. (2017) *Economics for the Common Good*, Princeton University Press.

Vogel, H. L. (2010) *Financial Market Bubbles and Crashes*, Cambridge University Press.

Wade, R. (1998) "From 'Miracle' to 'Cronyism': Explaining the Great Asian Slump," *Cambridge Journal of Economics*, 22:6, 693–706.

Wall, L. D. (2014) "The Adoption of Stress Testing: Why the Basel Capital Measures Were Not Enough," *Journal of Banking Regulation*, 15:3/4, 266–76.

Wolf, M. (2008) "The Rescue of Bear Sterns Marks Liberalisation's Limit," *Financial Times*, March 25.

Wolf, M. (2010) "Basel: The Mouse That Did Not Roar," *Financial Times*, September 14.

Woodall, P. (1995) "The World Economy: Who's in the Driving Seat?," *The Economist*, October 7.

World Bank (2001) *Finance for Growth: Policy Choices in a Volatile World*, World Bank.

Wyplosz, C. (1986) "Capital Controls and Balance of Payments Crises," *Journal of International Money and Finance*, 5:2, 167–79.

21 Monetary Unions

Imagine that you are the finance minister of a medium-sized country with extensive trade and investment relationships with fellow members of a **preferential trade agreement** of the type discussed in Chapter 9. Imagine also that you have responsibility for determining the future exchange rate regime of your country. One option you have is a flexible exchange rate regime (a float). If you chose this option, however, your country might be buffeted by destabilizing changes in the nominal (and hence real) exchange rate. A second option you have is a fixed exchange rate (or crawling peg). If you chose this option, however, your country might eventually stumble into a balance of payments and currency crisis, as we discussed in Chapter 20. What should you do? There is no easy answer.

There is a third option available to you, one we mentioned briefly in Chapter 9 on PTAs. You and the other finance ministers in the PTA could agree to do away with all the exchange rates between your countries by becoming a **monetary union** with a common currency. This is not a panacea, because you and your colleagues would still need to decide upon the exchange rate regime for the common currency against other major currencies. But at least you can hope to avoid exchange rate instability with your major trade and investment partners. As we will see, however, other kinds of instability can arise.

As it turns out, this common currency policy was adopted as a goal by the countries of Western Europe in 1971 and was implemented in 1999. Monetary union has also been a living reality for the Communauté Financière Africaine (CFA) franc zone, a group of African countries with ties to France, and for the rand zone in Southern Africa. In this chapter, we first take up the case of the European Monetary Union (EMU), assessing both its planning and implementation. Next, we assess the EMU in light of the theory of **optimum currency areas** (OCAs) and discuss its potential adjustment problems and how it fared during the global financial crisis. Finally, we briefly consider the cases of the CFA franc zone and the rand zone.

The European Monetary Union at a Glance

The European Monetary Union is a monetary union between 19 countries (as of 2019) in which the euro (€) serves as the shared currency. The euro is administered by the European Central Bank (ECB). The member countries are listed in Table 21.1.

Table 21.1 EMU membership

Country	Year joined	Original currency	Central government debt as percentage of GDP, year of entry	Central government debt as percentage of GDP, most recent year available
Original members				
Austria	1999	Austrian schilling	71	95 (2017)
Belgium	1999	Belgian franc	127	120 (2018)
Finland	1999	Finnish markka	53	69 (2018)
France	1999	French franc	74	124 (2017)
Germany	1999	Deutsche mark	61	72 (2017)
Ireland	1999	Irish pound	51	77 (2017)
Italy	1999	Italian lira	124	152 (2017)
Luxembourg	1999	Luxembourg franc	18	31 (2017)
Netherlands	1999	Dutch guilder	67	70 (2017)
Portugal	1999	Portuguese escudo	61	141 (2018)
Spain	1999	Spanish peseta	68	114 (2018)
Subsequent members				
Greece	2001	Greek drachma	126	189 (2017)
Slovenia	2007	Slovene tolar	30	89 (2017)
Cyprus	2008	Cyprus pound	162	103 (2018)
Malta	2008	Maltese lira	73	46 (2018)
Slovakia	2009	Slovak koruna	43	58 (2017)
Estonia	2011	Estonian kroon	10	13 (2017)
Latvia	2014	Latvian lat	46	47 (2017)
Lithuania	2015	Lithuanian litas	76	48 (2017)

Sources: European Central Bank, World Bank, World Development Indicators, Organisation for Economic Co-operation and Development, and tradingeconomics.com.

In 1999 there were only 11 members (Austria, Belgium, Finland, France, Germany, Ireland, Italy, Luxembourg, the Netherlands, Portugal, and Spain). Subsequently, accessions added Greece in 2001, Slovenia in 2007, Cyprus and Malta in 2008, and Slovakia in 2009. After a few years further accessions added Estonia in 2011, Latvia in 2014, and Lithuania in 2015.

During the initial years of the EMU the euro was "invisible," used only as a unit of account and for electronic transactions. But, beginning in 2002, it appeared "on the streets" in the form of notes and coins. The euro is legal tender in the EMU member countries for all types of transactions. It also plays a large role both in the EU and the world economy, as an important component of national governments' foreign reserves, for example. Further, there are some mini-states and territories that use the euro as their legal tender. Given the size of the EMU (over 340 million people), the bloc is also an important component of the world economy.[1]

As we will see below, there are three pre-1999 EU members (Denmark, the United Kingdom, and Sweden) that *chose* not to join the EMU. Denmark and the United Kingdom utilized an "opt-out" provision of the Maastricht Treaty. As we saw in Chapter 9, the United Kingdom's relationship with the European Union is in the process of dissolution through Brexit. Sweden joined the European Union in 1995 and does not have an official opt-out. Although the result of a 1994 Swedish referendum was in favor of joining the European Union, a 2003 referendum went against joining the EMU. Since then the Swedish government has respected that result.[2]

Table 21.1 lists the original currency of each EMU member country. It also lists the central government debt as a percentage of GDP both for the year of entry and for the most recent year available. As we will see below, these debt levels have proved to be an important aspect of EMU history, and they played a role in the spread of the GFC to the Eurozone.

Table 21.2 lists the EU members that are *not* members of the EMU and provides some information on their current exchange rate regime and readiness to join the EMU. With the exceptions of the United Kingdom and Denmark, with their opt-outs,

Table 21.2 In but out: countries that are members of the EU but not the EMU

Country	Currency	Exchange rate regime	Status as of 2019
Bulgaria	Bulgarian lev	Pegged to euro in a currency board arrangement	Seeking to join and meet convergence criteria. In process of joining the EU banking union. Not yet a member of the Exchange Rate Mechanism (ERM II).
Czech Republic	Czech koruna	Stabilized arrangement	Not yet a member of the Exchange Rate Mechanism (ERM II).
Denmark	Danish krone	Pegged to euro	Formal opt-out. Two referendums against joining. A member of the Exchange Rate Mechanism (ERM II).
Hungary	Hungarian forint	Floating	Not yet a member of the Exchange Rate Mechanism (ERM II).

[1] For further information on the euro, see Salvatore (2009).

[2] Another way this is sometimes stated is that Sweden's opt-out is de facto but not de jure.

Table 21.2 (cont.)

Country	Currency	Exchange rate regime	Status as of 2019
Poland	Polish złoty	Floating	Not yet a member of the Exchange Rate Mechanism (ERM II).
Romania	Romanian leu	Floating	Not yet a member of the Exchange Rate Mechanism (ERM II).
Sweden	Swedish krona	Floating	Referendum against joining. Not yet a member of the Exchange Rate Mechanism (ERM II).
United Kingdom	British pound	Floating	Formal opt-out. In the process of leaving the European Union. Not yet a member of the Exchange Rate Mechanism (ERM II).

Sources: ec.europa.eu and imf.org.

all EU members are expected to *eventually* join the EMU. As seen in Table 21.2, one question is whether a country has joined the Exchange Rate Mechanism (ERM), or, more precisely, the post-1999 ERM II. As we will discuss further, the ERM fixes a currency against the euro within a band of 2.25 percent around a central rate. The Danish kroner is the only currency in Table 21.2 that is part of ERM II. The Bulgaria lev is also pegged to the euro, however, in a currency board arrangement.[3]

Planning the European Monetary Union

The history of monetary integration in Europe has roots that go back to the period immediately after World War II.[4] In Chapter 9, we discussed the evolution of the **European Union** from 1951. For your convenience, Table 9.3 of that chapter is reproduced here as Table 21.3. Issing (2008: 4) notes that, after the formation of the European Economic Community in 1958, "there were occasional suggestions that work should also be undertaken towards monetary union." The real monetary union initiative began in 1970, however, when a commission chaired by the then prime minister of Luxembourg, Pierre Werner, issued a report providing a detailed plan for a step-by-step movement to a European Monetary Union by 1980. Some details regarding Pierre Werner are provided in the accompanying box. The European Council of Ministers of Economics and Finance (ECOFIN) endorsed the Werner Report in 1971.

---

[3] On this case, see Marinova (2016).

[4] See Gros and Thygesen (1992: chap. 1) and Dinan (2010: chap. 13).

Table 21.3 The evolution of the European Union

Year	Initiative	Treaty	Members added
1951	European Coal and Steel Community	Treaty of Paris	Belgium France Germany Italy Luxembourg Netherlands
1958	European Economic Community	Treaty of Rome	
1965	Institutional reform	Brussels Treaty	
1973	Enlargement		Denmark Ireland United Kingdom
1981	Enlargement		Greece
1986	Institutional reform	Single European Act	
1986	Enlargement		Portugal Spain
1992	European Union	Treaty on European Union (TEU) or the Maastricht Treaty	
1995	Enlargement		Austria Finland Sweden
1997	Institutional reform	Treaty of Amsterdam	
1999	European Monetary Union		United Kingdom, Sweden, and Denmark not included
2001	Institutional reform	Treaty of Nice	
2002	Common EMU currency: the euro		United Kingdom, Sweden, and Denmark not included
2004	Enlargement		Cyprus Czech Republic Estonia Hungary Latvia Lithuania Malta Poland Slovakia Slovenia

Table 21.3 (cont.)

Year	Initiative	Treaty	Members added
2007	Enlargement		Bulgaria Romania
2007	EU constitution	Lisbon Treaty	
2013	Enlargement		Croatia
2016	Brexit vote	United Kingdom votes to eventually leave the European Union	

Sources: Dinan (2010) and europa.eu.

Werner's vision of an EMU by 1980 was not to come to pass. Recall from Chapter 19 that the early 1970s were characterized by the demise of the Bretton Woods system of global monetary arrangements. During 1971 key European currencies, including the German deutsche mark, began to float, and US President Nixon closed the "gold window," signaling an end to a monetary era. In response to this crisis, a year later the members of the EEC decide to bind their exchange rates within 2.25 percent of each other. This became known as the "snake in a tunnel," or just "snake." During 1972, however, the British pound came under pressure and was forced out of the "snake." Later, the Danish krone also was forced to pull out of the "snake." The French franc was forced out in 1974, re-entered in 1975, and was forced out again in 1976. Despite these difficulties, the "snake" continued through 1978, and this time period represented one in which the EEC was attempting to deal with new global monetary realities.[5] As we discussed in Chapter 19, this was not an easy task.

In 1977 the European Commission president, Roy Jenkins, gave a lecture at the European University in Florence. In this lecture, he called for Europe to return to the Werner vision and adopt monetary union as a goal. As a result of this new impetus and other developments, negotiations began in earnest over the creation of a European Monetary System, or EMS, in 1978. The EMS came into being as a fixed-rate system in 1979. In a very real sense, the EMS was an attempt to replicate the fixed-rate Bretton Woods system between the countries of Europe.[6] A new currency was created, called the European currency unit, or ECU, defined as a basket of European currencies. The ECU had a role equivalent to that initially hoped for the special drawing right in the Bretton Woods system (see Chapter 19). Furthermore, the European Community acted in a role equivalent to the IMF, providing balance of payments credit to members.

[5] See Eichengreen (2008: chap. 5) for a history of the "snake."

[6] See James (1996: chap. 10).

The original hope was that each country would peg its currency to the ECU, but this hope did not come to pass. Instead, in the 1980s countries began to peg their currencies to the German mark.[7] The ECU continued only as a unit of account for official European Community business. In the early years of the EMS there was a great deal of instability. A number of parity realignments were necessary, with the French franc falling against the German mark. The latter was largely a result of the expansive macroeconomic policies of the Socialist government of President François Mitterrand. During a crisis in 1983 Mitterrand changed course, in order to keep France within the EMS.[8] Thereafter, stability was restored with less frequent parity changes.

In 1988 the European Council called upon then president of the European Commission, Jacques Delors, to study the steps required to move towards a monetary union. The subsequent Delors Report was issued in 1989. The report called for a single currency and an integrated system of European central banks. In 1991 a meeting of the European Community took place in the Dutch town of Maastricht. The Maastricht Treaty, agreed to at this meeting, was to serve as a constitution of the new European Union, replacing the Treaty of Rome. It was signed in 1992. Importantly for our purposes here, however, the Maastricht Treaty set 1999 as a target date for the EMU.

In 1994, as specified by the Maastricht treaty, a European Monetary Institute (EMI) came into being. Its purpose was to plan for the future European System of Central Banks, or ESCB, and to plot the course towards monetary integration. The EMI was to also monitor the progress of member countries towards meeting a set of *convergence criteria*. These criteria concerned price stability, levels of government deficits and debt, exchange rate targets, and interest rate targets. For example, government deficits (a flow) were required to be equivalent to less than 3 percent of gross domestic product, and government debts (a stock) were required to be less than 60 percent of GDP. These convergence criteria reflected the wishes (or demands) of the German government.[9]

---

[7] "Structurally, Germany...occupied within the EMS a situation analogous to that of the United States within the classical Bretton Woods par value system, and the deutsche mark constituted the European 'key currency'" (James, 1996: 482).

[8] The adjustment came under the guidance of the French minister of economy, Jacques Delors, who would later become a powerful president of the European Commission.

[9] Having experienced two periods of hyperinflation in the twentieth century, the German government and the German citizenry approached the EMU project with some caution. Issing (2008: 23) writes: "Without any doubt, a stable currency was to a very large extent the foundation that underpinned the economic reconstruction after the Second World War.... No wonder, then, that [Germans] saw little merit in the idea of abandoning their stable national currency." These considerations were also why the European Central Bank was located in Frankfurt, home to the German central bank. Eichengreen (2015) revisits this history, stating the following (40): "The hyperinflation was history. But it was not history that was quickly forgotten. This background explains how...the Deutsche Bundesbank continued to view the world through the lens of the 1920s...into the twenty-first century."

Pierre Werner

Pierre Werner was born in Luxembourg in 1913 and grew up in a bilingual family, speaking both German and French. His professional life spanned the fields of law and economics. Werner studied law at the University of Paris and economics and finance at the Paris École Libre de Sciences Politiques (Science Po). Unlike many leading citizens of Luxembourg, who fled the country, Werner spent World War II under German occupation, witnessing many horrors first-hand. As with many Western Europeans of this generation, Werner became passionate about European integration as an *antidote to war*. He was elected to the Luxembourg parliament in 1945 and befriended Jean Monnet, one of the architects of the European Economic Community, formed in 1958. To Werner, Monnet, and other leading integrationists of that era, "the central aim of European unity was to prevent war. Economic gain, though useful, was a secondary consideration" (*The Economist*, 2002b).

Werner became prime minister of Luxembourg in 1959 and remained in that post until 1974. He returned to that post in 1979, retiring from politics in 1984 to pursue a subsequent career in business. In 1993 he published his memoirs, entitled *Itinéraires Luxembourgeois et Européens*.

Werner first floated the idea of a common European currency in a 1960 speech at Strasbourg. In 1969 the EEC adopted the goal of monetary union and convened a High Level Group, under Werner's chairmanship, to develop a plan for an EEC monetary union by 1980. The plan, which became known as the Werner Report, was circulated in 1970 and endorsed by the EEC in 1971. Although it did not mention the adoption of a common currency per se, the Werner Report called for the "total and irreversible conversion of currencies, the elimination of fluctuation in exchange rates, the irrevocable fixing of parity rates and the complete liberation of capital accounts." A continued advocate of a common currency for Europe, however, Werner had to wait until January 2002 to witness the introduction of euro notes and coins. He died six months later.

Sources: Daily Telegraph (2002) and *The Economist* (2002b).

The evolution towards the EMU proved to be more difficult than envisioned in the Delors Report. In 1990 East and West Germany had reunified. This required unprecedented increases in public expenditure on the part of the German government. To prevent the German economy from expanding too quickly, the German central bank pursued a tight or restrictive monetary policy. This kept German interest rates high, caused international investors to favor deutsche-mark-denominated assets over other European assets, and put downward pressure on the value of other European currencies. The EMS par-value system consequently came under pressure.

In addition, difficulties in ratification of the 1992 Maastricht Treaty ruffled investors' expectations. In particular, there were growing predictions of a "No" vote (proved to be incorrect) in the French referendum on Maastricht in September 1992. That very same month pressure built against the British pound and Italian lira. Despite very large interventions by European central banks to support these currencies, they were forced out of the EMS.[10] The French franc came under a second-round attack in 1993. In response to these events, the margins around the EMS parities were expanded from 2.25 percent to 15 percent.

The EMS crisis was certainly an inauspicious transition to European monetary integration. The British government, which subsequently opted out of the EMU, was particularly irritated by its forced exit from the EMS. That said, however, most EU leaders resolved to *press on*, and so they did. In 1995 EU members meeting in Madrid committed themselves to introducing the euro in January 1999. They also adopted the EMI's plan for monetary integration, despite widespread misgivings. After the Madrid meetings, the EMU project proceeded in large part as an act of political faith, supplemented by technical competence in institutional design.[11]

Implementing the European Monetary Union

The day of reckoning for the EMU came in May 1998, when the European Council met in Brussels to determine which countries were to take part in the EMU on January 1, 1999. Recall that the first convergence criteria concerned *price stability*. Figure 21.1 plots inflation rates for the six countries ultimately included in the EMU with the highest inflation rates in 1990 (Austria, Finland, Germany, Italy, Portugal and Spain). As you can see in this figure, there was a significant degree of convergence in inflation rates between 1990 and 1998, a relatively short period of time. From the perspective of this first convergence criterion, then, prospects were good.

The second and third convergence criteria concerned central government *deficits* and *debt*. As it turned out, nearly all the candidates for inclusion in the EMU had

---

[10] The pound and lira crises were preceded by crises of the Finnish markka and the Swedish krone. Later, the Irish pound, the Portuguese escudo, and the Spanish peseta were also devalued. The franc peg survived thanks to intervention by the German Bundesbank.

[11] With regard to the political economy of the EMU, Walter and Sen (2009: 138) argue that "it is difficult to avoid the conclusion that the strong commitment of France, Germany, and other European governments (left and right) to monetary union has much to do with the broader goal shared by political elites of promoting deeper political integration."

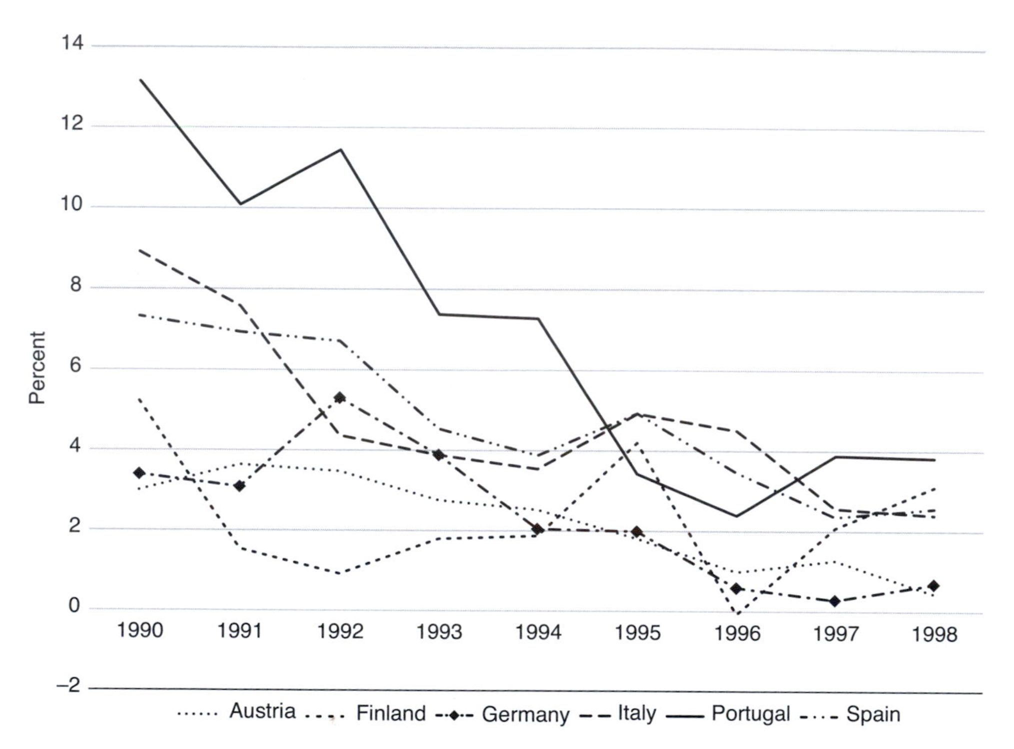

Figure 21.1 Inflation rates (GDP price deflator) in selected euro countries, 1990–1998
Source: databank.worldbank.org.

made significant progress in the area of government deficits, though in some cases this involved a bit of creative accounting. With regard to government debt levels, however, two countries stood out as *not* having met the convergence criterion: Belgium and Italy. As we saw in Table 21.1, these two countries had debts equivalent to 127 percent and 124 percent of GDP, respectively. No amount of creative accounting would move these statistics to the required 60 percent level!

In the event, the European Council chose to give Belgium and Italy a *pass*. As noted by Issing (2008: 16, emphasis added), "For both of these countries, founder members of the European Economic Community and in every respect at the center of European integration, a major effort at interpretation and ultimately a *political decision* were required to enable their entry." In other words, a key convergence criterion was *violated*. As a result of this political decision, the original members of the EMU were: Austria, Belgium, Finland, France, Germany, Ireland, Italy, Luxembourg, the Netherlands, Portugal, and Spain.

Greece was the one country that wanted to join the EMU at that time but was not allowed to. This decision was later reversed, and Greece joined in 2001 with a debt level of 126 percent of GDP, again violating the relevant convergence criterion. As mentioned above, the United Kingdom, Denmark, and Sweden opted not to join. At the time, *The Economist* (1998b) summed up the situation as follows: "A striking feature of the single currency arrangements is that they make no provision, legal or practical, for any participant's withdrawal or expulsion. In this adventure, Europe has left itself no choice but to succeed."

The centerpiece of the EMU is the Frankfurt-based European Central Bank. The charter of the ECB was modeled on the German central bank, and the former national central banks are related to the ECB in a structure modeled on the Federal Reserve System in the United States. As specified in the Maastricht Treaty, the primary objective of the ECB in its monetary policy decisions is to maintain *price stability* within the EMU. The ECB is required to maintain annual increases in a Harmonised Index of Consumer Prices (HICP, calculated by Eurostat—the statistical office of the European Union) at or below 2 percent. This is widely regarded as a very stringent rule, but one insisted upon by the German central bank in the run-up to the EMU.[12] In the conduct of this objective, the ECB is to maintain independence from political influence.

The ECB is headed by a president with an eight-year, non-renewable term. This proved difficult from the start. The European Council appoints the ECB president, and a battle ensued over who would initially fill this post. This inauspicious beginning is discussed in the accompanying box. The European Council also appoints the ECB vice president. The president, the vice president and four other individuals compose the ECB executive board. The executive board is responsible for *implementing* monetary policy within the EMU. Issing (2008: 70) describes the executive board as the "operational decision-making body of the ECB."

The executive board plus the heads of EMU member central banks compose the ECB Governing Council. The Governing Council is responsible for *formulating* monetary policy within the EMU. There is also a General Council, which adds the heads of the EU member central banks that are not part of the EMU. The four members of the executive board other than the president and the vice president do not have the right to vote as part of the General Council, however. The General Council is an *administrative* body that is responsible for the work previously undertaken by the EMI, with a focus on accession processes.

The ECB actually plays two roles within the European Union. This is illustrated in Figure 21.2. First, with regard to the European Union, it is the centerpiece of the European System of Central Banks. Originally it had been assumed that all EU members would be members of the EMU, but we now know that it is not the case. So, second, the ECB is the centerpiece of a subset of the ESCB that has become

---

[12] For more on the conduct of monetary policy within the EMU, see Issing (2008: chap. 3) and Micossi (2015). Issing notes (83): "With the Harmonized Index of Consumer Prices, Eurostat provided the most important indicator for the development of euro area prices on a timely basis." For a criticism of the 2 percent inflation ceiling, see Münchau (2011).

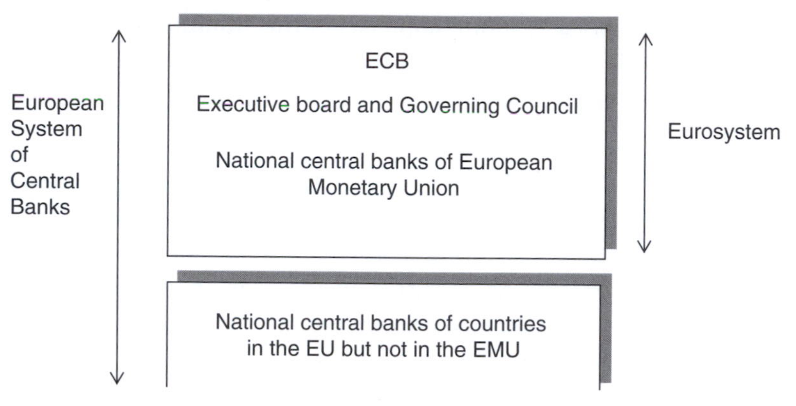

Figure 21.2 Organizational structure of the ECB
Source: European Central Bank.

known as the Eurosystem, consisting of the central banks of EMU members and the ECB. If, at some future date, all EU members are also members of the EMU, the ESCB and the Eurosystem will be one and the same.[13]

Battles over the ECB's Head

The European Central Bank had a rough start in the decision over who would serve as its president. Most members of the European Council favored Wim Duisenberg, a chain-smoking Dutch economist and former chair of the EMI. French President Jacques Chirac insisted on Jean-Claude Trichet, however, governor of the French central bank, despite the fact that Trichet had formerly endorsed Duisenberg! Finally, Duisenberg was appointed with the understanding that he would stand down during 2003 and that Trichet would then complete a full eight-year term. As Dinan (2010) states: "To everyone's surprise, Chirac pursued this nakedly nationalistic position to the end." Since this arrangement was against both the letter and the spirit of ESCB statutes, the ESC had a decidedly unglamorous start.

Wim Duisenberg had been appointed as head of the European Monetary Institute in 1997, having previously served very successfully as head of the Dutch central bank. He took over at the helm of the ECB in 1999 and called upon the European public to consider him their "Mr. Euro." But he ran into trouble in 2000 when he gave an interview to a newspaper in which he commented on the

[13] Given current sentiments among many EU members (e.g. euroskepticism), convergence of the ESCB and the Eurosystem seems increasingly unlikely.

Battles over the ECB's Head (cont.)

conditions under which the ECB might intervene to support the value of the euro. This comment violated a central banking taboo, and resulted in calls for—and rumors of—his resignation.

Jean-Claude Trichet ran into his own troubles. During 2000 Trichet was caught up in the French financial scandals surrounding the bank Crédit Lyonnais. These issues related to his career at the helm of the French Treasury, from 1987 to 1993, when he was responsible for the accounts of Crédit Lyonnais. He was cleared of wrongdoing in 2003 and eventually became head of the ECB during that year.

Trichet's term expired in 2011. Political maneuvering over the new ECB head began early that year. Names that were on the shortlist included Axel Weber and Klaus Regling of Germany, Mario Draghi of Italy, and Erkki Liikanen of Finland. In the end the Council chose Mario Draghi, previously governor of the Bank of Italy. It was Draghi who steered the EMU through the GFC. At a speech in London in 2012, Draghi said: "Without our mandate, the ECB is ready to do whatever it takes to preserve the euro. And, believe me, it will be enough." This decisive language helped to sooth jangled financial nerves.

In 2019 the ECB head was again up for grabs. Arguments were made that, with the previous ECB head being a "southerner," the next one had to be a "northerner," namely a German. In the end, however, Christine Lagarde, French former managing director of the International Monetary Fund, was chosen to replace Draghi.

Sources: Dinan (2010), *The Economist* (2019), Ewing and Castle (2011), and Sullivan (2000).

The euro was officially launched in January 1999, when EMU member exchange rates became "irrevocably" locked and monetary policy was transferred to the ECB. The value of the euro was initially set at €0.85/US$1, or US$1.18/€1, in a flexible exchange rate regime against other currencies, such as we discussed in Chapter 17. There was no going back.

In January 2002 the ECB introduced euro notes and coins and began the process of withdrawing old notes and coins from circulation. Amazingly, this huge logistical task was carried out with very few problems. The European Union now had its common currency in physical form. As you can see in Figure 21.3, the euro's value initially fell against the US dollar and the Japanese yen, despite predictions that it would appreciate. But, since then, it has more or less held its value through 2019. Although some Europhiles interpret movements of the euro against other currencies as reflecting the strength or weakness of "Europe," it is really a sign of the workings of the flexible exchange rate regime between the EMU and the rest of the world.

Figure 21.3 The euro/US dollar and euro/100 yen exchange rates, 1999–2019
Source: ecb.europa.eu.

What about the ECB's core mission, price stability? The HICP inflation rate in the euro area is presented in Figure 21.4. Note that the number of countries included in the HICP in this figure changes over time with changes in EMU membership. This figure shows that the ECB was able to maintain price stability through the 2008 GFC. Hereafter, it became something of a bumpy ride. From the anti-inflationary point of view, the ECB was able to keep the annual change in the HICP below 2.0 percent (with the exceptions of 2008, 2011, and 2012). But there were two near-deflationary episodes, the first in 2009 and the second from 2014 to 2016. These later periods were related to the GFC and its aftermath, and we will take them up shortly.

In some sense, since 1999 the EMU and its ECB have been a remarkable success. Monetary union on this scale is historically *unprecedented*, and much could have gone wrong in conducting this economic experiment. As noted by Aizenman (2018: 376), "Observers viewed the successful convergence of most EU countries towards the Maastricht Treaty criteria by 1999, and the subsequent launching of the euro and its rapid acceptance as a viable currency, as steppingstones toward a stable and prosperous Europe." Issues have arisen with regard to the conduct of monetary policy, however, during both periods of economic prosperity and in

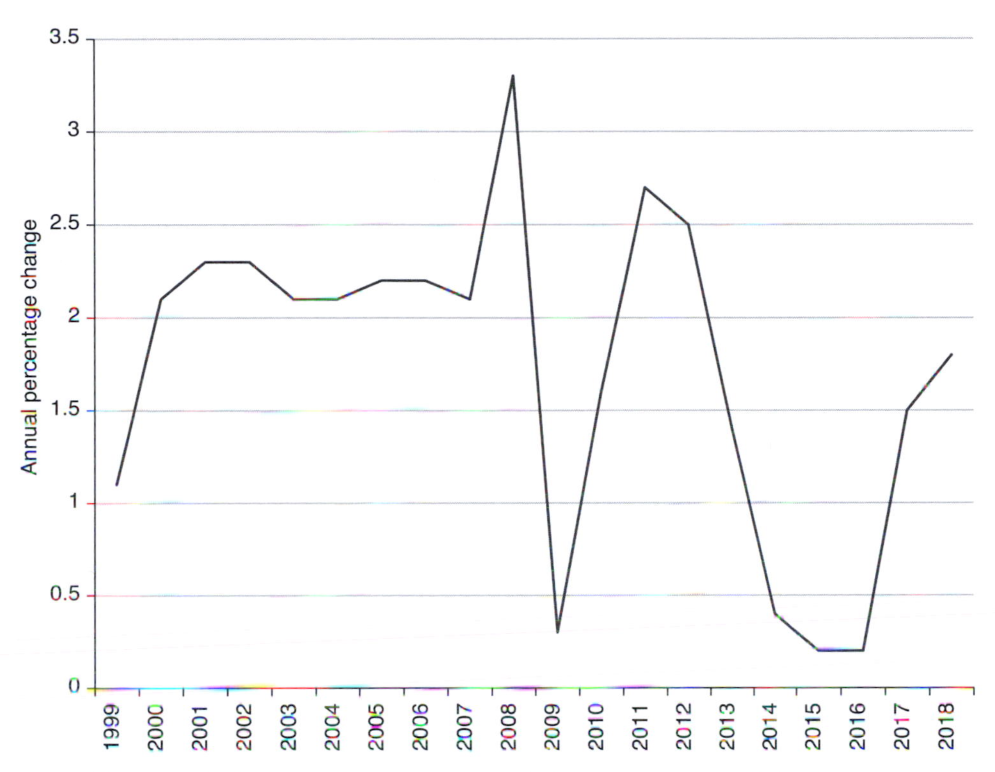

Figure 21.4 Annual inflation rate in euro area, 1999–2018 (percentage change in HICP)
Note: The number of countries included in the euro area changes over time with membership expansions.
Source: ec.europa.eu/eurostat.

downturns, particularly in relation to the GFC, as well as with fiscal policies in member countries. We consider these issues in the next two sections, on optimum currency areas and the GFC.

Optimum Currency Areas and Adjustment in the EMU

There is an idea in international economics that is important to our above discussion of the EMU. This is the notion of an *optimum currency area.*[14] An OCA is a collection of countries characterized by the following:

1. well-integrated factor markets
2. well-integrated fiscal systems
3. economic disturbances that affect each country in a symmetrical manner

[14] This line of thinking in international economics was started by Mundell (1961) and McKinnon (1963). See also Alesina and Barro (2002) and Aizenman (2018).

Most observers, for example, agree that the United States constitutes an OCA. Labor and physical capital are quite mobile between the states of the United States, and there is a great deal of integration of fiscal systems through the US federal government. Finally, cycles of recession and recovery tend to affect each region of the United States in a somewhat symmetrical (albeit not identical) manner.

In the case of the EMU, there seems to be significantly less evidence that it constitutes an OCA.[15] First, despite the fact that the EMU is a sub-component of the European Union, which is, in turn, a common market (see Chapter 9), both labor and physical capital are less mobile between the countries of the EMU than in the United States. Second, the budget of the European Union is relatively small in proportion to the size of the economies involved. This indicates a lack of fiscal integration on the part of the EMU economy. Third, business cycles among the members of the EMU are somewhat asymmetrical, with the potential for one country to experience an expansion while another experiences a contraction.

There is also the issue of potential OCAs in an era of the capital flows, discussed in Chapter 15. Aizenman (2018: 374), for example, points to the need to "reshape OCA criteria into the twenty-first century." Aizenman suggests that "financial globalization," including increased capital flows, can make monetary unions fragile because of the tendency of capital flows to exhibit "sudden stops" and capital flight. These shocks can trigger banking crises with accompanying prolonged recessions, as described in Chapter 15. For this reason, standard OCA analysis might not be sufficient to assess potential monetary unions.

The absence of an optimum currency area in the EMU leaves some room for worry over how economic adjustment can occur within it. In the face of a recession in one country, unemployment will rise. This rise in unemployment can be addressed in four ways:

1. an overall decline in wage rates, leading to increases in quantity demanded for labor
2. labor mobility out of areas of unemployment
3. expansionary monetary policy (at the EU level)
4. expansionary fiscal policies (at the member-country level)

The first of these potential remedies, declining wages, can in principle address unemployment problems. We can appreciate this better by looking at the following equation for the foreign (US dollar) real wage in EMU country i:

$$\text{Foreign currency real wage for member } i = \frac{1}{e} \times \frac{w_i}{P} \tag{21.1}$$

[15] For example, Issing (2008: 49) concludes that "the euro area that was to be created on 1 January 1999 fell quite a long way short of meeting the conditions for an optimum currency area."

We can use Equation 21.1 to consider how an EMU member country *i* can improve competitiveness in a downturn. Prior to the EMU it would have been able to increase its exchange rate *e* (devalue its currency), which would have decreased the foreign-currency wage. With the EMU in place, however, that is not an option for an individual country. That leaves only an increase in the EMU-wide price level *P* or a decrease in the nominal wage w_i. But the ECB's marching orders are to ensure that the EMU-wide price level increases only by two percentage points a year. Therefore, any further decrease in the foreign-currency wage needs to come about by a *decrease in the nominal wage*, a process sometimes called "internal devaluation." If there is one thing we know about EMU labor markets, however, it is that nominal wages tend to be downwardly inflexible.[16] So, the first remedy is not likely to be of help.

The second remedy, labor mobility (migration out of the country experiencing a recession), could likewise help achieve adjustment. As we have just mentioned, however, labor mobility within the EMU is not very strong overall.[17] The third potential remedy is the countercyclical monetary policy of the ECB. But, as just mentioned, the ECB is required to maintain annual increases in the Harmonised Index of Consumer Prices at or below 2 percent. It therefore has very little discretion to pursue other adjustment measures.[18]

The final potential remedy for unemployment is national fiscal policy, but this operates within two kinds of restraints. The first is the European Union's Stability and Growth Pact. This pact prescribes members to pursue balanced or surplus budgets during economic upswings and to limit deficits during downswings to an amount equivalent to 3 percent of GDP. Central government debt is also to be capped at 60 percent of GDP. Exceptions to the 3 percent rule exist for severe downturns.[19] The Stability and Growth Pact limits the extent to which the fiscal remedy for addressing unemployment can operate. But so do financial markets themselves. As EMU member countries issue government bonds to finance deficits, they are subject to differential interest rate spreads that reflect market expectations regarding the possibility of sovereign default. As we will see below, these bond spreads played a role in the EMU crisis that followed on the GFC beginning in 2009.

The European Central Bank, naturally, defends the Stability and Growth Pact, stating some time ago that it "represents an important commitment to maintaining

---

[16] *The Economist* (2009) notes that "workers have generally been reluctant to take wage cuts, at least in nominal terms, which has made real-wage adjustment slow."

[17] A key exception here is the case of Polish workers, who have been willing to work in many other EU countries. But Poland is not yet an EMU member.

[18] ECB monetary policy is enacted using a "two pillar strategy" of monetary targeting and inflation targeting. See Clausen and Donges (2001), ECB (2001), and Issing (2008).

[19] For further fiscal issues regarding the EMU, see Ferguson and Kotlikoff (2000).

fiscal policies conducive to overall macroeconomic stability" (ECB, 2001: 17). The truth of the matter, however, is that the pact has evolved into a *soft constraint*, with key EMU members (including Germany and France) exceeding the 3 percent deficit threshold and countries joining the EMU vastly exceeding the 60 percent debt threshold.[20] A more central issue, however, is that the EMU is a monetary union but a fiscal disunion. There is no *central* fiscal authority to match the ECB. That will always place limits on how well the EMU can function.[21]

The above considerations leave some observers worried about the future of the EMU, as a monetary union that falls substantially short of an OCA. Early on, some researchers (e.g. Sheridan, 1999) predicted political problems as a result of the absence of economic adjustment mechanisms.[22] As we will see, these political problems arose with the GFC.

The EMU in the Global Financial Crisis

The year 2009 was a tough one for the world economy as a whole, but the crisis from 2007 to 2009, discussed in Chapter 20, caused some particular difficulties in the EMU. By and large, the EMU was *not ready* for the crisis. As stated by Eichengreen (2015: 337):

> The Europeans had long been working to make things as difficult as possible. They neglected the problems in their banks. They neglected the deterioration of competitiveness across Southern Europe. They neglected the fiscal problems of Greece, which in their wisdom they admitted to the Eurozone in 2002.

As hinted at in our discussion of OCAs, adjustment to the GFC was difficult. A long quote, again from Eichengreen (2015: 337), gives a sense of this issue:

> In creating the euro, [the Europeans] closed off all avenues for resolving...problems. There was no possibility of devaluing the national currency because there was no national currency to devalue. There was no scope for regaining the devaluation option,

---

[20] *The Economist* (2009) writes that the "stability and growth pact is now too full of holes to be a binding constraint on fiscal policy."

[21] In this regard, Micossi (2015: 11) states: "In a monetary union without fiscal union, such as the Eurozone, national governments issue bonds, as it were, in a 'foreign' currency, since individually they have no control over its availability to counter a liquidity crisis in their sovereign debt market. The absence of such guarantee makes sovereign bond markets prone to liquidity crises and contagion, very much like banking systems lacking a lender of last resort."

[22] Tsoukalis (1997) also recognized this problem, writing (186): "EMU could divide the EU; it could destabilize it politically, if new institutions do not enjoy the legitimacy which is necessary to carry their policies through; and it could create economically depressed countries and regions. These are the main risks." Even more pessimistic views (e.g. Feldstein, 1997) involve scenarios of war.

> since there was no provision for exiting the Eurozone. There was no banking union to accompany the monetary union. In the absence of a single bank supervisor and a mechanism for winding up bad banks, there was no way of forcing national regulators to recapitalize or liquidate insolvent financial institutions.... There was no mechanism for providing emergency assistance to governments.... There was not even agreement that the European Central Bank should act as a lender of last resort, injecting credit as needed to stabilize the financial system.

Recall, from Chapter 20, that the GFC hit European shores in 2008 with the bankruptcy and rescue of the London-based AIG Financial Products. Despite the unfolding crisis in the United States, described in Chapter 20, the initial response of the ECB was to *tighten* monetary policy in the middle of 2008, with an eye to the HICP. Circumstances forced it to quickly change course as the Eurozone entered into recession.

The difficulties hit a sub-group of states known as the GIIPS countries: Greece, Ireland, Italy, Portugal, and Spain.[23] Recall from Chapter 20 that the GFC had its roots in a housing price bubble in the United States. As it happened, two of the GIIPS countries, Ireland and Spain, had also experienced housing (and construction) booms, which came to a rapid end in this crisis. Greece and Ireland became caught up in fiscal crises that to a lesser extent have characterized Portugal and Italy. The ramifications of these issues on external accounts can be seen in Figure 21.5, which reports GIIPS current account balances from 1999 to 2009. As you can see in this figure, with the exception of Italy, all these countries experienced significant current account deficits as a percentage of GDP.

The GFC began to impact the EMU in mid-2010, when first Greece and then Ireland were caught up in market speculation over government or sovereign default, of the kind we discussed in Chapter 20. Bond yield spreads widened, with Greece (at approximately 12 percent) and Ireland and Portugal (at approximately 6 percent) paying much higher rates than Germany (at approximately 2 percent) on new ten-year bond issues. It did not help that it had emerged that the Greek government had purposefully underestimated its annual fiscal deficit by many percentage points. What had been announced as an annual deficit equivalent to approximately 4 percent of GDP was more like 12 percent.

To address the developing crisis that year, the European Union set up the European Financial Stability Facility (EFSF) with funding of €440 billion to issue bond guarantees in order to help soothe the markets.[24] The International Monetary Fund committed a further €250 billion to this endeavor. In the event, bond issues were successful, albeit at high interest rates. But, as we discussed in Chapter 19,

---

[23] In some sources, these countries are also known by the unfortunate acronym PIIGS.

[24] The EFSF was subsequently renamed the European Stability Mechanism, or ESM.

Figure 21.5 Current account balances in the GIIPS countries, 1999–2017 (percentage of GDP)
Source: World Bank, World Development Indicators.

the IMF became involved in the Greek case. And, in late 2010, the European Union and the IMF had to rescue the Irish economy with an €85 billion package.[25]

The loans extended to Greece were accompanied by conditions that required fiscal consolidation. In the event, Greece entered into a recession that rivaled the Great Depression in the United States. Whereas in 2010 the IMF and the ECB were arguing that Greece's debt was sustainable, by 2012 restructuring had become inevitable. The restructuring that took place was one of the largest in history, being written down by no less than 75 percent.[26] Holders of Greek government debt underwent a "haircut," having to exchange old bonds for new worth less than half the original value. Recall from Chapter 20 that the definition of a "debt crisis" involved sovereign default or substantial restructuring of debt. The financial press often labeled the Greek haircut as the largest sovereign default in history, partly because bondholders were essentially *forced* to accept the deal.

[25] As was widely reported at the time, the German government was reluctant to "bail out" Greece. But it turned out that the German financial system had a significant exposure to Greek debt. That helped concentrate minds in the German government. The French financial sector was also exposed, as was the ECB itself.

[26] See, for example, Arghyrou and Tsoukalas (2011) and Zettelmeyer, Trebesch, and Gulati (2013).

Some years later *The Economist* (2013) reported on the Greek crisis as follows: "The crisis has left a terrible legacy. Five-and-a-half years of recession have wiped out over 25% of output and more than a million private-sector jobs. Tens of thousands of retailers and small manufacturers have gone under. Unemployment is above 27%, a record; for youths it is over 60%." The economic pain was therefore very real.

The Greek crisis, to put it mildly, called into question the advertised macroeconomic paradise of the Eurozone. It also set in motion an overreaction. Spain and Ireland, unlike Greece, had run budget *surpluses* up until the GFC. Nonetheless, fiscal consolidation became the go-to policy in the EMU, leading to EMU-wide recession.

In the case of Ireland, recall from the box in Chapter 12 that it had a lot going for it beyond a budget surplus. It had a banking sector that had over-borrowed abroad, however (capital flows in the form of commercial bank lending in Table 15.1), and had over-lent to the property and construction sector in response to a property market bubble. When the property bubble burst in 2007, a banking crisis ensued. During this time the Irish government also announced a promise to guarantee both the deposits and debts of six Irish banks.[27] Subsequently, this banking crisis morphed into a general financial crisis, Ireland fell into the IMF's hands, and the country entered into a significant recession.

Subsequently, all eyes fell on Portugal and Spain as the next potential EMU crises. Despite the fact that Portugal did not have the debt problem of Greece or the banking problem of Ireland, it entered into a recession. Spain did have an Irish-style property market collapse and entered into recession as well. In the case of Spain, it had to be bailed out by the European Stability Mechanism.

These events gave rise to a number of considerations. First, there was talk of centralized EMU bond issues, what came to be known as "blue bonds," as opposed to sovereign "red bonds."[28] Second, there were renewed discussions of whether adjustment in monetary systems should be the responsibility only of deficit countries (the GIIPS countries) or surplus countries (such as Germany and the Netherlands) as well. Finally, the crisis revealed cracks in the central project of the European Union, namely political integration. For example, the idea of contributing to the EFSF/ESM did not sit well with the German public. Why should they "bail out" the profligate Greeks, for example? These sorts of political issues will be on the EMU and EU agenda for some time to come.

---

[27] Pisani-Ferry and Sapir (2010) analyzed the rescue of Fortis and Dexia. The Irish bailout was repeatedly criticized by Krugman (2010), who states: "These debts were incurred, not to pay for public programs, but by private wheeler-dealers seeking nothing but their own profit. Yet ordinary Irish citizens are now bearing the burden of those debts."

[28] Arguments for and against are presented in *The Economist* (2010).

From 2010 to 2012 EU handling of what proved to be an ongoing crisis was not adept, seeming to lurch from one half-measure to another. A sampling of *Economist* headlines during this period conveys the mood at the time: "Beware of Falling Masonry"; "Is Anyone in Charge?"; "Europe on the Rack"; and "The Cracks Spread and Widen." These headlines do not describe a well-functioning EMU.[29]

One way to appreciate the intractable nature of the euro crisis is to begin considering it in light of macroeconomic adjustment. Financial columnists who have pointed us in this direction include King (2011) and Wolf (2012). King (2011), for example, notes that reducing Germany's current account surplus as a percentage of GDP required that demand increase in Germany, with potentially higher inflation there–an anathema to German sensibilities. Germany's exports could decrease substantially through a large recession in the GIIPS countries, but these recessions exacerbated some of the instability behind the crisis. Very few of the individuals managing the crisis proposed solutions to this adjustment problem. Wolf (2012) points out that, having removed one macroeconomic adjustment mechanism (currencies and exchange rates), the Eurozone has made credit crises more likely.

In 2012 events seemed to take a turn for the better. Germany's constitutional court gave its long-awaited approval of the ESM. The European Commission set out its plan for a long-called-for EU-wide banking union.[30] In addition, Mario Draghi, head of the ECB, announced that it would begin to purchase GIIPS bonds to aid in their adjustment and thus begin to act as a lender of last resort. Bond yields consequently began to decline. This initially seemed to have been the point at which the euro crisis began to resolve itself.

The crisis reasserted itself in 2013, however, with a banking crisis in Cyprus. As it turned out, Cypriot banks had assets worth eight times the country's GDP in 2011. Much of this total was owned by foreigners, including Russians who distrusted economic and legal conditions back at home. The government at first hoped to raise funds by imposing a levy on depositors (9.9 percent on deposits of over €100,000 but, controversially, also 6.75 percent on deposits below this threshold). In the face of protests and a bank shutdown, this initial proposal was modified and controls on capital outflows introduced. This event shed light on the role of banking within the European Union, particularly since Cyprus was not the

---

[29] *The Economist* (2011) predicts multiple sovereign debt crises within the EMU.

[30] James (2009: 183) notes: "Although banks were active across national frontiers in a single capital and money market, regulation and supervision remained national. Bank support operations, because they were so expensive, were also national affairs. The consequence of this national focus was heightened uncertainty when there was a need to unravel complex cross-national institutions."

only country with banking deposits out of proportion to its GDP (Luxembourg and Malta also fell into this league).

The effects of the crisis linger to this day. Consider Greece. *The Economist* (2018c) reports: "Output, in real terms, is a quarter below its peak in 2007 and investment is down by two-thirds. The share of people living in poverty has doubled. One in five of the workforce is unemployed.... Debt remains a crippling 180% of GDP." Problems such as this will take a long time to be resolved. Meanwhile, the EMU must cope with the "legacy of mistrust that haunts the euro zone today" (*The Economist*, 2017). This is a less than positive record.

Poland, the EMU, and the GFC

Poland has been a member of the European Union since 2004. For many years now it has met some central EMU convergence criteria with relatively low inflation and a debt-to-GDP ratio of under 60 percent. Officially, the accession of Poland to the European Union commits it to ultimately join the EMU, as it does not have an opt-out. The European Central Bank (2018) notes that "Polish law does not comply with all the requirements for central bank independence" required by the ECB. This would need to change if and when Poland adopts the euro.

This eventuality now seems a long way off. In effect, Poland has elected *not* to be a member of the EMU, and the Polish złoty floats against other currencies. The absence of Poland from the EMU does seem to matter. With a population of 38 million, Poland is large by EU standards (France's population is 67 million, Germany's 82 million). Poland has also been relatively successful from an economic perspective, with relatively high and stable growth rates. Its relatively low wages (about one-third of those prevailing in Germany) have contributed to a manufacturing boom.

A stumbling block to Poland's joining the EMU has been that the euro is not very popular in Poland. Indeed, under the Law and Justice Party, Poland's relationship to the European Union itself has been strained, with occasional talk of a "Polexit." This, thankfully, has not come to pass at the time of this writing.

During the GFC Poland fared relatively *well* outside the EMU. Indeed, it has often been pointed out that Poland was the one EU country that actually avoided recession in the wake of the GFC. Part of the reason for this was a comparatively large depreciation of the złoty, something that would not have been possible if Poland had been a member of the EMU. Maybe outsider status has some advantages.

Sources: The Economist (2018b), ECB (2018), and Sharma (2017).

Monetary Unions in Africa

Other than the EMU and what might be called mini-states, the only other examples of monetary union occur in Africa.[31] These are the CFA franc zone in central and West Africa and the rand zone in southern Africa. Both are relatively long-standing, if not entirely stable. We consider each in turn.

The Communauté Financière Africaine (CFA) franc zone is a complete and functioning monetary union between 14 member countries that have adopted the CFA franc as a common currency. It has been in existence since 1945, though a number of original members subsequently left to establish their own currencies. The CFA franc zone actually consists of two sub-unions, the West African Monetary Union (WAMU) and the Central African Monetary Area (CAMA), associated with the Central Bank for West African States and the Bank for Central African States, respectively. The membership in these two sub-zones is listed in Table 21.4.[32]

This long-standing monetary union was associated, at least until the mid-1980s, with economic performance no worse than and perhaps better than neighboring

Table 21.4 Members of the CFA franc zone

Member	Sub-zone	Former colonial power	Member since
Benin	West	France	1945
Burkina Faso	West	France	1945
Cameroon	Central	France	1945
Central African Republic	Central	France	1945
Chad	Central	France	1945
Côte d'Ivoire	West	France	1945
Equatorial Guinea	Central	Spain	1985
Gabon	Central	France	1945
Guinea-Bissau	West	Portugal	1997
Mali	West	France	1945, left 1962, rejoined 1984
Niger	West	France	1945
Republic of the Congo	Central	France	1945
Senegal	West	France	1945
Togo	West	France	1945

[31] See Pomfret (2009).

[32] For a history, see Giorgioni (2018). Analysis of the CFA franc zone suggests that it is not an OCA: see, for example, Loureiro, Martins, and Ribeiro (2012) and Zhao and Kim (2009).

countries that utilized floating or managed floating exchange rate regimes.[33] As part of the monetary union, the Central Bank for West African States and the Bank for Central African States maintain a foreign exchange reserve pool in which they keep approximately one-half with the French Treasury, an arrangement that is clearly a legacy of the colonial past.

In the case of a completed monetary union, the issue of how to manage the relationship of the common currency to the rest of the world still exists. In the case of the CFA franc zone, this was resolved in 1948 by means of a fixed peg to the French franc, the main trade partner. This management strategy proved workable up to the mid-1980s. Controls on the capital accounts of member countries and the backing of the peg by the French Treasury both helped to support the fixed rate.

Beginning in the early 1980s the world prices of the main CFA export goods declined significantly, and the countries involved found themselves in balance of payments difficulties. With devaluation not a possibility, adjustment was attempted by contractionary macroeconomic policies aimed at reducing import demand and maintaining high interest rates. A number of CFA members began to turn to the IMF for assistance, some of them under the programs described in Chapter 19. Following civil unrest in Cameroon and a withdrawal of support by the French prime minister, Édouard Balladur, both in 1993, a devaluation of 50 percent against the French franc was made in 1994. This devaluation sparked riots in a number of CFA franc countries.

With the launch of the euro in 1999, the franc peg became a euro peg, at 656 CFA francs to the euro. This change made some economic sense, since the European Union is the CFA franc zone's main trading partner. A key remaining question was whether the CFA franc/euro peg could be maintained.[34] As noted by *The Economist* (2018a), "To maintain the euro peg...these very poor countries must track the hawkish monetary policy of the European Central Bank."[35] Some notable change came in 2020, in the form of what *The Economist* (2020) calls "the most far-reaching changes to the currency area since its formation." The WAMU will replace the CFA franc with a new currency, called the "eco," also to be pegged to the euro, while the CAMA will remain unchanged. Instead of the French treasury, the eco will be supported by the Central Bank of West African States. Time will tell whether the fixed arrangements of the eco and the CFA franc will work in the long run. The history of fixed exchange rates suggests that there will be bumps in the road.

[33] See Eichengreen (2008: chap. 5) and James (1996: chap. 14).

[34] For a fuller discussion of this issue, see *The Economist* (2002a; 2018a).

[35] Of course, the CFA franc does have some flexibility, as the euro changes in value against other major currencies, but this is somewhat more remote from the CFA member countries' perspective.

The rand zone or Common Monetary Area (CMA) is a smaller endeavor than the CFA franc zone and includes South Africa, Lesotho, Namibia, and Swaziland.[36] The South African rand is legal tender in all CMA countries, but the countries also circulate their own currencies at a one-to-one par. The South African central bank operates as lender of last resort for the other three countries of the zone.[37] The origins of the rand zone go back to the 1970s, and, at one time, the zone also included Botswana as a member. Unlike the CFA franc, the rand *floats* against other major currencies, as South Africa pursues an inflation-targeting monetary policy. There is a significant amount of liberalization within the CMA. As reported by Nchake, Edwards, and Rankin (2018: 155), "There is a high mobility of capital between members as no restrictions are imposed on the transfer of funds between member countries, whether for current or capital transactions." This is another example of a long-standing monetary union.

Conclusion

In a previous era of capital controls, it was possible to pursue an independent monetary policy within a fixed exchange rate system. Capital controls have slowly and steadily been eroded, however, with only appropriate taxes on short-term flows possible remaining in some cases. In such a world, countries can choose between floating with an independent monetary policy (inflation targeting) and fixing their currency's value without an independent monetary policy. At the end of his history of global monetary arrangements, Eichengreen (2008: 232) concludes that "a floating exchange rate is not the best of all worlds. But it is at least a feasible one." But some groups of countries have pursued the rarer path of monetary union discussed in this chapter.

Monetary unions such as those discussed in this chapter are attempts to escape the limitations of both fixed and flexible exchange rate regimes. The EMU example has been an uneven success, but the two African examples are even more long-standing. Having pursued monetary union, however, member countries face other limitations. As currency areas are generally less than optimal, adjustment is always a concern. So is the relationship between the currency of monetary union and other major currencies. Should the common currency float (as in the case of the EMU and rand zone) or be fixed (as in the case of the CFA franc)? These are issues that need to be addressed in any attempt at monetary union.

[36] Adding Botswana to the rand zone gives the membership of the South African Customs Union, or SACU, with which the CMA has an association. The SACU is one of the oldest customs unions in the world.

[37] Grandes (2003) points out that the rand zone is actually a hybrid monetary union and currency board. See Chapter 18 on currency boards.

Review Exercises

1. Imagine that, suddenly, the US dollar was abolished and each state of the United States introduced its own currency (the Arizona, the Montana, the Wyoming, etc.). Would this alter economic life in the United States? How so? What problems would it entail?
2. Three European Union countries (the United Kingdom, Sweden, and Denmark) chose not to be part of the EMU. Can you think of any reasons why they would do so?
3. Have you or your classmates had any experiences with the euro or the CFA franc? What are they?
4. Do you have any ideas for how the adjustment problems and current crisis in the EMU could be better addressed?
5. One region in which there are many discussions of monetary union is Latin America. Are there any countries in Latin America that qualify as an optimum currency area?

FURTHER READING AND WEB RESOURCES

An important and accessible source on the European Union is Dinan (2010). See in particular chapter 13, on the EMU. For a history of the European Union, see Dinan (2004). For a discussion of the events leading up to the formation of the EMU, see *The Economist* (1998a), Eichengreen (2008: chap. 5) and Tsoukalis (1997: chaps. 7 & 8). An advanced treatment can be found in Hallwood and MacDonald (2000: chap. 5). An insider's account of the EMU, with numerous details on the conduct of monetary policy, is Issing (2008). For an account of the EMU's response to the GFC, see Eichengreen (2015: chaps. 24 & 25).

A useful website on the euro can be found within the European Union's website, at europa.eu. The European Central Bank's website is ecb.europa.eu.

REFERENCES

Aizenman, J. (2018) "Optimal Currency Area: A Twentieth Century Idea for the Twenty-First Century?," *Open Economies Review*, 29:2, 373–82.

Alesina, A., and R. J. Barro (2002) "Currency Unions," *Quarterly Journal of Economics*, 117:2, 409–36.

Arghyrou, M. G., and J. D. Tsoukalas (2011) "The Greek Debt Crisis: Likely Causes, Mechanism and Outcomes," *World Economy*, 34:2, 173–91.

Clausen, J. R., and J. B. Donges (2001) "European Monetary Policy: The Ongoing Debate on Conceptual Issues," *The World Economy*, 24:10, 1309–26.

Daily Telegraph (2002) "Pierre Werner," June 27.

Dinan, D. (2004) *Europe Recast: A History of the European Union*, Lynne Rienner.

Dinan, D. (2010) *Ever Closer Union: An Introduction to European Integration*, 4th edn., Lynne Rienner.

The Economist (1998a) "A Survey of EMU," April 11.

The Economist (1998b) "Euro Brief: Eleven into One May Go," October 17.
The Economist (2002a) "The CFA Franc and the Euro," February 9.
The Economist (2002b) "Pierre Werner," July 6.
The Economist (2009) "Holding Together: Special Report on the Euro Area," June 13.
The Economist (2010) "Fixing Europe's Single Currency," September 25.
The Economist (2011) "The Euro Areas Debt Crisis: Bite the Bullet," January 15.
The Economist (2013) "Greece's Government: Up, But Not Out," May 25.
The Economist (2017) "Rebuilding the House of Euro," June 3.
The Economist (2018a) "Africa's CFA Franc: Franc Exchange," January 27.
The Economist (2018b) "Flirting with Polexit? Poland's President Wants a Referendum on the EU," June 20.
The Economist (2018c) "Euro-Zone Austerity: The Greece-y Pole," August 4.
The Economist (2019) "The European Central Bank: Constrained Optimization," June 15.
The Economist (2020) "Francly Speaking: The End of the CFA," January 4.
Eichengreen, B. (2008) *Globalizing Capital: A History of the International Monetary System*, Princeton University Press.
Eichengreen, B. (2015) *Hall of Mirrors: The Great Depression, the Great Recession, and the Uses – and Misuses – of History*, Oxford University Press.
European Central Bank (2001) *The Monetary Policy of the ECB*, ECB.
European Central Bank (2018) "Convergence Report 2018," ECB, www.ecb.europa.eu/pub/convergence/html/ecb.cr201805.en.html#toc1.
Ewing, J., and S. Castle (2011) "Politics Will Determine the New ECB Head," *New York Times*, February 13.
Feldstein, M. (1997) "The EMU and International Conflict," *Foreign Affairs*, 76:6, 60–73.
Ferguson, N., and L. S. Kotlikoff (2000) "The Degeneration of the EMU," *Foreign Affairs*, 79:2, 110–21.
Giorgioni, G. (2018) "The CFA Franc Zone: A Political Re-Evaluation Twenty Years after the Advent of the Euro," *Journal of Contemporary African Studies*, https://doi.org/10.1080/02589001.2018.1481280.
Grandes, M. (2003) "Macroeconomic Convergence in Southern Africa: The Rand Zone Experience," Working Paper 231, OECD Development Centre.
Gros, D., and N. Thygesen (1992) *European Monetary Integration*, Longman.
Hallwood, C. P., and R. MacDonald (2000) *International Money and Finance*, Blackwell.
Issing, O. (2008) *The Birth of the Euro*, Cambridge University Press.
James, H. (1996) *International Monetary Cooperation since Bretton Woods*, Oxford University Press.
James, H. (2009) *The Creation and Destruction of Value: The Globalization Cycle*, Harvard University Press.
King, S. (2011) "Why the Eurozone Deal Will Fail," *Financial Times*, December 12.
Krugman, P. (2010) "Eating the Irish," *New York Times*, November 25.
Loureiro, J., M. Martins, and A. P. Ribeiro (2012) "Anchoring to the Euro (and Grouped Together)? The Case of African Countries," *Journal of African Economies*, 21:1, 28–64.
McKinnon, R. I. (1963) "Optimum Currency Areas," *American Economic Review*, 53:4, 717–25.
Marinova, T. (2016) "Comparative Study on Monetary and Fiscal Policy in the Eurozone and Bulgaria," *Economic Alternatives*, 10:3, 367–78.

Micossi, S. (2015) "The Monetary Policy of the European Central Bank (2002–2015)," Special Report 109, Centre for European Policy Studies.

Münchau, W. (2011) "Time to Get Real on Europe's Inflation Target," *Financial Times*, January 30.

Mundell, R. A. (1961) "A Theory of Optimum Currency Areas," *American Economic Review*, 51:4, 657–65.

Nchake, M. A., L. Edwards, and N. Rankin (2018) "Closer Monetary Union and Product Market Integration in Emerging Economies: Evidence from the Common Monetary Area in Southern Africa," *International Review of Economics and Finance*, 54, 154–64.

Pisani-Ferry, J., and A. Sapir (2010) "Banking Crisis Management in the EU: An Early Assessment," *Economic Policy*, 25:62, 341–73.

Pomfret, R. (2009) "Common Currency," in K. A. Reinert, R. S. Rajan, A. J. Glass, and L. S. Davis (eds.), *The Princeton Encyclopedia of the World Economy*, Princeton University Press, 188–91.

Salvatore, D. (2009) "Euro," in K. A. Reinert, R. S. Rajan, A. J. Glass, and L. S. Davis (eds.), *The Princeton Encyclopedia of the World Economy*, Princeton University Press, 350–2.

Sharma, R. (2017) "The Next Economic Powerhouse? Poland," *New York Times*, July 5.

Sheridan, J. (1999) "The Consequences of the Euro," *Challenge*, 42:1, 43–54.

Sullivan, R. (2000) "Duisenberg Tries to Rescue Reputation," *Financial Times*, October 20.

Tsoukalis, L. (1997) *The New European Economy Revisited*, Oxford University Press.

Walter, A., and G. Sen (2009) *Analyzing the Global Political Economy*, Princeton University Press.

Wolf, M. (2012) "Can One Have Balance of Payments Crises in a Currency Union?," *Financial Times*, February 16.

Zettelmeyer, J., C. Trebesch, and M. Gulati (2013) "Greek Debt Restructuring: An Autopsy," *Economic Policy*, 28:75, 513–63.

Zhao, X., and Y. Kim (2009) "Is the CFA Franc Zone an Optimum Currency Area?," *World Development*, 37:12, 1877–86.

22 Growth in the Open Economy

I once spoke with a Ghanaian student who had just taken his first course in international economics. He held a well-known book on globalization in his hand (I won't say which one), and was waving it at me. "Professor," he asked with some agitation, "what does all this *really* mean for my country? We are going nowhere!" His question was a profound one, and it is shared by many individuals who have similar feelings about their own countries' relationships to the world economy. The question was implicitly concerned with the processes of *growth* and *development* in open economies. Development per se is a field in itself beyond the scope of this book. But we want to say something about the smaller realm of growth in open economies, and that is the purpose of this chapter.

The Ghanaian student had a point. In 1960 Ghana's gross domestic product per capita exceeded those of South Korea and Thailand. It was only just below that of Malaysia. By 2015 it was approximately 30 percent of Thailand's, 15 percent of Malaysia's, and 7 percent of South Korea's. So, the question is: how can Ghana "get somewhere" rather than "go nowhere"?[1] What insights can we obtain into this possibility using the development as growth perspective? Finally, what roles might human capital, trade, and institutions play in this process? This chapter will help you to answer these questions.

Economists are increasingly concerned with explanations of levels of per capita GDP, as well as their rates of growth. For such explanations, economists turn to what is known as **growth theory**. In this chapter, we will consider two variants of growth theory: "old" growth theory and "new" growth theory.[2] Next, we will consider the interrelationships between human capital, trade, institutions, and growth. For the interested reader, an appendix to the chapter presents some of the algebraic details of growth theory.

Growth

In the realm of growth and development, we inevitably find ourselves engaging in what is called *outcome assessment*. This is the process of embracing some metric (or metrics) to judge the progress of countries over time and to compare

[1] Unknowingly, my student was echoing concerns voiced by Easterly (2001: chap. 2).

[2] We can only touch the surface of this important area of research. Interested readers can pursue this subject further in Jones and Vollrath (2013).

the progress of one country with others.[3] An early and persistent conception of economic development is in terms of the sustained increase in either per capita production or per capita income, or, in other words, **growth**. This concept begins with the circular flow diagram of Chapter 14 (Figure 14.2). In this diagram, **gross domestic product** is the same as **gross national income**. In most countries, there is a difference between GDP and GNI (described in Appendix 14.3). For the most part, we ignore this difference and work with GDP as our crucial variable. In the circular flow diagram, GDP, or Y, is divided by the total population to calculate GDP per capita, or y. GDP per capita is an important measure of the *level* of economic development, and the growth rate of GDP per capita is an important measure of the *pace* of economic development over time.

Why is growth considered to be such a central indicator of development? Rodrik (2007) echoes much of the field when he states (2): "Economic growth is the most powerful instrument for reducing poverty.... [N]othing has worked better than economic growth in enabling societies to improve the life chances of their members, including those at the very bottom." As Easterly (2001: 3) comments, however: "We experts don't care about rising gross domestic product for its own sake. We care because it betters the lot of the poor and reduces the proportion of people who are poor. We care because richer people can eat more and buy more medicines for their babies." As we see here, it is not the increase in GDP per capita per se that matter for development, but what can be done with it.[4]

The growth perspective, based as it is on GDP per capita, has a few limitations that are important to recognize. These include the following.

- Although it is sometimes used as such, per capita GDP is *not* a measure of welfare.[5]
- Per capita GDP does not account for *factor income flows* between the countries of the world. (This is the distinction between GDP and GNI that we took up in Appendix 14.3.)
- Per capita GDP includes only market activities, and many activities in low- and middle-income countries take place *outside the market*. For example, GDP does not include farmers' production of agricultural products for home consumption, only the amount sold on the market.
- Per capita GDP does not account for certain *costs* associated with development, such as the use of non-renewable resources, the loss of biodiversity, and pollution.

[3] As Szirmai (2015: 9) emphasizes, "Development is unavoidably a normative concept involving very basic choices and values."

[4] This point is emphasized by Reinert (2018), who stresses the provision of basic goods.

[5] In a review of the GDP concept, for example, Coyle (2014: 14) states: "GDP definitely does not attempt to measure welfare or well-being."

- Per capita GDP is an average measure that *hides the distribution of income* between the households of a country. If income distribution becomes more unequal as per capita GDP increases, the level of well-being of the poorest groups in the country could fall.[6]
- Per capita GDP is not always an accurate predictor of *human development*, such as in the form of education and health. As emphasized by Sen (1989: 42) many years ago, "Countries with high GDP per capita can nevertheless have astonishingly low achievements in the quality of life."
- The nominal or currency exchange rates used to convert GDP into US dollars for comparison between countries are misleading. A large part of economies consists of *non-traded goods*. Furthermore, a large part of non-traded goods consists of *services*. Services tend to be less expensive in developing countries, so a US dollar buys more in developing countries than in developed countries.[7]

There is another way to consider GDP and GNI. This is in terms of *deprivations*. Income deprivations are a central measure of **poverty**. As shown in Figure 22.1, income poverty is measured by the World Bank in *three forms*. These include those living on US$1.90 per day or less, US$3.20 per day or less, and US$5.50 per day or less. The good news is that the number of people living in the most extreme form of poverty, US$1.90 per day or less, declined from approximately 2 billion in 1981 to just above 700 million in 2015. In Ghana's case, however, this includes one in ten of its citizens (*The Economist*, 2019). There is broad agreement in the field that the global decline in the number of extremely poor individuals has been mostly because of growth and development processes in China. The less good news relates to the more expansive conceptions of poverty: the number of people living on US$3.20 per day or less shows a less dramatic decline, and the number living on US$5.50 or less per day *increased* to over 3 billion. The poverty challenge is therefore both large and persistent and exacerbated by the COVID-19 pandemic.

It is becoming clear that the relationship between income distribution and poverty is more important than ever. With the movement of some large countries from low-income to middle-income status (India and Indonesia, for instance), the majority of the world's extremely poor reside in middle- rather than low-income

---

[6] Income distributions are measured using the Lorenz curve and the Gini coefficient.

[7] The solution to the last of the above problems lies in what is now called the *purchasing power parity* methodology. This methodology is closely related to the purchasing power parity model of exchange rates that we developed in Chapter 16. The PPP methodology uses US dollar prices to value all goods in all countries. This has the effect of increasing the GDP of LMICs. One of the original attempts to examine the less expensive nature of services in LMICs was Bhagwati (1984).

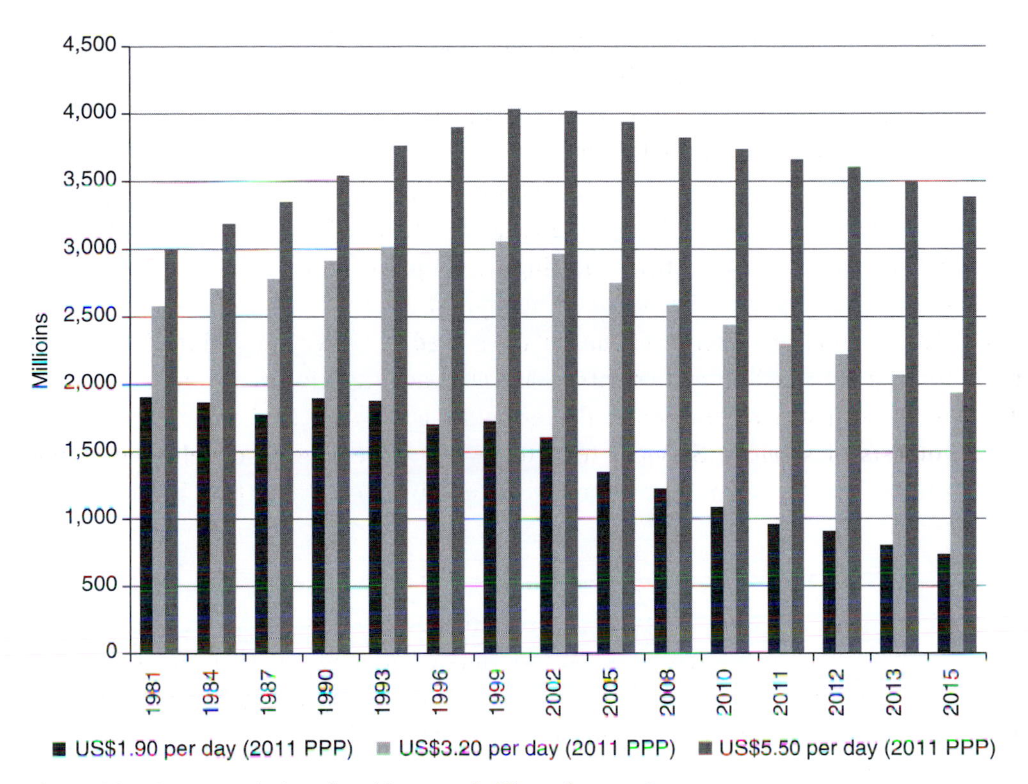

Figure 22.1 Recent evolution of world poverty (millions of persons)
Sources: databank.worldbank.org and author's calculations.

countries.[8] Therefore, along with growth, it is often the *distribution* of income within middle-income countries that is important for alleviating poverty.

Analyzing the relationship between growth and poverty takes note of the fact that poverty reduction depends on initial inequality levels and changes in inequality as well as growth itself. It also gives rise to what has come to be known as *pro-poor growth*.[9] This line of thinking considers what is known as the *growth elasticity of poverty*, namely the ratio of the percentage change in a poverty rate to the percentage change in a growth measure such as GDP per capita. This elasticity can vary by country, time period, and region within a country and can be influenced by a multitude of factors. But it is a first step in recognizing that the link between growth and poverty alleviation is not uniformly one for one, and it opens up a discussion on how to best increase the growth elasticity of poverty.[10]

---

[8] See Sumner (2010), who places the figure at three-fourth of the world's extremely poor living in middle-income countries.

[9] See, for example, Cord (2007) and Kakwani and Pernia (2000).

[10] Poverty and inequality compose a field of research in and of itself. Consequently, there is much, much more that can be said. See, for example, Clark, Fennell, and Hulme (2017), who identify the depth, breadth, and duration of poverty.

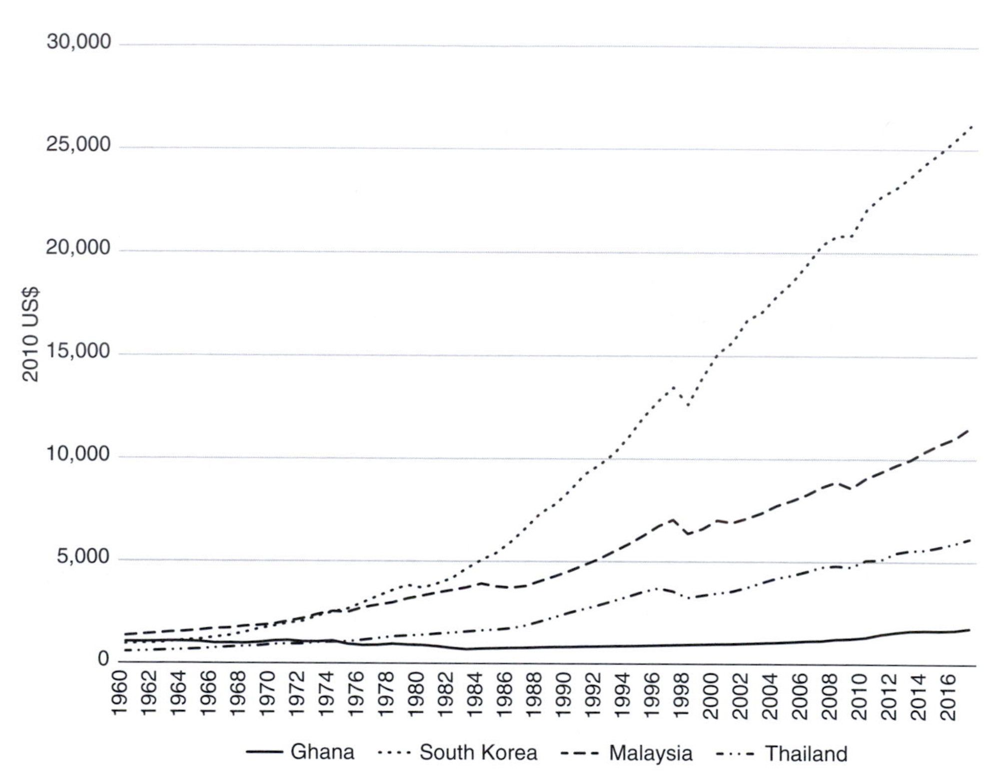

Figure 22.2 Real GDP per capita for Ghana, South Korea, Malaysia, and Thailand (2010 US$)
Source: databank.worldbank.org.

With the above considerations in mind, let us get back to growth and the Ghanaian student's comment mentioned in the introduction. That the student's observations have some merit can be seen in Figure 22.2. As mentioned in the introduction, in 1960 Ghana's GDP per capita exceeded those of South Korea and Thailand. It was only just below that of Malaysia. By 2015 it was approximately 30 percent of Thailand's, 15 percent of Malaysia's, and 7 percent of South Korea's. From the growth (and poverty) perspective, making Ghana more like South Korea is *what matters*. How exactly to do this, however, remains something of a mystery. Indeed, it is clear that what works for growth can differ significantly from one country to another.[11]

But can we can say *something* about where growth in an open economy may come from? Answering that question is the purpose of the rest of this chapter.[12] We will start with "old" growth theory.

[11] This is the point forcibly made by Rodrik (2007), among others.

[12] Here is a standard hint from Berg and Ostry (2017: 793): "Broadly speaking, countries should pursue market-friendly policies, open up to foreign trade and capital, introduce more competition in different spheres of economic activity, pursue macroeconomic stability…, and ensure appropriate regulation and supervision of the financial sector."

Old Growth Theory

Why was Ghana's 2017 real GDP per capita $1,756 rather than $10,756? An early attempt to answer this sort of question was provided by Nobel laureate Robert Solow (1956), in what is now known as "old" growth theory.[13] Growth theory begins with what economists call a **production function**. In particular, it utilizes the **intensive production function** illustrated in Figure 22.3. The intensive production function relates two economic variables. The first is per capita GDP and is denoted by $y = Y/L$, where Y is GDP and L is the labor force/population.[14] The second is the capital–labor ratio and is denoted by $k = K/L$, where K is the total amount of physical capital.

Figure 22.3 indicates that there is a *positive* relationship between the capital–labor ratio (k) and per capita GDP (y). For example, as the capital–labor ratio increases from k_1 to k_2, and each worker has more physical capital to work with, per capita GDP increases from y_1 to y_2. This is a process known as **capital deepening**. Figure 22.3 also indicates that the relationship between the capital–labor ratio and per capita GDP is *decreasingly positive* (the slope of the curve becomes flatter as k increases). This is the result of *diminishing returns* to labor and capital.[15] Consequently, increases in k at lower levels add more to per capita GDP than increases in k at higher levels.

Figure 22.3 indicates that increases in per capita income in a country such as Ghana can occur through capital deepening. There is a set of other possible sources of increases in per capita income, however. This we will refer to as *shift*

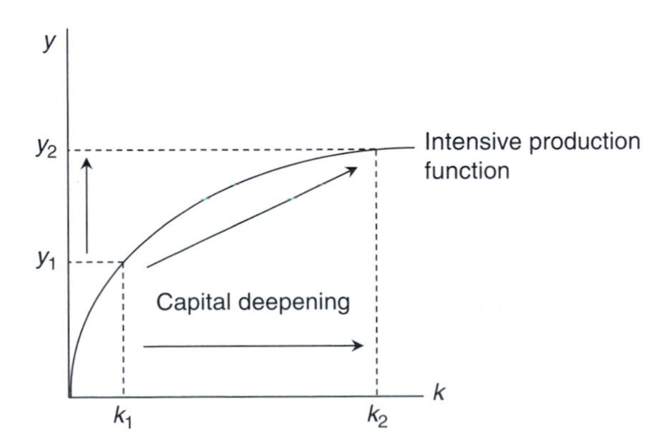

Figure 22.3 The intensive production function and capital deepening

[13] The Solow model replaced what was then called the Harrod–Domar model. See Sato (1964) and Easterly (1999).

[14] In more advanced models, the labor force and population can differ from one another.

[15] Diminishing returns to labor and capital appear as what is known as diminishing marginal products of labor and capital.

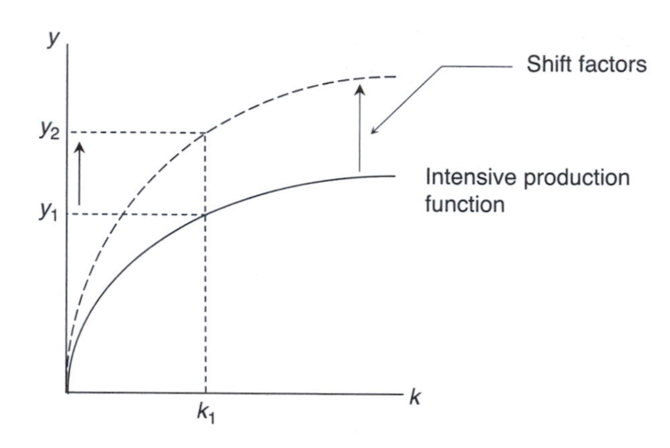

Figure 22.4 Shift of the intensive production function

factors, because they shift the intensive production function, as in Figure 22.4. Originally Solow had referred to this as *technological change*, but this turns out to be only one of a larger set of potential shift factors. In Solow's original analysis, technological change, involving a variable that does not appear on either axis of the intensive production function diagram, *shifts* the curve upwards, as in Figure 22.4. For example, at a given capital–labor ratio, k_1, per capita income increases from y_1 to y_2.[16]

Figures 22.3 and 22.4 tell us some important things about increasing per capita incomes in Ghana, or in any other country. Let us summarize them in a box.

> Increases in per capita incomes can come about through increases in the capital–labor ratio (capital deepening) or through other shift factors, including, but not limited to, improvements in technological efficiency.

We can use Figure 22.3 to understand some additional requirements for economic growth in Ghana based on capital deepening. To do this, however, we need to supplement it with some important relationships concerning Ghana's capital–labor ratio, k. Increases in k require increases in the capital stock that *more than offset* any increases in population. Increases in the capital stock, in turn, require *investment*. Finally, investment requires saving. The relationship between saving

[16] The contrast between Figures 22.3 and 22.4 is one of many cases of the important difference in economics between a *movement along* a line and a *shift of* a line, respectively. When a variable on one of the two axes changes, there is a movement along a line. When a variable *not* on one of the two axes changes, there is a shift of a line. This was true of the demand and supply graphs in Chapter 2, for example, as well as for the emigration supply and immigration demand graphs in Chapter 13.

and investment was depicted in the circular flow diagram of Chapter 14. In particular, we are going to rely on Equations 14.1a and 14.1b from that chapter, reproduced here as

$$I = (S_H + S_G) + S_F \tag{22.1a}$$

Or, in words:

$$\text{Domestic investment} = \text{Domestic savings} + \text{Foreign savings} \tag{22.1b}$$

How do these equations relate to our discussion in this chapter? Increases in GDP per capita through capital deepening require investment. Investment has two sources: domestic savings (household and government) and foreign savings. In the absence of shift factors such as technological improvements, increases in domestic and foreign savings are the only sources of growth in per capita incomes. As mentioned above, these increases in savings must be large enough to increase the capital stock sufficiently so that it more than offsets any increase in population. If the increase in the capital stock is not large enough, k and y will fall because of population growth. This phenomenon sometimes goes by the ugly term *capital shallowing*.[17]

Let us return to the sources of savings in Ghana or elsewhere. Increasing household savings is often a matter of making institutions available to the households of the economy to facilitate savings. Importantly, these institutions should be as broad-based as possible, being accessible to rich and poor, rural and urban. Increasing government savings is a matter of decreasing government expenditures and increasing government tax revenues, moving the government budget towards surplus. An important caveat here is that some types of government expenditures (e.g. education) can positively affect the level of technology (see below). In addition, some government investments (e.g. infrastructure) are *complementary* to private investments.

Finally, increasing foreign savings, as we saw in Chapter 14, is a matter of increasing the capital/financial account surplus on the balance of payments. Here, as discussed in Chapter 15, it is important to pay attention to the *form* and *magnitude* of the capital/financial account surplus. As we discussed in Chapter 20 on crises, large capital account surpluses based on short-term investments are risky and could be damaging to Ghana in the long run.[18] But these sources of savings are key to increasing GDP per capita.

"Old" growth theory contributes greatly to our understanding of how per capita incomes are determined. It draws our attention to savings and shift factors such as

---

[17] Recall that $k = K/L$, where K is the capital stock and L is the population, assumed also to be equal to the labor force. The algebraic condition for investment to increase k is given in Appendix 22.1.

[18] For a discussion of this, see also Goldin and Reinert (2012: chap. 4).

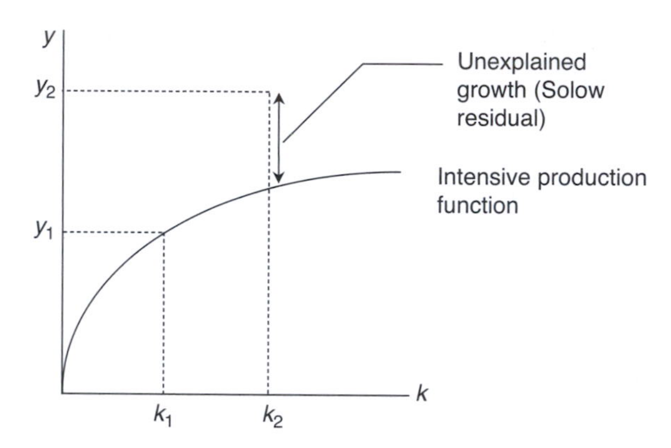

Figure 22.5 Unexplained growth in per capita incomes

technology as central variables that can be affected by various institutional and policy regimes among the countries of the world. It turns out, however, that this theory leaves a lot to be explained. This is represented in Figure 22.5. Here, in the initial year, we observe Ghana with a capital–labor ratio of k_1 and a per capita GDP of y_1. In the subsequent year, we observe a capital–labor ratio of k_2 and a per capita income of y_2. The vertical, double-headed arrow in this diagram indicates the amount of the *unexplained growth* in per capita incomes, which is known as the *Solow residual.*

In practice, these Solow residuals can be *quite large.* How can we begin to account for this unexplained growth? One explanation we have discussed already. As we showed in Figure 22.4, shift factors such as improvements of technology shift the intensive production function graph upwards. But technology is simply an *exogenous* parameter in the Solow model. How is it determined in the real world? This is the question that "new" growth theory attempts to answer.[19]

New Growth Theory and Human Capital

It is easy to say that Ghana needs to improve its technical efficiency to help improve per capita income, but what does this entail? "Old" growth theory has little to say about this. "New" growth theory provides us with some insights,

[19] For example, many years ago *The Economist* (1992) assessed the "old" growth theory, concluding that it is "patently inadequate – so much so that its teachings have had virtually no influence on policy-makers." The theory "supposes...that new technologies rain down from heaven as random scientific breakthroughs." We should remember, however, that, as stated by Singh (2017: 428), "a broader, though less formal, understanding of technological change had always been present in the work of economic historians."

however.[20] The models of the new growth theory are quite varied, and we cannot attempt a serious review of them here. Instead, we will consider a single approach that helps us understand its essence.

Many new growth theory models emphasize the role of a third factor of production in addition to labor and physical capital. This is **human capital**. Including this factor acknowledges that labor is more than just hours worked. It reflects skills, abilities, and education. In certain sectors, it might even reflect creativity. Because productive knowledge can be embodied in workers, there appears to be a positive link between human capital and technological efficiency. In other words, technological efficiency depends on levels of human capital. These considerations lead some economists to modify the intensive production function so that increases in human capital shift it upwards (as in Figure 22.4) through a positive impact on technological efficiency.

In this intensive production function of new growth theory, technology is an *endogenous* variable that can be influenced by levels of human capital, measured perhaps as literacy rates or years of education. The implication of this can be seen in Figure 22.6. In this figure, an increase in human capital from period 1 to period 2 shifts the intensive production function upwards. The amount of unexplained growth from Figure 22.5 (the Solow residual) declines, and changes in human capital are an important component in this decline.

Early attempts to address this possibility indicated that human capital was important. For example, Mankiw, Romer, and Weil (1992) and Hall and Jones (1999) show that including human capital in growth models can contribute to their ability to explain the variation of per capita incomes between the countries of the world. Subsequent work questioned the empirical importance of human

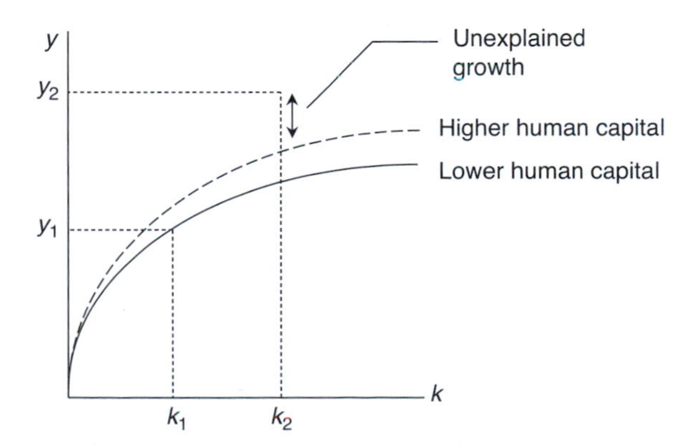

Figure 22.6 Human capital and unexplained growth in per capita incomes

[20] The "new" growth theory traces its roots back to Romer (1986; 1990). See also Lucas (1988) and Romer (1994).

capital as education in explaining development as growth. For example, Easterly (2001: 73) notes that "the growth response to the dramatic educational expansion of the last four decades has been distinctly disappointing. If the incentives to invest in the future are not there, expanding education is worth little.... Creating skills where there exists no technology to use them is not going to foster economic growth."

Why did the seeming importance of human capital as education not show up as significant in empirical investigations? Krueger and Lindahl (2001) suggest that it can be difficult to establish the role of education in growth because of *measurement errors*. This can relate to an important distinction to be made between educational *attainment* and educational *achievement*. Educational attainment refers to the number of years of education an individual has completed. At the level of an economy, educational attainment is often measured by average years of schooling. In the past, average years of schooling were taken to by *synonymous* with economy-wide human capital. This approach turned out to be mistaken.[21] Subsequent work by Cohen and Soto (2007) seems to have resolved the measurement error difficulties by establishing a non-linear relationship between education (years of schooling in their study) and human capital that allows for decreasing returns to years of education.[22] Once they did this they found that education does indeed contribute to development as growth. Further evidence of this is provided by Tamura et al. (2019).

Wößmann (2004), Hanushek (2016), and others emphasize that educational achievement can be best conceived of in terms of *cognitive skills*. The statistical analysis of Hanushek (2016) shows that educational achievement in the form of cognitive skills matters for growth and renders educational attainment much less important.[23] In the relationship between education and growth, achievement matters more than attainment.

---

[21] For example, Wößmann (2004: 23) states: "Although it is the most commonly employed measure, using the unweighted sum of schooling years linearly as a measure of the stock of human capital lacks a sound theoretical foundation. There are two major criticisms which render years of schooling a poor proxy for the human capital stock. First, one year of schooling does not raise the human capital stock by an equal amount regardless of whether it is a persons' first or seventeenth year of schooling. Second, one year of schooling does not raise the human capital stock by an equal amount regardless of the quality of the education system in which it takes place."

[22] This approach goes back to the work of Mincer (1974).

[23] This positive relationship does not apply to higher education, however. As stated by Hanushek (2016: 550), "Once knowledge capital as measured by international mathematics and science tests is taken into account, school attainment (or years of schooling) *per se* is unrelated to economic growth. In this, adding years of university provide no greater impact than added years of earlier schooling."

Further evidence on the importance of human capital in the form of education comes from research on the rate of return to education (RORE).[24] Standard results from this body of research suggest the following.

1. The private/market RORE is generally higher than the rate of return on physical capital investments.
2. The private/market RORE is generally higher at lower levels of education.
3. The private/market RORE is generally higher at lower levels of GDP per capita.

There is also a body of research looking at *female education*, which suggests that the human capital of girls and women is particularly important. For example, in a review, Schultz (2002: 212) reports: "There is a substantial empirical literature suggesting that adding to a mother's schooling will have a larger beneficial effect on a child's health, schooling, and adult productivity than would adding to a father's schooling by the same amount."[25] Additional evidence of this kind is presented in Tembon and Fort (2008).

We also need to recognize that human capital can also include *health* components. Quite some time ago, in a review of new growth theory, Pio (1994: 278) advocated devoting "particular attention...to the role of human capital with an emphasis on the adjective human; that is to say, on the levels of health, education, and nutrition of the population and the implications of changes in such levels for long-term growth." He concluded (297) that "the inclusion of a broader definition of human capital (encompassing health and nutrition as well as education) seems useful both in the construction of models and in their empirical verification." Statistical support for this intuition has been provided by Barro (2013).

Trade and Growth

Many development economists and international trade economists have suggested that countries' openness to international trade has a positive impact on growth in per capita GDP.[26] These researchers suggest that exports might be an important growth strategy for Ghana and other developing countries. This argument actually has a number of components.[27] First, increased exports can support increased

[24] See, for example, Psacharopoulos (1994; 2006).

[25] Schultz (2002: 207) also comments: "There are few instances in international quantitative social science research where the application of common statistical methods has yielded more consistent findings than in the area of gender returns to schooling."

[26] See Dollar and Kraay (2004), for example. An alternative view is given in Rodríquez and Rodrik (2001).

[27] See, for example, Goldin and Reinert (2012: chap. 3).

employment and wage incomes, with the latter being reinvested in increases in human capital. Examples of this include clothing exports from Bangladesh and rice exports from Vietnam, both of which have been shown to have had these effects. Second, increased trade (both imports and exports) can in some circumstances improve competitive conditions in domestic markets.[28] Some studies have confirmed the importance of this effect in Mexico and India, for example.[29] Third, and perhaps most importantly, exports can contribute to improved technological efficiency as a shift factor in the intensive production function diagram.

The notion here is that technological efficiency responds to two impulses. The first impulse is domestic innovation, which is positively affected by human capital accumulation in some new growth theory models. The second impulse is the absorption of new technology from the rest of the world.[30] It is thought that openness to trade, and exports in particular, facilitate this absorption of technology from abroad.[31] For this reason, exports are sometimes seen as having a *positive externality* for the exporting country. In other words, exports generate additional technology gains on the supply side of the economy.

The logic of export externalities is illustrated in Figure 22.7 in an absolute advantage diagram (see Chapter 2). P^G is Ghana's autarky price, and P^W is the world price. In the absence of a positive export externality, as the price increases from P^G to P^W in the movement from autarky to trade, quantity supplied increases from point A to point B, and exports of E_1^G appear. In the presence of export externalities, however, the process continues one step further. The initial export level, E_1^G, facilitates the absorption of technological knowledge from abroad, and the subsequent improvement in production technology makes possible an increase in supply, or a shift in Ghana's supply curve, from S_1^G to S_2^G.[32] Given P^W, Ghanaian firms move from point B to point C, and exports expand to E_2^G. In simplified form, this is how some international economists view the role of exports in the development process.

What is the evidence for the process depicted in Figure 22.7? The historical experience of East Asia, discussed in the accompanying box, is usually cited. More

---

[28] This possibility is known as the pro-competitive effects of trade.

[29] See, for example, Goldar and Aggarwal (2005), Grether (1997), and Kambhampati and Parikh (2003).

[30] See, for example, Romer (1993).

[31] For example, the World Bank (1999: 27) claims: "Trade can bring greater awareness of new and better ways of producing goods and services: exports contribute to this awareness through the information obtained from buyers and suppliers." Similarly, Rodrigo (2001: 90) notes: "By opening up a channel to the world market, trade...serves to promote specialization and sustain production tempos of goods in which learning effects are embodied; if constrained by domestic market size alone along with associated domestic business cycle uncertainty of demand, firms would be less willing to make the investments needed to capture gains from learning."

[32] Recall from Chapter 2 that reductions in input prices and improvements in technology shift the supply curve to the right, while increases in input prices and technology setbacks shift the supply curve to the left.

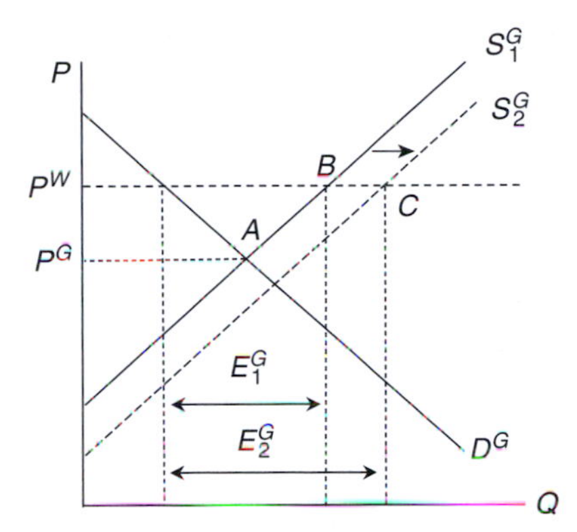

Figure 22.7 Export externalities for Ghana

formally, early studies, such as Sachs and Warner (1995) and Edwards (1998), deploy statistical techniques to show that the more open countries are to international trade, the faster their growth in per capita GDP. Another study, however, by Levin and Raut (1997), shows that these externalities are notably *absent* in the case of *primary product exports*, which characterize many developing countries, including Ghana.

These initial studies have been severely criticized by Rodríquez and Rodrik (2001), and subsequent revisits to the methodology of the studies (e.g. Wacziarg and Welch, 2008) show that such criticism had its merits. Nevertheless, statistical analysis based on extended and improved indicators does seem to support the trade and growth link. The results of Wacziarg and Welch (2008), for example, suggest that openness to trade can increases investment and growth rates by over 1 percent.[33] The results of Huchet-Bourdon, Le Mouël, and Vijil (2018) reinforce this conclusion but also suggest that the *variety* of export products (moving beyond primary product exports) also helps to support growth.

Trade and Growth in East Asia

The large increases in per capita GDP in the countries of East Asia were one of the most notable successes of the world economy in the era since World War II. One observation made about the East Asian economies is that the growth of per capita GDP was accompanied by a significant expansion of exports, especially in

[33] It is important to note that this overall result occurs within what Wacziarg and Welch (2008) describe as "considerable heterogeneity" in their country sample. For example, political instability can break the link between trade and growth. This opens up the way to institutional considerations, taken up in the next section.

Trade and Growth in East Asia (cont.)

Japan, South Korea, and Taiwan. Some observers, particularly those affiliated with the World Bank, concluded that the export promotion policies pursued by these economies explain a great deal of their growth and development successes. For example, this was the point of view expressed in a major World Bank report entitled *The East Asian Miracle: Economic Growth and Public Policy*, issued in 1993.

According to the World Bank (1993), export promotion positively affects per capita incomes via *technology effects*. These can arise in a few ways. First, exports help firms to earn the foreign exchange necessary to purchase new equipment from abroad. This new equipment can embody a more sophisticated technology than the older equipment of the firm. Second, the presence of exports signals to foreign firms that the country in question would be a good place in which to engage in export-oriented foreign direct investment. This FDI can bring with it new technology. Third, exports indicate that the exporting firms are competitive and are therefore taken seriously in technology cross-licensing schemes. Thus, the World Bank (1993: 317) claims that "the relationship between exports and productivity growth [arises] from exports' role in helping economies adopt and master international best-practice technologies."

Not all international economists agree with this interpretation. For example, Rodrik (1994) finds this export–technology link to be unconvincing. His interpretation of the East Asian development experience is that exports were largely a *result*, not a cause, of successful development. He attributes the increases in per capita GDP to levels of education and the equal distributions of income and land. He stresses the role of these *initial conditions* in the subsequent economic development of East Asia. With regard to the role of exports in improving countries' technological capabilities, Rodrik (1994: 48) states that "whether export orientation generates spillovers and productivity benefits…is still unclear."

More generally, Rodrik (1999: chap. 2) demonstrates that there are many instances when high export-to-GDP ratios are associated with *low* rates of growth. He goes further (1999: chap. 3) to demonstrate, for a sample of 47 countries, that increases in export-to-GDP ratios *followed* increases in investment-to-GDP ratios. The implication here is that exports were a *consequence* of East Asian growth rather than a cause of that growth.

Standard interpretations of the East Asian growth experience also leave out a couple of other important factors. Among these are broad-based education (e.g. Stiglitz, 1996) and broad-based asset redistribution via land reform (e.g. Davis, 2004). Indeed, *The Economist* (2017) states: "A voluminous literature ponders the causes of the East Asian miracle.… Most studies point to market-friendly

Trade and Growth in East Asia (cont.)

policies that encouraged exports of manufactures and the rapid accumulation of capital, including the human sort. Others emphasize the importance of institutions. Yet one crucial factor has been relatively underplayed: land reform." Much evidence suggests that broad-based education (the ownership of human capital) and broad-based ownership of land via redistribution positively affected growth in each East Asian country.

Sources: Davis (2004), *The Economist* (2017), Rodrik (1994; 1999), Stiglitz (1996), and the World Bank (1993).

There are other caveats to the role of exports in economic growth. There is some agreement that the accumulation of human capital (discussed in the previous section) is an important *prerequisite* to the absorption of technology from abroad.[34] Indeed, many statistical studies of the trade–growth link include educational measures along with trade measures as explanatory variables. There has also been some empirical evidence to support the conclusion that human capital and *manufactured* exports interact positively in supporting the growth of per capita incomes (e.g. Levin and Raut, 1997). This interaction is restricted to manufactured exports, however. Primary product exports do not necessarily generate the same effects. Finally, there is the additional role that institutions play—to which we next turn.[35]

Institutions and Growth

Although much attention has been given to the trade and growth possibility, increasing recognition has gone to the role of *institutions* in growth as an additional shift factor in the intensive production function diagram. This line

[34] For example, in its study of economic development in East Asia, the World Bank (1993: 320–1, emphasis added) acknowledges that "[a]ccess to international best-practice technology and rapid formation of human capital supplement and reinforce one another.... The externalities generated by *manufactured* exports in the high-performing Asian economies in the form of cheaper and more effective knowledge transfers would have undoubtedly been less productive had there been fewer skilled workers to facilitate their absorption."

[35] Rodrik, Subramanian, and Trebbi (2004) make a relevant distinction. They write (132): "It may be useful to distinguish between 'moderate' and 'maximal' versions of this [trade and growth] view. Much of the economics profession would accept the hypothesis that trade can be an underlying source of growth once certain institutional pre-requisites have been fulfilled. But a more extreme perspective...is that trade/integration is the major determinant of whether poor countries grow or not."

of thinking goes back to the work of North (1990), and has a long history in economic thought, but has only more recently been taken up in modern growth theory and its associated empirical analysis. As we mentioned in Chapter 8 on the World Trade Organization, North defines institutions as "humanly devised constraints that shape human interaction" (3). A less formal definition is as "the rules of the game." How can the rules of the game in a country affect economic growth?

Perhaps first and foremost, many developing countries had long histories as colonies of other (usually European) countries. In many instances, colonial institutions had a lasting impact. As North also emphasizes, institutional change is "overwhelmingly incremental," and independence from a formal colonial power does not necessarily bring about the termination of colonial institutions, just the slow modification of them. This phenomenon is known as *path dependence*: the notion that a country's institutions are strongly influenced by its history. For example, the work of Bolt and Bezemer (2009) shows that variations in colonial education investments within sub-Saharan Africa help to explain human capital levels as far forward as 1995. They further show that colonial educational investments help to explain current institutional quality in the form of measures of democracy and constraints on the executive. Banerjee and Iyer (2005) show similar results for colonial land tenure systems in India.[36]

But what are the relevant institutions from the perspective of growth? Table 22.1 presents some relevant institutional categories. The table begins with the *rule of law* in the elements of political representation, elections, an independent judiciary, civil liberties, and consistency. The rule of law helps to prevent violent conflict and provides for legitimacy in political decision-making. Clearly, conflict (either internal or external) involves productive asset destruction and is not good for growth. Issues of consistency in the rule of law are complex and under argument in the democracy and development research literature, but are clearly relevant.[37] For some time the role of civil liberties in growth was unclear, but the work of Benyishay and Betancourt (2010) shows that it does indeed matter.[38]

Property rights concern the ownership of productive assets that are involved in the growth and development process. The relevant elements here include the secure ownership or control of assets, the right to returns on these assets, and the distribution of the assets. As emphasized by Rodrik (2007: chap. 5), and many others, the private ownership (or, at least, control) of property has proved to be the

[36] Institutional path dependence can even impact the export and growth linkage we discussed above. As pointed out by Myint (2001), the export success of South Korea and Taiwan was in part attributable to the inheritance of rural and urban institutions from the (brutal) Japanese colonial period.

[37] For just one example, see Mansfield and Snyder (2005). But, on the positive role of democratic processes in institutional development and growth, see Rodrik (2007: chap. 5).

[38] This is in the form of personal autonomy and individual rights, as measured by Freedom House.

Table 22.1 Institutions and growth

Category	Elements	Relevance
Rule of law	Political representation Elections Independent judiciary Civil liberties Consistency	Prevents violent conflict and provides for legitimacy in political decision-making.
Property rights	Secure ownership or control of assets Right to returns on assets Asset distribution	Ensures that the use of productive assets will result in appropriable returns that will, in turn, provide incentives for further development and use.
Contract enforcement	Contract design Escape clauses Recourse	Allows for parties to enter into long-term productive arrangements with a minimum degree of certainty.
Regulation	Prudential regulation of finance Macroeconomic management Health and safety regulation	Addresses well-known instances of market failure.
Social insurance	Transfer payments Employment practices Traditional social arrangements	Ensures that market dislocations are managed so as not to impede human development.

Sources: Rodrik (2007) and others cited in text.

best institutional arrangement for growth.[39] That said, economists tend to downplay the importance of the *distribution* of asset ownership or control, but this can be quite important. For example, years ago Adelman (1980) stressed the importance of asset redistribution in Japan, South Korea, and Taiwan for their growth through export success. This point is also made by Alesina and Rodrik (1994) and Birdsall and Londono (1998). More recently, Berg and Ostry (2017) show that inequality *negatively* affects the *duration* of growth episodes.[40]

---

[39] Rodrik (2007: 156) rightly points out: "Formal property rights do not count for much if they do not confer control rights. By the same token, sufficiently strong control rights may do the trick even in the absence of formal property rights." This distinction is especially important in countries transitioning from formally socialist systems (e.g. Russia, China, and Ethiopia).

[40] Berg and Ostry (2017: 805) conclude: "Income distribution survives as one of the most robust and important factors associated with growth duration.... Remarkably, inequality retains a similar statistical and economic significance in...joint analysis despite the inclusion of many other possible determinants. This suggests that inequality matters in itself and is not just proxying for other factors.... Inequality is thus a more robust predictor of growth duration than many variables widely understood to be central to growth."

Contract enforcement is a third area of institutions for growth. Market systems rely on complex sets of contracts (both explicit and implicit), with varying degrees of intertemporality. If the process of entering into and exiting from these contracts is not regularized, confusion ensues. Relevant elements of contract enforcement include contract design, escape clauses for early exit, and legal recourse in the case of contract violation. As emphasized by Clague et al. (1999: 206), "Only countries where governments give private parties the capacity to make credible commitments that they could not otherwise make, and thereby achieve gains from trade that they could not otherwise obtain, achieve their economic potential."

Regulation is a fourth area of relevant institutions. Although the notion of regulation often has negative connotations, this area of government activity is actually essential for growth and development. Regulation's purpose is to address known market failures.[41] Important areas include the prudential regulation of finance to avoid the crises we discussed in Chapter 20, macroeconomic management, and basic health and safety regulation. As noted by Rodrik (2007: 157), "The freer are the markets, the greater is the burden on the regulatory institutions." This is not to deny the possibility of over-regulation, but to recognize the importance of minimum regulatory requirements for sustained growth.

Finally, *social insurance* is an important institutional realm. This includes transfer payments, employment practices, and traditional (family and community) social arrangements. Traditional family and community social insurance systems tend to break down as growth and development proceeds. As this occurs, they need to be replaced by other social insurance systems based on employment practices or transfer payments. Without these systems in place, the vicissitudes of the market system can undermine its effectiveness in allocating resources, improving technological efficiency, and accumulating physical and human capital. Even worse, the absence of effective social insurance systems can unleash varieties of ethno-nationalism that undermine market systems and international economic integration.

What is the evidence on the role of institutions in economic growth? At one level, this is a silly question, because the entire classical literature on economics from Adam Smith on, as well as the entire early development economics literature, both addressed precisely this question.[42] But, at another level, there has been a set of new quantitative studies of the role of institutions in growth, and, taken as a whole, they indicate that institutions (in multiple dimensions) do matter. This appears to be true of the rule of law (e.g. Hall and Jones, 1999: Rodrik,

[41] See, for example, Acocella (2005: chaps. 2 & 3).

[42] See Szirmai (2015: chap. 3).

Subramanian, and Trebbi, 2004: Benyishay and Betancourt, 2010), property rights (e.g. Rodrik, Subramanian, and Trebbi, 2004), and contract enforcement (e.g. Clague et al., 1999) to name a few.

Despite this important and emerging evidence, the task of actually constructing effective institutions is difficult given the "overwhelmingly incremental" nature of institutional change. Further, there is the choice to be made between home-grown and imported institutions. As Rodrik (2007: chap. 5) emphasizes, effective institutions are frequently hybrids between existing domestic institutions and imported institutions, often cobbled together in novel ways. So, having established the importance of institutions, we need to be aware that approaches can vary from place to place but still have positive effects on growth. There is room for variety and experimentation.

This and the previous section allow us to supplement the box at the beginning of the chapter with the following.

> Increases in per capita incomes can come about through increases in the capital–labor ratio (capital deepening) or through other shift factors, such as improvements in technological efficiency, improvement in human development (education and health), export expansion, and improvements in institutional quality.

Conclusion

What causes growth? The accumulation of both *physical capital* and *human capital* is part of the growth story, but so are *international trade* and *institutions*, with institutions probably being more important. Changing institutions is not easy, and there is no one formula for successful institutional design.

So what should Ghana do? We need to be careful in answering this question, because there is probably more than one potential answer. But it is difficult to imagine Ghana continuing to grow by neglecting human capital in its education and health aspects and ignoring institutional development. And exports will no doubt help to some extent. There are other, more idiosyncratic answers. For example, Braimah and Amponsah (2012) studied the effects of electricity blackouts on small enterprises in Ghana, and determine that blackouts had detrimental impacts on machinery, inhibited the ability of entrepreneurs to satisfy contracts, and substantially increased costs. Frimpong, Okoye, and Pongou (2016) draw attention to the nutrition of Ghanaian children. The growth agenda for Ghana (and all countries) is large.

Review Exercises

1. Given the discussion of this chapter with regard to trade, education, health, and institutions, what policies do you think countries ought to pursue to ensure that international trade supports increases in per capita incomes?
2. Are there any connections you can find between the discussion of this chapter and that on leveraging international production covered in Chapter 12? Look back at Chapter 12 and try to be as specific as you can.
3. The World Bank has suggested that there are important externalities associated with exports. In general, such positive externalities call for subsidies on the part of governments. Given our discussion of the GATT/WTO system in Chapter 8, do you detect any problems with the use of *export subsidies*?
4. This is one of the few chapters in which we mentioned *gender* issues in our discussion. Are there any other aspects of the world economy in which gender issues are important? How might these issues arise in the realms of international trade, international production, and international finance?
5. Consider a country with which you have some familiarity. Using Table 22.1 as a rough guide, what can you say about the institutional qualities of that country?

FURTHER READING AND WEB RESOURCES

Jones and Vollrath (2013) is a basic reference on the theory of economic growth. For a concise and informative summary, see Rodrik (2003). Szirmai (2015) and Cypher (2014) present the roles of education, health, and population in the growth and development processes in an accessible manner. The role of trade in growth and development is effectively reviewed by Bruton (1998) and in Goldin and Reinert (2012: chap. 3). On the role of institutions in growth and development, see North (1990) and Rodrik (2007).

The Groningen Growth and Development Centre, at rug.nl/ggdc, is a good source for data and research on growth and development. It is particularly known for having historical data on growth.

REFERENCES

Acocella, N. (2005) *Economic Policy in the Age of Globalization*, Cambridge University Press.

Adelman, I. (1980) "Income Distribution, Economic Development and Land Reform," *American Behavioral Scientist*, 23:3, 437–56.

Alesina, A., and D. Rodrik (1994) "Distributive Politics and Economic Growth," *Quarterly Journal of Economics*, 109:2, 465–90.

Banerjee, A., and L. Iyer (2005) "History, Institutions, and Economic Performance: The Legacy of Colonial Land Tenure Systems in India," *American Economic Review*, 95:4, 1190–213.

Barro, R. J. (2013) "Health and Economic Growth," *Annals of Economics and Finance*, 14:2, 329–66.

Benyishay, A., and R. R. Betancourt (2010) "Civil Liberties and Economic Development," *Journal of Institutional Economics*, 6:3, 281–304.

Berg, A. G., and J. D. Ostry (2017) "Inequality and Unsustainable Growth: Two Sides of the Same Coin?," *IMF Economic Review*, 65:4, 792–815.

Bhagwati, J. (1984) "Why Are Services Cheaper in the Poor Countries?," *Economic Journal*, 94:374, 279–86.

Birdsall, N., and J. L. Londono (1998) "No Tradeoff: Efficient Growth via More Equal Human Capital Accumulation," in N. Birdsall, C. Graham, and R. H. Sabot (eds.), *Beyond Tradeoffs: Market Reforms and Equitable Growth in Latin America*, Brookings Institution, 111–45.

Bolt, J., and D. Bezemer (2009) "Understanding Long-Run African Growth: Colonial Institutions or Colonial Education?," *Journal of Development Studies*, 45:1, 24–54.

Braimah, I., and O. Amponsah (2012) "Causes and Effects of Frequent and Unannounced Electricity Blackouts on the Operations of Micro and Small Scale Industries in Kumasi," *Journal of Sustainable Development*, 5:2, 17–36.

Bruton, H. J. (1998) "A Reconsideration of Import Substitution," *Journal of Economic Literature*, 36:2, 903–36.

Clague, C., P. Keefer, S. Knack, and M. Olson (1999) "Contract-Intensive Money: Contract Enforcement, Property Rights, and Economic Performance," *Journal of Economic Growth*, 4:2, 185–209.

Clark, D. A., S. Fennell, and D. Hulme (2017) "Poverty and Inequality," in K. A. Reinert (ed.), *Handbook of Globalisation and Development*, Edward Elgar, 487–512.

Cohen, D., and M. Soto (2007) "Growth and Human Capital: Good Data, Good Results," *Journal of Economic Growth*, 12:1, 51–76.

Cord, L. J. (2007) "Overview," in T. Besley and L. J. Cord (eds.), *Delivering on the Promise of Pro-Poor Growth: Insights and Lessons from Country Experiences*, World Bank, 1–27.

Coyle, D. (2014) *GDP: A Brief but Affectionate History*, Princeton University Press.

Cypher, J. M. (2014) *The Process of Economic Development*, Routledge.

Davis, D. E. (2004) *Discipline and Development: Middle Classes and Prosperity in East Asia and Latin America*, Cambridge University Press.

Dollar, D., and A. Kraay (2004) "Trade, Growth, and Poverty," *Economic Journal*, 114:493, 22–49.

Easterly, W. (1999) "The Ghost of the Financing Gap: Testing the Growth Model Used in the International Financial Institutions," *Journal of Development Economics*, 60:2, 423–38.

Easterly, W. (2001) *The Elusive Quest for Growth*, MIT Press.

The Economist (1992) "Economic Growth: Explaining the Mystery," January 4.

The Economist (2017) "Land to the Tiller," October 14.

The Economist (2019) "Ghana and the IMF: Never Gonna Let You Go," June 22.

Edwards, S. (1998) "Openness, Productivity and Growth: What Do We Really Know?," *Economic Journal*, 108:447, 383–98.

Frimpong, J., D. Okoye, and R. Pongou (2016) "Economic Growth, Health Care Reform, and Child Nutrition in Ghana," *Journal of African Development*, 18:2, 41–60.

Goldar, B., and S. C. Aggarwal (2005) "Trade Liberalization and Price–Cost Margin in Indian Industries," *The Developing Economies*, 43:3, 346–73.

Goldin, I., and K. A. Reinert (2012) *Globalization for Development: Meeting New Challenges*, Oxford University Press.

Grether, J. M. (1997) "Estimating the Pro-Competitive Gains from Trade Liberalization: An Application to Mexican Manufacturing," *Journal of International Trade and Economic Development*, 6:3, 393–417.

Hall, R., and C. I. Jones (1999) "Why Do Some Countries Produce So Much More Output per Worker than Others?," *Quarterly Journal of Economics*, 114:1, 83–116.

Hanushek, E. A. (2016) "Will More Higher Education Improve Economic Growth?," *Oxford Review of Economic Policy*, 32:4, 538–52.

Huchet-Bourdon, M., C. Le Mouël, and M. Vijil (2018) "The Relationship between Trade Openness and Economic Growth: Some New Insights on the Openness Measurement Issue," *World Economy*, 41:1, 59–76.

Jones, C. I, and D. Vollrath (2013) *Introduction to Economic Growth*, Norton.

Kambhampati, U. S., and A. Parikh (2003) "Disciplining Firms: The Impact of Trade Reforms on Profit Margins in Indian Industry," *Applied Economics*, 35:4, 461–70.

Kakwani, N., and E. Pernia (2000) "What Is Pro-Poor Growth?," *Asian Development Review*, 18:1, 1–16.

Krueger, A. B., and M. Lindahl (2001) "Education for Growth: Why and for Whom?," *Journal of Economic Literature*, 39:4, 1101–36.

Levin, A., and L. Raut (1997) "Complementarities between Exports and Human Capital in Economic Growth: Evidence from Semi-Industrialized Countries," *Economic Development and Cultural Change*, 46:1, 155–74.

Lucas, R. E. (1988) "On the Mechanics of Economic Development," *Journal of Monetary Economics*, 22:1, 3–42.

Mankiw, N. G., D. Romer, and D. Weil (1992) "A Contribution to the Empirics of Economic Growth," *Quarterly Journal of Economics*, 107:2, 407–38.

Mansfield, E. D., and J. Snyder (2005) *Electing to Fight: Why Emerging Democracies Go to War*, MIT Press.

Mincer, J. (1974) *Schooling, Experience, and Earnings*, National Bureau of Economic Research.

Myint, H. (2001) "International Trade and the Domestic Institutional Framework," in G. M Meier and J. E. Stiglitz (eds.), *Frontiers of Development Economics: The Future in Perspective*, Oxford University Press, 520–8.

North, D. C. (1990) *Institutions, Institutional Change and Economic Performance*, Cambridge University Press.

Pio, A. (1994) "New Growth Theory and Old Development Problems," *Development Policy Review*, 12:3, 277–300.

Psacharopoulos, G. (1994) "Returns to Investment in Education: A Global Update," *World Development*, 22:9, 1325–43.

Psacharopoulos, G. (2006) "The Value of Investment in Education: Theory, Evidence, and Policy," *Journal of Education Finance*, 32:2, 113–36.

Reinert, K. A. (2018) *No Small Hope: Towards the Universal Provision of Basic Goods*, Oxford University Press.

Rodrigo, G. C. (2001) *Technology, Economic Growth and Crises in East Asia*, Edward Elgar.

Rodríquez, F., and D. Rodrik (2001) "Trade Policy and Economic Growth: A Skeptic's Guide to the Cross-National Evidence," in B. Bernanke and K. S. Rogoff (eds.), *Macroeconomics Annual 2000*, MIT Press.

Rodrik, D. (1994) "King Kong Meets Godzilla: The World Bank and *The East Asian Miracle*," in A. Fishlow and C. Gwin (eds.), *Miracle or Design? Lessons from the East Asian Experience*, Overseas Development Council, 13–53.

Rodrik, D. (1999) *The New Global Economy and Developing Countries: Making Openness Work*, Overseas Development Council.

Rodrik, D. (2003) "Introduction: What Do We Learn from Country Narratives?," in D. Rodrik (ed.), *In Search of Prosperity: Analytic Narratives on Economic Growth*, Princeton University Press, 1–19.

Rodrik, D. (2007) *One Economics, Many Recipes: Globalization, Institutions and Economic Growth*, Princeton University Press.

Rodrik, D., A. Subramanian, and F. Trebbi (2004) "Institutions Rule: The Primacy of Institutions over Geography and Integration in Economic Development," *Journal of Economic Growth*, 9:2, 131–65.

Romer, P. (1986) "Increasing Returns and Long-Run Growth," *Journal of Political Economy*, 94:5, 1002–37.

Romer, P. (1990) "Endogenous Technological Change," *Journal of Political Economy*, 98:5, S71–S102.

Romer, P. (1993) "Two Strategies for Economic Development: Using Ideas and Producing Ideas," in L. H. Summers and S. Shah (eds.), *Proceedings of the World Bank Annual Conference on Development Economics 1992*, World Bank, 63–91.

Romer, P. (1994) "The Origins of Endogenous Growth," *Journal of Economic Perspectives*, 8:1, 3–22.

Sachs, J., and A. Warner (1995) "Economic Reform and the Process of Global Integration," *Brookings Papers on Economic Activity*, 26:1, 1–118.

Sato, R. (1964) "The Harrod Domar Model vs. the Neoclassical Growth Model," *Economic Journal*, 74:294, 380–7.

Schultz, T. P. (2002) "Why Governments Should Invest More to Educate Girls," *World Development*, 30:2, 207–25.

Sen, A. (1989) "Development as Capability Expansion," *Journal of Development Planning*, 19, 41–58.

Singh, J. P. (2017) "Technology," in K. A. Reinert (ed.), *Handbook of Globalisation and Development*, Edward Elgar, 426–43.

Solow, R. (1956) "A Contribution to the Theory of Economic Growth," *Quarterly Journal of Economics*, 70:1, 65–94.

Stiglitz, J. E. (1996) "Some Lessons from the East Asian Miracle," *World Bank Research Observer*, 11:2, 151–77.

Sumner, A. (2010) "Global Poverty and the New Bottom Billion: Three-Quarters of the World's Poor Live in Middle-Income Countries," Working Paper 349, Institute of Development Studies.

Szirmai, A. (2015) *Socio-Economic Development*, Cambridge University Press.

Tamura, R., J. Dwyer, J. Devereux, and S. Baier (2019) "Economic Growth in the Long Run," *Journal of Development Economics*, 137, 1–35.
Tembon, M., and L. Fort (2008) *Girls' Education in the 21st Century*, World Bank.
Wacziarg, R., and K. H. Welch (2008) "Trade Liberalization and Growth: New Evidence," *World Bank Economic Review*, 22:2, 187–231.
Wößmann, L. (2004) "Specifying Human Capital," in D. A. R. George, L. Oxley, and K. I. Carlaw (eds.), *Surveys in Economic Growth: Theory and Empirics*, Blackwell, 13–44.
World Bank (1993) *The East Asian Miracle: Economic Growth and Public Policy*, Oxford University Press.
World Bank (1994) *Adjustment in Africa*, Oxford University Press.
World Bank (1999) *World Development Report 1998/99: Knowledge for Development*, Oxford University Press.

Appendix 22.1: Growth Theory Algebra

This appendix presents some of the algebra behind the growth theory presented in this chapter.

Growth theory begins with what economists call a **production function**:

$$Y = A \times F(L, K) \tag{22.2}$$

This equation presents what is known as the *aggregate* production function. In this equation, Y is total output and total income, L is the aggregate labor force, and K is the aggregate stock of physical capital. A refers to an *exogenous* measure of technology.

"Old" growth theory assumes that production takes place according to **constant returns to scale**. The constant returns to scale concept means that a doubling of both L and K will lead to a doubling of Y. More generally, multiplying both L and K by some constant θ will increase Y by that same factor. In other words:

$$\theta Y = A \times F(\theta L, \theta K) \tag{22.3}$$

Solow's growth model uses Equation 22.3 and introduces a little trick. The trick is to set θ equal to $1/L$. This gives us the following equation:

$$\frac{1}{L}Y = A \times F\left(\frac{1}{L}L, \frac{1}{L}K\right) \tag{22.4}$$

Equation 22.4 is a little confusing. To make sense of it, we are going to consider each of its terms in turn. Let us begin with the term on the left-hand side of the equation, Y/L. This is *per capita GDP*. We are going to denote per capita GDP with a *lower-case* $y = Y/L$. The second term, A, we have seen before. It is just our technology term. Inside the parentheses, we next encounter L/L. This term is equal to one, a constant, and we can therefore ignore it. Finally, we have K/L. This is known as the *capital–labor ratio*. We are going to denote the capital–labor ratio with a lower-case $k = K/L$. Given all this, we can rewrite Equation 22.4 as follows:

$$y = A \times F(1, k) = A \times f(k) \tag{22.5}$$

This equation is the **intensive production function** used in this chapter.

New growth theory often works with a modified intensive production function of the form

$$y = A(h) \times f(k) \tag{22.6}$$

where h is a measure of per capita human capital, $h = H/L$. Trade issues in new growth theory involve adding an additional variable to this equation, as follows:

$$y = A(h \times e_M) \times f(k) \tag{22.7}$$

where e_M is manufacturing exports' share in gross domestic product. Note in Equation 22.7 that A is a function of the *product* of h and e_M. Therefore, the contribution of human capital depends on the level of manufactured exports, and the contribution of manufactured exports depends on the level of human capital.

Let us next call the rate of population growth in percentage terms n. Along with the percentage increase in the stock of physical capital, the rate of population growth determines changes in the capital–labor ratio k. Increases in y via capital deepening (increases in k) will require that

$$\frac{K}{K} \times 100 > n \tag{22.8}$$

The higher the rate of population growth, the less likely this will be.

Glossary

Absolute advantage. The possibility that, because of differences in supply conditions, one country can produce a product at a lower price than another country.

Adjustable gold peg. An international financial arrangement that was part of the Bretton Woods system. It involved pegging the US dollar to gold at US$35 per ounce and allowing all other countries to either peg to the US dollar or directly to gold. The currency pegs (other than the US dollar) were to remain fixed except under conditions that were termed "fundamental disequilibrium."

Anti-dumping. Trade policies that respond to exported goods sold at less than "normal" value.

Appreciation. An increase in the value of a currency under a flexible or floating exchange rate regime.

Asset price deflation. A rapid or substantial decline in the value of assets.

Assets. Financial objects characterized by a monetary value that can change over time and making up individuals' and firms' wealth portfolios.

Assets-based approach. A model of exchange rate determination that views foreign exchange deposits as assets held as part of an overall wealth portfolio.

Autarky. A situation of national self-sufficiency in which a country does not import or export.

Backward linkages. The purchase of goods from local suppliers by foreign multinational enterprises.

Balance of payments. A detailed set of economic accounts focusing on the transactions between a country and the rest of the world. Two important sub-accounts are the current account and the capital/financial account.

Balance of payments and currency crises. Large devaluations or rapid depreciations of the value of domestic currencies.

Banking crises. The occurrence of bank runs, mergers, closures, or government takeovers of banking institutions.

Binding. A major GATT/WTO principle. As negotiations proceed through the rounds of trade talks, tariffs are bound at the agreed-upon level. They may not, in general, be increased in the future.

Bond finance. A form of capital flow in which firms (private debt) or the government (public debt) issue bonds to foreign investors.

Brain drain. The loss of highly educated or skilled citizens to emigration.

Brain gain. The possibility that the emigration of high-skilled individuals can increase the overall level of education in the remaining population.

Brain waste. The possibility that immigrants fail to find a job in the destination country that is commensurate with their skill level.

Bretton Woods system. An international financial system introduced at the Bretton Woods Conference in 1944 involving an exchange rate arrangement known as the adjustable gold peg.

Bubble. A rapid increase in asset prices above what is to be expected by the underlying productive value of the asset.

Capital controls. Policies that attempt to influence (typically, dampen) capital flows between the countries of the world.

Capital deepening. An increase in the overall capital–labor ratio in a country.

Capital/financial account. A subsection of the balance of payments recording transactions between a country and the world economy that involve the exchange of assets.

Capital flight. A situation in which investors sell a country's assets and reallocate their portfolios towards other countries' assets. It tends to cause a capital account deficit for the country in question.

Capital flows. The annual flows resulting from the exchange of assets between the countries of the world.

Capital gain (loss). An increase (decrease) in the price of an asset.

Change in demand. A shift of a demand curve because of a change in income, wealth, preferences, expectations, and prices of related goods.

Change in quantity demanded. A movement along a demand curve because of a change in the price of a good.

Change in quantity supplied. A movement along a supply curve because of a change in the price of the good.

Change in supply. A shift of the supply curve because of a change in technology or input prices.

Circular flow diagram. A graphical representation of the flow of incomes and expenditures in an economy. It involves firm, household, government, capital, and rest of the world accounts.

Closed economy. Similar to autarky. An economy that does not have any interactions with the world economy.

Cluster. A collection of interrelated firms in a geographic area that engage in cooperative information sharing and, thereby, contribute to their collective efficiency and competitiveness.

Commercial bank lending. A type of capital flow consisting of lending within the commercial bank sector across national borders.

Common market. An agreement on the part of a set of countries to eliminate trade restrictions between themselves, to adopt a common external tariff, and to allow the free movement of labor and physical capital between member countries.

Comparative advantage. A situation in which a country's relative autarkic price ratio of one good in terms of another is lower than that of other countries in the world economy.

Compulsory licensing. The production of off-patent medicines under the Agreement on Trade-Related Aspects of Intellectual Property Rights.

Conditionality. Policies pursued by the World Bank and International Monetary Fund in which loans are made only to countries that promise to institute a set of prescribed policy changes.

Constant returns to scale. A condition of production in which a doubling of all inputs leads to a doubling of output.

Consumer surplus. The benefit accruing to consumers from the fact that, in equilibrium, the consumers receive a price lower than their willingness to pay for lesser quantities.

Contagion. The spread of a financial crisis from one country to another.

Contracting. A mode of foreign market entry whereby a home-country firm contracts a foreign-country firm to engage in production in the foreign country. Includes both licensing and franchising.

Countervailing duties. An import policy that addresses foreign subsidies.

Crawling band. An exchange rate regime in which the monetary authorities intervene to maintain the nominal exchange rate in a band of prescribed width around a central rate.

Crawling peg. An exchange rate regime in which a country fixes its nominal exchange rate in terms of another currency but changes this fixed rate gradually over time in small increments.

Crises. Any of a number of extreme difficulties faces by economies, including hyperinflation, balance of payments and currency crises, asset price deflation, banking crises, external debt crises, and domestic debt crises.

Currency board. A type of fixed exchange rate regime in which the monetary authority is required to fully back up the domestic currency with reserves of the foreign currency to which the domestic currency is pegged.

Current account. A subsection of the balance of payments recording non-official transactions between a country and the world economy that do not involve the exchange of assets.

Customs union. An agreement on the part of a set of countries to eliminate trade restrictions between themselves and adopt a common external tariff.

Depreciation. A decrease in the value of a currency under a flexible or floating exchange rate regime.

Devaluation. A decrease in the value of a currency under a fixed exchange rate regime.

Direct investment. An entry in the balance of payments that records the net inflows of foreign direct investment.

Dissemination risk. The possibility of a foreign-country partner firm obtaining technology or other know-how from a home-country firm and exploiting it for its own commercial advantage.

Domestic debt crises. Sovereign default on debt obligations to domestic creditors or the substantial restructuring of this debt.

Economic union. A monetary union that adopts a process of domestic policy harmonization in areas such as tax and spending policies and domestic regulation.

Effective exchange rate. An exchange rate weighted across a country's trade partners.

Efficiency seeking. One motivation for foreign direct investment, involving the pursuit of firm-level economies in which intangible assets are spread over a greater number of international productive activities.

Endogenous protection. A body of trade theory that uses political considerations to explain the presence and level of barriers to trade, particularly tariffs.

Equity portfolio investment. A type of capital flow consisting of international transactions in firm equities.

European Community/Union. A common market between European countries. The European Community was established in 1958, the European Union in 1992.

Exchange rate exposure. The loss of income denominated in a particular currency as a result of exchange rate changes.

Export processing zone. An area of a host country in which multinational enterprises can locate and in which they enjoy, in return for exporting the whole of their output, favorable treatment in the areas of infrastructure, taxation, tariffs on imported intermediate goods, and labor costs.

External debt crises. Sovereign default on debt obligations to foreign creditors or the substantial restructuring of this debt.

Financial intermediary. A financial institution, such as a bank, mutual fund, or broker, that receives funds from savers and uses these funds to make loans or buy assets, thereby placing the funds in the hands of investors.

Firm-level economies. Economies accruing to a firm from spreading the cost of firm-specific assets over larger numbers of production facilities, including production facilities in more than one country.

Firm-specific asset approach. An explanation of foreign direct investment based on the capabilities and resources possessed by a firm that contribute to its sustained competitiveness. The firm-specific assets can be tangible or intangible.

Fixed exchange rate regime. An exchange rate policy in which a country sets its nominal or currency exchange rate fixed in terms of another currency.

Flexible or floating exchange rate regime. An exchange rate policy in which a country allows the value of its currency to be determined by world currency markets.

Flexible manufacturing. A recent phase of manufacturing history in which information technology combines with machinery in a way to promote rapid switching between products and processes.

Foreign direct investment. Occurs when a firm acquires shares in a foreign-based enterprise that exceeds a threshold of 10 percent, implying managerial influence over the foreign enterprise. Contrasts with portfolio investment. FDI may be horizontal, backward vertical, or forward vertical.

Foreign market entry. Sales on the part of a firm in a foreign country via trade, contractual, or foreign direct investment modes.

Foreign savings. An inflow of funds into an economy from the rest of the world. It occurs when foreign investors buy the assets of the economy in question.

Forward rate. The rate of current contracts for transactions in currencies that usually take place one, three, or six months in the future.

Fragmentation. The breaking up of a production process into a larger number of stages, particularly across national borders; used to explain vertical *intra*-industry trade.

Free trade area. An agreement on the part of a set of countries to *eliminate* trade restrictions between themselves. In contrast to a customs union, it does not involve a common external tariff.

Fundamental accounting equation. Derived from the circular flow diagram, it appears in two forms. The first is Domestic investment - Domestic savings = Foreign savings = Trade deficit. The second is Domestic savings - Domestic investment = Foreign investment = Trade balance.

Gains from trade. Advantages that accrue to a country from engaging in importing and exporting relationships. In an absolute advantage framework, gains from trade are identified as a net gain between consumer and producer surplus effects. In a comparative advantage framework, gains from trade are identified as an increase in consumption of all goods.

GDP price deflator. A means of establishing a price level as the ratio of nominal to real gross domestic product.

General Agreement on Tariffs and Trade. Established in 1946, the GATT was to be part of an International Trade Organization. The ITO was never ratified, but the GATT and its Articles served as an international vehicle for trade relationships until 1995, when it became embodied in the Marrakesh Agreement establishing the World Trade Organization. As part of the Marrakesh Agreement, it is now known as GATT 1994.

General Agreement on Trade in Services. Part of the Marrakesh Agreement of 1994. Applies the GATT/WTO principles of non-discrimination and national treatment to services.

Global production network. A system of value chains linked together in buyer–supplier or ownership relationships across countries. Also known as global value chain.

Global value chain. A system of value chains linked together in buyer–supplier or ownership relationships across countries. Also known as global production network.

Gold standard. An international financial arrangement in existence from approximately 1870 to 1914. Under the gold standard, countries defined the value of their currencies in terms of gold and held gold as official reserves.

Gold exchange standard. An international financial arrangement introduced in the 1920s to replace the gold standard. It consisted of a set of center countries tied to gold and a set of periphery countries tied to the center-country currencies.

Gravity model. An empirical model of trade or FDI flows that uses an analogy to gravitational forces.

Gross domestic product. The value of all final goods and services produced within a country's borders during a specific period of time.

Gross national income. The value of all final goods and services produced by a country's factors of production (but not necessarily within the country's borders) during a specific period of time.

Growth. A sustained increase in per capita income over time.

Growth theory. In its "old" and "new" variants, growth theory is the explanation in economics of the sustained increase in per capita incomes over the long run. It is based on the intensive production function.

Grubel–Lloyd index. An index of the degree of *intra*-industry trade that varies between 0 and 100.

Heckscher–Ohlin model. A model of international trade based on differences in factor endowments between the countries of the world.

High-skilled migration. The movement of persons with significant education and/or training from one country to another.

Home base. The country in which a multinational enterprise is incorporated and holds its central administrative capabilities.

Horizontal intra-industry trade. Trade in differentiated products at the same stage of processing.

Human capital. Investments made in the education, training, and capabilities of a labor force.

Human development (index). A conception of economic development introduced by the United Nations Development Programme that stresses health and education levels along with per capita income. The Human Development Index (HDI) is reported in the annual *Human Development Report*.

Hyperinflation. A very large increase in the overall or aggregate price level in an economy on the order of 40 percent or more annually.

Illicit trade. International trade in goods and services that are deemed illegal.

Import licenses. A right to import under a quota given either to domestic importers or foreign exporters.

Impossible trinity. The inability of countries to obtain all three goals of monetary independence, exchange rate stability, and capital mobility.

Inflation. A substantial increase in the overall or aggregate price level in an economy.

Information and communication technology. A driver of economic globalization that is based on computer hardware and software as well as telecommunications.

Intensive production function. A production function expressed on a per capita basis.

Interest rate parity condition. The equilibrium condition in the assets approach to exchange rate determination models. It relates a country's interest rate to the expected rate of depreciation of its currency and the interest rate of another country. Appears in both "covered" and "uncovered" varieties.

Inter-industry trade. A pattern of trade in which a country *either* imports *or* exports in a given sector.

Internalization. The process of taking a transaction along a value chain and bringing it within a firm.

International development. A concept with many meanings, including increases in per capita income, improvements in health and education, structural change, and institutional "modernization."

International finance. The exchange of assets between the countries of the world economy.

International Monetary Fund. An international organization founded after the Second World War to manage the international financial system, primarily by making conditional loans to countries experiencing balance of payments problems.

International production. A production of a good or service with processes located in more than one country.

International trade. The exchange of goods and services between the countries of the world economy.

Intra-firm trade. Trade that takes place within a multinational enterprise.

Intra-industry trade. A pattern of trade in which a country *both* imports *and* exports in a given sector.

Knowledge capital. A particular type of firm-specific asset based on knowledge, such as intellectual property.

Low-skilled migration. The movement of persons without significant education and/or training from one country to another.

Managed floating regime. An exchange rate regime in which a country allows its currency to float but intervenes in currency markets to affect its value when it determines that such intervention will be desirable.

Market seeking. A motivation for foreign direct investment in which the multinational enterprise engages in FDI to better serve a foreign market.

Marrakesh Agreement. Signed in 1994, the Marrakesh Agreement concluded the Uruguay Round of trade talks, begun in 1986, and established the World Trade Organization.

Medical brain drain. The emigration of high-skilled doctors and nurses.

Migration. The movement of persons from one country to another, particularly outside the country of residence.

Monetary approach to exchange rate determination. A theory of long-run exchange rate determination based on purchasing power parity and the quantity theory of money.

Monetary union. A group of member countries in a common market all using a common currency. The most notable example is the European Monetary Union, or EMU.

Money demand. The amount of money households want to hold at any particular time.

Money supply. The amount of money set in an economy by a central monetary authority such as a central bank or treasury.

Most favored nation. A principle of the GATT/WTO system in which each member must treat each other member as generously as its most favored trading partner.

Multilateral environmental agreements. Agreements on any environmental issue negotiated and codified between a large number of countries.

Multilateral trade negotiations. Rounds of trade negotiations conducted under the auspices of the World Trade Organization and its predecessor, the GATT Secretariat.

Multinational enterprise. Also known as a multinational corporation or a transnational corporation. A firm operating production, sales, and service operations in more than one country.

National treatment. A principle of the GATT/WTO system, under which foreign goods within a country should be treated no less favorably than domestic goods with regard to tax policies.

Net factor income. An item in the current account of the balance of payments. It records the difference between factor income and factor payments, both of which reflect income earned on physical capital.

New trade theory. A body of trade theory based on increasing returns to scale (economies of scale) and imperfect competition.

Nominal exchange rate. The number of units of a country's currency that trade against a world currency such as the US dollar or the European Union's euro.

Non-discrimination. A major GATT/WTO principle achieved via the sub-principles of most favored nation and national treatment.

Non-tariff barrier. An import restraint other than a tariff. A quota is one example.

Non-tariff measure. An import restraint or export policy other than a tariff. An import quota is one example.

Non-traded goods. Goods such as local services that are not imported or exported.

Official reserves balance/transactions. The element of the capital account of the balance of payments that reflects the actions of the world's central banks.

Open-economy accounts. The accounting identities derived from the firm, household, government, capital, and rest of the world accounts of the circular flow diagram.

Opportunity cost. What has to be given up to gain something. Along a production possibilities frontier, there is an opportunity cost of increasing the output of one good in the form of less production of another good.

Optimum currency area. A collection of countries characterized by well-integrated factor markets, well-integrated fiscal systems, and economic disturbances that affect each country in a symmetrical manner.

Overvaluation. Under a fixed exchange rate regime, the value of a home currency above its equilibrium value causing an excess supply of the home currency.

Ownership requirements. A limit placed on the degree of foreign ownership of firms by a country's government.

Performance requirements. A large host of measures placed on the performance of multinational enterprises by a government. A subset of these is known as trade-related investment measures.

Pollution haven hypothesis. The notion that multinational enterprises locate environmentally damaging processes in low-income countries.

Poverty. Significant deprivation in terms of income.

Preferential trade agreement. An agreement by a number of countries to grant preferential access to their markets to other members of the agreement. Examples include free trade areas and customs unions. Also called a regional trade agreement.

Price level. A measure of the average or overall level of prices in a country. Includes the GDP price deflator and the consumer price index.

Producer surplus. The benefit accruing to producers from the fact that, in equilibrium, producers receive a price higher than their willingness to accept for lesser quantities.

Product differentiation. The differentiation of one product from another along any dimension used to help explain horizontal *intra*-industry trade.

Production function. A mathematical relationship between the output of a firm, sector, or economy and inputs such as labor and physical capital.

Production possibilities frontier. A diagram that illustrates the constraints on production in general equilibrium imposed by scarce resources and technology. It shows all the combinations of two goods that a country can produce given its resources and technology.

Purchasing power parity model. A long-run model of exchange rate determination based on the notion that nominal exchange rates will adjust so that the purchasing power of currencies will be the same in every country.

Quota. Usually applied to imports. A maximum amount of imports allowed by a government.

Quota premium. The increase in the domestic price of a good as a result of an import quota.

Quota rents. The income accruing to the holder of a right to import a good into a country.

Real effective exchange rate. A real exchange rate weighted across a country's trade partners.

Real exchange rate. The rate at which two countries' *goods* (not currencies) trade against each other. The real exchange rate adjusts the nominal exchange rate using the price levels in the two countries under consideration.

Regional trade agreement. An agreement by a number of countries to grant preferential access to their markets to other members of the agreement. Examples include free trade areas and customs unions. Also called a preferential trade agreement.

Remittances. The flow of money from emigrants to their countries of origin.

Resource seeking. One of the motivations for foreign direct investment, in which a multinational enterprise secures backward integration into resource supply in a foreign country.

Revaluation. An increase in the value of a currency under a fixed exchange rate regime.

Ricardian model. A model of international trade based on differences in technologies between countries.

Rules of origin. A means to determine whether a product is from a partner country in a preferential trade agreement.

Smithsonian Conference. A conference that took place in Washington, DC, in December 1971 to attempt to repair the damaged adjustable gold peg system of the Bretton Woods system.

Special drawing right. An international currency administered by the IMF and introduced in 1969. It is currently defined in terms of a basket of three currencies: the US dollar, the euro, and the yen.

Specific factors model. A model of trade theory that allows for factors of production that cannot move easily from one sector to another.

Spot rate. The current nominal exchange rate between two currencies.

Stolper–Samuelson theorem. A result of international trade theory concerning the political economy of trade. It states that an increase in the relative price of a commodity (e.g. as a result of trade) raises the return to the factor used intensively in the production of that good and lowers the return to the other factor.

Strategic asset seeking. A motivation for foreign direct investment in which the multinational enterprise wants to acquire productive assets as part of the *strategic game* between competitors in an industry.

Structural adjustment. The process of change in an economy that takes place in response to internal and/or external imbalances. It typically requires demand reduction and currency devaluation.

Systemic risk. The spread of a financial crisis among a large number of countries.

Tariff. A tax on imports, which can be either in ad valorem or specific form.

Tariffication. The process of replacing quotas by equivalent tariffs.

Tariff rate quota. An import restraint involving two tariff levels: a lower tariff, for levels of imports within the quota; and a higher tariff, for levels of imports above the quota.

Terms of trade effects. The effects of a country having an impact on the world prices of the merchandise and services it trades.

Trade creation. A potential outcome of a free trade area or a customs union in which imports switch from a high-cost source to a low-cost source.

Trade diversion. A potential outcome of a free trade area or a customs union in which imports switch from a low-cost source to a high-cost source.

Trade-related investment measures. A subset of performance requirements, including export requirement and domestic content requirements, some of which are now prohibited by the World Trade Organization.

Traded goods. Goods and services that can be imported or exported.

Transfer pricing. The manipulation of the prices of intra-firm trade by multinational enterprises to reduce their global tax payments.

Triffin dilemma. A critique of the gold exchange standard developed by Robert Triffin. It involves a contradiction between the requirements of international liquidity and international confidence.

Undervaluation. Under a fixed exchange rate regime, the value of a home-country currency below its equilibrium value causing an excess demand for the currency.

Value chain. A series of value-added processes involved in the production of a good or service.

Vertical intra-industry trade. Trade in differentiated products at different stages of processing.

Washington Consensus. A term used to define a set of common policies adopted by the International Monetary Fund and the World Bank and imposed on developing countries through structural adjustment lending.

World Bank. An international organization founded in 1944 by the Bretton Woods Conference that became a lender to low- and middle-income countries in support of development projects and structural adjustment.

World Trade Organization. The WTO was established in 1995 as part of the Marrakesh Agreement, ending the Uruguay Round of trade talks. It is an international organization with a legal foundation for managing world trading relationships.

Index

absolute advantage, 27–29, 30–33, 35–37, 38, 44, 46, 48, 50, 53–54, 55, 66, 68, 70–71, 73, 121–122, 136, 137, 138
accounting frameworks, 311, 351
activity composition effect. *See* comparative advantage
ad valorem tariff. *See* tariffs
adjustable gold peg. *See* Bretton Woods
administrative protection, 123
Africa, 34, 61, 85, 111, 127, 158, 161, 164, 214–215, 276, 284, 292, 357, 365, 435, 457, 479, 502–504, 524
African, Caribbean and Pacific (ACP), 161
aggregate measure of support (AMS), 152
Agreement on Agriculture, 142, 149, 150–152, 167, 184
Agreement on Basic Telecommunications, 154–155
Agreement on Textiles and Clothing, 148–149, 150
Agreement on Trade Related Aspects of Intellectual Property Rights (TRIPS), 194
air freight, 4
allocative efficiency, 451, 470
American Motor Corporation (AMC), 223
anti-dumping (AD), 111, 123–124, 133–134, 148, 162, 190
anti-globalization movement, 2, 436
apartheid regime, 215
Apple Corp., 217, 224, 245, 247, 274
applied general equilibrium (AGE), 136–137
appreciation. *See* exchange rates
Argentina, 127, 164, 179–181, 189–190, 194, 262, 357, 365, 413–414, 416, 435, 438, 442–443, 451, 452, 457–458
  Convertibility Plan, 413
  Fifth Summit of the Americas, 190
Argentine peso, 189
ASEAN Economic Community (AEC), 191
ASEAN Free Trade Area (AFTA), 191
  Common Effective Preferential Tariff, 191
ASEAN–Australia–New Zealand Free Trade Area, 191
Asian financial crisis. *See* crises
asset price deflation. *See* crises, bubbles, 454
asset-based approach, 376, 382, 391, 539
asset-based securities, 12
assets, 9–10, 11, 211, 215–217, 222, 239–240, 241–242, 244, 263, 312, 316, 317, 320, 323, 376, 378–379, 381–388, 389, 390, 394–397, 404, 454–456, 460–461–524, 525, 534–535, 536–537, 539
  financial, 19
  firm-specific, 207, 211, 221–222, 226, 238–240, 241–242, 244, 253, 272
  intangible, 211, 238–239, 242, 244, 252–253, 272
  property rights, 525
assets approach.
  capital gain, 383
Association of Southeast Asian Nations, 5, 191
asylum seekers, 284–285
autarky, 32, 35–36, 38, 43, 48, 49–50, 51–56, 67, 70–73, 76, 88, 97, 101, 104, 114, 122, 520
automobiles, 123, 126, 136, 177–178, 186–187, 188
average cost (AC), 86, 88, 161

backward linkages. *See* multinational enterprises
balance of payments, 261–263, 277, 325–326, 327–328, 336, 351, 376, 377–378, 381, 404–405, 415, 429–431, 451–452, 459–460, 461–462, 463, 534–535, 536, 540–541
balance of payments, official reserve transactions, 321
Balance of Payments and International Investment Position Manual (BPM6), 328
balance of payments crises. *See* crises
banana dispute. *See* dispute settlement process
bancor, 446, 448
Bangladesh, 437, 520
Bank for International Settlements (BIS), 10
banking crises. *See* crises
Basel Committee on Banking Supervision (BCBS), 471, 472, 474
Basel standards, 470
Baumol effect. *See* migration
Beijing Auto Works (BAW), 223
Beijing Jeep, 222–223
Belassa index (BI), 69

Berne Convention, 157
Berne Initiative, 301
best alternative to a negotiated agreement (BATNA), 165–166
Big Mac index (box), 364
bilateral investment treaties. *See* international investment agreements.
binding. *See* General Agreement on Tariffs and Trade
bond finance, 11, 334, 336, 339, 340–341, 342, 345–346, 351–352, 445
bonds, government bonds, 10, 316, 320–321, 335, 341, 495
brain drain. *See* migration, permanent high-skilled
Brazil, 111, 127, 164–165, 179–181, 189–190, 194, 214, 216, 343, 409, 438, 442–443, 451, 452, 454, 457, 458, 465–466
  balance of payments crisis in, 11
  Brazilian real (box), 409
  debt crisis in, 435
  opposition to intellectual property, 156
  steel exports of, 111
Bretton Woods, 146, 421, 424–427, 431, 433, 446–448, 484
Brexit, 1, 16, 183–184, 185, 481, 484
bubbles. *See* asset price deflation

Canada, 84, 112, 173, 185–188, 192, 261, 284, 290, 291, 297, 357, 365, 427
Cancún Ministerial Conference. *See* World Trade Organization
capital account liberalization, 334, 347, 349, 437, 463, 465
capital account surplus, 321, 323
capital adequacy ratio (CAR), 348, 471, 472
capital controls, 334, 349, 350, 352, 412, 440, 446, 451, 459, 472–474, 504
  unremunerated reserve requirement, 350
  variable deposit requirement, 350, 473
capital deepening, 513–515, 527, 533
capital flight, 11, 348, 434, 457, 458, 461, 463, 473, 474, 494
  sudden stops, 348
capital flows, 11
  financial capital, 11, 347
  push and pull factors, 344–345
capital gain. *See* assets approach
capital mobility. *See* impossible trinity
Central African Monetary Area (CAMA), 502. *See also* CFA franc zone
certificate of origin (CO), 177
CFA franc zone, 479, 502–504
change in tariff heading (CTH), 177–178
Chile, 127, 173, 189, 192, 224, 350, 357, 365
China, 5–6, 8, 12, 23, 34, 85, 91–92, 95–96, 191, 214–216, 219–220, 223–224, 245–248, 251–252, 262, 297, 325–326, 365, 406–407, 437
circular flow diagram, 312, 328, 378, 509, 515
clusters. *See* spatial clusters
Colombia, 127, 160, 189, 262, 350
commercial bank lending, 11, 321, 334, 335–336, 339, 340–344, 345, 346, 350–352, 437, 445, 499
commercial presence of foreign direct investment. *See* Mode 3
Committee on Regional Trade Agreements (CRTA), 176
Committee on Trade and the Environment (CTE), 163
Common Agricultural Policy (CAP), 148, 184
Common Effective Preferential Tariff. *See* ASEAN Free Trade Area
common external tariff (CET), 174
common market. *See* regionalism
Communauté Financière Africaine (CFA), 479, 502
comparative advantage, 27, 30–31, 37, 38, 46, 48–49, 50–56, 60, 61–76, 82, 90, 92, 97–98, 101–102, 105–106, 108–109, 114, 115, 136, 137
  environment
    activity composition effect, 74–75
    technique effect, 74
  revealed
    Belassa index, 69
comparative advantage. Ricardian model, 27, 44, 46–47, 49, 51–55, 60, 64, 66–67, 68–69, 70–71, 73, 75, 104, 113
competitive devaluation. *See* exchange rates
computers, 91
conflict, 15, 37, 193, 422, 430, 524–525
constant returns to scale, 532
consumer surplus, 35–36, 42–43, 128–129, 130–133, 141, 180
contagion. *See* crises
container shipping, 4, 8, 16
contract manufacturing organization (CMO), 206
contracting, 6–8, 17, 90, 146, 203, 207, 226, 228, 232, 234, 239, 241–243, 244–245, 253, 257, 270, 335, 367
Convention on Biological Diversity, 15
Convention on International Trade in Endangered Species of Wild Fauna and Flora (CITES), 15
cooperative equilibrium, 176
copyrights, 156–157

Corn Laws (British), 51, 115
Costa Rica, 13, 126, 160, 236–240, 244, 256, 266, 268
countervailing duty (CVD), 124, 133, 135, 137, 142
covered interest rate parity (CIP), 389
 See also interest rate parity condition
crawling pegs. *See* exchange rates
crises, 11–12, 334, 335–336, 342–343, 347–348, 415, 435, 437–438, 440, 454, 459, 462–463, 465–466, 467, 469, 472–475, 497, 499–500, 534, 536–537
 Asian crisis, 191, 465
 asset price deflation, 451
 balance of payments, 451, 457
 banking, 451
 bubbles, 454, 457, 468, 474
 contagion, 339, 458–459, 470
 currency, 451
 domestic debt, 451
 external debt, 451
  sovereign debt default, 457
 global financial, 1, 214, 299, 326, 338, 422, 451, 455, 468, 469, 479
 Great Depression, 414, 423, 459
 hyperinflation, 375, 413, 414, 451–454, 474
 subprime crisis, 440, 468, 470
cross-border trade. *See* Mode 1
cross-price elasticity. *See* elasticity of demand
culture, 14–15, 16, 18, 20, 97, 103, 121, 211, 222, 259, 265, 277, 295
currencies, 19
currency board. *See* exchange rates
currency crises. *See* crises
current account, 259, 263, 319–327, 343–344, 381, 385–386, 407, 409, 435, 439, 459–460, 461–464, 466, 468, 475, 497, 500
 balance, 319–320, 322, 497
 deficit, 320–321, 323–324, 326–327, 409, 439, 459–460, 461–464, 466, 468, 497
 surplus, 326, 407, 435, 500
customs procedures, 125
customs unions.
 See preferential trade agreements
Czech Republic, 29, 182, 215, 481, 483

de minimis rule, 178
deadweight loss, 129
deflation, 413, 451–452, 454–455, 457, 458, 465, 468–469, 474
demand, changes in, 41
demand diagonal, 45
demand-side factors, 42
 incomes, 42
 preferences, 42
depreciation. *See* exchange rates
devaluation. *See* exchange rates
development
 international, 12, 16, 20, 300, 301, 337, 539
development. *See* economic development
Dillon Round, 147
direct exporting. *See* foreign market entry
direct foreign investment. *See* foreign direct investment
direct investment, 7, 9, 19–20, 186, 256, 259, 263, 283, 320–321, 327, 334–336, 351, 436, 437, 536–537, 540, 542
Dispute Settlement Body, 150, 159
dispute settlement mechanism (DSM), 134
dispute settlement process, 150, 159–162, 167
 the "banana" dispute (box), 160
dissemination risk, 212, 226, 228, 239, 242
Doha Round, 1, 145–146, 147, 152, 155, 158, 164–165, 167, 190, 194–195, 302
domestic support, 150–152, 164–165
Dominican Republic, 115, 126
Dubai, 156
dumping, 111–112, 123–124, 133–135, 162, 190
 See also anti-dumping

East Asia, 85, 191, 213, 235, 248, 267, 274, 520–522
 trade and growth in (box), 521–523
economic development, 91, 253, 265, 289, 303, 327, 509, 522
 capabilities approach, 13
 growth, 508–509, 523, 528
 structural change, 439, 446, 459, 465–466, 539, 543
economic growth, 260, 274, 338, 347, 456, 509, 514, 518, 522, 523–524, 526, 528
 growth theory, 524
 human capital, 60–61, 75, 108, 211, 221, 235, 258, 260, 261, 290, 291–292, 299, 508, 520, 523–524, 526, 527, 533
 institutions, 523
 natural capital, 61
 path dependence, 524
 pro-poor growth, 511
 Solow residual, 516
economies, 31, 49, 64, 67, 86–87, 90, 135, 209, 219, 221, 222, 238–239, 413, 414, 446, 447, 508, 510, 521–522, 536–537
 firm-level, 209, 238–239, 244, 252
Ecuador, 127, 263
education, 13, 61, 108–109, 113, 259, 274, 277, 287, 288–289, 290, 292–294, 301, 436, 510, 515, 517–519, 522–524, 527–528
El Salvador, 194
elasticity of demand, 89, 141
 cross-price, 141

endogenous protection, 98, 104, 119–120
Enhanced Structural Adjustment Facility (ESAF), 439
environment, 14–16, 18, 20–21, 37–38, 74–77, 162–163, 186, 187–188, 207, 244–246, 258–259–261, 263, 264–265, 275, 277, 540, 541
environmental Kuznets curve, 75
equities, 10
equity portfolio investment, 335, 338
Ethiopia, 13, 439
  the IMF in Ethiopia (box), 439
ethno-nationalism, 16, 113, 167, 295
European Central Bank (ECB), 479, 489, 490
European Coal and Steel Community (ECSC), 183, 483, 486
European Council of Ministers of Economics and Finance, 482
European Economic Community (EEC), 182–183, 482, 483, 488
European Financial Stability Facility (EFSF), 497
European Monetary Institute (EMI), 485
European Monetary Union (EMU), 182, 185, 274, 441, 479, 483–484–485, 486–490, 491–497, 499–500, 501–502, 504–505
European Stability Mechanism (ESM), 499
European Union (EU), 12, 112, 155–156, 164, 167, 174, 177, 181–184, 186, 224, 273–274, 284–285, 287, 359, 482, 483–485, 505
  Maastricht Treaty, 183, 481, 485
exchange rate exposure. *See* exchange rates
exchange rates, 355–357, 358–359, 361–367, 369–371, 377, 381–382, 386–390, 392, 401, 402–404, 407, 408–412, 414–415, 418–419, 464, 475, 479, 491–492
  appreciation, 377
  assets-based model, 378, 381, 386–388, 390, 404
  crawling peg, 400, 412, 415
  currency board, 189, 400, 401, 413–416, 436, 458–481, 482
  depreciation, 402
  devaluation, 402
  effective, 359
    real, 361
  expectations, 386–388, 410, 412
  exposure, 355, 368
  fixed, 400, 414
  forward, 389
  nominal, 357, 359, 361–367, 370, 376, 378, 381, 386, 388, 390, 392, 394, 399–401, 404, 411–412, 454, 464, 510
  overvaluation, 364, 404
  real, 355, 357, 361–363, 366, 369–370, 371, 374–375, 388, 409–410, 415, 434
  revaluation, 403
  spot, 358, 369
  stability. *See* impossible trinity.
  trade-based model, 376, 378–380, 386, 390
  undervaluation, 403
    is China's currency undervalued? (box), 407
expectations. *See* exchange rates
export processing zone, 269
export promotion, 522
export subsidies, 148, 150–152, 167, 184, 528
Extended Credit Facility (ECF), 429, 430
Extended Fund Facility (EFF), 429, 430
external balance. *See* production possibilities frontier

fabrication, 233
factor endowments, 60, 61–63, 68–69, 70, 71–74, 76, 81, 101–102, 105, 108, 119
factor intensities, 62, 76
factors of production, 19, 60–61, 62, 71, 73, 76, 101–104, 110–111, 112–113, 319–320, 374
finance, 2, 8–14, 19–22, 283, 288, 292, 301, 311, 316–317, 327–328, 334, 339, 340–341, 342, 344–346, 351–352, 369–370, 411, 421–422, 445–446, 447, 458, 459, 475, 479
  international, 2, 8–12, 19–22, 245–246, 274, 283, 301, 311, 317, 327–328, 334, 337, 369–370, 411, 421–422, 445–446, 447, 458, 528, 539
financial capital. *See* capital flows
financial intermediary, 312
firm-specific assets. *See* assets, firm-specific
flexible manufacturing, 208
flows, 4, 7–8, 11–12, 72–73, 78–79, 185, 219–220, 227, 283–284, 288–290, 293, 298–300, 313–314, 320–322, 334–339, 341, 342–346, 348–349, 351–352, 366, 381–382, 398, 494, 509, 534–535
foreign direct investment (FDI), 1, 19–21, 78, 108, 153, 186, 283, 320, 327, 334–335–336, 351, 436, 437, 522, 536–537, 540, 542
  backward vertical, 236, 239, 240, 252
  forward vertical, 240
  greenfield investment, 207, 211–212, 222, 239
  joint venture, 203, 207, 222, 229, 266
  knowledge capital model, 211
  market seeking, 208–209, 228, 244, 540
  mergers and acquisitions, 207
  resource seeking, 208–209, 228, 244, 542
foreign exchange, 10
foreign market entry, 205–206, 207–208, 210–212, 215, 218, 226, 228–229, 236, 242, 286, 369

foreign market entry (*cont.*)
direct exporting, 205
indirect exporting, 204, 211
foreign outsourcing, 6, 17–18, 206
foreign savings, 313
forward exchange rate. *See* exchange rates
Foxconn, 245
France, 80, 84–182, 183, 216, 423, 428, 434, 445, 479–480, 483, 488, 496, 501, 502
franchising, 7, 204–206–207
free trade area. *See* preferential trade agreements
Free Trade Area of the Americas (FTAA), 190
fundamental accounting equation, 315
fundamental equilibrium exchange rate (FEER). *See* exchange rates

gains from trade, 27, 35–37, 44, 54–56, 69–71, 74, 76, 89, 97, 101, 108, 114, 157, 475, 526
net welfare increase, 35
General Agreement on Tariffs and Trade (GATT), 60, 517, 520, 523, 533, 539, 541
binding, 149
non-discrimination, 147
quantitative restrictions, 148
General Agreement on Trade in Services (GATS), 131, 134–135, 149, 150, 152, 156, 159–161, 162–163, 166–167, 168, 173–176, 194, 195, 268, 302, 528
General Arrangements to Borrow (GAB), 431
Geneva Convention, 301
geographical indications, 157
Germany, 5–6, 84, 115–182, 183, 216–217, 326, 423, 427, 428, 445, 480, 483, 486–488, 491, 496, 497, 499–500, 501
Global Commission on International Migration (GCIM), 301
global financial crisis (GFC), 338, 340–341, 342–343, 422, 440, 451, 455, 457, 468, 469–470, 472, 473–475, 479, 481, 491–493, 495–497, 499, 501 *See also* crises
global safeguard investigation, 112
Global Trade Analysis Project (box), 137
global value chain (GVC), 8–9, 15, 91, 92, 108, 217, 232, 236–237, 239–240, 241, 242–253, 256–257, 268–271, 277–278, 335, 538
globalization, 1–2, 4, 9, 14–17, 27, 69, 71, 113–114, 227, 228, 232, 252–253, 283, 290, 297, 303–304, 326–328, 346
economic globalization, 14, 15–16, 38, 60, 69, 208, 227, 232, 253, 256, 283, 290, 304, 328, 337, 346, 351
globally systemically important bank (GSIB), 472
gold standard, 423, 446, 447–448
gold-exchange standard, 422–423, 425, 447
government bonds. *See* bonds
government procurement, 127
gravity models, 78–79
Great Depression. *See* crises
Greece, 12, 182, 341, 440–442, 452, 457, 480, 488, 496–499, 501
greenfield investment. *See* foreign direct investment
gross domestic product (GDP), 3, 75, 78–79, 333, 485, 508
per capita, 508
Group of 10 (G-10), 471
Group of 20 (G-20), 164
growth elasticity of poverty, 511
growth. *See* economic growth
Grubel–Lloyd index, 84, 95–96, 344

Haiti, 126
health, 1, 18, 37, 124–125, 153, 157–159, 259, 263–264, 275, 277, 292, 436, 453, 485, 510, 519, 525, 526, 527–528
access to medicines (box), 158
Heckscher–Ohlin model, 27, 44, 60–64, 71, 72–73, 75–76, 82, 99, 101–102, 103–105, 109–110, 114–115, 119, 187, 269
heterarchy, 218–220
Honda, 203
Honduras, 126
Hong Kong, 85, 217, 464
housing mortgages. *See* United States housing market
human capital. *See* economic growth
Human Development Index (HDI), 13
Hungary, 215
hyperinflation. *See* crises

illicit trade, 15, 37–38, 99, 258
imperfect substitutes model, 122, 134, 136, 137
import licenses, 132
impossible trinity, 411, 414–416, 445, 511
capital mobility, 411
exchange rate stability, 411–412, 415, 445–446
monetary independence, 411–412, 415, 445–446
Inclusive Wealth Report, 61
income inequality, 109
India, 13, 16, 17–18, 113, 153, 156, 158, 164–165, 191, 219, 225, 248, 284, 291, 293, 443, 510, 520, 524
indirect exporting. *See* foreign market entry

Indonesia, 11, 85, 111, 113, 147, 191–192, 219, 246, 262, 357, 365, 437, 443, 451, 457, 464, 465–467, 510
the Indonesian crisis (box), 466
industrial designs, 157
Industrial Technology Research Institute, 235
inflation, 3–4, 402, 413–414, 423, 434, 439, 452–453, 457, 467, 469, 474, 487–488, 492–493, 500–501, 504
information and communication technology, 17, 33, 37, 108, 114, 154, 208, 228, 232, 290
institutionalism, 98–99, 114, 120
institutions, 145–146, 256, 258, 272, 274, 276, 292–293, 312, 421, 452, 455, 458–459, 469–470, 508, 515, 523–528, 534
intangible assets, 238
integrated circuits, 156, 157, 232
Intel, 149, 151, 155–156, 168, 194, 224, 226, 227, 234, 235–240, 244, 268, 273, 355
intellectual property, 145, 149, 151, 155–156, 157, 166–167–168, 186, 190, 192, 194–195, 226–227, 238
Intellectual Property Committee (IPC), 156
intellectual property rights, 149, 151, 155, 194, 226
interest rate parity condition, 388–389, 408, 460, 465
covered interest rate parity, 389
covered versus uncovered interest rate parity (box), 389
uncovered interest rate parity, 389
inter-industry trade, 80–81, 90, 91, 92–93, 95, 104, 108, 136, 187, 240. *See also* trade, inter-industry
internal balance. *See* production possibilities frontier
internalization, 232, 237–238
International Bank for Reconstruction and Development. *See* World Bank
international capital mobility, 99, 100
International Clearing Union (ICU), 421
international development. *See* development, international
international finance. *See* finance, international
International Financial Statistics, 326–327, 328, 371, 391
international investment agreements
regional investment treaties, 258
International Labour Organization, 301
International Monetary Fund (IMF), 146, 150, 326–327, 328, 347–348, 371, 391, 400, 416, 421, 451, 453, 463
International Organization for Migration (IOM), 301
international production. *See* production, international
International Stabilization Fund (ISF), 421
International Trade Organization (ITO), 146
intra-firm diffusion, 29
intra-firm trade. *See* trade, intra-firm
intra-industry trade. *See* trade, intra-industry
investor–state dispute settlement (ISDS), 192
Ireland, 12, 182, 215, 273–274, 440–442, 480, 488, 497–499
Italy, 6, 12, 84–182, 183, 217, 422, 428, 480, 483, 487–488, 491, 497

Jamaica, 126
Japan, 28–33–37, 44–50, 51–55, 62–68, 70–74, 84–85, 97, 101–103, 111–112, 121–122, 128–132, 138, 142–144, 191–192, 214, 216, 217, 248, 357–358, 454–455
consumer surplus and producer surplus in, 130
industrial robots, 29–30, 112
intra-industry trade in, 85
rice imports into, 97
steel exports of, 111
joint venture. *See* foreign direct investment
July 2008 Package, 165

Kennedy Round, 171
Keynes, John Maynard, 392, 421, 424–425, 431, 433, 434, 446, 448
Keynes Plan, 421, 431, 433, 434, 448
knowledge capital, 211
Kyoto Protocol, 15

labor-intensive good (LIG), 105
Latin America, 123
law, international, 15, 146, 160
lender of last resort, 497, 500, 504
licensing. *See* technology
life expectancies, 13–14
linkage, 271, 272, 327, 458
lobbying, 100, 111
local content requirement, 266
logistics, 3, 4, 91, 205, 234, 272
Lorenz curve. *See* income inequality
low and middle-income countries (LMICs), 7, 11, 148, 152, 155, 157–158, 164–165, 167, 168, 214–215, 257–258, 261, 302, 324–326, 337–339, 340–341, 435, 440–442, 467

Maastricht Treaty. *See* European Union
Malaysia, 6, 85, 191–192, 350, 437, 451, 464, 473, 508, 512

marginal cost (MC), 86–88
marginal revenue (MR), 87–88
market access, 150
market economy (ME), 135, 340
market failure, 238, 525
market-seeking foreign direct investment. *See* foreign direct investment
Marrakesh Agreement, 134, 145, 147, 149–150, 154–155, 159, 162, 176, 194, 267, 277
material injury, 133–134, 135
matrix management, 218
medical transcription services. *See* services
mercantilism, 28, 50
Mercosur, 127, 174, 189
mergers and acquisitions (M&A), 7, 204, 207, 213, 222, 336
Mexico, 11, 17, 84, 112, 127, 173, 186–188, 190, 192, 224, 262, 266, 299, 311–323, 356–357, 359–363, 365, 366–367, 373–374, 377, 379, 388–389, 394–398, 402, 406, 408–409, 416, 418, 434–435, 437, 443, 451, 452, 454, 457, 459–462, 520
  currency crash, 454
  FDI flows into, 186
  free trade agreements and, 174
  intra-industry trade with the United States, 84
  Summit of the Americas, 190
Middle East, 85
migration, 9, 14, 17, 21, 54, 73, 76, 113, 184, 185, 188, 225, 227, 283–288, 289–292, 293–296, 298–304, 346, 495
  Baumol effect, 294
  illegal, 285, 303
  migration hump, 289
  permanent high-skilled, 284
  refugees, 284, 286, 301
  undocumented, 285
miniaturization, 14
Mode 1, 153, 195, 302
Mode 2, 153, 302
Mode 3, 153, 154, 167, 195, 302
Mode 4, 153, 154, 302–303
mode of services supply, 152, 302
Modi, Narendra, 16
monetary independence. *See* impossible trinity
monetary policies, 387, 392, 395–398, 399, 418
monetary union, 176–177, 182–183, 185, 274, 415, 441, 479, 482–484, 485, 486–487, 492, 496–497, 502–503, 504–505
monopolistic competition model, 87–89, 92
Montreal Protocol on Substances that Deplete the Ozone Layer, 15
Morecambe Bay cockle tragedy, 297
mortgage-backed security (MBS), 468
most favored nation. *See* non-discrimination
movement of consumers, 302
Multilateral Agreement on Investment (MAI), 274–275
multilateral environment agreements (MEA), 23
multilateral trade negotiation (MTN), 1, 97, 142, 146–147, 173, 190, 193
multilateralism, 165, 173–174, 192–194
multinational corporation. *See* multinational enterprise
multinational enterprise (MNE), 7, 14–15, 19, 203, 207, 209–210, 212–213, 215–216, 218–222, 224–225, 227–228, 229, 239, 242–243, 256–257, 258–265, 266–268, 271–274, 275–277, 284, 293, 537, 541
multinational enterprises, backward linkages, 271
Myanmar, 127, 191, 457

NAFTA automobile ROOs (box), 177
national treatment (NT), 173. *See also* non-discrimination
natural capital, 61
Negotiating Group on Basic Telecommunications (NGBT), 154
net factor income, 333
net income, 263, 319–320, 405–406, 409, 415
Netherlands, the, 84, 182, 480, 488
New Arrangements to Borrow (NAB), 431
newly industrialized countries, 85
Nicaragua, 126
Niger Delta, 18
nominal exchange rate. *See* exchange rates
non-discrimination, 147, 148, 153–154, 156, 167, 173, 195
  most favored nation (MFN), 134, 147–148, 161, 173, 184, 195
  national treatment, 126, 155, 162, 173, 275, 446
non-governmental organization (NGO), 436
non-market economy (NME), 135
non-tariff measure (NTM), 123–128, 131, 133, 135, 175, 191
North American Agreement on Environmental Cooperation (NAAEC), 186
North American Agreement on Labor Cooperation (NAALC), 186
North American Free Trade Agreement (NAFTA), 5, 105, 174, 177, 185–187
North–South trade. *See* trade, North–South

official development assistance (ODA), 298
open-economy accounts, 311, 317, 321, 327–328, 329, 331, 378

open-economy macroeconomic model, 317
opportunity cost, 57, 65
optimum currency areas. *See* regionalism
Organisation for Economic Co-operation and Development (OECD), 37, 84, 250, 274
Organisation for European Economic Co-operation, 432
original sin, 342
other investment, 321, 335–336, 342
outsourcing, 7, 17–18, 204–206
overvaluation. *See* exchange rates
ownership requirements, 266
ozone layer, 15

Pakistan, 357, 376, 443
Paraguay, 127, 189, 457
patents, 156–157, 158, 211, 227, 228, 238, 272
perfect competition, 58
perfect factor mobility, 110
performance requirements, 267–268, 275, 277
Permanent Court of Arbitration (The Hague) (PCA), 264
Peru, 126, 189, 192, 264
Peterson Institute for International Economics, 21, 435
petroleum industry, 18
  the petroleum industry in the Ecuadorian Amazon (box), 263
Philippines, the, 11, 85, 191, 365, 451, 464
Poland, 182, 215, 399, 482, 483, 501
political economy, 37, 38, 48, 50, 55, 60, 93, 97–104, 109–110, 112–113, 114–115, 119, 304, 416, 421, 443, 448
politics, 14–15, 18, 20, 100, 115, 120, 303, 423, 486
pollution haven hypothesis, 263
portfolio investment, 320–321, 327, 334–335, 338, 341, 349, 437, 460
Portugal, 12, 182, 442, 457, 480, 487–488, 497–499, 502
post-Fordism. *See* Toyotism
poverty, 2, 21, 27, 303, 414, 436, 437, 440, 501, 509, 512
Poverty Reduction and Growth Facility (PRGF), 439
preferential trade agreements, 5, 127, 136, 148, 155, 173–175, 479
  customs unions, 174, 193, 258
  free trade area, 174, 190, 258
  regional trade agreements, 173
  spaghetti bowl, 193
pressure group models, 100
producer surplus, 35–36, 42, 129, 130–133, 141, 180
product differentiation, 81, 86, 89, 92–93, 136, 266
production, international, 4
production factors, 22. *See also* factor endowments
  production function, 60, 517, 520, 523, 533, 539, 541
  intensive, 533
production possibilities frontier, 44, 46, 57, 59, 62
pro-poor growth. *See* economic growth
protection, 98, 112
purchasing power parity model, 355, 362, 364, 370, 372, 374, 376, 390

quantitative performance criterion (QPC), 432
quantitative trade restrictions, 123
quantity demanded, changes in, 41
quantity supplied, changes in, 41
quota, 121, 124, 127, 133, 138, 142–144, 148, 150, 161, 291, 301, 350, 428–430, 435, 441–442
  rents, 132, 133, 143–144

Rapid Credit Facility (RCF), 430
Rapid Financing Instrument (RFI), 430
rare earth elements (REEs), 33, 99
rate of return to education (RORE), 519
real exchange rate. *See* exchange rates
realism, 98–100, 114–115, 312
recession, 299, 337, 410, 463, 494–495, 497–500, 501
refugees, 284, 286, 297, 301
regional trade agreements. *See* preferential trade agreements
regional value content (RVC), 178
regionalism, 173–174, 192–193, 194, 196
  common market, 177, 183, 196
  optimum currency areas, 479, 493–494, 496
remittances, 284, 286, 293, 297, 298–300, 304, 312, 320
research and development (R&D), 7, 203, 212, 218, 223–224, 261, 266
resource-seeking foreign direct investment. *See* foreign direct investment
Responsible Minerals Assurance Process (RMAP), 246
Restriction of Hazardous Substances (RoHS), 246
revaluation. *See* exchange rates
revealed symmetrical comparative advantage (RSCA), 70
Ricardian model, 27, 44, 46–47, 49, 51–55, 60, 64, 66–67, 68–69, 70–71, 73, 75, 104, 113

Ricardo, David, 27, 44, 48, 50–51, 56, 115
Romania, 183, 215, 440, 442, 482, 484
rule of origin (ROO), 177
Russia, 11, 111, 215, 357, 365, 438, 443, 451

sanitary and phytosanitary requirements, 125
Saro-Wiwa, Ken, 18
Seattle Ministerial Conference. *See* World Trade Organization
securitization, 339, 470
semiconductor industry, 99, 232–237, 239, 241, 243, 247, 253
Senegal, 1
services, 2–4, 8–9, 17–18, 37, 149, 151–155, 157, 166–167, 175, 185–186, 194–195, 209–210, 234, 248–249, 263, 273–274, 283–284, 294, 302–303, 316, 318–319, 323, 360–362, 364, 373, 538
  medical transcription services, 18
Singapore, 85, 164, 191–192, 275
skilled labor-intensive good (SLIG), 108
Slovakia, 111, 215, 483
smile curve, 247
Smith, Adam, 28–29, 36, 38, 44, 50, 526
Smithsonian Conference, 427
smooth adjustment hypothesis, 90–91
South Africa, 34, 111, 127, 158, 164, 214–215, 357, 365, 504
South Africa Breweries (SAB) (box), 215
South Korea, 13, 85, 112, 191, 365, 437, 440, 442, 451, 464–465, 508, 512, 522, 525
sovereignty, 286, 301, 304, 444
spaghetti bowl. *See* preferential trade agreements
Spain, 12, 182, 217, 480, 487–488, 497, 499, 502
special drawing right (SDR), 484
specialization in production, 66
specific factors model, 99–100, 110
specific tariff. *See* tariff
spiky globalization. *See* globalization
spillovers, 261, 522
standards and technical regulations, 125
Standby Credit Facility (SCF), 430
steel, 110
Stolper–Samuelson theorem, 99–100, 103–110, 112, 114–115, 119, 187
structural adjustment, 1, 439, 446
structuralism, 459, 539
subcontracting, 204–206
subsidies, 123, 135, 148, 150–152, 155, 163, 164, 167, 184, 190, 235, 467, 528
supply, changes in, 41
supply and demand model, 30, 35, 38, 40–42, 44
supply-side factors, 41
  factor prices, 41
  technology, 41
Swiss formula, 171–172
Swissair, 17
Switzerland, 17, 217, 365

Taiwan, 85, 91, 111, 235, 245, 247, 293, 464, 522, 525
Taiwan Semiconductor Manufacturing Company (TSMC), 235
Tanzania, 215
tariff, 5, 124, 127–133, 137–138, 141–144, 146–147, 149, 150–152, 161, 167, 171, 174–178, 179–180, 183–184, 191, 193–194, 251, 535–536, 541, 543
  ad valorem, 123, 128, 191
  specific, 123, 128, 132, 141
  within-quota, 142
tariff rate quota, 122, 124, 127, 137, 142–144, 161
tariffication, 167
technical barriers to trade, 124, 125
technology, 4–5, 16–18, 20–21, 22–23, 31, 37–38, 41–42, 57–58, 69–70, 72–76, 98–99, 107–109, 114, 157–158, 206, 208–209, 221–222, 226–227, 247, 259–262, 266, 272–273, 293–294, 515–516, 520, 522, 523
  endogenous, 517
  licensing, 206, 226, 235, 267, 522
  transfer, 158, 222, 227, 259, 261–262, 266, 267, 293, 520, 522, 527
terms of trade, 129, 141–142
Thailand, 11, 85, 111, 113, 191, 262, 350, 357, 365, 437, 451, 458, 462–466, 473, 508, 512
  the Baht crisis (box), 463
Tokyo Round, 171
trade
  inter-industry, 75, 80–81, 90, 91, 92–93, 97, 104, 108, 136, 187, 240–241
  international, 1, 2–5, 9–11, 12, 19–21, 27–28, 31–32, 54–55, 61–63, 68–70, 82, 88–89, 102, 104–106, 145–146, 159–160, 166–168, 228, 274, 300–301, 327–328, 337, 447, 527–528, 539
  intra-firm, 232, 240–241, 244, 252–253, 276
  intra-industry, 69, 76, 80–87, 89–93, 97, 104, 108, 136, 187, 191, 240–241, 344
    computer products trade (box), 91
    horizontal, 81–83, 84, 89–90, 92–93, 240
    vertical, 83–84, 85, 89–93, 191
  North–South, 98, 104–108, 116, 187

political economy of, 5, 37, 38, 55, 60, 93, 97–104, 109–110, 112–113, 114–115, 119, 131, 229, 304
trade creation, 174, 181, 184–185, 196
trade diversion, 174, 179, 180–181, 184–185, 191, 194, 196
Trade in Services Agreement (TiSA), 155
Trade in Value Added (project/database) (TiVA), 250–251, 253, 269
trade policy analysis, 60, 76, 121–122, 125, 136–138, 142, 252
trade related investment measures (TRIMs), 267, 277
traded goods, 467, 510
trademark, 156, 206
Trade-Related Aspects of Intellectual Property Rights (TRIPS), 155
transactions costs, 208
transfer pricing, 276
transnational corporation. *See* multinational enterprise
transnationality index, 215–217
Trans-Pacific Partnership (TPP), 192
transportation, 3–5, 8, 186, 188, 233–234, 239, 244, 269
Triffin dilemma, 427, 433
Trinidad and Tobago, 126
Troubled Asset Relief Program (TARP), 469
Trump, Donald, 16, 112, 188, 192, 251
Turkey, 111, 357, 365, 442–443, 458

Ukraine, 215
undervaluation. *See* exchange rates
undocumented migration. *See* migration
United Kingdom, 1, 6, 12, 16, 84, 182–184, 214–217, 291, 297, 357, 423, 428, 443, 445, 468, 481–482, 483–484, 488, 505
Brexit, 1, 16, 183–184, 185, 481, 484
United Nations Conference on Trade and Development (UNCTAD), 229, 258
United Nations Development Programme (UNDP), 13
United Nations Framework Convention on Climate Change, 15
United Nations High-Level Dialogue (HLD) on International Migration and Development, 300, 301
United States housing market, 12, 468
housing mortgages, 12
unremunerated reserve requirement (URR), 106–107, 350
Uruguay, 127, 147, 189, 262, 457
Uruguay Round, 97, 134, 142, 147, 149, 152, 156
US International Trade Commission, 111–112, 116
US steel protection (box), 135, 190

value chain, 239, 240, 241, 242, 243, 247, 251, 252, 271, 275
value of non-originating materials, 178
variable deposit requirements, 350, 473
Venezuela, 111, 127, 160, 189, 190, 262, 341, 414, 452–453, 457
Vietnam, 27–29, 30–33, 35–37, 44–50, 51–54, 62–68, 70–72, 80, 90, 97, 101–103, 110, 113, 121–122, 128–131, 138, 191–192, 203, 207–208, 246, 248–249, 251, 262, 437, 520
Vietnam, Honda in, 207
Vietnam Engine and Agricultural Machinery Corporation (VEAM), 208
voluntary export restraint (VER), 124, 127

wages, 104–109, 115, 187, 259, 287, 295–296, 333, 494–495, 501
in Latin America (box), 107
Washington Consensus, 437, 448, 466
Wealth of Nations, The, 36
wealth portfolios, 10
welfare, 12–13, 35–38, 43, 45, 54–55, 70, 74, 97, 125, 128–133, 136, 137–138, 141, 157, 179–181, 194, 195–196, 266
West African Monetary Union (WAMU). *See* CFA franc zone
White Plan, 421, 431, 433, 448
willingness to accept, 43
willingness to pay, 42
windows, 425
Wiwa, Owens, 18
women, 519
Working Group on Environmental Measures and International Trade (EMIT), 162
World Bank, 3, 6, 8, 10, 21, 274, 295–296, 299–301, 337, 338, 435, 437, 439, 456, 464, 466, 522, 523, 535–536, 543
Industrial Pollution Projection System, 187
institution for international economic development, 145
World Trade Organization, 4, 5, 131, 134, 138, 145, 147, 148–149, 173, 175, 250, 253, 301–302, 538, 540, 543
Cancún Ministerial Conference, 1
dispute settlement mechanism, 34, 134
Seattle Ministerial Conference, 1

Zimbabwe, 414, 452–454, 457